Early Childhood Development
Prenatal Through Age Eight

2nd Edition

Sandra Anselmo
Wanda Franz

West Virginia University

Merrill,
an imprint of Prentice Hall

Englewood Cliffs, New Jersey   Columbus, Ohio

Library of Congress Cataloging-in-Publication Data

Anselmo, Sandra.
    Early childhood development : prenatal through age eight / Anselmo/Franz.—2nd ed.
       p.   cm.
    Includes bibliographical references and index.
    ISBN 0-02-303607-9
    1. Childhood development. 2. Infants—Development   I. Franz, Wanda. II. Title
    RJ131.A655   1995   94-13382
    305.23'1—dc20   CIP

Cover art/photo: Elizabeth Hathon/The Stock Market
Editor: Kevin M. Davis
Production Editor: Patricia A. Skidmore
Photo Editor: Anne Vega
Text Designer: Bill Harrington
Cover Designer: Anne Flanagan
Production Buyer: Patricia A. Tonneman
Electronic Text Management: Marilyn Wilson Phelps, Matthew Williams, Jane Lopez, Karen L. Bretz

This book was set in Folio, Dutch and Swiss by Prentice Hall and was printed and bound by R. R. Donnelley & Sons. The cover was printed by Phoenix Color Corporation.

Earlier edition © 1987 by Merrill/Macmillan Publishing Company.

Photo credits: pp. 0, 10, 17, 26, 32, 40, 98, 116, 140, 158, 174, 183, 192, 212, 214, 219, 224, 244, 248, 262, 303, 315, 336, 342, 345, 350, 352, 356, 358, 421, 426, 445, 472, 497, 505, 507 by Anne Vega, Prentice Hall and Merrill; pp. 3, 24, 37, 49, 111, 265, 271, 328, 370, 382, 385, 415, 452, 504 by Todd Yarrington, Prentice Hall and Merrill; pp. 47, 71, 165, 198, 208, 226, 235, 274, 348, 391–393, 435, 443, 483, 502 by Sandra Anselmo; pp. 66, 287, 510 by Scott Cunningham, Cunningham/Feinknopf Photography; p. 81 courtesy of Riverside Hospital; p. 105 by Robert L. Craig; pp. 110, 401, 408, 447 by Barbara Schwartz, Prentice Hall and Merrill; p. 117 by Bruce Johnson, Prentice Hall and Merrill; pp. 126, 172, 176, 178, 273, 480, by Gunter Franz; pp. 147, 231 by Diane Elmer; pp. 284, 302, 323, 332, 441, 458 by Dan Floss, Prentice Hall and Merrill; p. 405 by Blaire Seitz; p. 430 by Julie Tober, Prentice Hall and Merrill.

Printed in the United States of America

10 9 8 7 6 5 4 3 2 1

ISBN: 0-02-303607-9

Prentice-Hall International (UK) Limited, *London*
Prentice-Hall of Australia Pty. Limited, *Sydney*
Prentice-Hall of Canada, Inc., *Toronto*
Prentice-Hall Hispanoamericana, S. A., *Mexico*
Prentice-Hall of India Private Limited, *New Delhi*
Prentice-Hall of Japan, Inc., *Tokyo*
Simon & Schuster Asia Pte. Ltd., *Singapore*
Editora Prentice-Hall do Brasil, Ltda., *Rio de Janeiro*

This revised edition is dedicated to the living memories of Sandra Anselmo, her two sons—Christopher Anselmo Cary and David Anselmo Cary.

About the Authors

Sandra Anselmo

Sandra Anselmo died from breast cancer at the age of 40 on November 10, 1986, just before the publication of the first edition of this book. She was a Professor of Education at the University of the Pacific and an award-winning teacher of child development classes. She published numerous articles on various aspects of early childhood development and a book, *R is for Rainbow: Developing Young Children's Thinking Skills through the Alphabet*. After graduating from Stanford University, she earned her doctorate at the University of Iowa. At both universities, she was associated with the early childhood laboratory schools in teaching and administrative capacities. She also consulted with public agencies and private corporations on matters of early childhood development and education. In honor of her life and contributions, the new Sandra Anselmo Head Start Center opened on the campus of the University of the Pacific in 1993.

Wanda Franz

Wanda Franz is Professor of Child Development and Family Studies at West Virginia University. She received her B.A. in Anthropology at the University of Washington, Seattle, where she worked in the Child Development Laboratory. Her thesis dealt with Piagetian interventions in the curriculum of early childhood education programs. She received her doctorate from the Department of Psychology at West Virginia University, where her thesis addressed the issue of neonatal learning ability. She has had over twenty years of teaching experience, working with students preparing for careers in early childhood education and related fields. Her research and service activities stress the importance of developmental principles in the preparation of professionals working with children and their families.

Preface

Early Childhood Development tells the amazing story of human development from the prenatal stage through age eight. The book's scope and structure are both important to the student of childhood development. First, job opportunities are expanding for students in child development and early childhood education. In addition to work with preschool children, there are opportunities for child development specialists to work in hospitals, mental health facilities, Head Start, and day care programs. Today's graduates will work with children in a wide range of ages, and this book provides developmental data from across the early childhood period. Second, the book's structure allows students to follow the developmental process longitudinally. This approach shows the interrelationship in development over a span of years and builds a bridge between the first years of life and the initial part of elementary education.

In addition to concentrating only on the formative early childhood years, *Early Childhood Development* has three other distinctive features. First, it combines the study of strategies for observing children with the study of theories and research about early childhood development. Readers take a process approach, learning to observe children's behaviors in natural settings and to record and summarize what they see. Throughout the book, exercises called "Activities to Enhance Learning" encourage systematic application of observational skills, on the theory that people will remember best what they discover themselves. Involvement with children through observation creates a meaningful context for studying the theories and findings of others.

Second, the book presents early childhood development within the context of our pluralistic society. Its ecological approach shows how strongly cultural factors influence development. Research conducted in many cultural groups is integrated throughout the book to help readers understand the multitude and complexity of cultural variables. Topics include black English, cultural differences in parent-child interactions, and culture and school success. All readers must realize that their own childhood experiences represent just one way of growing up in a pluralistic society. By understanding the richness of cultural differences, readers are better able to interact with families from a variety of backgrounds.

The third distinctive feature is the use of many vivid examples and illustrations to help readers understand early childhood development. Applications, often appearing in "Developmental Issues in Practice," accompany all chapters and make the book particularly appropriate for readers who are in or who plan to enter the helping professions and who want to learn to rear children more effectively. Applications include such topics as handling parent-child separations, encouraging cognitive development, stimulating creativity, and choosing day care.

ORGANIZATION OF THE BOOK

The first chapter gives an overview of major contemporary theories of early childhood development, and the second presents strategies for observing young children. After Chapter 2, the details of early childhood development are organized and presented chronologically. Part I (Chapters 3 and 4) discusses the events before and at birth. The focus then turns to the first year of life in Part II (Chapters 5, 6, and 7), ages one through three in Part III (Chapters 8, 9, and 10), and ages four through eight in Part IV (Chapters 11, 12, and 13). The book ends with a brief epilogue about middle childhood.

Because early childhood development is complex, Parts II, III, and IV are each divided into three chapters devoted to physical, psychosocial, and cognitive domains of development. *Physical development* deals with growth patterns, coordination, and body image; *psychosocial development* encompasses feelings, self-concept, and interactions within a broad social context; and *cognitive development* refers to thinking, problem solving, intelligence and language. For clarity and specificity, the three domains are presented separately, but interrelationships are frequently noted.

SPECIAL FEATURES AND CHANGES IN THIS EDITION:

- ❑ lists of books for recommended reading at the end of each chapter
- ❑ a summary statement of key points listed at the end of each chapter
- ❑ boxed "Developmental Issues in Practice," which apply the content to practical settings and situations in each chapter
- ❑ recommendations for hands-on projects and observations at the end of each chapter
- ❑ glossary of terms at the end of the book
- ❑ new and expanded "Developmental Issues in Practice," emphasizing practical applications
- ❑ expanded discussion of standardized and developmental test materials in addition to observation techniques
- ❑ new discussion of genetics and the nature/nurture controversy
- ❑ new information on premature birth and the characteristics of babies born prematurely
- ❑ expanded discussion of child abuse
- ❑ new discussion of theories of motor development
- ❑ new material on the Ainsworth attachment paradigm
- ❑ new discussion of preoperational logical abilities, including egocentrism and seriation
- ❑ new information on emotional development and intervention to enhance emotional expression
- ❑ new information on children with disabilities and the use of the Individual Education Plan (IEP)
- ❑ greatly expanded discussion of language development
- ❑ new material on preschool perceptual development and its implications for reading ability
- ❑ new information on moral development and self-concept

ACKNOWLEDGMENTS

I would like to thank my husband for his patience and assistance. I also thank my children, Anthony, Angela, and Erika. They have been my primary teachers and have also provided me with excellent anecdotal information, which has greatly enhanced this book. Angela deserves additional thanks for her editorial and research contributions.

The staff at Merrill have been of great assistance. I am especially grateful to Linda Sullivan, administrative editor; Patty Skidmore, production editor; and Anne Vega, photo editor, for their understanding and encouragement as well as their professional expertise during the book's production.

I would like to thank the reviewers of this book for their comments, criticisms, and suggestions on earlier drafts: Becky Bailey, University of Central Florida; Kathleen Fite, Southwest Texas State University; Elaine Goldsmith, Texas Woman's University; John R. Hranitz, Bloomsburg University of PA; Peg A. Ketron, Ball State University; Jeanne B. Morris, Illinois State University; Marcia L. Oreskovich, University of Northern Colorado; Donna Castle Richardson, Oklahoma State University; Deborah J. Smith, Appalachian State University; Kay Springate, Eastern Kentucky University; Jessie M. Zola, University of Wisconsin-Milwaukee.

Brief Contents

Contents

Chapter 10   **One- to Three-Year-Olds: Cognitive Development   342**

**PART IV   Early School Years [Ages Four through Eight]:
Exploring the World   381**

Chapter 11   **Early School Years (Ages Four through Eight):
Physical Development   382**

Chapter 12   **Early School Years (Ages Four through Eight):**
Psychosocial Development   426

CHAPTER 1

Introduction and Theories of Early Childhood Development

▼ KEY IDEAS

What Is Early Childhood Development?

Why Study Early Childhood Development?
- ❏ To Help Rear Children
- ❏ To Prepare for the Helping Professions

History of the Study of Early Childhood Development
- ❏ Perceptions of Children in History
- ❏ Beginnings of the Scientific Study of Children

Contemporary Theories in Early Childhood Development
- ❏ Cognitive Theory
- ❏ Psychoanalytic Theory
- ❏ Humanist Theory
- ❏ Maturationist Theory
- ❏ Behavioral Theory

Many different theories attempt to explain the dramatic changes that take place between birth and eight years of age. This chapter gives an overview of the five major contemporary theories in early childhood development. But first, early childhood development is defined, reasons for study are cited, and a brief history of the field is presented.

WHAT IS EARLY CHILDHOOD DEVELOPMENT?

This book defines **early childhood development** as the orderly psychosocial, physical, and cognitive changes that take place between the prenatal months and the early elementary school years. Specifically, this book chronicles the developments in human beings from before birth through age eight. Early childhood development begins the continuous process of human development.

The boundaries for the study of early childhood development are somewhat arbitrary. The book begins with the events that occur even before birth. But where should it end? Naturally, eight-year-olds do not "graduate" from early childhood; nor do they realize that they are suddenly different. Instead, their development continues in much the same incremental fashion as it did during the first eight years. The age of eight is designated as the end of early childhood because it usually marks a time of intellectual transition. After the age of eight, most children begin to be able to think in rather different ways: their approach to solving problems becomes more abstract and they can understand others' perspectives. The onset of a new type of logical thinking is as natural a marker for the end of early childhood as any other that might be chosen.

This book was written to help readers understand early childhood development within the context of a pluralistic, multicultural society. The following section presents some of the reasons for becoming knowledgeable about early childhood development.

WHY STUDY EARLY CHILDHOOD DEVELOPMENT?

An initial interest in early childhood development is likely to motivate readers to explore this book. There are many reasons to nurture that interest and to learn more about the early development of human beings. Two main reasons are discussed next.

To Help Rear Children

Parents, parents-to-be, or others in close contact with young children want to be able to rear children in positive ways. But they may not understand what developmental patterns to expect in the early years and how they might influence such patterns. The more that people know about the development of young children, the more they can help each child to achieve a full and rich potential. Parents want the best for their children, but many times parents cannot decide what to do in specific situations. Here is a sampling of puzzling situations that will be explained in this book:

Six-month-old Susan wakes up in the middle of the night. She has been sleeping through the night for some time, so her tired parents halfheartedly play with her because she seems to need comforting. The next night Susan wakes several times. What are Susan's needs and how should her parents help her?

Two-year-old Sammie shouts "No!" even when he wants what is offered to him. How should his parents respond?

Four-year-old Greg refuses to eat his fruit because he claims that his sister has more in her differently shaped bowl. Why does he perceive the situation in this way and what should his parents do?

Second grader Laura announces that an older child touched her in uncomfortable ways. The more she is questioned, the more upset she becomes. What happened and what should her parents do?

The everyday interactions of parents and children could yield further examples of such puzzlers. The problem is not that parenting is inherently difficult but that most parents are not completely prepared to take on the care of a relatively helpless infant and the young child who soon develops. When parents know about the normal developmental characteristics of infants and young children, they are in a better position to make good and effective decisions regarding care. If a child is truly delayed in development, the knowledgeable parent is better able to recognize the situation and seek help early.

Parents who know what to expect can relax and enjoy their children more. There is a special kind of pleasure in recognizing what a child is doing and understanding the meaning of the behavior for its importance to the child's development. For example, when an infant begins to be shy in the presence of strangers, this is an indication of the attachment to the mother. The knowledgeable parent recognizes this as a natural part of growing up, feels pride in the growth of the child, and has a sense of accomplishment in identifying an important growth marker. In addition, parents with this kind of knowledge are much less likely to be irritated with the behavior and fearful that the child might be developing a personality disorder.

There is evidence that this kind of positive attitude is important to good parenting. When parents understand the facts of child development, they are less likely to abuse their children (Wood-Shuman & Cone, 1986).

To Prepare for the Helping Professions

Those who aspire to one of the **helping professions** such as early childhood teaching, child care, parent education, social work, nursing, developmental therapy, or recreation need to understand early childhood development. The behavior of helping professionals is accepted by others as a model for interacting with young children. Professionals are asked about matters as diverse

Those who aspire to enter one of the helping professions need to understand early child-hood development.

as thumb sucking, discipline, nutrition, suspected child abuse and neglect, speech problems, and bed wetting. By setting examples, making recommendations, and giving advice, they guide young children and their families. The responsibility is enormous. It is absolutely essential that all who enter the helping professions have a thorough knowledge of the development of young children. Professionals must also be prepared to stay abreast of new information being obtained through research and intervention programs.

Helping professionals must understand not only the patterns of early childhood development in their own cultural groups but also those that are typical of other groups. In this book, research and examples illustrate the range of patterns of child rearing and development that exist in this multicultural society. It is essential for effective working relations with parents that those in the helping professions be sensitive to the special needs of families with different backgrounds.

An important role of those working with families is to provide reassurance when children behave in normal ways. They should understand why a child engages in certain behaviors—many of which can be irritating to parents and caregivers—and provide explanations to concerned parents. In addition, they should be prepared to emphasize the range of normal developmental patterns. Most children fall into the statistical norm for development. However, not all children mature at the same rate, and parents are exceptionally sensitive to variations in development when they see other children engaging in behavior that their own child has yet to acquire. They need reassurance that their own child is normal and that the child's development is not delayed.

Finally, our culture tends to encourage families to think of early child development as "simple," requiring little skill on the part of the professionals who care for these children. It is assumed that young children "just play" and do not require specialized care. For this reason, trained child care workers are often viewed as merely baby-sitters. Professionals can help to change that distorted view by preparing themselves to provide professional information to the public and parents in particular.

For example, perhaps Johnny is playing with a set of blocks. He is not only "playing," however—he is also learning about spatial relations, number concepts, seriation, and classification. Maybe Susie is "fighting" with her friend over the toys, but she is also learning interpersonal social skills, communication, and the natural consequences of her actions toward others.

Professionals need to demonstrate their competence in understanding and caring for children by describing the children's behavior in terms of human developmental principles. The major function of this book is to provide the basis for such ability for those who expect to work with young children and their families.

HISTORY OF THE STUDY OF EARLY CHILDHOOD DEVELOPMENT

The scientific study of children is a relatively recent phenomenon in human history. Only in the past 200 years have children been recognized as different from adults and worthy of study in their own right. Previously, life was harsh and the needs and expectations of society did not allow children to experience what is now called childhood. Children instead were thought to be miniature adults and were treated accordingly. Adulthood was frequently defined as beginning at 12 or 13 years of age.

Perceptions of Children in History

In earlier times, parents who gave birth to a dozen children might have seen only two or three live to adulthood. Thus, they needed to retain an emotional distance from the children who were likely to die in early childhood.

Although the diseases and malnutrition that resulted in so many deaths in early childhood have been largely eliminated, in previous centuries the high mortality rate had an important influence on the treatment of children.

Until fairly recently, there was no "childhood" as we currently define it. A human being from birth to about six years of age was considered to be an infant and was entrusted to the mother to be taught how to behave properly. By six or seven years, the person was apprenticed or otherwise put into gainful employment. Pictures of children in those days show them wearing cut-down versions of adult clothing and engaging in adult activities.

The interest in childhood as a unique phase of development had its roots in speculation about how adults acquire their ability to function. The English philosopher John Locke (1632–1704) suggested that children are born neither inherently good nor bad but are the products of their environment. He hypothesized that children are born with a mind that is a **tabula rasa** (blank slate), upon which is written by experience all that the adult eventually knows and feels. Locke's ideas represented a radical departure from the doctrine of basic human sinfulness and the belief that human traits were inherited "in the blood."

In this intellectual climate, Frenchman Jean Jacques Rousseau (1712–1778) wrote his famous book on education, *Émile*. Rousseau contended that the environment, not some original sinfulness, contaminates humans. His position was fundamentally different from Locke's in that he believed that children are essentially good and capable of correct development. They need only to be provided with a supportive environment in which to develop. He believed that the causes of development are inherent in the child. Rousseau's theory acts as the base for subsequent approaches that stress the importance of the individual's own nature in determining the outcome of development.

Locke and Rousseau presented the earliest examples of the controversy on nature versus nurture. Although these two theorists differed in some of their fundamental assumptions, both emphasized the importance of the environment in either shaping or supporting the development of the person. This orientation altered the way children were perceived by society in Europe and North America. People began to believe that it was important to organize the environment so that children could develop in the most effective way. Consequently, society began to allow a time for childhood—an interlude before it was necessary to assume adult responsibilities. This orientation was facilitated by the industrialization of society, which provided for better living conditions and more time for education and play for children. It is important to realize, though, that in most parts of the world industrialization came later than in Europe and North America, and the change in perceptions about childhood also followed much later. In fact, there are still a few cultures, generally in Third World countries, that initiate children as young as five or six years of age into the work force of the community.

Specialists in early childhood development are interested in studying children in a wide variety of cultural contexts in an attempt to discover which aspects of development are universal and which are influenced by culture. This book reports the results of research done in other parts of the world as well as research conducted in the United States with members of various cultural groups.

Beginnings of the Scientific Study of Children

The Swiss educational reformer Johann Heinrich Pestalozzi (1746–1827) is generally regarded as a pioneer in the modern scientific study of children. In 1774 he published a biography of his son, which was influential in calling attention to the process of development in the early years.

More than 100 years later, Charles Darwin (1809–1882) built on the work of Pestalozzi in writing the biography of his own young son. Because Darwin was a scientist, his book was written in more precise behavioral terms than was usual at that time. Darwin even included the results of simple experiments on how his child reacted differently to forward and backward movement, for instance. The publication of Darwin's book made baby biographies popular, opened the door to a method for scientifically studying children, and set the stage for modern research in early childhood development. Jean Piaget, for example, wrote baby biographies of his children that were the basis for his later research. His observations uncovered the surprising ability of even very young infants to organize their experiences and coordinate their actions to be more effective in responding to sets of environmental events.

The rapid expansion and improvement of scientific child study can be credited in part to the teaching, research, and vision of G. Stanley Hall (1844–1924), one of the first psychologists in the United States. Hall was the teacher of such leaders in child development research as Arnold Gesell, a physician who was instrumental in charting the maturation of young children and establishing the norms of development; John Dewey, an educator who led the progressive education movement to provide a more democratic school environment; and Lewis Terman, a psychologist who introduced the concept of intelligence quotient (IQ) after participating in the revision of the Binet tests of intelligence. In 1883 Hall wrote an influential book, *The Content of Children's Minds*, that represented a major step forward in the scientific study of children. He also founded the first scientific journal in which research on child development was published, the *Journal of Genetic Psychology*. And Hall was responsible for introducing Sigmund Freud to American psychologists by inviting him to Clark University for a series of lectures. Because of Hall's activities and his role in training others, he is generally regarded as a leader in the scientific study of children in the United States.

Before contemporary theories are described, a definition of **theory** is in order. A theory is an organized system of hypotheses or statements, based on observations and evidence, that explains or predicts something. In early childhood development, theories have been formulated to explain and predict various aspects of children's behavior.

Some people believe that theories are not practical. However, the saying "Nothing is as practical as a good theory" holds true here. Theories allow observations to be organized into a coherent system. For example, Jean Piaget's theory of intellectual development helps adults understand young children's perceptions about their world and how they organize these perceptions into systems of thought to help them solve problems. Theories also determine the kinds of questions that researchers will ask. For example, Piaget asks questions about how the child reasons, and behavioral psychologists ask questions about why the child behaves in a certain way.

One basic theme that underlies all the theories on childhood development is that of the role of genetics and environment. This has been called the **nature versus nurture** controversy (see Developmental Issues in Practice 1.1). It is important to recognize that each theory is based on underlying assumptions about the role of genetics in influencing the development of the child. Keep this controversy in mind as you read the following sections that describe the most important theories of early childhood development.

CONTEMPORARY THEORIES IN EARLY CHILDHOOD DEVELOPMENT

This book takes an **eclectic approach** to the many interesting contemporary theories in early childhood development. Methods, ideas, and research findings are incorporated from the whole spectrum of contemporary theoretical positions: cognitive, psychoanalytic, humanist, maturationist, and behavioral. Early childhood development seems too complex to be satisfactorily explained by any one of these positions. It is important to understand that each theory is based on underlying assumptions about the role of genetics in influencing the development of the child. In judicious combination, these contemporary theories explain and predict much of the behavior of young children. A general overview of these theories is presented in this section.

The theories in this chapter are arranged in two groups—developmental and behavioral—according to the underlying assumptions that determine the way the theories explain human functioning. The differences between the two groups are based on assumptions about human beings that cannot be proven true or false but that determine the way the theories are developed and researched (Overton & Reese, 1973; Reese & Overton, 1970).

Developmental theories are based on the notion that development is caused by internal, biologically based changes. The changes can be seen to evolve in stages in a **discontinuous** way, so that each stage represents the emergence of completely different patterns of behavior (e.g., the changes an infant goes through from crawling to standing to walking). The stages are always **sequential,** meaning that they must come in a particular order (e.g., you couldn't have walking before standing). They are also assumed to be **hierarchical;** that is, each new stage is integrated into the old stages so that nothing is lost (e.g., when a child begins to walk, crawling is still possible). According to developmental theories, the source for change comes from within, although the environment is important in encouraging the adapta-

▲ DEVELOPMENTAL ISSUES IN PRACTICE   1.1

NATURE AND NURTURE IN EARLY CHILDHOOD

Throughout many centuries, it was thought that a person's adult personality was largely determined by inherent, God-given traits. For example, in medieval England, the royal lords of the manor were assumed to be endowed with leadership capabilities as a birthright. People believed that traits were "in the blood." As a result of this belief, a rigid class system was maintained and was an issue of great importance to everyone.

The writings of Locke and Rousseau raised questions about how much of children's development is a result of the nurturing that they receive both before and after birth and how much is a result of natural, inborn tendencies. This issue has been debated by scientists ever since and has been called the nature versus nurture (or heredity versus environment) controversy. This issue is still very important because there are a number of important implications for whichever position is taken.

An example of the controversy that this issue still arouses can be found in the discussions regarding intellectual functioning. Arthur Jensen contended that there is a genetic basis for the lower-average scores on standard intelligence (i.e., IQ) tests of African Americans compared with those of white and Asian Americans (1969). The response of most scholars to Jensen's thesis was immediate and negative. Then and now, most experts disagree strongly with Jensen, citing as confounding factors the many differences between the environments of African Americans and other groups as well as the bias of traditional IQ tests toward information and patterns of thinking that are more familiar to whites and Asians than to African Americans. Expert opinion holds that each child is born with a hereditary endowment that has great influence on development but that, after conception, the child's development is influenced by diverse environmental factors.

tional changes in the child. Developmental theories mentioned in this chapter are those of Piaget, Freud, Erikson, Rogers, Maslow, and Gesell.

Behavioral theories are based on the belief that the environment controls the changes in children's development. It is assumed that these changes are **continuous** in that children learn more effective behaviors through environmental encouragement. Behavioral theorists discussed in this chapter include Skinner, Pavlov, and Bandura. These theorists have developed the basic theoretical constructions upon which subsequent research is being produced. (The specific work of current researchers is discussed in other chapters.)

Cognitive Theory

Eight-year-olds have learned a great deal during the years since they were born. **Learning,** defined as changes that occur in behavior as the result of

DEVELOPMENTAL ISSUES IN PRACTICE   1.1 (continued)

There is strong evidence that IQ has high **heritability,** which means that when comparing the relative effects of heredity and environment on intelligence, heredity plays a very important role. There are major political and social implications for whichever position is held. If we choose to accept the thesis that IQ is controlled largely by heredity, it follows that African Americans are doomed to having low IQs and must resign themselves to lower expectations for education and jobs. On the other hand, if IQ is determined primarily by environment, then the lower IQ scores found among African Americans can be explained by environmental events, and the potential for intervention and improvement of scores becomes possible.

It is possible, however, to reconcile these two issues. First, it is clear that some traits are more affected by heredity than other traits. Second, there is evidence that all traits are affected by both factors, so that heredity may set very broad limitations on the performance of an individual but the trait can be greatly affected within those limits. Third, we have to recognize that our evaluations of IQ are still limited. The standardization procedures are oriented toward middle-class white Americans. Furthermore, IQ tests measure only certain types of intellectual abilities, which are very useful for predicting school success but do not tell us everything there is to know about a person's intellectual potential.

In the debate over the IQ scores of African Americans, heredity may play a part in the lower scores. However, research on the effectiveness of Head Start programs has conclusively demonstrated that IQ scores can be raised as a result of the intervention program (Lazar & Darlington, 1982). High heritability in a trait should not prevent us from doing what we can to improve the environment of poor children in general. Both nature and nurture are essential to normal development. Parents and child care professionals must be able to respect the natural traits and talents of each individual child as well as do everything possible to maximize the effectiveness of the environment in which the child develops.

experience, is of interest to parents, helping professionals, and others who deal with young children. And learning has been the subject of a considerable body of research by specialists in early childhood development. **Cognitive theory,** in contrast to other theories, tends to place more emphasis on children's thought processes when they learn.

The theory of Jean Piaget (1896–1980) is the best known and most highly developed of the cognitive theories. Piaget's theory has profoundly influenced early childhood development in this country. Perhaps one of the reasons for the speedy acceptance of his theory is that it rings true to anyone who has spent time with young children. It is clear that Piaget carefully observed young children, and his theory shows that there are distinctive patterns to their thought processes. For instance, Piaget wrote about the behavior of his daughter, Jacqueline, when she was two years, seven months of age:

According to the theory of Jean Piaget, young children think in distinctive ways. For instance, they believe that a person can change identity by changing clothes.

Jacqueline, seeing her sister Lucienne in a new bathing suit, with a cap, asked: "What's the baby's name?" Her mother explained that it was a bathing costume, but Jacqueline pointed to Lucienne herself and said, "But what's the name of that?" (indicating Lucienne's face) and repeated the question several times. But as soon as Lucienne had her dress on again, Jacqueline exclaimed very seriously, "It's Lucienne again," as if her sister had changed her identity in changing her clothes. (Piaget, 1962, p. 224.)

Piaget explained many of the intriguing differences between the thinking of young children and that of adults. For example, he showed why children think that clothes can make people change or that the moon follows the car at night or that there is more milk in taller, thinner glasses than in shorter, wider glasses. Knowing about Piaget's theory changes the way we view young children and helps us understand them.

Piaget's observations of young children led him to propose that their thinking develops sequentially in four stages, three of which occur during the early childhood years. Table 1.1 briefly outlines the four stages: **sensorimotor, preoperational, concrete operational,** and **formal operational**. The first two are presented in considerable detail later in this book.

Table 1.1. *Piaget's Stages of Development*

Stage	Age
Sensorimotor	0–18 months
Children learn through their senses, beginning with reflexes, and through activity: touching, tasting, smelling, and manipulating materials.	
Preoperational	18 months–6 years
Children think with words and objects in an intuitive manner, with judgments based on perceptions rather than logic. Thinking is limited by the inability to deal with more than one variable at a time.	
Concrete operational	6–12 years
Children think logically and expand knowledge. They use reasoning rather than perceptions to justify their judgments. Their thinking is still limited, however, to concrete, tangible objects and familiar events.	
Formal operational	adolescence–adulthood
Young people think symbolically and hypothetically. Abstract thinking and concepts can now be used.	

Piaget observed that each stage tended to occur at about the same time in each person's life span, so he attached age **norms** to each stage. That is, he specified the normal time when developmental changes would occur. Since he first developed his theory, there have been many changes in the ways that children are raised, and the age norms have changed. For example, the norms for the beginning of the preoperational stage have changed over the years from 24 to 18 months. It is important to recognize that the individual child cannot be expected to meet each age norm exactly; rather, in normal children each stage will occur at approximately the same age but with wide variability.

Jean Piaget was a precocious Swiss youth who published his first scientific article at the age of 10. He received his doctorate in the field of zoology at the age of 22, but he never worked in that field. Instead, he followed his formal education with work in psychoanalysis. He then assisted in the project to refine Binet's intelligence tests. His experiences interviewing children led him to observe that children's thinking was different from that of adults. The IQ test was designed to measure the change in the number of questions the children could answer correctly; however, the test did not have the capacity to measure changes in the process of thinking. He gave up his work on the IQ test and began to study how children think. He did so by means of a **méthode clinique,** or clinical interview, in which he asked carefully worded questions to discover how children think and why they respond as they do.

As a biologist, Piaget recognized that children must organize their environment and must be able to adapt to changes in it if they are to survive.

Piaget identified two critical biological factors that affect development: the principle of **structures** (organized elements of actions on the environment) and the process of **equilibration,** which has two components, **assimilation** and **accommodation** (the way humans process or adapt to new information).

A structure refers to a person's ability to act in response to environmental events. For example, an infant grasps a rattle with the hand; a preschool child grasps an idea with the mind. Both are examples of structures. They are different in appearance because of the difference in developmental level of the two children being observed. Piaget used the word *scheme* to refer to a single structure. Additional terms are also found in the literature, including *schema* and *schemata*. All these words mean the same thing and refer to structures.

Assimilation is the attempt to make new information fit into existing structure, whereas accommodation involves restructuring one's thinking by adding new information. The concepts of assimilation and accommodation can be illustrated by the feeding activities of a newborn infant. Piaget believed that an infant is born with basic sensory abilities and reflexes such as sucking and grasping, that these basic reflexes represent basic structures, and that soon these develop into more elaborate structures. The infant sucks his mother's breast and then at some later time is given a bottle, which has a different kind of nipple. If the infant tried to suck the bottle in the same way he sucked his mother's breast, he would be attempting to make new information fit into the old structures—he would be assimilating. When the infant finds that he cannot obtain milk in this manner, he changes his way of sucking on the bottle, thus adding new information to the original structure—he is accommodating.

All knowledge, according to Piaget, is the result of expanding our structures from our original learning based on reflexes. Piaget considered his theory to exclusively emphasize neither the environment (nurture) nor the internal capabilities of the person (nature). Rather, he believed both were important, and he called himself an interactionist, stressing the child's actions on the environment. Because the child's actions were so important, he described the child as **constructing** structures out of his interactions with the environment. Thus, Piaget's theory is referred to as a constructivist approach to human development. Following are examples of preschool children's construction of structures:

Annie watches her mother exchanging money at the store. Later she tells her mother to "go to the store and get some money." Her structure (or explanation) for the event is that her mother is receiving, not giving, money.

Todd plays in a rushing stream. He builds a mud dam to create a small pool and then watches as the moving water washes away the dam. His structures (or explanations) for the event include primitive ideas about gravity, force, and pressure.

Children learn through a combination of maturation, social transmission, and the results of their own actions on the environment; structures thus

---

▲ DEVELOPMENTAL ISSUES IN PRACTICE   1.2

COGNITIVE THEORY

PIAGET: CLASSIFICATION

Five-year-old Dan likes to play with the button collection of his day care provider, Sara. At first he seemed to concentrate his attention on the tactile aspects of the buttons: he ran them through his fingers and felt individual buttons. Soon, though, he noticed that Sara was making some kind of arrangement with her buttons. She saw him watching her and asked, "Can you tell how all of these buttons are alike?" Dan did not know, but Sara showed him that all of the buttons in her arrangement were bigger than most of the others. At other times when Dan asked to play with the buttons, Sara arranged some of them into groups by color or by number of holes or by the material from which the button was made. It wasn't long before Dan began making his own groups to "trick" Sara.

Guided exploration of the buttons by Sara is what Piaget called the *méthode clinique*, and it helps Dan to learn to classify—to place objects into consistent, logical groups. Classification is one of the important structures developed during the years between ages four and seven. Piaget said that the ability to classify, like other types of learning, is gained through many opportunities to handle and manipulate objects in the environment. Active, curious children develop classification skills and other logical thinking skills gradually through their play. By interacting sensitively with Dan and asking him thought-provoking questions, Sara has facilitated his understanding of the process of classification.

---

become increasingly complex. In the two examples just presented, the structures are incomplete, reflecting the developmental level of the children involved. Children develop mental knowledge in this way. For example, children acquire the concept of numbers by first assimilating all numbers as though they have equal value, then gradually recognizing that numbers have an additive property that gives each number a value as a cardinal number, and finally accommodating their thinking to make counting possible. Basically, then, assimilation refers to the attempt to make new information fit into previous structures; accommodation occurs when mental processing must change to include novel information, thus expanding mental organization.

Piaget's theory can help explain the behavior of four-year-old Greg described at the beginning of this chapter. He believed that his sister had more fruit because the shape of her bowl made it look like there was more. Piaget claimed that this tendency to rely on perceptual observation, rather than intellectual analysis, is typical of the preoperational child.

Piaget said that children do not learn if they are intellectually satisfied at all times. The biological concept of homeostasis refers to the ability of animals to change when the environment requires it. This is what Piaget referred to as equilibration, the internal mental process of establishing equilibrium or balance in thinking. Young children can be quite happy (or at equilibrium) with some unique interpretations of experiences because they simply assimilate them into their existing structures. To adults, these interpretations may seem incorrect, but young children see no need to accommodate or change their thinking processes. (An example of this process is given in Developmental Issues in Practice 1.2.) As children grow older and have more experiences, however, they sense that something is not quite correct in their interpretations and feel the need for a new equilibrium reached through the assimilation-accommodation process. They gradually accommodate to new information by changing their structures through the mental process of equilibration. In this way, children learn by correcting their own thinking. The sense of disequilibrium or dissatisfaction with current explanations of events leads to mental growth, according to Piaget's theory. (Further examples of structural development are discussed in Chapters 7, 10, and 13.)

Psychoanalytic Theory

Sigmund Freud (1856–1939) developed the **psychoanalytic theory** of human development, which has made a major contribution to our understanding of human psychological functioning. Some of the principles he developed include the following:

1. Unconscious processes control human behavior.
2. Events that occur in infancy and early childhood can have a profound impact on the way a person functions as an adult.
3. Human beings develop in universal, predictable stages, which determine how they will function at each point in their life.
4. Human beings seek an equilibrium between inner needs and environmental demands.

Freud also postulated that personality is made up of three components: the id (that which seeks pleasure), the superego (the conscience) and the ego (the rational aspect). A healthy adult is able to maintain a balance among these three parts, with the ego controlling the whole system.

Freud organized his developmental principles into **psychosexual stages**. However, he put too much emphasis on the sexual aspects of the human being, which have not been supported by subsequent research. Erik Erikson, the major contemporary proponent of psychoanalytic theory, made use of the basic principles of Freud's theory but dropped the concept of psychosexual stages from his own theory.

Erikson was a student of Freud's daughter, Anna. After receiving his license to practice psychoanalysis, Erikson came to the United States, where he was affiliated with Harvard University and other institutions of higher learning. In addition to teaching and practicing child psychoanalysis, he investigated child rearing practices on Sioux and Yurok Indian reservations, and he studied World War II soldiers who suffered from what was then called shell shock. Erikson built on the theory of Sigmund Freud but modified it significantly by adding the component of social interaction. Erikson's version of psychoanalytic theory used **psychosocial** stages of development. Whereas Freud had built a theory around the biological development of the child, Erikson's theory considers the child within the family and the broader social context.

Erikson proposed that there are eight stages of psychosocial adjustment during the human life span, as shown in Table 1.2. The first four of these stages are helpful for understanding early childhood development. At each stage, a specific life crisis must be resolved in order for the child to move on to the next stage of development. If the social environment fails to provide the child with sufficient guidance to allow for a positive resolution of the stage, then the child emerges from the stage with psychological problems that make the next stage of crisis more difficult to resolve. The way the crisis is resolved at each level will determine the psychological outcome of the adult.

Erikson identified each stage by its contrasting outcomes:

❑ Trust versus mistrust
❑ Autonomy versus shame and doubt
❑ Initiative versus guilt
❑ Industry versus inferiority

Each pair of contrasting elements can be visualized as the two ends of a continuous line. According to Erikson, the desirable resolution of each stage falls toward the positive end of this imaginary line, with children ideally developing a sense of trust, autonomy, initiative, and industry.

In Erikson's theory, the stages are sequential. It is necessary for children to resolve one stage positively in order to be successful with the next. The sequential stages show the time of ascendancy of a certain pair of contrasting elements, but these same elements are also dealt with at all other stages in the life span. For instance, at ages four and five, initiative versus guilt is the most important psychosocial problem with which young children must deal.

Table 1.2. *Erikson's Stages of Psychosocial Development*

Age	Stage	Strength Developed
0–1 year	Trust versus mistrust	Hope
2–3 years	Autonomy versus shame and doubt	Willpower
4–5 years	Initiative versus guilt	Purpose
6–12 years	Industry versus inferiority	Competence
Adolescence	Identity versus role confusion	Fidelity
Young adulthood	Intimacy versus isolation	Love
Middle age	Generativity versus stagnation	Care
Old age	Ego integration versus despair	Wisdom

▲ DEVELOPMENTAL ISSUES IN PRACTICE   1.3

PSYCHOSOCIAL THEORY

ERIKSON: PRESERVING AUTONOMY

James found himself frequently at odds with his two-year-old daughter, Erika. She constantly said "no" when any request was made of her, even though she might like to do the thing being requested. She insisted on trying to dress herself, even though it was impossible for her to reach the buttons on the back of the dress. Any attempt to help was met with "Do it myself." She would throw a temper tantrum if anyone tried to force her to go to bed or pick up her toys. James decided to join a parenting class to see whether he could discover other ways of handling the challenges that Erika was presenting.

In the parenting class, James learned about Erik Erikson's theory. He learned that two-year-olds are well known for being "terrible" because they are at a stage in their lives when they acquire a strong sense of themselves as autonomous individuals and they need to express their autonomy in everything they do. James was relieved to find out that other parents had similar experiences with their two-year-olds and that he wasn't alone in being exasperated with this particular stage of development.

In the case of Erika's behavior, he learned to recognize it as a sign of emotional and cognitive growth, which is a positive sign that Erika is perfectly normal. He learned some skills to help Erika express her autonomy without creating chaos in the family. James learned to offer Erika more than one option, rather than just demanding one behavior from her. For example, when it was bedtime, he learned to say, "Would you rather brush your teeth first or put on your pajamas first?" When it was time to clean up the playroom, he would say, "Do you want to put the blocks away or the cars?"

This approach gives Erika choices and leads her to develop and practice autonomy, but it also assures her of learning what behaviors are expected in her family. Erikson emphasized that it is important for parents to find a "happy medium" between putting demands on the child and allowing the child to make the choices. Total permissiveness and total authority will both develop a sense of shame in children because they are not learning to be effective autonomous beings. By finding the happy medium, James will teach Erika what autonomous behaviors will be acceptable, and this will ensure her ability to leave the stage with a positive sense of success in making autonomous decisions.

But throughout the life span, children and adults have many additional encounters with initiative and guilt.

Erikson's theory has implications for how children are treated at home, in day care centers, at school, and in other settings. It helps adults understand the psychosocial needs of young children. For example, two-year-old Sammie, described at the beginning of the chapter, is in Erikson's stage of **autonomy versus shame and doubt.** His use of the word "no" is an attempt to assert his autonomy, as he comes to be aware of himself as a separate, independent person. Developmental Issues in Practice 1.3 gives an example of the use of this approach to manage the difficult behavior of a two-year-old.

Humanist Theory

The writings of the existential philosophers in the 1920s and 1930s introduced the **humanist** perspective as a way of looking at development. The existential philosophers believed that humans are creatures of choice—not passive with predetermined or programmed actions but active in making choices about how they will live.

Of the many prominent American humanists who have influenced early childhood development, Carl Rogers will be discussed here. Rogers (1902–1987) was a psychotherapist who had been trained as a psychoanalyst. In his practice of psychotherapy in the 1940s, he introduced a radical new approach based on the premise that humans are basically good and capable and have within themselves the potential to develop optimally. His own training in working with his clients led him to conclude that his counseling techniques could be of value to ordinary people who needed to communicate more effectively. For example, second grader Laura, described at the begin-

"I-messages" from adult to child communicate feelings about specific behaviors. In this case, the adult said, "I like the way you've made a design."

▲ **DEVELOPMENTAL ISSUES IN PRACTICE 1.4**

HUMANIST THEORY

GORDON: I-MESSAGES

Thomas Gordon teaches important principles of parent–child communication in his book *P.E.T.: Parent Effectiveness Training.* He encourages parents to focus their attention on the particular situation at hand, not on general personality characteristics of the child. Gordon would have parents banish from their verbal repertoire such comments as "You're such a slob" and "I've never seen such a messy child." It is natural for parents to become upset with some of their children's behavior, but although such comments can relieve anger they don't directly tell the child what the parent is feeling. Gordon suggests that parents instead use what he calls **I-messages,** which tell the child how parents feel about behavior.

For instance, the parent might say, "I feel upset when I see your brand new bedspread in a heap on the floor," or, "I get really angry when clean clothes are left out and not put away." According to Gordon, this type of communication allows children to view their parents as real people with their own valid needs and feelings because the statements are made within an atmosphere of mutual respect and understanding. Children are more motivated to change their behavior under such circumstances. Many parents have applied Gordon's humanist ideas with success.

ning of this chapter, found it difficult to communicate her fears to her parents. Her parents would have benefitted from knowing about "active listening" and "I-messages." To practice active listening with children, caregivers are encouraged to look for the feelings the children are expressing, not just the words being spoken. In addition, the active listener verifies the meaning of statements by asking for clarification and feedback. (Developmental Issues in Practice 1.4 gives an example of the use of I-messages.)

Rogers proposed no theory of development as such, but he was very influential in affecting the lives of children by encouraging an environment of empathy and understanding in which they can develop optimally. Followers of Rogers have included Haim Ginott, author of *Between Parent and Child* (1965); Don Dinkmeyer and Gary D. McKay, authors of *Systematic Training for Effective Parenting (STEP)* (1976); and Thomas Gordon, author of *P.E.T.: Parent Effectiveness Training* (1975).

Abraham Maslow, another important proponent of humanist theory, developed a hierarchy of human needs (1968, 1970). According to Maslow, humans have certain needs, called **deprivation needs,** that must be met before humans are free to develop their most creative characteristics (see Figure 1.1). The deprivation needs include physiological needs (basic needs for maintenance of the body); safety needs (shelter, protection from danger); belongingness needs (love, affection); and esteem needs (self-esteem and

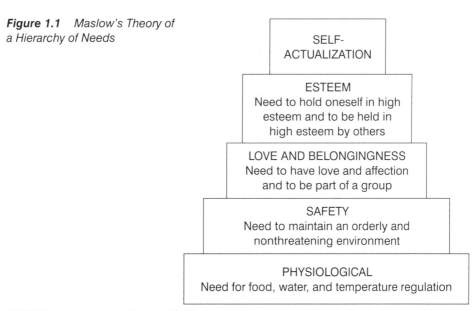

Figure 1.1 *Maslow's Theory of a Hierarchy of Needs*

SOURCE: Adapted from Abraham H. Maslow, *Motivation and Personality* (2nd ed.). Copyright 1954 by Harper & Row, Publishers, Inc. Copyright ©1970 by Abraham H. Maslow.

esteem from others). Only after deprivation needs have been satisfied can people be motivated by **being needs,** or the pursuit of values such as truth, honesty, beauty, and goodness. At the highest level of Maslow's hierarchy, people can test themselves, expand their horizons, and become **self-actualized.** Self-actualization involves reaching the highest possible level of functioning so that the individual's skills and abilities are brought to full potential. The assumption is that every person has a completely individual set of abilities. The goal of development should be to build one's abilities fully, rather than to be measured against the performance of others. When a person is self-actualized, he or she naturally assumes the position of being a truly creative, productive member of society. Maslow's major contribution to early childhood development was his contention that children will choose to do things that promote their own growth if their deprivation needs are met.

The humanists have made a significant contribution to the study of early childhood development. They have reacted strongly against the behaviorist position that humans are passively shaped by the environment. They have emphasized that much of behavior is determined by active choices.

Maturationist Theory

Maturationists emphasize the role of genetically determined growth patterns and deemphasize the role of environmental stimulation in early childhood development. They base their beliefs on the work of two Englishmen, Charles Darwin and Karl Pearson (1857–1936), who studied intellectual capacity and physical growth patterns. These men concluded that parents pass on their own traits. For example, parents who are bright in intellect and tall generally have children who are bright in intellect and tall, and parents who are dull in intellect and average in height tend to have children who are dull in intellect and average in height. G. Stanley Hall elaborated on the early studies and taught his students that development is determined primarily through a hereditary process of maturation. One of Hall's students, Arnold Gesell (1880–1961), and Gesell's colleagues at the Yale University School of Medicine have subsequently been leaders in articulating the maturationist approach to development.

To show the importance of maturation in development of specific skills, Gesell organized some experiments with twins. In one of these experiments, one of each pair of twins was given extensive practice in walking before the children would have been "ready" to walk, according to the norms established at Yale. The other of each pair of twins received no practice or training in walking. Gesell demonstrated in this experiment that, when the twins with no practice were "ready" to walk, they quickly equaled the skill in walking of the twins who had practiced. Gesell cited this experiment and similar ones as evidence of the importance of maturation in development.

Gesell and his associates determined the ages at which different physical, mental, and behavioral functions mature in children. They recorded detailed information about height and weight; age of teething, crawling, walking, and grasping objects; rate of vocabulary growth; and patterns of social interaction. The norms or average ages of attainment observed by Gesell were widely accepted beginning in the 1920s, 1930s, and 1940s (Gesell & Ilg, 1949), and Gesell became an influential leader in the area of early childhood development. The data that he gathered have been updated and are still used today. (Gesell's data are most appropriate, however, when applied to white, middle-class children, the group Gesell studied, and are not necessarily appropriate for application to children with other ethnic and cultural backgrounds.)

In the course of his research, Gesell enumerated some general principles of growth that remain important today. One of these is the **cephalo-caudal** principle, which states that growth proceeds generally from the head (*cephalo*) down toward the tail (*caudal*) area. Another is the **proximo-distal** principle, which states that the brain, nerves, and organs (located close, or *proximal*, to the body) develop earlier than the hands, feet, and other extremities (located at a distance, or *distal*, from the body).

The continuing influence of maturationists such as Gesell can be observed in strict age guidelines for school entrance and in casual remarks that characterize children by age: "terrible twos," "trusting threes," "frustrating fours," and "fascinating fives." Although research conducted in connection with other theories has shown that environmental factors are more

---

▲ DEVELOPMENTAL ISSUES IN PRACTICE 1.5

MATURATIONIST THEORY

GESELL: POTTY TRAINING

Paul wants his son, Bob, to be successful in potty training, and one of Paul's considerations is Bob's level of maturation. Paul has decided not to introduce the idea of using the potty to Bob until Bob shows several of the following signs of readiness:

- ❑ Stays dry for several hours
- ❑ Shows an awareness that he is about to urinate
- ❑ Understands simple instructions and directions

By taking Bob's maturation into account before expecting him to urinate on the potty, Paul is helping his son to be successful.

---

important than Gesell believed, maturation must be considered in the study of early childhood development. (Developmental Issues in Practice 1.5 shows how an understanding of maturation helps make potty training easier to accomplish.)

Behavioral Theory

Proponents of **behavioral theory** are not inclined to hypothesize about mental processes such as structural development, assimilation, and accommodation. Instead, they focus on the behaviors displayed by children when they are learning and afterward. Another major difference between behavioral theorists and cognitive theorists such as Jean Piaget is the concept of stages of development. Behavioral theorists view development as **continuous,** with no division into stages, whereas, as we mentioned earlier, cognitive theorists see it as **discontinuous**. To behaviorists, development occurs as children learn, and learning is a gradual, cumulative process. Learning is believed to lead to changes in observable behavior when the appropriate skills are learned.

The study of behavior has evolved over the years, and now there are three distinct types of behavioral theories: classical conditioning, operant conditioning, and social learning. Each of these behavioral theories is described separately.

Classical Conditioning.　Ivan Pavlov (1849–1936), a Nobel Prize–winning Russian physiologist, discovered a process of learning called **classical conditioning**. Pavlov noted that when food is given to dogs, the dogs give an unlearned response, salivation, which he called an unconditioned stimulus–response pair because it did not have to be learned (or conditioned).

In a series of experiments, Pavlov found that if he consistently rang a bell at the same time that he placed meat powder on dogs' tongues, eventually an association would be formed so that the bell alone would cause the dogs to salivate as if they were going to eat. Pavlov called the ringing of the bell a **conditioned stimulus** and the response of salivation in the absence of food a **conditioned response**. He had succeeded in conditioning the dogs to salivate on the cue provided by the bell. This reaction must be learned because it is not a natural response. (An example of this process in humans is given in Developmental Issues in Practice 1.6.)

In this country, Pavlov's theory of classical conditioning was popularized by the American psychologist J. B. Watson (1878–1958). Watson believed that psychology would not assume status as a science unless it dealt with strictly observable behaviors. He applied Pavlov's theory to children, with his most famous subject being an eleven-month-old named Albert.

Albert initially liked to play with white rats and would reach out if one were presented to him. Then Watson and his associates began striking a steel bar behind Albert just as the rat was presented. Albert, like most young children, responded to loud noises with fear behaviors such as crying (this is the unconditioned stimulus–response pair). After a few experiences with hearing the noise as he reached for the rat, Albert developed a fear of rats, even when no noise accompanied the presentation of a rat. Watson had conditioned the fear of rats in a child who previously had liked them. In fact, Albert's fear **generalized** to (or extended to include) other white furry animals, such as rabbits, and even to men with white beards.

Because this fear behavior could have been detrimental to Albert, it was important for Watson to try to **extinguish** (or remove) it. For example, extinguishing Albert's conditioned response could have involved repeated presentations of the rat without striking the steel bar. Gradually, the response of fear would have disappeared. It may also have been necessary to **desensitize** Albert from his fear reactions to furry white objects. Desensitizing is done by slowly reintroducing the feared object in circumstances not likely to elicit the full-blown fear response. For example, pictures of white rats could have been presented. If this was done under nonthreatening circumstances with pairing of positive experiences, such as cuddling, touching, and smiling on the part of the adult, it would have lessened Albert's fear sufficiently so that a white furry object other than a rat could be introduced. Slowly, Albert would be desensitized to having feelings of fear around the white furry objects because the fear would have been replaced by feelings of support. Finally, the white rats could have been introduced, and the desensitization would be complete.

Based on experiments like the one involving Albert, Watson asserted that children's behavior is totally determined by the events in their lives. In an article on child rearing, he declared:

> Give me a dozen healthy infants, well-formed and my own specified world to
> bring them up in and I'll guarantee to take any one of them at random and train
> him to become any type of specialist I might select—a doctor, lawyer, artist,

▲ **DEVELOPMENTAL ISSUES IN PRACTICE   1.6**

CLASSICAL CONDITIONING

PAVLOV: INFANT BOTTLE FEEDING

During childbirth classes, Mary and Joe Sherwin learned to apply the principles of classical conditioning to the care of their newborn baby. They learned that there are many natural unconditioned stimulus–response pairs. The most important ones are related to early reflexes. For example, when a baby is hungry, if you stroke the cheek the baby will engage in a rooting reflex, which involves turning toward the stimulation and trying to suck. If the baby is always given the breast, a conditioned response will be established where the smell and feeling of the breast will be associated with food.

  If this association is well established, the baby will expect to have the breast whenever there is a feeling of hunger. If Mary and Joe decide to go out to the movies and leave the baby with a sitter and a bottle of formula, they may be surprised to come home and find the baby crying for hunger but unwilling to take the bottle, because the nipple of the bottle was never associated with feeding. The baby is conditioned so that the feeling of hunger must always be associated with mother's breast. When a new nipple is introduced, the baby rejects it.

  Mary and Joe are told that this association can make it difficult for them to leave the baby when they need a well-deserved rest from child care. They are taught that they should introduce a bottle of formula to the baby occasionally, along with breast-feeding. They talked it over and decided that Joe would feed the baby a bottle at the nighttime feeding so that Mary could get some much needed sleep. It also gave Joe an opportunity to spend some special time alone with the baby.

merchant, chief, and yes, even into a beggarman and thief regardless of his talents, penchants, tendencies, abilities, vocations and race of his ancestors. (Watson, 1928, p. 104.)

According to Watson and other believers in classical conditioning, heredity plays an insignificant part in development, and experience is all important.

  Watson's recommendations about the environment on children resulted in some suggestions that were not of benefit to the child. Watson was particularly concerned about the potential for "spoiling" the child. He recommended against excessive handling and suggested that parents leave a crying baby to "cry it out." Recent studies, as discussed in Chapter 6, find that such practices have the potential for detrimental effects on the infant.

Operant Conditioning.   B. F. Skinner, an American psychologist at Harvard University, shared many of Watson's views about the importance of the environment. However, Skinner thought that classical conditioning alone was not adequate to explain how children learn, and he formulated a model of

The major premise of operant conditioning is that the consequences of children's behavior, such as receiving an award, determine whether the behavior will reoccur.

another type of conditioning: **operant conditioning.** It was Skinner's belief, and the major premise of operant conditioning, that the consequences of children's behavior, in the form of reward or punishment, determine whether a behavior will reoccur. In such conditioning, then, a child is put into a situation in which a desired response is likely to occur. When it does, the child is immediately **reinforced** or rewarded. For example, a young girl who often shouts inappropriately indoors might receive verbal praise each time she uses her "inside voice." If the verbal praise is rewarding to her, she will increase the use of her inside voice. If no consequence is paired with shouting, that behavior will disappear—that is, it will be extinguished. Because attention is one of the most powerful reinforcers, the withholding of attention to unwanted behaviors is an excellent way to lessen the chances that they will reoccur.

Six-month-old Susan, described at the beginning of the chapter, is waking up at night because she is being reinforced when her parents give her attention for doing so. If her parents wish to extinguish the behavior, they must avoid giving her attention when she cries at night.

Skinner (1974) and other proponents of operant conditioning make a strong distinction between reinforcement and punishment. They use **reinforcement** to increase the chances that desirable behavior will be repeated. **Punishment** involves introducing an aversive event following behavior, which discourages the reoccurrence of the behavior. Punishment can be anything

▲ DEVELOPMENTAL ISSUES IN PRACTICE   1.7

OPERANT CONDITIONING

SKINNER: BEHAVIOR MODIFICATION

Tia Garcia applied a type of operant conditioning, behavior modification, to teach her young son to react positively when placed in his car seat. Behavior modification is a way of using operant conditioning to change behavior. The steps in applying behavior modification are as follows:

1. Decide exactly what behavior you want a child to acquire.
2. Decide what reinforcers (rewards) will be meaningful to that child.
3. Shape the behavior; that is, divide progress toward the desired behavior into small steps that the child can successfully master, and then reinforce achievement of each step.
4. Continue to reinforce success occasionally even after the behavior has been changed as planned.

At the time that Tia began her program of behavior modification, her one-year-old, Georgio, had not had much experience with riding in his car seat. Tia attended a workshop that convinced her that his safety required use of the car seat, but each time she tried to place him in it, Georgio cried, kicked his legs, and thrashed his arms. Tia realized that it was too much to expect that Georgio would suddenly become a model passenger when in his car seat. She decided that it would be necessary to shape his behavior. She knew that he responded well to praise and that he liked frozen yogurt and fruit juice.

Tia made a plan for Georgio that included taking him to the car frequently to put him in his car seat. Before he had a chance to object, she praised him warmly for sitting quietly in his seat and gave him a spoonful of frozen yogurt or a sip of fruit juice. When Georgio attained success at sitting pleasantly in his car seat for a brief period, Tia gradually expanded the amount of time he would have to sit there for him to be reinforced. Eventually, Georgio learned to be an uncomplaining passenger in his car seat on short and then longer car trips. Tia could now feel more assured of his safety, thanks to behavior modification, an application of operant conditioning.

that is painful or unpleasant. Behavior can be changed using both reinforcement and punishment. However, behaviorists suggest avoiding the use of punishment because it only suppresses undesirable behaviors temporarily and does not change patterns of behavior.

One reason that punishment has been found to be ineffective is that it does not teach children what behavior is expected. Children may have some idea of what the adult does not want, and they often have negative feelings about the entire incident, but they do not necessarily know what the correct behavior should have been. Many behaviorists believe that, rather than punishing children, parents and other caregivers should help children demonstrate correct behavior and then reinforce the correct behavior.

Another reason that punishment is ineffective is that it is more difficult to control behaviors when punishment is used. For punishment to work, a negative response must be given on a **continuous schedule**—that is, every time the behavior is emitted. It is difficult for adults to be present every time the unwanted behavior occurs. Positive reinforcement can maintain behaviors on an **intermittent schedule**—that is, with occasional reinforcement. Adults find it much easier, and much more pleasant, to maintain positive behaviors with occasional praise and attention than to suppress negative behaviors by punishing the child every time the behavior occurs.

The theory of operant conditioning has provided specialists in early childhood development with a wealth of information about how children learn. It has also provided ways to analyze and change particular behaviors. Even though operant conditioning does not address children's internal mental functioning, it does make important contributions to knowledge about children's behavior. Developmental Issues in Practice 1.7 shows how behavior modification can be used, for example, to encourage safe behavior in a child.

At group time, the teacher uses social learning theory by encouraging imitation of the behaviors of the children pointed out by the teacher.

▲ **DEVELOPMENTAL ISSUES IN PRACTICE   1.8**

SOCIAL LEARNING THEORY

BANDURA: MODELING

Jeff Reynolds, a preschool teacher, applies social learning theory every day at group time. When one of the four-year-olds in his group speaks out of turn, bothers another child, or restlessly moves around, he calls attention to someone in the group who is behaving appropriately. His verbalizations in these situations point out positive behaviors and include comments like "I like the way Timmy is raising his hand," "Good, Lisa is keeping her hands in her own lap," and "I'm glad that most of you are sitting in our circle." Mr. Reynolds finds that children respond to his comments by imitating others who function as the appropriate behavioral models. When he calls attention to the desired behavior, the children are shown what is acceptable. Consequently, they imitate the desired behavior so they will be favorably noticed. Mr. Reynolds feels that he is very effective in managing young children's behavior by applying the principle of vicarious reinforcement.

Social Learning.   Social learning theorists consider themselves in the tradition of the classical and operant conditioning theorists, but they believe that neither classical nor operant conditioning is adequate to account for the rapidity and complexity of children's learning. **Social learning theory** proposes instead that there are internal cognitive processes that influence reinforcement and determine which behavior children model, or imitate.

According to social learning theorists, children learn from observing and modeling the behavior of people who are powerful and significant in their lives, and this modeled behavior can be learned without direct reinforcement. Instead, indirect reinforcement, such as observing another person being praised or acquiring power, can affect behavior. This is called **vicarious reinforcement**. Albert Bandura and his associates at Stanford University have been in the forefront of articulating a theory of social learning that goes well beyond operant and classical conditioning by modifying the role of reinforcement.

In their early research, Bandura and his associates showed how children can learn aggressive behavior (Bandura, Ross, & Ross, 1963) (see Figure 1.2). Bandura had one group of children observe an adult playing with toys, becoming frustrated, and beginning to hit a large inflatable doll while exclaiming, "Hit it. Pow." Another group of children observed an adult whose frustration was not followed by aggressive behavior. Bandura found that the children who observed the aggressive behavior demonstrated significantly more aggressive behavior in play than did the children who had not observed the aggression. This experiment and others that followed led Bandura and other social learning theorists to the conclusion that children can learn without reinforcement—they can also be encouraged to model positive behaviors

Figure 1.2 *Children Modeling Adult Behaviors.*
Bandura's research demonstrated that children first observe and then imitate the behaviors of adults who hit a doll with a hammer and then kick the doll.

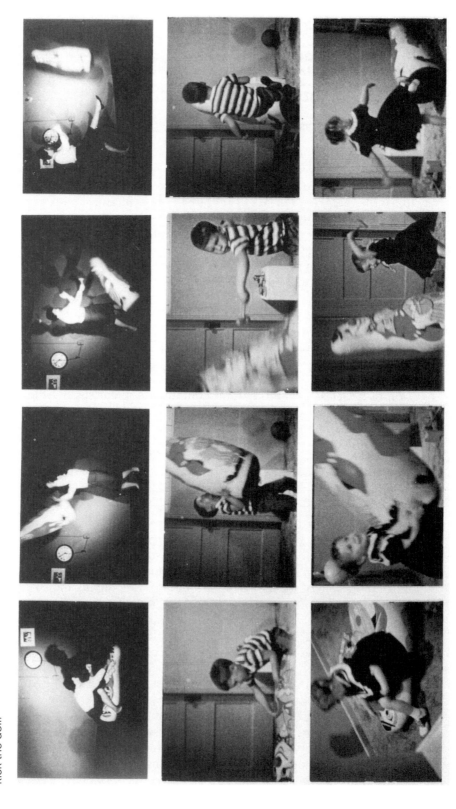

SOURCE: From A. Bandura, D. Ross, and S. A. Ross, Imitation of film-mediated aggressive models. *Journal of Abnormal and Social Psychology, 66,* 8 (1963). Reprinted with permission.

(as described in Developmental Issues in Practice 1.8). Social learning theory helps us understand aspects of children's behavior that cannot be explained in terms of conditioning.

This chapter has introduced the most basic theories used in developmental research today. In addition, it has demonstrated the importance of theory in guiding the decisions made by caregivers in responding to the needs and behaviors of children. Because each theory can be used to assist with different needs, this book takes an eclectic approach to presenting its discussions. In the following chapters, data will be presented from many researchers who rely on the basic underlying assumptions put forth by the early theorists described here.

SUMMARY

1. Early childhood development describes the changes in human beings from the prenatal period through eight years of age.
2. The study of early childhood development can help in rearing children and in preparing for the helping professions.
3. The scientific study of children has taken place within the past 200 years.
4. The views of John Locke and Jean Jacques Rousseau encouraged an awareness of the need for a time of childhood to occur before adult responsibilities were assumed.
5. Pioneers in the scientific study of children include Pestalozzi, Darwin, and Hall.
6. Theories are organized systems of hypotheses, based on observations, that explain or predict behavior.
7. The study of early childhood development is influenced by cognitive theory, psychoanalytic theory, humanist theory, maturationist theory, and behavioral theory. These theories of early childhood development can be viewed as complementary ways to understand how children change over time.
8. Jean Piaget has been the best-known proponent of cognitive learning theory. His theory explains development in terms of four stages: sensorimotor, preoperational, concrete operational, and formal operational thinking.
9. Erik Erikson, the major proponent of psychoanalytic theory, explains development in terms of eight ages, or stages, the first four of which take place in early childhood.
10. Humanists have emphasized the extent to which children's behavior is determined by active choices.
11. Maturationists, following in the footsteps of Gesell, emphasize the role of genetically determined growth patterns in shaping development.
12. Behavioral learning theory includes the theories of classical conditioning, operant conditioning, and social learning.
13. In classical conditioning, Pavlov and others succeeded in linking a conditioned stimulus, such as ringing a bell, with a conditioned response, such as salivation.
14. In operant conditioning, Skinner and others put children in situations in which a desired response was likely to occur and then rewarded that response.
15. In social learning theory, Bandura and his associates showed how much children learn from observing and imitating, without the necessity of a reward.

ACTIVITIES TO ENHANCE LEARNING

The discussion of nature versus nurture in Developmental Issues in Practice 1.1 describes the differences of opinion among professionals about this issue. Think of these two issues as falling on each end of a continuum. Take each one of the theories and mentally place the theorist on the continuum. Which factor, genetics or environment, is more important in explaining the development of the child according to each theory? Write a short paragraph on the position each theorist probably has on the importance of genetics versus the environment. Answer the following questions:

1. According to each theorist, what is the most important causative factor explaining the development of the child?
2. Are children affected primarily by events outside themselves, or do they have an inherent capacity to develop?
3. Does each theorist subscribe to the principle of readiness?
4. What kind of intervention program would each theorist develop?

FOR FURTHER READING

Cognitive Theory

Ginsburg, H., & Opper, S. (1988). *Piaget's theory of intellectual development* (3rd ed.). Englewood Cliffs, NJ: Prentice Hall.

Piaget, J., & Inhelder, B. (1969). *The psychology of the child.* New York: Basic Books.

Psychoanalytic Theory

Erikson, E. H. (1963). *Childhood and society* (2nd ed.). New York: W. W. Norton.

Erikson, E. H. (1982). *The life cycle completed.* New York: W. W. Norton.

Humanist Theory

Maslow, A. H. (1970). *Motivation and personality* (2nd ed.). New York: Harper & Row.

Dreikurs, R., & Soltz, V. (1964). *Children: The challenge.* New York: Hawthorn Books.

Maturationist Theory

Ames, L. B., Gillespie, C., Haines, J., & Ilg, F. L. (1979). *The Gesell Institute's child from one to six.* New York: Harper & Row.

Behavioral Theory

Bandura, A. (1977). *Social learning theory.* Englewood Cliffs, NJ: Prentice Hall.

Bijou, S. W., & Baer, D. M. (1961). *Child development* (Vol. 1). New York: Appleton-Century-Crofts.

Skinner, B. F. (1974). *About behaviorism.* New York: Knopf.

CHAPTER 2

Strategies for Assessing Child Development

▼ KEY IDEAS

Observational Methods
- ❏ Observing Behaviors as They Occur
- ❏ Observing Predefined Behaviors
- ❏ Case Studies

Standardized Measures
- ❏ Developmental Assessments
- ❏ Screening Test
- ❏ Skill Assessments
- ❏ The Ethics of Scientific Research

Assessment for Decision Making: Delays and Disabilities

Two very different observations were conducted simultaneously by Jeff and Tom, students of early childhood development:

Jeff: The boy was really angry at being removed from the storytime. The teacher had to send him to another room.

Tom: Carlos, age six, raised his hand when the teacher asked what might happen next in the story. He stood up and said loudly, "I know, I know!" The teacher called on Sarah, saying, "I like the way Sarah waited to be called on before speaking." Carlos jumped again to a standing position, shouted, "I raised my hand, too!" and continued talking so that Sarah's words could not be heard. The teacher asked Carlos to either sit down quietly or leave the group. Carlos chose to leave the group with another teacher but returned silently within two minutes.

Jeff and Tom were both in the same room at the same time, but they did not "see" the same things in the classroom scene that they watched. Jeff, the first of the observers, is a beginner in the scientific study of young children. He generalized about the events that he watched and left out many details that would help us to understand Carlos's reactions. Tom, on the other hand, has received some instruction in observing children and included considerably more information about what was happening. These two observations illustrate the importance of knowledge, skill, and practice in maximizing what is learned during time spent with young children. Jeff and Tom were making narrative observations, one of the strategies for observing the behavior of young children as it occurs, which is discussed below.

Observation is at the very core of most scientific endeavors. Biologists, physicists, chemists, astronomers, and other natural scientists observe and record phenomena, form hypotheses, and then devise experiments to test these hypotheses. The same methods are used in the study of early childhood development. By learning systematic strategies of observation, students become better able to understand children's behavior; gain insight into their psychosocial, physical, and cognitive development; and then generate hypotheses or ideas, answer specific questions, and plan appropriate activities.

In Chapter 1 it was pointed out that observation in natural settings provided the foundation for the early scientific study of young children. However, this strategy fell out of favor with researchers during most of the 20th century, and they came to use experimental methods that brought children into laboratories. This allowed the researchers to control as many variables as possible and to isolate causes and effects of behavior.

Much has been learned from experimental methods, but specialists in early childhood development have also rediscovered observation as a method of child study. And so, during the last part of this century, researchers find themselves at an intermediate point, using both observational methods and experimental strategies to study child development. There are several reasons for the resurgence of interest in the observation of children in natural settings. First, it has become clear that good observations of children have been the basis for very important research. For example, Piaget's (1963) observations provided the basis for later research on cognitive processes. Brown's (1973) research on the in-depth language development of three children was the beginning of an extremely fruitful research program that has changed our entire view of the language ability of children.

Second, the focus of early childhood development has shifted to the study of younger and younger children. Experimental methods that depended on the cooperation of children in laboratories have been found to be inappropriate to the study of newborns, infants, and toddlers. For example, young infants have a smaller behavioral repertoire for research, are more prone to interfering behaviors (such as crying and sleeping), and they have very short attention spans for research procedures.

Third, and most important, a movement in the field of early childhood development has been calling for ecological studies. Bronfenbrenner (1979) and others have pointed out that many experimental studies are so controlled and specific that they cannot adequately lead us to generalizations about the real environments in which children live. These researchers have noted that assessment is authentic only when it is done in a naturalistic setting. Children should be studied in their natural contexts: the immediate family environment, intermediate environments that impinge on them, and the larger social and cultural structure.

The observation strategies described in this chapter have a value beyond doing research. Observations can help us answer many questions about the behavior and development of young children. The applications contain some examples of the range of situations in which these strategies are appropriate. Further examples are found in the sections called "Activities to Enhance Learning" at the ends of the chapters of this book. These sections give guidance in applying each observation strategy to answer questions about young children of a particular age range. Making observations extends one's learning beyond the printed page into memorable life situations, facilitates an understanding of early childhood development, and provides a basis for becoming a confident and competent parent or helping professional.

Wood-Shuman and Cone (1986) found that mothers who had abused their children were significantly more likely to overestimate the developmental abilities of children. For example, these mothers were more likely to believe that a two-year-old could sit quietly through a meal without standing up, moving around, and spilling food. It appears that these abusive mothers had very high expectations for their children. It is possible that when the children failed to meet these expectations, the mothers became unreasonably angry and abused the children. Such mothers might benefit from learning to observe accurately the appropriate behaviors of children.

This chapter first presents strategies for observing the behavior of young children. This section is followed by discussions of strategies involving standardized measures and assessment for the purpose of decision making.

OBSERVATIONAL METHODS

Table 2.1 lists the eight strategies for observing young children that are described in this section of the chapter. The premise of this chapter is that all students of early childhood development can and should become scientific in their observation techniques. Learning how to observe young children while studying early childhood development enables the student to integrate theory

Table 2.1. *Strategies for Observing Young Children*

Type of Strategy	Strategy	Use
Observing behaviors as they occur	Narrative observation	Record continuously for a period of time. Show running account of all that happens.
	Vignettes	Record from time to time. Select incidents or behaviors that seem significant.
	Child diaries	Record regularly, perhaps daily. Note developmental changes.
Observing predefined behaviors	Checklists	Record regularly or from time to time (depending on objectives). Check presence or absence of behaviors.
	Interviews	Record responses to selected questions. Explore the reasons for responses.
	Time sampling	Record behavior taking place in short, uniform time intervals. Examine frequency and duration of behaviors that occur often.
	Event sampling	Record behaviors of a specified type. Gather information about behaviors that occur infrequently.
Summarizing observations	Case studies	Summarize development of a particular child. Provide a basis for conclusions and recommendations.

SOURCE: Adapted from D. M. Irwin and M. M. Bushnell, *Observational Strategies for Child Study.* New York: Holt, Rinehart & Winston, 1980. Copyright 1980 by Holt, Rinehart & Winston. Adapted with permission.

and practice. It also prepares future professionals to acquire the skills for accurate assessment of children. Accurate observations enable professionals to help children maximize their development.

It is important for professionals to learn to make continual observations of children in casual situations during the ordinary activities of the child care program. For instance, a child may insist on retaliating against a playmate for accidentally knocking down a block tower, even when it is obvious that the playmate had no intention of causing the damage. The teacher makes a mental note that this particular child is still egocentric with respect to social interactions. In the future the teacher can put special emphasis on such issues when working with this particular child.

Often, professionals working with children are called upon to provide input to assist parents with certain needs of the child. Effective, accurate observations are very important to the work of professionals concerned with children.

Observing Behaviors as They Occur

Observing the ongoing behaviors of young children is more challenging than may at first seem to be the case. Most beginners need considerable help in learning to give objective, descriptive accounts rather than their own judgments, inferences, and conclusions about what they have seen. The following examples illustrate effective and ineffective descriptive accounts of observations:

Effective: Beth leaned forward in her seat and fixed her eyes on the experiment. She remained nearly immobile in that position for the full five minutes of the teacher's explanation.

Ineffective: Beth seemed very attentive.

In the effective description, Beth's behavior is described in enough detail to make it possible to visualize her in the classroom environment. However, in the ineffective description, an inference is drawn but no substantiating data are offered. Inferences can be incorrect, and later, given only the observer's inference, it would not be possible to reconstruct what Beth did that led the observer to think that she was attentive.

This section provides guidelines for being descriptive, objective, and scientific in using narrative observations, vignettes, and child diaries. These strategies for observing young children enhance understanding of children and their natural environments.

Narrative Observations.   Narrative observation is an effective strategy for studying young children. The observations made by Jeff and Tom at the beginning of the chapter are examples of this method. They give an on-the-spot record of behavior at the time it occurs, including as much detail as possible. Narrative observation can be planned to take place at certain times of each

Narrative observation records a child's behavior as it occurs.

day or week and can provide a rich source of information. These observations consist of full descriptions of ongoing behavior and can include baby book entries, stories of particular key events in the life of the child, and descriptions of sample behaviors. These are the most meaningful to parents.

A series of narrative observations of a specific child can provide important information about that child's development. Parents, helping professionals, and others can draw conclusions from narrative observations to understand the course of an individual child's development. Learning to make accurate narrative observations is an excellent first step in studying young children.

Suppose that the director of a child care program wants to provide input to the parents of the children about the developmental changes occurring during the time the children are cared for at the center. A set of narrative observations taken at regular intervals during the year is an excellent method for passing on the information to nonprofessionals. This type of observation is rich in detail and provides entertaining reading. The untrained person can easily understand and follow important changes by reading narrative descriptions. They contain description only, with no judgmental comments that might be offensive to the parents. For this reason, they should be stated without personal references from the observer and should be written in the third-person format. Narratives can be shown to parents at any time during the year when they ask for meetings with the caregiver.

To conduct a narrative observation, an observer needs some time without direct responsibility for involvement with the child to be studied. Equipment can be modest or more complex: a notepad and a writing instrument is sufficient; however, a tape recorder can be used to record quietly dictated observations, and a video camera can capture selected activity. Children will be interested in what an observer is doing, and responses to their questions can be honest and simple, such as, "I'm writing down some things that I'm learning," or, "I'm doing some work for my teacher." These vague responses seem to satisfy young children and yet allow them to remain uninhibited by the knowledge that an observer is intently watching what they are doing.

The basic task in narrative observation is to record everything that happens during a certain time period in a certain setting. The setting should be described, and some details should be given of the activity that is taking place. Then the observer records all activities and the child's reactions to changes in routines, use of materials, and social interactions. The observer also records the passage of time; usually, noting one-minute intervals allows generalizations to be made later about the amount of time a child spent in various kinds of activities.

The language used in narrative observations should be as colorful as the child who is being observed. If that child moves across the room, observers select verbs and adverbs that show how the child moved: readily or reluctantly, quickly or slowly, purposefully or absentmindedly. Because of their choice of words, good narrative observers can make children seem to "come alive" on the written page.

It is important to know, however, that colorful language is very different from judgmental language. In narrative observations, the observer tries to avoid making judgments about how the child is feeling or what the child is thinking. Instead of saying, "She seemed unhappy," the narrative observer describes the child's actual behaviors: "Her eyes turned downward, she stopped talking in midsentence, and a tear rolled out of the corner of her eye." A good rule of thumb is to label the behavior, not the child. Using descriptive language means that the reader of a narrative observation can recreate the event rather than having to trust that the observer's judgments or conclusions were accurate. Developmental Issues in Practice 2.1 is an example of a narrative observation. Note the detail used and the lack of judgmental statements.

Vignettes.   **Vignettes** of child activity are similar to but more limited than narrative observations. Vignettes are defined as accounts of particularly meaningful events in children's development; such events may show attainment of particular developmental milestones. Vignettes are the form of observation most often recorded by parents in, for example, a baby book. Professionals may find that a collection of vignettes is more meaningful to parents and can be used in working with families to maximize the development of children. Selecting material for vignettes can help in recognizing salient aspects of children's behavior. By recording vignettes, the details of that behavior can be preserved for later analysis.

▲ DEVELOPMENTAL ISSUES IN PRACTICE   2.1

NARRATIVE OBSERVATION

After coming home from daycare, three-year-old Paige and her mother were stretched out on the couch in cozy conversation.

Time	*Observation*
12:32	Paige said, "When I grow up, I'm going to be a daddy." Her mother responded, "Well, the way it usually works, little girls grow up to be women who are mommies and little boys grow up to be men who are daddies. Since you are a girl, you will grow up to be a mommy."
12:33	Paige sat very still and stared ahead intently. Her forehead became furrowed.
12:34	Finally, Paige said, "But I want to grow up to be a man." Her mother responded, "People don't usually decide that; you just start out being a little boy or a little girl and then you just grow up." Paige's eyes got very wide. She looked at her mother and said, with strong emphasis at the end of the sentence, "You mean, no matter how many times I play football and no matter how many jeans I wear, I'll still grow up to be a girl?" Her mother smiled and said, "Yes, doing those things won't change it."
12:35	Paige became quiet for a moment, staring ahead. Her mother asked, "Are you ready for a snack now?" Paige jumped off the couch and said, "I want some milk and cookies."

If the director of a child care center wants to emphasize particular aspects of a child's development, or if a parent has expressed an interest in a particular aspect of his or her child's development, a vignette would be most appropriate. Explaining a child's behavior through a vignette provides a specific example of the child's behavior.

The events that form the basis for vignettes are unpredictable in their pattern of occurrence and can be recorded by adults who are participants with the children. For instance, in the following example, the teachers who noted Alice's disorientation were engaged in their usual duties:

> It was Halloween and all the teachers wore costumes. Tina and I were greeting the children as they arrived in the morning. Tina was dressed as a clown with whiteface and wig. I was dressed as Little Bo Peep with a big bonnet. Three-year-old Alice came running through the door with a big smile on her face; she was carrying a brown bag that contained her costume. When she saw us, she stopped and her smile changed suddenly to a serious expression. She stared at each of us for a few seconds. I said, "Good morning, Alice." She continued to stare without answering. She slowly moved away to the coat storage and sat down on the edge of the storage unit. I said, "I'm Mrs. Brown, your teacher.

Don't you recognize me? This is Tina." Tina said, "Hi Alice. I can't wait to see your costume." Alice broke her silence with a sigh, saying, "Hi." I said, "Do you want to come in and play?" She smiled slightly and moved restlessly on her seat. She said, "Well, I think I'll just sit here for a while." I said, "That's fine. Just come in whenever you're ready." We then went into the playroom. After a few minutes, Alice stood up, smiled, and ran into the playroom.

Because vignettes are recorded only when events seem meaningful, adults can interact with children rather than having to sit apart from them with pens poised. This vignette can be used to show the egocentric nature of Alice's thinking and her behavior in dealing with confusing events.

After the techniques of recording narrative observations are mastered, the same skills can be applied to recording vignettes. As with narrative observations, vignettes must describe the setting, time, and activity; include exact words used in conversations; include details of interactions with other people; and involve descriptive, objective language. A collection of vignettes can

Child diaries, kept over the years by the parent of these children, reveal the continuities of development and the uniqueness of each child.

▲ DEVELOPMENTAL ISSUES IN PRACTICE 2.2

APPROPRIATE AND INAPPROPRIATE VIGNETTES

Example 1: Vignette Using Judgmental Language

Sally wouldn't give Marion a block, so Marion pushed Sally as hard as she could, shouting, "You dummy!" Sally was very surprised.

Example 2: Vignette Using Descriptive, Nonjudgmental Language

Marion, age three, and Sally, age five, were together in the block corner. The two girls took turns placing blocks on a tower until they had used all the blocks except one, located near Sally. Sally began balancing the last block in a vertical position at the top of the tower. Marion turned to Sally and said, "Me. Give it to me." Sally did not respond verbally but pointed to the vertical block, now at the top of the tower.

Marion stood up, pulled back her shoulders, and pushed Sally against the tower, saying, "You dummy!" in a loud voice. Sally's eyes widened and her mouth opened as she silently looked from Marion to the toppled tower.

Commentary on Vignettes 1 and 2

The first vignette gives the conclusions or judgments of the observer but few details about what happened before and after the pushing episode. Certain words are inappropriate in vignettes. For example, the word "so" implies a cause-and-effect relationship that may or may not be accurate; "as hard as she could" is a judgment about which the observer is unlikely to have evidence; and "very surprised" is a conclusion that would be better expressed in terms of behavior.

Example 2 avoids the inappropriate words just mentioned and gives much more information about Marion's and Sally's responses to frustrated desires. Such a vignette, used by the day care teacher, could provide the basis for an interesting discussion during a parent–teacher conference.

---

provide insights about children that cannot be obtained in any other way. Developmental Issues in Practice 2.2 lists examples of both effective and ineffective observations using vignettes.

Child Diaries.   A **child diary** gives accounts of the day-to-day changes and milestones attained by a young child. Developmental Issues in Practice 2.3 gives an example of a child diary. Entries are made regularly, perhaps even daily, by someone who interacts frequently with the child. Usually, child diaries are kept by parents or close relatives who are excited by the process of early childhood development. Keeping such a diary requires discipline and commitment, but those who have succeeded report that they have become more alert to nuances of behavior and more sensitive to the needs of young children.

▲ DEVELOPMENTAL ISSUES IN PRACTICE   2.3

CHILD'S DIARY ENTRY

Observation 33—Having learned to direct his glance (Obs. 32), Laurent explores his universe little by little. At 0;1 (9), for example, as soon as he is held vertically in the arms of his nurse, he examines successively the various images before him. First he sees me, then raises his eyes and looks at the walls of the room, then turns toward a dormer window, etc. At 0;1 (15) he systematically explores the hood of his bassinet which I shook slightly. He begins by the edge, then little by little looks backward at the lowest part of the roof, although this had been immobile for a while. Four days later he resumes this exploration in the opposite direction. He begins with the hood itself and then examines a piece of veiling which extends beyond the edge of the roof, a part of the coverlet (in the same position), my face which he finds before him and finally empty space. Subsequently he constantly resumes examining the cradle but, during the third month, he only looks at the toys hanging from the hood or at the hood itself when an unwonted movement excites his curiosity or when he discovers a particular new point (a pleat in the material, etc.).

Observation made by Jean Piaget of his son and reported in *The Origins of Intelligence in Children.* New York: W. W. Norton, 1963. Used with permission.

Child diaries provide detailed, permanent accounts of development. They preserve information about the timing and circumstances surrounding various events—such as the child's first shaky independent steps, the first sentences spoken by the child, and the child's first solo ride on a bicycle without training wheels. Child diaries portray a wide range of a child's development, show continuity and change from month to month and year to year, and depict the child in settings that are comfortable and familiar. The written word can be supplemented with audio and video recordings.

Child diaries are useful to parents in answering questions that arise later during their child's development. Diaries can serve as useful adjuncts to parents' memories, especially when the passage of time may have caused them, for example, to exaggerate the precociousness of a first child and worry about the development of a second or third child. On the other hand, if parents are concerned that a child is showing too much or too little of some behavior, they can refer to past diary entries to determine whether their perception is accurate and whether a pattern exists. Most exciting, child diaries reveal the uniqueness of each child. Diary entries not only give a record of the regularities of development, but they also highlight the individual preferences and desires of children.

Child diaries have been shown to have two main disadvantages. First, entries in child diaries, especially if made by proud parents, are subject to many types of bias and may be unreliable. Second, being in close contact with a child over a long period is an inefficient research strategy for the non-parent, who isn't normally in contact with the child; it is very time-consuming. Even so, in the past several decades, researchers in the area of early language development in young children have made important discoveries by keeping detailed diaries of the language development of their own children. In the 1920s and 1930s, Jean Piaget, by carefully recording observations of his own children, worked out a theory of development that could then be tested by observing other children in other settings. In Developmental Issues in Practice 2.3, notice how carefully Piaget described the details of the infant's visual behavior. These observations formed the basis for later experiments to verify the findings on larger groups of infants. It is now clear that child diaries, even with their disadvantages, hold potential as a strategy for the study of young children.

Observing Predefined Behaviors

A different type of strategy involves observing **predefined behaviors**. This approach adds more specificity and structure to observations and is therefore more efficient. Also, such a strategy is more appropriate for collecting research data. For example, the observer may be interested in the amount of aggression shown by children in an early childhood program. It is necessary to predefine this construct so that the observer knows exactly what behaviors to count as aggression. We can assume, for instance, that hitting, kicking and biting would be counted as aggressive behavior, but what about threats and name calling? Obviously, it would be helpful to know exactly what behaviors to include. A vague construct can be defined more precisely before the observation begins, thus eliminating subjective judgments on the part of the observer. This section presents four tools for observing predefined behaviors: checklists, interviews, time sampling, and event sampling.

Checklists.   A **checklist** is a list of behaviors that have been deemed important to note or observe. In the hands of skilled professionals, checklists provide an efficient means of ascertaining the presence or absence of certain behaviors. For instance, a parent or teacher might use a checklist to find out whether a preschooler can count to 10 and line up objects in one-to-one correspondence. In the hands of beginners in the study of early childhood development, checklists give insights into behaviors that are appropriate for children of certain ages. Without a checklist to provide structure, it is difficult for beginners to know what is typical and what is atypical.

Experienced parents and professionals can make their own checklists. First, they decide what they want to find out. Then they phrase their objectives in terms of behaviors that can be observed as either present or absent. Finally, they check off the behaviors. This approach is based on developmental theory, which recognizes that behaviors can be used to mark important stages of development. Consequently, we check off the accomplishment as soon as we see it, indicating that the child has progressed one more step in the sequential order of development.

An example of a checklist can be found in Developmental Issues in Practice 2.4. Such a checklist has many advantages. Using it is a more systematic way to establish the child's developmental level. The procedure is quick and efficient, giving a great deal of information in a short period of time. And, if desired, the accomplishments on the checklist can be dated to provide a permanent record of when each behavior was first recognized.

Beginners in the study of early childhood development will probably want to use some of the excellent checklists developed by professionals in the field. (For example, see Beaty [1994] and Nicolson and Shipstead [1994].) These checklists give beginners a sense of the wide range of normal development at a given age level.

Checklists serve important functions: they tell whether certain behaviors are present or absent, and they provide a permanent record of when the many "firsts" of early childhood were achieved. However, it is important to be aware that, for all their advantages, checklists do not describe how the behavior occurred, nor do they tell about frequency or duration of the behavior.

Interviews. **Interviews,** or one-to-one verbal interactions between adults and young children, begin to be appropriate when children learn to express themselves comfortably in response to questions. A great deal of information can be gained by directly asking young children about their ideas and beliefs.

Interviews may be planned in many ways. One approach is modeled after the **méthode clinique,** which was used by Piaget to learn about the thinking processes of young children. As he gained experience in working with young children, Piaget began to build his interviews around the use of concrete objects that would stimulate young children to think. He and the children manipulated the objects and discussed the children's responses to his questions.

In the méthode clinique, the interview has a predetermined structure, which is related to the manipulations being carried out with the objects that the interviewer introduces to the child. For instance, in trying to ascertain a young child's understanding of number concepts, the interviewer might move red and black checkers in and out of direct visual one-to-one correspondence, repeatedly asking whether there are more red checkers, more black checkers, or the same number of each color, and questioning the child about his or her responses, as demonstrated in Developmental Issues in Practice 2.5. Although the interview is structured, the interviewer has the flexibility to probe to find the reasons for the child's responses. The purpose of the méthode clinique is to find out as much as possible about children's thinking. It involves careful questioning of the child to draw out the maximum amount of information. In Developmental Issues in Practice 2.5, notice how the interviewer carefully asks questions that appear to make the child think about the best answers.

To gain the maximum amount of information from an interview, keep in mind several general considerations. First, rapport with the child should be

▲ DEVELOPMENTAL ISSUES IN PRACTICE   2.4

DEVELOPMENTAL CHECKLIST: INFANT SOCIALIZATION

Age Level	*Behavior*	*Date Achieved*
Newborn	Stops crying or quiets when picked up and held.	
1 mo.	Eyes follow moving object or person.	
	Quiets to face or voice.	
2 mo.	Regards persons alertly. Excites, smiles, moves arms and legs, vocalizes.	
	Smiles at others besides mother.	
	Responds differently to different people.	
3 mo.	Looks at face and eyes of person talking to him or her.	
	Crying decreases dramatically.	
4 mo.	Laughs aloud in social play; wails if play is interrupted.	
	Vocalizes, smiles, and reaches for familiar persons more than strangers.	
6 mo.	Expresses protest (resists adult who tries to take toy).	
	Discriminates between strangers and those who are familiar.	
7 mo.	Smiles, pats, vocalizes to mirror image.	
9 mo.	Responds to name with head turn, eye contact, and smile.	
10 mo.	Responds to a verbal request, usually in regard to games.	
11 mo.	Repeats performance laughed at. Begins to establish the meaning of no.	
12 mo.	Gives a toy to adult upon request.	

Adapted from M. E. Glover, J. L. Preminger, and A. R. Sanford, *The Early Learning Accomplishment Profile for Developmentally Young Children, Birth to 36 Months*, pp. 86–89. Winston-Salem, NC: Kaplan Press, 1978. Adapted with permission.

established before beginning the interview (e.g., by talking with the child about favorite television programs or about family and school activities). Second, the interview should be conducted in a quiet place where there are unlikely to be disturbances. Finally, all the child's responses should be accepted with interest, even if they seem incorrect from an adult perspective. Developmental Issues in Practice 2.5 shows this approach. The child should be assured that there are no right or wrong answers to the questions that will be asked; the purpose of the interview is to find out how children think and why they think the way they do. Explanations can be probed, if necessary, by saying that another child responded in the opposite way and

▲ DEVELOPMENTAL ISSUES IN PRACTICE   2.5

INTERVIEW USING THE MÉTHODE CLINIQUE

After learning about Jean Piaget's theory, Charles Balch was eager to find out about his five-year-old daughter's understanding of number concepts. To do so, he lined up eight red checkers and eight black checkers on the table. The checkers were placed in direct visual one-to-one correspondence, as shown here:

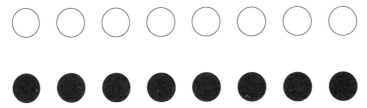

He began the interview by asking Allison, "Are there more checkers here [pointing to the red checkers] or more checkers here [pointing to the black checkers] or the same amount in both lines?" Allison looked carefully at the lines of checkers, counted them, and replied, "There are the same."

Charles said, "Now watch what I am going to do," and he moved the red checkers so that the distances between them were increased, as shown next:

Again he asked Allison, "Are there more here [pointing to the red checkers] or more here [pointing to the black checkers] or the same in both?" Allison looked at the two rows of checkers and answered, "There are more here [pointing to the red row]."

Charles asked, "Why do you think so, Allison?" Allison pointed and said, "You can see. It sticks out here." To an adult, this answer is obviously wrong, because no change was made in the number of checkers; only the placement on the table had changed. Parents are often surprised when a bright child makes such an obvious "mistake." However, this particular task clearly shows that Allison's concept of numbers is different from that of adults.

Charles did several other manipulations of the checkers and questioned Allison about each. In all cases, Allison's responses were based on how the checkers looked rather than on logical thinking about consistent characteristics of numbers. Before conducting this interview, Charles had believed that Allison understood numbers in the same way he did because she could count so well. Yet in the interview, he could see that counting did not help Allison to respond logically to the task: if the checkers were rearranged, one line of eight could seem to be more than the other line of eight. The interview helped Charles to understand his daughter's thinking process better and to have more appropriate expectations of her.

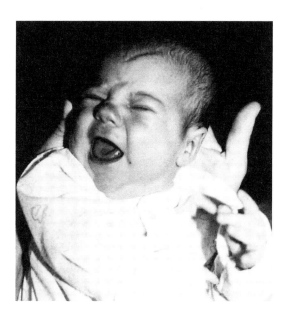

A time sampling study can determine how often and for how long infants cry.

asking about the reasons for this different response. Carefully conducted interviews with young children uncover interesting differences between their thinking processes and those of older children and adults.

When children are too young to be able to respond to questions, useful information can be gained by interviewing their parents. Many of the same considerations described above are relevant in these adult interviews.

Time Sampling. **Time sampling** is a strategy for observation that documents the frequency (and sometimes the duration) of certain behaviors. The behaviors that are observed are treated as "samples," or examples of usual behaviors, and predictions are made from the sample about the overall pattern of behavior. Time sampling does not yield a picture of the whole child but instead gives detailed information about specific behaviors of individuals or groups of children.

In time sampling, behavior is recorded at certain times rather than continuously. Depending on the behavior, the observations might be made for fifteen minutes in the morning and again for fifteen minutes in the afternoon or for one-half hour in the middle of the day. Within this schedule, a child might be observed for the whole time or for a certain unit of time, perhaps one minute, and all instances of specific behaviors would be recorded. Time sampling is useful for answering questions such as the following: How often does four-year-old Chris suck his fingers? What percentage of the time is eight-year-old Megan out of her desk chair? How often and for how long does one-year-old Sean cry?

Time sampling is usually used when the behavior to be observed happens frequently—at least once in a 15-minute period. For example, event sampling of aggression in the preschool can be easily recorded, since aggres-

▲ DEVELOPMENTAL ISSUES IN PRACTICE   2.6

TIME SAMPLING

Andrea Barnes wanted to find out how often her two-year-old bit her siblings or parents. She devised a time sampling study and recorded the following results.

Name of child: Betty Age: 2 years, 2 months
Dates of observation: 2/10–2/14
Times of observation: 10:30–11:00

Days	Tallies	Total
1	II	2
2	III	3
3	I	1
4	IIII	4
5	IIIII	5

Average per day: three biting episodes per day for the five days.
Trend: tendency for increasing number of episodes per day.

sive acts don't occur that often, but if the observer is interested in the sucking behavior of babies, it would be very difficult to mark each event, as an infant can suck continuously. It then makes sense to record sucking in 10-second bursts and record them as sucks per 10-second period. (Event sampling, to be described next, would be a more appropriate strategy for studying infrequent behaviors.)

Before a time sampling study begins, the purposes of the study must be decided, behaviors must be defined, and recording forms must be organized, as is shown in Developmental Issues in Practice 2.6. A good illustration of this preparation is one of the best known of the early studies using time sampling. Mildred Parten wanted to study differences in social participation in relationship to the age of the child (1932–1933). She first defined categories so that any social participation would be included in a category but none would be included in more than one category. The following is an example of her operational definition for parallel activity—one of six categories of social participation:

> The child plays independently, but the activity he chooses naturally brings him among other children. He plays with toys that are like those that the children around him are using but he plays with the toys as be sees fit and does not try to influence or modify the activity of the children near him. He plays beside rather than with the other children. There is no attempt to control the coming or going of children in the group.

After defining six categories of social participation, Parten memorized the definitions and their placement on her recording form so that she could record quickly and easily. And, before she could begin observing, she had to decide whom she would observe and for how long. She decided to observe two- to five-year-old children during their free play time (one hour each day) over a nine-month period. She observed each child in the group for one minute, according to a random ordering of names. By using time sampling, Parten was able to draw some interesting conclusions about children's play.

In time sampling studies using several observers, everyone must be consistently in agreement in their recording. In all such studies, it is important to know that each observer is recording the same behavior in the same way every time that behavior occurs. A training period using videotapes can give observers practice in recording and can provide a needed check on consistency, which is called **reliability**.

Time sampling yields important data on children's behavior. These data can provide the foundation for making parenting decisions and teaching decisions or for seeking professional referrals.

Event Sampling.   **Event sampling** provides a way to study behaviors that occur too infrequently for time sampling to be used. In event sampling, the

Event sampling can be used to study the incidence of pretending.

observer begins to record when a predefined event or type of behavior occurs. Event sampling is more efficient than narrative observation, more systematic than recording vignettes or child diary entries, and more descriptive of the natural context than when time sampling is used. In Developmental Issues in Practice 2.7, an example of event sampling is used to measure the occurrence of different kinds of preschool classification activities. The purpose is to show the number of times the event occurs.

In event sampling, the observer waits for an occurrence of an event that has previously been carefully defined (note the definition of the event in Developmental Issues in Practice 2.7). Each time the event occurs, the observer gathers information corresponding to categories that have been delineated on a recording form. When a sufficient number of events has been recorded, the data are analyzed to determine the frequency, context, and outcomes of that type of behavior.

An illustration of event sampling is provided by a classic study of children's quarrels (Dawe, 1934). Helen Dawe was working in a preschool and had made arrangements with other staff members to free herself from responsibility for dealing with quarrels among children. Over a period of time, she noted the following information about quarrels that took place during free play time: duration, gender, and age of participants; location; cause; and resolution. At the end of four months she had collected enough information to make some interesting generalizations about quarrels among preschool children.

The length of time needed for event sampling is not easy to specify in advance, and this ambiguity is a disadvantage of using this strategy. Event sampling is probably most useful to parents, teachers, and other helping professionals who are routinely in contact with children. For these people, event sampling allows the systematic collection of data, which can then be used to make decisions about children's behavior.

Any observable behavior can be studied using event sampling. Even very infrequent behavior, such as expressions of sympathy or altruism, can be studied if the behavior is carefully defined. And the type of paper-and-pencil work done by Dawe can be greatly simplified by modern technological advances. Audio and video recording makes noting behaviors relatively easy and allows later analysis of behaviors that are fleeting or subtle.

Case Studies

A **case study** is a report that summarizes many observations of a given child. The observations themselves provide an important link between theory and practice in early childhood development. Further learning is involved in the sometimes challenging process of summarizing and organizing a number of observations into a coherent study of a child.

Case studies are compiled from information gathered by means of all the strategies introduced so far: narrative observations, vignettes, child diary entries, checklists, interviews, time sampling, and event sampling. Writing a case study necessitates the pulling together of disparate bits of information on psychosocial, physical, and cognitive development. An example of an out-

▲ DEVELOPMENTAL ISSUES IN PRACTICE   2.7

EVENT SAMPLING STUDY

Tally Event Sampling of Preschool Classification Activities

Center: University Heights Children's Center
Date: 2/16 to 2/24   Time: 9:00–9:50 a.m.
Observer: Al   Teacher: Molly
                                     Children: Twelve 3– to 4–year-olds

Event: Classification—Ability to sort objects into classes and subclasses by their similarities and differences.
Classification Codes: G=sorts by graphic collections, I=sorts by identity, S/E=sorts by similarity with errors, S=sorts by similarity, S/R=sorts and re-sorts.
Initiator Codes: CI=child initiated, TI=teacher initiated.
Instructions: Make one tally mark in the appropriate box each time a child exhibits classification in one of the seven classroom areas.

Classification	G		I		S/E		S		S/R		
Initiator / Area	CI	TI	CI	TI	CI	TI	CI	TI	CI	TI	
Blocks	I		꠵ꠜ II		I		III				(12)
Art			꠵ꠜ				III				(8)
Dramatic play			꠵ꠜ								(5)
Music											(0)
Manipulatives	I		III				IIII				(8)
Language arts											(0)
Science	II						II			I	(5)
	(4)	(0)	(20)	(0)	(1)	(0)	(12)	(0)	(0)	(1)	

Comments:
Blocks: all CI-I at cleanup
Music was not available for 4 out of the 7 days.

Adapted from S. Nicolson and S. G. Shipstead, *Through the Looking Glass: Observations in the Early Childhood Classroom.* New York: Merrill/Macmillan, 1994. Adapted with permission.

▲ **DEVELOPMENTAL ISSUES IN PRACTICE   2.8**

CASE STUDY OUTLINE FOR PRESCHOOL CHILDREN

Name of child:

Report date:

Age of child:

Reporter:

Date of preschool entrance:

A. General description of child

B. Relationship of child to self
   1. Personal task accomplishment (dressing, toileting, washing, caring for personal property)
   2. Speaking capacity (articulation, structure, usage)
   3. Moving capacity (control of basic movement; patterning of walking, running, jumping, balancing, hopping, galloping, skipping)
   4. Pattern of affective expression (moods, responses to frustration)
   5. Situational responses (making choices, solving problems, having persistence)

C. Relationship of child to adults
   1. Adults as supporters of self-control
   2. Adults as resources for assistance

line for a case study is given in Developmental Issues in Practice 2.8. Because data come from more than one source, case studies give a more thorough description of development than does any single observational strategy.

The child whose development is summarized in a case study "comes to life" as an individual with unique strengths and needs. Insights gained from case studies help parents and professionals make decisions about children. Case studies, as used by educators and other helping professionals, are recognized as valuable tools for enhancing understanding of young children.

Consistent with Bronfenbrenner's (1979) views of environmental influences on children, case studies seek to portray children in as many different environments and situations as possible. Data can be obtained from many of the significant people in children's lives: parents, teachers, doctors, and other specialists. The influences on children are complex, and the more that is learned about these influences, the deeper the understanding of young children.

DEVELOPMENTAL ISSUES IN PRACTICE   2.8 (continued)

D. Relationship of child to other children
    1. General interactions (quality, quantity)
    2. Situationally specific interactions (conflict resolution, turn taking, sharing)

E. Relationship of child to groups
    1. Basic responsibilities (care of and respect for materials, observation of space boundaries)
    2. Participation in group activities (story, music, movement, trips, snacks)
    3. Conduct during transitions

F. Relationship of child to objects and ideas
    1. Objects manipulated as body extensions (tricycle, balls, pencils, scissors)
    2. Objects shaped or formed (clay, finger paint)
    3. Objects used for construction (blocks, building games, woodworking, pasting, gluing, puzzles)
    4. Drawing and painting
    5. Language activity (attending, observing, writing symbols, reading, concept usage)
    6. Concept development (causation, seriation, number, space, time, classification, measurement)

Adapted from S. A. Provence, A. Naylor, and J. Patterson, *The Challenge of Day Care*. New Haven: Yale University Press. Copyright 1977 by Yale University Press. Adapted with permission.

When writing case studies for class projects, the author should protect the child's privacy by substituting a fictitious name for the child's own. When case studies are written in educational settings, the child's rights are further protected by the Family Educational Rights and Privacy Act, passed by the U.S. Congress in 1974. Teachers should also refer to state laws, as most states have passed Open Meeting and Freedom of Information Acts. These acts give parents and students the right to inspect school records and to challenge any material that they feel is inaccurate. It also requires written permission before information from a student's school file can be released to others. Because of the privacy act, access to some information in children's files may be denied, and what is written in case studies may be made available to children's parents. Accurate recording of behaviors and conversations, rather than opinions or interpretations, will result in case studies that will be clear to parents and discourage challenges.

STANDARDIZED MEASURES

Standardized measures are evaluation tests developed to assess specific content areas called **domains**. These tests have been given to many children and have been found to be effective measures of the domains; they have been shown to have **validity** and **reliability**. If a test is reliable, it means that no matter how many times a child takes the test, the results will be the same. A test that is not reliable is useless because it will never provide the same score twice. If a test is valid, it means that it measures the domain it claims to measure. If it is called an IQ test, it should measure the child's intellectual capability, not verbal skill or assertiveness. If it is a test of cooperation, it should measure cooperation, not compliance or social inadequacy. Three types of standardized measures will be discussed here: developmental assessments, screening tests, and skill assessments.

Developmental Assessments

This book is about developmental issues primarily. Tests that measure development are based on the theories of human development. It is important to understand how developmental tests work because a thorough understanding is essential to grasping the practical implications of developmental theory. This section will focus on one of the developmental tests, which can serve as an example of the intent of all other such tests.

The most well-known **developmental assessment** is the Denver Developmental Screening Test (DDST). The revised edition is the Denver II. The test is broken into four domains: (1) personal-social, (2) fine motor-adaptive, (3) language, and (4) gross motor (see Figure 2.1). When you look at the adapted scoring sheet for the Denver II, notice that the behaviors being measured across time form a pattern that looks like stair steps. For example, in the gross motor domain, the item "head up 90°" comes before "sit–head steady," which comes before "sit–no support." It is developmentally necessary that abilities evolve in this particular order. You would never expect to see a child who could sit without support and not be able to hold the head steady. It is logical to expect physical development to occur in this order because each ability is necessary for the next one to occur. Research has shown that all the domains on the Denver II generally follow this same inherent law of development, including language and social development.

If an infant can "pull to stand," "stand holding on" and "sit–no support," it is assumed the child has already mastered everything below these items, including "pull to sit–no head lag" and "roll over." In addition, if the child misses three items in a row, it is assumed that he or she will fail all the more advanced abilities. These assumptions are inherent in developmental tests. The evaluator should enter the test at the age that is most appropriate for the child being tested and move up or down the scale to identify the spot that is the highest stage the child can achieve. Although most children acquire skills in the same natural order, each child matures at an individual rate or speed of acquisition. Each skill on the original test is represented by a bar that

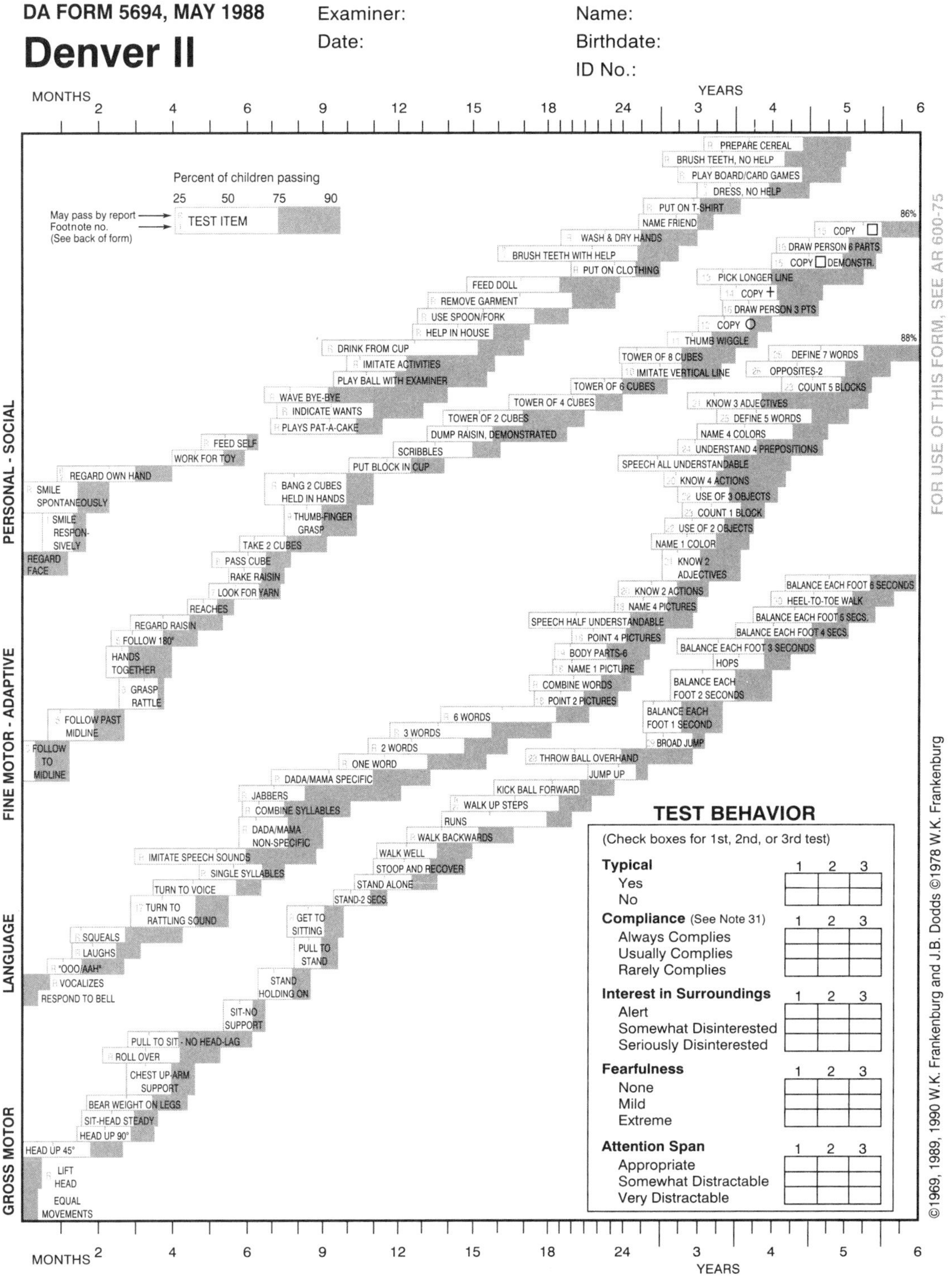

Figure 2.1 The Denver Developmental Screening Test

SOURCE: Denver Developmental Screening Test, ©1990 by W. K. Frankenburg and J. B. Dodds. Used with permission.

spans a number of ages in months and years at which normal children acquire the behavior.

Find the age line for 10 months and look at the cluster of boxes that it intersects in the "gross motor" domain. Most 10-month-old infants will have mastered the skills indicated by the boxes marked "stand holding on" and "pull to stand." On the other hand, a smaller number of children at 10 months of age will be able to "stand–2 secs" and "stand alone." For example, for the behavior "stand-2 secs," there is a one-and-a-half-month range during which most normal children acquire this ability. It is very easy to make comparisons between children, and it is important for professionals and parents to realize that individual differences in children are normal and to be expected.

Screening Tests

The Denver II is also a good example of a **screening test,** which is an important tool but limited to very specific purposes. It is very important for us to identify children who have developmental delays so that intervention can begin as early as possible. To accurately identify children with delays, testing must be done. In-depth testing is time-consuming and expensive. It is obviously not possible to test every single child at length to find out which ones are delayed. Screening tests are used to screen out the children who are clearly normal. Children who are left are then identified as "at risk" for delays. On the Denver II, if the child fails an item that 75% to 90% of children in his age group can pass, this is considered to be of some concern or a "caution." If the child fails an item that more than 90° of children in his age group can pass, this is considered more serious or a "delay." If the child has one or more "delay" items and/or two or more "caution" items, this is considered a suspect test result for developmental delay. However, such children are not necessarily actually delayed; to determine exactly which children are in need of intervention, additional testing is necessary.

The Denver II is less expensive to administer than other tests, in part because there is no need to use physicians and psychologists. Instead, the Denver II can be administered in about 15 minutes by a trained paraprofessional. Thus, the Denver II could potentially reach all children, although that goal has not been achieved. Dr. William K. Frankenburg, author of the DDST and the Denver II, has also written a Prescreening Developmental Questionnaire (PDQ), revised in 1986, which is even more efficient than the DDST and the Denver II. The revised PDQ (R-PDQ) is derived from the DDST but is designed to be completed by parents who have at least a high school education. The questionnaire is designed for use by parents with a wide variety of ages of children. The parents answer age-appropriate questions until three questions are answered "no," and then the answers are reviewed by trained paraprofessionals.

Instruments such as the Denver II and R-PDQ can help to identify infants who should receive intervention services. The sooner that particular needs are identified and met, the better for the child, family, and society. Such instruments also give professionals an assessment of children's unique strengths and weaknesses, which can be used to guide program planning. Screening tests should never be used for the following functions:

❑ As a measure of IQ

❑ To diagnose disabilities or handicaps

❑ To predict future performance

❑ To label a child without using further in-depth testing

Many different kinds of screening tests are in use. They are used to evaluate speech and hearing ability, children's understanding of language, large and fine motor skills, and the health and well-being of newborns.

Skill Assessments

There are two general types of **skill assessments**: readiness tests and achievement tests. These are used to measure different types of abilities. **Readiness tests** are used to predict performance, whereas **achievement tests** measure the accomplishments of the child. Examples of such tests include the following:

❑ Brigance Diagnostic Inventory of Early Development (Curriculum Associates)

❑ Learning Accomplishment Profile (LAP) (Kaplan School Supply)

❑ Portage Guide to Early Education (Portage Project; Portage, Wisconsin)

❑ Illinois Test of Psycholinguistic Ability (ITPA) (University of Illinois Press)

❑ Peabody Picture Vocabulary Test (PPVT) (American Guidance Service)

❑ Cognitive Skills Assessment Battery (Teachers College Press)

One distinction between readiness tests and achievement tests is the time at which they are given. Readiness tests are given before a program begins to see whether the child has the necessary competencies to enter the program. Achievement tests are given afterward to see what the child has accomplished. A second distinction involves developmental theory. The idea of readiness implies that the child must master a set of abilities that are inherently necessary before being able to move on to more complex content areas. For example, developmentalists have shown that before children can master basic mathematics, it is necessary for them to understand such pre-math concepts as seriation, classification, one-to-one correspondence, and number conservation.

Assessment tests are extremely valuable when they are reliable and valid and when they are used correctly by trained professionals. It is unfortunate, however, that tests are often misused by well-meaning adults who can do great damage to children (Cryan, 1986; Kamii, 1990; Wortham, 1990). For example, tests are often culture biased and language biased and have been validated on middle-class, white populations. Great caution must be used in interpreting the results of such tests when given to minority children, such as African Americans and Hispanics. Furthermore, tests are designed for specific purposes. They should be given and used only for those purposes. Tests should never be given just to see how "smart" a child is.

Most tests are designed to measure intellectual functioning, as there is a great deal of interest in that area. However, many other domains are of equal or greater importance to understanding the functioning of children. For example, social skills, creativity, and emotional traits should not be overlooked. In addition, when tests of intellectual ability are used by teachers, there is always the temptation to "teach to the test." That is, teachers plan their program around the test rather than around the needs and abilities of the children.

Finally, it is essential that the results of a single test are not used to make serious, far-reaching decisions about the child's future. A number of different assessments must be used, including observations as well as standardized tests. Professionals must avoid the temptation to "label" a child and must always use the results of testing to describe interventions and define appropriate short-term goals for the child (Beaty, 1994). The younger the child is when tested, the less accurate the prediction will be for future success. Properly developed programming can powerfully influence the developmental course of the child. Tests can help to guide such programming but should never be used as an end in themselves to label the child.

The Ethics of Scientific Research

The kinds of tests just discussed are also used in research projects. Findings from such projects will be presented in the subsequent chapters of this book. It is important to remember that the findings are always limited by the effectiveness of the tests in assessing the group being studied. Because research is generally based upon group findings, the results cannot be applied directly to any particular child. On the other hand, research can be very helpful in guiding the expectations of those in the helping professions.

Some questions about young children cannot be answered without violating the **ethics of science**. Making observations to collect data about such questions would sanction placing children in situations that would cause them bodily or psychological harm. For example, here are a few questions that should not be answered by experiment and observation: How much pain can a one-year-old endure? How hard does a beating have to be in order to be called "abusive"? How does the social behavior of eight-year-old children change as a result of school failure?

In earlier years, ethical concerns about research with children were not given as much attention as they now receive. As just one example, recall John Watson's experimental conditioning of Albert's fear of white rats, described in Chapter 1. Obviously, Albert had been personally affected by the experiment.

Children have rights and deserve to be treated with the same respect and consideration as do adults. The child's right to privacy and bodily integrity must always be protected.

Because of studies such as Watson's, Congress passed a law requiring that all institutions that receive federal funds for research involving human beings certify that no physical or psychological harm will come to participants. The Society for Research in Child Development and the National Association for the Education of Young Children have their own set of standards, which delineate the rights of children and the responsibilities of researchers and journal editors. These standards assert that children's rights supersede those of researchers, that children have the right to refuse to participate in any research, and that informed consent is required of children's parents or guardians before any research can be undertaken.

All students of early childhood development have the responsibility to see that the children who are observed are in no way harmed. The privacy of children and their parents must be respected by reporting results so that the subjects are not recognizable. Ethical observers work to protect the rights of children and their families. Taking the time to consider important ethical issues is a small price to pay for the excitement of making discoveries about how children develop.

ASSESSMENT FOR DECISION MAKING: DELAYS AND DISABILITIES

There are times when one's goal is to find a diagnosis for a child for the purpose of identifying certain needs. Once particular needs are identified, program planning can begin to intervene and ensure maximum developmental potential for the child. Under the Education for All Handicapped Children Act (P.L. 94-142), now called the Individuals with Disabilities Education Act, passed by Congress in 1992, all early childhood programs must be prepared to serve children who have so-called special needs—such children include those who have developmental delays or developmental disabilities. Ten diagnostic categories are used to place children in certain programs: mental retardation, serious emotional disturbance, hearing impairments (including deafness), visual impairments (including blindness), orthopedic impairments, speech or language impairments, other health impairments, specific learning disabilities, autism, and traumatic brain injury. Sometimes the term *developmental delay* is used to describe these disabilities.

Once a diagnosis is made, it is important to understand what it means for a particular child. First, every disability can appear on a range of effects—from mild to moderate to severe/profound. Second, the diagnosis does not necessarily result in a specific treatment. The determination of treatment must take account of the benefit to the particular child, other developmental skills of the child, and the goals and values of the family. Third, in most cases, the diagnosis does not result in a prediction of long-term outcome. The effects of family and intervention programs are more important in determining the child's subsequent development. Fourth, each condition can occur alone or in combination with other conditions. Fifth, the major purpose of the categories is to determine eligibility for program services (Bredekamp & Rosegrant, 1992).

Because certain children must be placed in the special educational programming, it is essential that appropriate assessments are performed to assure the child of appropriate placement. The National Association for the Education of Young Children has developed guidelines for the use of evaluation procedures. These guidelines state that assessment activities must be carried out for the purpose of making specific decisions. The law requires that an **Individual Education Plan (IEP)** be prepared for each child once the results of the assessments are known. The law also requires that the IEP be established with the involvement of the family. Continuing modifications should be made to the IEP in consultation with the parents. Table 2.2 lists seven types of assessments to be made, the decisions that need to be considered in each case, and the appropriate measurement practices for each decision.

As listed in Table 2.2, screening tests are used first, but only to determine whether **diagnostic testing** should be undertaken. Such testing provides

Table 2.2.   *Assessment for Decision Making*

Assessment	Decision	Measurement Practices
1. Screening	Determine whether to refer for assessment	Use of norm-referenced, reliable, valid, nondiscriminatory developmental screening measures
2. Diagnostic	Determine whether there is a disability	Standardized measures conducted by professionals in clinical settings
3. Eligibility	Determine whether disability criteria are met	Use of diagnostic assessments and other criteria to determine eligibility
4. Instructional Program planning	Determine level of functioning	Observations in natural situations; informal testing; interviews
5. Placement	Determine needs and services	Direct observation, rating scales, interviews, and formal assessments by professionals
6. Monitoring	Determine usual performance	Observations in natural contexts
7. Program evaluation	Determine extent of progress of child	Developmental performance and measurements based on intended outcomes of program

SOURCE: Adapted from M. Wolery, P. S. Strain, and D. B. Bailey, Jr. Reaching potentials of children with special needs. In S. Bredekamp and T. Rosegrant (Eds.), *Reaching Potentials: Appropriate Curriculum and Assessment for Young Children* (Vol. 1), pp. 98–99. Washington, DC: National Association for the Education of Young Children, 1992. Copyright 1992 by NAEYC. Adapted by permission.

the diagnosis of the child's condition. There is a wide range of diagnostic tests available, associated with various disabilities. These tests can be administered by specialized professionals only. The diagnosis obtained from the testing is used, in conjunction with other criteria, to determine eligibility for programming. Monitoring and program evaluation are used to be certain that the child is progressing appropriately. Many different kinds of professionals must be involved in the diagnostic assessment. However, the early childhood specialist must also help to provide assessment for decision making. As can be seen from Table 2.2, both observational and standardized assessments can play a part in the decision-making process.

This chapter has provided an overview of the major techniques for assessing child development. The succeeding chapters will describe uses and applications of these methods for each of the age groupings from the prenatal months to eight years.

SUMMARY

1. Learning systematic strategies of observation enables us to understand children's behavior and gain insight into their psychosocial, physical, and cognitive development.
2. Strategies for observing the ongoing behavior of young children—including narrative observation, vignettes, and child diaries—use objective, descriptive language.
3. Narrative observation involves writing down everything that happens in a certain period in a certain setting.
4. Vignettes are accounts of particularly meaningful events in a child's development.
5. Child diary entries are made regularly by parents or others in close contact with a child; they give accounts of day-to-day changes and milestones.
6. Specific predefined behaviors can be observed efficiently by using checklists, interviews, time sampling, and event sampling.
7. Checklists are lists of behaviors. They can be used for systematically observing whether the listed behaviors are present or absent in a given child.
8. Interviews provide opportunities for one-to-one verbal interaction with children. Researchers conduct interviews to find out about children's thinking processes.
9. Time sampling is a method of documenting the frequency and duration of certain behaviors.
10. Event sampling is a method of recording the occurrence of specific types of predefined behaviors.
11. Case studies are reports that summarize many observations of a given child.
12. Strategies of observation answer questions about the behavior and development of young children.
13. Ethical observers must safeguard the rights and privacy of young children at all times.
14. Standardized measurement tests have been administered to many children and have been found to be both reliable and valid.

15. Reliability refers to the ability of a test to produce the same score every time it is given to the subjects.
16. Validity refers to the ability of a test to measure the domain it claims to measure.
17. Developmental assessments are based on the idea that children progress through an inherently ordered set of competencies, each being necessary for the development of further abilities.
18. Each child matures at his or her own individual pace; there are often wide age ranges in acquisition of abilities among normal children.
19. Screening tests are relatively short, simple tests that can be given by paraprofessionals to identify children who then qualify for in-depth testing.
20. Skill assessments can be used as readiness tests to ascertain a child's competencies for anticipated programs. Achievement tests measure ability following intervention.
21. Assessments for decision making involve screening and diagnostic testing of children suspected of having developmental delays or disabilities.
22. If a child qualifies for services by fitting into one of the 10 diagnostic groupings, an Individual Education Plan (IEP) must be written in consultation with the child's parents.

ACTIVITIES TO ENHANCE LEARNING

Test a child using the Denver Developmental Screening Test. Draw a line down the page at the age of the child you are testing. Observe the child's ability to complete the developmental skills specified in each box that your line intersects.

❑ If the child fails to perform the specified behaviors in any domain, move down the scale (to the left) to identify the performance level of the child.

❑ If the child can perform each task at his or her age level, move up the scale (to the right) to find the level at which the child fails to perform.

Answer the following questions:

1. Is the child delayed in development, or is the child advanced in development? Check each domain separately.
2. Which domain is the strong point for this child?
3. Which domain is the weak point for this child?
4. What kind of developmental assistance would you recommend for this child to enhance the child's overall development? (The type of assistance should focus on the child's areas of weakness.)

FOR FURTHER READING

Beaty, J. J. (1994). *Observing development of the young child* (3rd ed.). New York: Merrill/Macmillan.

Bredekamp, S., & Rosegrant, T. (Eds.). (1992). *Reaching potentials: Appropriate curriculum and assessment for young children* (Vol. 1). Washington, DC: National Association for the Education of Young Children.

Grace, C., & Shores, E. F. (1991). *The portfolio and its use: Developmentally appropriate assessment of young children.* Little Rock, AK: Southern Association of Children Under Six.

Nicolson, S., & Shipstead, S. G. (1994). *Through the looking glass: Observations in the early childhood classroom.* New York: Merrill/Macmillan.

Strategies of Experimental Research

Vasta, R. (1979). *Studying children: An introduction to research methods.* San Francisco: W. H. Freeman.

PART I

Before Birth, Birth, and the Expanded Family

Mary Johnson has just been informed by her doctor that her pregnancy test is positive. She came to the doctor suspecting that she might be pregnant but is nevertheless amazed and even apprehensive now that she knows for sure. Without Mary even knowing about it, complex processes have been going on inside her body, even though she is only about eight to nine weeks pregnant. She is sharing in the mystery of the beginnings of life. It is amazing that all the essential external and internal structures are beginning to form in her baby. Although one cannot see that Mary is pregnant by just looking at her, many of the most important prenatal developments have already taken place.

Mary Johnson is experiencing a complex set of sometimes conflicting emotions. Many expectant parents are excited about the new life they have created, but their excitement can be tinged by worry, fear, uncertainty, or similar emotions. Parents-to-be can assuage some of these feelings by obtaining accurate, understandable information about what they are experiencing and what lies ahead. The well-being of the developing child is directly affected by the ability of the family to accept the realities and responsibilities of caring for the child and to deal effectively with the new roles involved in parenthood. For that reason, it is important to consider pregnancy in the context of the family.

Part I of this book provides information about a wide spectrum of events that precede, accompany, and immediately follow the birth of an infant. Chapter 3 deals with the months before birth—genetics, prenatal development, prenatal care for the mother, congenital malformations, and preparation for childbirth. Chapter 4 explains the birth process itself and explores issues raised by the addition of an infant to the family.

Before Birth

▼ KEY IDEAS

Genetics: The Hereditary Basis of Life
- ❑ Chromosomes and Genes
- ❑ Genetic Effects on Development
- ❑ Twins
- ❑ Genetic versus Environmental Effects on Traits
- ❑ Gender Development

Prenatal Development
- ❑ Fertilization
- ❑ Implantation
- ❑ Embryonic Stage
- ❑ Fetal Stage
- ❑ Behavioral Consistency from Prenatal to Newborn Periods

Prenatal Care of the Mother
- ❑ Medical Supervision
- ❑ Nutrition

Causes of Congenital Malformations
- ❑ Genetic Screening
- ❑ Genetic Factors
- ❑ Environmental Factors
- ❑ Interaction of Factors

A baby is born looking very small and fragile. And yet, a healthy newborn baby is a miracle of organization and adaptive ability. Approximately nine months before the baby's birth, fertilization occurs and a single-celled organism is formed. In an amazing burst of growth, within just nine months, the single cell develops into one of the most complex biological systems on earth: a fully functioning human baby. How does this miracle occur? How is a baby made? Modern science doesn't have the complete answers to these questions, but in these sections we will explore some of the issues concerning the origins of life. We will discuss genetics, prenatal development, and prenatal care of the mother. We will then look at some of the causes for congenital malformations, which result in the baby not being normal and healthy at birth. The chapter will end with a discussion of preparation for parenthood.

GENETICS: THE HEREDITARY BASIS OF LIFE

The characteristics of each person and the way each person develops depend on genetic information contributed by both parents at the time of fertilization. A whole range of characteristics, from hair color to structure of the heart, is programmed by one or more pairs of genes that are contained in chromosomes at the very center (nucleus) of all the cells of our bodies.

Chromosomes and Genes

Chromosomes are threadlike structures that contain genes. Different species can have different numbers of chromosomes. Normal human beings have 46 chromosomes, arranged in 23 pairs. All of the cells of the body, except the nerve cells, constantly reproduce themselves to make new cells as the old ones die off. When the cells reproduce (in a process called **mitosis**), the exact genetic code for the individual person is passed along in the **genes**. The **genetic code** describes the chemical components of DNA (discussed later in the chapter), which can be reorganized into an infinite variety of combinations. It is this potential for infinite variation that makes it possible for every single fertilization to produce a unique new human being.

The sex cells (i.e., the sperm and egg cells in the reproductive organs of mature men and women) are different in that they each contain 23 unpaired chromosomes. This reduction in the number of chromosomes takes place through the process of **meiosis,** which involves two cell divisions. In meiosis the two chromosomes in each of the 23 pairs are separated and distributed to different cells. After meiosis, each mature sperm or ovum contains one member of each pair of the chromosomes. Sperm and egg then fuse at conception to form a single cell with 46 chromosomes, 23 from each parent. This process makes each new infant a unique individual with his or her own combination of traits from both parents.

Genetic Effects on Development

Children often wonder why their hair or eye color, body type, or some other characteristic differs from that of their parents or siblings. As described earlier, each infant is genetically unique because of the new chromosomal makeup resulting from the process of meiosis and fertilization. To understand these processes, it is necessary to know something about genetic transmission of traits, as studied by Gregor Mendel.

In 1866 Gregor Mendel, an Austrian botanist and monk, published his paper on the theory of inherited traits. The work received no attention at the time but was rediscovered 30 years later, and Mendel was then hailed as the father of modern genetics. He developed the **Mendelian laws of heredity** by studying the variations in the traits of pea plants in his monastery garden (the traits included size, color, and shape). For example, he found that parent plants that were both either white or red passed their color onto the offspring. If each parent plant were a different color, Mendel found that both traits were passed down to future generations and the appearance of each one occurred with mathematical regularity in each succeeding generation. The Mendelian laws of heredity are as follows:

1. The law of dominance. When organisms with differing traits of a pair are crossed, only one trait, the **dominant trait** of the pair, appears in the first generation. The red color in the example above is dominant; therefore, the first generation is red. The trait that does not appear (white color) is the **recessive trait**.

2. The law of segregation. The characteristic that was hidden (recessive) in the first generation is not lost, since it reappears in later generations. The recessive trait of white color will be passed on to the future generation of flowers.

3. The law of independent assortment. Every characteristic is inherited independently of every other characteristic. According to this law, new combinations of traits are possible in succeeding generations. In the pea plants, it was possible to produce every combination of the trait's size, color, and shape in future generations by appropriate cross-breeding.

The Mendelian laws can be seen operating in every family, as the following example demonstrates.

Both Joan and Andrew Green had brown hair and brown eyes. These are dominant traits, so all the Greens' friends expected Joan's first pregnancy to produce a baby with brown hair and brown eyes. When their first baby was born with blond hair and blue eyes, everyone was surprised.

The Greens had moved away from their home community, so their new friends hadn't met any other members of the Greens' families. An examination of the two families of origin can explain the appearance of the baby with recessive traits. Joan's mother is dark, but her father is fair, with blond hair and blue eyes. Joan must be carrying a blond, blue-eyed recessive trait from her father, because those are the only kind of genes he has (if he were carrying the dark genes, he would be dark because that is the dominant trait). Because Andrew's parents are both dark, it was not known whether they were carrying recessive genes until they had children; the presence of Andrew's two blond, blue-eyed siblings was evidence of the recessive trait in both parents. Andrew had a chance of receiving one of the recessive traits but couldn't know for sure until his blond, blue-eyed baby was born.

With the preceding example we can illustrate the use of genotype and phenotype to make predictions about possible reproductive outcomes. The **genotype** is the totality of a person's genetic heritage and includes all the genes that are inherited from both parents. The genotype includes recessive genes, which are never expressed because they happen to be paired with dominant genes. This would include the blond, blue-eyed traits discussed in the preceding example. The **phenotype,** on the other hand, is a description of a person's actual traits that result from interaction of genes with each other and the environment.

The distinction between genotype and phenotype sometimes explains the appearance of certain traits and diseases. Hemophilia, a disease that interferes with blood clotting, is caused by a recessive gene that appears only on the X chromosome. If one of a woman's two X chromosomes carries the recessive gene for hemophilia, she will not be afflicted but will be a carrier of the disease. Sons receive only one X chromosome from their mother. Thus, if the son of a **carrier** receives an X chromosome that carries the recessive gene for hemophilia, that son will inherit a serious disease that leads to profuse bleeding even from slight wounds. Daughters of carriers cannot inherit the disease unless their father has the disease, but they may carry the disease as part of their genotype. It has been found that 120 traits, including color blindness, myopia, and juvenile muscular dystrophy, are also transmitted as part of the genotype through X chromosomes. Information about such traits can be obtained from genetic counselors, who specialize in helping families to understand their own genetic inheritance and reproductive capacity (Developmental Issues in Practice 3.1 discusses genetic counseling).

Most complex human characteristics, such as intelligence, are **polygenic,** or caused by the interaction of many genes and not just a simple pair. Quantitative traits such as intelligence and size are also influenced by interaction with the environment. The best evidence for the effect of environment on the development of these traits comes from the study of identical twins. Twins with exactly the same genotype may differ considerably in phenotype, especially if they develop in different surroundings.

Only since the 1960s have scientists begun to understand how genetic information is transmitted. An exciting account of the clues that researchers

▲ DEVELOPMENTAL ISSUES IN PRACTICE   3.1

GENETIC COUNSELING

The example of the Green family demonstrates the approach used in **genetic counseling.** No one would use genetic counseling for a trivial matter such as hair color and eye color, but the issues and the approaches involved in determining such traits are similar to those involved with more serious matters. Usually the parents have a serious problem in the family or they have already had children who had a serious genetic disorder. They go for genetic counseling to get an idea of the mathematical probability of having a child with a similar problem. The counselor uses the medical and family facts about illnesses to assist the family in understanding the genetic mechanisms of disease and the risk of recurrence involved.

Genetic counseling usually has five main phases. First, the counselor gathers information about the family and then communicates the medical facts, including diagnosis, cause of the disorder, and management. Second, the counselor explains how heredity contributes to the disorder and to the risk of recurrence. Third, the counselor outlines alternatives for dealing with the risk of recurrence. Fourth, the counselor offers guidance and support in choosing a course of action that would be compatible with family values and beliefs. Finally, the counselor helps the parents adjust to their child's disorders and to the risk of recurrence (Benirschke et al., 1976).

Information about careers in genetic counseling can be obtained from the American Society of Human Genetics, P.O. Box 6015, Rockville, MD, 20850.

followed in trying to determine the structure of genes was written by Watson (1968). Years of research revealed that each chromosome contains thousands of genes. **Genes** in turn are composed of **deoxyribonucleic acid** (**DNA**), the substance through which biological information is transferred. Researchers found that the molecular structure of the chemical **DNA** is in the form of a coil, or double helix. When the fertilized egg divides and subdivides, the two strands in the DNA double helix uncoil, and each of the strands takes with it the exact pattern of chemicals that it needs to reproduce itself.

Some human traits require the involvement of many pairs of genes, and some need only one pair. In all cases, DNA contains complicated information that allows formation of chains of protein that develop into tissue and organs, control other genes, and regulate body processes.

Recently, researchers have found that traits may develop differently depending on whether the genetic material has come from the mother's genes or from the father's genes (Hoffman, 1991). This has led to a theory postulating that genetic material is imprinted as coming from one or the other parent (Moore & Haig, 1991). Thus an additional complication is added to the laws of inheritance, which have yet to be fully understood.

Twins

An infant's genetic endowment is like no one else's, unless that infant has an identical (**monozygotic**) twin. In the case of identical twins, the zygote formed by the union of sperm and egg splits, and the two identical halves begin to develop independently. These twins look alike and share identical inherited characteristics. But not all twins are identical. Fraternal (**dizygotic**) twins are twice as common as identical twins. Fraternal twins develop when two ova (rather than the usual one ovum) are released and are fertilized by different sperm. Fraternal twins do not share any more inherited characteristics than do any other two siblings. They can look very much alike, somewhat alike, or very different, and the same is true for other traits. Fraternal twins can be either the same gender or different genders. However, fraternal twins differ from ordinary siblings in that they have shared the first environment: the womb. They will therefore share in factors that could affect congenital outcome, including congenital malformations.

Genetic versus Environmental Effects on Traits

Scientists have found that twins can provide very useful information about the kinds of traits that are strongly affected by genes and those that are not. Research on monozygotic twin pairs raised apart has provided the most interesting findings (Holden, 1980) (see Developmental Issues in Practice 3.2 for a story of such twins). It has been found that IQ and temperament are powerfully affected by genes (Bailey & Revelle, 1991; McClearn, 1970). In addition, twins have similar patterns of psychiatric problems, such as

The nearly identical appearance of these twins confuses teachers and friends.

▲ DEVELOPMENTAL ISSUES IN PRACTICE   3.2

IDENTICAL TWINS RAISED APART

In 1980 an unusual event was made public. Robert Shafran went to New York College as a freshman. From the day he stepped on campus, he was confronted with students who treated him like an old friend. When he denied that his name was Eddy Galland, the students assumed he was joking around. The students were so certain that Robert was Eddy that the two young men decided to meet. When Robert and Eddy met, it was clear that they were monozygotic twins who had been separated at birth. The publicity generated by the incident was noted by David Kellman, who turned out to be the triplet of the other two. The three boys had been separated at birth and raised in three different families.

What was surprising was the striking resemblance among the three in characteristics usually thought of as being socialized by environmental effects. These triplets of identical genetic endowment, but raised apart, had strikingly similar personalities. They were outgoing and gregarious. They enjoyed people and had lots of friends. They were known as being fun loving and always good for a laugh. They liked the same kinds of foods and music and wore the same kinds of informal dress (Battelle, 1981). These are all characteristics that are thought of as learned behaviors. Is it possible that they have their roots in the genetic similarity among the three men?

migraine headaches, depression, phobias, and other lesser emotional disturbances. An important factor in these twin similarities may be the similarities found in brain tracings from the twins, as well as their general medical histories. Even personality characteristics such as temperament and altruism have been found to be influenced by genetic inheritance (McClearn, 1970). Neurochemical similarities caused by genes might be responsible for a wider range of human behaviors than originally thought.

Some of the similarities between twins might be due to **indirect genetic effects**. That is, the genes create patterns that the environment tends to respond to in specific ways. For example, two female twins raised apart each wore seven rings. It happened that they had both inherited very attractive hands, and in our culture it is likely that we would respond to having pretty hands by wearing rings to show them off.

As it happens, every trait is influenced by both the environment and by one's genes. For that reason, scientists speak of the **heritability rate** of a given trait. Heritability is a statistic computed as a percentage of genetic effect in relation to the total (Dobzhansky, 1973). Table 3.1 lists high heritability estimates for a number of traits in a number of different species. For example, stature, IQ, and weight have the highest heritability in humans. These average around 80%; however, approximately 20% of the trait's expression is due to environment. In human beings, environment plays an important role in most characteristics, even height and weight.

Table 3.1.   *Some Estimates of Highest Heritability in Various Animals and Plants*

Organism and Trait	Heritability
Spotting in Friesian cattle	0.95
Slaughter weight in cattle	0.85
Stature in man	0.81
IQ in man	0.81
Weight in man	0.78
Cephalic index in man	0.75
Plant height in corn	0.70
Egg weight in poultry	0.60
Weight of fleece in sheep	0.40
Milk production in cattle	0.30
Yield in corn	0.25
Egg production in poultry	0.20
Egg production in *Drosophila*	0.20
Ear length in corn	0.17
Litter size in mice	0.15
Response to light in *Drosophila*	0.09
Conception rate in cattle	0.05
Response to gravity in *Drosophila*	0.04

SOURCE: Reprinted with permission from T. Dobzhansky, *Genetic Diversity and Human Equality*. New York: Basic Books, 1973, p. 18.

Sometimes people are uncomfortable with findings that a trait such as IQ is largely inherited. They fear that this knowledge will result in an assumption, for example, that there is nothing that can be done in the environment to help children with low IQs. However, Dobzhansky (1973) has pointed out that such people are confusing equality with identity. Dobzhansky says that "human equality pertains to the rights and to the sacredness of life of every human being, not to bodily or even mental characteristics." A low IQ may be due largely to genetic effects, but a negative attitude toward a person with a low IQ is due to the environment. If a child is discouraged from trying new things because the parents perceive him to be slow, this is due to parental attitudes, not to the child's genes.

Furthermore, Dobzhansky points out that genes really determine the range of ability that a person has, not the specific IQ level. For this reason, it is important to help every person to develop to the full capacity of his or her given genetic inheritance. Every child must be treated equally in that sense. Children with a low IQ can be helped to improve. It has long been known that good intervention programs can raise IQ as much as 20–30 points (Heber, 1968), and children from adoptive homes tend to have IQ rates that are more like their adoptive families than their families of origin (Schiff et al., 1978).

A person's sex is assumed to be almost entirely determined by genes; however, even here there is room for environmental effect. The next section explores the development of a person's gender. By studying gender development, one can see the kind of role played by the environment in the expression of our genetic traits.

Gender Development

Each person has a **gender identity,** which is the belief we have about our individuality as a male or female. We experience our gender identity as a matter of self-awareness, which results in specific kinds of behaviors. Our gender identity is the private expression of our **gender role,** which in turn involves everything that we do to indicate to others the degree to which we are either male or female. This includes what we say and do and is the public expression of our gender identity (Money & Ehrhardt, 1972). In most cases, our gender identity and our gender role are the same. That is, we have a sexual identity that is expressed in our gender role. However, in the rare cases of sexual hermaphroditism or confusion of sex, these two will not be the same. Research on these cases has given us a great deal of information about the source of our sexual identity. The actual cases are extremely rare and they are being discussed here because they illustrate important principles about inheritance. Figure 3.1 provides a schematic guide to the following discussion on the development of gender identity.

A person's **gender** is determined at the time of fertilization by the kind of sperm that fertilizes the ovum. Each ovum carries one X chromosome, but some sperm carry an X chromosome and some carry a Y chromosome. If the ovum is fertilized by an X-bearing sperm, a female (XX) will develop; if the ovum is fertilized by a Y-bearing sperm, a male (XY) will develop. Thus, it is the father's sperm that determines the gender of the child. A detailed understanding of the role of the X and Y chromosomes in sexual development is still poorly understood (Gordon & Ruddle, 1981). However, it is known that one role of the XX and XY chromosomes is to pass the message of inherited sexuality to the fetal gonads, which are the sex glands. The sex glands then send out hormones to the fetus during normal development, giving the message as to whether the child will develop testes and a penis or a uterus, ovaries, and a clitoris. If no hormonal messages are passed to the gonads, the child will develop as a girl (Haseltine & Ohno, 1981). For a boy to develop, two hormonal events must occur: the female development must be suppressed and masculinizing hormones must be sent to develop the male sex organs (Wilson, George, & Griffin, 1981).

The hormones are also responsible for brain formation (MacLusky & Naftolin, 1981; McEwen, 1981). For the body to carry out behaviors, central nervous system signals must exist; in the adult person, these include signals of sexual arousal, or eroticism. The pattern for such programs is laid down in the fetal brain during brain development. It is believed that this process is also responsible for the development of right- and left-brain dominance, which may cause some of the sex-linked traits. The brain contributes to the internal confirmation of the sense of appropriate sexual identity, which is articulated by the

Figure 3.1 *Diagram Illustrating the Sequential and Interactional Components of Gender Identity Development*

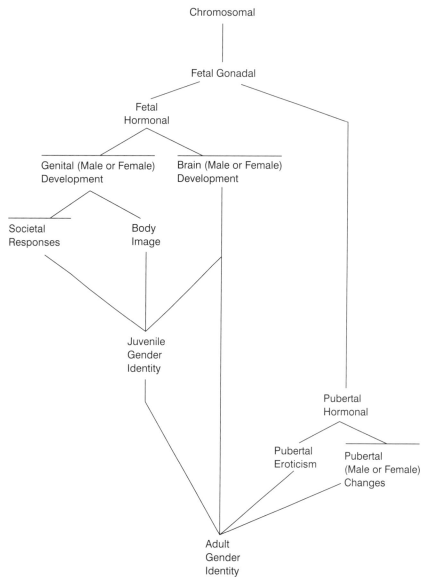

SOURCE: Adapted from J. Money and A. A. Ehrhardt, *Man and Woman, Boy and Girl*. Baltimore: Johns Hopkins University Press, 1972, p. 3. Adapted by permission.

society around us. If a person is told that she is a girl and her brain confirms that she has the responses of a girl, then normal gender identity can progress.

Thus, a very important part of the development of gender identity comes from social reactions to the child. Everyone has a set of expectations associated with the sex of the newborn baby. It is so important for parents to know what sex their baby is because that knowledge fundamentally affects the perception of the new baby. When a baby is born, the trigger that sets off this fundamental reaction is the appearance of the external genitalia. This reaction is so obvious that we tend to forget how important it is unless there is a problem in determining the sex of the child. Occasionally a baby is born with ambiguous external genitalia, which means that the genitalia are abnormal, with such variations as an enlarged clitoris or poorly formed penis. This is very rare, but when it does happen, it raises questions about the most important causative factors in the development of our gender identity.

There are three important causative factors in the development of our gender identity: (1) chromosomes, which are the genetic factor; (2) fetal hormones; and (3) socialization. The latter two are environmental factors; one occurs before birth and the other occurs after birth. These three factors contribute to the child's gender identity, which, taken together with pubertal changes, contribute to the adult gender identity. Each of these factors will be discussed separately.

Chromosomes.   It is possible for an incorrect number of chromosomes to be passed on to a child at fertilization. If at least one X chromosome is present, the child can survive. If only a Y chromosome is present, it is lethal and the child will not survive. The most common forms of chromosome errors are Turner's syndrome, in which only one X is present, and Klinefelter's syndrome, in which there is an extra X. The Turner's syndrome child is raised as a girl; the Klinefelter's syndrome child is raised as a boy. Both are always infertile.

Fetal hormones.   Normally, the fetal gonads produce the hormones appropriate to the chromosome pattern of the child. If a Y chromosome is present, a male pattern will occur. However, it is possible for the fetus to be exposed to hormones that are incorrect for the genetic material present. This can happen if there are genetic errors also transmitted from the chromosomes, blocking the ability of the body to receive the correct hormones. It can also happen if a tumor on the fetal gonad causes incorrect hormones to be released or if extra hormones are introduced into the mother's body because of tumors or medical intervention. In the past, male hormones were sometimes given to women to prevent miscarriage. These would affect the development of both physical genitalia and the brain. Various researchers (Money & Ehrhardt, 1972; Reinisch, 1977; Rubin, Reinisch, & Haskett, 1981) report that fetal hormones may be responsible for feminizing and masculinizing conditions, which we consider to be associated with traditional stereotypes.

Socialization.   If a baby is born with ambiguous genitalia, it creates great difficulties for the family. Parents will be confused, because they need to know the sex to know how to respond to the baby. They won't know what to name the baby, what to tell friends and relatives, and so on. Ideally, the child should be evaluated, and a decision as to sex should be made as soon as possible. In most cases, these children will continue to be ambiguous in their development and will be infertile. However, they can be helped to adapt to this kind of disability, and most grow into normal, functioning adults. Special counseling and assistance are usually required for all members of the family to help them adapt (Money & Ehrhardt, 1972).

Which of these factors is the most important? The answer is *all of them* are important. Money and Ehrhardt (1972) agree with this, although their clinical work with Turner's syndrome families has led them to argue that socialization is probably of greatest importance to the ultimate development of gender identity. Fetal hormones can also play an important role in the expression of gender. Money and Ehrhardt have worked with Turner's syndrome children, who are genetic girls. If such children are masculinized in utero but are correctly diagnosed at birth and then raised as girls, they represent cases where both the genes and the socialization process are feminizing but the fetal hormones are masculinizing. These children always develop a female identity; however, they have a high probability of having the following behavior patterns:

❑ Athleticism
❑ Self-assertion in seeking dominant social positions
❑ Preference to conservative clothing
❑ Engagement in very little doll-play as children
❑ Career orientation
❑ High IQ
❑ Responsiveness to visual sexual eroticism

Money and Ehrhardt (1972) theorized that these more masculine characteristics may be caused by the fetal hormones.

There is a great deal of interest in the effects of fetal hormones on the development of the brain. Scientists (de LaCoste, Horvath, & Woodward, 1991; Kolata, 1979; vom Saal & Bronson, 1980) are investigating the different patterns of neural connections that develop in male and female brains as the result of fetal hormones. It is clear that male and female brains are different and are affected by fetal hormones. However, the exact role of hormones in behavior is unclear and has not been conclusively demonstrated in human beings (Ehrhardt & Meyer-Bahlburg, 1981).

In summary, our genes are important in determining the outcome of our development (including our physical and personality development) and gender identity. However, each of our traits has a heritability quotient, which is an estimate about the amount of effect that the environment can have in the expression of the trait. Every trait, even our gender identity, can be affected by environmental factors, which begin in the womb during the fetal period.

The full expression of our genetic potential will not be known until development is complete. For example, gender identity, height, and bone structure are not complete until puberty, and IQ develops well into young adulthood. Regardless of genetic endowment, environmental conditions can be adjusted to maximize the genetic potential of each individual.

PRENATAL DEVELOPMENT

Prenatal development is divided into stages in various ways. Obstetricians and prospective parents often divide pregnancy into three equal periods of three months each, called trimesters. More descriptive, however, is another type of division made by embryologists (scientists who study prenatal development). Embryologists refer to three stages that correspond to developments after fertilization. The first stage covers the period from fertilization to implantation. In this stage, the **zygote,** or **conceptus,** travels into the womb, where it is implanted in the wall, which has been prepared for it by hormonal changes in the mother's body. The second stage begins after implantation and extends through the first eight weeks following fertilization. During the second stage, the developing life is called an **embryo.** The third and final stage begins at nine weeks after fertilization and continues until birth, at approximately 38 weeks. From the beginning of this stage, the **fetus** (from the Latin term for "young one") is clearly recognizable as having human characteristics.

There are two different ways of identifying the ages of the developing child before birth. Doctors often refer to **menstrual age,** which is the age figured from the last menstrual period the mother had before becoming pregnant. Of course, fertilization occurs approximately two weeks after the last menstrual period. The actual age of the developing child can be computed by subtracting two weeks from menstrual age to obtain the actual age since fertilization occurred, called **gestational age.** The gestational age method is used in this chapter for assessing age during prenatal life.

Mary and Brett Johnson are eager to understand the development of their baby. As soon as the pregnancy is confirmed, they ask their doctor about human development in the womb. A great deal of information is available to them to explain developmental processes. They are especially excited by their doctor's promise that they will have an ultrasound. It is hard to believe that through the technology of ultrasound it will be possible to actually see the baby moving inside's Mary womb.

In the following sections, prenatal development will be described. Information on physical, sensory, and psychological development will be given. Various sources have been used for this information, including explanations from Nilsson, Ingelman-Sundberg, and Wirsen (1981) and Moore and Persand (1992), the early work on movement from Hooker (1939), and the summary of psychological and preferential behavior reported in Verny (1981). In addition to traditional research, the new technologies associated with ultra-sound imaging have added tremendous knowledge to our understanding of prenatal development. With these new techniques, it is possible to observe developments in the earliest weeks of pregnancy and to observe organ develop-ment so that we can understand the nature of malformations and imple-ment medical interventions, such as fetal surgery (Timor-Tritsch, Peisner, & Raju, 1990; Timor-Tritsch & Rottem, 1988). Real-time ultrasound allows us to actually see the fetus moving in the womb in a way never before possible. (See Developmental Issues in Practice 3.3 for information on the effect that the availability of ultrasound imaging has had on parents.)

Fertilization

Fertilization is the process of beginning a new life. It starts with contact between sperm and ovum and ends with intermingling of paternal and mater-nal chromosomes. The result of the fusion between sperm and egg is a single cell, containing a completely unique set of genetic material, which is called a **zygote**. This zygote is the first cell of a new, developing human being.

Besides creating a new life, fertilization performs three other significant functions. First, the union of sperm and egg, each carrying 23 chromosomes, restores the usual number of 46 chromosomes in the zygote. Second, the process of fertilization ensures variation among human characteristics. Half of the chromosomes coming to the zygote are from the mother and half are from the father; the zygote consequently has a unique intermingling of char-acteristics. Third, the gender of the zygote is determined by the kind of sperm that fertilizes the ovum.

The zygote spends the early part of the first week after fertilization in the fallopian tube on the way to the uterus. Signals from the ovary control muscles in the fallopian tube as the fertilized ovum moves toward the uterus.

In the fallopian tube, the zygote undergoes cell division. Before the entire cell divides, each chromosome is duplicated precisely. Then the two like chromosomes separate from each other and move into two new cells, called blastomeres. Other cell divisions follow rapidly in an orderly fashion, producing smaller and smaller blastomeres. The mechanism of duplication enables an infinite series of new cells to receive the same genetic material.

By the third day after fertilization, a ball of about 16 blastomeres is formed. At about five or six days after fertilization, the zygote reaches the uterus. At this time, two different parts can be recognized: an inner cell mass, which gradually differentiates into a human being, and outer cells, which later become the **placenta** (the organ that permits the exchange of materials carried in the bloodstreams of the mother and the developing new life).

Until two weeks after fertilization, there is great flexibility in the cells, and normal human development will occur in spite of major environmental assaults. However, at two weeks, **gastrulation** occurs, which turns the ball of cells inside out to form a hollow ball surrounded by three layers. Each layer now has a specific purpose and will mature into cells of a specific type, such

▲ **DEVELOPMENTAL ISSUES IN PRACTICE   3.3**

ULTRASOUND IMAGING

The use of **ultrasound** imaging has dramatically changed the way new parents view the pregnancy. It is becoming routine for mothers to have an ultrasound performed to check for malformations and to estimate an accurate date for the delivery of the baby. The procedure is entirely noninvasive and is not associated with any known dangers or side effects.

Ultrasound utilizes high-frequency sound waves, which are transmitted into the mother and reflected back through a transducer. A computer then takes the signals and creates the image on the screen. In the 1970s, real-time ultrasound was developed, making it possible to see moving images of the unborn baby. Originally, these signals were poor and created vague images on the screen, which were difficult to interpret. However, during the 1980s, new developments made it possible to get much better resolutions of the image, which has had a great impact on fetal medicine.

From the point of view of the parents, the procedure is quite simple. The pregnant mother lies comfortably on a table and a gel is placed directly on her skin over her uterus. This facilitates transmission of the sound waves from the transducer, which is a small hand-held object the sonographer moves about on the woman's stomach to obtain the best images. It is very rewarding for the father and other members of the family to watch the developing baby on the ultrasound screen. Many families have their first baby picture before their baby is even born. (Later in the chapter, Figure 3.5 shows such a picture at 10 weeks gestational age.)

as muscle, nerve, and blood cells. This eliminates the flexibility of the earlier developmental period. The entire future development of the organism depends on a correct process of gastrulation occurring. The processes of cell development and pattern formation (i.e., putting the cells into proper form to create body parts) are controlled by chemical messages sent out from the genes.

Recent research has identified a **homeo box** in the genetic material, which controls the timing of the sending of the genetic messages during the prenatal period. The homeo box is a discrete grouping of genes, which occur in the DNA of every species of animal. It appears to function as an executive controller. The homeo box has the same appearance whether it occurs in a fish, fruit fly, or human being. It is possible for chemicals in the environment to interfere with the chemical messages sent out by the homeo box, causing malformations in the developing child. The most critical time for such problems occurs between 15 and 60 days after fertilization.

Figure 3.2 presents a schematic illustration of the critical periods during prenatal development. As can be seen from the chart, during the first two weeks the zygote is not affected by teratogens. However, beginning at three

DEVELOPMENTAL ISSUES IN PRACTICE   3.3 (continued)

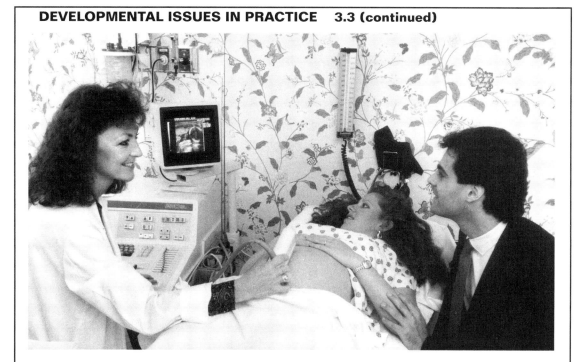

In this picture, the ultrasonographer holds the transducer on the mother's stomach, while the father looks on. The computer and the screen with the ultrasound image can be seen beside the bed.

weeks after fertilization, as each major organ system develops, the zygote becomes susceptible to major abnormalities in form, called morphological abnormalities. Once the organs are fully formed, the defects that can occur are relatively minor or are those affecting the functioning of the organ (these problems will be discussed in the section on congenital malformations).

Implantation

Implantation is the embedding of the zygote into the wall of the womb, where it can be nourished and can grow. The process of implantation is completed by the end of the second week after fertilization. At implantation the zygote is a sphere consisting of outer cells that burrow into the uterine wall and form a placenta to nourish growth. The inner cells are forming into the specialized cells that develop into the human being.

Embryonic Stage

The **embryonic stage** begins after implantation and extends until the end of the eighth week after fertilization. During the embryonic stage, all the major

Figure 3.2 *Critical Periods in Human Prenatal Development.*
Schematic illustration of the sensitive or critical periods of human development. Dark shading denotes highly sensitive periods; lighter shading indicates stages that are less sensitive to teratogens. Note that each organ or structure has a critical period during which its development may be deranged. Physiological defects, functional disturbances, and minor morphological changes are likely to result from disturbances during the fetal period. Severe mental retardation may result from exposure of the developing human to high levels of radiation during the 8–16-wk. period.

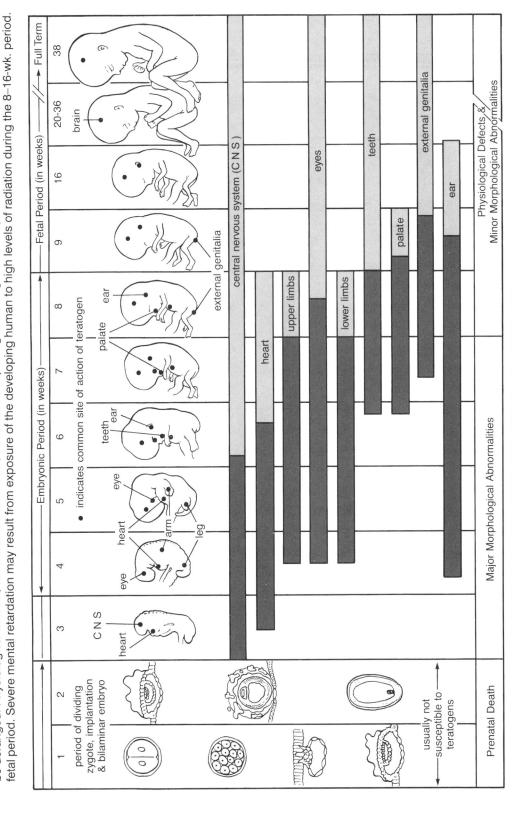

SOURCE: From K. L. Moore, *Before We Are Born*, 2nd ed. Philadelphia: W. B. Saunders, 1983, p. 111.

82

organ systems begin to form, although their function is still minimal. Because the organs are developing, exposure of an embryo to certain dangerous substances can cause major congenital malformations.

Dramatic changes in the appearance of the embryo occur during this stage. During the third week after fertilization, the embryo resembles a disk. By the eighth week, though, the embryo has taken on a distinctively human appearance. Because of the importance of changes during this stage, we chronicle them week by week, beginning with the third week after fertilization.

Week 3. The third week after fertilization often coincides with the first missed menstrual period. Most pregnancy tests establish the presence of a hormone, human chorionic gonadotropin (HCG), which originates from the placenta. This hormone goes into the mother's blood to prevent menstruation, is excreted through the kidneys, and can be detected by testing the urine. Although cessation of menstruation may be the first sign of pregnancy, it does not necessarily follow that bleeding at the expected time of menstruation rules out pregnancy. There can be some bleeding from the area where the zygote is implanting.

The third week is important because some critical structures form. The basis is laid for the skull, the sternum, and the vertebral column; the central nervous system; and a primitive cardiovascular system. In fact, the primitive heart is believed to begin beating by the end of the third week, making the cardiovascular system the first to function.

Week 4. By the fourth week the placenta is well enough developed to facilitate exchanges between embryo and mother. From maternal blood to embryo come water, nutrients, and hormones. Wastes pass from embryo to mother through the placenta. During week four, the umbilical cord begins to form.

Although the basis for organ development is laid in the first three weeks, it is only during the fourth week that major organs begin to be definitive in form. The nervous system, cardiovascular system, and renal system undergo rapid expansion. The first sensory organs appear: the precursors of the inner ears, the lenses of the eyes, and the tongue. Lung buds form and the esophagus and stomach are delineated.

The rapid development of internal organs affects the external structure of the embryo. During the fourth week, the embryo changes from a disk-shaped form to a tubular structure. The head and neck regions are disproportionately large. Late in the fourth week, arm and leg buds appear.

Week 5. At the start of the fifth week of development, the embryo measures 7 millimeters (mm), about the same diameter as most pencils. Even though the embryo is small, most of its organ systems are already present. In the fifth week, organ systems continue to rapidly grow, and new structures appear, such as the cerebrum, cerebellum, and spleen.

The most striking change during week five is the development of the face of the embryo. Expansion of the cerebral hemispheres creates a forehead, and lens pits and nasal pits are visible. By the end of the fifth week, the face seems recognizable as human.

There are other highlights of the fifth week. Limb buds show signs of hand and foot development. Spinal nerves, cranial nerves, and olfactory pits form. The esophagus elongates and the stomach rotates. The liver mass enlarges and the heart changes from having two chambers to having four. Internal and external genitalia form, but there is as yet no differentiation between males and females.

Week 6.   As the sixth week begins, the embryo is about 14 mm long. The most important milestone of the sixth week of development is that the neuromuscular system is operational, although at a primitive level. Touching the skin around the mouth of the embryo can evoke a movement response in its body, which is the first indication of activation of the neural system by the environment. Note from Figure 3.2 that the arms are still very short during this period of development, causing the hands to rest directly in front of the mouth. It is quite likely that this placement facilitates stimulation of the mouth, the only area susceptible to activation of the neuromuscular response system (Franz, 1981).

In the sixth week, facial changes are again notable. The upper lip forms, the eyes move to face forward, the ears become defined, and the nose now has a tip. The face appears quite human with these changes.

Changes also take place in the urogenital system. In week six, the internal genitalia become distinctly either ovaries or testes. The external genitalia, however, do not differentiate until later in development.

Weeks 7–8.   The seventh and eighth weeks mark the last part of the embryonic stage of development. For the most part, the continuing development of organs is rather modest in comparison with the development that took place earlier. A few external changes occur: the proportions of the limbs begin to approximate those found in adults, fingers and toes develop further, eyelids develop, and all body contours become more rounded. By the end of the seventh week, establishment of organs and organ systems is complete and there is the first production of bone cells.

The embryo is still small, measuring 23 mm at the start of the eighth week and 30 mm at the end of the week. Before the end of the eighth week, the first spontaneous movements can be observed, which generally involve whole body movement from side to side. It is also at this time that the first brain waves can be detected and monitored.

This marks the end of the embryonic period, an important phase because all the parts of the body that will appear in the adult person are already present. In addition, the embryo has the definite external appearance of a baby. Most congenital malformations will have occurred by this time. The

mother will have just missed her second menstrual period. Thus, most important development occurs before the mother even knows she is pregnant.

Fetal Stage

The term *fetus* means "young one." The fetal stage begins at the point when
the new life has become recognizable as a human being. Week nine, counting
from the time of fertilization, is usually considered to be the beginning of this
stage. The fetal stage ends at birth, which usually occurs 38 weeks after fertilization.

The fetal stage is characterized mainly by growth and differentiation of
tissues and organs. Few new structures appear during the fetal stage, but
there are dramatic changes in size and weight (see Figure 3.3 for a description of the size changes that occur during the fetal stage). In addition, sensory

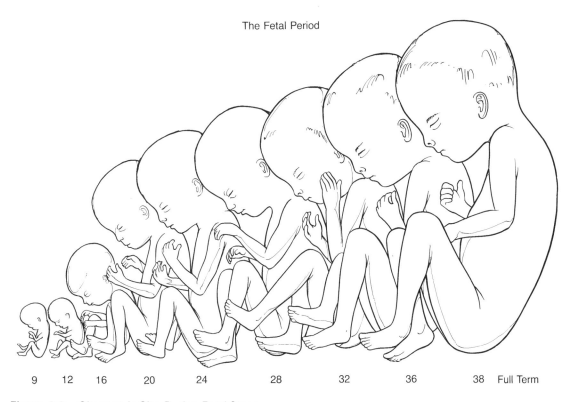

The Fetal Period

9   12   16   20   24   28   32   36   38   Full Term

Figure 3.3 *Changes in Size During Fetal Stage.*
The embryonic period ends at the culmination of the 8th week; by this time, the beginnings of all essential structures are present. The fetal period, extending from the 9th week
until birth, is characterized by growth and elaboration of structures. Sex is clearly distin-
guishable by 12 weeks.
SOURCE: From K. L. Moore, *Before We Are Born*, 2nd ed. Philadelphia: W. B. Saunders, 1983, p. 5.

organs develop and the fetus develops individualized responses to the environment. Development in the fetal stage is described in units of four or five weeks.

Weeks 9–12.   During the first four weeks of the fetal stage, the length of the fetus more than doubles. At the end of 12 weeks from fertilization, the arms have reached appropriate proportions, and the individualized fingerprints that will identify this person as an adult are already present. The legs are less well developed and are still somewhat shorter than their final length relative to the body. Growth of the head now slows in comparison with the growth of other parts of the body. (See Figure 3.4 for a diagram of the body proportions during the fetal stage.)

   External genitalia of males and females seem similar at the start of the 9th week. However, by the 12th week, mature genital form is apparent.

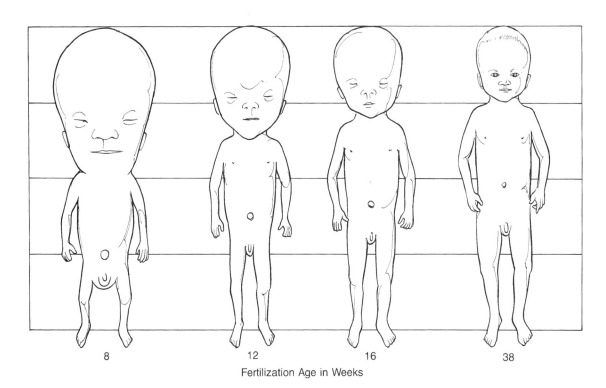

Fertilization Age in Weeks

Figure 3.4   *Changes in Body Proportions During Fetal Stage.*
Diagram illustrating the changing proportions of the body during the fetal period. By 36 weeks the circumferences of the head and the abdomen are approximately equal. After this, the circumference of the abdomen may be greater. All stages are drawn to the same total height.
SOURCE: From K. L. Moore, *Before We Are Born*, 2nd ed. Philadelphia: W. B. Saunders, 1983, p. 70.

Figure 3.5 *Ultrasound Picture of a 10-Week-Old Fetus*

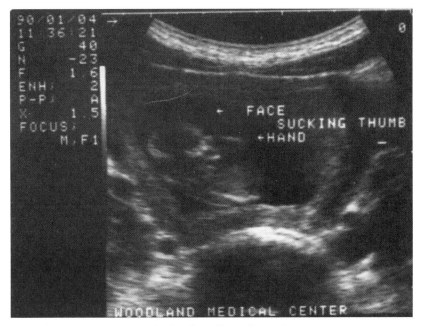

SOURCE: Used with permission from Soundwave Images.

The spontaneous movements of the sixth week evolve into organized patterns of jumping, rolling, and twisting during the 9th to 12th weeks. However, the mother cannot yet detect the movement because the fetus is too small to cause sufficient pressure on the mother's body. Ultrasound images show the incredible spontaneous activity of the fetus at this stage of development. (See Figure 3.5 for a picture of a 10-week-old fetus taken with ultrasound methods.)

At 9 weeks, responses to stimulation become differentiated and localized. That is, if the hand or foot is stroked, only the hand and foot, not the entire body, respond to the sensation. Although these movements are avoidant at this stage, they are the beginnings of important reflexes, such as grasping and the plantar flexion of the toes, which will be well developed at birth. By 12 weeks, stimulation of the area around the mouth causes movements that resemble the rooting reflex, including swallowing motions, which are essential to the newborn's ability to find the nipple and suck. In addition, all other newborn reflexes are present in rudimentary form.

It has been found that there are two major periods of brain growth by cell division. The division of nerve cells takes place between the 10th and 20th weeks of prenatal development. It is not possible to add cells later in life, so this is a critical period of development. The growth of glial cells occurs between the 20th week and four months after birth (Werner, 1979).

By 12 weeks, the eye is completely formed. The eyelid closes over the eye and will not open until the seventh month in the womb.

Weeks 13–16.   During weeks 13 and 16, the most dramatic changes in size will occur, as shown in Figure 3.3. By the 16th week, the lower limbs have lengthened, and the head, limbs, and body are closer to achieving mature relative proportions. Bones are developing, and if X rays are taken, the general skeleton shows clearly.

By 14 weeks, the reflex movements of the fetus are responsive, not avoidant. For example, if the face is stroked, the fetus will turn toward the stimulus and seek it out. If the hand is stroked, the hand will move toward the stimulus.

By 16 weeks, the ears are completely developed and the fetus can hear. Traditionally, it was thought that the world of the womb was silent and that babies were first introduced to noise upon delivery. It has been conclusively shown that the fetus can hear during the last months in the womb and that the inside of the mother is a very noisy place. The fetus can hear the rumblings of the stomach, the sound of the heart beating and the blood pulsing through the arterial system, the regular sound of the diaphragm moving air through the lungs, and the sound of the mother's voice. Research has shown that newborn infants prefer to listen to the sounds that are familiar to them from the prenatal environment, including the sound of the mother's voice and specific stories she may read or songs she may sing (DeCasper & Fifer, 1980; Stickrod, Kimble, & Smotherman, 1982; Verny, 1981). See Developmental Issues in Practice 3.4 for an example of the effects that fetal auditory ability can have on the new parents.

Weeks 17–20.   During weeks 17 through 20, the fetus becomes large enough and strong enough for fetal movements, called quickening, to be felt for the first time by the mother. Growth slows during these weeks, but fat forms, which will provide a source of heat for infants in the period after birth.

By 18 weeks, the grasping ability of the hand is present. The fingers flex independently and the thumb can move in opposition to the fingers. The fetus is capable of grasping the hands or the umbilical cord, sucking the thumb or fingers, and scratching the face.

The skin is covered with a greasy, cheeselike coating called vernix caseosa, which protects the skin of the fetus from the effects of amniotic fluid. By the 20th week, the body of the fetus is covered with fine downy hair, called lanugo, which perhaps serves to hold the vernix on the skin. Hair also appears on the scalp and eyebrows.

The growth of glial cells in the brain takes place from the 20th week of prenatal development to four months after birth (Werner, 1979). Glial cells appear in response to environmental stimulation and mark the storage places for learned material. The density of glial cells is directly related to levels of intellectual ability. This is a critical period for development of these brain cells. If they fail to develop during this time, intellectual impairment can

▲ **DEVELOPMENTAL ISSUES IN PRACTICE   3.4**

FETAL AUDITORY ABILITY

Most parents have a story about the responses of their unborn baby to sound stimuli. For example, one young mother reported having to leave a rock concert during her eighth month of pregnancy because the baby kicked so much at the loud sounds. Another mother, who played the bass guitar in the local orchestra, was forced to quit at seven months into her pregnancy because of the kicking of the baby when she attempted to play. Another mother reported that during her ninth month of pregnancy her baby woke up and kicked her during an especially bad thunderstorm one night.

There is evidence that this ability to hear sounds during the last months of pregnancy may provide the baby with comfort after birth. We know that the mother's voice can calm the baby best. Now we have found that the mother can calm the baby after birth with stories she read every day during the fetal period or with songs she has sung. One mother reported that her baby relaxed when listening to piano music she had played during the last months of her pregnancy.

Because the heartbeat of the mother is the most common sound heard by the baby in the womb, this sound should soothe the baby after birth. Some mothers make a recording of their heartbeat using the special equipment used by obstetricians to listen to the baby's heart during the pregnancy. This recording can then be played in the baby's room after birth to help facilitate sleeping. Parents can also buy commercial recordings of "sounds from the womb," which have been found to calm babies during the newborn period.

All this information helps to explain why a newborn baby will be comforted and go to sleep when the mother holds the baby next to her heart and talks to him or her. It also helps us to appreciate the importance of the events that the mother experiences during the last months of pregnancy.

result. However, because this critical period crosses over from prenatal into postnatal life, if there is deprivation during the fetal period it can be made up by good care immediately following birth.

Weeks 21–25. Weeks 21 through 25 are a time of substantial weight gain in the fetus. All organs are well developed, but fetuses born at this point are at great risk because their respiratory systems remain immature. The final maturation of the lungs occurs just prior to birth. Meanwhile, the diaphragm functions and breathing movements occur; however, the lungs cannot bring oxygen to the fetus. Oxygen is provided by the mother's body through the umbilical cord.

It has long been known that fetuses at this stage are capable of learning. In a classic study (Spelt, 1948), a vibration was paired with a loud noise that made fetuses kick. After repeated exposures, the fetuses kicked when presented with the vibration but not the noise. Research with animals is confirming these findings (Smotherman, 1982).

During these weeks, the fetus will begin to respond to many stimuli, including tactile pressure, general pressure, kinesthetic sensation, temperature, pain, vestibular movement, sound, taste, and light. These responses cause the development of glial cells in the developing brain. Mothers notice that their babies develop preferences. For example, if the mother slumps in her chair or turns over during the night, the baby will begin to move about until finding a more preferred position. Loud noises will cause startle responses in the baby, and certain kinds of music, especially very loud music, will cause a great deal of kicking, usually assumed to indicate stress. Sudden changes in temperature, such as when one steps into a cold swimming pool, also cause momentary stress reactions.

Weeks 26–29.   During weeks 26 through 29, the respiratory system gradually completes development, and the nervous system becomes capable of directing breathing movements and providing some control of body temperature. Thus, fetuses born prematurely after the 26th week have a higher survival rate than premature babies born before the 26th week. (See Chapter 4 for further discussion of respiratory development.)

More fat forms under the skin, giving a smoother, rounder appearance. Often, fetuses begin to assume an upside-down position as birth approaches. In males, the testes begin to descend.

During this time, it is possible to measure the tracing of brain waves (i.e., an electroencephalogram, or EEG). It is possible from these measurements to identify sleep/awake cycles in the fetus. In addition, active sleep can be measured, which indicates that dreaming occurs.

At 28 weeks, the eyelids, which have been closed since the third month, open again. The fetus has the capacity to see, even in this dark environment. Eye movements begin to occur and are associated with the waking state and the active sleep of the fetus, which is similar to the behavior of adults. Neonates have visual preferences that appear to correspond to images that could most likely be seen in the womb: black/white patterns with rounded edges.

Weeks 30–34.   By the end of weeks 30–34, the fetus's arms and legs often have filled out. At 30 weeks after fertilization, the fetus's pupils reflexively change in size when exposed to light. Newer techniques of photography in the pregnant womb demonstrate that the fetus finds bright lights aversive and attempts to avoid looking at the light by turning the head and holding up a protective hand.

Weeks 35–38.   At 35 weeks after fertilization, fetuses have a firm grasp and can grip an adult's finger with sufficient strength to lift their own weight. Growth slows, but most fetuses are already rounded by this time. The average size of a fetus at birth is seven pounds and 19.5 inches. At the time of birth, both male and female fetuses have prominent genitals and protruding breasts, due to hormones present in the fetal environment.

Birth is expected at about 38 weeks after fertilization, and most infants are born within 10–15 days of this time. Second and later pregnancies last longer than first pregnancies; infants of these later pregnancies are usually larger at birth than their older siblings.

Behavioral Consistency from Prenatal to Newborn Periods

It has been known for many years that extreme emotional stress in the mother causes stress reactions in the fetus, which consist of extraordinary kicking and prolonged movement (Carmichael, 1970; Sontag & Wallace, 1934). Extreme emotions in the pregnant woman, such as the stress brought about by war, famine, or death of a spouse, can bring about changes in her body chemistry, which may affect the fetus's body (Van den Bergh, 1990). According to researchers such as Verny (1981), intense and ongoing emotions can change an unborn child's normal biological rhythms. Verny presents data from animal research that there may be certain times in development when the fetal brain and nervous system are most vulnerable to overflows of maternal neurohormones.

The evidence for such specific effects in humans is still primarily anecdotal. However, Van den Bergh (1990) found correlations between maternal anxiety and fetal movement. The effects continued into the neonatal period. Other data show that there are many continuities between the prenatal and newborn periods, which suggests that events during prenatal life may well influence later development. For example, it has been found that fetal and newborn heart rates are very similar (Lewis, Wilson, Ban, & Baumel, 1970). This is important because a slowing of the heart rate is an indication of attention and thus provides information on the attention span of the individual. It has also been found that cardiac levels taken during the prenatal period predict differences in cognitive style in childhood (Lacey, Kagan, Lacey, & Moss, 1962). Furthermore, amounts of fetal activity can be related to performance on developmental tests (Walters, 1965) and on measures of temperament (Eaton & Saudino, 1992) during the early months after birth. We will discuss these issues further in Chapter 4 in the sections on birth and adaptation to the new environment.

PRENATAL CARE OF THE MOTHER

Mary Johnson is finding that pregnancy requires that she make adaptations in her routine. It is important that she care for herself, because her health and well-being are essential to the good outcome of the pregnancy and the optimal health of her baby. It is best if Mary has been taking good care of herself even before pregnancy; it is really too late for her to begin after she finds out she is pregnant, because so much of her baby's development has already occurred by then.

Appropriate prenatal care of the mother involves two key components: medical supervision and good nutrition. Both components are important to the healthy development of the fetus. Information about these components is presented, and then the effects of poverty on prenatal care are described.

Medical Supervision

A woman should schedule an appointment with a doctor or medical clinic at the first signs of pregnancy. Usually, absence of menstruation is the first clue, but other bodily changes sometimes also take place (e.g., increased need for rest, tenderness of breasts, and nausea in the morning). The complexity and importance of this early embryonic growth highlight the need for women in the child-bearing years to take good care of their bodies—if not for themselves, for the baby that could be developing. Good health habits and good nutrition are necessary at all times.

At a woman's first visit to a doctor or clinic, the pregnancy is confirmed by one of several tests. A complete medical history is taken, and some current information is recorded: weight, blood pressure, and general health. Blood tests determine whether the woman is anemic; has syphilis, rubella, or HIV; or can anticipate Rh blood incompatibility. A pelvic examination adds additional information about the probable duration of the pregnancy.

Nutrition

The importance of good nutrition has been underscored in recent years as more is understood about fetal development. For many years, it was assumed that almost any woman would be able to supply the needs of her fetus. Evidence now shows that infants of malnourished mothers may be born with permanent disabilities.

Research indicates that undernutrition during pregnancy may cause permanent damage to the fetal central nervous system; in these cases, the person's lifelong capacity for intellectual functioning is reduced. If undernutrition takes place during periods of growth by cell division, the actual number of cells in the brain (and other parts of the body) may be reduced. Later behavioral problems can be related to malnourishment during pregnancy, and damage from malnutrition after birth is more likely if there was poor maternal nutrition before birth (Simopoulos, 1986; Winick, 1976). The possible long-term effects of poor nutrition during pregnancy are sobering.

Many poorly nourished fetuses have been assumed to be premature—that is, they appear underdeveloped as though they had been born early—but in reality they are born malnourished. Because of this confusion, the use of the term *premature* is being discontinued in medical circles. Instead, infants are called **preterm** if they are born early and **small for date** if they are born at term but have not grown as would be expected. Poor maternal nutrition is one major cause of infants who are small for date and have low birth weight. Infant mortality and incidence of disabilities are directly related to low birth weight.

Nutritional supplementation before and during pregnancy is recommended for high-risk women (Newman, Lyon, & Anderson, 1990). These can be very effective in increasing birth weights and later functioning levels of individuals. Cross-cultural research has demonstrated that providing nutritional supplementation during pregnancy is related to improved performance on psychological tests during the first three years of life (Werner, 1979) and into late adolescence (Pollitt, Gorman, Engle, Martorell, & Rivera, 1993).

It is recommended that women gain at least 25–35 pounds during pregnancy and more weight (28–40 pounds) if there is a previous history of undernutrition. There is evidence that excessive weight gain (more than 200 pounds) is also associated with high-risk pregnancy and compromised newborn condition, but weight reduction is not recommended during pregnancy (Whitney & Rolfes, 1993). A balanced daily diet during pregnancy should include 4 servings of milk and milk products, 3 servings of protein foods, 3 to 4 servings of fruit, 4 to 5 servings of vegetables, and 7 to 11 servings of grain products (Food and Nutrition Board, 1992).

It is unfortunate that not all Americans have equal access to the resources needed for healthy prenatal nutrition. When families have limited economic resources, prenatal well-being is compromised (Gould & LeRoy, 1988). Myron Winick (1976) has made the following dramatic statement about the economic basis for differences in birth weights: "If birth weights are equal, poor babies survive as well as rich babies, black babies as well as white babies" (p. 98). His underlying point, of course, is that birth weights are not equal and neither are survival rates. The social costs of poor nutrition and low birth weight are great because those who survive have a higher than average incidence of various developmental problems. William Frankenburg (Brown, 1981) reports that half of the infants born into poverty circumstances will have problems in school. However, nutritional problems in these populations are confounded with many other social problems, so it is difficult to tell which variables create the greatest effect (Simopoulos, 1986; Whitney & Rolfes, 1993).

CAUSES OF CONGENITAL MALFORMATIONS

Congenital malformations are structural or anatomical abnormalities that are present when an infant is born. These malformations may be visible on the body, limbs, or head of an infant or may be hidden within the infant's body. About 20% of deaths in the period just before and just after birth can be related to congenital malformations, and later they are the single greatest cause of severe illness and death in infancy (Moore & Persand, 1993).

We will discuss the causes of congenital malformations, including genetic factors, environmental factors, interaction of factors, and maternal–fetal blood incompatibility. The primary sources of information about congenital malformations are excellent books on embryology and heredity by Moore and Persand (1993) and Gardner (1983). Before discussing the specific categories, some issues will be addressed regarding genetic screening, which is a method for prenatal identification of malformations.

Genetic Screening

Testing for carriers.   It is possible to use tests to identify potential **carriers** of genetic defects before they start their families. Simple blood tests are run to identify the diseases in the parents that would damage a child born to two carriers with the same harmful trait or to a mother who has an X-linked defect. It is possible to identify carriers of traits such as sickle-cell anemia and thalassemia. Eight percent of African Americans are carriers of the defective sickle-cell gene, and 1 in 600 African American children has the resulting disease, sickle-cell anemia. The disease causes fatigue, shortness of breath, pain, low resistance to infections, and clogged blood vessels in internal organs. Frequent blood transfusions can keep some patients alive, but there is as yet no cure for this disease. In the case of thalassemia, about 1 in 25 individuals of Italian or Greek ancestry are carriers, and 1 in 2,500 babies develops the most severe form of the disease. Infants with thalassemia seem normal at first, but during the first year or two they develop frequent infections, enlarged liver and spleen, and brittleness of bones. Blood transfusions are necessary for life to continue; and, again, there is no cure.

Enzyme levels in blood and skin cells can be measured to identify carriers of Tay-Sachs and related diseases. Tay-Sachs strikes Ashkenazi Jewish descendants, with about 1 in 30 being carriers of the defect. There is no treatment or cure when an infant is born with Tay-Sachs. From about six months of age, the brain and nervous system stop functioning, leading to deterioration and death in early childhood.

Amniocentesis.   An analysis of the genetic makeup of the fetus can be obtained by a method called **amniocentesis,** which involves the extraction and analysis of the amniotic fluid in the uterus. Amniocentesis is usually done after the 16th week of pregnancy. The amniotic fluid is obtained by inserting a needle through the abdominal wall into the woman's uterus (see Figure 3.6). The amniotic fluid contains fetal cells and can be used for genetic analysis. Amniocentesis is suggested only when a woman has a higher than normal chance of having a child with a defect, such as Down syndrome. This is because there is a chance (approximately 3–3.5% risk) of fetal damage and miscarriage from the procedure itself (O'Brien, 1984). Nearly 100 chromosomal disorders can be detected prenatally by analyzing fetal cells. Other nongenetic problems, such as spina bifida (open spine) and anencephaly (absence of the upper cortex of the brain), can also be diagnosed by testing the amniotic fluid for high levels of fetal proteins such as alpha fetoprotein (AFP). In addition, amniocentesis gives incidental information on the gender of the fetus.

Amniocentesis must usually be postponed until about 16 weeks after fertilization, when there is sufficient amniotic fluid for a safe procedure. Several weeks are then required for analysis, which means that a pregnancy can be in its fifth month before results of analysis are available. Waiting until midpregnancy for this information can extract an emotional toll from the prospective parents.

Figure 3.6 *Amniocentesis.*
A needle is inserted through the
lower abdominal wall and the
uterine wall into the amniotic
cavity. A syringe is attached and
amniotic fluid is withdrawn for
diagnostic purposes (e.g., for
cell cultures or protein studies).
Amniocentesis is relatively
devoid of risk, especially when
combined with ultrasonography
for placental localization. The
risk of injuring the fetus with the
needle is also minimized by
using ultrasound. The technique
is usually performed at 15 to 16
weeks of gestation. Prior to this
stage of development, there is
relatively little amniotic fluid, and
the difficulties in obtaining it
without endangering the mother
or the fetus are consequently
greater. There is an excessive
amount of amniotic fluid (polyhy-
dramnios) in the case illustrated
in this figure.
SOURCE: From K. L. Moore,
Before We Are Born, 2nd ed.
Philadelphia: W. B. Saunders, 1983,
p. 78.

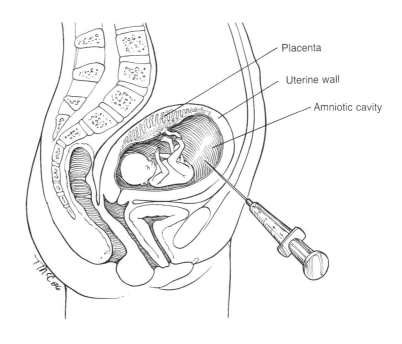

Placenta

Uterine wall

Amniotic cavity

Ultrasound tests.   Ultrasound can confirm some diagnoses and is also used
to ascertain the presence of hydrocephalus, a buildup of fluid in the brain. It
can also be used to examine structural malformations of the placenta, the
embryo, fetal heart, limb development, organ development, the central nervous system, and the genitalia. Ultrasound is also used to accompany surgery
in which the fetus is temporarily removed from the womb for the procedure
and then returned.

Newborn screening.   Screening programs have also been developed for
newborns. Phenylketonuria (PKU), a disease resulting in retardation, is transmitted by a recessive gene and occurs once in about 18,000 births. PKU cannot be detected prenatally but is treatable if a special diet is given from birth
until five or more years of age. Nearly all states require routine screening of
all newborns for PKU.

Screening programs raise many ethical problems for families. Some of
these concerns are discussed in Developmental Issues in Practice 3.5, which
examines the counseling used in genetic screening programs.

Genetic Factors

Genetic factors seem to predominate as causes of congenital malformations. About 1 in 200 newborns has abnormalities in either the number or structure of chromosomes.

Numerical abnormalities.   Numerical abnormalities of chromosomes usually take place as a result of errors in cell division. Ordinarily, chromosomes exist in 23 pairs: 22 ordinary chromosomes plus 2 X chromosomes for females and one X and one Y chromosome for males. Most embryos lacking one or more chromosomes die. However, some embryos lacking a sex chromosome survive and show symptoms of Turner's syndrome, including small size, webbed neck, and absence of sexual maturation.

In another, more frequent type of numerical abnormality, three chromosomes are in the place of the usual pair. The disorder, called trisomy, is caused when chromosomes do not separate and a sperm cell or an egg cell has 24 rather than the usual 23 chromosomes. If that sperm or egg is involved in fertilization, there are 47 rather than 46 chromosomes. The most common condition of this type is trisomy 21, or Down syndrome, in which a third chromosome (number 21) is present. The incidence of Down syndrome is 1 in 800 births. Symptoms include mental retardation, a characteristic facial structure, and congenital heart defects. Trisomies increase in frequency of occurrence with increases in maternal age. Down syndrome, for instance, is present in 1 in 2,000 births to mothers under 25 years of age but is present in 1 in 100 mothers over the age of 40. Trisomy of sex chromosomes leads to impaired sexual development and sterility. Rarely, infants are born with four or five sex chromosomes; they are usually mentally retarded and physically impaired.

Structural abnormalities.   Structural abnormalities of chromosomes, sometimes called Mendelian disorders, result from submicroscopic defects, usually in the DNA of one gene. Mendelian disorders are thought to take place by mutation, which occurs when DNA is not replicated accurately, causing permanent genetic changes that can be transmitted from parent to child. Mendelian disorders can remain unexpressed (hidden) for many generations, as is the case when only one chromosome carries the abnormality. Or they can be expressed and seen, as when both chromosomes of a pair carry the defective DNA. About 2,000 Mendelian disorders have been identified. Examples include cystic fibrosis, Tay-Sachs disease, thalassemia, and sickle-cell anemia. Individual Mendelian disorders are rare, but some ethnic groups have frequencies as high as 1 in 100 births.

Environmental Factors

Teratogens.   For a long time, scientists assumed that genetic factors were responsible for most congenital malformations, but now it is known that certain agents present in the environment of the embryo and fetus can cause

▲ DEVELOPMENTAL ISSUES IN PRACTICE   3.5

COUNSELING AND GENETIC SCREENING PROGRAMS

Screening programs and genetic counseling can involve participants in making some very difficult ethical decisions. If the results of an amniocentesis indicate that a fetus has multiple disabilities because of a genetic defect, does the couple choose to continue or to terminate the pregnancy?

Elkins, Stovall, Wilroy, and Dacus (1986) interviewed parents of children with Down syndrome. Although 28.6% of the families reported increased marital stress as a result of the birth of their Down syndrome child, 74.3% said it brought the marriage closer together and 72.7% said it brought the family closer together. In addition, 84% reported that having such a child was a rewarding experience overall. When asked about the use of amniocentesis as a means for determining that an abortion should be performed, the overwhelming response was negative. Most thought that amniocentesis should be available to women, but only 7.3% thought that abortion should always be performed if Down syndrome was detected and 34.7% thought abortion should not be allowed if it were detected.

The reason given by half of the women having amniocentesis was to make it possible for the family to prepare for a child with "special" needs. These parents reported frustration and anger that counselors and medical personnel focused so heavily on the negative aspects of living with a Down syndrome child and assumed that parents having amniocentesis did so with the intention of having an abortion. In this study, only 25% said they would have had an abortion had the test been positive. The parents indicated that counseling should include the positive as well as the negative aspects of caring for a child with Down syndrome. They also indicated that counseling should recognize the fact that most parents having amniocentesis do not do so with the intention of having an abortion.

Green-McGowan (1985) reported that doctors and other specialists who work with these parents are generally poorly informed about the potential life outcomes for children with so-called special needs. Parents report that they receive very little information about the potential for these children and they often feel pressured to make decisions with inadequate information.

Abortion has been legal in this country since a Supreme Court decision in 1973, but its legality does not ease the pain of deciding whether to terminate a pregnancy that is desired. Indeed, evidence indicates that terminating the pregnancy of a child with disabilities can cause psychological problems. It has long been known that the birth of such a child can cause family problems, including divorce. However, there is also evidence that family disruption, including communication disorders, family violence, and divorce, can occur as a result of terminating the pregnancy (Rue, 1985).

These children have Down syndrome, a numerical abnormality of chromosomes recognizable by delayed development and a characteristic facial structure.

malformations. These agents, called **teratogens,** include drugs, viruses, and other environmental factors that increase the incidence of congenital malformations. A new field of scientific study, teratology, has emerged in the past few decades. Teratology is the study of abnormal development and the causes of congenital malformations.

There are three factors that affect the impact of teratogens. One is the mother's body. The mother must process the teratogens before they reach the fetus. If she is not highly susceptible to them, they may be passed out of her body, doing little or no damage to the fetus. A second problem that complicates teratology is that the same agent can have varying effects, depending on when during pregnancy exposure is received. For instance, exposure to teratogens during the first two weeks may interfere with implantation or cause abortion of the embryo. Exposure to teratogens during the 15th through 16th days after fertilization can lead to conditions that alter the basic internal or external structure of the embryo. Each organ has a critical period of rapid cell division during which teratogens have the most damaging effect on development (refer again to Figure 3.2). Introduction of teratogens during the later fetal period does not usually alter basic structure, except of teeth, genitals, or the central nervous system, but it can affect growth, intellectual development, and other important aspects of functioning. A third complication involves the level of teratogen. A very small amount may do little damage; however, we have poor understanding of the direct effects of varying amounts of different teratogens.

Teratogenic effects. Some of the damage done by teratogens is difficult to identify at birth. For example, children may appear normal, but as they enter early childhood, learning disabilities may begin to appear. Various drugs have been associated with learning problems (Gray & Yaffe, 1986). Table 3.2 provides a summary of the relative risks for learning difficulties associated with certain drugs; the risks of the baby being born with learning difficulties and with more "severe" learning difficulties are listed separately for nine different types of drugs the mother could take.

Some of the damage done by teratogens during the fetal period may not be apparent for many years. The situation involving diethylstilbestrol (DES) illustrates the delayed effect that a teratogen can have. DES is a hormone that was given to pregnant women in the 1950s and 1960s to prevent miscarriage. At the time, DES was thought to be harmless, but in the mid-1960s doctors began to discover cases of vaginal cancer in teenage girls. These unusual cases were eventually linked with the mothers' use of DES to prevent miscarriage of those pregnancies.

Table 3.2. *Relative Risks for Learning Difficulties and Severe Learning Difficulties Associated with Drugs Taken During Pregnancy*

	Risk for Learning Difficulties	Risk for Severe Learning Difficulties
Antidiabetic drugs		1.99*
Antihistamines and antinauseants	0.83**	0.81**
Antidepressives	0.72*	
Barbiturates	1.13**	1.15*
Local anesthetics		0.77*
Parasympatholytic drugs		0.77*
Progestational agents	0.74*	
Technical aids	0.72**	
Topical antimicrobial agents	0.83**	

*p<.05
**p<.01

Note: Values of more than 1.00 indicate drugs used in pregnancy are associated with learning difficulties.

SOURCE: From D. B. Gray and S. J. Yaffe, "Prenatal Drugs and Learning Disabilities." *In* Michael Lewis (Ed.), *Learning Disabilities and Prenatal Risk*. Chicago: University of Chicago Press, 1986, p. 7. Used with permission.

Teratogenic drugs.   As in the case of DES, drugs prescribed during pregnancy can reach an unintended recipient (i.e., the developing embryo or fetus) and act as teratogens. The medical community once believed that the placenta insulated the fetus from any effects of drugs taken by the mother, but it is now understood that almost all drugs can cross the placenta to reach the fetus. Pregnant women who require medication for the maintenance of their own health should have specialized medical care to minimize the risks of congenital malformations.

The case of the drug thalidomide alerted physicians to the need for special safeguards in prescriptions written for pregnant women. In 1960, West German doctors noted a particularly high incidence of births of infants with severely deformed limbs and other problems. Cases also were reported in other parts of Europe. Investigation revealed that the mothers of all afflicted infants had taken the drug thalidomide early in pregnancy.

Most experts in teratology recommend that drugs other than those absolutely necessary for the health and welfare of the pregnant woman and her fetus be avoided. However, studies of drug usage show that the average pregnant woman takes four different medications, many prescribed by her physician, and that only 6% of pregnant women take no drugs at all (Gray & Yaffe, 1986). In the case of specific over-the-counter and prescription drugs, there has not yet been adequate research showing the short- and long-range effects on pregnant women and their offspring. In one study, benzodiazepine (a tranquilizer) was shown to cause low birth weight and pre- and perinatal complications (Laegreid, Hagberg, & Lundberg, 1990).

Alcohol.   Alcohol abuse, affecting 1–2% of women of child-bearing age, has been shown to lead to intrauterine growth failure, joint abnormalities, congenital heart disease, and withdrawal symptoms in newborns. This set of symptoms is known as **fetal alcohol syndrome** (see Figure 3.7). Alcohol also affects motor development (Autti-Ramo & Granstrom, 1991), cognitive ability (Autti-Ramo et al., 1992; Autti-Ramo & Granstrom, 1991), and growth capability (Day & Richardson, 1991; Day et al., 1990). Even moderate alcohol consumption may have adverse effects, especially in the first trimester of pregnancy (Raymond, 1987; Warren & Bast, 1988); however, the disabilities increase with patterns of increasing consumption.

Addictive drugs.   Maternal drug addiction can lead to low birth weight in infants (Lester et al., 1991; Woods, Eyler, Behnke, & Conlon, 1991). In addition, the infants of women addicted to crack cocaine, heroine, methadone, and morphine are addicts at birth and experience difficult withdrawal symptoms, which can lead to death (see a discussion of this in Chapter 4). The long-range effects of the use of LSD and marijuana before and/or during pregnancy have not been conclusively demonstrated, but our current knowledge leads to the hypothesis that there may be damage. Smoking during pregnancy produces infants with low birth weight. In addition, research indicates

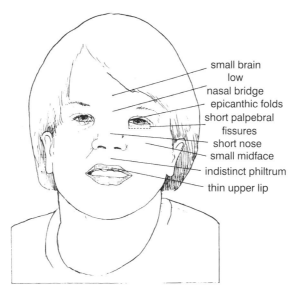

small brain
low
nasal bridge
epicanthic folds
short palpebral
fissures
short nose
small midface
indistinct philtrum
thin upper lip

Facial features that are characteristic of FAS

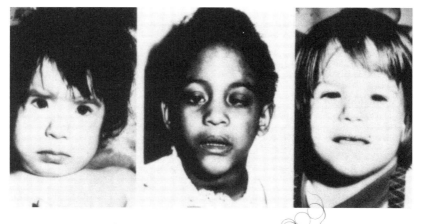

Figure 3.7 *Facial Characteristics of Children with Fetal Alcohol Syndrome*
SOURCE: Reprinted with permission from A. P. Streissguth, S. Landesman-Dwyer, J. C. Martin, and D. W. Smith, "Teratogenic Effects of Alcohol in Humans and Laboratory Animals," *Science 209* (1980):355. Copyright 1980 by the AAAS.

many long-range problems associated with maternal smoking during pregnancy (see Table 3.3).

Interaction of Factors

Some congenital malformations are not linked with specific defects in genes or chromosomes. Instead, they seem to result when two or more genetic factors interact. Individually, these genetic factors would be considered vari-

Table 3.3.   *Summary of Studies of the Effects of Maternal Cigarette Smoking During Pregnancy*

Findings	Authors
In the Fetal Stage	
Increased heart rate	Sontag and Wallace (1935)
Decreased breathing	Sontag and Wallace (1935)
In Infancy	
Apgar score	
Decreased score[a]	Garn et al. (1980, 1981)
No effect	Streissguth et al. (1982)
Auditory habituation and orientation	
Decreased function[a]	Saxton (1978)
No effect	Streissguth et al. (1983)
Mental and motor skills	
Decreased function[a]	Garn et al. (1980)
No effect	Streissguth, Barr, et al. (1980)
In the Preschool Years	
Attention	
Increased errors	Streissguth et al. (1984)
No effect	Landesman-Dwyer et al. (1981)
Hyperactivity	
Increased activity	Denson et al. (1975)
IQ scores	
Decreased function[a]	Dunn et al. (1977)
No effect[b]	Hardy and Mellits (1972)
In Childhood	
Decreased general abilities[a]	Goldstein (1977)
Decreased reading ability[a]	Butler and Goldstein (1973)
Decreased mathematics ability[a]	Butler and Goldstein (1973)
Increased hyperactivity/impulsivity[a]	Nichols and Chen (1981)
Increased neurological soft signs[a]	Nichols and Chen (1981)
Increased learning difficulties[a]	Nichols and Chen (1981)
IQ scores unaffected[b]	Lefkowitz (1981)
In Adolescence	
Decreased reading ability[a]	Fogelman (1980)
Decreased mathematics ability[a]	Fogelman (1980)

Note: Unless otherwise indicated, these studies adjusted for alcohol plus at least one sociodemographic variable or did not use a design that required adjustment.

[a]Study did not adjust for the effects of alcohol but did adjust for at least one other important environmental variable such as maternal education, socioeconomic status, or birth order.

[b]Study either did not adjust for at least one important sociodemographic variable in analyzing for smoking effects or had smoking effects wash out when demographic variables were adjusted.

SOURCE: From A. P. Streissguth, "Smoking and Drinking During Pregnancy and Offspring Learning Disabilities: A Review of the Literature and Development of a Research Strategy." *In* Michael Lewis (Ed.), *Learning Disabilities and Prenatal Risk.* Chicago: University of Chicago Press, 1986, p. 57. Used with permission.

ants rather than defects, but in combination they cause problems. In other cases, malformations occur because of the relationship between genetic factors and environmental agents. Examples of congenital malformations arising from an interaction of factors include spina bifida and anencephaly, congenital heart disease, cleft lip and palate, club feet, and congenital dislocation of hips. Neither the genetic nor the environmental factors involved in these disorders have been conclusively identified. It is fortunate, though, that many of these disorders can be corrected by surgery following birth, including spina bifida, cleft lip and palate, and club feet. Following special diets to prevent the development of severe symptoms can correct such disorders as diabetes and PKU.

Maternal–Fetal Blood Incompatibility

Incompatibility of maternal and fetal blood cells can cause congenital malformations. The most serious malformations occur if the mother's red blood cells lack a component called the **Rh factor** (named after the rhesus monkeys in which it was discovered) and if the father's blood cells have this component. The mother is then said to be Rh negative and the father Rh positive. Problems arise when the fetus of an Rh negative mother inherits Rh positive blood from the father. If blood from that fetus enters the mother's bloodstream, as often happens through the rupture of small blood vessels in the placenta, the mother's blood produces antibodies against the blood of the fetus. The production of antibodies typically does not affect the first fetus, but later fetuses can be killed or injured by these antibodies. Rh incompatibility is responsible for about 5,000 stillbirths and 20,000 congenital malformations each year (Gardner, 1983).

The Rh factor in blood cells is controlled by a dominant gene. The genetic structure cannot be altered, but there are two possible forms of treatment. The first involves replacing the blood supply of the fetus in the uterus before birth or at the time of delivery. The second form of treatment involves giving mothers a vaccine, Rhogam, designed to protect them from inflicting Rh disease on their fetuses. This vaccine must be given within days of the birth of the first Rh positive infant. Both forms of treatment show promise in reducing the incidence of congenital malformations or death due to Rh incompatibility.

PREPARATION FOR PARENTHOOD

In addition to having concern for Mary's physical well-being, Mary and Brett find that the pregnancy is a time of adaptation for them. They are especially concerned with their new roles as parents, which will require many changes in their daily routines. Many social and emotional changes can cause tension, but also excitement. They find that it is a time that requires all their good humor, love, and support for each other.

Adaptation to the Pregnancy

Pregnancy provides a time of transition for prospective parents as they anticipate new roles. Ellen Galinsky (1981) has used the theory of Erik Erikson as a framework for analysis of this transition. She believes that reactions during pregnancy can be divided into three stages, with each stage having its own unique tasks. In all three stages, parents are forming images to help them prepare for the birth of a new child. These images are based on their own experiences as children and on their own and other people's experiences with children. As the pregnancy progresses, the parents reject some images and elaborate on others.

According to Galinsky, the first stage takes place during the first three months of pregnancy. The task of this stage is acceptance of the pregnancy. This task is more immediate and compelling for women because of the daily changes in their bodies; men can delay dealing with this stage because the development of the pregnancy seems more distant from them.

The second stage begins when fetal movement is felt. Movement of the fetus brings about a focus on the realistic details surrounding childbirth, such as planning to take time off from work. Fantasies also intensify and the parents reassess their own upbringing. The main task of the second stage is recognition of the developing child as an individual who is part of the parents but also separate.

The third stage encompasses the last three months of pregnancy. Two conflicting feelings often coexist during this period: impatience to get on with the birth and dread of giving up the closeness and unity with the fetus. Many parents feel that they are experiencing one of the few inevitable events in their lives. The infant will come, whether they will it or not, ready or not. The key task of the last stage of pregnancy is to prepare for the physical separation from the fetus caused by the birth and for life with the infant afterward. Fantasies become more complete, including impressions of hair and eye color and other characteristics.

Feelings of support, protection, and care during this last trimester have been found to be related to the number of drugs given to women during labor. A lack of social support can lead to fear, depression, tension, and irritability during the last trimester. This in turn can lead to increased discomfort during labor, and the medical staff usually respond to this discomfort by increasing medication. It is well documented that increased medication during labor and delivery results in depressing the performance of infants on various tasks after birth. In fact, some studies have shown negative effects of drugs given in childbirth on infants up to seven months old (Yang, 1981). Helping families deal with problems and worries during pregnancy can help prevent a series of events that is likely to put the parent–child relationship at a disadvantage. The single most important factor for the pregnant mother is the presence of a caring, supportive partner.

Research has shown that the degree of parental involvement with the fetus during pregnancy can be used to predict later feelings toward the infant

(Valentine, 1982). Given these research findings, it seems important for professionals to assist parents in dealing with sources of stress so that the pregnancy can fulfill its function as a time of preparation.

Parents faced with the birth of a child with congenital problems need additional assistance in adapting to the special role they must play in the life of their child. Children with special needs deserve the opportunity to learn, to make personal choices, and to take as much responsibility for their lives as possible. Parents should be encouraged to play an active role in determining the educational needs of their child. The best possible care for the child occurs when parents work with professionals to meet the needs of the individual child.

Physicians are expected to provide assistance to new parents in preparing them for the special care required of these children. It is unfortunate, however, that they often do not have the time or expertise to provide support to the family, which is of such importance to the well-being of the child (Brumback, Bodenstein, & Roach, 1990). Many support groups have been founded by family members and professionals who have personal experience working with children with various special needs. When families are faced with the birth of such a child, it is important that they be provided with

A child with cerebral palsy, shown here with his father, fulfills his potential as a member of a supportive family.

▲ **DEVELOPMENTAL ISSUES IN PRACTICE   3.6**

SUPPORT GROUPS FOR FAMILIES WITH CHILDREN WHO HAVE DISABILITIES

Following is a list of some of the many support groups available to parents with children who have disabilities. Additional names of groups can be found in Brumback, Bodensteiner, and Roach (1990).

Alliance of Genetic Support Groups
1001 22nd Street, N.W., Suite 800
Washington, DC 20037
(202) 331-0942

American Council of the Blind
1010 Vermont Avenue, N.W., #1100
Washington, DC 20005
(202) 393-3666

American Speech-Language-Hearing Association
Consumer Affairs Division
10801 Rockville Pike
Rockville, MD 20852
(800) 638-8255

Association for Children with Down Syndrome
2616 Martin Avenue
Bellmore, NY 11710
(516) 221-4700

Association for Retarded Citizens of the U.S.
2501 Avenue J
P.O. Box 6109
Arlington, TX 76006
(817) 640-0204

Autism Society of America
1234 Massachusetts Avenue, N.W., Suite C1017
Washington, DC 20005
(202) 783-0125

DEVELOPMENTAL ISSUES IN PRACTICE 3.6 (continued)

Epilepsy Foundation of America
4351 Garden City Drive
Landover, MD 20785
(301) 459-3700

Hydrocephalus Parents Support Group
610 Verdant Place
Vista, CA 92084
(619) 726-0507

Muscular Dystrophy Association
810 Seventh Avenue
New York, NY 10019
(212) 586-0808

National Center for Learning Disabilities
99 Park Avenue
New York, NY 10016
(212) 687-7211

Spina Bifida Association of America
1700 Rockville Pike, Suite 540
Rockville, MD 20852
(301) 770-7222

United Cerebral Palsy Association
7 Penn Plaza, Suite 804
New York, NY 10001
(212) 268-6655

From R. A. Brumback, J. B. Bodensteiner, and S. Roach, "Support Groups for Pediatric Neurological Disorders." *Journal of Child Neurology* 5 (1990): 344–349.

resources for contacting these support groups. Developmental Issues in Practice. 3.6 contains a partial list of such resources.

Fetal and Newborn Death

When a child dies, the loss is staggering to the parents. This loss seems greater than any other. It leaves the parents feeling empty and "not quite whole." It raises feelings of guilt because a child is the responsibility of the parent—the death leaves the parents feeling like failures. When a child dies, the parent loses the future. The expectation of continuity is lost. There can be great anger because of the strong sense of impotency. It is often thought that a very young child will not be mourned as much as an older child. This assumes that the child has value only as a contributing member of the society. But to the parent, each child represents an entirely unique relationship. Even a miscarriage brings up the same feelings of loss and pain as the death of a newborn baby or an older child (Arnold & Gemma, 1983; Tengbom, 1989).

When a mother gives birth to a child with abnormalities, there is a loss of the healthy fantasy child. Parents in this situation may go through some of the same feelings of loss and mourning as those parents who grieve the death of their child.

It is unfortunate that after parents have experienced the death of a very young child, they are not encouraged to mourn. Friends, and even medical personnel, often show little compassion and understanding for their feelings. People often say such things as, "You will have another baby," or "You'll get over it; after all, he [or she] was very small." However, the parents are grieving the loss of their unique, individual child and they need the sensitive consideration of their friends and families. Because this is often not forthcoming, self-help groups have been developed to assist parents. One such group is called SHARE. Developmental Issues in Practice 3.7 describes the work of such self-help groups.

Training for Childbirth

Expectations about parental roles in childbirth have seemed to come full circle in the past century. Before modern medications were available, like it or not, the key adult in dealing with labor and delivery was the mother, perhaps assisted by a physician, nurse, or midwife. Change took place when general anesthetics came into wide usage, and the mother's role began to be considered to be more passive: she was sedated and the physician and other hospital personnel were the principal adult participants in the delivery of the baby.

Many parents have felt dissatisfied with their forced passivity during childbirth, and these parents have been joined by health care personnel in founding the prepared childbirth movement. There are various approaches to prepared childbirth, and one of the most prominent is the **Lamaze method.**

The Lamaze (Karmel, 1959) method uses conditioning principles to teach the mother to handle pain and discomfort by breathing in certain pat-

▲ DEVELOPMENTAL ISSUES IN PRACTICE   3.7

SUPPORT FOR BEREAVED PARENTS

SHARE is a national organization with local groups around the country. It is a source of help for airing and resolving death experiences for parents. The philosophy and approach of SHARE is described as follows:

> In our society, grief at the loss of a child or after a miscarriage is not acceptable, especially after a week or two has passed. The thought that the infant was never held, cuddled, fed, or perhaps embraced causes pain to the parents but is often seen by others as a reason for not feeling a loss. Well-meaning relatives and medical personnel may try to protect the grieving mother by not talking about the baby; by making plans without including her (putting away the baby clothes and crib, making funeral arrangements, etc.); by not letting her see or hold the baby; or by avoiding naming the baby.

> No parent should have to go through this experience alone. The basic reason for SHARE is to provide the comfort and mutual reassurance that parents who have had this experience can offer each other.

> The mother and father experiencing this loss need as much (if not more) pampering, concern, affection, and attention to their needs as the new parents whose baby has survived. They need to be able to put an identity on the baby, by naming it and by talking about it as though it is a member of the family.

> The mother needs, through her treatment by the people around her, to be assured that this is something that happened to her, that she is not in any way to blame, that she is not incompetent as a woman. She needs to be encouraged to take good care of herself physically, even though it may be very difficult to love herself in this situation.

> The father, too, may tend to blame himself. He needs an opportunity to share his feelings and to receive understanding and support.

> Through the local SHARE meetings, members can share their experiences, thoughts, and feelings. Parents learn that the intensity and longevity of their feelings are normal. They gain a sense of wholeness when they realize their problems are not unique to them alone but are rather problems that most bereaved parents are struggling to manage.

> SHARE is not a therapy group, nor are the meetings considered therapy sessions. Yet healing is slowly and gently promoted as parents gain insight and understanding and have an opportunity to ventilate their feelings in an accepting atmosphere.

Adapted by permission from SHARE of Morgantown, West Virginia.

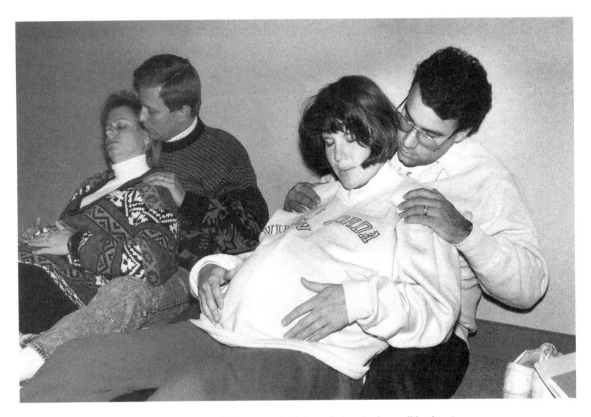

The Lamaze method of prepared childbirth uses principles of classical conditioning to teach the mother-to-be to handle pain by breathing in certain patterns.

terns. The father or other companion has an important role as "coach" and provider of support. The mother and coach practice breathing techniques together during the last months of pregnancy. During childbirth, these breathing techniques allow the woman to control her pain. Proponents of the Lamaze approach are not opposed to the possibility of a woman's request for medication during delivery, but women with this preparation use less medication than do unprepared women.

Other approaches to prepared childbirth are based on the Lamaze approach. Most are effective in bolstering the confidence of parents and giving them a sense of control.

Many parents seek to make decisions about the location as well as the circumstances of birth. Some choose home birth, citing as advantages the naturalness of the surroundings and the possibility of increased control over events. However, the medical community is almost unanimous in its negative response to the idea of home births. The most important disadvantages of

According to Galinsky's theory, parents-to-be form images to help them prepare for child-birth.

home birth involve danger to mother and child because of the difficulty of obtaining medical intervention in the event of an emergency. No one can know in advance when either the mother or child may suddenly be at risk and in need of the life supports that a hospital can offer. In partial compromise, many hospitals now offer "home birthing" rooms, which are furnished in a cozy manner but have the most advanced medical technology close at hand. In hospital birthing rooms, sometimes the entire family is present to assist in welcoming the infant.

SUMMARY

1. A person's development is determined by genetic information contained in the chromosomes and genes.
2. The DNA provides the genetic code that is passed on in each cell of the body during mitosis.
3. A person's development is determined by genetic information contributed by both parents at the time of fertilization when meiosis occurs.
4. Monozygotic twins develop from the same zygote and have the same genetic heritage; dizygotic twins do not share any more inherited characteristics than any other siblings but share the same environment in the womb.
5. Mendelian laws of heredity explain the presence of dominant and recessive traits.
6. Genotype is the totality of a person's genetic heritage; phenotype is a description of a person's actual traits.
7. Different traits have different heritability rates, determining the proportion of effect caused by the genetic code and the environmental influences.
8. Gender identity is the belief we have about our sexuality, while gender role is everything we do to express our sexuality.
9. Fetal hormones, chromosomes, and socialization all play an important role in the development of gender.
10. Prenatal development is divided into the stages of the zygote, embryo, and fetus.
11. Fertilization is the origin of a unique new life, which passes on the combined genetic contribution of both parents to the zygote.
12. By two weeks after fertilization, implantation and gastrulation occur and development begins to occur under the control of the homeo box.
13. The embryonic stage begins after implantation and extends until the end of the eighth week. During this stage, all the organ systems are laid down, the external structure is formed, and the face takes on a human appearance.
14. The fetal stage begins at the 9th week and continues until birth at about 38 weeks. By the end of 16 weeks, the fetus is completely formed and sensory organs begin to function, contributing to the growth of glial cells in the brain.
15. Individual patterns that develop in the last few months of fetal life predict development in the neonatal period.
16. Appropriate prenatal care includes regular medical supervision and good nutrition.
17. Congenital malformations result from genetic factors, environmental factors, interaction of factors, and maternal–fetal blood incompatibility.
18. Teratogens include any environmental factor that causes congenital malformations, including hormones, drugs, alcohol, cigarette smoke, and addictive drugs.
19. Genetic counseling is based on genetic screening, amniocentesis, and ultrasound imaging, which can help parents assess the risks of giving birth to infants with certain types of genetic problems.
20. Pregnancy is a period of adaptation for the parents to the role of parenting.
21. Fetal and newborn death create the need to mourn.
22. Parents can participate in childbirth using the Lamaze method.

ACTIVITIES TO ENHANCE LEARNING

1. Interview your mother or another woman who has experienced a pregnancy. Ask the following questions and compare the answers with the information given in the textbook.
   a. Did you have a sonogram? How did the experience make you feel about yourself, your pregnancy, and your baby?
   b. Describe your feelings when you were told you were pregnant. What were the positive feelings? What were the negative feelings?
   c. Describe the changes in your feelings over the course of the pregnancy. What kinds of feelings did you have? At what points in the pregnancy did you experience each type of emotion?
   d. What events in your life affected your feelings during the pregnancy?

2. In this chapter, the genetic traits of the Green family were described. In that example, the dark hair and eyes were dominant and the light hair and eyes were recessive and it was possible to guess at the genetic traits being carried by each of the parents in the family. Use your family, or interview someone from another family, to obtain three generations of information on the hair and eye color of the family members. After examining the appearance of various eye and hair patterns across the generations, determine the genetic traits being carried by each family member. In some cases, it may not be possible to determine the genetic traits. In those cases, indicate the possible genes that could be present in the individual.

FOR FURTHER READING

Prenatal Development

Gardner, E. J. (1983). *Human heredity*. New York: John Wiley & Sons.

Moore, K. L., & Persand, T. V. H. (1992). *The developing human* (5th ed.). Philadelphia: W. B. Saunders.

Nilsson, L., Ingelman-Sundberg, A., & Wirsen, C. (1981). *A child is born*. New York: Dell/Seymour Lawrence.

Preparation for Childbirth and Parenthood

Arnold, J. H., & Gemma, P. B. (1983). *A child dies: A portrait of family grief.* Rockville, MD: Aspen Systems.

Elkins, V. H. (1976). *The rights of the pregnant parent*. New York: Schocken Books.

Galinsky, E. (1981). *Between generations: The six stages of parenthood*. New York: Times Books.

Macfarlane, A. (1977). *The psychology of childbirth*. Cambridge, MA: Harvard University Press.

Videotape Presentations of Prenatal Development

Soundwave Images (Producer). (1990). *Ultrasound: Eyewitness to the earliest days of life.* Harness Union Lake, MI: Soundwave Images.

WGBH-TV, Boston (Producer). (1983). *NOVA: Miracle of life.* Distributed by WGBH-TV, P.O. Box 2284, South Burlington, VT, 05407-2284.

Birth and the Expanded Family

Birth renews the human species and often evokes in us a sense of hope and expectation. This chapter deals with the events surrounding birth and the adjustments families make following birth. The first part of the chapter describes the three stages of labor, the childbirth experiences of two families, and the ways in which the well-being of newborns is assessed. The second part examines the expanded family and looks at cultural factors, bonding of parents with the new baby, and the needs of fathers and siblings. The third part deals with some medical complications that can occur during and immediately following birth, including infant mortality and drug addiction; this section concludes with a discussion of the most common birth problem—the preterm birth—including a discussion of the prevalence and characteristics of early birth and its long-term effects on the child and the parents. The chapter ends with a discussion of legislation to assist families with infants who have so-called special needs.

BIRTH

Childbirth is the culmination of months of development during which a single cell becomes a complex human being. Researchers do not yet understand precisely how a hormonal signal sets off uterine contractions and the birth process, but with this signal the fetus starts its entry into the world. Labor and delivery can be a risky time for both the mother and child. For this reason, certain medical precautions are taken. The development of good medical

The doctor assists the new baby to be born as the mother watches joyfully.

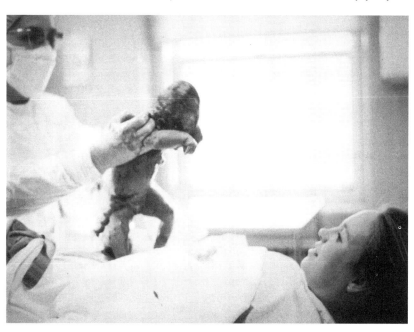

practice and antibiotics has had a positive benefit on infant survival. Since 1915 the rate of infant mortality has dropped 90% (U.S. Bureau of the Census, 1991). This is largely because good medical facilities have become more widely available.

Another aspect of good childbirth is the amount of support and emotional consideration given to the mother. Prepared childbirth, such as use of the **Lamaze method,** helps give the mother a role in the experience. An important component of the Lamaze method is the presence of a supportive partner to help with labor. Traditionally, fathers were not welcome in the labor and delivery rooms, but experience with couples using techniques such as the Lamaze approach have shown that the father has a beneficial impact on the progress of birth.

Tanzer and Block (1976) did a ground-breaking study on this topic at a time when the Lamaze approach was not as common as it is today, so a good random sample of families could be obtained. They compared couples who had taken prepared childbirth classes with those who did not. They found that couples who had taken the classes were more satisfied; the mothers had shorter labors, used fewer drugs, and reported less discomfort; and the wives perceived their husbands as more "in control" and helpful. These findings pointed to the importance of a helpful partner in speeding up labor and delivery but also emphasized the value of using the birth experience to help build family cohesiveness.

Traditionally, mothers always had support during labor from a knowledgeable and competent woman, usually a midwife, who also assisted in or performed the actual delivery. Doctors and nurses have replaced the midwife in most cases, and fathers are welcome in most labor and delivery rooms. However, the role of the experienced woman to provide emotional support has been lacking in most modern deliveries. Klaus, Kennell, Berkowitz, and Klaus (1992) have demonstrated that when such a woman is present in the labor room, there are a number of benefits to both mother and infant. See Developmental Issues in Practice. 4.1 for a discussion of this issue.

All of these considerations tend to reduce the mother's need for drugs during labor and delivery. This is important to the well-being of the baby because it has been found that drugs can have a negative effect on the child (Rosenblith & Sims-Knight, 1985). Drugs delivered to the mother during labor will reach the baby through the placenta. However, the drug dosage that is appropriate for the mother's body weight is much greater than that which would be appropriate for the baby. Consequently, the baby receives a much greater amount of drugs relative to newborn size. Furthermore, because of the immature organ system of the newborn, the drugs are inadequately processed and tend to stay in the baby's body much longer than is normally true of the adult.

The research on the effects of maternal drugs on the newborn child has produced a wide variety of results, largely because it is difficult to do good research. There are so many different factors that affect the outcome of the birthing process that it is hard to isolate the drug effect from all the others.

▲ DEVELOPMENTAL ISSUES IN PRACTICE   4.1

THE USE OF A DOULA

Klaus, Kennell, Berkowitz, and Klaus (1992) describe the value of having an experienced woman to help with childbirth. They call the woman who serves this role the childbirth *doula* (the Greek word *doula* means "a woman caregiver of another woman"). Her role is to provide emotional support during labor, make suggestions for coping with labor and delivery, answer questions about breast-feeding, and assist with the family's adaptation to the new baby.

In an international series of studies comparing groups of women with and without a *doula*, benefits of the *doula* could be clearly demonstrated. The presence of a *doula* reduced the length of labor by 25% and significantly reduced the odds of having a cesarean section or needing analgesia, oxytocin, or forceps assistance. In one study, 11% of mothers with a *doula* requested epidural anesthetic, while 64% of mothers in the control group did so. Clearly, the presence of the *doula* resulted in a more positive birth experience. In addition, the positive aspects of the experience occurred in part because of the less intrusive medical intervention.

There is also evidence that the presence of a *doula* increases the bonding process during the neonatal period. The following results occurred in the South African study:

	With Doula	*Without Doula*
Breast-feeding at six weeks	51%	29%
Demand feeding	81%	47%
Breast-feeding problems	16%	63%
Average hours per week away from the baby	1.7	6.6
Days needed to develop feeling of relationship with the baby	2.9	9.8

There is no evidence that the *doula* replaces the father in his role. Rather, the *doula* supports both parents and frees the father to act as the primary emotional support for his wife. Because of the reduction in medical costs due to shorter labor, fewer drugs used, and less of a need for cesarean delivery, the use of a *doula* more than pays for the cost of hiring extra personnel. Nonindustrialized countries have routinely used *doulas*, and there is good evidence that their use would benefit women in the West.

However, it is clear that the amount of damage to the newborn is due largely to the type of drug used. The following list summarizes some of the types of drugs available to the mother:

❑ **Oxytocin** is used to induce labor.

❑ **Analgesics** (including tranquilizers and sedatives) are used to make pain more tolerable, but they do not kill pain.

❏ **Anesthetics** are used to eliminate or greatly reduce pain. **General anesthetics** affect the whole body and are inhaled or injected. **Local anesthetics** are injected into the spinal cord, causing one to lose a sense of feeling below the point of injection.

Of these drugs, the one with the greatest amount of evidence for danger is oxytocin, which is used to speed up labor or induce labor. It tends to cause stronger contractions during labor and may be responsible for cutting off oxygen to the baby (the dangers of this are discussed in the section below). Oxytocin is also associated with psychomotor deficit in the newborn and with lower achievement scores when the children reach school age. The inhalant anesthetics are also associated with psychomotor and neuromotor deficits in the first year. Research on local anesthetics has produced mixed results. When negative effects were found, they usually lasted only a few days after birth and the effects were fairly small. There is some evidence that, overall, lower levels of drugs used by the mother result in benefits to the newborn infant (Rosenblith & Sims-Knight, 1985).

One of the greatest concerns of physicians is the problem of maintaining oxygen to the brain of the infant. A drop in oxygen to the brain is referred to as **anoxia**. During the fetal period, oxygen has been supplied by the placenta, which will begin to be less effective as the end of the prenatal period draws near. In addition, in some circumstances, the umbilical cord, which transports the oxygen, can be compressed during the contractions of labor and delivery. Any limitation of oxygen to the brain can cause brain damage in a very short period of time. For this reason, physicians will use a **fetal monitor** to look for signs of distress, especially if the labor is long and difficult. The mother can facilitate oxygen transport to the infant during labor by performing proper breathing techniques. The Lamaze method encourages the mother to breathe deeply to be sure that large amounts of oxygen are inhaled and provided to the infant throughout labor and delivery. Sometimes, the physician may recommend a cesarean section if it appears that the infant may be having problems.

Stages of Labor

The birth process, or period of **labor**, is often divided into three stages: (1) opening of the cervix, (2) delivery of the infant, and (3) delivery of the placenta. A description of these stages of labor follows.

Stage 1.   In the first stage of labor, contractions of the uterus dilate, or enlarge, the **cervix,** the opening of the uterus, to a diameter of about 10 centimeters. During this stage (or, occasionally, before), membranes rupture to allow amniotic fluid to escape from the amniotic sac. Once the membranes have ruptured, the baby is exposed to possible contaminants in the environment and the mother is usually confined to bed. The contractions that accompany the cervical dilation begin as mild sensations of muscle tightness, but they become increasingly intense as labor progresses. There is a great deal of discomfort associated with the contractions, but this can be greatly alleviated by the use of rhythmic breathing. The breathing distracts the mother from focusing on the discomfort and helps to relax her body so that dilation can proceed more easily.

Mothers are often very concerned about taking drugs at this point because of the evidence that they can harm the baby. However, small amounts of drugs do not appear to have a negative effect, especially if taken close to the time of delivery, when the discomfort is the greatest. Often, a mother benefits from receiving something to help her relax. Sometimes parents become so concerned about the effects of drugs that they feel like failures if the mother finds she must use something during labor. Having to use drugs should not be seen as a failing. The goal of the parents should be to reduce the stress for both mother and baby.

The first stage of labor is the longest, lasting from 8 to 16 hours in a first childbirth. The length will vary widely depending on a number of factors. One of the most important factors is the ability of the mother to relax and to assist her body in responding to the changes of childbirth. The amount of support she receives and the ability of those around her to assist in relieving stress are of greatest importance.

Stage 2.   During the second stage of labor, the baby emerges from the mother's body. Contractions of the uterus increase in frequency, forcing the baby through the cervical canal and vagina. During this stage, the mother is encouraged to push the infant out using techniques learned in childbirth class. As the infant emerges from the mother's body, mucus is removed by suction from its nose and mouth.

After delivery of the infant, the obstetrician clamps and cuts the umbilical cord. Nurses add drops to the infant's eyes to prevent infection, give the infant an identification bracelet to match the mother's, and weigh and measure the infant. Generally, in a first birth, the second stage of labor lasts several hours.

The position of the infant can make a difference in the progress of labor during the second stage. Normally, infants present themselves for delivery head first, with the crown of the head facing forward and down. Sometimes, however, delivery is complicated because the fetus is in another position. Labor is then extended, as the movement through the birth canal is slowed. Physicians have found that some fetuses can be manually turned before delivery, some can be delivered with instruments (forceps) even in their unorthodox positions, and some must be delivered by cesarean section.

Stage 3.   The third stage of labor is the time from delivery of the infant to delivery of the placenta. Contractions continue after the birth of the infant, and usually the placenta is expelled spontaneously within one-half hour from the end of the second stage of labor. Usually the parents barely notice this event because they are preoccupied with their new baby.

It has been found that comments made by staff during this time immediately following birth can have a big impact on the feelings and attitudes of the parents toward their new baby. Strong support from the staff can help parents develop a good attitude that can affect their later positive adaptation to the new family member. It is during this time that bonding can be encouraged.

It is important to realize that every birth is entirely unique. The number of children the mother has had before, the position of the baby in the birth canal, social and emotional circumstances surrounding the birth, and the age of the mother can all create variations in the experience. Consequently, no description of childbirth can account for the actual variations that occur, even for the same mother. However, there are two common patterns, which will be described here using the experiences of two couples. In the first, Donna and Paul delivered their daughter vaginally without much medication. In the second, Pat and Jose delivered their son by emergency cesarean section.

"Normal" Delivery

Donna and Paul went to the hospital when they thought that Donna's contractions were coming about five minutes apart but found it difficult to monitor them accurately. They were met at the emergency room by members of the hospital staff, who then took Donna to the maternity ward in a wheelchair, which made her feel strange because she was not in any distress at that point in labor. In the maternity ward, Paul completed paperwork while Donna was taken to the labor room. The doctor examined her and found that she was three centimeters dilated. Labor progressed slowly and Donna was encouraged to move about the labor room and relax as much as possible. After a few hours, Donna's doctor, Dr. Reynolds, suggested that they "break her waters" to encourage labor to progress more quickly. This involves cutting the membranes to allow the amniotic fluid to escape. The procedure was entirely painless, and the contractions picked up after it was completed. At that point, Donna was not allowed to get out of bed.

Both Donna and Paul wanted to limit the use of drugs and to make good use of the breathing exercises they had been taught. They followed instructions about using abdominal breathing and focusing on something in the labor room during contractions. Paul had not originally been enthusiastic about being part of the labor process but was participating because Donna had wanted him to do so. Once labor started, Paul began to appreciate being a part of this important event in both of their lives.

Donna's labor lasted throughout the night. She discovered that her pains did not continue to grow more severe over time, even though they occurred more frequently. Dr. Reynolds looked in regularly, and at one of his visits, Donna cried in alarm that the baby had stopped moving. Dr. Reynolds assured her that it is normal for the movements to be greatly reduced during labor. The cushioning amniotic fluid is gone, and the contracting uterus is moving the baby into position.

Toward morning, the contractions were close together and there were real feelings of pain, but Donna found she could "ride out" the pain by working hard at her breathing. She began to feel very tired and worried that she would not be able to keep working so hard if labor continued for a long period of time. After talking with Dr. Reynolds, Donna agreed to have something to help her to relax, which would not affect the baby in a negative way. Finally, her cervix was fully dilated and she was given permission to push. She had very much wanted to give in to the temptation to push earlier, but the doctor explained that pushing too early would damage the incompletely dilated cervix, which could extend labor even longer.

Donna was prepared to be taken to the delivery room. Once she was there, the anesthesiologist explained the options for medication. At this point in the delivery, the drugs would not have time to reach the fetus before the impending delivery. They chose a cervical block, a local anesthetic. Paul and Dr. Reynolds helped Donna to pant instead of giving in to the pressure to push the baby out while Dr. Reynolds made a small incision at the opening of the vagina, called an **episiotomy.** Then Donna was allowed to push. The purpose of the controlled incision of the episiotomy is to make room for the delivery of the baby's head and prevent dangerous tearing.

Donna squeezed Paul's hands with great intensity, and with one contraction the infant's head appeared. Dr. Reynolds removed the mucus from the infant's nose and mouth, and with the next contraction the infant's body appeared. With another contraction Dr. Reynolds carefully assisted Donna and Paul's daughter into the world. As the parents watched, their daughter began to cry loudly. Dr. Reynolds placed the baby on Donna's stomach, where she and Paul could hold and examine her. She stopped crying almost immediately and began to be attentive to her surroundings, especially her parents. Dr. Reynolds then cut the umbilical cord. With several more contractions, the placenta was expelled.

The staff commented to Donna and Paul on how healthy and beautiful their new daughter was. They made some preliminary observations of the baby, wrapped her in a blanket, and handed her to Donna, who held her gently. Their daughter seemed to look right at them, and they thought that she was the most beautiful thing they had ever seen. Donna felt a surge of energy she did not think she had left, and she found that she just wanted to look at her new baby and enjoy the moment of satisfaction and joy with Paul.

Cesarean Delivery

Pat and Jose had taken Lamaze prepared childbirth classes during the last months of pregnancy and felt very strongly about going through childbirth without unnecessary medication. They had found an obstetrician who would apply some of Dr. Frederick Leboyer's (1975) ideas about gentle childbirth in a dimly lit delivery room (see the section below for a description of this type of atmosphere).

Pat and Jose easily handled the early stages of labor at home and went to the hospital only when Pat's contractions were regular and close together and her waters had broken. Once in the labor room, they began using the techniques they had learned in the Lamaze classes. However, in routine monitoring of the baby's vital signs, a nurse noted signs of distress and notified the obstetrician. Dr. Adams immediately began to monitor the baby's condition with electrodes placed on its scalp through Pat's cervix. Dr. Adams stopped in frequently, watching the pattern of vital signs during each of the contractions of Pat's uterus. Pat and Jose, even as well trained and resolute as they were, had difficulty continuing their breathing patterns with the distraction of the activity around them and their fear for their baby. Pat found it difficult to ignore the discomfort caused by the contractions.

Dr. Adams discussed the options with them: they could have an immediate cesarean or they could adopt a wait-and-see approach. Pat and Jose were aware that some cesarean deliveries are viewed as being unnecessary, resulting from an overly cautious interpretation of the feedback from fetal monitoring. They opted to wait for more information before having a surgical delivery.

As Pat's labor progressed, though, Dr. Adams advised Pat and Jose that he felt that the baby was in danger. They nodded their assent, and Pat was prepared for surgery while Jose and Dr. Adams scrubbed up. Pat was given a spinal anesthetic rather than a general anesthetic, which would have put her to sleep, so that she could witness the birth of their child. The anesthesiologist stood near her head, and Jose held her hand on the other side. Soon after, their son was delivered through a low abdominal incision. Pat and Jose fully expected to hold their son right after birth, but because of the baby's distress the staff wanted to observe him carefully. His cord had been wrapped around him in such a way that his oxygen supply had been reduced with the action of each of the contractions of his mother's uterus. Once the staff members were satisfied that the baby was adapting to the new environment, they brought him to Pat and Jose so they could enjoy some time with him before he was put into the nursery, where his vital signs could be monitored. Pat and Jose felt as though they had failed their son. They felt let down after all their preparation and anticipation.

The arrival of their caring Lamaze instructor, Sarah, made the difference for Pat and Jose in regaining control of their feelings. Sarah reminded them of their preparation for this possibility and assured them that they had done everything that they could. She also told them that mothers who had cesarean sections were not at risk of poor bonding with their infant. Furthermore, it was quite possible that they could have a vaginal delivery for any subsequent pregnancies. This helped reassure the new parents that there would not be any long-term negative effects of the experience on the family.

Assessment of Newborns

All parents are most concerned that their baby be born normal and healthy. The most common way of reporting the condition of a newborn to parents is by explaining the Apgar score. A second way, supplementing the Apgar, is by showing parents the newborn's behavioral strengths in the days after birth, using the Brazelton Neonatal Behavioral Assessment Scale. The Apgar score and the Brazelton scale will both be described.

Apgar score.   In the past, some high-risk infants died because no one in the delivery room focused attention on the condition of these infants right after delivery. Now, thanks to Dr. Virginia Apgar, an **Apgar score** is quickly and easily computed by carefully observing an infant at one, five, and sometimes fifteen minutes after delivery. Five aspects of a newborn's ability to function can be quickly and reliably rated, with zero, one, or two points given to each. The five aspects of functioning can be remembered easily because the first letters spell *Apgar:* appearance (skin color), pulse (heart rate), grimace (reaction to slight pain), activity (motor responsiveness and tone), and respiration (breathing adequacy).

The generally accepted scoring guidelines for the Apgar are as follows: a score of seven or above indicates that there is no immediate danger, a score below seven indicates a need for specialized assistance, and a score below four indicates a life-threatening situation requiring immediate intervention. To put Apgar scores into perspective, they can be applied to Donna and Paul's daughter and to Pat and Jose's son. Donna and Paul's daughter's Apgar scores were 9, 9, and 10 at one, five, and fifteen minutes, respectively, after delivery. The change from 9 to 10 indicated improvement in the baby's color, but no problems whatsoever were apparent at any point. Pat and Jose's son, in contrast, had scores of 6, 8, and 9. His first score reflected his distressed status, but he responded well to emergency efforts and was already out of danger when the five-minute score was calculated.

Apgar scores, taken at most hospitals, give an indication of how well the infant is adjusting to the stress of delivery and the need to breathe independently. Taking an Apgar score achieves the important purpose of directing the attention of delivery room professionals to the well-being of the infant immediately after birth. Many infants have received life-saving assistance because of danger signals that were communicated by their low Apgar scores.

Brazelton Neonatal Behavioral Assessment Scale.   The Neonatal Behavioral Assessment Scale (Brazelton, 1973), usually called the **Brazelton scale** after its primary developer, T. Berry Brazelton, gives information about a wide range of behavioral strengths that newborns bring to their early interactions. The Brazelton assesses 16 reflexes and 27 behavioral items. The behavioral items simulate a variety of situations faced by newborns in the early days and weeks of life. Administration of the Brazelton requires considerably more training than does administration of the Apgar because, in the Brazelton assessment, the examiners try to elicit each infant's highest level of performance rather than an average. To do so requires sensitivity to an infant's signals and flexibility in the order in which items are presented.

Brazelton was able to demonstrate that newborn babies use their upper cortex to control their responses to environmental events. This baby scans the edge of the bassinet.

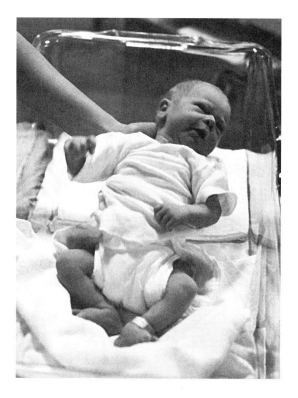

The Brazelton scale, developed over a period of 20 years, was the first major behavioral assessment designed for use with newborns. The 27 behavioral items, shown in Figure 4.1, assess infant responses to the environment, which are controlled by the upper cortex, the part of the brain responsible for thinking. Originally, it was thought that newborn babies did not use the upper cortex, but Brazelton was able to demonstrate that they do. In addition, he was able to show that newborns can control states of being. There are six different states of being in newborns: sound sleep, active sleep, drowsiness, quiet awake, active awake, and crying (Chapter 5 covers this in more detail). Brazelton was among the first to recognize that state control is important to effective development.

The Brazelton scale measures the infant's responses to different kinds of stimulation: sights, sounds, and pleasant and unpleasant touch. Some infants respond more to one kind of stimulation than to others. An important sign of self-control in the infant is the ability to respond less when sights, sounds, and touches are repeated. This is called response decrement, or **habituation** (discussed in more detail in Chapter 7). Researchers have shown that habituation is poorly developed in brain-damaged newborns, so it is a very important indicator of well-being in the newborn. The Brazelton scale also measures how mature the infant's motor skills are; the amount of reactivity exhibited toward various auditory and visual stimuli; how state, color, and

Figure 4.1 *Behavioral Items on the Brazelton Neonatal Behavioral Assessment Scale.* The states for assessment are (1) sound sleep, (2) active sleep, (3) drowsiness, (4) quiet awake, (5) active awake, and (6) crying.

1. Response decrement to repeated visual stimuli (2,3).*
2. Response decrement to rattle (2,3).
3. Response decrement to bell (2,3).
4. Response decrement to pinprick (1,2,3).
5. Orienting response to inanimate visual stimuli (4 only).
6. Orienting response to inanimate auditory stimuli (4,5).
7. Orienting response to animate visual stimuli—examiner's face (4 only).
8. Orienting response to animate auditory stimuli—examiner's voice (4 only).
9. Orienting responses to animate visual and auditory stimuli (4 only).
10. Quality and duration of alert periods (4 only).
11. General muscle tone—in resting and in response to being handled, passive and active (4,5).
12. Motor activity (4,5).
13. Traction responses as baby is pulled to sit (3,5).
14. Cuddliness—responses to being cuddled by examiner (4,5).
15. Defensive movements—baby's reactions to a cloth over his or her face (4).
16. Consolability with intervention by examiner (6 to 5,4,3,2).
17. Peak of excitement and baby's capacity to control himself or herself (6).
18. Rapidity of buildup to crying state (from 1,2 to 6).
19. Irritability during the examination (3,4,5).
20. General assessment of kind and degree of activity (alert states).
21. Tremulousness (all states).
22. Amount of startling (3,4,5,6).
23. Lability of skin color—measuring autonomic lability (from 1 to 6).
24. Lability of states during entire examination (all states).
25. Self-quieting activity—attempts to console self and control state (6,5 to 4,3,2,1).
27. Hand-to-mouth activity (all states).

*Numbers in parentheses refer to optimal state for assessment.

SOURCE: From *Cultural Perspectives on Child Development* by Wagner and Stevenson. Copyright 1982 by W.H. Freeman and Company. Reprinted with permission.

activity level vary; how well the infant can self-quiet; and how the infant responds to cuddling and other social interactions. Developmental Issues in Practice 4.2 describes three sample test items from the Brazelton scale. Such information is obviously of great interest to parents in helping them adapt to the behavior patterns of the newborn baby.

Assessing an infant's responses with the Brazelton scale serves two useful purposes. First, when the assessment is conducted in the parents' presence, the parents gain a sense of the infant's competence and ability to interact. In one relevant study (Myers, 1982), parents were taught to administer the Brazelton to their own infants. Attention was drawn by the researcher to the infants' most positive interactive and other abilities. Four weeks later the

▲ DEVELOPMENTAL ISSUES IN PRACTICE   4.2

SELECTED ITEMS FROM THE BRAZELTON SCALE

Orienting Response to Inanimate Visual Stimuli

The ability of the baby to follow the stimulus (a red ball) with the eyes

1. Does not focus on or follow stimulus.
2. Stills with stimulus and brightens (widening of eyes and brighter look).
3. Stills, focuses on stimulus, little spontaneous interest, no following.
4. Stills, focuses on stimulus, follows for 30° arc, jerky movements.
5. Focuses and follows with eyes horizontally for at least a 30° arc. Smooth movement, loses stimulus but finds it again.
6. Follows for 30° arcs with eyes and head. Smooth movement.
7. Follows with eyes and head for at least 60° horizontally.
8. Follows with eyes and head 60° horizontally and 30° vertically.
9. Focuses on stimulus and follows with smooth, continuous head movement horizontally, vertically, and in a circle. Follows for 120° arc.

Traction Responses as Baby Is Pulled to Sit

Examiner places a forefinger in each of the infant's palms. With the arms extended, the infant's automatic grasp is used to pull him or her to a sitting position. The infant attempts to right the head and hold it steady, using shoulder strength.

1. Head flops completely, no attempts to right it.
2. Futile attempts to right head but some shoulder tone increase is felt.
3. Slight increase in shoulder tone, seating brings head up, not maintained but there are further efforts to right it.
4. Shoulder and arm tone increase, seating brings head up, not maintained but there are further efforts to right it.
5. Head and shoulder tone increase as pulled to sit, brings head up once to midline by self as well, maintains for one to two seconds.

researcher found that the parents who had become acquainted with their newborns' abilities through the Brazelton scored higher than parents without that experience on measurements of knowledge about infants, confidence in handling infants, and satisfaction with their interactions with infants. It was also found that fathers who had used the Brazelton were more involved with their infants than were fathers who had not.

A second purpose for administering the Brazelton is to identify infants whose responses may make it difficult for parents to care for them. During administration of the Brazelton, the examiner moves the newborn from sleep

---

DEVELOPMENTAL ISSUES IN PRACTICE   4.2 (continued)

6. Head brought up twice after seated, shoulder tone increases as comes to sit, maintains for more than two seconds.

7. Shoulder tone increases but head not maintained until seated, then can keep it in position 10 seconds.

8. Excellent shoulder tone, head up while brought up but cannot maintain without falling, repeatedly rights it.

9. Head up during lift and maintained for one minute after seated, shoulder girdle and whole body tone increases as pulled to it.

Cuddliness—Responses to Being Cuddled by Examiner

Measures infant's response to being held

1. Actually resists being held, continuously pushing away, thrashing or stiffening.

2. Resists being held most but not all of the time.

3. Doesn't resist but doesn't participate either, lies passively in arms and against shoulder (like a sack of meal).

4. Eventually molds into arms, but after a lot of nestling and cuddling by examiner.

5. Usually molds and relaxes when first held (i.e., nestles head in crook of neck and elbow of examiner). Turns toward body. When held horizontally on shoulder seems to lean forward.

6. Always molds initially with above activity.

7. Always molds initially with nestling, turning toward body, and leaning forward.

8. In addition to molding and relaxing, nestles and turns head, leans forward on shoulder, fits feet into cavity of other arm, all of body participates.

9. All of the above, and grasps hold of the examiner to cling to him or her.

Used by permission from T. Berry Brazelton, *Neonatal Behavioral Assessment Scale*. Philadelphia: J. B. Lippincott, 1973, pp. 19, 27–30.

---

to alert states and then back to quiet again. The ability of newborns to control and regulate their states is viewed as an important indicator of maturity. Premature or ill infants have fewer clear states, and for all infants the states become easier to interpret over time as the central nervous system matures. Infants with few clear states who cry frequently, cannot easily quiet themselves, and are unresponsive or negative about cuddling present real challenges to parents. The Brazelton can identify infants whose parents could benefit from ongoing professional support to learn to recognize and build on their infants' strengths.

BIRTH AS A TRANSITION FOR THE NEWBORN

Physical Adaptation

The Apgar score and the Brazelton scale are intended to evaluate the ability of the baby to make an adequate transition from fetal life to extrauterine life. Many adaptations are being made. Some profound changes in the circulatory system begin to take place when newborns first breathe air into their lungs. Vessels and structures that received oxygen through the umbilical cord during prenatal development are no longer needed and are transformed in the days and weeks after birth. There is a gradual transition from a fetal pattern to an adult pattern of circulation.

It must also be remembered that while the baby was in the uterus, moving in a watery environment, the sensations of movement were quite different than those that are felt out of the uterus. After birth, the baby has its first exposure to the feelings of gravity. Movements that were smooth and easy, such as moving the thumb to the mouth for sucking, suddenly become more difficult because of the weight of gravity on the baby's body. Thus, the baby has to relearn his or her movements, which may take a few days or weeks.

In addition, the womb provided a rich environment of sensory stimulation during the last three months of fetal life. There were the noises of the mother's body, including heart rate, sounds of the diaphragm moving the lungs, blood pulsing through the cardiac system, and the sounds of the digestive tract. In addition, the fetus could hear the mother's voice and many other sounds coming from outside the mother's body, but they were muffled. After birth, all the sights and sounds become intense. In particular, bright lights hurt the baby's eyes, and most neonates keep their eyes tightly closed whenever the lights are turned on.

While in the womb, the fetus was held at a constant temperature. One of the most important adjustments that the neonate must make is to begin to regulate body temperature in response to the colder air. One of the measures of the Brazelton scale involves undressing the baby to see how quickly the body's pink color returns, indicating the ability of the body to warm itself by sending blood into the cooler body parts. It is extremely dangerous for a newborn's body to cool down too much, and great efforts are made to make sure that the baby is kept warm, which is why the baby is wrapped in blankets and even a cap. Oftentimes, warming lights are used in the incubators and neonatal nursery to make sure the baby's body temperature is kept at a normal level.

Leboyer (1975) developed a method of childbirth intended to minimize some of these stresses for the newborn. The **Leboyer method** involves making changes in the environment to provide an easier transition for the new baby. Leboyer advocated delivering an infant in a dimly lit, warm room to limit the harshness of the transition; putting the newborn on the mother's abdomen to provide maximum contact with the sounds of the mother's body that are familiar from the womb; and putting the newborn in a warm bath to simulate the conditions of the womb. Infants delivered by these methods behave differently from infants who are delivered by traditional methods. They do not cry, except for a brief period immediately after birth; they are much more relaxed; they open their eyes and examine the environment; and they spend time looking at their parents and listening to their voices. Leboyer encourages the father's participation by suggesting that the father put the baby into the warm bath.

Critics of the Leboyer method claim that the immature baby will not benefit from these activities over the long run and that the procedures involved will interfere with the ability of the medical staff to monitor the newborn's health and well-being. Families that have used the method report feeling very satisfied with the approach, because they feel that the baby is happier and more content, and they report feeling closer to the newborn after delivery. There is no evidence that these methods put the healthy, normal newborn at risk for medical problems.

Social Adaptation

One issue raised by use of the Leboyer method is the need for parents to feel a tie to the infant. This is called bonding and will be discussed in more detail later. Bonding is the expression of social needs. It is important to keep in mind that human beings are social organisms, and the ability to receive and respond to social stimulation begins as soon as the family makes contact. This ability is probably already developing in the womb, but it can be clearly seen and measured (using the Brazelton scale) once the baby is born. A detailed discussion of the infant's perceptual skills is presented in Chapter 7; it is important to recognize that these perceptual abilities are closely tied to the development of social relationships (Brazelton, 1973).

The newborn infant can see objects clearly if the room is dimly lit. The best resolution for seeing things is at a distance of 9 to 12 inches away from the eyes. This is approximately the distance that exists between the parent's eyes and the baby's eyes when the infant is being held in the crook of the arm. When the mother holds the baby so that the two faces are aligned and the eyes can make contact, this is called the ***en face*** position. It is very important to the baby because it allows full viewing of the parents' faces for recognition and later attachment. Figure 4.2 shows one picture of a woman in a close, *en face* position with the feeding baby and one picture of the same mother and baby without the *en face* position. It is easy to see the value of the position—in the right-hand picture the mother and child seem detached and poorly bonded. Comparing the two pictures, one can see why a breast-feeding mother is more likely to engage in *en face* gazing, because breast-feeding would force the faces into proper alignment.

The newborn infant prefers to listen to human voices, particularly those of the parents. Research has shown that newborns are capable of distinguishing all the complex components of the human voice, including distinctions among sound, rhythm, timbre, and so on. The baby will **quiet** to the sound of the human voice. This means that the baby stops all movements, the eyes

Figure 4.2   *Parent–Infant Bonding.*
A posed mother in two different caretaking positions. (A) Infant is held in close contact (mother's body touching infant's), mother is looking at infant *en face,* bottle is perpendicular to the mouth, and milk is in the tip of the nipple. (B) Infant's trunk is held away from mother, mother is looking at infant but not *en face,* and bottle is not perpendicular to the mouth.

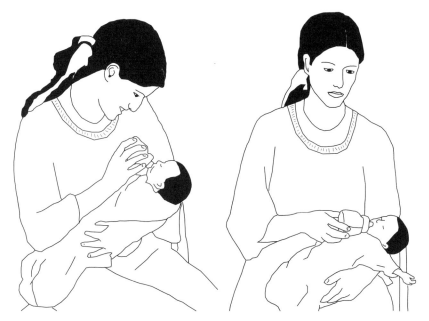

SOURCE: Adapted with permission from Klaus, M.H. & Kennell, J.H. (1982). *Parent-Infant Bonding.* St. Louis: The C.V. Mosby Company, p. 174.

become somewhat fixed, and frequently the baby attempts to turn toward, or **orient** toward, the voice (Brazelton, 1973). It is clear that the newborn is already learning about the sounds and voice characteristics of the parent's particular language.

The newborn infant has a well-developed sense of smell. It is believed that the early contact with the mother facilitates later identification of the mother by using smell. It is clear that the newborn learns to identify the smell of the mother's milk and shows a preference for the mother's breast pad even if the mother herself is not present.

The newborn infant also has a well-developed sense of touch and feeling of movement. In the womb, the fetus was constantly receiving stimulation from the swaying created by movements of the mother and from the amniotic fluid against the skin. The newborn clearly responds to being held and carried and will relax when being stroked and caressed.

The ability of the newborn to respond to the parents is very important in making the parents "feel good" about the baby and about their own ability to be successful parents. Most parents aren't specifically aware of the behaviors in the infant that cause them to feel this way about the baby. Klaus and Kennell (1976) have presented a clear case for the incredible complexity of the interaction between the newborn and the mother. All of the socially important response systems work together to provide this extraordinarily rich interaction. When everything is normal, it is hardly noticed. It is only in the absence of such positive stimulation that problems show up.

When a baby is born early, it is necessary to place the vulnerable infant in a **neonatal intensive care unit** (**NICU**) for special medical treatment. The NICU provides the baby with continuous care and is essential to preserve life, but it is not the same environment that would be available to the baby still in the womb; nor is it the same as the environment that is typical for the normal full-term infant (Graven et al., 1992). It is important that the preterm infant receive physical and social care that minimizes the trauma of the early birth experience. (These issues will be discussed more fully in the section entitled "Preterm Birth.") Anything that interferes with the ability of the neonate to respond to the parents can interfere with the ability of the family to develop good social interactions (this is the basis of the concern about bonding, which is discussed later).

THE EXPANDED FAMILY

Parents react to their newborns in a wide variety of ways, as demonstrated by the comments in Developmental Issues in Practice 4.3. This part of the chapter discusses factors that influence the reactions of parents and other family members to the birth of an infant: cultural factors, bonding, bonding with high-risk infants, and the needs of fathers and siblings.

Cultural Factors in Parent–Infant Interaction

Cross-cultural studies have demonstrated that newborns from the same cultural group behave similarly to each other and that they behave differently than newborns from other cultural groups. The unique characteristics of newborns from particular cultures have been shown to influence the reactions of their parents, and vice versa. Two examples of this influence will be discussed here: the responsive nurturing by Zinacanteco and the use of cradleboards by Navaho. Cradleboards are like small portable infant seats; infants can be easily transported in them. However, the Navaho cradleboard requires that the babies be bundled and tied into the board so that they cannot move.

Study of Navajo newborns has disclosed distinctive motor and muscular patterns, as compared with newborns from other cultural groups. For example, these infants show less resistance in muscle tone when legs or arms are straightened, less straightening of the legs to support the body, and an absence of walking movements when the infant is leaned forward. The argument has been made (Lester & Brazelton, 1982) that these motor patterns of

▲ **DEVELOPMENTAL ISSUES IN PRACTICE   4.3**

PARENTAL REACTIONS TO NEWBORNS

A teacher of a class for parents of newborns has observed a wide range of parental reactions to the responsibilities that follow childbirth. Here are examples of some of the remarks that she has heard over the years:

> I looked at him and thought that he was the most perfect, divinely crafted creature ever to be born. When I came home from the hospital with him and carried him for the first time to the crib I had prepared, I thought that I would explode with happiness and pride.

> I wanted her. I really did. I needed someone to take care of, someone to love. But when I got her to myself she cried all the time. I tried everything but she wouldn't stop. It wasn't like I thought it would be.

> When labor started so early, all I could think about was that I might have to go home from the hospital alone. I'll never forget my first look at her in intensive care; tubes and wires were everywhere and she was so tiny. At first I couldn't stand to visit her, but as she got stronger, a little hope began to grow in my heart. Now that she's home I still feel as though she's a gift on loan for now, but so fragile.

> He was so much more helpless than I had expected. I knew that my life would change when he was born but I hadn't expected that I would get so little in return for the night feedings, lack of freedom, fatigue, and intrusion on my life. These aren't the "right" things to say, I know, and my wife wouldn't understand them.

> She had her own little personality and approach to life from the first. I was amazed at how competent she was. She let me know when she wanted something and I thought that she recognized my voice.

Navajo infants long ago influenced the development of the practice of putting infants on cradleboards. The motor patterns of Navajo newborns seem to make them more likely to accept placement on a cradleboard than would be true for more active infants. (See Chapter 5 for more discussion of this issue.)

Observers of Zinacanteco Indians in Mexico have found that newborns have a low birth weight and are alert both in an auditory way and visually. The low birth weight probably results from maternal undernutrition, infection, and low oxygen due to the high altitude in which the Indians live. Zinacanteco newborns are slow and quiet in their reactions as compared with newborns in the United States. Again, reactions of Zinacanteco parents tend to be consistent with these predispositions. Zinacanteco infants are given a quiet environment immediately following delivery and are thereafter responded to immediately, being rocked, breast-fed, and cradled rather than allowed to cry or become frustrated. This responsive nurturing of Zinacanteco parents seems to reinforce the birth characteristics of the infants. With the Zinacantecos and the Navahos, it seems that infant characteristics shape and in turn are shaped by their parents' reactions.

Bonding

Bonding is defined as a complex psychobiological tie of the parent to the infant (Klaus & Kennell, 1982). (The tie of the infant to the parent is called attachment and is described in Chapter 6.) In 1976, two pediatricians at Case Western Reserve University School of Medicine, Marshall H. Klaus and John H. Kennell, wrote a landmark book, *Maternal–Infant Bonding*. Klaus and Kennell pointed out that events occurring during and immediately following birth are likely to have a big impact on the evolution of the relationship between parent and child. It is obviously of great importance that this relationship begin in a positive way so that the parents develop a strong bond that inspires ongoing care and protection of the vulnerable newborn child. They recommend that 30 to 60 minutes of private contact between parents and the infant should be provided right after birth.

Klaus and Kennell pointed out that immediately following unmedicated childbirth, both mother and infant are extraordinarily alert for approximately one hour. Thus, it appears that the conditions for the first parent–infant contact are most effective when they coincide with the period of calm alertness right after birth. Later on, both mother and infant will need to rest and recuperate from the birth experience and there will not be another opportunity for intense contact for a week or so. Klaus and Kennell also reported research suggesting that this close contact would lead to improved parent–infant interactions in the period of early infancy. A number of factors could increase the effect, including providing nude contact between the baby and the mother's body, leaving the parents alone with the infant, and providing additional close contact in the days after birth.

To understand the impact of the research on bonding presented by Klaus and Kennell, typical hospital procedures following childbirth in the early 1970s must be known. Because epidemic diarrhea and respiratory infections had historically been problems among newborns, hospitals developed the practice of grouping full-term infants for care in a central nursery. Parents and others were often treated as outsiders who might bring germs into the nursery and endanger the infants. Within this context, then, in most hospitals in the early 1970s, newborns were taken to the nursery soon after birth and were returned periodically to their parents only after a time of observation and examination. To be sure, there were exceptions to these procedures, especially among parents who had experienced various forms of prepared childbirth and who were requesting that their infants "room in" with them throughout their hospital stay. But the predominant experience soon after birth was of parent–infant separation.

Klaus and Kennell's recommendations were based on a series of studies. In a key study (Klaus et al., 1972), for example, mothers in one group were given early and extended contact with their infants, and mothers in the second group experienced the usual hospital procedures at that time (a glimpse of the infant at birth and 20 to 30 minutes of contact every four hours for feeding). When the infants were one month old, the mothers who had had early and extended contact stayed closer to their infants, made eye contact more often, and soothed and fondled their infants more. When the infants were one year old, these same differences persisted. And, when the children were two years old, the mothers in the early contact groups showed a different pattern of verbalization, using fewer commands, twice as many questions, and more adjectives.

In a critical examination of a number of carefully controlled studies of parent–infant bonding, Siegel (1982) concluded that early contact between parents and their infants, even if it is not supplemented with extended contact, has favorable effects on parental feelings about the infants in the days after birth. These findings are consistent even among various socioeconomic and cultural groups. Siegel also concluded that there are significant intermediate-term positive effects from this early contact: a longer duration of breast-feeding; increases in maternal behaviors (e.g., making eye contact, smiling, kissing, and vocalizing); and changes in such infant behaviors as responsiveness and alertness. According to Siegel, research findings on the long-term effects of early contact are not conclusive because there are so many other factors that influence the baby in the early years after birth that it is impossible to find any one factor that acts alone to affect the parent–child relationship.

The research of Klaus, Kennell, and others was positively received by many parents and medical professionals and led to the creation of a task force, which made recommendations in 1978 that were endorsed by the American Hospital Association. These recommendations specifically encouraged breast-feeding and handling of the infant by parents right after delivery. The recommendations resulted in a gradual process of hospital reform of maternity practices. It is now possible in many hospitals for parents to request and receive time with their newborns right after birth. Observations of parents and infants at first meeting show that parents interact with and get to know their infants in three primary ways: (1) by touching with fingertips and then palms, (2) through eye-to-eye contact, and (3) by talking in a higher-pitched voice than usual (Klaus & Kennell, 1982).

Some researchers have argued that the case for bonding has been overstated by making it appear to be an instantaneous process whose absence will have terrible effects on the developing child (Lamb, 1982). However, other researchers (Anisfeld et al., 1983) have emphasized that early contact has been demonstrated to be effective in increasing bonding, which parents find very satisfying; that lack of early contact does not have extremely negative effects, except in families at risk for child abuse; and that at-risk families show the greatest benefit of the early contact. Thus, it appears that strong families can overcome the effects of a poor beginning, but at-risk families may be less able to do so. On the other hand, even strong families deserve the very best possible experience, which research indicates includes an opportunity to have early contact at birth with their new infant.

Klaus, Kennell, and others (Anisfeld et al., 1983) clearly state that humans are too resilient and complex to be governed in bonding strictly by the timing set by hormones, as are some other animals. The moments after birth seem to be a good time to begin parent–infant contact, but factors such as cesarean births and premature or stressed infants sometimes make that particular timetable unworkable. All parents, but especially those who cannot interact with their infants right after birth, need to be told that bonding is not a simple, adhesive joining but is instead the result of a dynamic process of interaction that begins during pregnancy and continues in the days after birth. Parents need to know that prior experiences—such as the acceptance of the pregnancy, thoughts of the fetus as an individual, and contact with the infant—together determine bonding.

The Needs of Fathers and Siblings

Newborns profoundly alter the course of their parents' lives and influence other lives in families that are likely to include **siblings,** grandparents, and others. This section focuses attention on the reactions of two groups of family members who are often forgotten in the interest usually accorded mother and infant at birth: fathers and siblings.

Engrossment is the term coined to describe the intense interest of fathers in their infants.

Fathers.   Much of the research on bonding has investigated the bonding of mother to child. As recently as 1976, the first edition of Klaus and Kennell's book was called *Maternal–Infant Bonding*. The title of the second edition, *Parent–Infant Bonding* (1982), however, reflects a new interest in the role of fathers in child development. A term for the absorption that fathers have with their newborns, **engrossment,** was coined by Greenberg and Morris (1974). Research has demonstrated that early involvement of fathers with newborns leads to the same nurturing and vocal behaviors in fathers as in mothers (Greenberg & Morris, 1974). It also leads to the same positive changes in interaction patterns over time that were found with early involvement of mothers (Klaus & Kennell, 1982).

Becoming a father requires considerable adjustment. When a man becomes a father for the first time, his concerns center on the added financial responsibilities and other responsibilities of having a child, changes in his relationship with his wife, health of mother and child, and unknown aspects of the new role. When a man already has children, he usually feels added anxiety about how another child will fit into the family and how the sibling(s) will react. Fathers of newborns may need attention paid to their needs as they assume new roles in the expanded family.

Siblings.   Research indicates that concern about sibling relations is well founded. The least joyful response to the arrival of a new infant is often from the sibling(s). In fact, the birth of an infant can be one of the most stressful experiences of the early childhood years. Troubling reactions to the birth of an infant may include strenuous efforts to get attention from parents and others; regression in eating, sleeping, toileting, or other behaviors; and aggression toward parents and/or the infant. The intensity of any negative behavior seems to vary with age (with negative reactions found in 89% of children under three years but in only 11% of those over six years) and gender of the new infant (with infant brothers causing more negative reactions than sisters) (Trause & Irvin, 1982).

Helping siblings cope with the arrival of a new infant requires first of all an understanding of the sources of stress and worry. For young children, separation from their mothers during birth and the subsequent period of hospitalization is disruptive of established routines and worrisome even when the children are prepared for the separation by careful explanation. A study of separations for childbirth suggests that the distress of young children can be significantly reduced by having the children visit mother and infant in the hospital at least one time (Trause & Irvin, 1982). In recognition of the need for contact, some hospitals conduct parties in honor of the siblings whose mothers have just given birth: siblings and parents join to celebrate the arrival of a new family member.

The second major source of anxiety for siblings involves possible changes in their relationships with parents when a new infant arrives. One troubled six-year-old demanded to know why his parents would want an additional child if he, the first, had been entirely satisfactory. Research reveals a basis for the rejected feelings that older siblings sometimes have. Studies document mothers' usage of more angry commands with their older children in the weeks after the birth of a new infant than before childbirth and also a decrease in expressions of warmth toward older children after the birth of an infant (Trause & Irvin, 1982). Many mothers are fatigued after childbirth, and the roles of other adults therefore become important in helping older siblings make a satisfactory adjustment, both to temporary separation from the mother and to arrival of the infant in the family. The father or other adults can provide continuity and emotional support at a time when both may be needed by the siblings. Developmental Issues in Practice 4.4 provides some approaches to helping older siblings adjust to the birth of the new baby.

Birth and the days following it represent a new beginning for mother, father, infant, siblings, and important others. Together they encounter the challenges and rapid changes that are to come.

MEDICAL COMPLICATIONS OF BIRTH

Neonatal Mortality

The **neonatal period** is defined as the time from birth through the first month of life. This is a period when the infant is at greatest risk of death. Although there has been a great decrease in mortality in infants, the death rate for infants in the first year of life is the highest of any age period, and two-thirds of these deaths occur in the first month of life. Statistics about death rates during the first month of life are referred to as neonatal mortality, whereas infant mortality refers to death rates in all infants up to one year of age. When the statistics are divided between neonatal mortality (in the first month) and postneonatal mortality, an interesting pattern emerges (see Figure 4.3).

As can be seen in Figure 4.3, mortality has decreased since 1930. However, beginning in the 1960s, neonatal mortality has risen relative to postneonatal mortality. This is due in part to the newer technology that makes it possible for babies to be delivered alive, whereas in the past they would not have survived birth. In addition, in the United States, physicians advocate that every effort should be taken to assure a newborn baby of care; if the infant lives, early care assures the child of the best chance of having limited developmental problems as a result of a distressed delivery (Rhoden, 1986).

Another factor in the decline of infant mortality is the ability of very-low-birth-weight babies to survive with very few complications. For example, Grogaard, Lindstrom, Parker, Culley, and Stahlman (1990) found that infants born at 1,200–1,500 grams (normal birth weight is considered to be above 2,500 grams, or 5.5 pounds) can survive without any increase in disabilities. U.S. physicians have lowered the threshold of viability to 500 grams with ges-

▲ **DEVELOPMENTAL ISSUES IN PRACTICE   4.4**

HELPING SIBLINGS ADJUST TO NEWBORNS

Parents can help their older child adjust to the birth of an infant by following these suggestions:

❑ Talk with the older child about the needs and desires of the infant.
❑ Include the older child in making decisions about the infant.
❑ Interpret the infant's actions and reactions for the older child. Call attention to the infant's interest in the older child.

Involving siblings in the care of a newborn can ease the adjustment process.

tational ages at 24 weeks. It has been found that aggressive intervention will assure those babies who survive a chance of being normal. However, although these babies can survive, they are at higher risk for death, which is reflected in the overall statistics for neonatal mortality.

DEVELOPMENTAL ISSUES IN PRACTICE   4.4 (continued)

In an interesting study (Dunn and Kendrick, 1982), researchers showed that children of parents who followed these suggestions had more harmonious relationships 14 months after an infant's birth than did children whose parents had not followed them. When these suggestions were followed, firstborn children averaged 26.7 friendly advances to the infants (per 100 10-second observation units) and the infants averaged 26.8 friendly advances to their older siblings. In contrast, in families in which these suggestions were not followed, the comparable figures were 11.1 friendly approaches from firstborn children to infants and 14.4 from infants to first-born children.

This study also showed differences in the likelihood that firstborns would join mother–infant interactions in a friendly way. In cases where parents had followed these suggestions, the average friendly joining of interactions was 19%, compared with only 8% if these suggestions had not been followed. The study indicates that parents can positively influence the relationships of siblings by using suggested language patterns and including older children in the responsibility of caring for infants.

Addicted Newborns

When pregnant mothers use drugs, they put their infants at risk for a number of congenital problems, as discussed in Chapter 3. An additional problem occurs for the infant if the mother is addicted to drugs. The drugs are transferred to the fetus through the placenta and the fetus becomes addicted to the drugs just like the mother. After the baby is born, the drug use is removed and the baby goes through withdrawal. The withdrawal of drugs causes physiological and emotional stress. The set of characteristics associated with drug withdrawal is called **neonatal abstinence syndrome** (**NAS**).

The characteristics of NAS include extreme fussiness and irritability. These babies cry with a piercing, unpleasant sound and have difficulty responding to normal social interactions. They appear to be excessively aroused by touch and handling, do not make normal eye contact, and are overwhelmed by the sight of human faces (Dixon, 1989; Finnegan, 1984). While the symptoms at birth may be severe, there is relatively little information on the long-term effects from the drugs once the children have recovered from NAS. One reason for this is the difficulty of separating out all the factors that make drug use a problem for the baby and the family. For example, it is known that babies in homes where drugs are abused often receive poor care and poor nutrition. In addition, addicted parents have difficulty providing the appropriate social stimulation for their babies. Thus, it is difficult to know which of these factors is most important in causing the lower level of functioning of babies born to addicted mothers (Boyd & Mieczkowski, 1990; Egeland, Kalkoske, Gottesman, & Erickson, 1990; Kelley, Walsh, & Thompson, 1991; Woods, Eyler, Behnke, & Conlon, 1991).

Figure 4.3   *Decline in Five-Year Mean Neonatal and Postneonatal Mortality Rates, 1930–1988*

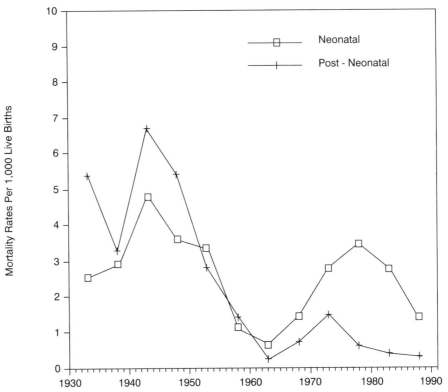

SOURCE: From A. L. Wilson & G. Neidich, "Infant Mortality and Public Policy." *Social Policy Report* 5 (1991): 13. Used with permission.

Cocaine is the drug abused most by women of child-bearing age and is therefore of greatest concern (Schutter & Brinker, 1992). Some studies of the results of prenatal cocaine use on infants have found lower scores in drug-exposed infants on the Brazelton scale (Chasnoff, Griffith, MacGregor, Dirkes, & Burns, 1989; Dixon, 1989; Eisen et al., 1991). However, other studies have found no differences on the Brazelton scale between babies with and without prenatal drug exposure (Day & Richardson, 1991; Woods et al., 1991). Long-term studies of children at two and three years of age have generally revealed no significant differences in drug-exposed children on formal tests of infant development, such as the Bayley Mental Development Index. However, these studies have found that drug-exposed children have subtle differences that are not measured directly by the tests. These include a difficulty in attending to several objects at the same time, poorer ability to structure play activities, and an inability to engage in representational play, fantasy play, or curious exploration (Chasnoff, Griffith, Freier, & Murray, 1992; Rodning, Beckwith, & Howard, 1989).

In summary, infants exposed to drugs prenatally are at risk for problems associated with addiction in families. They are particularly sensitive to bonding failures because of the behavioral characteristics associated with drug withdrawal. In addition, there is some evidence that there are subtle performance decrements in these children that could affect their long-term development. However, most studies do not find significant differences on regular developmental tests between groups of drug-exposed infants and the controls. It is clear that more research is needed to uncover the effects of drugs. In addition, it is clear that these families need special help in dealing with their addiction and in learning to work with their infants afflicted with NAS.

PRETERM BIRTH

Prevalence and Characteristics

Early birth is the most common birth abnormality. Most babies are born at **full term,** which is between 38 and 42 weeks. These normal babies weigh more than 2,500 grams (5.5 pounds). In the United States, 5–7% of all births occur before the baby reaches full term. This involves approximately 150,000 babies each year. Most of these babies develop normally, but they are at higher risk for having problems and therefore require more medical attention than full-term newborns. Newer medical techniques have made it possible for babies born early to survive in greater numbers in recent years. In addition, younger and younger babies are more able to survive than previously. Statistics for babies born before term at weights of 1,000–1,500 grams (2.25–3.25 pounds) indicate that 80–85% will survive; of those weighing 750–1,000 grams (1.50–2.25 pounds), 50–60% will survive (Goldberg & Divitto, 1983).

Preterm births are caused by a number of different factors. Some result from malformations and abnormalities due to genetic inheritance or other disease entities. Chronic illness of the mother can contribute to shorter pregnancies; general living conditions, including nutrition and medical care, can also have an effect on the mother's ability to carry the baby to term. Multiple births generally result in early delivery because of limited ability of the mother to carry the additional size and weight of more than one baby. Various poor health habits, such as smoking, drinking, and the use of dangerous or illegal drugs, are directly related to early delivery.

Because there are many different reasons for early delivery, the expected outcome for each of these conditions can vary greatly. Obviously, if the baby has medical problems in addition to being born early, the outcome is less positive than if the baby is fundamentally healthy but is born early because of twinning, for example. Babies born early are prematurely developed compared with full-term babies; that is, they have had less time to develop since the time of fertilization and will not be as capable developmentally as full-term babies. Prematurity produces problems that can be exacerbated by any additional illness.

One of the biggest problems for babies born early is **respiratory distress syndrome** (**RDS**). This condition occurs because the final maturation of the lungs does not happen until about 34 to 35 weeks, near the end of the fetal period. At that time, a substance called **surfactant** is stored in the walls of the lung, which holds the air spaces in the lung open and prevents the lung from collapsing. If the baby is born before the surfactant has fully developed, there is a much higher risk of developing RDS. Of infants born at 24–26 weeks, 60–70% develop the disease, whereas of those born at 34–35 weeks, only 5–10% develop the disease. This is important because RDS causes the majority of deaths in preterm babies. In addition, RDS is responsible for many diseases that put the baby at risk for death (Boyle, 1993).

It has been discovered that surfactant can be introduced artificially into the baby's system. Surfactant therapy is very effective in bringing about lung maturity. It has been demonstrated that it improves the functioning of the lungs and greatly reduces the death rate. The greatest effects are seen in the youngest infants. In one study of infants weighing 600–750 grams at birth, 53% of the treated infants survived with a normal outcome, compared with 25% of the control infants. However, these infants are still susceptible to other long-term abnormal outcomes, including developmental delay. Once the babies survive the birth period, they are no different from other babies in their tendency to develop problems (Boyle, 1993).

Long-Term Effects of Early Birth

Studying the long-term effects of early birth is very difficult for a number of reasons. First, it is important to compare a normal group of infants with a comparable group of preterm babies. However, the preterm babies have not had an opportunity to develop biologically for as long a time as the full-term babies. One-day-old preterm babies are many weeks younger in gestational age than one-day-old full-term newborns. Many researchers argue that comparisons are useful only if the preterm baby is allowed to "catch up" with the full-term baby by waiting until he or she is 38–40 weeks gestational age. The problem with this approach is that the preterm baby then has many weeks of postnatal environmental experience. Perhaps this time spent outside the womb then gives the preterm baby an advantage over the full-term baby (Siegel, 1982).

In fact, it appears that different developmental abilities are affected differently by biological and environmental events. This shouldn't be surprising, because we learned in Chapter 3 that some traits are more affected by heredity than others. Some of these traits have rigid timetables for developmental expression and they require a specific amount of time after gestation to reach full development. Thus, they should be measured using gestational age. An example of such a measure is the Bayley Scale of Infant Development, which assesses the motor and sensory ability of the infant. Some selected traits can be greatly affected by environmental experience. One of these is the interest in looking at three-dimensional shapes; this trait is best measured using age since birth (Goldberg & Divitto, 1983).

Some researchers have pointed out that the physical development of the preterm baby is probably different from that of the full-term baby because the preterm baby doesn't develop the same tightly flexed (or curled) position typical of the full-term baby. This may be because the baby born early doesn't have an opportunity to experience the very tight, cramped environment of the full-term infant, which might have an important impact on subsequent motor development (Harris, Simons, Ritchie, Mullett, & Myerberg, 1990).

As a group, preterm infants perform at lower levels than newborn infants on most skills. However, these are group means. In fact, many preterm infants perform better than many full-term infants. In addition, most babies recover from the effects of early birth and catch up with the full-term infants by the age of two. Some research shows that by school age, the groups are virtually the same (Grogaard et al., 1990; Sameroff, 1981).

Concerns are often raised that the larger survival rates of preterm infants will increase the number of children with developmental delays and retardation. The research shows that this fear is unwarranted. In fact, even among the most severely affected group (infants born at weights of 750–1,000 grams), 74% are normal or have only very mild disabilities, 15% are moderately impaired, and only 11% are left with serious problems, such as blindness, mental illness, or cerebral palsy (Goldberg & Divitto, 1983). There is evidence that very-low-birth-weight children may be at higher risk for problems such as school problems (Smith & Knight-Jones, 1990), hyperactivity (McCormick, Gortmaker, & Sobol, 1990), and social competence (Hoy et al., 1992). However, the outcome for most children born before term is extraordinarily good and the intervention for those with disabilities has become much improved. See Developmental Issues in Practice 4.5 for a discussion of some of the ethical issues involved.

The Effects of the Preterm Infant on the Parents

When a baby is born early, parents are put in a crisis situation. They are unprepared for the birth, psychologically and physically. Instead of the healthy baby they have dreamed about, they are faced with a sickly infant with an unknown future. These families need extra help in adapting to their preterm baby. First of all, these babies look very different from what the parents expect. They do not have the full, fat face of the full-term infant. This makes them less "cute" and appealing to parents. Second, they tend to sleep more and respond less well to parental interaction than full-term babies. Parents often feel less effective because they feel that their baby is not interested in them. Third, preterm babies have a different kind of cry from full-terms, which is more piercing and therefore more aversive to the parents. Fourth, preterm babies are small and thin and look very vulnerable. Parents are often fearful of handling them because they look so fragile.

Families whose infants are preterm or ill or have disabilities need special help in forming bonds with their infants. In the past decades it has become

ETHICAL CONCERNS INVOLVING NEWBORNS

Medical advances have raised ethical concerns involving newborns. One of these deals with the survival of infants with serious disabilities. Until the past several decades, newborns with very serious problems usually died. In those days, the infants who survived often had the fewest difficulties and the best chance of developing satisfactorily. In recent decades, development of neonatal medicine has brought an increase in the survival rate of infants in distress, although many survivors have had major disabilities. In one news report, the *San Francisco Chronicle* (1983) indicated that the number of infants born with a physical or mental disability has doubled in the past 25 years. According to the report, the idea of providing intensive care for newborns was called into question because this care resulted in an increase in the number of children with disabilities. The ethical issue being raised reflects concern about the quality of life available to infants with severe disabilities.

However, the follow-up research on very young preterm infants suggests that these concerns are misplaced. Aggressive medical intervention coupled with family support produces highly functioning infants with excellent prognoses (Shonkoff, Hauser-Cram, Krauss, & Upshur, 1992). A failure to intervene would actually produce more infants who survived but suffered with developmental delays. In addition, it is clear that most preterm babies develop quite normally. Physicians have every reason to expect a good outcome if they offer medical assistance. Furthermore, the decision not to intervene would require that the physician have a good expectation that this particular baby would certainly die, regardless of intervention, or would survive but be left with a severe abnormality. Our current level of knowledge about distressed babies and their ultimate outcome is insufficient to allow us to make accurate predictions of their future development. It is impossible to know in advance which babies would benefit most from medical intervention.

Thus, it would appear that the financial benefits to society of medical assistance for vulnerable, distressed infants can be substantiated. However, the ethical issues are the more compelling reasons for doing so. Each child really deserves the best that our medical capability has to offer. Jack Shonkoff (1992) has summarized this notion very well:

> The costs and benefits of early intervention services must be measured and analyzed in terms of both dollars and moral values. In many cases, the monetary costs of early intervention can be shown to be off-set by later savings in special education or family support services. For some individuals, however, the benefits of investing public resources are reflected primarily in the moral imperative to provide assistance for those whose needs exceed their own adaptive capacities. In such cases, the monetary costs of service must be weighed against the moral costs of abandoning those who depend on public support. . . .[S]ervices for young children with more severe disabilities are provided not necessarily because it will save money later, but because it is the right thing to do.

Jack P. Shonkoff, M.D., Early Intervention Collaborative Study Division of Developmental and Behavioral Pediatrics, University of Massachusetts Medical School, "Early Intervention Research: Asking and Answering Meaningful Questions." *Zero to Three* 12 (3) (February 1992): 9. Used with permission.

▲ **DEVELOPMENTAL ISSUES IN PRACTICE   4.6**

THE PHILLIP BECKER STORY

The process of bonding between parents and infants with disabilities requires extensive support from hospital and other personnel. Considerable media attention was accorded the story of Phillip Becker, now an adult, who was born in 1968 with Down syndrome and an accompanying heart defect (Ganz, 1983). Phillip's parents did not take him home after birth but instead chose an institutional upbringing for him. Meanwhile, a family named Heath became involved with Phillip through their volunteer work at his board-and-care home. Phillip's parents and the Heath family engaged in a long court battle over his parents' right to keep Phillip institutionalized instead of relinquishing custody to the Heath family. During the litigation, Phillip's parents refused permission for necessary heart surgery for Phillip and indicated in court testimony that they thought that it was better for Phillip not to form attachments to them or to other people. The courts ultimately upheld the Heaths' custody.

This case illustrates what can happen when bonding between a parent and a child who has a disability does not take place. Phillip's parents related to him only in terms of abstract parental rights; they did not see him as a human being who could engage the love of the Heath family, the judge, and various caregivers along the way.

clear that problems in family relationships frequently occur when infants are at risk at birth. Space age technology has progressed to the point at which the lives of preterm or ill infants can be saved in intensive care nurseries, but if their families are not given appropriate help, some of these infants return to the hospital weeks, months, or even years later as battered children (Klaus & Kennell, 1982). The problem of forming family relationships when infants are at risk is an important one; children who are abused are twice as likely as the general population to have been preterm infants (Helfer, 1982). Developmental Issues in Practice 4.6 describes a true story about the difficulty of families to become attached to children with special needs.

Traditionally, infants at risk have been "untouchable" in that they have been whisked away to intensive care nurseries and connected to life-support systems there. Parents and other family members have felt like outsiders. But, in studying families of infants at risk, researchers have found that early parent–infant contact in the intensive care nursery positively affects parental behavior, which in turn has favorable consequences for the child's later development. In one study (Kennell & Klaus, 1971), mothers in one group were encouraged to touch their preterm infants in the first week, but mothers in another group did not touch their infants until 21 days had passed. When the children were tested at 42 months of age, the children of mothers in the early-contact group had significantly higher scores on an intelligence test. In another study, mothers with early contact had more eye contact with their preterm babies and cuddled them more (Kennell, Trause, & Klaus, 1975). In addition, it has been found that mothers who could care for their infants in the nursery were more self-confident about their role as parents (Leifer, Leiderman, Barnett, & Williams, 1972). The impact of early contact on the parents was powerful and has led to many changes in the ways these facilities respond to parents.

It is important to recognize that preterm infants are cared for in the neonatal intensive care unit. The NICU is very different from the usual hospital nursery. The babies are kept in isolettes, which are enclosed cribs that protect the baby and provide the proper temperature. The baby always has many tubes attached and monitors that help the staff to watch for problems in the baby's health. All of this is very frightening for the parents. They see their baby as a prisoner of the medical care that is essential to preserve life. They are fearful of touching or handling the baby and need help in knowing how to hold and stimulate the very small child.

The NICU is the source of a great deal of abnormal stimulation for the premature infant. Infants receive a great deal of handling, but it is almost entirely within the context of caregiving and is often painful and aversive. Thus, newborn premature infants may be deprived of social contacts that encourage emotional well-being. Thoman and Ingersoll (1989) have developed a model of care that recognizes the premature infant as a social organism with strong emotional responses to the environment. The emotional reactions of the infant can mediate the effect of any stimulation. If the handling of the preterm infant is rough and painful, social interactions will be viewed in negative terms because emotional aversion occurs in the presence of social stimulation. This represents the well-understood process of learning. It is important for parents and caregivers to recognize that these small and vulnerable preterm infants have a well-developed capacity to experience all of these social and emotional events.

It is for these reasons that more care is being taken now to alleviate the pain of some of the procedures necessary to sustain the preterm infant's life. The American Academy of Pediatrics (1987) has recommended that neonates be anesthetized whenever surgery is performed. Positive benefits to the infant's medical well-being have been demonstrated in a number of studies that have examined pain reduction techniques for newborns (Field & Goldson, 1984; Porter, Miller, & Marshal, 1987; Williamson & Williamson, 1983). Various types of interventions have been developed to assist newborn, preterm infants in receiving appropriate stimulation. Developmental Issues in Practice 4.7 summarizes some of these intervention techniques.

Graven et al. (1992) have made a number of recommendations for using the social environment and the caregiving context to provide stimulation for high-risk infants:

1. Care should be provided with attention to the infant's state, behavior, physiological condition, and maturity.

2. Staff should provide contingent social input whenever possible while administering nursing and medical care.

▲ DEVELOPMENTAL ISSUES IN PRACTICE   4.7

INTERVENTIONS FOR FAMILIES OF PRETERM CHILDREN

The preterm infant may have a number of health problems and require extensive medical intervention, which can be very stressful to the immature biological system. For example, Anderson (1986) reports painful levels of noise and tactile stimulation due to medical instrumentation. In addition, the infant suffers for being in an environment that is inappropriate for his or her developmental level. Thus, the issue of appropriate environmental stimulation must take account of what the infant is missing by being outside of the womb during this period of development. Because the preterm baby is also a social organism with social and emotional responses to the environment, it is essential that social stimulation be integrated into the care of the infant. Finally, it is clear that the newborn infant is part of a family and the family must learn to accept and care for the baby. Any intervention must include the family as a whole (Goldberg and Divitto, 1983).

One type of intervention involves helping the babies to make a successful adaptation to the new environment by providing ways to simulate the womb that they should be experiencing. The womb contains regular, systematic sounds; rhythmic movements; muted sounds; and extensive touch and movement stimulation. To help the infant make maximum use of the environment, without undue stress, special intervention programs have been developed. Anderson (1986) describes the primary goals of one such program:

1. To provide specific sensory input to infants deprived of coordinated, positive sensory experiences due to the effects of medical intervention, prolonged stay in the NICU, or both.

2. To facilitate the occurrence of more mature developmental patterns through specific stimulation approaches.

3. To effect change in muscle tone, movement patterns, or both, through specific sensory input during handling.

Various types of sensory systems should be stimulated. These include the following:

❑ Visual stimulation, including the placement of mobiles in the isolettes

❑ Tactile input—encouraging the infant to produce self-generated stimulation by moving the hands of the infant to the mouth, face, head, ear, nose, and eyes

❑ Proprioceptive input—providing contact with blankets and the sides of the incubator to encourage pressure on the muscles and joints

❑ Vestibular input—providing rocking movements through handling or placement in swings

❑ Auditory stimulation—providing soft, high-pitched voice and soothing music

3. Efforts should regularly be made to minimize the stress and discomfort of traumatic and painful procedures.
4. Procedures should be timed to avoid sleep deprivation.

Parents are included in an effort to encourage appropriate social interaction. The following recommendations for parents are included:

1. Obtain sufficient sociodemographic information on parents to permit individualizing their care.
2. Document frequency of parental visiting.
3. Parents who visit infrequently should receive assistance and encouragement to visit more often.
4. Demonstrate to parents the behavioral capabilities and limitations of their infant.
5. Involve parents in planning and executing their infant's nursery care.
6. Provide parent support groups.
7. Involve parents fully in discharge planning.
8. Encourage sibling and extended family visitation, where appropriate.

The pediatricians and other health professionals who care for infants at risk find that families go through five predictable stages in learning to relate to the infants (Brazelton, 1982). At first, most families seem able to relate to their ill infants only in terms of medical diagnoses and terminology. Second, they gradually begin to see reflexive behavior but think of it as being directed at someone else, usually a medical person. Third, they begin to see glimpses of what seems like more human behavior, but it still seems directed at someone outside of the family. Some researchers report success at this point in involving volunteers intensively with these infants; the volunteers may spend three or four hours each day with the infants, who then begin to make eye contact, smile, and respond in other ways that cause them to become more appealing to their families (Klaus, Leger, & Trause, 1982). Fourth, family members finally begin to see their infants' responsive behaviors in terms of themselves, if they have received encouragement in involving themselves in their infants' care. And, fifth, the families relate behaviorally as well as verbally to their infants, picking them up and otherwise caring for them. Before families take their infants home from the hospital, they need help in working through the five stages of their grief, denial, and fear to become comfortable and involved parents.

It is sad that not all children are born healthy and whole. Helping professionals have the task of facilitating the bonding process between parents and high-risk infants or infants with disabilities. These families often require support as they move through the five stages of relating to their infants.

Individuals with Disabilities Education Act

The federal legislation originally called the Education for All Handicapped Children Act was amended in 1986 to include Part H, the infant/toddler section, which in turn was reauthorized in 1991 as part of the Individuals with Disabilities Education Act (IDEA). Two features of the IDEA include the requirement for service coordination to more effectively assist families and the requirement for an Individualized Family Service Plan (IFSP). These requirements reflect the realization that the well-being of young children with disabilities is directly dependent on the ability of the family to make adequate responses to their needs. Part H of the IDEA is specifically designed to meet those needs.

It is clear that parental involvement can be of great benefit to the professionals in the testing and identification of infants with disabilities. Henderson (1991) found that the effectiveness of the Early Screening Inventory to identify infants with disabilities could be enhanced when used in conjunction with parental evaluation. This is especially important when identification errors involve overreferrals. An overreferral means that a child will be identified as needing intervention even when he or she is "normal," which points up the great difficulty of making decisions about at-risk infants from testing procedures.

Indeed, we do not yet have the ability to test infants in such a way as to predict whether they will function normally as they mature. Even the most distressed infant can have an excellent outcome. Honzik (1983) has demonstrated that assessments given in infancy have no ability to predict later functioning; McCarton, Vaughan, and Golden (1988) have shown that it is impossible to make predictions for individual patients from evaluations made during the perinatal period. Lewis (1983) found that cognitive functioning cannot be predicted from early testing, especially in very-low-birth-weight infants. Thus, it is very important that professionals avoid making predictions that will only confuse and may frighten parents about the potential outcome of their preterm infant.

Interventions for High-Risk Newborns

The most important factor in planning programs of intervention for the at-risk child is the need to include the family (Hostler, 1991). Improvement in early development for infants can occur best in the context of a nurturing and supportive family (Brooks-Gunn, Klebanov, Liaw, & Spiker, 1993). This means that professionals must not only defer to the wishes of the family but also work closely with families to communicate the variety of services available so that families can make the best decisions for their at-risk infants. There is a need for an interdisciplinary approach to caring for these children, which incorporates psychology, physical and mental health services, early childhood education, family life education, and social work. The purpose of the family-centered approach mandated by Part H of the IDEA is to help families gain a sense of control over their own lives (Dunst, Trivette, & Deal, 1988).

The role of parents in this approach includes that of (1) supportive guardians, (2) primary decision makers about services, (3) service coordinators of their own children, (4) service coordinators of other children, (5) parent educators, and (6) social policy advocates. The notion of parents as service coordinators is new and was once reserved only for the professional. However, it is possible for parents to take on the role of organizing and identifying services, once these parents have been brought into the process (Berman, 1992). Various states have begun to implement Part H programs and to collect ideas about the role of professionals involved in the overall coordination of such programs.

SUMMARY

1. Childbirth culminates months of prenatal development.
2. Childbirth is enhanced when mothers have social support and when fathers can be present in the labor and delivery rooms.
3. Some drugs can have a negative consequence on the newborn baby, especially oxytocin and general anesthetics; but most analgesics and local anesthetics appear to produce no special problems.
4. The birth process, or period of labor, is divided into three stages: opening of the cervix, delivery of the infant, and delivery of the placenta.
5. Cesarean delivery has been found to have no detrimental effects on the baby but can induce feelings of failure in the parents, which should be addressed.
6. Newborns are assessed right after birth by computing Apgar scores, which show how well the infant is adjusting to the stress of delivery and the need to breathe independently.
7. Another assessment, the Brazelton Neonatal Behavioral Assessment Scale, shows infant reactions to a variety of situations and the ability to control states and engage in social behavior.
8. The newborn infant must make a variety of physical adaptations to the new environment.
9. The newborn infant is already a responsive, social organism and has the capacity to engage in complex social interactions with caregivers.
10. The Leboyer method is designed to help ease the transition of the newborn into the new environment.
11. Unique characteristics of newborns from particular cultures influence the reactions of their parents, and vice versa.
12. Bonding, the complex tie of parent to infant, is influenced by prior experiences and contact with the infant.
13. Fathers become fully absorbed in their newborn infants in a process referred to as engrossment.
14. Siblings have special needs that must be met to make a good adjustment to a new baby in the family.

15. Neonatal mortality has decreased because of better medical care for the mother and infant.
16. Newborn infants whose mothers used addictive drugs during pregnancy are subject to suffering from neonatal abstinence syndrome, which makes it very difficult for bonding to occur during the neonatal period.
17. Families with preterm or ill infants or infants with disabilities may need special help in forming bonds with their infants.
18. Preterm infants are at risk of respiratory distress syndrome, which can be alleviated by the use of surfactant therapy.
19. Current medical practice makes it possible for most preterm infants to survive without any developmental difficulties.
20. Preterm infants are sociable and require attention to their social and emotional needs.
21. The Individuals with Disabilities Education Act has been expanded to include infants and toddlers.
22. Intervention for high-risk newborns is facilitated by the inclusion of parents in the management of the infant.

ACTIVITIES TO ENHANCE LEARNING

1. Developmental Issues in Practice 4.2 contains three items from the Brazelton Neonatal Behavioral Assessment Scale. Follow the directions given and test two infants in the neonatal period. Or ask the parents to do the assessment, while you score the infants. Assess each baby and obtain the score. Compare the differences between the infants.
2. Locate a parent with a neonate. Observe the interaction between the parent and infant during caregiving and feeding. Answer the following questions:
   a. How often did the baby initiate interactions with the parent? What method did the baby use (looking, crying, excessive body movement, etc.) to get the parent's attention?
   b. What was the parent's response to the baby's actions?
   c. How often did the parent initiate interactions with the baby? What method did the parent use (looking, talking, rocking, etc.) to get the baby's attention?
   d. What was the baby's response to the parent's actions?
   e. Which type of attention did the parent display more of toward the infant: verbal or physical?
   f. Did the baby respond better to certain types of actions on the part of the parent?
   g. How would you assess the quality of the interaction you have observed? Was it well synchronized between parent and infant? Was there use of the *en face* position?

FOR FURTHER READING

Bonding

Klaus, M. H., & Kennell, J. H. (1982). *Parent-infant bonding* (2nd ed.). St. Louis: C. V. Mosby.

Klaus, M. H., & Robertson, M. O. (Eds.). (1982). *Birth, interaction and attachment: A roundtable*. Skillman, NJ: Johnson & Johnson.

Smeriglio, V. L. (Ed.). (1981). *Newborns and parents: Parent–infant contact and newborn sensory stimulation*. Hillsdale, NJ: Lawrence Erlbaum.

Sibling Relationships

Lamb, M. E., & Sutton-Smith, B. (Eds.). (1982). *Sibling relationships: Their nature and significance across the lifespan*. Hillsdale, NJ: Lawrence Erlbaum.

Fathers

Robinson, B. E., & Barret, R. L. (1986). *The developing father: Emerging roles in contemporary society*. New York: Guilford Publications.

Infants with Disabilities

Goldberg, S., & Divitto, B. A. (1983). *Born too soon: Preterm birth and early development*. San Francisco: W. H. Freeman.

Raver, A. (1991). *Strategies for teaching at-risk and handicapped infants and toddlers: A transdisciplinary approach*. New York: Merrill/Macmillan.

PART II

The First Year of Life

Four alert, healthy infants wait in a pediatrician's reception area. Newborn Agnes sucks on a pacifier and gazes intently at her father's face. The movement of her body slows and her eyes widen as she centers her attention on his words. The interlude soon ends, however, when a five-year-old slams the nearby door. Agnes gives a startled reaction and cries vigorously.

Four-month-old Ted sits on his grandmother's lap. He alternately plays with his wiggling bare toes and watches the antics of some older block builders. When the tower of blocks collapses, Ted wrinkles his brow at first but then smiles as the older children go into gales of laughter.

Eight-month-old Justin sits on his mother's lap and looks at the simple, bright pictures of animals in his baby book. He looks at a picture of a dog and exclaims, "Gok." His mother responds, "Yes, that's a dog." Justin then repeats "Gok" with enthusiasm and begins to slap the book with his open hand.

Twelve-month-old Lena rides a rocking horse while making an engine noise: "Rmm-mmm, rmmmmm!" She laughs and claps when her mother pretends to feed the horse a plastic apple. When she finally tumbles off the horse, Lena toddles up and down the room, holding onto chairs and knees for support and smiling at anyone who will pay attention to her.

The dramatic differences among Agnes's, Ted's, Justin's, and Lena's development are characteristic of infancy. Part II of this book gives detailed information about the changing capabilities of infants during their first year of life. The contents are designed to increase understanding of infant development and generate ideas about how to apply that understanding to make a positive impact on infants.

Much of the information in this part reflects recent research findings. Until the past few decades, the development of infants has not been well understood even by specialists in the field. Because infants cannot use words to tell adults what they see, hear, or feel, their physical, psychosocial, and cognitive development has been more a matter of conjecture than fact. Now, however, through the use of innovative techniques of investigation, more is understood about the fascinating ways in which infants interact, grow, and learn.

This part is divided into three chapters, devoted respectively to information about physical, psychosocial, and cognitive development. Through all three chapters, research on cultural variables in child development is explained and job opportunities for child development specialists are highlighted. Ideas about developmental issues in practice are also included.

Physical development is described in Chapter 5, beginning with the states of alertness of newborns. Information is then given about reflexes, with an emphasis on the strengths with which infants enter the world. Other topics include theories about motor development, milestones of physical development, nutrition, and health and safety.

Psychosocial development is described in Chapter 6. Attention is given to the importance of a basic sense of trust, communication between adults and infants, secure attachments and separations, infant crying, and social understanding. The effects of the infant's temperament and of parental employment are also explored.

Part II of this book concludes with Chapter 7, which describes cognitive development. The chapter starts with new findings about the sensory competence of newborns. Piaget's theory of cognitive development is then considered, as is the nature of infant intelligence. The chapter concludes with the topics of language development, cultural differences in language interactions with infants, and early intervention programs.

Infant Physical Development

▼ KEY IDEAS

States of Alertness
- ❏ Sound Sleep
- ❏ Active (REM) Sleep
- ❏ Drowsiness
- ❏ Active Awake
- ❏ Crying
- ❏ Quiet Awake (Alertness)
- ❏ Managing States of Alertness

Reflexes and Competence in Early Life
- ❏ Tonic Neck Reflex
- ❏ Rooting and Sucking Reflexes
- ❏ Burst–Pause Pattern
- ❏ Babkin Reflex
- ❏ Walking Reflex
- ❏ Placing, Babinski, and Grasping Reflexes
- ❏ Moro Reflex
- ❏ Protective Reactions

Theory of Motor Development

This chapter was written with James William Younge, Ed.D., Western Illinois University.

Newborns do not closely resemble the smiling one-year-olds chosen for baby product advertisements. Their heads are large—comprising one-fourth of their body length, compared with one-eighth in adulthood—and their necks are not yet well developed enough to support the weight of their large heads. They have round faces and cheeks, which are often considered "cute" configurations of appearance and may trigger inborn nurturing responses in adults (Brazelton, 1981).

Newborns have a number of distinctive physical characteristics. Their skin tends to be wrinkled and covered with peach fuzz hair, the **lanugo**. A white, greasy **vernix caseosa** has collected on their skin to protect it from the surrounding amniotic fluid and provide lubrication during birth. Their heads may be misshapen because the bones constricted during the birth process as the head was squeezed through the mother's pelvis. Such constricting or molding is possible because of open spaces in the head, called **fontanelles.** During the first weeks of life, the lanugo and vernix caseosa disappear and the head becomes more rounded. The fontanelles usually close in the first two years of life. Until they close, they leave the vulnerable brain open to damage; care should thus be taken to protect the baby's skull.

Important physiological developments take place during the weeks after birth. Living outside the uterus requires the infant to move against gravity, breathe air, regulate body temperature, receive and process new kinds of stimulation, digest food, and eliminate wastes through kidneys and intestines. Because of the importance of developments in the first weeks of life, these weeks have their own designation: the **neonatal period**. The accomplishment of the neonatal period can be summarized by just one word—*adjustment*. The neonatal period is a period of adjustment to living outside the uterus.

Much change takes place between the neonatal period and an infant's first birthday. This chapter provides an overview of physical development in the first year of life. Attention is given to various levels of alertness; reflexes;

milestones of physical development; nutrition, health, and safety; and child abuse.

STATES OF ALERTNESS

Suppose a father tries to play with his newborn infant and in response the infant closes his eyes tightly or starts to fuss and cry. Should the parent feel rejected and unhappy? No, and this father would be helped by an understanding of the different levels of alertness that can be expected in infancy. With this knowledge, he can plan his play times to coincide with the best times in his infant's cycle of states. Six different **states** make up the infant's cycle: sound sleep; active sleep, characterized by rapid eye movement (REM); drowsiness; active awake; crying; and quiet awake, or alertness (Wolff, 1959). In the case of the parent–infant dyad just described, the infant appeared to be ready for sleep and unable to respond to the father's bid for play. The father should wait for the quiet awake state in the infant.

Sound Sleep

In **sound sleep** the infant is unaware of the sights and sounds of the surrounding environment. Breathing is regular and the eyes are tightly shut. Every so often there is a startled movement, a break in breathing pattern, and then a return to the same deep breathing. If a light goes on or if there is a loud noise, the infant will usually be able to shut it out. Even if disturbed briefly, the infant will go back to sound sleep without really waking. For most infants, then, it is not necessary for adults to tiptoe during their sleeping time. The infant is able to control the amount of noise or light that is received.

Premature infants have shorter and less consistent periods of sound sleep than do mature infants. Premature infants are less able to shut out sights and sounds and are more likely to be disturbed by them. Parents of premature or stressed infants need to provide a more controlled setting for sleep than do parents of full-term infants. On the other hand, premature infants spend more total time sleeping than do full-term infants. Full-term infants spend about 75% of the day (approximately 18 hours) sleeping. Premature infants are found to sleep around 88% of the day (Holmes, Reich, & Pasternak, 1984). Small infants also sleep longer than larger infants at the same age during the first months of life (Bamford et al., 1990).

Active (REM) Sleep

Active sleep can be identified by body movements and vocalizations, including grunts and bursts of sucking. **Rapid eye movement** (**REM**) also characterizes this phase of sleep, which regularly alternates with sound sleep in newborns, just as is the case in adults. In adults, this state is characterized by dreaming and includes a discharge of electrical energy in the brain. It is assumed that infants have periods of dreaming. The REM phase of sleep accounts for about 60% of total sleep in newborns. During **REM sleep,** infants are more restless and more easily roused than during sound sleep. Gradually, between birth and adulthood, both the amount of REM sleep and its ratio to total sleep diminish (Holditch-Davis, 1990).

Drowsiness

The state of **drowsiness** is characterized by a glazed, unfocused look in the eyes, with eyelids closing and opening. Infants in this state are generally ready to go to sleep and should be encouraged to relax. Attempts to rouse the infant during this stage often lead to fussiness and agitation.

Active Awake

In the **active awake** state, the infant is restless, with much body activity. The eyes do not focus on anything in particular. Very little learning can occur in this state because of the inability to focus attention.

Crying

Crying is the most difficult state for parents to handle. Parents are highly responsive to the crying of their own infant, and the way that they handle infant crying is important for the parent–infant relationship (Thompson, Harris, & Bitowsk, 1986). Infants have a tendency to be fussy late in the day when they are most tired (Pinyerd & Zipf, 1989). Some infants are very fussy and suffer from colic, which is assumed to be related to digestive discomfort. Babies usually outgrow this tendency by around six weeks to three months of age. The amount of time a normal baby spends crying each day is in some dispute; estimates range between 30 minutes and three hours (Carter & Mason, 1989).

Quiet Awake (Alertness)

Attractive sights and sounds can help infants move from sleep to a transitional state between sleep and full alertness. This **quiet awake** state is very important to infants because it presents the prime opportunity for the infant to learn from the environment. Adult sensitivity to infants' cues is extremely important in helping infants attain and maintain alertness. Sometimes in the transitional periods the infant fusses and cries. The crying can discharge energy and then, with comforting of adults, move the infant into alertness. The adult's role is to be soothing and calm, letting the infant be involved in his or her interaction but not overloading the infant so that an excessive motor response throws him or her back into a transitional state.

Managing States of Alertness

The six states of the infant's cycle are experienced at intervals throughout each day and night. An adult who observes carefully can choose appropriate play times that will lead to mutually positive experiences. The all-important quiet awake state occurs for only approximately 10% of the day in the new-born but increases in length as the infant matures. It is important for infants to learn to organize these states. Early, effective state organization has been shown to have a beneficial effect at eight months (DiPietro & Porges, 1991) and at one year (Fajardo, Browning, Fisher, & Paton, 1992).

Parents have a role in helping the infant to organize and define the states. Brazelton (1981) suggests that the "ideal" adult response is to provide encouragement to the infant—to extend gratifying periods of alertness as well as periods of sound sleep. Sometimes overzealous parents interfere with the infant's organization of these cycles by trying to bring the infant to alertness during periods of REM during the night. But for an infant to sleep for a long period of time at night, which is desired by most parents, the infant needs to learn to handle the REM periods that come regularly between times of sound sleep. Sensitive parents can help their infants master and extend parts of this cycle by encouraging daytime alertness and by not being too quick to intervene during nighttime REM. For this reason, parents sometimes find it better to put their infant to sleep in a separate room to prevent the infant from being aroused and to prevent themselves from interfering with the infant's sleep. To the great relief of parents, the cycle of states becomes increasingly easy to interpret with each passing month of infancy.

Premature infants or infants with a low sensory threshold have to be handled especially patiently and carefully. These infants may cry and sleep a great deal, as if to shut out the outside world, and parents need to be very gentle in reaching out to communicate with them when they are alert. Over time, these sensitive infants become better able to manage stimulation.

Sleep patterns change during the first year of life. The number of sleep episodes is reduced by 50%, but the total sleep time is reduced by only about two hours (Bamford et al., 1990). Average sleep time for infants younger than three months old was found to be 15.2 hours; for infants over nine months old, the average was 13.4 hours (Michelsson, Rinne, & Paajanen, 1990). Infants waken regularly at night during the first year of life (Scher, 1991). In a telephone survey of parents of infants and toddlers, parents reported that 42% of their infants resisted going to bed and 35% woke or cried during the night. About half the parents reported that changing the schedule of the child improved the situation (Johnson, 1991).

REFLEXES AND COMPETENCE IN EARLY LIFE

During infancy, motor development is often gauged by the appearance of new skills. The rate at which these skills emerge will vary from child to child because of individual differences in physical growth and maturation. Many of the movements of the fetal period and the postnatal period are reflexive (Haywood, 1986). **Reflexes** are automatic responses to specific environmental stimuli. For example, stimulation of the cheek triggers the sucking reflex. Infants will exhibit about 27 reflexive actions. As the nervous system matures, control of reflexive movement shifts from the subcortical area to the mid-brain and brain stem. Reflexes at birth are mostly primitive and deal with helping the infant survive in a new environment. By six months of age, in a normally developing child, most reflexes disappear; only a few (like coughing, blinking, and sneezing) linger past the first birthday (Gabbard, 1992). Ultimately, movements come under the conscious control of the child. For example, the child decides when and under what circumstances sucking will occur.

Textbooks often discuss reflexes in isolation from other aspects of development, leaving the impression that infants are bundles of undifferentiated reflexes. This book, however, follows the approach of Brazelton (1981) by describing reflexes as part of the competence with which infants approach even their first encounters in the world. Following is a discussion of some of the most commonly seen reflexes.

Tonic Neck Reflex

Anyone involved in fencing recognizes the position characteristic of the tonic neck reflex: the face turns to one side and the arm and leg on that side extend away from the body, the body arches away from the face, and the opposite arm and leg flex at the elbow and knee. Newborns can often be observed working very hard to get into this position. The turning of the head triggers the reflex, causing the arm on the side the infant is facing to extend and the opposite arm to flex. Newborns then may work to overcome the reflex and bring a hand to the mouth. Their eyes show an alert seeking of sights and the origins of sounds in the environment. Infants are active in wanting to get acquainted with what surrounds them.

Rooting and Sucking Reflexes

Newborns also have strong rooting reflexes, which can be activated by gently touching the cheek around the mouth. Infants turn toward the touch, grasp the finger in their mouth, and start sucking. The strength of the suck is often a surprise to adults, as is the sensation of separate movements of the infant's mouth. Sucking effectively involves the integration of three separate movements: suction from the esophagus, rhythmic movement from the back of the tongue, and up-and-down movement from the front of the tongue. At first, infants need time to coordinate their movements. By the third day, most infants suck efficiently even at the start of a feeding. Exceptions are brain-damaged and premature infants, who take longer to integrate the sucking movements.

Burst–Pause Pattern

Related to the rooting and sucking reflexes is the burst–pause pattern of feeding that most infants have at birth. They suck at first on the breast or bottle quite steadily. But when their initial hunger is satisfied, they move into a pattern of 10–20 sucks and then a pause. This behavior can be interpreted as a communication used by infants to get a response from adults. During these pauses, most adults move the nipple, jiggle, talk, or touch the infant with the intention of making the infant comfortable and continuing the feeding. Brazelton (1981) studied the length of the pauses of infants under two conditions: when mothers responded and when they did not respond. He found that the infants' pauses were shorter when the mother did not respond. When the mother did respond, infants lengthened the pauses and extended the communication. This study seems to demonstrate that burst–pause sucking is an example of the way a pattern of behavior can help the infant to establish communication.

Babkin Reflex

Another related reflex is called the Babkin. This reflex can be observed when an infant's cheek is stroked. The infant's hand on that side of the body forms a fist and the infant gradually brings it to the mouth. The Babkin reflex can be observed even before birth by physicians who work with ultrasound equipment.

Walking Reflex

Newborns have a walking reflex, even though voluntary walking does not occur until about a year later. The walking reflex can be produced by supporting the infant in a standing position with feet planted firmly on a flat surface such as the couch. Then the infant is bent slightly forward over an adult's hand; gradually the infant will "walk," alternating feet. The infant loses this reflex at about six months of age, when similar but more controlled movements begin to prevail.

Placing, Babinski, and Grasping Reflexes

A placing reflex can be activated by holding an infant upright and stroking the upper part of the foot. The infant will flex from the hip, reach out the foot, and spread and grasp with the toes. A related reflex is the Babinski, bringing about a spreading of the toes when the sole of the foot is stroked. The grasping movement can be produced with the infant's hand if the palm of the hand is stroked. With this grasping reflex, an infant can hold onto a finger or object with a surprisingly firm squeeze.

Moro Reflex

Infants also have a startle reflex called the Moro, which is set off if the infant's head falls quickly backward or if there is some other disruption. In reaction, the infant extends arms and legs and then pulls them back to the body with a hugging motion.

A walking reflex is present from birth until about six months of age.

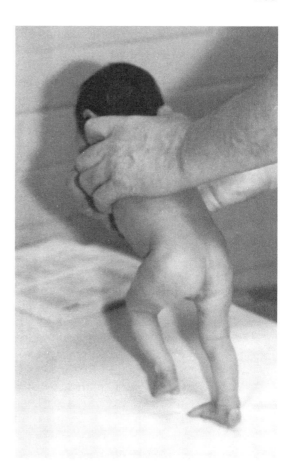

Protective Reactions

From birth, infants instinctively take action to protect themselves from suffocation under a blanket during sleep. When a blanket does cover an infant's face, the infant usually moves the head actively from side to side. If that movement does not dislodge the blanket, the infant brings the arms alternately to the face to knock the blanket away.

When adults play with infants to produce these reflexes or observe infants to see them, the adults gain a sense of the real competence with which infants enter the world. Certainly an infant is helpless compared with an adult, but an infant is born with surprising ability to guide adult efforts at caregiving with actions and reactions.

THEORY OF MOTOR DEVELOPMENT

The study of motor development as a specified field is relatively new. Originally, emphasis had been placed on studying achievement-oriented norms.

Recently, the focus has shifted to studying the underlying developmental processes that make motor behavior possible. Piaget's theory has been the most useful for studying the development of motor behavior over time. See Chapter 2 for a discussion of the theory.

Piaget's theory is useful because it is sequential; that is, it evolves in increasingly complex stages with age. Piaget developed the notion of structure, also referred to as **schemes,** to define innate capabilities of the individual. A scheme is the smallest unit of coordinated action that the individual makes. These coordinated actions become more and more complex with age. The actions are always understood to occur in response to environmental demands. In addition, the actions consist of the coordination of all the individual's available domains, including physical and intellectual actions.

A hungry infant turns toward the mother's breast, grasps the nipple, and begins to suck. This seemingly simple action is made up of the complex coordination of many subsystems. A partial list of such subsystems includes (1) identification of the breast by sight and smell, (2) perceptual and motor orienting toward the breast, (3) movement of the head toward the breast, and (4) the complex interaction of lips, tongue, and throat needed to suck and swallow the milk.

In motor development, Schmidt (1991) used certain terminology to explain how we perform a novel task. Schmidt used the term *schema* to refer to generalized motor programs based on past experiences. Common features of past performance are stored in the central nervous system and retrieved as movement is required. For example, a six-month-old infant is seated on the floor playing with toys. She is attracted by a certain toy. Using schemes already developed and her past experience in such situations, she coordinates her eyes' visual assessment of the distance with her hand's reach to try to make contact with the toy. The schemes available to the child are sufficient to accomplish the tasks. The child's functioning is driven by schemes motivated by the desire to obtain the toy. However, should the toy be too far away for the child to reach it from a seated position, the child has insufficient schemes at this stage of development to move into a crawling position and retrieve the toy.

An important point is that there is a value in giving the child an opportunity to experience the scheme in a number of different situations with a variety of different objects. For example, if a toy rolls behind the infant, the infant must rotate his or her body to reach for it. Such variations strengthen the scheme and make it possible for the infant to transfer the skill to new schemes, such as reaching while in a crawling position. Thus, it is important for effective motor development for the child to have sufficient time and opportunity to practice using schemes, allowing for endless repetition. Caregivers can provide interventions to encourage opportunities to practice motor skills in a variety of conditions.

Recently, researchers have investigated the active, ongoing interaction of the child with the environment. This approach is called **dynamical systems theory** (Ray & Delprato, 1989) and involves the notion that an organism uses

---

▲ DEVELOPMENTAL ISSUES IN PRACTICE   5.1

INFANT EXERCISE

Levy (1973) has developed a series of exercises for parents to do with infants to learn about infant competency and to feel comfortable with handling their infants. In the first three months, exercises are based on relaxing infants' bodies. From three to six months, exercises prepare infants for the sitting position. And from six to twelve months, exercises include a variety of movements and prepare for standing. The following example is a relaxation exercise:

Position: Put the child flat on his or her back on a table covered with foam rubber.

Aim: To make the hand open by relaxing the shoulder.
Begin the loosening-up at shoulder level, making regular pats. Progress gently to the hand. Toss the arm gently up and down. When the child has opened his or her hand, relax the other arm and hand.

Adapted by permission of Pantheon Books, a Division of Random House, Inc., from *The Baby Exercise Book for the First Fifteen Months,* (pp. 10–11), by Dr. Janine Levy, translated by Dr. Hermina Benjamin. Copyright 1973 by William Collins Sons Ltd.

---

all systems collectively to accomplish coordination of a task. The individual attempts to become self-organizing in interaction with the environment. This approach is consistent with Piaget's but is in opposition to Schmidt's, since the central nervous system is seen as only one of the many systems and not the controlling one.

In a normal environment, the average child will have an opportunity to explore and "play." However, motor development can be enhanced by using systematic interventions to strengthen motor schemes. An example of one such intervention is found in Developmental Issues in Practice 5.1. It is important that such training programs are carried out in the natural sequential order of human development, that they be treated as games with positive emotional tone and high affect, and that the individual developmental rhythm of the child be respected. The next section contains a description of the developmental milestones of the first year of life. How does the child move through the stages of increasingly complex structures?

MILESTONES OF PHYSICAL DEVELOPMENT

Many infants are taking their early wobbly steps at about the same time that their first birthday candles are being lit. It is clear how far they have come when it is remembered that at birth they were not capable of voluntary locomotion. In no other one-year period until puberty are there so many physical changes. The changes in infancy are measured in terms of days and weeks rather than in terms of months and years.

Physical development has an orderly sequence from the top to the bottom of the infant's body. The infant first gains control over the head, then gradually the arms and body, and finally the legs and feet. This progression from head to toes is called **cephalo-caudal** development. In addition, there is an orderly progression from the center of the body outward toward the ends, called **proximo-distal** development. The infant gains control of arms first, hands next, and fingers last. What is gratifying about watching infants gain mastery over their movements is their obvious delight in each milestone. They work hard to accomplish each new feat and then practice repeatedly. Rather than producing boredom, the repetition seems enjoyable. As infants feel successful with one feat, they build their confidence for the next.

A significant developmental task to be achieved during the first year of life is gaining control of the body. Three categories of movement represent the control skills to be mastered in infancy: stability, locomotion, and manipulation. **Stability** includes gaining control of body parts and muscles as they struggle with the force of gravity (standing and walking). As the control skill of stability develops, it allows various forms of **locomotion** to be mastered (crawling, creeping, cruising, upright walking). The third control skill of **manipulation** involves reaching, grasping, and releasing. The control skills of infancy allow for exploration and therefore lay the foundation for infant learning (Gallahue, 1989).

To become acquainted with the course of physical development in the first year of life, we will follow the changes in Anna, a composite of many infants. The age ranges given for Anna's activities are only averages (adapted from Glover, Preminger, & Sanford, 1978; White, 1990); some infants will do these things earlier and some will do them later. It is important to keep in mind that a wide time variation exists in what is known to be typical development.

The First Three Months

Even in the first hours after birth, Anna has a lively interest in the world. She can distinguish light, dark, and some colors; she prefers simple patterns; and she can use her eyes to follow slowly moving objects. She does all these things best if sights are placed within 12 inches of her. Anna is interested when someone brings a rattle to her or takes her over to look at the wallpaper. She relies on her parents to help her get to know them and the other things that surround her.

In Anna's first six weeks, her hands are usually held in tight fists when she is awake. Like most infants in the first months, Anna can be induced to use her hands for a strong reflex grasp. When she sleeps, her hands sometimes open and relax. Anna's mom can help relax her baby's body by gently massaging body parts. (See Developmental Issues in Practice 5.1.)

When Anna is about four weeks old, she becomes able to lift up her head when she is lying on her front side. She can stay in that position only briefly, but she seems very pleased with the new perspective. The kinds of circumstances that facilitate the acquisition of the specific skills of the early months simultaneously seem to result in a more interested, cheerful, and alert child (White, 1990).

From birth, Anna is alert to sounds and seems to like rhythms. In her first weeks of life, Anna smiles in response to her mother's high-pitched voice. At four weeks, her mother can still get her to smile most effectively by talking to her, but Anna also shows her first signs of smiling at someone's face when no words are spoken. Anna seems to scan her parents' and caregiver's faces, make eye contact, and then smile widely. Adults begin to spend even more time playing with her now, although they cannot explain why.

Anna has more control over her hands by the time she is six weeks of age. She keeps them more open when she is awake, and voluntary grasping movements replace her earlier reflexes. Her father worries that Anna is becoming weak, because for a while she cannot hold on as tightly or for as long as when her grasping was part of a reflex, but he relaxes as he watches Anna learn to bring objects to her mouth. Anna studies, mouths, and amuses herself with these objects. Anna's mouth is extremely sensitive and she learns a great deal about objects by feeling them with her tongue and lips; therefore, her parents must be careful that she does not have access to objects that she might swallow.

Anna's world expands when she is six weeks old. Her caregivers notice that she can visually follow the movement of people and things that are several feet away. From the time that she is two and a half months old, she begins to swing her arms at the activity gym that is suspended just over her crib. When she makes contact and moves it, she seems surprised and pleased.

By two months of age, Anna can lift her head and chest for a longer time when she is on her front side. That increased strength in her neck and back makes it comfortable for her to sit with support in an infant seat or on someone's lap. At three months of age, she looks at everything around her and definitely wants to be in the hub of family activity. She is now experiencing more and more periods of wakefulness (White, 1990). Her body is now moving away from the influence of flexion (the curled fetal position) to more extension in body movements. When she is looking around, she often kicks her legs.

Anna can swim when placed in the water. This is a period of reflexive swimming. Ingestion of water and coughing are less common at this stage because of the breath-holding reflex. These reflexive movements, which disappear by the fifth month, are under subcortical control (McGraw, 1963). See Developmental Issues in Practice 5.2 for a description of this field of motor development.

In her third month, Anna is able to locate where sounds originate. Her mother reports that Anna also seems to know what some different adult tones of voice mean.

▲ **DEVELOPMENTAL ISSUES IN PRACTICE   5.2**

INFANT SWIM PROGRAMS

Linda Illuzzi (1991) has studied the benefits of early water experiences for young children. She emphasizes that the primary goals are for the child to enjoy the experience and to become acquainted with the water. Activities should be based on the physical, cognitive, and social development of the child. Children learn about the buoyant characteristics of water and improve their body awareness through their play, exploration, and interactions in the water. The goals in placing children in early swimming programs should be to teach children water safety, to teach them aquatic "readiness" skills such as bubble blowing, and to provide experience in being on the stomach and back in the water, as prerequisites for later swimming and aquatic activities.

Children should never be asked to do something that they fear. The Council for National Cooperation in Aquatics (CNCA) and the American Academy for Pediatrics do not endorse forcible submerging, prolonged or frequent submersion, or dropping a child from a height into the water. These practices are dangerous and have the potential to cause psychological trauma. When the child becomes comfortable in the aquatic environment, he or she will readily place the face in the water and explore and play.

Goals for adults who enroll with their children in aquatic programs include learning about water safety, proper holding positions, flotation devices, and supervision of children. They should learn that at no time is a young child ever considered water-safe. According to the National Swimming Pool Safety Committee (1987), drowning is the third leading cause of accidental death for children under five. Children must be carefully supervised in the bathtub, backyard pool, and other aquatic facilities because it is not a lack of supervision but a lapse in supervision that could lead to a water emergency.

Many adults are concerned about the effect of water in the ears and the possibility of ear infections, which can occur often in young children. The frequency of this condition among young children is related to their tendency to have narrow and short eustachian tubes, which do not permit middle ear drainage when moderate inflammation of mucus membranes is present (Langendorfer, 1989). It is unfortunate that the tendency has been to associate swimming with ear infections even though the problem is primarily anatomical. Pediatricians differ in their recommendations regarding exposure to water for children who have a tendency to get ear infections or who have typanostomy tubes (tubes placed in the ear drum to help regulate the pressure between the inner ear and the outer ear to relieve infections and prevent hearing loss).

Three to Six Months

When Anna is four months of age she learns to roll from her front to her back side. The first time she succeeds, she seems surprised. Then she repeats the movement with relish. Her waking-up routine changes after that. Rather than calling her mother by crying, she rolls over from front to back and awakens her mother by the sounds of the activity gym above her in the crib. In another month, Anna masters rolling from her back to her front side. Anna enjoys her new freedom and sometimes rolls herself from one part of the room to the other.

Her increased movement now causes her to notice her hands and feet. On her back, she studies her hands and feet and gradually brings their movements under her control. A great deal of pleasure comes from the sheer joy of exercise of large muscles (White, 1990).

Anna's father extends his hands to her, and she is strong enough to pull herself into a sitting position. Anna explores objects as she sits, but her father tries to anticipate when she is getting tired because at first Anna cannot get herself out of the sitting position.

Anna reaches for interesting things and can move them up and down and from side to side. Her eyes sparkle and she exclaims in pleasure when she is able to make noises with a rattle.

When she is five months of age, she opens her hands as she reaches for objects. She has had enough experiences to begin to estimate size by opening widely for a large object and narrowly for a small one. She receives more tactile information from her fingertips than from the whole-hand approach that she used earlier in handling objects. Eye–ear coordination is much improved and is demonstrated when eyes turn toward nearby sounds (White, 1990).

Six to Nine Months

Anna gets herself up on all fours in a crawling position and rocks back and forth as if she has an idea but cannot quite implement it. Her first crawling movements are backward, but she gradually learns to move forward. Delight registers on her face as she discovers that she can get anywhere she wants to go. Movements enhance new motor skills and satisfy curiosity, which encourages Anna to conduct first-hand investigation of her environment (White, 1990). Anna likes to be put into a standing position. She especially likes jumping up and down on her mother's lap.

Anna's play is much more complex than it was earlier. She shows that she knows what is coming by starting to clap her hands when her father suggests playing "Pat-a-Cake." She puts smaller objects into larger ones and understands how to use simple hammers or other tools. She explores everything and seems particularly to like things that change and move according to her actions. Activities that now use newly emerging motor skills—such as doing arm and leg exercises, turning over, sitting unaided, dropping, throwing, and banging objects—are continuous in the infants' play (White, 1990).

By six months of age, infants eagerly explore their feet. Their mouths give them the most information about objects at this age.

At this age, Anna's swimming patterns become disorganized. This is because the reflexive patterns of the earlier swimming skill are beginning to dissipate. Movements of the extremities are of a struggling nature, and coughing and ingestion of water do occur. This is a transition to more voluntary types of swimming activity.

Anna needs to have careful adult supervision and some redirection of her interests. For instance, her mother redirects her interest in the television set by providing bright, colorful toys for manipulation.

Nine to Twelve Months

As Anna's crawling becomes more efficient, the need for adult management of her environment increases. She is enticed by the challenges of the stairs in her building but can be safe on them only with close adult supervision. At other times, a gate is put between her and the stairs. (See Developmental Issues in Practice 5.3 for a discussion of positive discipline for infants.)

Feeding Anna becomes a bit of a tug-of-war. Anna wants to use the cup and handle the food herself. Her mother compromises and feeds some things to her and gives her some chunks of cheese and other finger foods to feed herself. By twelve months, she perfects the process of grasping small objects between the tips of her thumb and index finger. Anna can also point with her index finger.

▲ DEVELOPMENTAL ISSUES IN PRACTICE 5.3

POSITIVE DISCIPLINE FOR INFANTS

Before infants gain mobility, it is relatively easy to be positive in interacting with them. However, the time when they first begin to crawl and climb presents special challenges and many opportunities for decisions about their activities. Some of these decisions are likely to convey positive messages to infants, and some may convey negative messages.

Consider the following situation and responses: A nine-month-old succeeds in opening a cabinet and removing all the pots and pans.

Response 1: "You're into everything! What am I going to do with you?!"

Response 2: "You must have really worked hard while I was in the other room. I need these for cooking but you can use those over there."

In this situation, the infant has achieved mastery of something new and has opened up a set of novel possibilities for exploration. When the adult returns to the room, the infant is delighted with the noise that the lids make when banged together. However, seen through the first adult's eyes, the infant is an exasperating person who makes extra work for adults. The infant is given no options besides stopping and will probably return for further exploration at the first unsupervised opportunity. When that happens, there is likely to be a similarly negative but somewhat more annoyed response.

In contrast, the second adult sees the infant as a hard worker who stays with a problem until it is resolved. Like the first adult, the second also does not want the infant in that particular cabinet but instead is willing to set aside another area with safe and interesting similar items for the infant to explore. The infant can return for further exploration and will probably receive additional positive feedback at that time.

The second adult has communicated a positive message to the infant: "Your interests are valid and worthy of pursuit." Yet the adult has also redirected the infant's activities. Providing interesting alternatives is an important aspect of positive discipline for infants.

It is important to note that in some instances the child chooses to play in areas that are unsafe. When this happens, it is essential that the parents change the environment by adding locks or by moving dangerous substances. Parents cannot expect an infant to understand their cause for concern for safety.

Anna controls several objects at one time, building block towers and putting smaller things into larger ones. She drops and throws almost everything, both to practice the letting-go motion and to see what will happen. Peas are tossed off the high-chair tray and toys are tossed from her crib. She is a small scientist and her environment is her laboratory.

In this last quarter of the first year, Anna begins to pull herself into a standing position. She progresses to walking while holding onto furniture.

The first independent steps, taken at about one year of age, are cause for excitement.

Finally, she sets off on her own. She has had an eventful first year and, just as she will never be the same again, her parents will never view infants in the same way that they did before getting to know Anna.

Maturation and Experience

Could Anna's parents accelerate her development or teach her to walk early? What roles do maturation and experience play in the developmental process? McGraw (1935) studied the effects of early training on two twins. One twin had special training sessions several times a day, whereas the other twin had the practice sessions withheld. The trained twin's performance increased temporarily over the untrained twin's performance. However, the untrained twin quickly caught up with the other twin, and there were no differences between them in development of motor skills. McGraw concluded that the **phylogenetic** behaviors (i.e., independent sitting, crawling, and walking), which are characteristic of the species, are not modified by early practice. The **ontogenetic** behaviors (i.e., roller skating and bike riding), which are characteristic of the individual and not necessarily evident in everyone, are enhanced with practice.

Many skills in the first year of life emerge automatically within the maturation process and are fairly resistant to modification by practice. In addition, individual patterns develop in a fairly stable way. For example, early crawling in infants has been shown to be related to the later accomplishment

---

▲ DEVELOPMENTAL ISSUES IN PRACTICE   5.4

HOPI CRADLEBOARDS

How much of physical development is determined by maturation? What is the effect of experience? A classic study by Dennis (1940) relates to these questions. Dennis studied two groups of Hopi infants. One group was raised in the traditional Hopi manner, tying infants on cradleboards for much of the first nine months of life. The other group was raised in a more typically Western manner. On the cradleboard, infants are restricted in raising their bodies, moving their arms, and rolling over. Dennis was interested in determining whether the group of infants raised without the restrictions imposed by the cradleboards would learn to walk sooner than the group that had used cradleboards.

Dennis found that both groups of infants started to walk at about 15 months of age. He concluded that walking is maturationally determined, and his conclusion was accepted for a period of time. However, the evidence is less convincing than Dennis believed because use of the cradleboard was discontinued when infants were about 9 months of age. Even the infants who had used cradleboards, then, had the opportunity to exercise without restriction between 9 and 15 months of age. A cautious interpretation of Dennis's study is that restriction of movement before infants reach 9 months of age does not seem to affect the age of walking. Although the maturationist case could have been stronger, Dennis's study shows the importance of maturation in walking but does not rule out the importance of experience.

---

of selected motor skills (McEwan, Dihoff, & Brosvic, 1991). Skills that are not species-specific are highly influenced by environmental experiences and practice. See Developmental Issues in Practice 5.4 for a further discussion of the importance of maturation and experience; this example is particularly interesting because it involves cross-cultural issues.

NUTRITION

Breast-Feeding versus Bottle-Feeding

The food most ideally suited to infants is breast milk. There are many nutritional, health, practical, and emotional advantages to breast-feeding. From the perspective of nutrition, human milk contains just the right nutrients that infants need for growth and activity. Breast milk does not "come in" until a few days after the birth of the baby. Before that, the human breasts produce a substance called **colostrum**. The composition of colostrum is different from that of breast milk; colostrum appears to provide some essential nutrients not found in breast milk. In particular, colostrum contains **immune factors** that will protect the baby from getting sick from the illnesses that the mother has had. It also contains substances that will inhibit the development of intestinal

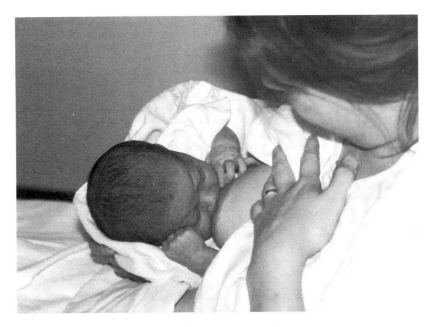

The food most ideally suited to infants is breast milk.

infection. Breast milk also provides some immunity to a variety of infections if the mother herself carries immunity. Breast milk is matched to the capabilities of an infant's digestive system and is less likely than substitute formulas to trigger allergic reactions in the infant.

Breast-feeding has been associated with positive benefits for the infant. It has been found that breast-fed infants have different sleep cycles than bottle-fed infants (Butte, Jensen, Moon, Glaze, & Frost, 1992). The breast-fed infants slept better than bottle-fed infants. In addition, breast-fed infants have been found to have higher cognitive scores at the age of three years than a control group of bottle-fed infants (Bauer, Ewald, Hoffman, & Dubanoski, 1991).

The practical advantages of breast-feeding are numerous: there are no formulas to mix, no refrigeration or sterilization to ensure, no expense (except that of assuring the mother of a good diet), no bottles to warm, and no worry about how much an infant drinks. The emotional advantages of breast-feeding involve a special feeling of closeness when a nursing mother realizes that she is the source of something that her infant needs and that she alone can provide. Because of the many advantages, most pediatricians recommend breast-feeding. Support groups, such as the La Leche League, are available to provide practical advice and caring guidance.

Sometimes women have every intention of breast-feeding their infants but find it difficult to be successful. There are various reasons why our modern life-style might interfere with breast-feeding success. It has been found that the amount of milk produced by the mother's breasts is directly related to the frequency of feeding. The more often the mother feeds the baby, the more milk is produced for use by the baby; length of each feeding is not related to milk production. For this reason, mothers should be encouraged to feed the infant whenever the baby wishes and not on prearranged schedules as has often been recommended for bottle-feeding babies in the past (Klaus, 1987). Another factor that influences success is the critical importance of the mother's comfort and feeling of relaxation. Breast-feeding is most likely to be successful if education in lactation can be given while the mother is still in the hospital and if she can have access to an experienced breast-feeding consultant (Saunders & Carroll, 1988). If the mother is tense or stressed for any reason, she will produce less milk; there will be less milk available for the baby to suck because tension inhibits the ability of the breast to "let down" the milk (Newton, 1973).

Family traditions of not breast-feeding, less formal education, and working outside the home are also reasons given for not breast-feeding (Ruiz & Cravioto, 1989). Working can be an important factor in preventing breast-feeding. Even mothers who intend to breast-feed often find that the complications of working prevent them from carrying out their intention (Morse & Bottorff, 1989).

Bottle-feeding is the method of choice in certain circumstances. If the mother is in poor health or taking medications that would be transmitted to the infant through breast milk, bottle-feeding is often recommended. In addition, premature infants have insufficient development of mouth muscles to make breast-feeding possible. Some employed mothers breast-feed, but others, especially those with inflexible working hours, decide to "express" breast milk and arrange to have it fed to the child from a bottle.

Feeding Infants

Feeding infants is essential to their physical well-being, but eating also entails dangers. Choking is a serious concern and care must be taken to avoid problems. Feedings should be kept within the developmental capabilities of the infant (Satter, 1984). Newborn babies are limited in the amount of muscle strength and coordination they have, and they do not acquire adult levels until the preschool years. The food given to infants must conform to these developmental limitations (Satter, 1984). The following list provides a guide to the needs of infants as they develop from birth to two years.

Birth to Six Months	*Five to Seven Months*
Roots for nipple	Begins to sit
Suckles	Follows food with eyes
Six to Eight Months	Begins to swallow runny solids
Moves tongue laterally	Lips close over spoon

Six to Eight Months (continued)	*Twelve Months*
Controls position of food in mouth	Sociability increases
Controls swallow	Interest in solids increases
Munches	Cup drinking improves
Seven to Ten Months	*Second Year and Beyond*
Bite matures	Circular rotary chews
Rotary chews	No pause in side-to-side transfer
Transfers food from side to side	Begins to use utensils
Curves lips around cup	

From Ellyn Satter, "Developmental Guidelines for Feeding Infants and Young Children." *Food and Nutrition News, 56* (1984):21–26. Published by National Live Stock and Meat Board. Reprinted with permission.

During the first six months of life, the only appropriate food for infants is breast milk or fortified infant formula. The newborn baby is capable of rooting for the nipple and sucking. It has been shown that infants use the smell of their mother's milk to help identify their mother. However, infants will orient to any breast-feeding woman for milk (Porter, Makin, Davis, & Christensen, 1992). The tongue makes a front-to-back motion that transfers the liquid to the back of the throat for reflex swallowing. This movement is not appropriate for solid foods; if solid food is given, it will be pushed out onto the chin. A very runny solid can be taken if it is placed on the back of the

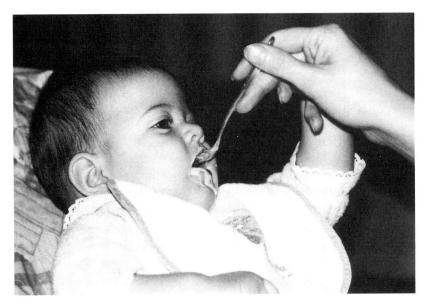

When placed in a semireclining position, a young infant can eat soft, runny solids to facilitate swallowing.

tongue and if the infant is in a semireclining position to facilitate swallowing. Infants have a very strong gag reflex to guard against choking, which generally begins to fade at around four months of age.

Between five and seven months of age, the infant is ready for practice with solids. At this age, the infant can sit up, open the mouth in anticipation of the spoon, and close the mouth around the spoon, scraping off the contents. Soft semisolids can be transferred to the back of the mouth with an up-and-down movement of the tongue, a movement that begins to develop at this age. It requires coordination for the infant to process this movement; choking can be prevented by having the child in an upright position and facing forward. It is essential that the child is not startled or frightened in any way during this process, because such events cause sudden breathing movements that disrupt swallowing behavior. Feeding times should always be calm and quiet.

The only food that meets both the feeding and the nutritional needs of infants at this age is iron-fortified cereal mixed with formula, breast milk, or water (cow's milk should not be used until one year of age). This provides all the essential nutrition, especially the additional iron that is required. Iron deficiency is a major nutritional deficit, and iron is an essential component of the growth needs of children at this age. See Developmental Issues in Practice 5.5 for additional information about the importance of iron.

This a good age at which to introduce a variety of textures and flavors to the baby. Most pediatricians suggest that after about six months of age, new food or juice should be introduced every three to four days to begin to accustom the infant to them. These are just "for fun," and the approach should be accordingly low key. In this regard, it is important to remember the temperamental need of the infant, who is slow to warm up to new experiences; such infants need more time and patience. For all infants, the pattern of giving three to four days between adding new foods allows the adult to detect any allergic reaction to something new. If many new foods were introduced all at once, it would be difficult to isolate the one responsible for any reaction. It is essential that parents take the advice of their pediatrician in deciding which foods to give infants in the first year of life, because infants are more prone to develop life-long allergies to foods if they are introduced at this time. In addition, some foods should be avoided, including canned vegetables (which contain too much sodium), sweetened desserts (which contain too much sugar), and honey (because of the risk of botulism poisoning, which can cause death). Initially, a tablespoon of food is sufficient. Infants should not be forced to finish food if they are satisfied with the amount they've eaten.

At around seven to ten months, babies can begin to chew foods; this is the time to introduce finger foods and soft solids, such as cooked carrots or bananas, as the baby can begin to pick up objects with a pincer grasp. The infant can begin to curve the lips around the edge of a cup. Food is taken from side to side in the mouth so that there is better control; however, the chewing pattern is still not fully mature, and choking is still possible if the child is startled or distracted (Satter, 1984). At eight to twelve months the infant will want to join in the social aspects of eating by being a part of the

▲ **DEVELOPMENTAL ISSUES IN PRACTICE   5.5**

IRON-DEFICIENCY ANEMIA

Iron-deficiency anemia is a worldwide phenomenon. Research from many parts of the world has confirmed that this is the most severe nutritional deficiency. Even in technologically advanced countries it is a problem. For example, in the United States, Japan, and Europe, 10–20% of women are anemic. In Third World countries this problem is greater because of lower levels of meat in the diet (Scrimshaw, 1991).

Low iron in the diet has severe health implications. When a pregnant mother is anemic, her baby is born with the high probability of being light in weight and having health problems. There is insufficient understanding of all the biological causes of iron's role in good health. However, it is clear that iron is essential for health and for adequate cognitive development. In research from many countries (including Egypt, Indonesia, Guatemala, Costa Rica, and Chili), it has been found that anemic children show cognitive limitations. Even when infants suffer from low levels of iron deficiency, there are clear test score deficits in their performance. There is a tendency for these children to be slow and listless. There is also an indication that iron deficiency is associated with behavior problems (Johnson et al., 1992). It has been found that infants improve with an increase in iron supplements if the intervention occurs early enough. If the intervention is delayed until the preschool years, it isn't effective in raising test scores.

Research has also shown that infants born with iron deficiency are more likely to be sick and have more difficulty surviving illnesses. They are more likely to have infections, including bronchitis and gastroenteritis. In studies performed in Africa, iron helped to protect against malaria. It has also been demonstrated that children can survive illnesses more effectively if they are not iron deficient.

It is for these reasons that infants must receive breast milk from a healthy mother. If infants are on formula, it must contain iron supplements. When adding solid food to the diet, iron-enriched cereal is recommended, and it is important for older infants to receive meat in diets that include finger foods. The World Health Organization is cooperating with the United Nations to develop a plan to eliminate iron-deficiency anemia in less developed countries.

family meal time. Parents should watch for signs of this interest and begin to provide the baby with plain food from the family table. Infants want to feed themselves at this age, which is always a very messy process.

At around a year, the infant begins to have a nutritional need for non-milk protein. Usually, milk becomes a smaller part of the total diet. Meat protein is preferred because it is most easily absorbed and because it contains trace elements and vitamins that are not found anywhere else in the same amounts. Meats should be soft and cut into small pieces. Ground meat is eaten easily, as is flaked fish. Hot dogs are popular; however, they are high in fat and can lodge in the throat. For this reason, it is best to cut them lengthwise into four strips and then into small pieces. To prevent choking, it is important for infants to always eat while seated and not be allowed to run around with food in their mouths. Excitement and sudden changes in breathing patterns can still be dangerous. It is not until around 25–36 months of age that the chewing and swallowing abilities reach full development with circular rotary chewing and no pause in the side-to-side transfer. This pattern eliminates the greatest concerns of choking (Satter, 1984). However, even at this time, it is difficult to chew firm or large pieces of food; care should be taken to cut up all food, as even preschool children do not have the dexterity to cut food into the appropriate sizes for eating. It is important to allow children at this age to monitor the amount of food they can handle. Children should not be forced to eat huge amounts of food. As long as they are eating at regular times and have a well-balanced diet, they will be getting enough.

Malnutrition

Protein-calorie malnutrition in infants is a worry for those in health care professions. Severe cases are seen in clinics or hospitals, but there are also infants who suffer malnutrition without any noticeable signs except poor physical growth. One type of malnutrition that occurs in infants 6–18 months of age is called **marasmus** (from the Greek word meaning "to waste"). Marasmus is caused by a restriction in total food intake, including protein. The symptoms of marasmus include poor physical growth, severe wasting of muscles, anemia, diarrhea, lack of subcutaneous fat, wrinkled skin, and drawn face. Marasmus is on the increase, especially in developing countries, because of the movement toward shorter periods of breast-feeding or total reliance on bottle-feeding under inadequate conditions of supply, sanitation, and sterilization.

Malnutrition can also occur in our own culture. When it does, it is most likely related to the development of the relationship between the mother and the infant. Research has shown that mothers who are sensitive to their children's needs and are synchronous in establishing interactions, have infants who gain weight faster and are in better general health because of effective feeding patterns (Pollitt & Wirtz, 1981). (See the section on child neglect for further discussion of this issue.)

Concern about adequate nutrition in infancy is particularly acute because of the brain growth that occurs at this time. Brain cells multiply during two periods: the first is at 10–20 weeks of gestation and involves the division of nerve cells; the second is from 20 weeks of gestation to four months after birth and consists of growth of glial cells (see Chapter 3 for a discussion of this topic). Growth of the brain by cell division is almost completed by 18 months of age; further growth occurs but is due to other causes, such as increases in cell size. The weight of the brain increases 200% in the first three years of life, and study after study has shown direct links between nutrition and brain growth (Lynn, 1989; Werner, 1979).

Research indicates that the long-term effects of undernutrition in early life include impaired functioning of the central nervous system and reduced thinking capacity. Emmy Werner (1979) reviewed a number of cross-cultural studies and concluded that nutritional supplements, combined with medical care, have the most powerful effect on cognitive development if given during pregnancy and the first years of life. Pollitt, Gorman, Engle, Martorell, and Rivera (1993), in a long-term cross-cultural study, have demonstrated that providing protein supplements in the first years of life gives cognitive advantages to children that continue even in adolescence and young adulthood (11–24 years of age).

When malnutrition occurs after age three, the effects on brain development are less noticeable and are almost absent after age five. It seems that infants can grow to become fully functioning adults only if great care is taken to meet their nutritional needs in infancy. Normal growth curves can be used to monitor growth. To use the growth curve, the child is placed on one of the curves and growth should follow that particular curve. It is assumed that there is a problem if the child's weight or height suddenly drops below the curve that is being followed.

HEALTH AND SAFETY

Health and well-being of infants depends entirely on the care provided by parents and caregivers. This section discusses issues of importance to the health and safety of infants, including dental care, immunizations, safety, and abuse and neglect.

Dental Health

An infant's first tooth usually breaks through the gums at about seven months of age, and the set of 20 teeth is complete by about two and a half years of age. The typical pattern is for the two lower middle incisors to come in first, followed a few months later by the four upper incisors. At the end of the first year, most infants have these six teeth.

Infants vary greatly in the amount of discomfort teething seems to give them. Some chew on everything, sleep fitfully, and seem fretful for days at a time. Other infants surprise their parents with a suddenly visible tooth after no noticeable change in behavior.

Fluoride in the diet of children from infancy through age 12 is known to aid the formation of strong teeth that resist decay. In some areas of the country, fluoride is found naturally in or is added to the water. In other areas, fluoride drops can be given daily for infants up to one year of age. The incidence of tooth decay is lowered substantially when fluoride is taken as teeth develop.

Immunization

A major societal concern is the number of children who are unprotected by immunizations against some of the major childhood diseases. Perhaps part of

A twelve-month-old shows his displeasure at receiving an immunization. He will feel only momentary discomfort and will be protected from diseases that can cause disability or death.

the reason for the relaxed attitude of many parents today is that they are too young to remember what it was like when many children did suffer disabilities or death from diseases for which immunizations are now available. The importance of immunizations has not diminished, however; they should be given in infancy and throughout the early childhood years.

The first inoculation is usually the combined DPT—diphtheria, pertussis (whooping cough), and tetanus—given at about two months of age. A total of three combined shots are administered at two-month intervals during the first year. It is unfortunate, however, that these combined shots often cause reactions, including fever, soreness near the location of the shot, fussiness, and loss of appetite. The physician can prescribe medication to relieve the symptoms.

Also at two months of age, administration of oral poliovirus vaccine is started. This vaccine is given by mouth three times during the first year, usually separated by two-month intervals. A combined vaccine protects against the three viruses that are known to cause polio.

Other vaccinations are recommended at about one year of age, and they are often given in a combined form, immunizing against measles, mumps, and rubella. Although many people have had these diseases without complications, there can be serious consequences, such as ear infections, encephalitis, or brain damage from measles; sterility in males from mumps; and birth defects during the first three months of pregnancy from rubella. Parents have an important responsibility to protect their infants from the very severe complications that can result from these diseases.

Safety

Adults are responsible for creating an environment within which infants can be active and safe. In the early months, infants have limited mobility; finding appropriate places for them to eat, play, and sleep is relatively easy. In fact, some parents take their newborns wherever they go and feel that their lives have altered very little with the infant's birth. This perception and the ease with which an environment for the infant can be managed both change as the infant gains mobility. Once infants can move themselves at will from place to place, setting up their environments becomes more challenging. Adults need to take an infant's-eye view of each room and remove small objects that might be swallowed, sharp objects, breakable or delicate objects, and poisonous plants and other substances. All medicines and household cleaners and soaps should be stored in high, locked containers. Special caps should be put over electrical outlets to eliminate the danger of electrical shock if the infant gets the idea of sticking an object into the outlet.

Exploration is important to an infant's development. By "child proofing" the environment, adults free themselves to be relaxed and encouraging of the infant's interests and movements. The alternative is to surround the infant with saying no, a situation that is exhausting to adults and frustrating to babies. Some families find it particularly helpful to set aside a child-proofed room, where the child can play without fear of danger. This is important because parents cannot watch the child every minute. Yet there is no substitute for constant supervision, because no environment can be made completely safe. However, a safe room and fenced-in play yard can give infants the space to explore while allowing caregivers the freedom to leave the child for brief periods.

Major causes of death for infants include house fires and traffic accidents. General safety precautions that benefit families also protect infants. Developmental Issues in Practice 5.6 includes an important discussion on infant vehicle safety.

Abuse and Neglect

Definitions.   In recent years the media have emphasized the growing problem of **child abuse** in our society. In infants under the age of six months, abuse is second only to sudden infant death syndrome as a cause of death. After the age of 12 months, it is second only to actual accidents (Lloyd-Still, 1976). This is naturally a cause for concern, as it appears that there are many families in which the ability to interact normally with infants breaks down. Originally, child abuse was defined as physical battering that could be identified by medical evaluation. The primary method of detection was the X-ray

> **▲ DEVELOPMENTAL ISSUES IN PRACTICE   5.6**
>
> ## INFANT VEHICLE SAFETY
>
> Traffic accidents are a principal cause of death and injury in childhood; yet relatively few infants ride safely in appropriate car seats each time they travel. Being in an approved car seat prevents infants from being thrown out of the car onto the road and from hitting the windshield or the inside of the car with great force. Safety experts agree that all occupants should be properly restrained every time even a short car trip is taken.
>
> Infant car carriers are designed so that the infant faces the back of the car and is in a semireclining position. The infant wears a snug harness, and the carrier attaches to the seat of the car with a car lap belt. Car carriers designed specifically for infants should be used from the first ride home from the hospital until the infant weighs 17–20 pounds. At that time, the child can graduate to a conventional car seat, which should be used until the child weighs 40 pounds or is four years old. The U.S. Department of Transportation has a set of standards (upgraded in 1981) that all safety restraints should meet. Some states now require the use of these restraints.
>
> Parents might be more inclined to restrain their infants in approved car seats if they knew how unsafe their usual practices were. Consider these comments and the facts that follow them:
>
> "But I hold her on my lap."
>
> An adult's lap is one of the most dangerous places that an infant can ride. In a sudden stop or crash, the adult's body would crush the infant. Even if the adult is restrained, the force of a crash would make it impossible to hold on to the infant.
>
> "I'm a safe driver, and this is a short trip."
>
> Many accidents are caused by the mistakes or problems of other drivers, and many accidents take place close to home.
>
> "He won't like being placed in one of those."
>
> Like anything else, the adult's attitude is important. Children who have always been safely restrained usually accept it as the usual way to travel in the car. Adults can teach by their own example, too, and always buckle up.
>
> "I put them all in seat belts."
>
> Until a child weighs about 40 pounds, a seat belt can exert dangerous pressure on the abdomen in a crash. A seat belt may be better than no restraint whatsoever, but, particularly with infants, an appropriate infant car carrier is the safest choice of all.

machine, which revealed multiple fractures in the bones of children, some improperly set, indicating repeated damage to the child. It soon became evident to the doctors that the battering of the children had been carried out by the parents; they called the pattern of abuse "the battered child syndrome" (Kempe, Silverman, Steel, Droegemueller, & Silver, 1962).

However, it was found that abuse could take many forms, involving more than the breaking of bones. These include burning, whipping with implements, and lacerations caused by jerking the arms or ears. One definition given by Gil in 1973 is as follows: "Intentional, non-accidental use of physical force, or intentional, non-accidental acts of omission, on the part of caretaker, aimed at hurting, injuring, or destroying the child." This definition is supposed to cover child abuse and neglect. However, there are those (Parke and Collmer, 1975) who have argued that this is a poor definition. First of all, it could conceivably include disciplinary actions, accepted as appropriate by many in our culture. There is one belief system that holds that it is essential for the child to feel some pain in order for disciplinary acts to be effective. In addition, the notion of "intentional" implies guilt on the part of the abusing parent. The need to include "intentions" can be bad for two reasons. First, most parents probably abuse their children in a state of uncontrolled anger, not as intentional disciplinary action. Second, the presupposition of guilt may be an incorrect assessment of the parent's situation. The parent may be a victim of circumstances that lead to abuse or may have inappropriate developmental expectations of the child. In any case, it is probably counterproductive to begin by accusing parents of guilt.

Thus, the definition of *abuse* is not agreed upon by everyone. Even among professionals working in the field, there is variation in what each would define as a case of child abuse. Gelles (1982) did a study that involved a group of professionals, including physicians, counselors, principals, private social workers, public social workers, emergency room physicians, and police officers. All agreed that "willfully inflicted trauma" and "willful malnutrition" constituted abuse. However, when the statement eliminated the issue of intentional action by simply stating "injured when struck too hard," between 72% and 75% of counselors, principals, and social workers would identify this as a case of abuse. Only 44% of emergency room physicians and 66% of general physicians identified nonintentional damage to a child as a case of abuse.

The question "What is child abuse?" is obviously not an easy one to answer. It requires a great deal of information from both the abused children and their parents. This is particularly true because the issue of intentional desire to hurt the child seems to be so important to the thinking of many professionals. The Child Abuse Prevention and Treatment Act of 1975 (42 U.S. Code 5101) avoids the problem of intentionality by defining child abuse and neglect as "the physical or mental injury, sexual abuse, negligent treatment, or maltreatment of a child under the age of eighteen by a person who is responsible for the child's welfare under circumstances which indicate that the child's health or welfare is harmed or threatened thereby." According to this approach, abuse results from an adult's nonaccidental action toward a child.

Neglect is the absence of action when action is necessary. Although experts do not understand why, in cases of abuse there is usually one child in the family who receives the brunt of the violence. In cases of neglect, all children in a family are usually involved.

To receive federal assistance in developing, strengthening, and carrying out programs for the prevention and treatment of child abuse and neglect, states must meet the following criteria: provide for the reporting of known and suspected instances of child abuse and neglect; investigate such reports; train personnel to work with abused and neglected children and their families; appoint a guardian to represent the child in any judicial proceeding; preserve the confidentiality of all records; provide for cooperation of law enforcement officials, the courts, and state agencies providing human services; and disseminate information about abuse and neglect to the public. In some states, professionals, such as teachers and physicians, are guilty of a misdemeanor if they do not report incidents of suspected child abuse to the appropriate authorities.

Of great interest and concern to readers of this chapter on infancy is that many of the reported cases of child abuse involve infants under one year of age. It may be difficult to imagine that anyone would beat, burn, or otherwise injure a defenseless infant. However, this abuse does take place; all who are interested in child development need an understanding of the phenomenon. Many parents damage their infants out of frustration over crying or other difficulties. For example, they may shake a child who continues to cry, inadvertently causing brain damage when the weight of the head puts stress on the spine. Parents need help in coping with the stresses of parenting. Developmental Issues in Practice 5.7 gives suggestions for working with parents to help them cope with frustration.

Nonorganic failure to thrive.   Doctors began to receive infants who were not doing well into their emergency rooms. They were malnourished, underweight, and unresponsive. When the doctors looked for a medical or organic cause for the problem, they could not find one. If they kept the baby in the hospital, brought him or her back to a healthy weight, and sent him or her home, the infant would frequently return some time later with the same symptoms. This pattern has been referred to as the syndrome of **nonorganic failure to thrive** (Barbero, 1975). To be identified as having this syndrome, the infant and family must have the following qualities:

1. Weight below third percentile for age
2. No evidence of disease entity
3. Developmental retardation with rapid recovery in hospital
4. Signs of deprivation, which decrease in the hospital
5. Significant disruption of attachment between infant and family

There is fairly good medical agreement on the definition of nonorganic failure to thrive; and it is generally observed in hospital settings. It occurs because the infant is totally dependent on his caregivers for survival. If the

▲ **DEVELOPMENTAL ISSUES IN PRACTICE   5.7**

ASSISTING PARENTS WHO USE EXCESSIVELY HARSH BEHAVIOR

The following strategies were presented by Bromwich (1981).

We listened empathetically as the parent
- talked about how angry she felt when the child expressed negative feelings.
- talked about how frustrated she often felt, having to deal with this child 24 hours a day.
- talked about how badly she felt after she had punished the child more harshly than she had meant to.

We asked the parent whether she could pinpoint the areas of the child's behavior that made her particularly angry and upset and then find ways of avoiding situations that evoked these behaviors.

We also discussed with the parent
- how easy it is to feel frustrated and angry with a young child when one is isolated and has no one to talk to.
- that there are groups in the community where parents who feel isolated and frustrated with their young children can share their experiences and help each other.
- that it is important for parents who tend to punish their children more severely than they intend to get help from groups in the community because harsh punishment can inflict injury to the child without the parent being aware of this.
- particular resources in her community where she could get help.

(When there is sufficient evidence to suspect child abuse, state laws dictate that physicians, nurses, teachers, and other professionals contact the Protective Services division of the Department of Public Social Services or, in the case of an emergency, the Protective Services division of the local police department.)

We encouraged the parent
- to call us or a friend when she was faced with a particularly difficult problem with her child, or when she felt especially tense and upset with the child.
- to get out of the house with the child occasionally
- to keep tensions from building up.
- to try to find a baby-sitter so that she could occasionally get away from the child.
- to follow up on one or more of the resources provided for her before she loses control over her angry feelings and does something she might regret.

infant is not cared for, he or she will die and any evidence of poor care shows up as nonorganic failure to thrive. It differs from other cases of neglect in that it occurs at a time in the life of the child when he or she is totally vulnerable. To cure this problem obviously requires treatment for the parents as well as the child.

Size of the problem.   The estimates for child abuse vary widely depending on the study and its methods (Gil, 1973). One reason is that there is a high number of unreported cases, so all of our figures are only "best guesses" or estimates of the actual number. Once states passed laws requiring that child abuse cases be reported, the numbers of cases increased dramatically. However, there are those who believe that, in addition to the reporting increase, the actual numbers of cases are increasing in America (Parke, 1982). Some writers believe that the actual number, including unreported cases, could range into the hundreds of thousands (Nagi, 1973). Heins (1984) has suggested that the number could be as high as six cases per 1,000 births.

Prevention.   Can child abuse and neglect be prevented rather than stopped only after it has happened? In fact, certain projects have attempted to do just that. These parent–infant intervention projects have goals such as encouraging positive parent–infant interactions, helping parents to feel adequate and important, and communicating information to parents about development and community resources. When skilled, empathic professionals are in close touch with families under stress, they can provide positive suggestions about outlets or solutions for the frustrations of life that seem overwhelming. Belsky, Lerner, and Spanier (1984) have pointed out that interventions must take account of the child, the family, and the community in order to be successful.

SUMMARY

1. Physical changes are greatest during the first year of life than at any time until puberty.
2. Infants' daily cycles include the states of sound sleep, active sleep, drowsiness, active awake, crying, and quiet awake.
3. A series of reflexes is part of the competence that infants have at birth, which helps them interact successfully with the environment.
4. Newborn reflexes include tonic neck reflex; rooting and sucking reflexes; burst–pause pattern; Babkin reflex; walking reflex; placing, Babinski, and grasping reflexes; Moro reflex; and protective reactions.
5. The theory of motor development is based on the concept of motor schemes to explain the increasing complexity of behavioral development.
6. In movement and coordination, infants achieve voluntary control in a progression from head to toes (cephalo-caudal development) and from center to exterior (proximo-distal development).
7. During the first six months, infants learn to control their hands, develop the ability to roll over and sit up, and expand their ability to handle objects.
8. Between six and nine months, infants learn to crawl, play simple games such as "Pat-a-Cake," and begin to use simple tools.
9. Between nine and twelve months, infants learn to stand and then walk, attempt to feed themselves, use finger/thumb grasp, build towers, and put objects into containers.

10. Phylogenetic behaviors cannot be easily modified, but ontogenetic behaviors can be.
11. Nutrition is essential to the ability of the child to develop normally; milk is the most appropriate food for an infant. Breast milk has been found to meet the needs of the infant better than other forms of milk.
12. Feedings should meet the developmental abilities of children and care should be taken to provide calm environments for eating in order to prevent choking.
13. Severe malnutrition is called marasmus and can result in poorly developed brain growth with consequent lowering of intellectual ability.
14. Infants begin to cut their first teeth at around seven months.
15. Immunizations during the first year of life are essential to protect children from dangerous childhood diseases.
16. It is essential that adults protect infants from dangerous environments by "child proofing" their homes and child care centers.
17. Child abuse and neglect have increased in America. Extreme cases of neglect in infants are referred to as nonorganic failure to thrive.

ACTIVITIES TO ENHANCE LEARNING

To complete these exercises, it will be necessary to make observations of infants. Obtain permission from family, friends, or an infant daycare center to observe an infant between the ages of birth and one year.

1. State observation. Observe an infant and caregiver while the infant is between birth and four months of age. Use a diary approach to write down the various states of the infant over the course of a one-hour period. Note the following:
   a. How does the infant respond to caregiver communication in the different states?
   b. What methods are used by the caregiver to change the state of the infant?
   c. Are some methods more effective for changing particular states?
2. Developmental Checklist. Using the information in the chapter, set up a developmental checklist for the age of the infant you are observing. Observe the infant over the course of a week, indicating the skills performed on your checklist. Write a statement about the performance of the infant, indicating whether the performance is developmentally appropriate.

FOR FURTHER READING

Early Development

Capian, F. (1978). *The first 12 months of life*. New York: Bantam.

White, B. L. (1990). *The first three years of life*. New York: Prentice Hall.

Sensory and Perceptual Competence

Bower, T. G. R. (1977). *The perceptual world of the child*. Cambridge: Harvard University Press.

Bower, T. G. R. (1982). *Development in infancy* (2nd ed.). San Francisco: W. H. Freeman.

Parenting Support Programs

Bromwich, R. (1981). *Working with parents and infants: An interactional approach.* Baltimore: University Park Press.

Infant Exercise

Bailey, R. A., & Burton, E. C. (1982). *The dynamic self: Activities to enhance infant development.* St. Louis: C. V. Mosby.

Levy, J. (1973). *The baby exercise book for the first fifteen months.* New York: Pantheon.

Nutrition

Satter, E. (1991). *Child of mine: Feeding with love and good sense.* Palo Alto, CA: Bull Publishing.

Psychosocial Development of Infants

The term **psychosocial** refers to one's traits, feelings, attributes, and interactions. It refers to the ways that individuals feel about themselves and the ways that they relate to other people. According to Erik Erikson, John Bowlby, T. Mary Ainsworth, Berry Brazelton, and other experts whose ideas are presented in this section, infants' psychosocial development is of great importance. Later development is influenced by how infants establish a sense of trust, communicate with their parents, form attachments, understand social information, and show characteristics of temperament. The more that is understood about the psychosocial development of infants, the more likely people are to create growth-enhancing environments for them.

A SENSE OF BASIC TRUST

An infant is brought into a strange home. The strange family gathers around to "meet" the baby. Does the infant respond with trust or mistrust? Is there sufficient trust to allow the infant to interact, explore, and learn, or will the infant withdraw in fear and mistrust and fail to benefit from the new experience?

The term **trust versus mistrust** comes from the theory of Erik Erikson (1963, 1977, 1982) (see Chapter 2 for an introduction to this theory). Erikson built on the thinking of Sigmund Freud, developing his ideas during years of practice in child psychoanalysis. His young patients were brought to him because of their inabilities to cope with interpersonal relationships. In the process of helping his young clients, Erikson created a theory about the challenges, or crises, that occurred in their psychosocial development. He found that, at each developmental level, it was necessary for the children to meet and resolve these crises.

According to Erikson, in the first year of life infants need to establish a sense of trust. This sense of trust develops gradually from the time of birth if the infant's needs for food and comfort are met relatively promptly and consistently. When the infant feels hunger, is appropriate nourishment provided? When the infant is tired, can someone interpret this feeling and allow rest? When the infant is alert, does someone take the time to play? Through it all, does someone give the infant the feeling of being a person who is loved? If the usual answers to these questions are affirmative, the infant is probably developing a sense of trust. Of course, no one is able to respond instantly to every need of any infant, nor do even the most caring individuals always know how to interpret each cry of distress or discomfort. Erikson refers to typical responses to infants' needs as being important in establishing a relationship of trust.

In understanding Erikson's theory, it is helpful to imagine a continuum of feelings that ranges from absolute and total trust to absolute and total mistrust. Erikson indicates that interactions with the infant should establish feelings that are toward the trust end of the continuum. Research has supported Erikson's theory by demonstrating that when mothers respond quickly and efficiently to their infants' needs, babies end their first year as happier, more sociable and well-adjusted children (Damon, 1983).

Developing a basic sense of trust is the infant's primary psychosocial task during the first year of life, according to Erikson. When adults have responded promptly and in an appropriate manner, infants develop a sense of trust and behave as if adults will be available to them in times of need. That kind of trust characterizes secure relationships and forms the basis of all later social interactions. When adult responses have been less predictable or negative, infants show mistrust, which appears as patterns of avoidance in social situations.

To understand how some adults create an environment in which basic trust is established, and why others do not, researchers study the mutuality of the parent–infant relationship. Parent responds to infant and infant responds to parent. It is relatively easy to study only the parent or the infant or the rest of the infant's environment. Studying the interrelationships is more accurate but also much more complex. In an attempt to learn more about the dynamic parent–infant relationship, researchers have studied parent–infant rhythms.

PARENT–INFANT RHYTHMS

The term **parent–infant rhythms** refers to the mutual coordination of behavior according to the interest and attention of both parent and infant. At first, parents make most of the adjustments as they attempt to sustain interaction with their infants. The details of the adjustments would normally be too subtle and fleeting to be observed by the unaided eye. But painstaking, frame-by-frame analysis of high-speed motion picture film has revolutionized research on early parent–infant interactions by revealing rhythmic changes in expression and behavior in the interactions of parents and infants. Here is what the camera might show as one-month-old Nathan and his mother interact:

> *The mother turns to face Nathan, and their eyes meet. Nathan's eyes widen and his legs and hands move toward the mother and then gently curl back according to a rhythm. Nathan's eyes are alternately brightly interested and dull or averted. His mother adjusts her pattern to his so that she talks when his interest is high and quiets while he recovers.*

Because Nathan goes through four or more interest/recovery cycles in a minute, the film must be viewed in slow motion to see the rhythm of the games that Nathan and his mother play. When Nathan averts his eyes, he signals that he is overstimulated and must have time to recover. Nathan's physiological systems are immature and easily overloaded, so he needs these periodic rests. Researchers have found, for example, that young infants have a great deal of heart rate variability during highly emotional displays of interest, joy, and look-away behaviors when interacting with adults (Stifter, Fox, & Porges, 1989). In addition, high-intensity smiling of both mother and baby are associated with the frequency and duration of the baby's look-away behaviors (Stifter & Moyer, 1991). The baby's mother can sense this tension and attempts to match her responses to her baby's; in this way, she gradually introduces her baby to new experiences and more complex interactions. The first part of Developmental Issues in Practice 6.1 shows a schematic figure of such a rhythmic interaction pattern—the graph represents the mother's responses following the infant's lead. On the other hand, some mothers are less successful in responding to their infants' cries. An example of poor maternal response appears in the second graph in Developmental Issues in Practice 6.1.

T. Berry Brazelton (1981) found that mothers could be trained to be more sensitive to their infant's needs. By carefully responding to the child, the mother could maintain the child's involvement over longer periods, thus increasing attention span. Brazelton and his colleagues at Children's Hospital in Boston are pioneers in the analysis of films of parent–infant interaction. They believe that the parent's ability to achieve a satisfactory rhythm with the infant forms the basis for early communication. Parent and infant experience a rewarding mutuality, which is an important step in the infant's development of social skills. This mutuality and the satisfaction of communicating with another human being are certainly instrumental in the process of developing a sense of trust and attachment.

Various studies have confirmed that when the mother is sensitive and responds with speed and accuracy to the needs of the infant, the attachment between mother and child is enhanced (Ainsworth, 1978; Ainsworth, Bell, & Stayton, 1971, 1974; Belsky, Rovine, & Taylor, 1984; Isabella, 1993; Pederson et al., 1990; Smith & Pederson, 1988). Lamb, Hopps, and Elster (1987) found that poor attachment in a group of toddlers was related to infrequent caregiving, poor ability to engage the babies, and less tendency to respond to the babies' cues. In a similar study, Isabella and Belsky (1991) confirmed that well-attached infants had mothers who engaged in well-timed, synchronous interactions. Both intrusive and unresponsive mothering patterns resulted in significantly more poorly attached toddlers.

Rhythms with Fathers versus Mothers

The interactions between mothers and infants generally follow a definite pattern:

1. Engagement occurs, where either mother or child initiate face-to-face communication.
2. Interactive synchrony occurs between mother and infant, with mother's behavior characterized by wide-opened eyes, smiles, and high pitched, repetitive verbalizations, which become increasingly complex.
3. Infant looks away and a pause occurs until the infant reengages.
4. Cycle continues.

This is the typical pattern for white, middle-class mothers. Brazelton's research has demonstrated that infants as young as three or four weeks have

▲ **DEVELOPMENTAL ISSUES IN PRACTICE 6.1**

INTERPRETATION OF INFANT CUES

The rhythmic parent–infant interactions that have been described would be graphed in the following manner:

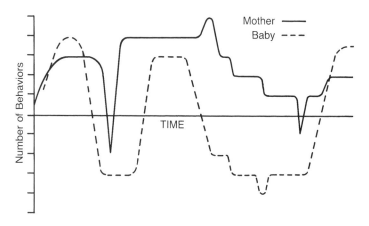

The graph shows that the parent pauses when the infant looks away, allows time for the infant to recover, and then gently initiates another round of interaction. In these cases of appropriate parent–infant rhythms, parents receive rewarding feedback that gives them energy to continue to meet the demands of parenting. The infants, in turn, establish a gratifying sense of reciprocity with the environment and gain feelings of competence.

It is unfortunate that not all parents seem able to establish appropriate rhythms with their infants. The following graph shows an interaction in which the infant

different social interaction patterns with different people. By the time infants are three weeks of age, they show such different kinds of interactions with their mothers and fathers that observers can view videotapes of the infant's movements and tell immediately whether mother or father was present.

Brazelton (1981) has found that infants in two-parent families typically respond to their fathers with movements that are less rhythmic than those they use when they are in interaction with their mothers. Fathers are likely to interact playfully, in a physical way with tickling or bouncing, and using movement rather than vocal rhythms. At first the infant's shoulders hunch, eyebrows raise, and movement stops. When movement begins again, it is jerky. As the infant grows, excited laughter accompanies the movements. Both parental forms use repetitive patterns with increasing complexity and heightened excitement. The difference between them is in the use of verbal as opposed to motor stimulation. Sometimes mothers feel envious of fathers'

DEVELOPMENTAL ISSUES IN PRACTICE 6.1 (continued)

spends most of the time looking away and the parent lacks sensitivity in "reading" this cue to reduce stimulation:

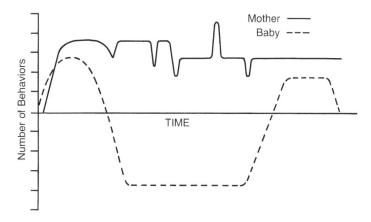

Left on their own, these parents may reject their infants because they do not find a "fit" in their interactions. One such parent said, "I never could reach him."

T. Berry Brazelton (1979), whose research is the source of these graphs, believes that professionals have a responsibility to assess parent–infant rhythms. Professionals could then volunteer support to parents who need help in interpretation of infant cues.

Graphs from T. B. Brazelton, "Behavioral Competence of the Newborn Infant." *Seminars in Perinatology, 3* (1979):35–44. Copyright 1979 by Grune & Stratton, Inc. Reprinted by permission.

ability to communicate "Let's play!" by eye contact and voice tone. However, there is obviously a value to the baby in receiving different kinds of input from each parent. What is most important is that each parent communicate to the baby "You are a special person to me." The infant receives these communications and the sense of trust is built between parent and infant.

Rhythms in Various Cultures

When parents and infants from different cultural groups are observed, different rhythmic patterns are apparent. For example, white, black, and Navajo mothers and their three- to five-month-old infants were videotaped in face-to-face interaction. Each mother was instructed to obtain her infant's attention in whatever way she wished. The mothers from the three groups had distinctive patterns of interactions with their infants. The white mothers used vocal rhythm to entice the infant into interaction. If the infant did not respond, the

This mother communicates "Let's play!" by putting her six-month-old in a face-to-face position, raising the pitch of her voice, making eye contact, and bouncing the baby.

mothers paused and then returned to the vocal rhythms, which sometimes seemed to be overstimulating. Black mothers used similar vocal rhythms, but they continued even if the infant did not respond. If the infants persisted in turning away, black mothers tended to stop the interaction abruptly. Black mothers seemed less intrusive than white mothers, perhaps because they seemed more involved in their own performances. Navajo mothers, in contrast, did not use vocal rhythms to sustain interactions with their infants. Navajo mothers were quieter and seemed to rely on infants' capacities for self-soothing and self-regulating (Fajardo & Freedman, 1981).

The differences found in this study correspond with patterns of behavior of newborns from each of these groups. Evidence suggests that white newborns are more irritable and have a lower tolerance for stimulation, black newborns are less irritable and have a higher tolerance for stimulation, and Navajo newborns are the least irritable and the most capable of organizing their own responses without structuring by the mother (Callaghan, 1981). The fact that infants from different groups seem to show different reactions to stimulation indicates that no one pattern of interaction can be advocated for all (Fajardo & Freedman, 1981).

The universal rule in establishing parent–infant rhythms seems to be the need to observe and follow the infant's cues. Comparable "rules" do not appear to govern the details of interaction, such as the amount or type of vocalization, touching, movement, and distance.

Given the different rhythms in various cultural groups, do parents use these interactions to teach cultural values to infants? To answer this question and others, a study examined the games that parents from four cultural groups play with their infants (Van Hoorn, 1982). The researcher found that parents prefer traditional games that are passed on from generation to generation and are known to others from their cultural group. This finding holds true even for parents with Chinese, Filipino, and Mexican backgrounds who have lived in the United States for many years.

With such traditional preferences, it is interesting to find that the games themselves are similar across cultures. Regardless of culture, adult–infant game sessions seem to occur with a single partner at a time. The adult communicates "This is play" by changes in tone of voice and facial expression and by actions particular to games. Across cultural groups, games are characterized by moderate tempo and rhythm, interrelated responses, face-to-face position, eye contact, position within a foot of each other, and manipulation of the infant's body. (Van Hoorn, 1982).

Barbara puts three-month-old Shawn on her lap, propping him with her arms so that he is facing her. In this position, the two faces are very close together. Barbara smiles broadly, opens her eyes wider, and says with enthusiasm, "How is Shawn? Do you want to play?" Shawn responds immediately by smiling, widening his eyes, and squirming with excitement. Shawn's excitement leads Barbara to continue. "What a pretty baby . . .pretty, pretty baby . . .pretty, pretty, pretty baby." As she says this, she uses her right hand to wiggle Shawn's foot in rhythm with her words.

The similarities across cultures of infant games can be explained by hypothesizing that the purpose of infant games is not so much to communicate cultural values as to communicate human values, such as trust, as described earlier, and attachment, a concept to be explained in the following section.

ATTACHMENT

Attachment refers to strong bonds of affection directed toward particular people, usually those who are viewed as stronger or wiser than oneself. Attachment theory was first proposed to psychologists and later refined by John Bowlby (1958, 1982). The theory describes both the tendency of humans to want to be close to preferred individuals and the emotional distress and personality disturbance that can result from unwilling separation or loss of these special people.

In many family situations that researchers have studied, the mother is the first person with whom infants form an attachment. Cross-cultural studies (Ainsworth, 1967) have found that attachment can be measured by the following kinds of behaviors of infants toward mothers during the first year of life: crying when held by a stranger but not when held by mother; more frequent smiling and vocalizing with mother than with a stranger; turning and looking at mother when near her; protest and attempts to follow mother if she leaves; body contact with mother; greeting of mother when she returns; and exploring the environment when mother is present as a secure base.

Freud had suggested that satisfaction from being fed was the source of these feelings. However, Bowlby has theorized that infants form attachments primarily by having personalized contact with adults and not just by being fed and physically cared for.

Evidence of the importance of contact is found in a classic series of experiments with rhesus monkeys (Harlow, 1961; Harlow & Zimmerman, 1959). In these experiments, infant monkeys were removed from their mothers at birth and were provided with two types of model mothers: one made of wire and the other covered with soft cloth. The infants were fed from a bottle that could be placed with either model mother. By setting up the experiments in this way, the effects of food could be separated from the effects of having something comfortable to hold onto. In all experiments, infant monkeys developed attachment to the cloth model mother. For instance, infant monkeys spent an average of 15 hours a day clinging to the cloth model but only 1–2 hours with the wire model, even when their food came only from the wire model mother (Harlow & Zimmerman, 1959).

Recent research on people with low socioeconomic status confirms the value of physical contact (Anisfeld, Casper, Nozyce, & Cunningham, 1990). In this study the experimental group was given soft baby carriers, which promote closer body contact. There were more well-attached infants in this group than in the control group, who were given infant seats. These findings certainly suggest that mothers should have as much physical contact with their infants as possible. Leaving them in infant seats, cribs, and playpens does not promote attachment.

Bowlby (1982) delineated four phases in the development of attachment in human infants, which were amplified by Mary Ainsworth. Description of these phases is presented in the form developed by Damon (1983). This is followed by discussion of responses to separation, effects of attachment, negative reactions to strangers, and cultural differences in attachment.

Attachment Phase 1: Preattachment

The first phase, **preattachment,** lasts from birth to about 8–12 weeks of age. During this phase, infants behave in certain characteristic ways toward people. They turn toward people in their vicinity, follow people with eye movements, smile, vocalize, and often cease crying when people are nearby. Each of these behaviors is attractive to most adults and causes adults to want to spend time near infants. At one time, it was thought that this lack of discrimination between important adults and strangers was a sign that the child couldn't recognize the uniqueness of the mother. There is evidence from recent research, however, that newborns can recognize their mothers (see Chapter 7 for studies on infant perceptual ability). Thus, there is a difference between recognition and attachment. Attachment figures are important, even in these early days, when it appears that the infant behaves the same way toward the mother and toward others.

Attachment Phase 2: Attachment-in-the-Making

The second phase, **attachment-in-the-making,** lasts until about six months of age. In this phase, infants continue to show friendly interest in people who are around. The main change from Phase 1 is that infants begin to differentiate their responses. Infants are noticeably more enthusiastic in interactions with the person to whom they are forming their primary attachment. They show differentiated responses by looking more at mother, being more soothed by her, and following her with eyes and body movements. In traditional literature, it was reported that the primary attachment was assumed to be with the mother. But in these changing times, when the mother may not be the primary caregiver, an infant's primary attachment may be to father, grandparent, or some other person. During this phase, it is still relatively easy to introduce new caregivers to the infant. The infant can be in contact with strangers without showing great distress. For example, visits to the doctor do not unduly stress the infant.

Attachment Phase 3: Clear-Cut Attachment

Phase 3 usually begins at six or seven months of age and continues through the second year of life. The onset of this phase is delayed if there has not been one consistent person in an infant's life, as is sometimes the case in institutions or with frequent changes in foster care. During Phase 3, children become increasingly discriminating in the way they interact with people. They show continuing strong interest in the primary attachment figures. In addition, they use the mother as a base from which to explore. In this behavior, the baby moves away from mother to explore the environment. If something unusual happens, such as a stranger entering the room, the infant immediately returns to his or her base: the mother.

Research has shown that there is more exploration when the mother is present, presumably because the baby is encouraged by the emotional security she provides. Infants at this phase include other people in subsidiary attachments, but strangers are treated with increasing caution and sometimes alarm. The peak for **stranger anxiety** occurs between 10 and 12 months but can continue into the toddler period. All children show wariness around strangers, but some become very distressed. Less distress tends to occur in infants with larger families, those who are in infant group care, and those exposed to wider experiences with other people. This stage can be difficult for both infant and caregivers, especially if the infant must be exposed to strangers. For example, this is not a good time to change baby-sitters or day-care facilities or to begin sending a child into an alternate care facility.

A group of mothers is sitting on the floor at the Parent's Place with their infants, ranging in age from 10 to 14 months. Josh sits on his mother's lap, but he eyes a toy nearby. He moves away from his mother, retrieves the toy, and plays with it from the safety of his mother's lap. Muriel leaves her mother's lap to examine a toy. She remains playing with the toy on the floor, about five feet from her mother. She occasionally looks at her mother and is reassured by her presence. Tad sits on his mother's lap and looks at a toy, which obviously intrigues him greatly. He starts to reach for it, but his mother, noticing his interest, grabs the toy first and gives it to Tad. Tad's attempts to use his mother as a base from which to explore are short-circuited by her. If Tad's mother continues this pattern, she may delay his normal exploratory development.

Attachment Phase 4: Goal-Corrected Partnership

The fourth phase, **goal-corrected partnership,** begins after a child's second birthday. In this phase, children develop a greater understanding of the goals and plans of the adults to whom they are attached. Their behavior becomes more flexible, and they are able to develop more complex relationships, even partnerships, with adults. (This stage is further discussed in a later chapter.)

Factors Affecting the Level of Attachment

It has been suggested that personality factors of the mother and infant could affect the strength of infant attachment. There is no clear evidence that infant temperament alone is associated with strength of attachment. Calkins and Fox (1992) found that certain types of insecurely attached infants at 14 months were more inhibited at 24 months. This study found that the relationship was for attachment to influence temperament, not the other way around. Mangelsdorf, Megan, Kestenbaum, Lang, and Andreas (1990) found no relationship between infant temperament and strength of attachment but did find that the infants' behaviors were related to maternal behavior and personality.

Cohn, Campbell, and Ross (1991) also found no relationship between attachment and infant proneness to distress. They did, however, find that the infant's response to the mother's still face during testing, when the mother is asked not to respond to the infant's cues, was related to later secure attachment. This suggests that it is not the baby's fixed traits that affect attachment but rather the patterns learned in interaction with the mother that are important.

On the other hand, there do appear to be maternal characteristics that are related to attachment outcome between mother and child. In one study (Fonagy, Steele, & Steele, 1991), mothers were tested on their personal representations of attachment while they were pregnant with their first child. The responses predicted attachment at the baby's first birthday in 75% of the cases. Thus, maternal attitude was related to security of attachment even before the baby was born, indicating that the baby's characteristics and temperament played a less important role in the attachment outcome than did the mother's personal attitude and beliefs. Other studies have confirmed this finding (Izard, Haynes, Chisholm, & Baak, 1991) by showing a relationship between attachment outcome and the mother's emotional experiences, expressive behaviors, and personality traits.

If attachment is determined largely by the mother, it would suggest that improvements can be made by establishing intervention programs for the mothers. Programs (such as the Parent's Place mentioned earlier) can be used to help mothers be more effective at encouraging attachment.

Responses to Separation

Researchers have found some consistent patterns of responses when children in Bowlby's third or fourth phases are separated from the adults to whom they are attached. At first, children usually **protest** strongly. For as much as several days, children cry and storm for the return of their special person. Then they fall into **despair**. They become quieter but still preoccupied with the absent person. Hope seems to fade. Sometimes protest and despair alternate, but eventually, children enter a period of **detachment**. They seem to forget the special person and may not appear to recognize that person when they are reunited. During all these three phases, the child experiences what seems to be unrelated tantrums and episodes of destruction.

How children respond when reunited after a separation from an attachment figure depends on whether they are experiencing protest, despair, or detachment. Children in the stage of protest eagerly welcome the caretakers back. They are able to express their sadness with tears but also their pleasure in the return of the caretaker. They return fairly quickly to a normal interactional relationship with their caregivers.

Twelve-month-old Jean's parents were forced to leave her behind to drive out of state to a funeral. Jean was very unhappy when her parents left her with the sitter, and, although she generally adapted well to the situation, she occasionally showed fussiness and anger during the three days that her parents were gone. When her parents came home, Jean was joyful and happy to see them. She hugged them and didn't want to be put down. While the family was spending time together for the first time in days, a neighbor came by to welcome the parents home. Jean immediately began crying and clung to her mother. She was obviously fearful of another separation. Her distress was so great that the neighbor was forced to leave. However, the next day, Jean seemed to be back to normal and the family didn't experience any long-term problems.

The reunion is the most difficult if children have entered the period of despair. When the caregiver returns, the children may show anger and have difficulty in reestablishing a relationship.

Fifteen-month-old Ronnie was unhappy when his father left for the summer for a college course. He showed greater and greater distress whenever his father called home. When his father was scheduled to return home, Ronnie showed little interest in the plans to meet him at the airport. When his father arrived, Ronnie kicked him in the shins. He refused to greet him and reacted with anger when his father tried to approach him. It took several weeks for the father to reestablish his relationship with his son.

If children have entered the period of detachment, this produces the most long-lasting damage. Children are unresponsive at the reunion and can be unresponsive for days or even weeks afterward. When the detachment ends, children often show intense clinging and rage if left. Children demonstrate their anger at being deserted and yet their strong need for the person's presence, according to Bowlby. This ambivalence comes about as part of the grieving process that children undergo when they are separated against their will. Military families are particularly prone to such problems, because the father may be away on ship or at training programs for months at a time. Such families need special support programs to help them cope with the constant disruption.

Parents find that separating from their children is very traumatic. Any separation during this time can be especially difficult, and unnecessary separations should be avoided. It is unfortunate that work responsibilities, hospitalizations, and family emergencies often cannot be avoided. It is important for parents to be aware of the potential problems and, upon their return, focus on responding in a calm and loving way to their unhappy children. Working parents often find the process of separating from their child very difficult, especially when the child is brought to a child care center. Developmental Issues in Practice 6.2 gives some helpful suggestions for making the separation as smooth as possible.

Effects of Attachment

Researchers have found that they can set up laboratory situations that successfully identify infants who have formed strong attachments and infants who have not. Moreover, researchers have been able to predict future behavior from differences in attachment.

Researchers study attachment by placing an infant and the child's attachment figure into a room that is equipped with toys. A stranger enters and interacts with the infant, first in the adult's presence and then in his or her absence. Meanwhile, unseen observers (usually on the other side of a one-way-vision mirror) record the reactions and interactions. The laboratory conditions are so standard that in the research literature they are referred to as the "strange situation" (Ainsworth & Bell, 1970). This approach allows assessment of a wide range of reactions under a number of conditions. There are eight different episodes that can be scored for information on the security of attachment:

- ❏ Episode 1: Mother and baby are introduced into the room.
- ❏ Episode 2: Baby explores the room with mother present.
- ❏ Episode 3: Stranger enters and approaches baby.
- ❏ Episode 4: Mother leaves stranger and baby in room alone.
- ❏ Episode 5: Mother returns and stranger leaves.
- ❏ Episode 6: Mother leaves baby alone in room.

▲ DEVELOPMENTAL ISSUES IN PRACTICE 6.2

MANAGEMENT OF SEPARATIONS

Jimmie Peters is already behind schedule in getting to work. Anticipating that his seven-month-old will fuss, he slips away while the alternate caregiver greets the infant.

Is this an effective strategy? Thinking about basic trust, attachment, and stranger reactions, the response to this question is clearly no. The father may avoid a scene at that moment, but he arouses the infant's suspicions that he is going to disappear whenever he is momentarily out of sight. A preferable approach, then, is the following:

1. Try to let the infant become familiar with the new person (and new place, if care is outside the home) before it is necessary to leave the infant.
2. Be sure that the alternate caregiver is familiar with the infant's routine and preferences.
3. If the infant gains comfort from a special blanket or toy, have that available.
4. Let the infant know when the time of departure arrives. Establish a routine pattern (e.g., hug, kiss, give warm good-bye) that precedes the departure.

Then depart, knowing that the infant will probably cry momentarily but that the transition has been made as smoothly as possible. With an older infant, parents can verbalize about the time of return in terms of the infant's schedule (e.g., "I'll be back after nap time").

Parents can prepare their infants for separations by carefully handling the many momentary separations within the home. When an infant protests as the parent leaves the room briefly, the parent can continue talking to the infant to keep constant voice contact. A parent's sensitive approach to these many short separations gradually builds the child's confidence that the parent always does come back.

❑ Episode 7: Stranger enters room and is alone with baby.
❑ Episode 8: Mother returns and stranger leaves.

Infants' behavior in the strange situation depends on the way they have been treated in the previous months and on the strength of attachment to the adult present in the strange situation. When adults have behaved positively and consistently, infants turn to them for security in a strange situation. When adults have been negative or inconsistent, infants avoid them or show ambivalent patterns in a strange situation.

Ainsworth and her associates have found that children can be divided into three different groups: (1) **securely attached** infants (70%), (2) **anxious/avoidant** infants (20%), and (3) **anxious/resistant** infants (10%) (see Table 6.1 for a description of these three patterns of infant–caregiver attach-

Table 6.1.   *Three Patterns of Infant–Caregiver Attachment*

Ainsworth Episodes	Securely Attached Infants	Anxious/Avoidant Infants	Anxious/Resistant Infants
1.	readily separates to explore toys	readily separates to explore toys	difficulty separating to explore toys
2.	extensive exploration	extensive exploration	little exploration
3.	affective sharing of play	little affective sharing	little affective sharing
4.	distressed but rapid recovery	little distress, easily comforted by stranger	great distress
5.	active seeking of contact with caregiver * seeks caregiver * shows pleasure	active avoidance of caregiver * turns away * mixes avoidance with proximity	difficulty settling with caregiver * shows striking passivity * continues to cry and fuss
6.	distress expressed	no negative reaction	great distress
7.	Same as for Episode 4.		
8.	active greeting behavior, happy	avoidance more extreme on second reunion	mixes contact seeking with resistance

ment). The securely attached infants showed extensive exploration behavior, recovered quickly from mother's absence, and showed relatively little distress. The anxious/avoidant infants showed relatively little distress upon separation but, unlike the securely attached infants, did not show pleasure at the return of the mother and could be comforted by the stranger as well as by the mother. The anxious/resistant infants showed the greatest distress upon separation and were very difficult to comfort upon the return of the mother. They were most disturbed by the stranger and showed the least inclination to play with the toys.

Belsky has pointed to an interaction between temperament and maternal sensitivity. If a mother is sensitive, the infant will be securely attached regardless of whether there is a high degree of emotional reaction to stress. On the other hand, if the mother is unresponsive and insensitive, the attachment will differ depending on the infant's sensitivity to stress. An infant highly sensitive to stress will develop an insecure/resistant attachment; whereas the infant who has low sensitivity to stress develops an insecure/avoidant attachment (Belsky, Rovine, & Taylor, 1984; Isabella, Belsky, & von Eye, 1989).

In addition, the behaviors of mothers in interaction with their infants are closely related to the infants' attachment behaviors. For example, in one study, mothers who tended to be dismissing in their behavior had infants who could be classified as avoidant, and mothers who were autonomous had infants who could be classified as secure (Zeanah et al., 1993).

Knowing an infant's behavior in the strange situation has been found to have value in predicting the future behavior of children. Research has demonstrated that the patterns of communication established early in life have long-range consequences for interactions with attachment figures and with other people. For instance, in a longitudinal study it was found that infants who were securely attached at 12 months of age, compared with those who were less securely attached, were significantly more compliant and cooperative with other adults with whom they interacted at 21 months of age (Londerville & Main, 1981). Another study reported that infants who were securely attached to a parent at 12 months of age were rated as more competent socially in preschool two years later (Lamb, Thompson, & Frodi, 1982). Researchers have also reported that securely attached infants are more enthusiastic, happy, and persistent in problem-solving situations.

Negative Reactions to Strangers

The development of negative reactions to strangers follows the general pattern of development of attachment to certain individuals. Infants in Bowlby's first phase of attachment show no differences in their reactions to familiar people and to strangers. In the second phase, infants initially respond positively to familiar people but not as positively to strangers. Then there is a period of four to six weeks during which infants sober at the sight of a stranger and stare. Finally, at about eight or nine months of age, infants show behavior typical of fear. They move away from the stranger, cry, and/or change facial expression. As mentioned earlier, these behaviors are sometimes referred to as **stranger anxiety**.

While behavioral distress doesn't occur until late in the first year, research has shown that infants as young as two months show physiological signs of distress around strangers (Mizukami, Kobayashi, Ishi, & Iwata, 1990). In another study (Roe, 1991), three-month-old infants were shown to give very different vocal responses to their mothers, compared with the vocal responses they gave to a stranger. The differences were stable across four days, suggesting that the infants were actually aware of the differences in the stranger and were reacting differently, even though there were no overt signs of distress.

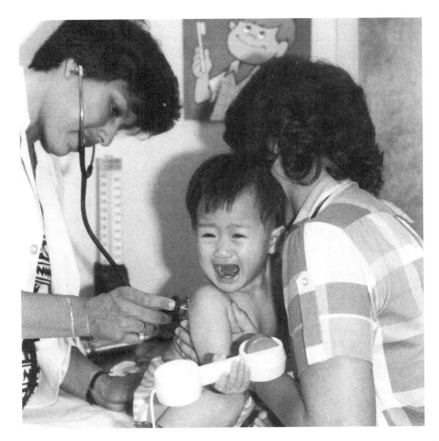

This 11-month-old shows "stranger anxiety" typical of attachment phase 3: moving away from the stranger and toward the parent, crying, and showing a fearful facial expression.

Stranger anxiety is influenced by various factors, such as how much experience the infants have had with other adults and individual differences in infants. Attributes of the stranger also modify the negative reaction. Small adults (such as midgets) and infants are perceived less negatively than are larger or older strangers. And a quiet, slow approach of a stranger is preferred to a loud, rapid approach (Reed & Leiderman, 1981).

The time at which negative stranger reactions become significant depends on the definitions used. If crying is used as the distinguishing criterion, negative stranger reactions become significant at 10 months of age. But when all kinds of negative responses are observed and combined, wariness of strangers is present in 23% of infants at 8 months, 35% at 9 months, and 59% at 10 months. On the other hand, only 10–15% of 5- through 7-month-old infants show negative reactions. It is important to note that only 14% of the 10-month-olds showed what can be labeled as extreme distress (Waters, Matas, & Sroufe, 1975). Wariness of strangers is certainly not universal but tends to occur at this developmental period. However, discussion of such wariness sometimes overshadows the positive, gregarious interest that infants have in others.

Cultural Differences in Attachment and Separation

Are attachment patterns different among different cultures? Should the same behaviors be expected in a large extended family as in a small nuclear family? Researchers have observed cultures in which many adults interact with infants and have found that the development of attachment follows a pattern similar to that observed in cultures in which few adults interact regularly with infants (Reed & Leiderman, 1981). These researchers suggest that attachment is determined by an interaction of behaviors exhibited by infants from the time of birth and the responses of adults to these behaviors. As partial evidence, researchers point to the fact that, in all cultures studied, infants have developed and show strong attachments by about 9–11 months of age.

There is some evidence that culture values are used by parents to determine whether a "good" attachment has been made by an infant. Harwood (1992) found that Anglo mothers showed the greatest concern over the ability of the child to maintain individual autonomy. The Puerto Rican mothers in the study were more concerned about the proper behavior of the child in public. Parental attitudes could have an impact on the expression of attachment in different cultures.

Ainsworth (1967) found that attachment patterns occurred in other cultures and also observed the presence of separation anxiety. However, she noted that in her observation of Ugandan infants, there was less indication of separation anxiety than is normally observed in the United States. A study of Japanese infants by Takahashi (1990) also revealed a number of differences in separation reaction. The Japanese infants showed more extreme reactions and there were no examples of anxious/avoidant infants in the Japanese sample. The variations across cultures have been studied to see whether the differences found are due to differences in the way the observations were scored (van Ijzendoorn & Kroonenberg, 1990). No differences in scoring were found, further supporting the evidence that there may be actual differences in separation reactions across cultures. Although attachment appears to be universal, separation patterns appear to vary, suggesting that separation anxiety may be more conditioned by the child-rearing characteristics of a particular culture.

INFANT CRYING

Crying is the means by which infants communicate their needs. Crying is extremely effective: when adults hear an infant in distress, they do everything they can to soothe and comfort. Because crying is so unsettling to adults, they have considerable concern when their most conscientious efforts do not diminish it. Both mothers and nonmothers respond with nurturing behavior toward a crying infant, and the cry itself is more important in triggering such behavior than any information about the specific causes of the crying (Gustafson & Harris, 1990). If parents have difficulty in controlling the crying, then at the next episode of crying, adults often wonder whether they should respond to it or ignore it. Some interesting research on crying lends insights to appropriate action.

Susan Crockenberg (Crockenberg & McClusky, 1982) studied the ways in which infant temperament is interrelated with mothers' attitudes about crying and spoiling. She found that some infants fuss and cry more during the first days after birth; these infants continue the same patterns throughout the first months of life and might be described as having a "difficult" pattern of temperamental characteristics. Their crying is not caused by the mothers' attitudes, and mothers and other primary caregivers of these infants need support from family members and others because infants who cry a great deal take considerable time and attention.

Even though mothers' attitudes do not cause the initial patterns of crying, adult attitudes and actions affect future developments. Parents who respond promptly to crying and engage the infants in frequent interaction gradually find that their infants cry less than infants of parents who believe that they spoil their infants by responding when they cry. Fish, Stifter, and Belsky (1991) also found that the mother's personality traits, marital quality, and sensitivity to the infant were related to a change in crying at five months in those infants, who cried a great deal as neonates. Thus, it appears that the mothers conditioned the behavior.

Sometimes it may seem that infants cry most of the time. Researchers (Bell and Ainsworth, 1972) have found a consistent average of about four fussing or crying spells per hour throughout the first year of life. But the amount of time spent in crying changes over this period. In the first three months of life the average amount of time spent in crying is just under eight minutes per hour; in contrast, in the last three months of the first year, an average of only four minutes per hour is spent in fussing or crying.

These researchers also noted the effects of early responsiveness to an infant's crying. They found that the infants who cry and fuss the most after three months of age are the ones whose parents did not respond to their early crying or did so only after a delay. When infants learn that adults meet their needs, they seem to be able to find a variety of ways to communicate other than by crying.

Infants respond best to certain kinds of comforting. In the first three months, infants are soothed best by being picked up and held. The next most useful strategies include being fed and given a pacifier or toy. By the last quarter of the first year, however, infants are comforted by having a familiar adult nearby and attentive.

SOCIAL COGNITION

Social cognition is defined as the way individuals understand and perceive other people. Until recent decades, infants were rarely included in studies of social cognition because it was assumed that they simply acted and reacted. Now, however, researchers credit infants with having a more constructive role in social interactions. Accordingly, the study of infant social cognition has expanded to explore the reasons why infants behave as they do. This section presents some recent findings about the origins of social understanding, the ability of infants to interpret the emotions of others, and the self-understanding of infants.

Origins of Social Understanding

Michael Lamb (1981) has traced the origins of social understanding to the first months of life. Infants show distress by crying, and, if adults respond by picking up the infants to relieve their distress, important social learning can take place. Often an infant who is picked up and soothed moves into a state of quiet alertness and looks intently at the adult. Simultaneously, the infant hears the adult's voice and experiences touch and unique odors. Repetitions of a sequence of distress followed by relief allow infants to develop nonverbal concepts of the adults who respond to them. They also learn that distress predictably leads to relief, what Erikson meant by basic trust.

Infants' sociability is enhanced in three ways when the distress–relief sequence is predictable. First, infants are able to form expectations concerning adults' responses. Second, adults begin to establish positive relationships with infants by helping them move from unpleasant distress to pleasant calmness. And third, infants gradually gain a sense that they are effective individuals who can exert partial control over their experiences by summoning adult relief. This sense of effectiveness is a critical early cornerstone of self-concept.

Lamb (1981) has asserted that infants' social understanding is relatively sophisticated and complicated by the time they reach one year of age. Because social understanding develops as a consequence of each infant's particular experiences, infants vary widely in their expectations of people.

Perception of Emotions

During the first year of life, infants become more sensitive to and perceptive about the facial expressions of the people around them. Campos and Stenberg (1981), for instance, report on research that designates three levels in the reactions of infants to information from facial expressions. The first level extends from birth to three months of age and is characterized by similar reactions to all facial expressions. Researchers report that infants at this age are as likely to smile at angry faces as at friendly faces. Some researchers speculate that the tendency of young infants to respond positively to faces, regardless of expression, might be adaptive in the sense that it helps in the development of secure attachments.

The second level extends from three to seven months. During this time, infants begin to be able to discriminate certain facial expressions from others. Research has shown that infants at this age can distinguish surprise from sadness and happiness, joy from anger and neutral expressions, and fear from happiness.

Well before their first birthdays, infants can recognize and act on the emotions of adults who care for them.

The third level begins at seven months of age and is differentiated from the second in the following way: infants now not only discriminate facial expressions but also react in different emotional ways to them. For example, infants in the last part of the first year respond with more negative emotion to angry and sad faces than to happy and neutral ones.

The developmental sequence presented by these researchers indicates that infants can recognize and act on information about the emotions of other humans. Well before their first birthdays, infants are attuned to the emotions of people who interact with them. This is important for adults to remember, because infants will use adult expressions as a guide for their own reactions to situations. We can cause a child to show fear, excitement, or anticipation depending on our reaction to events.

Marcella is eleven months old and just starting to attempt to walk. The first time she falls down, she simply gets up and starts to try her wobbly legs again. Her mother comes into the room and sees her fall. With great agitation and concern, she rushes over to her baby and checks to be certain that she is not hurt. She then proceeds to hover around the baby with an expression of great concern on her face. The next time Marcella falls, she looks first at her mother and only then begins to cry. She is learning to be cautious and fearful by following her mother's lead in giving her emotional messages.

We must guard against inducing emotional states in infants, such as fear, which might cause them to develop inappropriate caution in situations where they need to be encouraged to experiment and try new experiences. This sometimes happens more with girls than with boys because of parents' unconscious and misplaced fear that girls may be more delicate or sensitive than boys.

Hirshberg (Hirshberg, 1990; Hirshberg & Svejda, 1990) has observed the effect of parental emotions on twelve-month-old infants. When parents gave happy signals, the infants showed more positive emotions and spent more time with toys than when parents gave fearful signals. When the mothers and fathers gave conflicting signals, the infants showed greater negative emotional tone and decreased toy exploration, presumably as a response to the conflict they were experiencing over the conflicted signals they were receiving. Daycare workers have also been shown to influence play behaviors of infants (Camras & Sachs, 1991). Infants showed more approach toward toys when daycare workers gave enjoyment/joy signals than when they gave fear/avoidance signals. In addition, infants can discriminate the emotional tone in vocal expressions of adults, but facial expression provides additional information for infants in discriminating vocal input (Walker-Andrews & Lennon, 1991).

Self-Understanding

Infants are very sensitive to others, but when do they begin to know themselves? In a creative approach to answering this question, Lewis and Brooks-Gunn (1979) put a dot of rouge on the infants' noses as they looked at themselves in a mirror. Infants beginning at age nine months show surprise and amusement. If the infants think the rouge is on another child (the one in the mirror), they stare and point at the image. If they realize that the rouge is on their own noses, they touch them. Under the age of one year, none of the infants touched their noses. Between 12 and 15 months, the infants began to touch their own noses, demonstrating that they knew the image they saw in the mirror was their own. By 24 months, most of the infants touched their noses.

This study demonstrates that infants begin to show visual self-recognition by 15 months of age. The infants have two clues to recognizing themselves: (1) facial recognition and (2) visual and proprioceptive feedback (the feeling of the movement of their own bodies) from their moving image in the mirror. In an extension of this study, Lewis and Brooks-Gunn used video images on TV screens. There were three conditions: (1) live video, which gave a similar visual–proprioceptive experience as the mirror, (2) videotape of child filmed earlier, and (3) videotape of another child. In addition, an adult was filmed sneaking up on the infant from behind during the live taping. At every age, the children tended to turn toward the approaching adult in the "live" condition. On the other hand, when the two taped conditions were compared, it was not until 15 months that the infants started to treat the strange child differently from the taped version of themselves. Thus, it wasn't until 15 months that the infants could distinguish themselves by facial recognition.

TEMPERAMENT

Temperament is an individual's unique way of dealing with people and situations. Referring to characteristics of temperament, parents and others are often heard making comments such as the following:

"She's never still—the most active child I've ever seen."

"I could set the clock by his hunger."

From birth, infants show distinctive differences in characteristics of temperament.

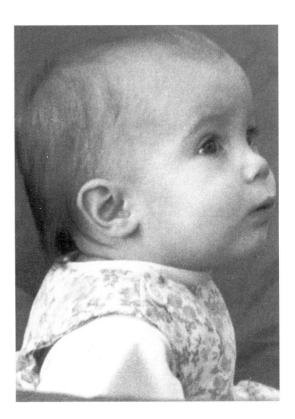

"He's a real ray of sunshine."

"She adapts so well to our changing schedules."

Is there any scientific basis for attributing such characteristics to infants? Are these characteristics consistent over time? According to the New York Longitudinal Study (Thomas & Chess, 1981), distinct characteristics of temperament can be observed soon after birth. The New York study, which began in the late 1950s and still continues, has observed infants from birth through adulthood. The researchers assert that there is consistency of temperament over the years.

The New York Longitudinal Study has identified nine categories of temperament. The temperamental characteristics of a particular infant vary independently of each other. That is, in each category, a given infant's temperamental characteristics may fall anywhere within a range. The categories are as follows:

1. *Activity level*. Some infants do not seem to move around very much. They can be covered up at nap time and will still be covered when they awaken. Infants who are very active, on the other hand, never seem to rest. An active infant might already push her whole torso up with her arms even in the first days after birth.

2. *Regularity*. Some infants fall into a fairly regular schedule by the second or third week of life. They seem to be hungry at regular times, to sleep in a certain pattern, and to have bowel movements at similar intervals. Other infants are predictable only in their unpredictability.

3. *Approach or withdrawal*. At first, almost all experiences are new for infants, and this category refers to an infant's typical initial response to new situations. The "approaching" infant is agreeable about experiences such as the first bath at home. The "withdrawing" infant may actually physically pull back from the bath; considerable coaxing is necessary for this type of infant.

4. *Adaptability to change*. When the routine changes in some way (e.g., new formula, a vacation schedule), some infants adjust without apparent effort. Others do not modify their routines easily; these infants need ample time and a gradual approach in order to make any transition.

5. *Level of sensory threshold*. Some infants can sleep when their siblings are arguing, ignore being wet, overlook movement of the crib, and continue sleeping when a light is turned on. These infants have a high sensory threshold, which means that they are less sensitive in all ways than infants who have a low sensory threshold. The latter awaken with the arguing or movement or light and may scream in discomfort over a wet diaper.

6. *Positive or negative mood*. Positive infants spend much time in behaviors such as smiling and cooing as soon as they learn how. Negative infants spend proportionately more time in behaviors such as fussing and crying.

7. *Intensity of response.* This category describes the energy with which the other responses occur. One infant might be described as being very intense either happy or upset with gusto; perhaps he spit out his first taste of carrots. Another infant of milder temperament let carrots he did not like just trickle down his chin.

8. *Distractibility.* Some infants, even if they are sensitive, continue in their feeding or other activity in proximity to many sights and sounds; these infants are not easily distracted. Distractible infants shift their attention at the first noise or stirring.

9. *Persistence.* The persistent infant continues to suck on a nipple that may be partly plugged or will pay attention for a long period of time to a mobile blowing in the breeze. The nonpersistent infant gives up on the slow nipple and attends only briefly to the mobile.

From these nine categories of temperament, the researchers from the New York Longitudinal Study have identified various patterns (Thomas & Chess, 1981). Identifying infants according to three of these patterns helps in predicting whether parents will feel a need for professional help: (1) regular/easy/positive, (2) difficult/irregular, and (3) slow to warm up/likely to withdraw in new situations. If most parents were ordering an infant according to specifications of temperament, which pattern would they choose? With which kind of infant would it be easiest to form an attachment? Developmental Issues in Practice 6.3 gives information on how to determine patterns of temperament and provides suggestions for the optimal kind of caregiver interactions for each of the three temperament types.

A recent study of 200 pairs of twins assessed the role of genetics on temperament (Emde et al., 1992). Twin studies can be used to examine the degree to which genes function as causative factors in the expression of traits (see Chapter 3 for a discussion of this approach). The study by Emde et al. (1992) confirms the claims that temperament is a genetic, inborn trait, which is most likely to be stable across the life of the individual. A similar study with 70 twin pairs (Saudino & Eaton, 1991) produced similar findings.

For years, researchers studied communication patterns and social development in infancy primarily from the perspective of the behavior of adults toward the infant. The findings of the New York Longitudinal Study clearly demonstrate the additional need to observe and note the temperamental predispositions of infants. Those who interact with infants need information about differences in temperament and support in dealing with difficult/irregular and slow to warm up/likely to withdraw infants.

EFFECTS OF PARENTAL EMPLOYMENT

The "traditional" family, composed of the nonworking mother, working father, and children, was never as idyllic as it is sometimes portrayed, but statistics show that only 23% of U.S. households now fit that pattern (Lamb, 1982). In

▲ DEVELOPMENTAL ISSUES IN PRACTICE 6.3

IDENTIFICATION OF AND RESPONSES TO PATTERNS OF TEMPERAMENT

Regular/easy/positive infants signal moderately when hungry or satisfied; eat steadily without being easily distracted; have regular patterns of eating, sleeping, and elimination; show interest and pleasure in new experiences. Infants with this temperament need caregivers who remember their need for attention and stimulation. This kind of infant is so undemanding that it is possible for adult needs to take too much priority.

Difficult/irregular infants cry loudly when hungry; reject food when full; eat actively but are easily distracted; have irregular patterns of eating, sleeping, and elimination; refuse new foods or other new experiences; only gradually adjust. Infants with this temperament need caregivers who are patient and flexible in their responses and who control pressures from visitors or new experiences. These infants may cry a good deal; caregivers of difficult/irregular infants need assurance that it is not their fault if their best efforts at soothing fail to be effective.

Slow to warm up/likely to withdraw infants show moderate reactions; refuse and withdraw from new experiences. Infants with this temperament need caregivers who provide a calm, slow introduction to new experiences. This infant should not be pressured to put her head into the swimming pool water or to join the group at the park. Pushing makes this infant balk more, but holding the child on your lap gives the child a chance to set his or her own pace.

About 60% of infants seem to fall into one of these patterns. The remaining 40% have temperaments that combine categories in other ways that are less likely to bring them and their families to the attention of helping professionals.

two-parent families, more and more women are working outside of their homes. In 1990, more than 50% of mothers with children under six years of age were in the labor force (U.S. Bureau of the Census, 1990).

In single-parent families, the custodial parent is usually employed. This parent, whether female or male, tends to have higher levels of stress and fatigue when the parent is single than occurs when another parent is available in the home to take on responsibilities or to participate in day-to-day decisions. When the single parent is a woman, she faces economic pressures stemming from being paid less than male workers who have been employed for the same length of time.

The difficulties caused by parental employment patterns lie not in the family nor in the place of employment but in the interplay between the two. Research (Lamb, 1982) has indicated that employed mothers are more likely to have insecurely attached infants than are unemployed mothers. But when the group of employed mothers is divided into two subgroups—those who value work highly and those who value both parenthood and work—it is

▲ **DEVELOPMENTAL ISSUES IN PRACTICE 6.4**

INFANT DAY CARE

More and more infants are born to single parents or to two employed parents. In these cases and others, there is often the need for daycare while parents are at work. In deciding on a child care arrangement, the three major questions are When? Who? and Where?

When?

Many pediatricians view the period after birth as one of potential stress for parents. Parents are often far away from their own extended families, and there are few societal supports to act as substitutes in helping parents meet their infants' and their own needs. In addition, until about 10 weeks of age, infants' nervous systems predispose them to be very sensitive to tension and stimulation. Infants often react by crying, which can increase parents' sense of frustration and incompetence.

By the third month, infants' systems are more mature. Smiling, cooing, and other behaviors give positive feedback to parents. Many pediatricians therefore recommend that alternate child care arrangements not begin until the end of the third month. The stronger the bond between parent and child, the more positive their long-term relationship is likely to be. If, on the other hand, parent and infant are separated for long periods of the day while the parent still feels unrewarded by any positive feedback from the infant, parents can later feel a sense of competition with alternate caregivers. The competition can be especially strong if "good" behaviors, such as smiling and cooing, are associated with the child care situation.

Sometimes parents are not able to wait to return to work until mutually rewarding attachment takes place. In these cases, alternate caregivers need to be particularly sensitive to verbal and nonverbal indications of parents' feelings. Alternate caregivers require special training in acting as supports to the parent–infant relationship.

Another consideration in timing involves the period at the end of the infant's first year. Some pediatricians and researchers advise against placement during the height of "stranger anxiety."

Who and Where?

In most locations, infant daycare centers are rare. Most parents' main options for alternate caregiving include care by either a relative or a family daycare home provider. A family daycare home provider gives care in his or her own home for four children. Often these homes are licensed by or registered with the state.

By far the most important consideration in choosing a child care arrangement involves the personal and professional characteristics of the alternate caregiver:

1. Caregivers should be patient and warm toward children.

2. Caregivers should like and enjoy children and be able to give and receive satisfaction from what infants give.

DEVELOPMENTAL ISSUES IN PRACTICE   6.4 (continued)

3. Caregivers should be energetic, in good health, and not excessively moody or irritable.

4. Caregivers should understand the basic needs of children, including affectional, intellectual, and physical needs.

5. Caregivers must be flexible and understanding of feelings.

6. Caregivers should be acquainted with, accept, and appreciate the children's different cultures, customs, and languages.

7. Caregivers should respect infants and their parents, no matter what their backgrounds or particular circumstances are.

This alternate caregiver demonstrates patience, warmth, enjoyment of infants, and pride in children's developmental accomplishments—important personal and professional characteristics for this type of work.

SOURCE: Adapted from "Selection of Staff" (pp. 69–72) by M. Jorn, B. Persky, and D. S. Huntington, in *The Infants We Care For* (rev. ed.), edited by L. S. Dittman, 1984, Washington, DC: National Association for the Education of Young Children. Copyright 1984 by the National Association for the Education of Young Children. Adapted by permission.

found that mothers in the second subgroup have infants who are securely attached. In a related study, Crockenberg and Litman (1991) found that the adverse effect for working mothers who did not value their work occurred in the laboratory but not in the home. Employment per se, then, is only one of many factors that influence the course of child development. In fact, in a related study (Farel, 1980), researchers found that the most poorly adjusted children were those whose mothers were not employed outside the home but wished to be. Most recent research has controlled for factors such as income, and in this research there is no difference between working and nonworking mothers on attachment and separation behaviors of their infants (Rogers, Rahman, & Casertano, 1991; Zaslow, Pederson, Suwalsky, & Rabinovich, 1989).

Working mothers tend to take responsibility for children, even in two-parent families (Leslie, Anderson, & Branson, 1991). This presumably leads to greater stress for working mothers than for those who stay at home to raise their children. The most frequently reported stress for employed mothers comes from conflicts about returning to work (Walker & Best, 1991). The problems for working mothers affect the mothers more than the infants.

Whether parents are employed outside the home or not and whether parents live together or not, the infant's development is most significantly affected by the quality of parent–infant interactions and by the quality and consistency of alternate caregiving. Research conducted in Bermuda has demonstrated that differences in the quality of daycare environments influence the language, social, and emotional development of very young children (McCartney, Scarr, Phillips, Grajek, & Schwarz, 1982).

Choosing an alternate caregiving situation is one of the most challenging and difficult decisions that the employed parent makes. Developmental Issues in Practice 6.4 responds to three common questions about infant daycare: when, who, and where?

SUMMARY

1. Psychosocial development is fundamental in determining the future quality of an infant's life.
2. According to Erik Erikson, basic trust can be established if the basic needs of the infant are met promptly and consistently.
3. Parent–infant rhythms in communication contribute to a basic sense of trust and vary according to gender of the parent.
4. Patterns of interactions may vary between cultures, but some maternal–infant behaviors are universal and represent a human need to communicate.
5. John Bowlby showed that attachment of infants to adults begins with undifferentiated interest in all people and develops through four phases to differentiated preference for a primary caregiver.
6. The development of attachment is not affected by infant temperament; it is, however, affected by the mother's personality, attitudes, and communication style.

7. Between 10 and 12 months of age, stranger anxiety emerges as part of the stages of attachment.

8. Prolonged separation of infants from their primary caregivers leads to protest, despair, and detachment.

9. The "strange situation" consists of eight separate episodes and can be used to assess the level of attachment of infants.

10. Ainsworth identified three levels of attachment: securely attached, anxious/avoidant, and anxious/resistant.

11. Attachment behaviors appear in all cultures; however, the expression of stranger anxiety appears to vary greatly across cultures.

12. Early responsiveness to infant crying seems to lead to less crying later in the child's development.

13. Social cognition refers to the way that other people are perceived. Early recognition of other people occurs in the earliest months of life.

14. Infants become more capable of understanding facial expressions at the beginning of the first year.

15. Infants develop a sense of self between 12 and 24 months.

16. Nine distinct categories of temperament can be observed soon after birth. It is possible to classify infants into three general categories by temperament: regular/easy/positive, difficult/irregular, and slow to warm up/likely to withdraw in new situations.

17. By 15 months, an infant can distinguish himself or herself by facial recognition.

18. Temperament appears to be genetically determined and is relatively stable throughout the child's development.

19. Parental employment is only one of many factors that influence psychosocial development.

ACTIVITIES TO ENHANCE LEARNING

The following exercises are designed to help students apply what has been learned and to increase understanding about social and emotional development in infants. To complete these exercises, it will be necessary to make observations of infants. If friends or neighbors do not have infants in their families, the following are some possible ways to arrange observations: visit a public place that attracts families, such as a busy store, park, or zoo; request permission to observe at a daycare center or family daycare home. These exercises require the use of observational techniques discussed in Chapter 2. Plan to review the relevant section before beginning the observations.

1. *Narrative Observation.* Write down everything that an infant who is in the first six months of life does for a 10-minute period. Repeat the observation at approximately one-hour intervals for three times. (Remember to use descriptive, nonjudgmental language.) Answer the following questions about the infant's behavior:

   a. What are some examples of parent–infant interaction? Are there any differences between mothers and fathers? If so, what are they?

   b. Make a note of any signs of attachment between the caregiver and the child. Is the infant comforted more by the caregiver? Does the infant show wariness when the caregiver leaves?

    c. What signs of temperament do you see in the infant? Could you identify the child's temperament from the information you have collected?

2. *Vignettes.* Plan a one-hour observation time with an infant between 6 and 12 months. During this time period, watch for examples of separation anxiety. Write down as many examples as possible. Answer the following questions about the infant's behavior:
    a. Is the infant engaging in behavior appropriate for his or her age?
    b. What would you tell the parent about the child's functioning, based on the vignette recorded?

3. *Child Diaries.* Maintain a daily diary of an infant's emotional expressions. Note the signs of joy and fear. Describe the role the adults play in encouraging emotional reactions with their own behaviors.
    a. List the emotions you see being portrayed.
    b. Describe the events in the environment that triggered them.
    c. What role did the adults play in encouraging the emotional expression?

4. *Checklists.* Prepare a developmental checklist for attachment. Use the information in this chapter to make up the list of behaviors in developmental order. The checklist should be appropriate for the age of the child being observed. Observe the child and use the checklist to assess performance.
    a. Did the child perform as expected based on his or her age?
    b. Is the child functioning at the appropriate developmental level?

5. *Interviews.* Design a questionnaire and use it to interview the parent of an infant about the baby's temperament.
    a. Based on the interview, can you place the baby into one of the categories of temperament as described in the chapter?
    b. Is the parent responding to the infant's temperament in a positive way?
    c. How does the parent interpret the infant's behavior?
    d. Does the parent have a correct perception of the infant's functioning?

6. *Time Sampling.* Adapt the recording form given as an example in Chapter 2 (Developmental Issues in Practice 2.6) for attachment development. Use the recording form to observe an infant in the first year of life. Write a few paragraphs describing what you learned about the baby's functioning.

7. *Event Sampling.* Adapt the recording form given as an example in Chapter 2 (Developmental Issues in Practice 2.7) for interactional synchrony observations between infant and caregiver. Use the recording form to observe an infant's responses to the interactional patterns of the caregiver. Write a few paragraphs describing what you learned about the baby's functioning.

FOR FURTHER READING

Attachment

Bowlby, J. (1982). *Attachment and loss* (2nd ed.). New York: Basic Books.

Brazelton, T. B. (1981). *On becoming a family: The growth of attachment.* New York: Delacorte/Seymour Lawrence.

Fraiberg, S. (1977). *Every child's birthright: In defense of mothering.* New York: Basic Books.

Social Development

Greenspan, S., & Greenspan, N. T. (1986). *First feelings.* New York: Penguin Books.

Smith, C. A. (1982). *Promoting the social development of young children: Strategies and activities.* Palo Alto, CA: Mayfield Publishing.

Temperament

Chess, S., Thomas, A., & Birch, H. G. (1972). *Your child is a person: A psychological approach to parenthood without guilt.* New York: Viking Press.

Cognitive Development of Infants

Cognitive development is defined as the process of mental activity and reasoning; factors involved with such development include perception, thinking, problem solving, creativity, and language. Cognitive development is highly valued in our society. Many parents are willing to spend money (even in excess of their budgets) to purchase toys and other materials for infants if lasting cognitive benefits are promised. But such promises can be evaluated sensibly only in the context of an understanding of the changes in infant cognition during the first year of life.

It must be remembered that in all of human development there is interplay among the various aspects of development. Cognitive development doesn't happen in a vacuum. For instance, psychosocial development is fundamental to cognitive functioning because of the vital importance of the psychosocial bonds that link infants with adults. If infants develop secure attachments, mutual communication with adults, and a basic sense of trust, then their cognitive needs are probably also met. The inverse is not so likely to be true, however. An infant could receive what is judged to be adequate cognitive stimulation, but if it was received in a mechanical fashion without attachment, mutual communication, and a growing sense of trust, the infant's cognitive and psychosocial development can be negatively influenced. This can sometimes be seen in abused children. Psychosocial stability is the base upon which other aspects of development build. In addition, motor processes in infants appear to be closely linked to cognitive functioning.

Many people believe that babies cannot see and hear; however, recent research has demonstrated the incredible sensory abilities that babies have at birth. These abilities form the basis for cognitive functioning. This chapter will begin with a description of these perceptual abilities of newborns, followed by discussions of Piaget's theory of cognition; infant intelligence; language development; and early intervention programs.

SENSORY CAPABILITIES OF NEWBORNS

In examining some of the findings about the sensory competence of young infants, special attention is given to the research designs that have increased our knowledge from the level achieved by William James (1890) a full century ago. James described the infant psychological state in the following way: "Assailed by eyes, ears, nose, skin, and entrails at once . . .all is one great booming, buzzing confusion." The description of infants given in this book is radically different from James's.

Not only are infants born with an extraordinary sensory capability, but this capability is surprisingly organized and complex. An important question regarding perceptual development has been whether these complex abilities are inborn or must be learned. As we shall see, most of the perceptual skills that characterize human beings are already fully formed at birth and appear to have developed as part of genetic inheritance.

Vision

One of the most exciting discoveries about infants is that their vision is well developed at birth. When newborns are shown a red or yellow object within about 12 inches, they become alert and gradually focus on it. If the object is slowly moved from side to side, they will follow the object with their eyes and sometimes with head movements (Brazelton, 1981). Infants tend to prefer turning to the right side; one should take this into account when placing mobiles and other visual stimuli nearby.

Not only can newborns see, they can also distinguish shapes and forms (Slater, Mattock, & Brown, 1991). They are particularly interested in looking at human faces (Johnson, Dziurawiec, Ellis, & Morton, 1991). This ability to distinguish faces appears to be part of the perceptual capability present in the human brain. It is probably an important part of the infant's social development.

Research has found that visual attention in the early months predicts cognitive functioning at two years of age.

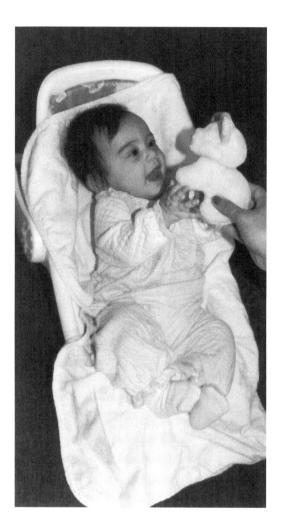

It has been found that, as infants mature, they generally look longer at something they have not seen before than they do at something that is familiar. Also, they look longer at a flashing light than at a steady one, and they look longer at a pattern of dots than at a blank square. Using this information, researchers can find out whether infants can tell one shape or pattern from another by measuring how long they look at it. For example, an infant might be shown a screen on which a shape or pattern is projected. She is at first interested and gazes with bright eyes. Then the novelty wears off, her interest wanes, and she glances away or otherwise shows disinterest. Researchers (e.g., Spelke, 1985) say that at this point the infant is habituated to (used to seeing) that one shape or pattern. When a second shape or pattern is shown, if the infant increases gazing time, then that increase reflects a perception that something new is being viewed. If, on the other hand, the infant looks only briefly at the second shape or pattern, it can be assumed that she has not noticed anything new and therefore has not seen a difference between the two items.

The principle of **habituation** has been used to determine that infants as young as two weeks can distinguish their own mothers' faces. Infants from one to eight weeks of age were shown the following sights for one minute each at a porthole in the wall: face of mother; face of a female stranger; face of a store manikin; and a flesh-colored colander with knobs for ears and nose. From the second week on, the infants showed that they distinguished their mothers by their attention time and their behavior. The infants paid proportionately less attention to their mothers than to the other sights in the porthole. This is because they are familiar with their mother and are learning about the new stimuli, so they look longer at the new things. Moreover, the infants' behavior seemed to show that the nonresponding and isolated face of the mother was so different from their typical experience that it was disturbing. The younger infants tried to control the situation by looking at the mother's face and then looking away. Older infants fussed, smiled, and cried in an apparent attempt to change the mother's behavior (Carpenter, Tecce, Stechler, & Friedman, 1970).

Using the habituation approach, researchers have demonstrated that infants have an innate ability to recognize the sizes of objects (Slater, Mattock, & Brown, 1990). When an object is moved away from us, it begins to look smaller than it is. Slater et al. (1990) have shown that the newborn baby can control for distance and will recognize the size of the object as constant, even when it is moved many different distances from the eye. This is the evidence needed to demonstrate that babies can discriminate distances; however, it does not mean that the baby recognizes the danger if seated on the edge of a high place or that the baby can control behaviors in such a way as to prevent falling.

A great deal of time has been spent trying to find out about infants' **visual preferences**. What do they like to look at? Fantz (1961) was the first to investigate this question. He showed two-month-old infants six types of disks and found that they stared longer at patterned than plain disks and longest of all at a disk of a smiling face. More recently, Sherrod (1981) presented 26 research papers and found that infants of all ages prefer looking at people to looking at things; by two months, they prefer looking at actual faces to looking at drawings of faces; by three months, they prefer looking at animate faces (moving, talking) to looking at inanimate faces (still, silent); and by five months they prefer looking at familiar faces to looking at unfamiliar faces.

Other vision studies (Bornstein, 1985) have shown that infants not only can discriminate between colors, they can also divide them into categories: blues, greens, yellows, and reds. Four-month-olds were habituated to a color in the middle of the blue wavelength in the spectrum. Then they were shown a color of shorter wavelength that adults would still call blue and a color of longer wavelength that adults would call blue-green. Both of the test colors differed from the first blue by the same number of wavelengths. Infants did not increase their gazing time when shown the second blue, but they did for blue-green and for similar transitional colors within groupings. Researchers therefore assume that infants see the spectrum as divided into color categories even though it is actually continuous. This interesting study raises the question of whether the ability to classify color is natural, later requiring only the adding of the names of the colors (Bornstein, 1985).

Taste

Some aspects of taste seem to be as sensitive in newborns as in adults. In one study, one- to three-day-old infants were given varying concentrations of sugar three to five hours after their previous feeding. The four concentrations were put into a bottle with a cleverly designed nipple that measured the sucking patterns of the infants. The researchers found that the average intake pressure on the nipple increased directly with the sweetness of the sugar solutions. Infants can discriminate among different levels of sweetness and prefer the sweetest (Nowlis & Kessen, 1976).

Smell

In an often cited study, researchers (Lipsitt, Engen, & Kaye, 1963) showed how the sense of smell develops in the first days of life. Under the infants' noses researchers waved cotton swabs that had been treated with seven concentrations of an odor that is offensive to adults. The researchers measured changes in movement or breathing patterns to note the reactions of the infants. They found that a 60% concentration was needed to get a response from infants on the day after birth. But the concentrations necessary for a reaction diminished to 30% on the second day of life, 15% on the third, and 12–13% on the fourth.

In a related study, Russell (1976) found that breast-fed infants were awakened more quickly by the smell of a cloth worn next to their mother's breast than by the smell of a cloth worn by another breast-feeding mother. Smell may be important to mother–infant relationships. Infants appear to use their sense of smell to identify their mother (Porter, Makin, Davis, & Christensen, 1992).

Hearing

Hearing seems well developed at birth, as can be verified by anyone who has held an infant startled by a loud noise. In fact, there are anecdotal reports of infants who seemed after birth to recognize music or other sounds to which they had been exposed before birth. Newborn infants will reliably "turn toward" a sound (Zelazo, Weiss, Papageorgiou, & Laplante, 1989). They are particularly likely to listen to sounds that are related to language production. For example, newborns can already discriminate language sounds at birth (Marean, Werner, & Kuhl, 1992; Molfese, Burger-Judisch, & Hans, 1991), and young infants can detect syllable clusters (Jusczyk, Bertoncini, Bijeljac-Babac, Kennedy, & Mehler, 1990) and classify tones on the basis of timbre differences (Trehub, Endman, & Thorpe, 1990).

Researchers have investigated whether two-month-old infants perceived sound rhythms. The researchers used the premise of habituation; that is, if attention decreased to a particular rhythm but was renewed when another was played, the infant had noted the difference. Researchers played three pairs of rhythms, and, under all three conditions, infants were skillful in perceiving the differences in rhythmic patterns (Demany, McKenzie, & Vurpillot, 1977). Adults often play rhythmic games (such as "This Little Piggy") with infants or try to soothe them with singing. These research findings explain why these approaches are often successful.

PIAGET'S THEORY OF COGNITION

Jean Piaget's theories have been among the most influential in modern psychology. He carefully observed his own three infants earlier in this century and found that they were active, using both motor skills and perception, in learning about the world around them. Note the excitement with which Piaget (1962) told about the imitation of one of his infants at six months of age:

> J. invented a new sound by putting her tongue between her teeth. It was something like *pfs*. Her mother then made the same sound. J. was delighted and laughed as she repeated it in her turn. Then came a long period of mutual imitation. J. said *pfs*, her mother imitated her, and J. watched her without moving her lips. Then when her mother stopped, J. began again, and so it went on. Later on, after remaining silent for some time, I myself said *pfs*. J. laughed at once and imitated me. There was the same reaction the next day, beginning in the morning (before she had herself spontaneously made the sound in question) and lasting throughout the day. (p. 19)

Piaget was one of the first scholars to realize that exploration and play serve important purposes in helping infants learn. He saw the infant as an integrated entity in which motor, social, and cognitive functions worked together to make it possible for the infant to learn about and adapt to the environment. According to Piaget, the sensorimotor stage characterizes most infants' thinking between birth and about two years of age. Within the sensorimotor stage are six substages, four of which typically fall within the first year of life, as shown in Table 7.1.

Piaget's Substage 1: Birth to 1 Month

In the first substage, much of an infant's activity centers on the area around the mouth, which has the greatest amount of neural connection and sensitivity. Accordingly, Piaget devoted considerable attention to showing how reflexes, such as sucking, can provide a basis for later development. Piaget's contention was that infants, far from being helpless or passive, are active in seeking stimulation through their own behavior. To illustrate the way newborns often initiate their own activities, Piaget (1962) described how his child Laurent made sucking actions between meals. Piaget discarded the possibilities that Laurent's sucking was activated only by objects, hunger, or the desire to repeat earlier satisfaction. Instead, Piaget interpreted Laurent's between-meal sucking as evidence that infants seek opportunities to exercise movements that are useful or interesting.

Piaget also showed ways in which infants in the first substage use their experiences to learn about the world. Again using the example of sucking, Piaget described a series of events illustrating that Laurent recognized his

Table 7.1.   *Piaget's Sensorimotor Stage of Development*

Sensorimotor Substage	Age	Accomplishments
Substage 1 (Reflexes)	Birth–1 month	Builds on reflexes
Substage 2 (Primary circular reactions)	1–4 months	Repeats interesting movements of the body (primary circular reactions) Anticipates familiar events (e.g., feeding) Coordinates senses
Substage 3 (Secondary circular reactions)	4–8 months	Repeats interesting actions on objects (secondary circular reactions) Imitates sounds and actions in repertoire Attempts search for hidden object
Substage 4 (Coordination of secondary schemes)	8–12 months	Uses goal-directed behavior Begins to be able to uncover hidden objects Imitates many behaviors
Substage 5	12–18 months	(See Chapter 10.)
Substage 6	18–24 months	(See Chapter 10.)

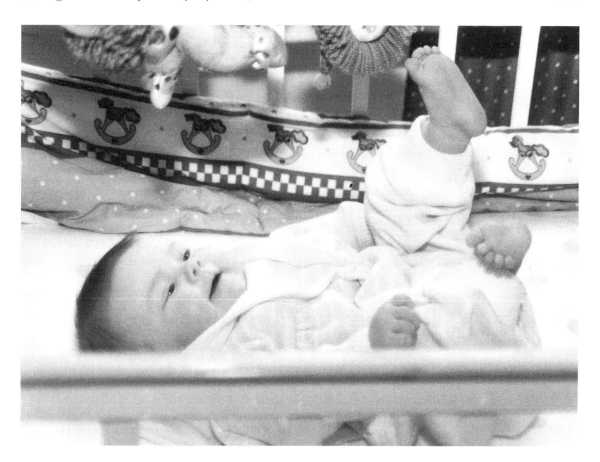

This infant discovered that by kicking her legs, she could cause the mobile to jingle. Her joyful repetition of the kicking is an example of primary circular reactions.

mother's nipple and knew where to look for it. Laurent adjusted to disturbances in the feeding process; in these adjustments, Piaget noted the roots of later intelligent behavior.

Piaget's Substage 2: 1–4 Months

According to Piaget, one of the most important intellectual advances in the second substage is the ability of infants to repeat interesting movements that first occur by chance. For example, the accidental contact of an infant's hand with her mouth may set off a series of trial-and-error efforts to return the hand to her mouth. Often she eventually succeeds. Piaget called this phenomenon a **primary circular reaction,** defined as active reproduction of actions that were first produced by chance. The term *primary* reflects the focus on the infant's own body; *circular* refers to the endlessly repetitive nature of these reactions.

Two-month-old Aaron spends a great deal of his waking hours watching his hands. This is easy because when lying on his back, his hands tend to float right in front of his face. However, in the beginning he doesn't seem to understand that his hands are part of his body. He hasn't learned to control them. If his hands float into view, he eagerly grabs them with his eyes and studies them intently.

Later, he experiments with moving his hand and following the movement with his eyes. He watches his hand intently as he moves it slowly toward his face until he hits himself in the face. This startles him so much that he jumps and his arms fly apart. He stares blankly, not knowing what to do to get the hand back. As he relaxes, it automatically floats back into view. He is noticeably excited at seeing it again and immediately starts moving it toward his face. Once again he hits himself in the face, is startled, and loses sight of the hand. Once again the hand floats back into his line of sight. This time he slowly moves it and then stops it before it hits his face. He is learning to control it. He then spends much time moving it forward and backward, but without hitting himself again.

This is an example of the learning of **proprioceptive** control—that is, the feeling in the body that provides feedback as to what the body is doing. It is learned by noticing what feelings in the body correspond to an event. For example, Aaron is learning to associate certain sensations of the muscles of the arm with the appearance and movement of the hand.

Another milestone of the second substage is the anticipation by infants of familiar events, such as feeding. Adults notice that infants in the second substage may begin to suck immediately when placed in the feeding position, rather than waiting for contact with the nipple as they did previously. Infants thus begin to make more accurate predictions about events that they have experienced.

A third development in this substage is that infants start to be able to coordinate their senses. They can use their eyes to follow objects. They can turn to look in the direction of interesting or surprising sounds. And they often manage to become more active in exploring their environments. See Developmental Issues in Practice 7.1 for ideas on interacting with infants at this stage of development.

A fourth characteristic of infants in the second substage involves their behavior when someone or something disappears from their view. Piaget demonstrated that, if someone in interaction with an infant suddenly disappears, the infant stares at the spot and then turns his or her attention elsewhere. Piaget called this a failure to show **object permanence,** defined as the understanding that things and people continue to exist even though not in view. At this early stage, infants do not search and they do not seem surprised about the disappearance. Piaget has asserted that infants in this second substage do not protest when people or things disappear because the infants have not begun to retain consistent mental images of people or objects. The baby behaves as though "out of sight" is "out of mind."

There are several practical implications of this behavior. First, infants in

▲ **DEVELOPMENTAL ISSUES IN PRACTICE 7.1**

SENSORIMOTOR ACTIVITIES FOR COGNITIVE AND LANGUAGE GROWTH

From about four months of age, infants show great pleasure in social games. They smile and laugh in anticipation of the climax of the games that adults play with them. Each culture has its own games. Here are three common ones:

❑ "Peekaboo, I see you"—An adult alternately covers and uncovers his or her face, making the excited exclamation,

   Peekaboo, I see you!

❑ "Round and round the garden"—An adult moves his or her finger around the infant's hand, up the infant's arm, and then tickles under the infant's arm, saying,

   Round and round the garden, went the teddy bear. One step, two steps, tickly under there!

❑ "This little piggy"—Starting with the largest toe, an adult grasps each toe in turn, saying,

   This little piggy went to market. This little piggy stayed home. This little piggy ate roast beef. This little piggy ate none. And this little piggy cried, "Wee-wee-wee," all the way home!

These social games give infants experiences with auditory sequencing, anticipation of outcomes, search for a hidden person, and imitation (as they begin to initiate the games). The games also encourage a special closeness and warmth between infants and adults.

this second substage usually require little adjustment when parents leave them in alternate child care arrangements. Second, they stop fussing to have an object as soon as it is removed from view. Third, they are easily distracted from a negative situation by removing them from the context.

> *Three-month-old Laura tries to grab her mother's glasses. She finally gets a good grip on them and is immediately in a tug of war with her mother. The interference in her plans causes frustration, and Laura begins to fuss. She thrashes around, trying to get the glasses as her mother takes them firmly away from her grasp. Laura's mother quickly slips the glasses into her pocket. As soon as the glasses disappear from sight, Laura settles down and is easily drawn into a game of peekaboo.*

Piaget's Substage 3: 4–8 Months

Piaget indicated that infants expand their horizons dramatically during the third substage. Crawling brings infants into wider contact with the environment, and they manipulate and explore whatever they find. Infants continue to try to repeat interesting actions, but their focus expands. Piaget called these endeavors **secondary circular reactions,** with the word *secondary* indicating that these actions center on objects rather than on the infant's own body. For instance, infants show great pleasure at being the cause of the delightful noises that occur when they pound a rattle.

Piaget showed that in this third substage, infants' imitation becomes more systematic than it was earlier. Infants can imitate sounds and expressions already in their repertoires, and they enjoy games that involve repetition of familiar patterns.

Infants' wider contact with the environment leads to growth in their understanding of the permanence of people and objects. Now, if someone or something disappears from sight, infants try to search. They may search in a new location, as if understanding that movement could continue even if the object is not in view. Or, if an object is partly visible, infants may attempt to uncover it. These search procedures show that infants are developing a more complete understanding of the existence of people and objects in the environment. However, infants' attempts at retrieving lost objects only repeat actions that they have already performed in the past rather than introducing any novel strategies. For example, if an infant had been looking at an object before it vanished, he would tend to search visually but not use his hands to try to find it. Piaget has said that infants at the third substage still think of everything in relationship to their own actions rather than as having independent, individual existences.

Piaget's Substage 4: 8–12 Months

Piaget has said that an infant's major intellectual accomplishment in the fourth substage is the onset of goal-directed behavior, which occurs because the infant can coordinate action subschemes. He called this stage **coordination of secondary schemes.** Until this last part of the first year, infants accidentally discover goals, which they then pursue. In contrast, in the fourth substage, infants have goals in mind from the beginning and work purposefully to achieve them. Piaget has said that behavior in the fourth substage can be called "intelligent" because infants are able to overcome obstacles by using strategies that differ from the strategies initially applied to reach the goal.

Michelle sees her bottle in the middle of the table. She reaches for it, but it is out of reach. As she continues to reach across the table, she inadvertently pulls on the tablecloth. She begins to notice that her actions of pulling on the cloth are causing her bottle to move closer to her. Eventually, the bottle comes within her reach. Repeated experience with this situation gives her confidence in exactly how much force is required to move an object by pulling on the tablecloth.

Eventually, in a later developmental stage, she will be able to walk up to the table with calm assurance, grab the edge of the tablecloth, and, with one sharp pull, bring the bottle to the edge within easy reach. This is what Piaget called goal-directed behavior.

An infant in Piaget's substage 4 demonstrates goal-directed behavior.

Another accomplishment in the fourth substage is increased understanding of the relationships between and among objects. Infants realize that someone's hand might need to be pushed open to obtain a toy. They are able to keep the goal in mind and to remember that the hand encloses the toy. Infants will push an adult's hand toward something the child wants but cannot reach.

Correspondingly, the ability to imitate expands dramatically. Infants initiate familiar games such as peekaboo and find success in imitating sounds and gestures that are new. Toys can be an important component of helping children to develop in an optimal way. Toys should thus be chosen carefully to help develop such abilities in children.

According to Piaget's theory, it is also during the fourth substage that infants develop a sense of object permanence. They demonstrate this ability by finding hidden objects. They can lift a cloth that is covering the object. When someone or something disappears, infants in the fourth substage use a variety of systematic strategies to search for what is missing. Infants now seem to realize that objects and individuals have an independent existence, whether or not they can be seen at the moment. When a ball rolls under the sofa, infants look carefully for it. Piaget has said that infants come to understand that objects have permanence by having been provided with many opportunities to manipulate and observe the movement of things around the house.

T. G. R. Bower (1977, 1982), of the University of Edinburgh, disagrees with Piaget about explanations for infants' behavior in the object permanence task. The differences between the views of Bower and Piaget center not so much on their interpretations of how infants act and react but on their explanation about why.

Bower has indicated that infants under five months of age do not search for lost objects or people because they are unable to understand that the same objects or people can appear in different places and that objects and people must move to get from one place to another. Bower has illustrated his point with two experiments. In the first, infants were presented simultaneously with three images of their mothers. Before five months of age, infants interacted pleasantly with all three, lending support to Bower's idea that infants think that there is a different mother for each location in which she appears. After about five months of age, infants registered shock and protest at seeing multiple mothers, indicating that this sight violated an understanding that they had achieved. In the second experiment, infants were shown the movement of a toy train. When the path of the train changed and the train stopped on another side of the track where it was still visible, infants younger than five months of age were unable to locate the train. Bower explained this finding by saying that infants do not associate the moving train with the stationary one.

Bower and Piaget are in agreement that, even when infants reach about five months of age and have resolved some of the problems in their understanding of location and motion, their reactions to disappearances of objects or people show unique aspects of their thinking processes. Bower has explained infants' behavior by saying that they still do not grasp the spatial relationships between and among objects. When an infant at six months of age does not lift a handkerchief to search for a hidden ball, Bower has indicated that the failure to search is not due, as Piaget said, to a lack of a consistent mental image of the object. Rather, according to Bower, the infant lacks an understanding of spatial relationships such as under, on, in, in front of, and behind. Bower has concluded that infants do not realize until the end of the first year that objects can be in these relationships with other things (e.g., a block on top of another block) and still remain separate and separable. However, if there are more than one type of cover or if the object is moved spatially from one place to another, they will have difficulty recovering the object.

The development of a sense of object permanence is related to infants' strong attachment to parents and alternate caregivers at these ages. Piaget uses the word *object* to include people as well as things. The important people in infants' lives are the first "objects" to which they attribute permanence. And they now often protest vigorously when they are left behind. This makes possible the behavior referred to as stranger anxiety, which is discussed in Chapter 6.

INFANT INTELLIGENCE

It is clear from the examples of infant behavior discussed so far that infants do not have the same kind of intellectual abilities that older children have. They do not talk, so it is difficult to tell what is going on in their minds. For many years, researchers have been attempting with little success to predict later cognitive functioning by administering intelligence tests to infants. By studying other skills and activities of infants, researchers have found that some perceptual and motor abilities are related to later intellectual functioning. However, there has been an ongoing debate in the literature about what kinds of infant behaviors constitute intellectual functioning. Rose (1981) has pointed out that it is difficult to obtain correlations between infant functioning and IQ scores taken when children begin school. Several different kinds of infant behavior are being studied to see whether they correlate with later IQ scores.

Cross-modal transfer of information may be a useful measure of intellectual functioning in infants (Rose, 1981; Rose, Feldman, & Wallace, 1992). This is the ability to use a number of sensory modes to process the same information. For example, an infant can learn about an object by looking at it (vision) and by feeling it with hands or mouth (tactile). Hand–eye coordination is an example of this ability and has been discussed in Chapter 5. Another example is that of the theory of **active intermodal mapping** (Meltzoff & Moore, 1985). This theory attempts to explain imitation abilities of infants, in which infants can compare information received by two different modalities (vision and their sense of their own movement). This is used to explain the finding that young infants who have never seen their faces can imitate facial expressions of others.

Visual information processing has been measured by studying attention abilities in infants. McCall and Carriger (1993) have reviewed the literature and concluded that recognition memory in infants is a better predictor of IQ than are standardized infant tests. Visual information processing has been found to correlate with later adolescent attentional skills related to efficiency in information processing (Sigman, Cohen, Beckwith, Asarnow, & Parmelee, 1991). Visual recognition memory in seven-month-old infants correlated with six-year-old IQ, language proficiency, early reading, and perceptual ability (Rose, Feldman, & Wallace, 1992). Lecuyer (1989) found that habituation is a good measure of attention in infants and may be an important component of what is being measured by IQ tests. The Brazelton Neonatal Behavioral Assessment Scale measures habituation. If a light is shined on the closed eye of a sleeping baby, the baby will respond by squeezing both eyes tightly shut and by making some restless body movement. The second time the light is shined, the eyes will tighten some and then relax. By the third time, most babies will not respond at all. The stimulus has been habituated.

Motor functioning was thought by Piaget to be the primary way infants processed information from the environment. It was for this reason that he named his first stage of development the **sensorimotor stage**. Uzgiris and

Hunt (1975) have developed a widely used scale based on Piaget's theory, and they provide evidence that sensorimotor abilities in infancy correlate with later IQ scores. The measure of object permanence provides the best relationship with IQ (Rose, Feldman, & Wallace, 1992). Following is a discussion of visual information processing, imitation, and motor functioning.

Visual Information Processing

Visual attention might be viewed as belonging in the domain of physical development; yet, as a measure of information processing, it seems to predict later cognitive competence. Lewis and Brooks-Gunn (1981) presented three-month-old infants with redundant visual stimuli interspersed with novel ones. Infants who were likely to habituate to redundant stimuli and recover interest when presented with novel stimuli were likely to have higher IQs at 24 months than infants who did not behave in this manner. The researchers have viewed their findings as supporting the stance that differences in attention are related to functioning of the central nervous system and that the ability to process information in the first months of life can provide a useful measure of intellectual capability.

Sontheimer (1989) studied information processing in normal infants and infants with disabilities, observing their visual preferences for novel objects. The normal infants showed a greater preference for looking at novel objects, indicating that they were trying to familiarize themselves with the objects. This provides further evidence of the link with central nervous system processing and suggests that this is a useful measure for studying intellectual functioning in infants.

Short attention times (Colombo, Mitchell, Coldren, & Freeseman, 1991) were associated with superior ability to process the information and identify objects. When infants of 6 and 10 months were given an opportunity to look at novel objects, they preferred those that were in the same category as the familiar ones. This suggests that infants process information in groupings, or classes. Catherwood, Crassini, and Freiberg (1990) found that the color of the novel objects was an important factor in helping children to attend to the objects' novelty. These studies suggest that visual attention and habituation are important components of IQ because they measure the ability of the babies to process information in a fast, efficient way by using categories and color to help make identifications of novelty. The babies are thinking by processing information.

Imitation

Meltzoff and Moore (1985) have demonstrated that infants as young as 42 minutes of age can imitate the facial gestures of mouth opening and tongue protrusion. The experiments were recorded on videotape for later analysis by observers who did not know which adult gesture preceded any infant gesture. Infants produced significantly more mouth openings in response to adult mouth opening and significantly more tongue protrusions to the adult tongue protrusion gesture. Thus, imitation appears to be an inherited trait.

Meltzoff and Moore (1985) propose that this early imitation reflects a process in which infants use equivalences between gestures they see and gestures they perceive themselves to be making—that is, proprioceptive feedback. The researchers call this process **active intermodal mapping** and have concluded that infants can compare information received by two different modalities (vision and their sense of their own movement). Meltzoff and Moore have summarized their experiments by postulating that human newborns have an innate ability to appreciate equivalences between their own actions and actions they see. An interesting example of complex cross-modal behavior is presented in the following quote from a parent's diary:

> Danny (eight months, two weeks, six days) has been fascinated by the sound that I make by emitting a long vowel sound, while at the same time rapidly moving my tongue in and out of my slightly opened mouth. This makes a "burbling" sound, and Danny has been imitating it quite well. However, he makes the sound in a different way than I do, by moving his tongue along his lips rather than in and out. Today, while sitting on my lap, he became very excited when I made the sound. He immediately jumped up close to my face to watch my mouth. He really wanted me to repeat it, so I did. He then made the sound and felt both his mouth and my mouth. He kept trying to do it my way until he finally moved his tongue in and out the way I was doing. He then seemed satisfied and has continued to make the sound using the method that he learned from me. I was amazed because he had used both touch and vision to figure out how to make his mouth work, though he can't even see his mouth!

Legerstee (1990) has substantiated this research by studying intermodal activities directly. He presented infants with the sound of a vowel, either "a" or "u." For half of the infants, an adult silently articulated the same vowel as it was being played for the infant to hear. For the other infants, the adult articulated the opposite vowel sound. It was found that infants imitated only the adult who articulated the same sound as they heard. This presents strong evidence that the infant is coordinating the sound of the verbalization with the appearance of the mouth of the model. This behavior is very important to later language development, because the imitations of mouth movements would obviously facilitate imitation of the language sound system. In other research, Meltzoff and Moore (1985) have found that infants imitate other kinds of behaviors, including head turning. Thus, the imitation capabilities of infants undoubtedly contribute to language development but also go beyond language to other motor movements.

These abilities have been described as having their origin in an innate ability of infants to transform externally perceived stimuli into their own actions. However, there are environmental factors that play a role in encouraging the repetition of imitated behaviors. For example, Poulson, Kymissis, Reeve, Andreatos, and Reeve (1991) have shown that when parents reinforced infant vocalizations by giving social praise (such as smiling, looking, and talking), it increased the amount of vocal imitation in 9–13-month-old infants.

Motor Processes

Piaget has had the greatest influence on the idea that infants learn through motor processes. His first stage, which he called sensorimotor (referring to the child's ability to learn using the senses and motor skills), has been described earlier.

Piaget recognized that the readiness of a person for a new stage of development must be due to neurological changes in the brain that make new development possible. Fischer (1987) has shown that there are spurts of development in **synaptogenesis** in the brain that correspond to the stages observed by Piaget. Synaptogenesis refers to increases in the synapses, which are the electrochemical connections between cells. All behavior depends on these synapses; and the greater the density of synaptic connections, the greater the behavioral repertoire of the person.

Fischer identified synaptogenesis peaks, which appear to be associated with "windows of opportunity" when the child's actions have the effect of generating large numbers of new synapses. Greenough, Black, and Wallace (1987) have suggested that during peak periods of development, an excess of synaptic connections is formed. Over a period of time, experience determines which of the synapses are valuable enough to survive. This thinning out process appears to be controlled by the upper cortex, which is the thinking part of the brain. Thus, the repetitive behavior of children as new skills are learned corresponds to synaptogenesis, and the consolidation of the most efficient and adaptive behaviors corresponds to the systematic loss of over-learned synaptic connections.

This is demonstrated by the example, given earlier, of Michelle's developing ability to reach her bottle by pulling on the tablecloth. Her initial efforts require a burst of physical activity. Many of her actions are unnecessary, but her trial-and-error behavior leads to success. With experience, she learns to drop all of the reaching and struggling behaviors. She retains only the simple, fast, efficient jerk of the cloth, thus refining and consolidating her skill.

Developmental Issues in Practice 7.2 provides a listing of the various motor structures that infants exhibit along with a list of the objects that can be used to encourage the use of the structure. These objects provide an essential mechanism for encouraging cognitive development in infants.

LANGUAGE DEVELOPMENT

Because the word *infant* is derived from the Latin *infans*, meaning "not speaking," it may seem strange to discuss language development in infancy. Yet research shows that the groundwork for language competence begins to be laid in the first year of life. Research relating to infant language develop-

▲ **DEVELOPMENTAL ISSUES IN PRACTICE 7.2**

MOTOR ACTIVITIES IN THE FIRST YEAR

During the first year, children learn by exercising their sensorimotor structures and acting on objects in the environment. Following is a list of exploratory activities with suggested objects to encourage exploration.

1. Looking and inspecting: mobiles, stabiles, pictures, photographs of known persons and places, magazines, catalogs, cloth books, safety mirrors, living people (considered as objects by the child)

2. Listening: Metronome, ticking clock, bells on booties, variety of rattles, musical kicking toys, music boxes, records or tapes of music and familiar sounds, people's activities, verbalizations

3. Touching and fingering: hand-sized objects differing in texture, shape, and edges; miniature copies of large objects; piano keys and guitar strings; simple-form boards and shape-sorting boxes; people

4. Turning: book and magazine pages

5. Hammering and pounding: drum or other percussion instruments, wooden pegboard with one-inch thick pegs or dowels, cube blocks, modeling materials such as clay or play dough

6. Emptying and filling: sand, water, buckets, blocks, containers, nesting toys, one- or two-piece puzzles

7. Threading: wooden beads, empty thread spools, heavy cord or shoelaces

8. Opening and shutting: doors and drawers, boxes, pots and pans with lids

9. Stacking and knocking down: cube blocks, color cones

10. Picking up: counters, bottle caps, checkers, cotton balls, paper scraps

11. Twisting: knobs and switches, lock and lever boards

12. Bouncing: mattresses, "baby bouncers" (preferably, people)

13. Rolling and retrieving: balls, beanbags, round bell rattles

14. Dropping: spoons, cereal bowls, anything loose

15. Scribbling: crayons, newspaper, paper bags

16. Creeping or crawling through or under: boxes, barrels, classroom furniture

17. Pulling and perhaps pushing: pull-string wagon, toy animals on wheels, wheel-less wooden cars and trains, pop-beads

SOURCE: From Margaret G. Weiser, *Infant/Toddler Care and Education* (2nd ed.). New York: Merrill/Macmillan, 1991. Used with permission.

ment is presented in chronological sequence using the following categories: newborn, first six months, and second six months. When ages are given, they represent averages. There are two aspects of language—the receptive and the expressive. Receptive language develops first. It is easier to understand than to produce language.

Newborn

Newborns have been said to be genetically programmed for receptive communication, both visually and auditorily (Owens, 1984). Newborns attain their best visual focus at about 8–12 inches, the distance from them of parents who are providing food. Also, the mutual gazing that takes place during feeding is an early form of communication. Cooper and Aslin (1990) have shown that when adults directed their speech toward the newborn, the baby paid more attention than when adults directed their speech toward others in the environment. Newborns can discriminate between speech directed at them and speech directed at others, a function that is necessary for later language communication.

Newborns are known to be able to track the voices of their mothers and to distinguish them from those of other women (Mehler, 1985). Even 12-hour-old infants change their sucking rates when the rates controlled the tapes of the voices of their biological mothers (DeCasper & Fifer, 1980), and they are especially attentive to their mothers' speech (Moon & Fifer, 1990). Analysis of high-speed motion picture film has indicated that within hours of birth, infants respond uniquely to human speech sounds (Condon & Sander, 1974). As adults speak, infants make continuous slight movements of toes, fingers, head, eyes, shoulders, arms, and hips. This is called **speech entrainment.** These movements change with each separate sound of speech. Infants move in this manner when they hear male and female speakers in English and Chinese, but they do not synchronize to the sound of disconnected vowels or the sounds of tapping.

Infants participate in the rhythm of normal adult speech months before they begin to babble and two or more years before their own speech falls into these fluent rhythms. This suggests that language learning involves an important motor component. The movements in synchronization to speech are too subtle to be observed by the unaided eye, but frame-by-frame analysis of film is giving researchers a new view of the human newborn as a receiver of language stimulation. Selective attention to language is shown in other ways also: newborns stop crying to attend to human voices (Owens, 1984).

First Six Months

Most infants begin to coo in the second month of life. Cooing involves making vowel sounds, often in response to a human face, eye contact, or a voice. The development of **cooing** is parallel to that of social smiling and seems part of the process of communication between infants and adults even in the earliest months. Cooing is stimulated by human attention; in fact, 12-week-old infants are twice as likely to revocalize if an adult responds verbally rather than with a smile, a look, or other nonverbal gesture (Owens, 1984).

By four months of age, infants initiate communication with adults by smiling or coughing to attract attention. They participate in rituals and game playing, all the while learning to take turns in communication, to share attention, and to communicate their intentions. In the sixth month, infants have the ability to reflect a full repertoire of emotions in their vocalizations, including pleasure, anger, and surprise (Owens, 1984).

Toward the end of the first six months, infants begin to babble. **Babbling** includes both vowel and consonant sounds (*ma, da, pa*) and is therefore more complex than the earlier cooing. Table 7.2 shows the relationship between phonetic development and anatomic changes in the infant's mouth, nose, and **larynx** (voice box). Infants continue to babble until about a month or so before they use their first meaningful words, and then their babbling diminishes.

Table 7.2. *Relationship Between Infant Phonetic Development and Significant Physical Changes*

Age of Infant	Phonetic Development	Related Anatomy and Physiology
0–1 month Phonation stage	Nasalized vowels	Nasal breathing and nasalized vocalization because of engagement of larynx and nasopharynx; tongue has mostly back-and-forth motions and nearly fills the oral cavity
2–3 months Cooing stage	Nasalized vowels plus g/k	Some change in shape of oral cavity and an increase in mobility of tongue
4–6 months Expansion stage	Normal vowels	Increased separation of oral and nasal cavities, so that nonnasal vowels are readily produced
	Raspberry (labial)	The necessary air pressure in the mouth can be developed because of disengagement of the larynx from the nasopharynx.
	Squeal and growl	Contrasts in vocal pitch heightened perhaps because descent of larynx into neck makes the vocal folds more vulnerable to forces of supralaryngeal muscles
	Yelling	Better coordination of respiratory system; larynx permits loud voice
	Marginal babble	Alternation of full opening and closing of vocal tract enhanced by larynx–nasopharynx disengagement

SOURCE: From A. P. Reilly (Ed.), *The Communication Game: Perspectives on the Development of Speech, Language, and Non-Verbal Communication Skills: A Round Table*, p. 42. Skillman, NJ: Johnson & Johnson, 1980. Copyright 1980 by Johnson & Johnson Baby Products Co. Reprinted by permission.

By the time this baby is a year old, she will be able to turn the pages of books as she "reads" all by herself.

Second Six Months

Researchers have found that six-month-old infants can categorize the sounds of speech. Kuhl (1980, 1985) showed that infants by the age of six months can recognize that a specific speech sound that they hear is the same (e.g., a sound like *u*, *t*, *ch*, etc.) even though it is actually acoustically different because of variations in speakers, intonation, or context. These findings demonstrate that infants can recognize basic constancies of speech even when the words are spoken by either males or females, are whispered or shouted, or are said in anger or affection. Thus, their discrimination ability is very similar to that of adults.

In the second six months, infants begin to assert more control within interactions. They try to imitate new sounds and, toward the end of this period, they demonstrate selective listening and compliance with simple requests. They respond when asked to perform simple motor behavior ("Wave bye-bye") and show their understanding of names of family members and caregivers. Infants may demonstrate comprehension of other words, such as *ball, baby, more,* and *no.*

The context of language events is very important to learning the meaning of words. Nonverbal cues are used and mastered by babies during this period of language development. Allen (1991) found that gestures were an important influence on language responses in children by 18 months of age. In addition, children point as a means of signaling intentional communication (Yamane, 1989).

Harding (1983) has proposed a model to explain the development of **intentional communication** in infancy (see Figure 7.1). According to this model, as infants' behaviors become goal directed (during Piaget's fourth substage), adults interpret infants' actions as intending to communicate. Harding has said that intentional communication develops gradually, beginning with infants' cognitive awareness of goals in general and ending with

Figure 7.1 *Proposed Developmental Sequence of Prelinguistic Communication*

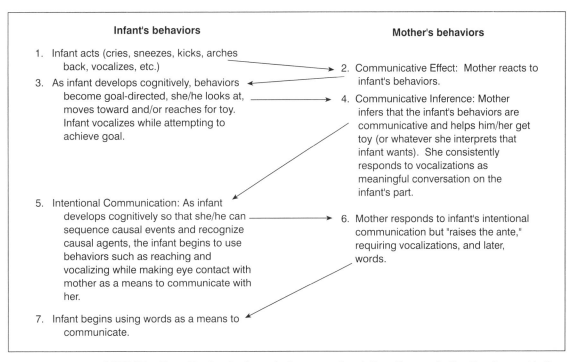

SOURCE: From "Setting the Stage for Language Acquisition: Communication Development in the First Year" by C. G. Harding, in *The Transition from Prelinguistic to Linguistic Communication* (p. 95) edited by R. M. Golinkoff, 1983, Hillsdale, NJ: Lawrence Erlbaum. Copyright 1983 by Lawrence Erlbaum Associates. Reprinted by permission.

infants' having communication as a goal. Harding has indicated that, when infants realize the usefulness of communication as a goal, they also recognize the utility of words as a vehicle for communication. Most infants produce their first words early in the second year of life. This is the beginning of expressive language.

By the end of the first year of life, infants have become communicators. They have learned how to influence the behavior of others, understand some language, use behaviors intentionally to signal others, and may have uttered their first words. The stage is set for further language development.

An important part of this language development is the development of literacy. McLane and McNamee (1991) have discussed the observation that literacy has its roots in the earliest development of the child. This **emergent literacy** is part of the behavior of infants and does not appear to have direct relevance to reading and writing as we know it in school-age children. Care-givers encourage these processes by engaging in interactive vocalizations with the infant. It is as important to listen as it is to speak. An essential part of assisting the child in literary experiences involves reading to the child, beginning in the first half of the first year of life. Developmental Issues in Practice 7.3 presents recommendations on reading to infants.

CULTURAL DIFFERENCES IN LANGUAGE INTERACTIONS WITH INFANTS

There are many individual differences in the language interactions of adults with infants. There are also systematic cultural and social class differences (Schieffelin & Ochs, 1983). The existence of differences is not surprising in a pluralistic society, but the implications of these differences deserve discussion.

Researchers have suggested that talking to infants is a feature of interaction mainly among middle-class groups in North America and Western Europe (Schieffelin & Ochs, 1983). Talking to infants seems to occur when adults believe that infants are separate individuals with whom communication is possible. Adults with this belief hold infants face-to-face, gaze at them, and address, greet, and question them. Conversations are established using a dyadic, turn-taking model. Parents take the perspective of infants, adapting and simplifying adult speech and making interpretations of infant vocalizations.

Researchers have found that vocalization levels of adults speaking to infants are low in many countries (e.g., Mexico, Kenya, Guatemala, Japan, Zambia, and New Guinea) and among Americans classified in lower socioeconomic groups (Snow, deBlauw, & Van Roosmalen, 1979; Schieffelin & Ochs, 1983). For example, the Kaluli people of the tropical rain forest of Papua New Guinea describe their infants as "having no understanding" and say that they care for infants because they "feel sorry for them," (Schieffelin & Ochs, 1983). The Kaluli do not treat infants as partners in dyadic communication, do not gaze into infants' eyes, and do not modify adult language

▲ DEVELOPMENTAL ISSUES IN PRACTICE   7.3

READING BOOKS TO INFANTS

One of the most interesting discoveries verified over the past few years is that the first steps in learning to read actually begin shortly after birth, when infants hear language spoken around them. When books are added to warm physical encounters, the child associates pleasure with reading.

Hold the baby comfortably in your lap and turn the pages of a book that has large, simple pictures. Point to different objects in the picture and name them for the child. Tell the child something about the picture, such as, "Look, Heather, here is a doll. It looks just like your doll." Do so in a pleasant voice so that everything will add up to a comfortable experience. Remember that the baby's listening vocabulary will become much larger than his or her speaking vocabulary; therefore, long before the child is able to say the word, he or she will be able to point to a picture if you say the word for the child. For example, if you say, "Heather, show me the kitty," she will proudly point to the picture.

By the time the baby is about one year old, he or she will be able to turn the pages of appropriate-sized books while "reading" all by himself or herself. Babies find books containing large pictures of familiar single objects, animals, or people most stimulating. Try making a texture book, a book that contains pictures and shapes made from materials of various textures. These books appeal to the infants' sense of touch as well as to their sense of sight, inviting them to explore and experience each page.

Sturdy picture books are most appropriate for infants, but their awareness of the printed word should not be limited only to such print media. Print surrounds the infant each day. Television commercials, cereal boxes, newspapers, billboards, letters in the mail, greeting cards, calendars, and a variety of other sources naturally introduce children to the printed language. Of course, the baby will not read these things, but exposure to print greatly influences the child's eventual acquisition of reading skills.

SOURCE: From George W. Maxim, *The Sourcebook*. New York: Merrill/Macmillan, 1990. Used with permission.

according to infants' abilities. They believe that the responsibility for clear speech rests with the speaker, even if that speaker is a young child. Although the language learning environment does not emphasize dyadic interactions between parent and child, infants in Papua New Guinea hear language and learn to speak.

Toda, Fogel, and Kawai (1990) studied mothers talking to three-month-old infants in the United States and Japan. They found that mothers in the United States were more information oriented than were Japanese mothers and used more question forms, especially yes/no questions. Japanese mothers

Talking to infants seems to occur when speakers believe that infants are separate individuals with whom communication is possible.

were affect oriented, and they used more nonsense, baby talk, and babies' names. Fernald and Morikawa (1993) found that mothers in both Japan and the United States adapted their speech to the needs of their infants by simplifying language and making frequent repetitions. On the other hand, mothers in the United States labeled objects more frequently, while Japanese mothers used objects more often to engage their infants in social interactions. The differences in maternal speech appear to reflect characteristic culture-specific communicative styles as well as beliefs and values related to child rearing.

Research within this country has found cultural differences in the amount and type of language directed by adults to infants. A study by Field and Widmayer (1981) found that Cuban mothers typically spent 82% of their time talking to their three- to four-month-old infants; black mothers spent 14% of their time doing so. The amount of talking by Puerto Rican and South American mothers was found to be between those two extremes. All mothers were from families classified at a low socioeconomic level, based on education and occupation.

Another report of differences in adult–infant interaction is from a study of families from the same cultural group but different educational and occupational levels. Observing in the homes of white 10-month-old children, Tulkin (1977) found more middle-class than working-class mothers to be very involved in talking with their infants. The significant differences between the two groups pertained to the amount of the mothers' spontaneous talk, their responses to infants' talk, and their imitation of infants' language. Mothers with working-class backgrounds spent as much time caring for infants as did mothers with middle-class backgrounds, but there were differences in the language used.

Talking with infants has been demonstrated to have a positive effect on language development. Feiring and Lewis (1981) observed parents and their children when the children were 3, 12, and 24 months of age. Researchers found great variability in how much parents talked to infants. Even more important, the researchers found that talking to infants may not have made a measurable difference at 3 and 12 months of age, but the 3- and 12-month-old infants who were talked with the most were the most capable with language and concepts when they reached 24 months of age. This finding reveals an apparent "sleeper" effect of early talking with infants. In another longitudinal study (Goldfield, 1993), mothers' use of nouns in talking to their infants during toy play was related to the tendency of the children to use more nouns later as first words were acquired. Clearly, the adults in the child's environment have an important impact on long-term language development. It is important for them to be aware of the kinds of responses that should be given under different circumstances. Developmental Issues in Practice 7.4 presents ideas for adults to use to turn an infant action into an adult–child interaction.

Certain aspects of verbal interaction with infants (e.g., engaging them in dyadic "conversations" as in the Harding [1983] model) tend to be characteristic of middle-class families. These interaction patterns have been found to have positive effects on language development. Morisset, Barnard, Greenberg, Booth, and Spieker (1990) studied children in high-risk environments, where *risk* was defined as family social status and mother's psychosocial functioning. They found that competence in these children was greatly improved by a high quality of dyadic involvement between mother and infant. Thus, this skill has been shown to be of assistance to the optimal development of children and it can be taught, even to families at risk. Research into cultural variation in language interactions can be very helpful in identifying interventions that might be of value to various groups.

EARLY INTERVENTION PROGRAMS

Infants with Disabilities

Often infants or their families have certain needs that can best be met with support, instruction, and help from outside the family. Programs that provide this support, instruction, and help to young children and their families are usually called **early intervention programs.** One such program has been described by Jablow (1982) in a book about her daughter, Cara.

▲ **DEVELOPMENTAL ISSUES IN PRACTICE   7.4**

SELECTED ACTIONS AND INTERACTIONS BETWEEN INFANT AND ADULT

Age	Infant-Toddler	Adult
0–3 months	Makes baby noises; gurgles and coos	Imitates; uses conversation; makes new sounds with changes in pitch
	Engages in mouth play	Allows baby to chew hand; kisses baby's hand; lets baby grab a finger or two
	Shows surprise at a change in the usual	Makes faces and different vocal sounds
	Moves arms and legs	Pushes gently on soles of baby's feet; raises and lowers baby's arms
	Responds to rhythmic sounds or movements	Dances with baby in arms; gently rocks the baby
	Visually explores	Provides things (patterns, bright colors, movement) and persons to look at
3–6 months	Plays with food	Supplies finger foods
	Recognizes familiar things	Provides stability in objects and persons
	Shows surprise at novelty in the context of the familiar	Gradually introduces slightly different objects and persons and activities
	Engages in object play and power play	Provides toys that do something as a result of the child's action
	Is excited by movement and rhythm	Dances, sings, and plays with baby; bounces baby on knees; holds baby up in the air
	Enjoys predictable excitement	Plays " This little piggy," "Pat-a-cake," and "Rock-a-bye baby"
	Explores environment visually and tactilely	Provides objects to look at and touch; positions baby in visual range of ongoing activities
6–12 months	Explores visually, tactilely, and motorically	Permits reasonable and safe exploration; introduces new objects; places baby in different locations in the room
	Imitates new sounds or sights	Converses with vocalizations, verbalizations, and facial expressions, including funny faces and sounds
	Wants an audience	Is a frequent observer and appreciative responder; makes "mirror" faces
	Enjoys total body movement	Gently roughhouses
	Enjoys predictable surprises	Plays "peek-a-boo" and "hear-a-boo"
	Enjoys fun and games	Makes baby laugh; plays with baby

SOURCE: From Margaret G. Weiser, *Infant/Toddler Care and Education* (2nd ed.). New York: Merrill/Macmillan, 1991. Used with permission.

Cara was born with Down syndrome and entered an early intervention program when she was one month of age. She attended four mornings per week for her first two and one-half years and engaged in a curriculum of challenge, stimulation, exercise, and language development. Cara gradually became able to participate in playground activities with her peers from a regular classroom in a regular school. Cara remains a retarded child with limitations, but her involvement in early intervention is believed to have raised her performance over what it would have been if she had not participated.

Programs such as Cara's do not help just the infant who is enrolled. Parents are involved, too, in helping to meet the program goals. Parents and brothers and sisters receive support and assistance. Interactions with other families help to relieve guilt and despair and to promote acceptance and nurturing.

In 1986, the federal legislation originally called the Education for All Handicapped Children Act was amended to include Part H, the infant/toddler section, which was reauthorized in 1991 as part of the Individuals with Disabilities Education Act (IDEA). Two features of this act include the requirement for service coordination to more effectively assist families and the requirement for an Individualized Family Service Plan (IFSP). These requirements reflect the realization that the well-being of young children with disabilities is directly dependent on the ability of the family to make adequate responses to their needs. Part H of the IDEA is specifically designed to meet those needs.

It is clear that parental involvement can be of great benefit to the professionals in the testing and identification of infants with disabilities. Henderson (1991) found that when the Early Screening Inventory, used to identify disabilities, was used in conjunction with parental evaluation, the ability to identify infants in need of referrals was greatly enhanced (see Table 7.3). This is especially important when the errors involve overreferrals. An overreferral means that a child will be identified as needing intervention even when in fact he or she is "normal." This points up the great value of involving parents in the intervention process.

Table 7.3. *The Effects of the Parent Questionnaire and Early Screening Inventory on the Number of Misclassifications of Infants at Risk of Developmental Problems*

Number of misclassifications:	
Early screening inventory	14/90 (all overreferrals)
Parent questionnaire	22/90 (all but one overreferrals)
Inventory and questionnaire	6/90 (all but one overreferrals)

SOURCE: From L. W. Henderson, "Parental Involvement in the Developmental Screening of Young Children: A Multiple Risk Perspective." Doctoral dissertation. Ann Arbor, MI: University of Michigan, 1992. Quoted in Meisels, "Early Intervention: A Matter of Context," *Zero to Three* 12(3), February 1992. Used with permission.

Some early intervention programs have been designed to compensate for possible problems with cognitive functioning. For instance, in the 1960s there was great enthusiasm for intervention programs aimed at infants born in families designated as economically disadvantaged. However, many of the components of these programs were based on questionable assumptions about development and have not been validated by research. After an extensive review of research related to early intervention programs, Wachs and Gruen (1982) described components of early intervention programs that have been shown to relate to cognitive and social competence in the first and second six months of life.

Wachs and Gruen (1982) concluded that two components are important in facilitating development between birth and six months of age: availability of visual stimulation and high level of physical contact between adult and infant. Visual stimulation seems to give infants something to attend to, and physical contact seems to increase infants' capacity to attend.

Wachs and Gruen also found that after six months of age, development is enhanced by frequent contact with a small number of adults who provide a range of experiences. Wachs and Gruen have said that the optimal low adult–infant ratio is most likely to be found in home-based rather than center-based early intervention programs. According to research reviewed by Wachs and Gruen, the physical environment in the second six months should allow for extensive exploration. It should also include a variety of perceptually stimulating colors, shapes, and textures that can be explored by all the senses and that are responsive to infant actions (e.g., making noises when moved). The work of Wachs and Gruen can help those who design programs to ensure that both physical and social environments are highly responsive to infants' needs and behavior.

Hostler (1991) has stated that the most important factor in planning programs in intervention for the at-risk child is the need to include the family. Improvement in early development for infants should occur in the context of a nurturing and supportive family. This means that professionals must defer to the wishes of the family, but it also means that professionals must work closely with families to communicate the variety of services available, so that families can make the best decisions for their at-risk infants. The purpose of the family-centered approach mandated by Part H of the IDEA is to help families gain a sense of control over their own lives (Dunst, Trivette, & Deal, 1988).

The roles of the parents in this approach include the following:

❑ Supportive caregivers

❑ Primary decision makers about services

❑ Service coordinators of their own children

❑ Service coordinators of other children

❑ Educators

❑ Social policy advocates

The notion of parents as service coordinators is new and was once reserved only for the professional. However, it is possible for parents to take on the role of organizing and identifying services once they have been brought into the process (Berman, 1992). In addition, there is a benefit for the child when an interdisciplinary approach can be used, which incorporates psychology, physical and mental health services, early childhood education, family life education, and social work (Bithoney et al., 1991). A number of states have implemented Part H programs and have begun to collect ideas about the role of these professionals involved in the overall coordination of such programs. The professional job skills and training for the job of Part H coordinators are presented in Developmental Issues in Practice 7.5.

Infant Daycare

In 1988, 56% of children younger than six years had mothers in the labor force (Galinsky, 1990). This number is increasing, and there will be continuing demand for programs to meet the needs of these children. The majority of parents prefer to arrange for child care in their own homes, preferably under the supervision of family members (Hofferth, 1989). Figure 7.2 shows the distribution of changes in child care arrangements for the years 1965–1985. In 1985, family daycare and child care centers combined made up nearly 50% of the settings in which children stayed. For this reason, there has been increasing interest in the impact of such programs on the development of young children, especially infants.

Figure 7.2   *Types of Child Care Arrangements, 1965–1985*

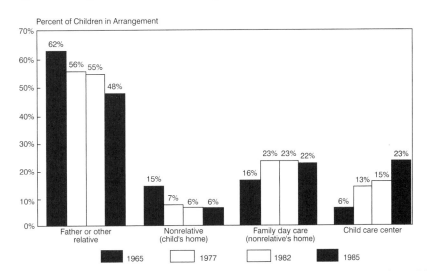

SOURCE: From Sandra L. Hofferth. Public Policy Report. "What Is the Demand for and Supply of Child Care in the United States?" *Young Children, 44* (1989):30. Copyright 1989 by the National Association for the Education of Young Children. Used by permission.

▲ **DEVELOPMENTAL ISSUES IN PRACTICE   7.5**

JOB SKILLS FOR PART H PROGRAM COORDINATORS

Carol P. Berman, Ph.D., of the National Center for Clinical Infant Programs, has discussed the professional job requirements and competencies of those individuals who have coordinated Part H programs (the infant/toddler section) of the IDEA (Individuals with Disabilities Education Act) (Berman, 1992). The coordinators have developed programs for infants and toddlers with disabilities and their families. A survey was disseminated to obtain information on the preparation for these jobs (1992). The majority of the coordinators had master's degrees. They tended to feel that job experience was more important than academic training. However, it was noted that academic backgrounds in early childhood, special needs, or family-centered approaches were helpful because this training helped the professionals to understand the rationale for the program and gave them professional credibility with some constituencies.

The specific skills that helped them meet their work responsibilities include facilitation, communication, negotiation, administration, long-range planning, budget development, grant writing, board and committee management, and policy planning. Personal qualities that coordinators found helpful in their work included flexibility, the ability to defer immediate gratification and set long-term goals, life experience and maturity, sensitivity to the needs of families, leadership, tolerance for the cultures of various disciplines and agencies, and the ability to work within state government.

The coordinators reported a wide range of job features. These included the following: direct contact with the families; planning and implementing research; conducting meetings; maintaining contact with legislative staff, legislators, and governor's staff; supervising personnel; and enjoying extensive opportunities for creativity. Job satisfaction was highest for those coordinators who had the personality characteristics best suited to demanding, creative work, with a high tolerance for job ambiguity and an ability to feel a strong sense of personal accomplishment from the development of a successful program.

SOURCE: From Carol P. Berman, "Part H Coordinators: Stresses, Satisfactions, and Supports." **Zero to Three,** February 1992.

There have been widely differing opinions about the value and/or detriment of child care programs. Belsky and Steinberg (1978) published a review of these differences and concluded that more study was needed to fully understand the implications of child care programs. In 1988, Belsky analyzed the data again and suggested that extensive time spent in daycare could have negative effects on the well-being of the children. In particular, he pointed to evidence of insecure attachment between mother and infant and tendencies for children to develop higher levels of aggression as preschoolers.

Clarke-Stewart (1988) has studied Belsky's analysis and drawn the conclusion that evidence against infant daycare is not strong and conclusive. She points out that maternal factors (including attitude toward the infant, sensitivity, and feelings about working) are more important than whether the child is in infant daycare. She recommends that more research be conducted, looking at these factors.

One other issue of concern is data indicating that children under the age of three in child daycare programs have significantly more respiratory illnesses than children cared for in the home (Wald, Guerra, & Byers, 1991). Such illnesses can have a negative effect on behavior and on speech development. (See further discussion of this issue in Chapter 8.)

Recent research suggests that infant daycare programs do not negatively affect the intellectual development of children and may enhance it in those children who come from economically disadvantaged homes. Burchinal, Lee, and Ramey (1989) found that high-quality daycare programs for disadvantaged infants were related to increases in IQ when the children reached the preschool years. A more extensive analysis (Andersson, 1992) of Swedish schoolchildren at 13 years of age demonstrated that IQ and school functioning were positively affected by daycare but only for those children who started daycare as infants. This is strong support for the value of infant daycare. It is clear, however, that more research is needed to fully answer the questions regarding infant daycare programs.

SUMMARY

1. There is interplay among psychosocial, physical, and cognitive aspects of development.
2. Perceptual abilities are highly developed at birth and appear to be part of genetic inheritance.
3. Newborn babies can focus on objects within 12 inches of their eyes. They can distinguish patterns and human faces and have specific visual preferences.
4. Newborns can recognize size constancy in objects and can discriminate color groupings.
5. Newborn babies show taste preferences for sweetness.
6. Newborn babies can discriminate a wide range of smells and can identify their own mother's breast milk by smell.
7. Newborn infants can hear and orient themselves toward sounds (especially human speech) and are sensitive to rhythm patterns.
8. Habituation is used to study infant sensory abilities.
9. Piaget's stages of sensorimotor development have been verified by studies of synaptogenesis.
10. Object permanence is Piaget's theory describing infants' inability to find hidden objects.
11. Piaget described four substages of sensorimotor cognitive development in the first year of life.
12. Piaget's first substage involves primarily the elaboration of inborn reflexes.

13. Piaget's second substage is called primary circular reactions because it involves repeated actions on the infant's own body.

14. Piaget's third stage is called secondary circular reactions because actions are focused on external objects.

15. Piaget's fourth stage is called coordination of secondary schemes because the infants organize their motor skills to reach goals.

16. Infant intelligence may be made up of a number of components, including inter-model transfer of information, visual information processing, and motor functioning.

17. Visual habituation and rapid visual processing are associated with high levels of intellectual functioning.

18. Active intermodal mapping allows young infants to imitate actions they see others perform.

19. Newborn infants can engage in mutual communication using speech entrainment and vocalizations.

20. Infant language development is characterized by cooing, babbling, and intentional communication.

21. Cultural differences in language with infants are based on the attitudes and values of the culture.

22. Early intervention programs can benefit the cognitive and language development of children.

ACTIVITIES TO ENHANCE LEARNING

The following exercises are designed to help students apply what has been learned and to increase understanding about cognitive development in infants. To complete these exercises, it will be necessary to make observations of infants. If friends or neighbors do not have infants in their families, the following are some possible ways to arrange observations: visit a public place that attracts families, such as a busy store, park, or zoo; request permission to observe at a daycare center or family daycare home. These exercises require the use of observational techniques discussed in Chapter 2. Plan to review the relevant section before beginning the observations.

1. *Narrative Observation*. Write down everything that an infant in the first six months does for a 10-minute period. Repeat the observation at approximately one-hour intervals for three times. (Remember to use descriptive, nonjudgmental language.) Answer the following questions about the infant's behavior:

   a. What are some examples of vocalizations? Write down the number of different sounds the baby can make.

   b. Make a note of the number and kinds of looking behavior the baby engages in. What does the baby look at? How long does the baby look at an object?

   c. What kinds of active attempts at object manipulation does the baby make? At what age is this kind of behavior to be expected?

2. *Vignettes*. Plan a one-hour observation time with an infant who is between 6 and 12 months of age. During this time, watch for examples of imitation. Write down as many patterns (both motor and language) as you observe. Answer the following questions about the infant's behavior:

    a. Is the infant engaging in behavior appropriate for his or her age?

    b. What would you tell the parent about the child's functioning, based on the vignettes recorded?

3. *Child Diaries.* Maintain a daily diary of an infant's speech patterns. Write down the number of sounds and sound combinations the child can make. Describe the caregiver–infant interactions that make use of language.

    a. Make a list of the sounds and sound combinations.

    b. Count the number of sounds.

    c. Describe the language interactions. Did they include motor and gesture patterns?

    d. Note the examples of intentional communication on the part of the infant.

4. *Checklists.* Prepare a developmental checklist for either language or cognitive functioning. Use the information in this chapter to make up the list of behaviors in developmental order. The checklist should be appropriate for the age of the child being observed. Observe the child and use the checklist to assess performance.

    a. Did the child perform as expected based on his or her age?

    b. Is the child functioning at the appropriate developmental level?

5. *Interviews.* Design a questionnaire and use it to interview the parent of an infant about the baby's ability to engage in intentional communication with the other members of the family.

    a. Based on the interview, is the infant's functioning appropriate to his or her age?

    b. At what substage is the infant functioning?

    c. How do the parents interpret the infant's behavior?

    d. Do the parents have a correct perception of the infant's functioning and developmental level?

6. *Time Sampling.* Adapt the recording form given as an example in Chapter 2 (Developmental Issues in Practice 2.6) for either cognitive or language development. Use the recording form to observe an infant in the first year of life. Write a few paragraphs describing what you learned about the baby's functioning.

7. *Event Sampling.* Adapt the recording form given as an example in Chapter 2 (Developmental Issues in Practice 2.7) for either cognitive or language development. Use the recording form to observe an infant during the first year of life. Write a few paragraphs describing what you learned about the baby's functioning.

FOR FURTHER READING

Piaget's Sensorimotor Stage of Development

Piaget, J. (1976). *The psychology of intelligence.* Totowa, NJ: Littlefield, Adams. (See especially Chapter 4).

Uzgiris, I. C., & Hunt, J. McV. (1975). *Assessment in infancy.* Urbana, IL: University of Illinois Press.

Language Development

Garvey, C. (1984). *Children's talk.* Cambridge, MA: Harvard University Press.

Owens, R. E. (1984). *Language development: An introduction.* New York: Merrill/Macmillan.

Curriculum for Infants

Fowler, W. (1980). *Curriculum and assessment guides for infant and child care.* Boston: Allyn & Bacon.

Weiser, M. G. (1991). *Infant/Toddler Care and Education* (2nd ed.). New York: Merrill/Macmillan.

One- to Three-Year-Olds: Energy and Determination Mobilized

At a park on a warm day, two young children venture into the crowded sand area. Melissa, age one, sits in the sand at her father's feet. Her hands are occupied with the sand, but she is looking at the other children. Her gaze darts from child to child as their voices or actions catch her attention. When one of the children falls and cries, she points and vocalizes with a look of concern on her face. However, the single word she uses is unintelligible to everyone except her father, who appears to understand what she is expressing.

Nikolas, age three, finds his friend Robbie, sits beside him, and begins to make a system of roads in the sand for his toy cars. However, Robbie does not collaborate with Nikolas in his play activities. Nikolas directs a steady stream of verbal commentary at Robbie: "Here goes the car. Oh, now I need a bridge. This stick is good. Here we go. . . ." Nikolas does not seem to expect Robbie to respond to what he says.

The sand play of these two children highlights the many changes that occur between one and three years of age, a period often identified as the toddler stage. In the area of physical changes, the stage is marked by the development of confident, independent locomotion. These toddlers are active and need a safe, healthy environment within which they can establish a positive physical image. Concomitant changes in psychosocial development include establishing a sense of autonomy and beginning to have social relationships. In cognitive development, toddlers move through the last of Piaget's substages of sensorimotor thinking and complete the first substage of Piaget's state of preoperational thinking. This period is characterized by rapid language development.

Part III is divided into three chapters, devoted to information about physical, psychosocial, and cognitive development, respectively. Research on the importance of the family and social/cultural variables is stressed throughout, and ideas about applications are included.

Physical development is described in Chapter 8, beginning with a discussion of milestones of physical development. Information is then given on the need for a safe and healthy environment and forming a positive self-image. The chapter concludes with a discussion of the role of the professional in identifying and preventing child abuse.

Psychosocial development is described in Chapter 9, beginning with a discussion of the development of autonomy. This is followed by discussions of emotional development, the importance of play, the influences of the family environment, and the social influences outside the family.

Part III of this book concludes with Chapter 10, which describes cognitive development. The chapter starts with a discussion of Piaget's stages of intellectual development. Other topics include a description of environments that help in developing cognition; language development; and language learning environments.

The period of the toddler is a transition between infancy and the early school years, when the child is physically, socially, and cognitively ready to venture out into the world. This stage normally begins between three and five years of age and is discussed in Part IV.

One- to Three-Year-Olds: Physical Development

This chapter was written with James William Younge, Ed.D., Western Illinois University.

> *Two-year-old Tad sits obediently on the potty in his diaper. When he stands up, his mother hugs him and exclaims, "Good! You sat on the potty in your diaper. Soon you can sit without your diaper. You're getting so grown up!" Tad beams.*
>
> *Several days later after snack and juice, Tad sits on the potty without his diaper. A bit of urine trickles out. Tad's ability to urinate on the potty is indicative of recent changes in his physical development.*

In this chapter, you will read that many of the changes in Tad and other one- to three-year-old children can be explained in terms of milestones of physical development (including large muscle skills, small muscle skills, drawing, perceptual–motor integration, maturation versus experience in physical development, and gender differences). This chapter also gives attention to other topics: the need for a safe environment, the need for a healthy environment, and the formation of a positive physical image. The chapter ends with a discussion of child abuse.

MILESTONES OF PHYSICAL DEVELOPMENT

One- and three-year-old children move very differently from each other. The changes that take place during this stage of development are gradual, and they make possible a wide variety of new activities. The motor milestone that signifies the beginning of toddlerhood is upright locomotion. Walking, accompanied by active manipulation and exploration of the environment, allows toddlers to learn about objects, themselves, and their relationships. Almost all of the basic motor skills emerge by the time the child is four. Therefore, the child is responsive and receptive to instruction in locomotor skills and fundamental skills such as striking, throwing, jumping, and catching. The developmental processes of large muscle skills and small muscle skills are described separately. Norms are adapted from Sanford and Zelman (1981) and White (1990).

Large Muscle Skills

Large muscle skills are the markers that many people use in talking about development. Is Bobby walking yet? At what age did Nina crawl? Is Jane peddling her tricycle? Look at how well Elmo balances!

Large muscle skills include **dynamic balance,** which is used in walking, running, and climbing; **static balance,** which enables a child to stand on one foot; **projecting,** the skill used in jumping and hopping; and throwing and catching. This section describes the changes taking place from one to three years of age by presenting the story of a hypothetical child, Joe. Average ages are used, but remember that the range of normal development is wide. For instance, Joe is said to take his first shaky independent steps at one year of age, the average. However, the range of ages at which most normal children walk extends all the way from 9 months to 17 months and beyond. Each child has his or her own timetable, which may well differ from Joe's.

One to two years.   Joe begins walking just weeks after his first birthday. These early attempts consist of only a few steps before he plops himself down again. But he practices his new skill often, sometimes clapping for himself afterward. Soon, walking replaces crawling as his primary way of moving from place to place. As he becomes steadier, he is confident enough to try to pull a duck on a string and to push a toy vacuum cleaner. Joe learns to squat, play for a while, and then return to standing. Later he is able to bend from the waist to pick up a toy. He can get from a sitting position to a standing position easily also. By his second birthday, Joe can walk on a line in the general direction indicated, and he prefers running to walking.

Joe's grandparents have stairs in their home, and Joe learns first to creep upstairs and then to walk upstairs with help. Going downstairs remains challenging and he continues to creep down, feet first. He has a rocking chair, which he likes very much and learns to use. He has no trouble climbing into adult chairs to sit down and manages small chairs well, too.

One of his favorite games is "roll the ball." Played on the floor, the game consists of rolling a ball from one person to another. Joe does not always aim accurately, but he is able to participate enthusiastically. Joe also enjoys making movements to music such as clapping and marching.

Two to three years.   Watching Joe in active play, his father notes that he seems to enjoy large muscle activities for their own sake and not just as a means of reaching some goal. His climbing improves. One day his mother hears a small voice calling, "Help!" and finds Joe on top of the refrigerator!

Joe can jump in place, using both feet, and he learns to kick a large stationary ball. He walks backward and seems amused by the changed perspective that he gets. After several attempts, he begins to walk downstairs with help. When Joe throws a ball, he brings the ball back behind his head and steps and throws using the same side of the body. He will use a straight leg action when he attempts to kick a ball. Joe catches a ball by trapping it against his chest with his arms. With his brother's encouragement and help, he masters a forward somersault. His balance improves, and he is able to stand on one foot briefly and he will side-step or shuffle-step forward on a balance beam. He receives a pounding toy from a friend and is able to ham-

Two- and three-year-olds are able to demonstrate many self-help skills, such as washing hands before meals.

mer in all five pegs. He likes the activity itself and is the only one who seems to tolerate the noise.

Three to four years.   Joe begins walking upstairs using alternating feet on subsequent steps. Joe has become interested in much of the equipment at the local park. He can swing if someone gets him started, and he climbs up and slides down the six-foot slide, if given assistance. He executes these feats over and over again during his visits.

When Joe runs, his legs and arms are well coordinated and his arm movements alternate. He can walk on tiptoes and now does not need his brother's help in doing a forward somersault. He marches in parades that he organizes, with either real or imaginary friends. Joe has learned to ride a tricycle and likes to go with an adult for excursions on it around the neighborhood. He can kick a ball by bending the leg at the knee. Joe's throwing has improved. He now steps using the arm opposite to the one he uses to throw. He can now catch the ball by bringing it into his chest with his hands. Joe's balance has also improved—he can now walk on a beam using alternate foot stepping.

Motor skills are emerging in Joe during early childhood. This happens through the natural process of maturation. Without the proper learning experiences and opportunities for practice, Joe may develop inefficient movement patterns, which will delay or prevent his refining the basic skills into game and sport skills. It is very important that, as their motor skills emerge and develop, children receive proper instruction and ample practice opportunities for each of the fundamental skills. See Developmental Issues in Practice 8.1 for a description of one program that provides such instruction.

Small Muscle Skills

Changes in **small muscle skills** are usually not accompanied by as much adult fanfare as are changes in large muscle skills, but the development in small muscle skills in these early years is nevertheless impressive. This development is in the proximo-distal direction. This term means that the parts of the body closest to the center become capable of differentiated movement first, and those parts farthest from the center are differentiated last. For example, the child first controls movement of the shoulder, followed by movement of the elbow, the wrist, and finally the fingers. To show how these skills change over time, a fictitious child, Amy, has been created from a cross-section of actual children. The account of Amy's development is followed by presentation of typical stages of a particular small muscle skill, drawing.

One to two years.   As might be expected at a time when Amy is developing a sense of autonomy, many of Amy's new small muscle skills are applied to achieving increased independence. She learns to use a spoon to feed herself at the table, and she drinks from a cup using one hand. She helps with getting herself dressed, putting on her own hat and taking it off repeatedly. In fact, undressing is really her forte at this point. She pulls off her socks easily and also her shoes, pants, and coat.

At the daycare center, Amy shows an interest in the pegboards and is able to take out and put in the one-inch pegs. She builds a tower of three blocks and then pushes it over to watch it fall. She uses crayons and marking pens on paper, often making dots or circular motions.

Two to three years.   During Amy's third year, her ability to manipulate utensils and clothing allows her to be increasingly independent. She scoops her food with a fork, learns to drink her milk with a straw, and pours her milk from a small pitcher into her glass. (She usually drinks more when thus in control of the quantity that she receives.) After meals, Amy wipes her own hands and face. She begins to put on her own socks, pants, and shirts but requests help if she has trouble. One morning her father hears a muffled, "Stuck! Stuck!" and finds her all tangled up in her shirt.

At the daycare center, Amy strings together four or sometimes more large beads. Her block towers now have as many as six blocks piled on before she pushes them over. She is able to turn the pages in a book one at a time with care, and practices this skill. Amy figures out how to turn doorknobs and handles, which gives her access to parts of the daycare center and her home that previously required adult assistance to enter.

▲ **DEVELOPMENTAL ISSUES IN PRACTICE   8.1**

FACILITATING PERCEPTUAL–MOTOR TRAINING

Walking and running are the most common large muscle activities, and games can be devised to help young children bring these activities under perceptual control. For instance, a young child can be asked to walk to the bed and stop when she reaches it. Perceptual information is provided for her to determine when to stop; but, if she does not use the perceptual information, the bed itself stops her. Playing tag games with a base requires the same perceptual–motor relationship as did stopping at reaching the bed, but tag games offer the additional excitement and distraction of being chased by the person who is "it."

At the next level of perceptual–motor training, children can be asked to control walking and running by perceptual information alone. A child can be asked to walk up to a line but to stop before stepping over it. The line is a perceptual element rather than a concrete object, such as a bed. In a tag game, the base could be marked with chalk on the ground.

At a more complex level of large muscle perceptual–motor training, children use perceptual information to give continuous control to an activity. Children can be asked to walk along an alley, which has been formed with two parallel chalk marks on the ground. The width of the alley can be modified to suit the coordination of each child, and eventually children can be asked to walk along a line without stepping off.

Jumping is another total body activity that can be used for perceptual motor training. Children can be asked to jump down from and then up onto a step, into and out of a circle drawn on the ground, and over a rope on the ground.

Arm and hand activities occupy a middle position between these total body activities and later classroom activities that require precise coordination between eye and hand. The most common arm and hand activities involve throwing balls or beanbags toward targets. The targets provide the perceptual information that governs the direction of the throw; accordingly, the targets should be moved to various heights and to a number of different positions relative to the child. Children should have opportunities to throw objects of various sizes with their right and left hands and with both hands together. In related arm and hand activities, children can roll balls to targets, push carts along alleys or lines, and hit a suspended ball with their hands or bats.

From N. C. Kephart, *The Slow Learner in the Classroom* (2nd ed.), pp. 234–241. Columbus, OH: Merrill, 1971. Adapted by permission.

Three to four years.   By this time, Amy is able to feed herself a whole meal with minimal assistance. She still needs to have help cutting up meat at meal times. She also dresses herself, requiring help mainly with pullover shirts and some fasteners. She brushes her teeth by herself, although her father makes sure that he also has a turn once a day, and she combs and brushes her own hair.

Amy develops an interest in puzzles and learns how to do those with three and four pieces. She uses a variety of art materials and is able to manage a pencil well enough to trace around objects. She builds complex structures with a snap-together construction set and learns to unscrew a set of nesting toys. Amy rolls play dough into balls and sausage shapes and seems to gain satisfaction from the pounding and shaping. Clearly, Amy has gained a great deal of control over her small muscles in the past three years.

Drawing

No one needs to teach one-year-olds to draw. Part of their play with crayons is to make marks—usually dots and lines at first. Gradually their drawings change, and researchers have shown that the changes follow a regular progression. Chappell and Steitz (1993) have demonstrated that young children's level of drawing human figures changes with increases in cognitive development. Thus, changes in children's drawings are of interest because they reflect changes in cognitive development.

Rhoda Kellogg (1969) attracted widespread attention to the drawings of young children. In her research she collected thousands of children's drawings from all over the world. She decided that children's drawings are composed of 20 types of forms, such as dots, vertical lines, horizontal lines, diagonal lines, curved lines, circles, crosses, and so on. Kellogg's work is well known and has generated great interest, but other researchers (Brittain, 1979; Lansing, 1970) have failed to find in children's drawings the 20 basic forms in the elaborate sequence of development that Kellogg described. This section presents instead a developmental sequence explained by Brittain (1979).

Brittain's system divides very early drawings into two levels: random scribbling and controlled scribbling (see Figure 8.1). The research that provides the basis for the system of classifying children's drawings has been conducted over a period of years at Cornell University.

Random scribbling.   Brittain has said that **random scribbling** is not really random, but it looks that way to adults. As early as one year of age and continuing until two or two and a half years of age, children make definite dots and lines with simple, whole-arm movements. The swing of the arm determines line length, and arm movements propel the crayon in arcs across the piece of paper. Over time, there is a gradual increase in movement of the wrist, which leads to more curves and loops in the drawings. The crayon is gripped tightly either in the fingers or with the entire hand, like a hammer. The child may look away from the drawing but often watches the movement of the crayon with interest. The process brings pleasure; often the drawing itself is of less interest than the fun of creating it. The drawing provides a visible record of motor coordination and shows that the foundations are being laid for more complex drawing and writing.

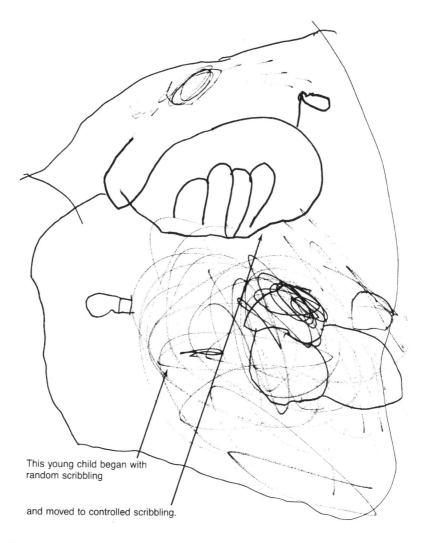

This young child began with random scribbling

and moved to controlled scribbling.

Figure 8.1 *Scribbling in Toddlers*

Controlled scribbling.   Brittain has described **controlled scribbling** as lasting for a bit more than a year perhaps from when children are 30 months until they are nearly four years of age. The finished drawings may resemble those completed earlier, but the process has changed. Children now consistently watch the movement of the crayon carefully as they form a scribble. They seem to have visual control over the crayon and produce a more intricate pattern of loops and swirls. The wrist is more flexible than it was earlier, and crayons are held in a fashion closer to the usual adult grip. In their scribbling, young children practice making basic shapes and lines that are necessary for later drawing and writing. By age three, children spend twice as long on their drawings as they did at age two—an average of two minutes. Some children begin making open and closed figures with attempts at representing objects and people. Most children show interest and stirrings of pleasure and pride as they survey their completed drawings. "See what I made!" is a common exclamation.

Sometimes adults are tempted to hurry children along from scribbling to representational drawing. However, Whitener and Kersey (1980) have asserted that scribbling is to writing as babbling is to talking. These commentators believe that trying to teach young children to draw before they have moved naturally through the scribbling stage is just as inappropriate as it would be to require infants to talk before they babble.

Copying geometric shapes is a task that often appears on developmental inventories and intelligence tests for young children. Usually three-year-olds are expected to be able to copy circles. The circle is the first shape children master because it is conceptually the simplest to draw. Drawings appear to be controlled by cognitive processes that determine the kinds of mistakes that children will make. It has long been recognized that children make specific, systematic errors, which decrease with age (Piaget & Inhelder, 1956; Werner, 1957). For example, children tend to draw chimneys rising at an angle from the roof because chimneys are perpendicular to the sloping roof, not to the ground. The presence of these systematic errors suggests that drawing shapes is controlled more by cognitive and intellectual factors than by motor factors. These systematic changes will be discussed in Chapter 11.

Perceptual—Motor Integration

At a library story hour, three-year-old Bud is learning a simplified version of the "Simon Says" game. The children's librarian waves her hand and asks the children to imitate her, but Bud does not respond with a hand wave. Bud understands the game but cannot yet move his body appropriately.

Bud's difficulty is in the realm of **perceptual–motor integration.** What this means is that Bud can visually perceive what the librarian is doing, but he cannot process that perception and integrate it with the appropriate motor response of giving his own hand wave in return. At Bud's age, this difficulty is not unexpected, and adults can plan a variety of experiences and activities to develop a basis for perceptual–motor integration. Developmental Issues in Practice 8.2 provides some examples of ways that perceptual–motor integration can be encouraged. Note the wide range of behaviors that are dependent on this integration, thus emphasizing its importance.

Perceptual–motor integration will be very important to Bud's effective functioning in the future. Perception through visual, auditory, and tactile-kinesthetic modalities provides the information upon which behavior is based. Motor responses lead to movement, which is the visible aspect of behavior. If Bud's perceptions and his motor responses are not integrated, there is little connection between information and behavior. For example, imagine a communication between Bud and his mother about a household task. His mother gives a detailed explanation about what is to be done, and

Children imitate their teacher in an exercise of perceptual–motor integration.

Bud indicates his understanding. But if Bud does not follow through on the task, the reason may be that he has an isolated body of perceptual information (the explanation) with no appreciation of how to translate this information into action.

Perceptual–motor development provides a link between children's perceptual functions and motor functions. Newell C. Kephart (1971) is most frequently associated with demonstrating the importance of this type of development. To pick up a cup, for example, the child must coordinate the view of the cup with the ability to reach for it. The hand must be aimed in the right direction and must reach far enough to contact the cup without knocking it over. Perceptual–motor development is obviously a critical skill for most environmental interactions.

Gallahue (1989) has emphasized two additional areas of perceptual awareness: **temporal** and **spatial**. **Temporal perceptual awareness** involves the development of adequate time structures in which to move the body. Rhythm is crucial in the performance of any act in a coordinated manner. Rhythm refers to the ability to change and control the pattern of movements, as in dancing, where there are slow and fast steps. Walking, for example, involves the intri-

▲ **DEVELOPMENTAL ISSUES IN PRACTICE   8.2**

SKILL ACQUISITION

Young children value motor skills and the opportunity to practice them. Practice can be perceived as fun playtime if activities are selected that will guarantee multiple successes and foster positive feelings about fundamental movement. Carson (1992) has summarized developmental characteristics and appropriate activities in an educational video designed for parents and teachers of preschool children. Here are some suggestions for making motor activities appropriate for young children:

Throwing, striking, and kicking activities should utilize large oversized targets, and emphasis on accuracy should be minimized.

Catching activities should utilize large, colorful, soft-textured balls.

Jumping activities should emphasize variations of big jumps, whether vertically, horizontally, or up and over.

Balance can be practiced on planks of wood, called balance beams, which vary in width of wood, height from the floor, and angle of incline.

In this approach, parents and teachers assume an important role as play partners by encouraging and modeling proper motor skills. When properly managed, they will lay the foundation for specialized skill development, positive self-concept, and pleasant feelings toward activity.

SOURCE: Adapted by permission from by Linda M. Carson, *KinderSkills.* Morgantown, WV: PlaySkills Video, 1992. Copyright 1992 by Linda M. Carson.

cate rhythm pattern of ordering the movement of arms and legs. Moving to various forms of music can be an important contributor to temporal awareness. Temporal awareness also refers to eye–hand and eye–foot coordination. This involves the coordination of various muscle and sensory systems, which form the basis of the movements needed for playing sports and dancing.

Spatial perceptual awareness involves the knowledge of how much space the body occupies (personal) and the ability to project the body effectively into external space (general). Young children tend to egocentrically locate everything in external space relative to themselves. They need to develop an objective frame of reference in which they can have a third-person image of themselves moving about in a given space. Appropriate movement experiences designed for them to learn about their bodies and how they move in personal and general space are essential during early childhood.

Sensorimotor development begins with large muscle activities in which children's whole bodies or major parts of their bodies are controlled in terms of perceptual information. This plays an important role in developing and refining the child's movement abilities. Ball texture is important to consider

Spatial awareness includes the knowledge of the amount of space the body occupies. Children delight in fitting themselves into containers.

in catching and kicking. Foam, fleece, or soft rubber will have a more positive effect on the child's level of skill and success than hard rubber or tightly inflated balls. Color and size of the object will have an impact on the skill being performed. For example, to facilitate the development of catching, begin with large, lightweight, brightly colored balls and gradually reduce the ball size (Gallahue, 1989). Young children also begin to learn to intercept objects, as in playing tag. As they mature they will be able to judge the future location of the moving object and move their bodies to meet it (Cratty, 1986).

Maturation versus Experience in Physical Development

A Sunday school teacher asked her group of three-year-olds to cut out a circular shape. Debbie handled the task easily, but Marcia did not know how to put her fingers into the holes of the scissors. The teacher cut out the circle for Marcia and remarked to her teenaged assistant, "There are big differences in maturity at this age."

The teacher was correct in saying that there are maturational variations in physical development in these early years. But her remark did not take into account the important role of experience in a skill such as cutting. Here is an account of the experiences with scissors that three-year-old Debbie had with her mother in the month before that Sunday school class:

One day Debbie's mother, Mary, was cutting coupons from the newspaper when Debbie reached for the scissors and tried to stick her chunky fingers into the holes as she had seen her mother do. "So you want to cut?" Mary asked.

Debbie nodded, and Mary went to get some safer scissors from a drawer in the kitchen. Mary patiently showed Debbie how to put her fingers in the holes, and she guided Debbie's hand in snipping through thin strips of paper. Debbie felt very proud when she snipped all by herself.

Mastery of skills such as cutting with scissors requires a combination of maturation and experience.

During the next weeks, Debbie practiced cutting. When she was consistently successful in snipping thin strips of paper, her mother gave her a series of increasingly challenging cutting tasks, by designing a sequence of appropriate learning experiences for her. Debbie began with snipping, a task with which she could feel successful from the start. Only gradually did she move from snipping to cutting out shapes.

In contrast to Debbie, Marcia had never held scissors until that day at Sunday school. Rather than giving instructions, the teacher completed the task for her.

The scissor example can easily be related to other motor skills such as throwing or striking. Without adequate opportunities for proper instruction and practice of the skill, the child may not develop to his or her fullest potential and find it difficult to learn complex skills required for games and sport activities.

The experiences that young children have with parents and other adults vary widely. What a child can do with large or small muscles depends on the experiences that the child has had as well as on the level of development that she has reached. If Marcia's teacher had tried to give Marcia instruction in using scissors, the teacher might have found that Marcia could eventually be as successful as Debbie. On the other hand, she might have found that Marcia needed a foundation of more activities that involved her whole body before she could be successful in using the small muscles in her hands for manipulating scissors. Sequential instruction in learning physical skills is not appropriate if children have not had the foundation of prerequisite activities; and children will not necessarily succeed in physical skills, even if adequate foundations have been built, unless they are given sequential instructions at their level of understanding. Both maturation and experience are important in physical development.

Gender Differences

Comments such as the following can be heard when parents of young children gather:

It'll take longer to potty-train Greg than it did Stephie.

Little girls cut better than little boys.

Are these comments examples of gender stereotyping? Not entirely; they do have some basis in fact. In the early childhood years, girls tend to develop more rapidly and be more advanced than boys in exhibiting certain behaviors (Ames, Gillespie, Haines, & Ilg, 1979). Not every girl will be more advanced than any boy at a given age, but when the abilities of girls are averaged and compared with the boys' average, the girls tend to be more advanced at the same age.

What explains differences in physical abilities between girls and boys? Some researchers find the cause in the different expectations that parents have for their daughters and sons. Other researchers believe that the cause lies totally in the faster maturation of girls. Present evidence is insufficient to offer a definitive explanation, but it seems unlikely that parental expectations alone explain why girls walk earlier, hop on one foot sooner, cut with scissors earlier, and copy *V* and *H* strokes sooner than boys (Ames et al., 1979). In many large and small muscle activities, girls are as much as six months ahead of boys, on average. This difference needs to be taken into account by parents, educators, health workers, and others who are in contact with young children and their families.

THE NEED FOR A SAFE ENVIRONMENT

Accidents are the leading cause of death for children between one and four years of age (U.S. Bureau of Census, 1982). See Table 8.1 for data on leading causes of death. This section discusses prevention of injury at home and in automobiles and the prevention of poisoning, burns, and drowning.

Young children are accident prone because of four factors. First, these children are now mobile: they can walk, climb, and reach many objects that were not accessible earlier. Second, their small muscle development allows them to grasp and open containers that they previously could not have explored. Third, they are curious, persistent, and eager to gather information through all of their senses. Many interesting things go into their mouths, despite taste or appearance. Fourth, they lack the experience and ability to predict dangerous outcomes of situations. It is no wonder, then, that the possible risks for young children are staggering.

Some accidents, like the one that led to the loss suffered by Mr. and Mrs. J. G. (see Developmental Issues in Practice 8.3), are particularly distressing because they can be prevented. There is no substitute for careful supervision of young children during all of their waking hours. The probability of many acci-

Table 8.1. *Leading Causes of Death in Toddlers Aged One to Four Years*

Causes of death	Deaths per 100,000 population
All causes	69.2
Accidents	28.8
Congenital anomalies	8.4
Malignant neoplasms	4.9
Influenza or pneumonia	2.9

SOURCE: From U.S. Bureau of the Census, *Characteristics of American Children and Youth: 1980*, p. 8. Washington, DC: U.S. Government Printing Office, 1982. Used with permission.

▲ **DEVELOPMENTAL ISSUES IN PRACTICE   8.3**

DEAR ABBY: PREVENTING DROWNING

In a poignant letter to Dear Abby (Van Buren, 1982), Mr. and Mrs. J. G. reported the drowning of their young daughter in the toilet bowl of her grandparents' home. Mr. and Mrs. J. G. had done many things to safeguard their daughter's life but did not imagine that a common household fixture could endanger her. The child toddled off during a visit and was found face down in the toilet bowl. Attempts to revive her failed.

dents, however, can be reduced by taking action to prevent injury in homes and automobiles and to prevent poisoning, burns, and drowning. When considering child safety, it is important to think in terms of the things that families can do to prevent death and other physical problems rather than to think that injuries occur only from accidents that are not under our control.

Preventing Injury at Home

It helps to think about the physical development of toddlers when examining some of the kinds of problems that can occur in the home. Toddlers have a large head, short arms, and unstable legs. The very term *toddler* defines their movements, which are wobbly because they are "top heavy." They have a high **center of gravity,** which means that the point in their body at which there is equally as much mass above as below is very high, unlike in adults. Adults can bend over a railing to look to the ground, but toddlers do not have enough body mass in the lower part of their body to do this without falling. If they can see over the edge, they are unbalanced enough to fall. Consequently, it is essential that temptations such as dangerous railings do not exist in the child's home. Windows must be closed at all times or be fitted with protective screens. Protective screens and gates must be put on all balconies, stairs, and porches.

In addition, having short arms makes it very difficult to push the body out once the infant has fallen into something. The toilet and bathtub, therefore, are particularly dangerous because the child can fall in while having no strength to push themselves out once they become unbalanced (this is the reason for the problem described in Developmental Issues in Practice 8.3). Toilet seat covers should be kept down to limit curiosity. Bathrooms should be off limits to young children, unless parents are with them. It is possible to buy fittings to attach to doorknobs to make them difficult to open for small hands. It is important for parents to provide opportunities for exploration that are safe for toddlers. Developmental Issues in Practice 8.4 provides an example of such controlled exploration.

Preventing Injury in Automobiles

Of all the types of accidents, those in automobiles affect the most children. Over one-third of all accidental deaths among one- to four-year-old children take place in automobiles (U.S. Bureau of Census, 1982), and many other children sustain serious injuries each year. Safety experts assert that a high percentage of these deaths and injuries could be prevented if children were put into approved safety restraints during each car ride. The evidence concerning benefits to children of the use of automobile safety systems has convinced some states to pass legislation requiring that children younger than four years of age or lighter than 40 pounds be placed in them.

For children between one and four years of age, three kinds of safety restraints are recommended by the U.S. Department of Transportation, National Highway Traffic Safety Administration (1980). The three recommended systems are child safety seats, protective shields, and safety harnesses. These systems are illustrated in Figure 8.2.

Child safety seats are designed for young children who are able to sit up without support. This type of seat faces forward and uses an automobile seat belt as well as a special safety harness. The harness redistributes the force of a crash over the child's shoulders and hips and protects the child's abdomen from receiving too much pressure. Some child safety seats also require the use of a top tether that attaches to the frame of the car.

Protective shields fit in front of children's laps and chests to cushion them in accidents. A shield is held in place with the automobile seat belt and has energy-absorbing padding as part of the design. Shields spread the force of collisions or sudden stops evenly over children's heads and upper bodies.

Child harness systems are designed to be worn when children sit normally, preferably in the center of the rear seat of the automobile. The harness is attached to an automobile lap belt and a top tether strap. In an accident, the child harness system redistributes the impact in a manner similar to that of the child safety seat.

A 1980 federal law requires that children's automobile safety restraints meet specified standards of strength and performance. The key problem, though, is in educating parents and other adults to put children in these devices.

Preventing Poisoning

The temptation is strong for young children to explore new things with their mouths. Even substances with bad tastes, smells, or appearances are ingested by children in dangerous amounts before unpleasant sensations seem to register. In addition to carefully supervising young children, adults must take precautionary measures in each household and child care facility where young children spend time.

The most important precaution against poisoning is the removal of all dangerous substances from children's reach. Medicines should be placed in a

▲ **DEVELOPMENTAL ISSUES IN PRACTICE 8.4**

CONTROLLED EXPLORATION

One of the givens in working with one- to three-year-old children is that they investigate every inch of their environments, even those areas or objects that have been placed off limits. They empty drawers, drop all the tissues down the stairs, play "sink and float" in the bathtub with their toys, climb up cabinets to look at fragile figurines, and so on. This persistent curiosity sometimes overwhelms parents into saying no automatically whenever children move toward something that is not designated as a toy. But frequently saying no reduces the learning potential of the home and robs parents and children of some of the fun that they could be having. The middle ground between saying no to everything and allowing exploration of absolutely anything involves establishing children's interest areas in the parts of the home where adults and children spend the most time.

In two-year-old Al's apartment, the kitchen tends to be the hub of activity during much of the day. Al is allowed free exploration of the cabinet that holds canned foods. Note Al's activity with the cans:

> Al leans far into the kitchen cabinet and pulls out the remaining several cans. The floor around him is strewn with soup, vegetable, fruit, and sauce cans of assorted sizes and shapes. When he has systematically emptied the cabinet, Al turns his attention to making a tower of cans, putting the largest at the base.

The cans are as good as any expensive, commercially available set of cylinders for stacking, comparing sizes and shapes, and sorting by color, size, or shape. And the cans allow Al to relate the pictures (and later the words) on the labels to his own food experiences. Al is also given access to another cabinet with muffin tins, cookie sheets, plastic containers, and empty oatmeal, margarine, yogurt, and other interesting cartons. All other cabinets have been closed off to Al by the installation of special childproof latches. Al seems to relish the availability of a variety of objects that parallel those that he sees his mother and grandmother use.

---

locked cabinet, cleaning products should be moved from under the sink to a high shelf or locked cabinet, cosmetics and personal products should be placed out of the reach of curious youngsters, and garage and workshop items should be placed in locked cupboards or cabinets. Indoor and outdoor plants should be checked for toxicity. Even very young children should be taught that they should not eat anything, whether indoors or out, that has not been approved by an adult.

A related precaution involves adjustments in the context in which medication is given and taken. Adults should never talk about medicine as candy or as a magic product. They should, instead, be matter-of-fact about the necessity for taking medicine when it is prescribed, talk with children about taking medicine only from certain people, and tell children that taking too

Figure 8.2 *Approved Automobile Safety Systems for One- to Four-Year-Olds*

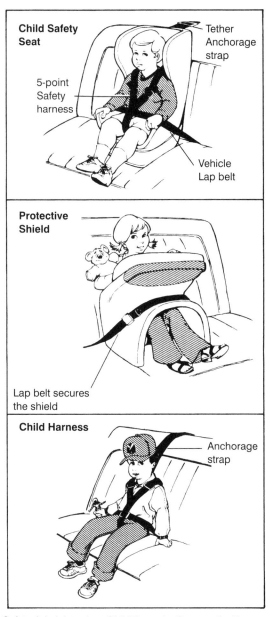

SOURCE: From National Highway Traffic Safety Administration, *Child Restraint Systems for Your Automobile.* Washington, DC: U.S. Department of Transportation, 1980. Used with permission.

much medicine can make them as sick as not taking it when needed. Adults should also be careful of the example that they set and should try to avoid taking medications in the presence of young children.

Children who have been poisoned show changes in behavior, stains or burns near the mouth, vomiting and stomach pains, unconsciousness, drowsiness, convulsions, and/or rapid breathing. Adults who suspect that their child has been poisoned should try to identify the poison and call a poison control center, hospital, doctor, or paramedic unit. If instructed to take the child to a hospital, an adult should bring the suspected poison.

Preventing Burns

Children can be protected from most of the major causes of burns if adults adjust the environment. One important adjustment involves keeping matches and lighters out of children's reach at all times. Another adjustment involves turning the handles of pots and pans so that they do not extend over the edge of the stove; also, one should be sure that children are not under foot when hot substances are being moved from one part of the kitchen to another. Similar adjustments involve safety with electricity, fire, and hot water. Special caps should be placed on unused electrical outlets, cords on appliances should not be left dangling, and children should be kept away from heaters, fireplace inserts, and fireplaces. The temperature of hot water should be set as low as is feasible for the household, and adults should test bath water before children enter it.

Preventing Drowning

Young children have drowned in bathtubs, pails, wading pools, and other small containers of liquid, as well as in swimming pools, rivers, lakes, and other large bodies of water. The key precaution in preventing drowning is to supervise children around any quantity of water. The supervision must be continual: there is no time off for phone calls or other distractions. Children are attracted to water, and it takes only moments for drowning to occur. It is important to follow safety precautions for safeguarding home swimming pools. It is possible to purchase life preservers for infants, and these should be worn at all times when in boats. They can also be used for other family outings around water. Even when parents are present, boating accidents can hinder parents' ability to help their children.

THE NEED FOR A HEALTHY ENVIRONMENT

If children do not feel well, their psychosocial, physical, and cognitive development may be impaired. A healthy environment is one of the most basic needs that young children have. This section considers the following topics: the relationship between health and behavior; physical growth and food intake patterns; the relationship between nutrition and development; and the maintenance of health.

Health and Behavior

Research has demonstrated the close link between health problems in the early years and developmental and behavioral disorders. Two perspectives on this link are presented here. First, a study (Bax, 1981) conducted in two inner-city areas in London showed that children who have frequent infections are more likely than other children to have developmental and behavioral problems. Second, research (Will, 1983) conducted in the United States pointed out the relationship between lead poisoning in young children and behavior and learning problems.

Infections and behavior.   Young children have various kinds of infections, the most common of which include those of the upper respiratory tract (e.g., colds and sore throats), lower respiratory tract (e.g., bronchitis and croup), and ear (e.g., otitis media). Of these infections, young children are more susceptible than are older children or adults to problems with the part of the ear behind the eardrum. It is estimated that one in three visits to doctors by children under six years of age results in a diagnosis of infection of the middle ear (Bax, 1981). Pediatricians explain that young children's eustachian tubes are smaller and at a different angle than will be the case later. Secretions from the nose and throat can back up into the middle ear and cause pressure if the eustachian tube becomes blocked. Ear infections are usually treated with antibiotics. If left untreated, or if prescribed dosages of antibiotics are not taken, these infections can lead to more serious medical problems, hearing loss, and language delays.

In studying two-year-old children, Bax (1981) found a significant relationship between ear infections during the previous six months and delayed language. In the same study, children with speech problems at two, three, and four and a half years of age showed a disproportionate number of behavior problems. Researchers hypothesized that the interactions among chronic ear infections, speech delays, and behavior problems begin with a temporary mild hearing loss due to an ear infection. The hearing loss in turn leads to a delay in speech development of six months to one year. The behavior problems then stem either from the pain and discomfort of the illness or from children's frustration over their difficulties in hearing and speaking. Bax (1981) also discovered that young children with frequent colds were more likely to be described by parents as difficult to manage and were more likely to have frequent temper tantrums. Children with a history of ear infections had a significantly greater tendency than other children toward persistent night waking long after infections have subsided.

In Great Britain, a 36-year longitudinal study was done of more than 5,000 people identified as chronically ill as children. By 36 years of age, those in the lower socioeconomic group showed poorer life outcomes than did controls (Pless, Cripps, Davies, & Wadsworth, 1989). Neumann, McDonald, Sigman, and Bwibo (1992) found that frequency of mild illness was associated with poorer school performance among African children. In addition, those with frequent mild illness were more likely than the healthy children to have lower developmental levels and lower cognitive performance and were less happy, active, and social in peer group settings.

These findings indicate that physical illness can be closely related to delayed development and behavior problems. Regular pediatric examinations and treatment lower the rates of speech and language delay and of behavior problems. Yet, according to researchers, only half of the young children in the United States are under medical supervision of any kind (Bax, 1981).

Lead poisoning and behavior.   George F. Will (1983) has pointed out that the synonym for *leaden* is *dull*. Lead poisoning in children can cause learning problems, retardation, brain damage, anemia, seizures, hyperactivity, and death (Wasserman et al., 1992; Will, 1983).

The most dangerous source of lead for young children is paint. Structures built before 1950 may have some coats of lead-based paint, which tastes sweet to children. Even a flake of paint the size of a fingernail can be dangerous; therefore, many cities have programs to detect and remove lead-based paint from older buildings.

A second major source of lead poisoning is gasoline. The average level of lead in children's blood has declined 25% since the inception of restrictions on lead in gasoline (Will, 1983).

Young children are particularly susceptible to lead poisoning because of their high metabolic rates. Not all children, however, are at equal risk of lead poisoning. Poor children are more likely than others to be deficient in iron, calcium, and zinc; these deficiencies predispose them to absorb lead. Inner-city dwellers are apt to live in older buildings that were painted with lead-based paint and to breathe air into which lead from gasoline has been emitted. Studies have indicated that there are excessive lead levels in the blood of one-fifth of African American children from low-income families; six times as many African American preschoolers as white preschoolers have excessive lead levels. Will (1983) has estimated that the government spends more than $1 billion yearly on children with lead poisoning, 80% of which goes to support special education programs for those with learning disabilities. Lead poisoning affects behavior and learning capacity and has a high cost in terms of human resources.

Physical Growth and Food Intake Patterns

Physical growth tapers off in the second year of life. At this time, children gain only about 3.5–4.5 kilograms; after that, weight gain is reduced still further, to 1.8–2.2 kilograms per year (Pipes, 1981). Children grow taller but without the increases in weight that characterized the first year of life. Children lose their roundness, and their bodies and limbs seem to stretch out.

Children obviously cannot continue to double their body weights within a span of months, as infants do, or they would become giants. Even so, many parents worry about declines in their children's appetites and food consumption. The decreased growth rate of this period and the struggle for autonomy combine to make negativism and confrontations over food intake almost

Small first servings are appropriate at meals, because children's rate of growth tapers off and their appetites decline.

inevitable. It is helpful for children to be presented with amounts of food that are appropriate to their age. It is a good idea to use the following formula: portions of meat, grains, fruits, or vegetables should equal one tablespoon per year of age (Whitney & Rolfes, 1993). Thus, in a given meal, a two-year-old child should receive approximately two to four tablespoons of fruits and vegetables, one to two ounces of meat, half a slice of bread, and one-half to three-quarters of a cup of milk.

Children's appetites are unpredictable in these early childhood years, and their likes and dislikes can change from one day to the next. For a week, Heather might eat only peanut butter sandwiches, but after that she might refuse to eat peanut butter at all. Matthew eats with apparent hunger at one meal but skips the next entirely.

The evening meal is usually the one in which young children are least interested. Nutrition experts (Pipes, 1981) believe that some children may meet their energy and nutrient requirements by consumption of only two meals and snacks. An alternative explanation for problems with the evening meal is that children are overstimulated by the social interaction that often accompanies it. If children feel that they cannot both eat and interact, they may choose to interact. Some modification of the social atmosphere at the evening meal may improve young children's food intake.

Young children often prefer foods that are high in carbohydrates because they are easiest to chew. Bread, crackers, and cereal may be preferred over meat and other foods that are high in protein. Children can be offered chicken, ground meat, cheese, and yogurt as easily chewed sources of protein if steaks, roasts, and other fibrous meats are refused. Children like raw vegetables better than cooked ones; warm food rather than hot; mild flavors; and smooth foods (Whitney & Rolfes, 1993).

Children may stop eating when their energy needs are met, even if needed nutrients have not been received (Pipes, 1981). For this reason, children's choices should be made from foods that provide nutrients as well as calories. The unpredictability of preferences can be frustrating, but adults can nonetheless try to give attention to children when they are eating or trying something new rather than when food problems occur.

Nutrition and Development

In some families, worries about food intake are much more fundamental than those that we have been describing. Cross-cultural studies have investigated the relationship between inadequate nutrition and development in the early childhood years.

A condition called **kwashiorkor** has been identified in cross-cultural studies. Kwashiorkor results when food intake is deficient in protein even if adequate in calories. The word *kwashiorkor* comes from the language of a tribe in Ghana and means "sickness that the older child gets when the next child is born." As might be expected from the definition, kwashiorkor develops most frequently in children between one and two years of age when they are weaned. Kwashiorkor is a severe form of malnutrition and leads to growth failure, anorexia, muscle wasting, and lack of interest and exploratory desire. Such severe malnutrition causes death or major disability.

Calvin and Hobbes　　　　by Bill Watterson

The decreased growth rate of very young children and the struggle for autonomy combine to make confrontation over food intake almost inevitable. However, some modification of the social atmosphere can help improve food intake.
SOURCE:　CALVIN AND HOBBES 1989 & 1990 Watterson. Dist. by UNIVERSAL PRESS SYNDICATE. Reprinted with permission. All rights reserved.

Even mild to moderate nutritional problems may negatively affect the development of young children. The Institute of Nutrition of Central America and Panama (INCAP) undertook a study in rural Guatemala to ascertain the consequences of chronic mild to moderate protein-energy malnutrition (Townsend et al., 1982). In this study, villages were randomly assigned to an experimental condition in which a high-energy, high-protein beverage was made available. In the control villages, a low-energy, no-protein beverage was made available.

The study design controlled for the effects of confounding social and economic variables that often accompany poor nutrition. Children in the INCAP study were observed and tested from conception to five years of age. At three, four, and five years of age, children in the experimental group (i.e., those who were given the high-energy, high-protein beverage) were found to exceed the mental test performance of children in the control group (i.e., those who drank the low-energy, no-protein beverage) (Townsend et al., 1982). The researchers concluded that inadequate nutrition inhibits mental development of young children and that adding protein supplements can enhance development in the early years.

A follow-up study done on these children compared a group that began nutritional supplements at birth with those who received the supplements only after 24 months of life. As adolescents, the early intervention group scored significantly higher on the psychoeducational tests (Pollitt, Gorman, Engle, Martorell, & Rivera, 1993). The researchers conclude that the only plausible explanation for the difference between the groups is the presence of the nutrition supplements in early infancy.

Findings from research on malnutrition and undernutrition in the United States parallel the findings reported by Townsend and Pollitt. Research (Stevens & Baxter, 1981) has indicated that adequate nutrition is necessary for the full development of the capabilities of young children. Researchers suggest that children at risk nutritionally be identified by testing for iron anemia and by collecting dietary intake data about calories, calcium, vitamin C, thiamine, and vitamin A. Once high-risk children are identified, appropriate nutritional supplementation can be provided. Research shows that correcting nutritional deficiencies is not enough (Lozoff, 1989). It is also necessary to provide social and emotional support to the families, particularly mothers. It is clear that lower socioeconomic status puts children at higher risk for such problems. When dealing with children from poorer families, it is important to consider the possibility of malnutrition as a contributing factor to social and academic problems.

Maintaining Health

The years from one to three present new challenges in health maintenance. Parents need to ensure that children receive adequate rest, continue the pattern of medical examinations and immunizations established in the first year of life, and receive dental care.

Health care.   Children should continue to receive immunizations on an established schedule. A booster DPT inoculation is needed at fifteen months, or about one year after the first three shots were completed. The fourth dose of the trivalent poliovirus vaccine is usually given at the same time as the DPT booster. Other immunizations may also be necessary.

Routine well-child medical examinations are important for ensuring the health of young children. Blood tests, tuberculin tests, and hearing and vision screening can help in diagnosing any possible problems; parents should also answer questions about their children's developmental milestones. When problems are found, referrals for assistance can be made.

Dental care.   Most young children acquire 20 teeth during their first two and a half years. Children's reactions to teething vary widely, with the most universal discomfort occurring between 12 and 18 months of age, when the first molars come in. Some children lose their appetites and wake at night; however, not much can be done to soothe them except to offer something cool for sucking. If a child has a fever as high as 101 degrees, a physician should be contacted.

Dentists disagree about how soon children's teeth should be brushed. Some advise beginning when the first molars come in. Others advise waiting until children are around two years of age because at that age they have a strong desire to imitate what they see adults and other children doing. This latter position, in combination with a restriction of sweets in the early years, seems sensible. When children show an interest, they should be given their

The visit of a pediatric dentist to a daycare center helps children develop positive attitudes about dental care.

own toothbrushes, placed in convenient locations. Children can take a turn with brushing and then an adult should have a turn after each meal.

Fluoride supplementation during these years is important for the formation of strong teeth. Some communities have fluoride in the water; in areas where there is none, a physician can prescribe drops for children to take each day, sometimes in combination with vitamins.

Dental examinations should begin when children are about three years of age. These early dental visits should be carefully planned so that children are rested and relaxed. The confidence that is built in the first appointments can make a positive difference later if fillings must be put in or other dental work must be performed.

Good dental care in the early years is important in building appropriate habits and preventing problems. The last of the "baby teeth" are not lost until children are 12 years of age. If these teeth become so decayed as to require removal, children not only have considerable pain, but the other teeth grow out of position and leave inadequate room for the permanent teeth.

FORMING A POSITIVE PHYSICAL IMAGE

Young children in the years from one to three begin to form a physical image of themselves. At this stage of development, the child's personal self-concept is closely tied to body concept. Three aspects of a positive physical image include body awareness, awareness of bodily functioning, and successful toileting experiences.

Body Awareness

Body image, laterality, and directionality are key aspects of the growing awareness that young children have of their bodies. One of the goals of physical experience during the early years is for children to find out how much space their bodies require and where their bodies are located in comparison with other things.

Body image.   Children form a body image by observing the movement of their body parts and noting the relationships of the body to other objects. They become aware of the relaxation or contraction of different muscles of their bodies. They see the movement of their limbs. They hear their arms or legs hit the wall when they move in the night. They learn how much space their bodies take up if they sit on the floor among toys. All of these sensations and learning merge into children's body images.

Play provides the vehicle for forming a reliable body image. Note how John receives feedback from the environment about the size and shape of his body.

John crawled through the large tire but got stuck in a smaller one. He had underestimated how much space his body would need.

▲ **DEVELOPMENTAL ISSUES IN PRACTICE   8.5**

PREVENTING "BOTTLE MOUTH" CAVITIES

Judd, a two-year-old, unexpectedly made his first trip to the dentist when his front tooth broke off at the gum line. Judd's father was skeptical of the story that Judd told of biting into a banana and having his tooth break. But the dentist told him that the story was plausible because Judd's tooth was decayed throughout, as was the other front tooth. Dr. Vasquez recommended that a number of teeth be capped or filled, with Judd under a general anesthetic at a hospital.

Dr. Vasquez explained that Judd's problem is called **bottle-mouth syndrome.** It usually occurs when adults allow children over one year of age to go to sleep while sucking on a bottle of juice or milk. When children do so, the undiluted liquid pools around the upper front and side teeth. During sleep, the flow of saliva and the swallowing reflex are both reduced, and the pooled juice or milk can cause serious tooth decay.

To prevent bottle-mouth cavities, children should be offered only water in bottles that they take to bed with them. Otherwise, young children may require the kind of expensive restoration of the mouth that Judd must have.

John backed up toward a chair with the intention of sitting on it, but he sat down before reaching the chair and landed on the floor. He misjudged the amount of space between his body and the chair.

Children at this age have difficulty negotiating the environment and manipulating things within it—for example, they back into things and fall off of furniture. By developing his body image, John will have a consistent frame of reference within which to organize his other perceptions and motor responses. Developmental Issues in Practice 8.6 presents suggestions for activities that will promote an awareness of the body and how it functions.

Laterality.   **Laterality** refers to an internalized awareness of the two sides of the body and their differences. Children develop a sense of laterality by experimenting with the two sides of their bodies and with the relationships of these two sides to each other. Activities that involve balance are useful in bringing about a differentiation of the two sides of the body. As children try to achieve balance, they learn which side of the body has to move, how it should move, and how the other side should compensate for that movement. For this reason, crawling, walking on balance beams, and hopping are important activities.

Even preschool children have difficulty with tasks that require left–right discriminations, but laterality is more basic than just knowing how to attach the labels "right" and "left" to the sides of the body. In fact, the sense of laterality within the body is what allows children to make sense of the directionality that they find in the world.

▲ DEVELOPMENTAL ISSUES IN PRACTICE   8.6

ACTIVITIES ENCOURAGING DEVELOPMENT OF BODY CONCEPTS

Charles Smith (1982) has developed a number of activities that encourage children to have a better awareness of their bodies. Following are some examples of these activities, which promote understanding of growth and development, establish awareness of body parts, increase awareness of the ways the body can move, and promote sensitivity to touch and taste.

Space Person (four years +)

Purpose	To help children develop an awareness of their bodies, especially its spatial dimensions. Key concepts are *body* and *space*.
Setting	A large, open space to allow for movement activity
Materials	None
Activity	**1.** Have the children move away from each other so they have sufficient space between them. Ask them to get down on the floor and curl up into a tight ball. **2.** Ask them to stick one arm out slowly and, without moving their bodies, to reach out as far as they can. Then ask them to move the other arm, then a leg ... and so on until they are completely spread out to take up the empty space. Reverse the process. **3.** Ask the children to stand up and make themselves as small (taking up the least space) as possible. Then ask them to take up slowly as much space as possible, making themselves as big as they can get. **4.** When finished, discuss how bodies can take up space in various places (e.g., theaters, cars, buses, etc.).
Suggestion	Find different size large containers or closed-in areas (e.g., a refrigerator box, a closet, under a table, etc.) and have the children find out how many of them can fit in each area. Use different combinations of children to see if the final count is affected.

Finger-licking-good Finger Paint (three years +)

Purpose	To promote children's sensitivity to touch and taste. Key concepts are *smooth, sweet,* and *awareness*.
Setting	Learning center arrangement in kitchen area
Materials	Vanilla pudding Finger-painting (slick) paper Food coloring Aprons
Activity	**1.** Make several different colors of pudding in separate bowls and encourage the children to finger paint with the pudding and to lick their fingers. (Make certain they have washed their hands.) **2.** As they are engaged in this experience, call their attention to how the pudding feels and tastes. When everyone is finished, discuss the experience and make certain to point out the special circumstances, such as the fact that food usually is not used this way.

DEVELOPMENTAL ISSUES IN PRACTICE   8.6

Me and My Shadow (three years +)

Purpose	To help children understand and accept their physical characteristics as well as their similarities to and differences from others. Key concepts involve various body parts such as *face, hair, neck,* etc.
Setting	A room that can be darkened.
Materials	Large sheets of white paper Paint Table lamp with shade or filmstrip Crayons projector or flashlight Collage materials Table and chair
Activity	**1.** Tape a large piece of white paper to the wall, and place a chair in front of it very close to the wall. Turn the chair sideways and have a child sit on it. Darken the room and shine a light from a filmstrip projector or a bright flashlight on the side of the child's face. Next, trace the silhouette or shadow that appears on the paper. **2.** Take the paper down and have paint, crayons, and collage materials set out so the children can decorate their "self-portraits." Discuss the various parts of the face that might be included or added to the shadow. **3.** Tape all the portraits around the room at a later time and ask the children to identify who matches each portrait.
Suggestion	Because the teacher is working with one child at a time, this activity may not be suitable for large groups (more than six children).

Body Drawing (three years +)

Purpose	To help children understand the physical similarities and differences between people and to help them identify and accept their own physical characteristics. Key concepts are various body parts.
Setting	Individual activity either inside or outdoors
Materials	Large sheets of paper Collage materials Crayons Chalk (if outside) Paint
Activity	**1.** Ask each child to lie down on a large sheet of paper so that you can draw around the contour of his or her body. **2.** Set out crayons and paint for decoration. **3.** Discuss and relate various body components to the picture.

SOURCE: C. A. Smith, (1982). Promoting the social development of young children: Strategies and Activities.

Directionality.   **Directionality** refers to the projection beyond the body of the laterality that children feel within their bodies. The intermediate step between laterality and directionality involves the ability to control eye movements and to know where the eyes are pointed. If children can match their internalized understandings with what they see, they can develop concepts of right, left, up, and down as applied to the world around them. Establishment of directionality allows older children to differentiate between symbols such as *p* and *q*.

Awareness of Bodily Functions

Sexual image/gender awareness.   By the age of two years, children understand the concept that human beings are either male or female. They have also identified themselves as either a boy or a girl. This is the beginning of sex role development. The child doesn't know what it means to be a boy or a girl, but from two years on the child will begin to form a self-concept based on sexual differences.

Children are very curious about their bodies and will explore themselves to learn about their body parts. Toddlers will also explore each other's bodies. It is important for adults to recognize that this is normal, healthy curiosity. If adults become excessively upset with such behavior, it can send a message that the child's body is "bad." One of the most important things for the adult to do for the child at this age is to send positive messages about the toddler's body to enhance good self-concept.

Angela, age two, stared pointedly the first time she helped her mother change baby Nick's diaper. "What dat?" she asked, touching his penis.

Sex education in these early years usually comes in response to questions about children's bodies and about how babies are born. These questions should be answered simply but accurately. Angela's mother, for instance, told her: "Nick is a boy, and boys' bodies are different from girls' bodies in some ways. Nick uses his penis to urinate."

The goals of early sex education are to help children feel comfortable with their bodies and to establish open communication patterns between parents and children. Children will consider their parents "askable" if parents can respond in a relaxed manner to questions. It is a good idea to clarify the question first (e.g., "Do you mean 'How does the baby get out of the mother's body?'") because sometimes children's questions are not what they initially seem to be. A familiar story features a mother who rushes through a detailed account of conception, prenatal development, and birth, only to have her son reply, "No, I mean what town was I born in?" Once the question is clarified, the parent should give the information requested and then stop to allow the child time to assimilate the information.

Interior body and illness.   Children have difficulty imagining the interior of their bodies at this age. They are normally not aware of the interior unless they become sick. Then they are apt to feel pain or discomfort. When children under the age of three were asked to explain what the inside of their bodies looked like (Crider, 1981), they made vague reference in the general vicinity of the upper torso to organs that they could name. They did not understand that the various organs had specific functions. When asked, "What makes a person sick?" (Bibace & Walsh, 1981), these young children talk in magical terms of contagion, in which mere proximity can cause illness. They obviously do not understand the notion of germ theory. When they are sick, they blame an outside event, usually the most recently occurring phenomenon, such as falling down. This has been referred to as "phenomenism." For example, a child may say, "I got sick because Mommy got mad at me."

Toileting

Success in toileting can give young children a sense of growth. Tad's first experiences on the potty, described at the beginning of this chapter, helped him to understand its function. He felt proud to be able to perform in a way that pleased his mother. However, learning to use the potty and later the toilet is not always such a positive experience, whether for the child or for the adult. Problems can center on the timing of the training process and the method of training. These potential problem areas are discussed next.

Timing of training. Some parents claim to have trained children as young as one year of age to use the potty. Usually, however, these children are very regular in their pattern of elimination and the adults are themselves "trained" to encourage use of the potty at certain times of the day. There is some speculation that children whose parents have "caught" them in the first 18 months rebel later because using the potty seems to be too much a part of an adult plan. For most children it is prudent to wait until after age two, when several kinds of readiness are established.

The most obvious kind of readiness involves physical maturation. Parents notice that young children begin to stay dry for several hours and then urinate in quantity, rather than urinating in small amounts more frequently. And, at a certain point, children seem able to show anticipation of urination by their body positions or facial expressions. Having prolonged dryness, urinating in quantity, and anticipating urination are all signs of physical readiness. Children should also be far enough past the first excitement of walking that they are willing to sit still for short periods of time.

Another kind of readiness involves psychological and intellectual development. Children should not be asked to sit on the potty if they are in a period of strongly oppositional behavior. And children should be able to understand simple directions and instructions. If they are asked to use the potty before they are ready, they will not be likely to be successful. If unpleasant associations form, it can take months to undo the harm done.

Method of training. These days, most pediatricians advocate a relaxed approach to potty training. For instance, T. Berry Brazelton suggests an approach to training that focuses on children's own decisions to gain control because they want to be grown up. He has advocated his approach to the parents of over 1,000 children in his private practice and has attained nearly 100% success with day and night control by age five (Brazelton, 1962).

Brazelton has suggested that parents wait to begin training until after age two and until signs of readiness appear in young children. Children are introduced to the potty as an interesting, child-sized piece of furniture. They are asked but not forced to sit on the potty with their clothes on. After children become accustomed to the potty, adults explain about urinating or having a bowel movement there. When children seem willing, they sit on the potty without their diapers at times when they are likely to urinate or defecate. Praise should be offered but not overdone because children at these ages do not like to think of themselves as being too much under adult control. After children seem to have the idea, they can wear thick absorbent underpants, called training pants, when at home.

With the Brazelton approach, daytime bowel and urine training come at about the same time. If children show any disinclination to continue, they are put back into diapers with no signs of disapproval, and training is resumed only when children again show interest in the process. According to Brazelton, nighttime dryness follows daytime dryness when the bladder is sufficiently mature, usually around three years of age (boys are somewhat later than girls). Children should be allowed to feel comfortable wearing diapers at night until they are consistently dry for a period of time.

For the impatient, there are quicker training methods than Brazelton's. Two behaviorists have written a book called *Toilet Training in Less Than a Day* (Azrin & Foxx, 1981). Children over 20 months of age who show signs of readiness are taught by imitation and rewards to use the potty. The success rate is high for daytime dryness, but two-thirds of the children who are trained in this manner continue wetting at night.

Some of the problems that occur with training are caused by coercive or shaming practices used by adults. Adults who try to impose their wills on children find that children can learn to hold on to their urine or bowel movements until they get off the potty. More positive approaches, such as Brazelton's and the behaviorists', enlist children's cooperation and their interest in being grown up. All training methods should allow children to feel good about themselves and their bodies.

CHILD ABUSE

It is recognized that abuse is a problem that must be addressed, to protect children. In every state, laws mandate that suspected cases of child abuse be reported by professionals in contact with the child. Because parents do not come forward with their problems, those working with children must be aware of abuse situations. The laws have put the burden on professionals working with families to identify possible cases of child abuse. This raises many questions for the child care specialist who might suspect a case of abuse. What does child abuse look like? How should the parents be dealt with? What if they are paying for the professional's services? Should abuse be reported before talking with the parents about the apparent problem? What should professionals do if parents deny the possibility of child abuse and withdraw the child from the program? This section will discuss the issues involved in recognizing cases of child abuse; characteristics of the child being abused; and characteristics of abusive parents.

Recognizing Cases of Child Abuse

An important point to remember is that child abuse always involves multiple characteristics, including physical signs of abuse, personality characteristics of the child, and characteristics of the abusing family. Each of these is discussed next. First, it is necessary to know the physical characteristics. When evaluating injuries, we must keep in mind that children, especially toddlers, do have accidents and do get bruises. It is important to be able to separate abuse from normal childhood injury. This becomes more difficult after 18 months, when the child is walking and falling more often. In infancy, almost any injury is apt to be caused by abuse. The following injuries are most likely to be caused by abusive behavior:

> Bruises that require medical attention
>
> Multiple bruises
>
> Bruises on a child less than one year of age
>
> Bruises on the face
>
> Bruises inflicted with closed fist
>
> Bruises from implements (cords, wooden spoons, etc.)
>
> Repetitive marks from implements
>
> Bruises from kicking
>
> Damage from burns
>
> Burns from cigarettes (round burns)
>
> Bruises around mouth (caused by gags to stop crying)
>
> Rope burns around ankles and wrists (from tying)
>
> Burns caused by household implements, such as irons
>
> Scalding in lower extremities from being lowered into hot water
>
> Bald patches on head caused from pulling the hair

Injuries to the skin are the most common in child abuse. Accidental burns occur frequently in children 18 months to five years of age. Burns in younger infants are most likely due to abuse. Ten percent of all injuries from abuse are due to burns. Shaking children can induce whiplash, which can cause bleeding in the skull (Zepp, Bruhl, Zimmer, & Schumacher, 1993). In young infants, the only sign that such damage has occurred may be a coma or seizures. Abdominal injuries are the most common cause of death in abused children. These occur when the child is struck. Any bruises or lacerations to the genitals are most likely due to sexual abuse. These injuries have been observed in even very young infants.

Characteristics of the Child Being Abused

It is not always easy to determine when bruises are caused by abuse. However, if the child is being abused, there are certain personality and developmental characteristics that are almost always present. Even in the youngest infants, the impact of abuse results in poor attachment to the important caregivers. The abused baby has a vacant, unresponsive gaze. He or she avoids eye contact and takes no pleasure in physical contact. At two years, these children are more apt to be negative and show frustration and anger than are nonabused children. They are apt to show developmental delays relative to their nonabused peers (Egland & Stroufe, 1981). At 19 months, abused infants have been shown to be more insecurely attached to their abusing parents but not to others and to have poorer development of self-recognition (Schneider-Rosen & Cicchetti, 1984).

By three years of age, abused children have a negative pattern of social interaction with others. They are more likely to be aggressive and to avoid contact with others, and they are less likely to seek comfort from adults (George & Main, 1979). These children tend to use approach patterns toward adults that tell with body language of their fear and insecurity—that is, they back up or walk in a side-stepping pattern. Over the course of development, maltreated children show cognitive deficits, especially poor language development (Hoffman-Plotkin & Twentyman, 1984; Reidy, 1977). School-age children show poorer peer and social interaction, being rated as more aggressive and less cooperative by peers and as more disturbed by teachers (Salzinger, Feldman, & Hammer, 1993). They also have high levels of depressive symptoms (Toth, Manly, & Cicchetti, 1992).

Characteristics of Abusive Parents

In identifying a case of abuse in a nonverbal child, the behavior of the parent will be one clue. If the parent cannot give an adequate explanation of the injury, this is one indication of possible abuse. The parent may be either overly concerned or inadequately concerned about the child. In addition, the parent may be unwilling to take the injured child to a physician for examination (McNeese & Hebeler, 1977).

A great deal of research has been done on the abusive family. It is important to recognize that abuse occurs in every social and economic class. However, poor families are most apt to come to the attention of the welfare system and to become part of the research, because wealthier families can afford to hide their abusive behavior. Shapiro (1979) reviewed a number of large-scale studies from many sections of the United States. He found the following variables to be represented in the samples of abusive families to varying degrees:

> On public welfare: 50%
>
> Mother working full-time: 19%
>
> Housing inadequate: 71%
>
> Below-average housekeepers: 28%
>
> No contact with neighbors: 26%
>
> No organizational affiliation: 56%
>
> No social life: 27%

The following attitudes on parenting roles were expressed by the reported abusers:

> Rejected their parenting role: 10%
>
> Considered parenting a mixed blessing: 43%
>
> Care of home most important part of parenting role: 34%
>
> Strongly agreed that spanking was important: 8%
>
> Were highly organized with regular routines: 100%

The characteristics of the mother's childhood among the abusing families included the following:

> Excessive restriction: 40%
>
> Actual or psychological absence of parent: 30%
>
> Marital problems of parents: 57%
>
> Continuous childbearing: 46%
>
> Alcoholism: 36%
>
> Unemployment: 35%
>
> Insufficient income; 35%

With these characteristics taken together, it is possible to construct a general portrait of the abusing family, one that is familiar to professionals. The abusing parent (1) tends to be isolated, (2) has a history of personal life stress and poor family organization, (3) was abused or neglected as a child, (4) shows behavioral rigidity, and (5) distrusts "outsiders." These are **contextual characteristics,** which put the parent at risk for abuse. However, note that not one of the family characteristics is a perfect predictor of abuse. Having an alcoholic parent puts the child at risk of being an abuser as an adult, but the vast majority of all such children will not abuse their children.

These background, contextual characteristics must be differentiated from the immediate **triggering event,** which is responsible for the particular act of abuse. The triggering events that cause abuse were summarized by Gil (1973). In a nationwide study, these percentages were found in cases of abuse:

63% occurred during an extreme act of discipline

34% were an act of rejecting the child, triggered by a specific behavior of the child

25% were provoked by the child by an act of defiance or chronic hyperactivity

46% were associated with mental-emotional deviation in the parent

59% involved mounting stress on the perpetrator because of life circumstances

From these data, it is clear that there are characteristics of the child that can trigger parental attacks. In addition, life stress and health problems can be associated with triggering a specific episode. In comparing the contextual characteristics and the triggering events, the two types of causative factors can give a very different picture of the abusing parent. For example, in the contextual retrospective studies, very few (8%) abusing parents agreed that spanking was an important part of the parent's disciplinary role. Yet in studying the triggering events for the abuse, it was found that 63% of cases occurred during an extreme act of discipline. What parents appear to want for themselves and their children is not necessarily manifest in what they will do under stress.

A recent national survey (Wolfner & Gelles, 1993) confirmed earlier findings. Abuse was more apt to occur in mothers who were young or fathers who were unemployed; in homes with low socioeconomic status with larger families; and where the parents abused drugs or alcohol. Connelly & Straus (1992) also found that the age of the mother at the time of the birth of the child was an independent factor in child abuse and more important than the age at which the abuse actually occurred.

Research has shown that parents often assume that children are more capable then they actually are. For example, parents may have very high expectations about a toddler's ability to manage food and feed himself. When the child engages in typical immature eating patterns, the parents become angry. Wood-Shuman and Cone (1986) have shown that abusive parents have the most inappropriate expectations for the behavior of young children. It is hypothesized that parents with high levels of inappropriate expectation become the most frustrated and are more apt to engage in abuse of their child. However, it is unlikely that such triggering events would cause abuse in such situations without the presence of other contextual characteristics that put the parents at risk of acting on the triggering event.

The professional must use care in evaluating all the possible variables in determining whether there is a case of child abuse. The child's physical and emotional/social characteristics are the most important, but information on the family background and current situation can also provide important information for assessing a particular case. Before reporting a case as potential child abuse, a number of different variables should be present. Finally, it is important to remember that the law does not require that the professional be certain that the child is being abused before calling in the social service agencies. To request an investigation, one needs only to have probable cause. In a recent study in Washington State (Sabotta & Davis, 1992), it was found that children who have been reported to the child abuse registry have a significantly higher probability of suffering a fatality than do comparably matched controls. This same group of children was 20 times more likely than the controls to die from homicide. Thus, once families have been reported, there is a need for continued vigilance for the well-being of the child. The professionals caring for the child will most certainly continue to be involved.

SUMMARY

1. Many physical changes take place in the years from one to three.
2. With large muscle development, children learn to walk, run, climb stairs, kick balls, throw balls, somersault, and ride tricycles.
3. With small muscle development, children learn to feed themselves, undress, dress, build block towers, turn the pages of books, and draw with pencils and crayons.
4. Perceptual–motor integration involves the ability of the child to see a relationship between information taken in through the senses and the child's behavior.
5. Maturation and experience are important in physical development.
6. In some large and small muscle skills, girls are six months ahead of boys, on average.
7. Young children are accident prone and need to be provided with a safe environment.
8. Children should be placed in an approved safety restraint every time they ride in an automobile.
9. Many poisonings can be prevented by placing dangerous substances out of the reach of children.
10. Burns and drownings can be prevented by making adjustments to the environment and by closely supervising young children.
11. Physical illness is related to delayed development and behavior problems.
12. Young children are particularly susceptible to lead poisoning, which causes learning problems, retardation, other problems, and even death.
13. In the second year of life, physical growth tapers off and appetites become unpredictable.
14. Adequate nutrition is necessary for the full development of the capabilities of young children.
15. Adequate health care and dental care are important in maintaining children's wellness.
16. Body awareness consists of the formation of body image, senses of laterality and directionality, and sexual and bodily awareness.
17. The goals of early sex education are to help children feel comfortable with their bodies and to establish open communication patterns.
18. Children have a poor understanding of the interior of their bodies and therefore have difficulty understanding the nature of illness.

19. Children's feelings of success in toileting are related to timing of training, method, and children's particular characteristics.
20. It is important for professionals to be able to recognize cases of child abuse; the law requires that suspected cases be reported.
21. Children who are being abused manifest physical, psychological, and social characteristics of the abuse.
22. Abusive families come from every social and economic class of people, but they all tend to share some elements, including contextual characteristics and triggering events.

ACTIVITIES TO ENHANCE LEARNING

1. Assume that you are running a program for two-year-old children and the parents come to you for help in dealing with toilet training. Prepare an outline for a presentation on the most effective ways to help parents toilet train their children.
   a. Include a discussion of maturational factors in the timing of toilet training.
   b. Include information on the importance of children's personality characteristics in determining methods for toilet training.
   c. Include information on signs of readiness.
   d. Discuss the various methods available to parents for toilet training their children.

2. Assume that a parent is very upset because her toddler doesn't eat the way she expects. Prepare an outline of the kinds of information you would use to explain to her the nutritional needs of toddlers.
   a. Include information on nutritional issues.
   b. Include information on eating patterns and appetite.
   c. Include information on how to facilitate good eating patterns.

3. A parent asks you to make a presentation to a group of parents with toddlers about providing a safe environment.
   a. Include information on the various safety problems that threaten toddlers.
   b. Include information on the developmental characteristics of toddlers that make them accident prone.
   c. Include information on how to childproof a home.

FOR FURTHER READING

Movement Activities

Gilliom, B. (1970). *Basic movement education for children: Rationale and teaching units.* Reading, MA: Addison-Wesley.

Sullivan, M. W. (1982). *Feeling strong, feeling free: Movement exploration for young children.* Washington, DC: National Association for the Education of Young Children.

Drawing and Writing

Brittain, W. L. (1979). *Creativity, art, and the young child.* New York: Macmillan.

Lamme, L. L. (1984). *Growing up writing.* Washington, DC: Acropolis Books.

Toilet Training

Azrin, N. H., & Foxx, R. M. (1981). *Toilet training in less than a day.* New York: Pocket Books.

Explaining Difficult Subjects

Brett, D. (1988). *Annie stories: A special kind of storytelling.* New York: Workman Publishing.

Nutrition

Satter, E. (1991). *Child of mine: Feeding with love and good sense.* Palo Alto, CA: Bull Publishing.

Endres, J. B., & Rockwell, R. E. (1993). *Food, nutrition, and the young child* (4th ed.). New York: Merrill/Macmillan.

Videotape Presentation of Child Safety

Promedion (Producer). (1991). *Childproof: Home safety checklist.* Austin, TX: Promedion.

CHAPTER 9

One- to Three-Year-Olds: Psychosocial Development

▼ KEY IDEAS

Autonomy
- ❏ Erikson's Concept of Autonomy
- ❏ Oppositional Behavior
- ❏ Effects of Temperament
- ❏ Transitional Objects

Emotional Development
- ❏ Range of Emotions
- ❏ Education About Emotions
- ❏ Fears

Play
- ❏ Importance of Play
- ❏ Definition of Play
- ❏ Pretense
- ❏ Peer Interactions and Play

Influences of the Family Environment
- ❏ Attachment and Separation
- ❏ Prosocial Behavior
- ❏ Awareness of Individual Differences

Social Influences Outside the Family
- ❏ Effects of Child Care
- ❏ Effects of Television

In the last half of their first year of life, infants gain an understanding of the expectations of adults and, if relationships are trusting, infants tend to try to please. The adults in the infants' lives often respond positively to compliant, dependent infants and may be jolted by what happens next in psychosocial development. In marked contrast with children in infancy, children from one to three are, for a time, uncooperative with adults and other children as they attempt to establish a sense of autonomy and control over events that affect them.

Children's struggles with autonomy tend to dominate any treatment of psychosocial development in this age range. This chapter thus begins with a discussion of autonomy, including issues of temperament. Then consideration is given to emotional development and the importance of play, followed by various family influences relating to attachment and separation, prosocial behavior, and awareness of individual differences, including gender and racial differences. Important social influences outside the family that affect psychosocial development are also presented: daycare arrangements and television.

AUTONOMY

Erik Erikson (1963) first used the term **autonomy** to describe the process of becoming a separate person with a separate will. During the years from one to three, the period between about 15 and 30 months is especially turbulent as young children work on developing a system of inner controls. Some peo-

These toddlers are at a stalemate, with the child in the front exerting autonomy by refusing to give up the chair and the child in the back exerting autonomy by climbing aboard.

ple call this period the "terrible twos" because of the challenges presented, but it is more exciting than it is terrible if the developmental processes are understood. Clearly, if adults were as dependent as infants, they too would have difficulty making their ways in the world. Children begin to make the necessary transition toward eventual independence during the years from one to three. Considered in this light, children's struggles for autonomy can be thought of as inevitable and healthy rather than as a problem to be endured.

Erik Erikson's theory provides the basis for this section. We begin with a summary of his ideas. An exploration of the relationship of autonomy to oppositional behavior, temperament and transitional objects follows the description of Erikson's concept of autonomy.

Erikson's Concept of Autonomy

According to Erik Erikson's theory (1963, 1977, 1982) of psychosocial development, autonomous behavior is normal and necessary. The infant's task in the first year of life was to develop a basic sense of trust. The child needs the sense of trust based on a safe predictability in the environment to move on to take the risks of autonomy. Just as the infant changes, the developmental task also changes. In the second and third years of life, children need to begin to develop a sense of themselves as separate individuals with unique desires.

A brief interchange between two-year-old Danny and his mother illustrates the exercise of autonomy:

Danny, you've hardly eaten anything. Can I help you with your dinner?

No.

This is your favorite dinner. Don't you want any chicken?

No.

Do you want any potatoes?

No.

Do you know what "no" means?

No.

According to Erikson, Danny's "no" responses, even sometimes to suggestions of activities that he enjoys, are affirmations of his emerging power to make his own decisions. Danny's ability to stand and walk and his new understanding of language increase his interest in self-reliance and lead to experimentation with the boundaries of what is acceptable behavior. Danny established trusting relationships in infancy and receives warmth and love now, but he is nonetheless very assertive of his wishes. He seems to have difficulty feeling his separateness from his parents unless he can make the decision to "do it myself."

Children will emerge from this stage with a sense of individual self-identity if they are given the opportunity to make some decisions on their own. Complete autonomy in a child of one, two, or three would be neither possible nor desirable. At this stage, children do not have the capacity to make effective decisions in all areas of their lives. How the adults in the child's life respond to these irrational demands determines whether the child emerges with a sense of autonomy or a sense of **shame and doubt** about his or her own capabilities.

If the child is given the opportunity to make decisions that are successful and effective, then he or she will emerge with a sense of autonomy. If the parents are overly controlling, the child will not have an opportunity to act autonomously. On the other hand, if the parents are overly permissive, the child will be "out of control" and autonomous actions will provide a sense of failure rather than success. Shame and doubt occur when the child is made to feel incompetent—that is, made to feel that he or she can't function on his or her own. The overly controlling parent sends the message that the child can't be trusted to do anything right. The overly permissive parent allows the child to take control of situations that cannot be managed, and the child's failure confirms that he can't do anything right. It is important to recognize that shame refers to a person's belief in his or her personal incompetence. It is not the task itself but the sense of failure that the child uses at this age to measure self-worth.

Erikson and others believe that culture can have an effect on the development of autonomy. Although the universal psychosocial task of children in this age range is to establish a sense of autonomy, there is a tendency for children to develop autonomy according to the way the society encourages and enhances autonomous actions. Thus, autonomy undoubtedly varies by culture. For instance, Erikson (1963) has said that native American children, in contrast with children from the majority culture, emerge from these years with much trust but only a small amount of autonomy.

In his landmark studies of Yurok and Sioux child-rearing practices, Erikson (1963) showed that young children in both tribes are trained in systematic ways that prepare them to uphold traditional concepts and ideals. The training is different in Yurok and Sioux tribes, as would be expected from an examination of their different patterns of life. The training in both tribes leads native American children to experience conflicts with expectations when they enter boarding schools that are provided for them by the majority culture.

Summarizing common native American values, B. J. Burgess (1980) emphasized brotherhood, personal integrity, generosity, and spirituality. Burgess has indicated that native American children are taught that wealth is measured by the amount that is shared with others rather than by what is kept. Certainly native American parents want their children to be successful but in a manner that is consistent with the cooperative and noncompetitive tribal community. In the years from one to three, native American children learn that they should not expect praise for what is required of them. They develop a sense of shame as a balance for autonomy. Shame among native Americans is expressed in terms of the community: "What will people say?" Shame is a common disciplinary tool.

Among the dominant American culture, while young children like Danny are establishing their autonomy they are trying to make sense of the prohibitions and rules set and enforced by adults. Successful resolution of the struggle for autonomy leaves young children with the resources for mobilizing the independent effort necessary for handling the tasks of childhood, adolescence, and adulthood. Only when young children have been able to define the boundaries between themselves and others can they develop their own code of behavior, which incorporates the prohibitions and rules of adults.

Oppositional Behavior

When young children are developing a sense of autonomy, much of their behavior may seem to be in opposition to that of others. Researchers have observed that **oppositional behavior** ranges from direct (making loud "no" responses) to indirect (leaving the room) to passive (staring silently) (Haswell, Hock, & Wenar, 1982). When young children exert their autonomy by oppositional behavior, they are trying to act as though they have the power and authority of the important adults in their lives.

Even at the times when young children's oppositional behavior is at its most flamboyant, one senses that they do not know precisely what they want at the end of the struggle. Indeed, some of their demands would be impossible to gratify because they embody conflicts and contradictions. For instance, in a given situation, children may say "no" to going to the park, to staying home, and to every other feasible alternative.

Crockenberg and Litman (1990) have analyzed the difference between **defiance** and **self-assertion**. They point out that in toddlers, autonomy is expressed by self-assertive behavior in which the children seek to fulfill their own goals. Defiance, on the other hand, involves behavior aimed at resisting the adult. When children give up their goals, they give up their autonomy to focus full attention on being defiant.

Crockenberg and Litman (1990) also report that defiant behavior has been associated with abuse and insecure attachment. Such behavior tends to occur when parents are highly controlling and power assertive, using techniques such as physical punishment. Self-assertion, on the other hand, is associated with developmentally mature children who engage in negotiation with their mothers and are more securely attached to them. The research of Crockenberg and Litman confirmed that defiance and self-assertion are separate factors triggered by different kinds of child-rearing practices. Defiance was associated with "negative control," defined as "control that is intrusive on child's person or conveys negative feeling toward child"; such control includes anger, annoyance, criticism, nonempathic behavior, force/restriction, undermining, punishing, spanking/slapping, and threatening.

Self-assertion was associated with "guidance" in the mother, defined as "attempts to direct child's behavior nonintrusively"; self-assertion includes asking or needing help, persuading/explaining, suggesting/asking, standing or sitting next to, and verbal assistance. The tendency of children to comply with their mother's wishes was associated with "control," defined as "telling" (a directive or prohibition providing no choice) and "bribing" (a reward offered contingent on compliance). When guidance was combined with control, greater compliance resulted. That is, the mothers with compliant children established firm limits but negotiated within those limits.

These findings were interpreted to mean that children need to feel that their personal needs are being considered and that they are given the impression that they are loved and valued. In such a setting, a child will use "no" to establish a point for negotiation. Children are prepared to comply when they have satisfied themselves that caregivers are concerned about them and willing to take the time to discuss the situation and offer explanations. This process gives them the sense of self-autonomy that is essential to their healthy development.

There is support for Crockenberg and Litman (1990) in a British study (Achermann, Dinneen, & Stevenson-Hinde, 1991) in which mothers and their two-year-old children were observed in a free-play setting, followed by clean-up of the area. The children, who were securely attached to their mothers and complied with requests to clean up, had mothers who were constructively involved in play and approached the clean-up period in an enthusiastic and positive way.

Compliance to adult requests is very important for making peace and harmony in the home and, ultimately, for the development of autonomy. Developmental Issues in Practice 9.1 gives parents three techniques to gain compliance during this developmentally difficult period.

An important question concerns the issue of how much children actually understand. Perhaps they have poor comprehension of adult requests. Kaler and Kopp (1991) have studied this issue by examining comprehension and compliance in a group of toddlers 12–18 months of age. They found that for the majority of the time, the youngest children did not understand requests and did not comply with them. When toddlers did comprehend a request, they tended to comply with it. Thus, Kaler and Kopp (1991) demonstrated that children do not do things they don't understand, which may explain why there appears to be oppositional behavior in young children. Furthermore, by 18 months, for the majority of the time the toddlers comprehended requests and complied with them, indicating that, with increasing age, there is an increase in comprehension. At no age was there a tendency for children to fail to do something they understood. What may appear to adults to be oppositional behavior was shown to be merely a result of the cognitive limitations of the toddlers. Adults must always keep in mind that toddlers require sufficient time to carry out requests. It is also important to avoid overloading the limited memory of toddlers. It is likely that the reactions of adults to this early noncompliance determines the tendency of children to engage in either defiant or self-assertive behavior as they enter the period of the "terrible twos."

Tantrums are more frequent during the months of the struggle for autonomy than at any other time in childhood. Temper tantrums signal that

▲ DEVELOPMENTAL ISSUES IN PRACTICE   9.1

DEALING WITH OPPOSITIONAL BEHAVIOR

Three techniques help parents and other adults deal with oppositional behavior: getting children's attention positively, giving time for compliance, and offering choices.

Get attention positively.   Molly's father needs to take her to a medical appointment. He could wait until it is time to leave and give a request or a command. If he does, however, his request or command is likely to be met with opposition from Molly, who is unwilling to stop her play. But, if he begins to organize the departure a bit earlier when Molly turns her attention to him during a lull in play, he could tell her about something interesting that they will see during the trip to the doctor's office. With his preparation he has laid a foundation that later eases the transition. Right before departure, he can follow up with a verbal reminder about what they will soon see. If he shows respect and consideration, Molly will have the sense of being a participant in the activities of the day.

Give time.   Research (Haswell, Hock, & Wenar, 1981) has shown that the strongest opposition from children comes within seconds after an adult makes a request. Researchers found that if adults wait at least 10 seconds before repeating a request or taking further action, children often surprise them and comply. Patience and a good sense of timing seem to be important attributes of adults who interact with young children.

Offer choices.   Children can be encouraged to comply if they are given many opportunities for choice during their struggles for autonomy. Young Jeff might be asked, "Do you want to eat with a spoon or a fork? Wear a red or blue shirt? Walk on this side or that? Fix your hair with a brush or comb?" When given such choices, Jeff can assert his will within a structure that is acceptable to him and to his parents. The decision-making focus is moved from whether or not to eat, get dressed, walk, or fix his hair to how each of these things will be done.

When opposition has already occurred, offering a very limited choice can help Jeff "save face." If it is time to go home and Jeff is resisting, his parent can say firmly, "It is time to go," and then offer a limited choice: "You may walk or hop or I will carry you." If Jeff chooses either of the first two alternatives, he is actively participating in the process of going home. If he continues to balk, he has chosen the third alternative and his parent should carry him out.

the young child has lost the ability to negotiate any further. They provide a way to release tension and a last desperate attempt to keep from losing the confrontation at hand. The screaming, kicking, thrashing, and hitting that take place during tantrums are all-consuming, blotting out the past and future. Although tantrums often begin in response to parental control, they bring a peacefulness in their wake that is sometimes surprising. Afterward, children are often willing to do what they have just refused. They want the reassurance that they are still loved and that, though they have been out of control, their parents are still strong and in control. Developmental Issues in Practice 9.2 describes how parents can handle such problem behavior.

Self-assertive behavior is a normal part of a toddler's need to establish autonomy. Saying "no" is a healthy sign of good development. If parents respond with consideration of the child's personal needs, then defiant behavior is less of a problem. Children learn that they can be autonomous and also compliant. Children who have been treated with firm balance, neither winning nor losing all the time, grow beyond their arbitrary and absolute need to control and dominate. Sometime around 30 months of age, the oppositional behavior diminishes and most young children begin to show that they have internalized the prohibitions and rules that they earlier resisted so actively.

Effects of Temperament

The process of establishing a sense of autonomy is influenced by the differing temperaments of children. Researchers in the New York Longitudinal Study (Thomas & Chess, 1981) think that **temperament** can explain the "how" of behavior (this concept is discussed at length in Chapter 6). They believe that infants come into the world with behavioral characteristics that shape their reactions and the responses of adults. These researchers believe that young children whose temperaments can be described as "difficult" or "slow to warm up" need special handling during the years from one to three when they are struggling with autonomy. For example, Rende (1993) found that highly emotional infants and toddlers were more apt to be high in anxiety/depression later in life. In addition, the boys were also more apt to have attentional problems.

To determine whether children from one to three years of age are "easy," "difficult," or "slow to warm up," a Toddler Temperament Scale (Fullard, McDevitt, & Carey, 1978; 1984) has been developed. Information is collected by parental response to 97 behavioral descriptions that relate to nine basic characteristics of temperament. Some examples from the Toddler Temperament Scale follow:

To find out about activity level, the parent is asked whether the child fidgets during quiet activities such as storytelling.

To learn about approach or withdrawal, the parent is asked whether the child's first reaction to seeing the doctor is acceptance.

To investigate adaptability, the parent is asked whether the child accepts delays of several minutes for snacks or treats.

To gather data about persistence, the parent is asked whether the child plays with a favorite toy for 10 minutes.

To investigate sensory threshold, the parent is asked whether the child reacts to a disliked food even if it is mixed with a favorite food.

▲ DEVELOPMENTAL ISSUES IN PRACTICE   9.2

DEALING WITH TANTRUMS

When Damon was two years old, he managed to gain complete control of the household. He did this by holding his breath whenever he was displeased, angry, or overtired. Turning blue and passing out produced a very dramatic effect. His parents were afraid he would die or suffer brain damage if they didn't give in to his demands. The result was that the parents were angry and resentful of him; and although Damon managed to get whatever he wanted, he was frustrated and unhappy. Being completely out of control did not satisfy his need for effective autonomous decision making but only confirmed in him his sense of shame and doubt at not being able to anything right.

Intervention and an establishment of a more moderate sense of autonomy came unexpectedly to this family when Damon's parents heard how another student in a parenting class had handled a similar situation. From that friend Damon's parents learned that children do not damage themselves by holding their breath; as soon as they momentarily lose consciousness, the involuntary breathing mechanism takes over. If adults are calm and unswayed by these collapses, breath-holding incidents gradually diminish in frequency and then stop entirely. This knowledge and the encouragement of their class allowed Damon's parents to begin to set firm limits for him.

Damon's parents found that they could help their son establish personal self-control by following a few rules whenever Damon had a temper tantrum:

1. They remained calm and avoided any show of panic or fear. It is important for Damon to know that, although he is out of control, his parents are in control of themselves and the situation.

2. They isolated Damon and avoided giving him any attention during his temper tantrums. Damon's parents learned that the tantrum was designed primarily to engage their attention. If they ignored it, Damon simply stopped doing it.

3. They made a point of giving Damon special attention and affection when he stopped a tantrum on his own or avoided having one. This reinforced Damon's "good" behavior and gave him a sense of accomplishment in achieving truly effective autonomy.

These examples are selected from the 8–13 questions to which a parent responds for each of the nine characteristics of temperament. Once a parent has completed the Toddler Temperament Scale, the child's temperamental characteristics can be compared with the following diagnostic clusters:

1. Easy: combines the characteristics of rhythmicity, approach, adaptability, mildness, positive mood

2. Difficult: combines the characteristics of unrhythmicity, withdrawal, slow adaptability, intensity, negative mood

3. Slow to warm up: combines characteristics of low activity level, withdrawal, slow adaptability, mildness, negative mood

Researchers have found that across ages, about 40% of children can be described as "easy," 10% as "difficult," and 15% as "slow to warm up" (Thomas & Chess, 1981). Difficult and slow-to-warm-up children present special challenges when they are struggling to establish their autonomy. They need more sensitive introductions to new things and people, and they need more time to make transitions than do easy children. Experiences involving such things as child care placement, play group involvement, and medical appointments have to be approached carefully when children are difficult or slow to warm up. A recent study (Bagley, 1991) suggested that it might be possible to analyze temperament according to two general components involving behaviors associated with (1) sociability and (2) difficult behaviors. No matter how temperament characteristics are measured, they appear to be relatively stable across ages.

Of course, temperamental style per se is not the only factor influencing the development of autonomy. Especially with difficult or slow-to-warm-up children, a key factor in children's adjustment is the fit between their temperaments and the context in which they find themselves. To illustrate this point, researchers (Thomas & Chess, 1981) use examples from various cultures. They point out that a child with irregular sleep patterns may be an annoyance in Boston, where sleeping through the night is emphasized; on the other hand, in a Kenyan farming and herding community, children sleep in skin contact with their mothers and are fed whenever they awaken. Other differences in perspective about sleeping "problems" exist between Puerto Rican working-class and Anglo middle-class parents in New York. The Puerto Rican group experiences few sleeping problems because children set their own sleeping and waking times; in the Anglo group, though, irregular sleep patterns are perceived as problems because the parents have certain expectations about appropriate schedules for their children.

Another factor to consider is the change that occurs in caregiver expectation as the child grows. There is a similarity in temperament across ages. However, the behavioral demands of each age change. For example, distractible infants can be easier to feed and change because they can be distracted from crying. This is also very helpful during the two-year-old period, when oppositional behavior is easier to handle in distractible toddlers. However, once a child enters preschool, distractible behavior can be detrimental to performing effective school work. Up until then, the distractibility trait may have been viewed in a positive way, but it may take on negative connotations when the caregivers find the children having difficulty with school work.

Transitional Objects

With all the turbulence that begins at about a year and a half, it may not be surprising that this is a time when children develop special attachments to objects, such as blankets, rag dolls, towels, teddy bears, and pieces of satin fabric. These objects are familiar, faithful things that are full of memories of past comfort. Psychologists call these **transitional objects** because they represent a transition from the parents and everything that seems familiar and safe to a wider, uncharted environment. If parents are not close at hand, transitional objects give children a sense of security and comfort. Arthur Kornhaber, a child psychiatrist, calls transitional objects a "portable mommy" that children can take along when separated by sleep, exploration, or child care placement (Burtoff, 1982).

Many psychiatrists and psychologists agree that children's attachments to transitional objects are normal and helpful in providing reliable comfort. Parents who are supportive of children's attachments to transitional objects allow their children to feel in control of themselves and what they need. During a period when there are tugs of war over eating, bedtime, and other routines, the transitional object should not be another cause of conflict. The need for transitional objects gradually diminishes and is often gone by the time children are seven or eight.

During the time of involvement with transitional objects, certain boundaries can be set for their use so that children have both hands available for exploration. Rather than taking the object along to the play group, the child could perhaps leave it in the car where it would be waiting when the session is over; or it could stay in the child's bed where it would remain clean and fresh for nap time; or it could stay in the child's cubby or locker at daycare until nap time. Reasonable boundaries depend upon the child's needs and the particular situations. Children's needs for comfort and reassurance are greater on the first than on the one-hundredth day of daycare placement, for instance.

EMOTIONAL DEVELOPMENT

Range of Emotions

Chapter 6 describes the basic emotions that can be seen in infants. Charles Smith (1982) has pointed out that all emotions are present and functioning in children by at least two years of age. Adults have a tendency to think of emotions as falling into categories of "good" and "bad." For example, we generally think of happiness as good but anger as bad. Smith points out that all emotions are valid and play a necessary role in the ability to function normally. Each one provides a positive and beneficial mechanism for assisting the child in learning and interacting. The following list is adapted from Smith (1982):

1. Ecstasy–joy–serenity dimension: defines situation as positive and encourages child to seek out similar situations

2 Adoration–liking–acceptance dimension: defines situation or person as capable of meeting child's needs; enables child to identify with another person

3. Terror–fear–apprehension dimension: defines situation as dangerous and helps child to seek protection

4. Amazement–surprise–distraction dimension: defines situation as strange and orients a child toward a situation for exploration and investigation

5. Grief–sadness–pensiveness dimension: defines a sense of loss and helps child admit to and adjust to losses in life

6. Loathing–disgust–boredom dimension: defines something as repugnant and helps child reject unpleasant things

7. Rage–anger–annoyance dimension: defines a situation in which a child experiences frustration; helps child to overcome or remove obstacles

8. Vigilance–curiosity–anticipation dimension: defines a situation as novel but safe and encourages children to explore unusual surroundings

Adults must be very careful not to discourage an emotion simply because of preconceived notions of its value. For example, it is not helpful to tell a child: "You're not really angry at mother; you love mother." The child cannot help having angry feelings. It is important that parents provide the child with reality-oriented observations. For example, the mother could say: "You're really angry at me for making you stay in out of the storm. I understand that you would feel angry, but I am doing it because it is dangerous outside now and I don't want you to be hurt." This helps the child to define his feelings and learn that his feelings don't make him a "bad" person—that he is loved in spite of his momentary emotional reactions to situations.

Education About Emotions

It is helpful to allow the child to learn to differentiate between feelings and actions. Emotional reactions are involuntary and cannot be controlled. However, our behaviors in reaction to emotions can and should be controlled. For example, a child may be angry at a younger sibling for interfering in the older child's play. The anger is natural, but the child needs help in acting on the anger. One reaction is to hit the sibling with the toy. However, there are many other socially approved responses. The child can be taught to use alternative responses, which are more functional than violent reactions. The caregiver can say: "It really makes you mad when Timmy messes up your games, doesn't it? I remember when my little brother used to do that to me and I really got angry. Let's see if we can find something for Timmy to do that he really likes so he won't bother you for a while." This approach has a number of advantages:

1. It allows the adult to accept the child's emotions.

2. It validates the child's feelings and person as important.

3. It separates the feelings from the reaction to the feelings.

4. It provides positive guidance for finding effective reactions.

It is important for caregivers to avoid using stereotyping in dealing with children's emotions. For example, it is common to hear adults say to boys, "Big boys don't cry," or to girls, "It's not nice to get angry with your friends." These reactions are often based on unconscious beliefs about the characteristics of boys and girls. Males can feel sad and should be given permission to cry when they are unhappy, just as girls should be given permission to express anger. These sex-role stereotypes are dangerous because they suggest to children that there is something "bad" about their feelings. An inability to express emotions distorts our social relationships and causes physical and emotional problems in later life. There are many other stereotypes as well—based on age, race, disability, and so on—and these should also be avoided.

Emotions are an essential part of our life. They help us to understand and respond to our environment. We can handle our emotions most effectively if we can identify them, understand the relationship between emotions and social behavior, and communicate emotions in a constructive way. These skills also make us more effective at responding in a sensitive way to the feelings of others (Smith, 1982).

We can facilitate this process by sharing our own feelings. Adults must be careful not to frighten or upset children. An effective approach is to share personal experiences similar to ones the child is having (e.g., "I remember how sad I felt when my goldfish died"). Second, adults can identify and define a child's feelings (e.g., "You sure are angry"). Third, adults can help children find the cause of their feelings, thus linking them to environmental events and making them understandable (e.g., "You really are happy now that Christmas is finally here").

Fears

At about 18 months of age, children become intellectually able to retain and manipulate mental images. This growth in cognitive ability is often accompanied by the advent of fears. An illustration is provided by the comments of the father of Pedro, age two:

Pedro was never afraid of the dark, but now he will go to bed only if the light is on. If I turn it off and he awakens in the night, he screams until I turn it on again.

Pedro is afraid of the dark; other children at his age develop fear of bathtubs, dogs, trucks, monsters, and so on. These new fears are a sign of the development of a new level of intellectual ability. Troubling fears are not possible until children form permanent mental images. Along with having fears, children are apt to have nightmares. When children receive reassurance and support, nightmares have no known long-term negative effects.

Children's fears are real and upsetting to them. If adults laugh at these fears, they communicate a lack of respect for children's concerns. Adults do not need to share or magnify children's fears to be sympathetic in seeking solutions that make children comfortable. If children participate in these

A thumb provides reliable comfort for this three-year-old as nap time approaches.

solutions, the process can sometimes be surprisingly simple. Pedro might pick out his own night light at a variety store. Sally might put Teddy Bear on guard for monsters who want to enter her room at night. Mitchell might decide to get out of the bathtub before the stopper is removed. Creative solutions often result when children and parents work together. Developmental Issues in Practice 9.3 discusses some other ways to deal with emotions in children.

PLAY

Play is very important to the development of young children. A number of distinctive characteristics of play differentiate it from other activities. This section will begin by discussing the significance of play. Then play will be defined, pretense will be described, and peer interactions and play will be discussed.

Importance of Play

Piaget emphasized the importance of play as an opportunity for children to incorporate new information into the framework of what they already know. He referred to this process as assimilation. Researchers have supported Piaget's assertions about the intellectual importance of play. Johnson, Ershler, and Lawton (1982) found that IQ scores were related to levels of play in children. Block play helps children learn about the concept of equivalence

▲ DEVELOPMENTAL ISSUES IN PRACTICE   9.3

METHODS OF HANDLING FEARS

Barbara was afraid of dogs. The family couldn't own a dog because of Barbara's allergies; furthermore, Barbara had had limited experience with dogs. Barbara's mother thought that a dog might have frightened her at one time. Whatever the cause, she didn't want to be around dogs. Barbara's mother wasn't too unhappy about that because Barbara's fear kept her out of dangerous situations with strange dogs the family didn't know. However, it was increasingly difficult because Barbara would not play in a room where there was a dog, and many of her friends who had dogs did not play with her because she simply couldn't stand to be in their houses.

Barbara's parents learned about desensitizing Barbara to her fear. The assumption behind **desensitization** is that a person can be conditioned to have a particular emotion under specific circumstances. For example, whenever Barbara saw a dog, she became frightened. The goal is to help Barbara have a different set of feelings around dogs to replace the fearful ones. This is done by making contact with dogs under positive circumstances and reinforcing Barbara's new responses. For example, Barbara's mother sat down with Barbara in a cozy way and read books about dogs. The stories were about dogs who were loving and helpful to their mistresses. Barbara's mother encouraged Barbara to talk positively about the dogs and to touch the pictures.

When Barbara appeared to be able to associate dogs with positive events, her mother arranged for a small, friendly dog to visit Barbara at her home. This allowed Barbara to make contact with the dog in her own familiar environment. At this time, Barbara's mother modeled behavior that she wanted Barbara to acquire. For example, the mother talked in very positive ways about the dog and how much she liked it. Then she touched and handled the dog, pointing out how the dog liked to be scratched behind the ears. She stressed how good it made her feel to be able to pet the dog. The goals of the first visit should be limited. Barbara's mother only wants to see closer approximations to the desired behavior. If Barbara stays in the room, that may be enough. On subsequent visits, Barbara can be encouraged to touch the dog and finally to play with it.

Barbara's mother desensitized Barbara to her fear by exposing her to very distant versions of dogs, in pictures and stories. She then exposed her to the real dog in a highly controlled and predictable way. She chose a dog that was known to be gentle and friendly. Then she used modeling to show Barbara how she could touch the dog. It is important in using modeling to express pleasure in the action that is being conditioned. Every step must be taken slowly, and Barbara's own reactions should serve as the sign that she is ready for the next step. In the end, Barbara's fear is replaced by pleasure in being around dogs.

and size (Cartwright, 1988). Free play experience increases problem-solving ability (Sutton-Smith & Roberts, 1981). Fantasy and sociodramatic play increase the intellectual skills of three-year-olds (Saltz, Dixon, & Johnson 1977). Sociodramatic play helps children learn to abstract out the important qualities of other social roles from the role being played and appears to contribute in many other ways to children's development. When teachers intervened to encourage sociodramatic play among poor children (Sutton-Smith & Roberts, 1981), there were various benefits, including improvements in intellectual ability, greater innovation and imaginativeness, reduced aggression, and increases in receptive and expressive language skills (a more in-depth analysis of such play is discussed in the section on pretense).

Support for the relationship between play and language production and competence has been found in a study of one-year-old children (Tamis-LeMonda & Bornstein, 1990). Flexible language comprehension and competence in play were related. Further support for the relationship between fantasy play and language use comes from a study on preschool children in Guyana (Taharally, 1991), in which children were encouraged to engage in fantasy play. Pellegrini (1980) found that language was particularly enhanced through play in the housekeeping corner of the nursery school. Hendrick (1992) has discussed a number of excellent ideas for dramatic play, which are summarized in Developmental Issues in Practice 9.4.

Other benefits of play include helping children to expand their attention spans and to increase their persistence. Children's play is also an important preparation for reading and writing. Play has in common with reading and writing the necessity of using something (gestures and mental images in the case of play and words in the case of reading and writing) to stand for actual objects or events.

Definition of Play

A group of early childhood educators (Almy, Monighan, Scales, & Van Horn, 1984) identified six characteristics of children's **play** that set it apart from other pursuits. These characteristics include intrinsic motivation, attention to means rather than ends, nonliteral behavior, freedom from external rules, exploratory base, and active engagement.

The first characteristic of play is **intrinsic motivation,** which is motivation that comes from within. Children who devise a game called "lava monster" show intrinsic motivation. Other children who build a wood collage also show intrinsic motivation. In both cases, the children are self-motivated to participate. Intrinsic motivation can be contrasted with **extrinsic motivation,** which is motivation that comes from outside. If children play games or participate in activities to receive an adult's approval or a sticker as a reward, the motivation is extrinsic.

A second characteristic of play is attention to the means or processes rather than the ends or goals. A child might begin play with the loosely defined goal of being "father," join a frisky group of "puppies," and then

---

▲ DEVELOPMENTAL ISSUES IN PRACTICE   9.4

ENCOURAGING DRAMATIC PLAY IN CHILDREN

Teachers can enhance play in the child care program by making suggestions that include bringing other children into the dramatic play situation. For example, an adult can suggest to the child who is "driving" a car that a bystander watching could fill the car with gas. It is also important to give children enough time for play to develop. Johnsen and Peckover (1988) found that dramatic play increased substantially in the later portion of the time available for the children to play. Children also need a background upon which to build dramatic play activities. Field trips, science projects, school visitors, and experience with diverse people can enhance dramatic play among children (Woodard, 1986).

Equipment is very important in encouraging dramatic play in child care programs. Some suggestions about play equipment include the following:

Buy equipment that encourages the use of imagination.

Select a wide variety of basic kinds of equipment.

Change equipment frequently to encourage new ideas.

Rearrange equipment and recombine it in appealing ways.

Store equipment in convenient, easy-to-reach places.

Provide safe areas that are large enough for play.

SOURCE: From Joanne Hendrick, *The Whole Child*, chap. 14, "Fostering Creativity in Play." New York: Merrill/Macmillan, 1992. Used with permission.

---

return to the original role. The goals of play are subject to change during the activity itself and are less important than the experiences and interactions of the moment.

A third characteristic of play is nonliteral, or make-believe, behavior. In play, children pretend to be parents, kings, "ninjas," or characters from favorite television programs. They can turn disobedient subjects into stone toads or dazzle the world by solving all problems with magical powers. (Pretense is described in more detail later in this section.)

A fourth characteristic of play is that any rules come from the children themselves. Children may have some implicit rules that govern how certain roles are played, but these rules are set by the participants and not by anyone outside. (Participation in rule-based games, such as checkers or board games, is considered to fall outside the category of play as defined at this point.) Children often change the rules "as they go along."

A fifth characteristic of play is free exploration of new objects or environments. Children feel, smell, touch, and look at new puppets as they prepare to play with them. If children are not allowed time to explore as part of

Calvin and Hobbes   by Bill Watterson

The first characteristic of play is intrinsic motivation—that is, the child is motivated to action by his or her own desires, not by those of someone else.

play, they tend to behave in stereotyped ways, perhaps only as an adult has demonstrated.

A sixth and final characteristic of play is that children are actively, sometimes almost passionately, involved. Children resist distraction and show their interest by the intensity of their engagement.

Pretense

Chip, 15 months old, sits on the rug and lines up several plastic cups. He pretends to drink from one, laughs, and tries to draw his brother's attention to his activity. Chip is pretending to drink and is seeking to get his brother to participate too.

Pretense is a theoretical term, used in the study of child development and defined as behavior that is not literal and is in an "as if" mode (Fein, 1981). Much research has focused on levels, advantages, incidence, and reality base of pretense in early childhood. Most researchers acknowledge that Jean Piaget's work in this area provided the impetus for their investigations. Accordingly, a description of Piaget's ideas about pretense begins this discussion.

Levels of pretense. According to Piaget, young children move through two levels in their pretend play. The first level, called **solitary symbolic play,** begins between 12 and 15 months with pretend gestures such as Chip's. Cross-cultural research shows that the appearance of pretense is rather abrupt. Only 8% of Guatemalan infants produced one or more pretend acts between 11 and 13 months, but 64% did so between 13 and 15 months (Fein,

1981). The findings from studies of infants in the United States are similar to those from Guatemala.

Chip's pretense is self-referenced—that is, he is the one who is pretending to do something that has to do with himself. In the next months, he will begin to involve others in his pretense, possibly by "feeding" a doll or a parent. At first the doll or parent will probably be treated as a passive participant. When Chip is in the last part of his second year, he will learn to take into account the possibility that others can bring their own motivations into pretend activities.

The transition to Piaget's second level of pretense occurs when young children become able to think of one set of objects as standing for another set of objects. For instance, two-year-old Marsha uses a wooden cylinder as an ice cream cone. By 24 months of age, three-quarters of children use substitution behaviors (Fein, 1981).

Piaget called the second level of pretense **collective symbolism**. At this second level, beginning by the latter part of the third year of life, children begin to interact with other children in playing roles. Research has shown that at all ages in early childhood, roles portraying family relationships are most prevalent. Three-year-olds portray themselves predominantly in relationship to their parents. By age four, some children create imaginary companions. The estimates of how many children have these imaginary playmates range from 12% to 65% (Fein, 1981). Only later, at age five or so, do children begin to incorporate into their play other relationships that they have observed.

Piaget has said that pretend play forms a bridge between sensorimotor and preoperational thought. Pretend play has its foundation in imitation and exploration, both of which are characteristics of sensorimotor thinking. But pretend play also uses sequencing, categorizing, and generalizing of symbols. Thus, pretend play provides a way to put imitation and exploration into a symbolic mode, and it gives young children opportunities to experience the interaction between their actions and their thoughts.

Advantages of pretense.   Most investigators attribute various cognitive and psychosocial advantages to pretense. According to researchers, children who pretend often develop acute observational skills. They watch important adults in their lives and then imitate what they interpret as salient characteristics and details. Children who pretend also have opportunities to use interesting language patterns and, in interpersonal pretend play, to receive feedback on their comments, requests, and ideas. In addition, children who pretend can work out their fears and frustrations in a safe and usually acceptable format. They can call a stuffed dog a "dummy head" in play, working through their earlier confrontation with a parent over a forbidden activity. Furthermore, children who pretend can develop an idea, work out the sequence of events, and assign characters and motivations. Dealing with such a scenario can be an important creative outlet for young children. And, finally, children who pretend can learn about the give-and-take necessary in sharing imaginative play with others. Gradually, children realize that other people may have different ideas and perspectives that can be coordinated and integrated to enrich the play.

How often children engage in pretend play relates to family and background variables. Reviewing the research in this area, Fein (1981) found four consistent generalizations about incidence of pretense. First, children who are securely attached at 18 months of age show higher levels of pretend play at 24 months than do children who are ambivalent to or avoid their parents. Second, children whose parents use physical punishment for discipline and those who come from homes in which there is marital discord show low levels of imagination in their play. Third, the children most likely to engage in pretend behavior have considerable contact with parents (especially fathers), have little sibling contact, and have parents who encourage conversation and varied experiences. Fourth, children who watch a great deal of television play less imaginatively than those who do not.

This research showed that parents do not teach or model pretense, but they indirectly encourage or discourage it by the kind of environment that they create for young children. On the other hand, Haight and Miller (1992) demonstrated that until about 36 months of age, most toddlers engage in pretend play with their mothers. These researchers found that the mothers encouraged pretend play and modeled it for their children. Developmental Issues in Practice 9.5 gives some ideas for encouraging pretense.

Pretense versus reality.   Young children sometimes have a tenuous hold on the boundary between pretense and reality, as illustrated by the behavior of three-year-old Virginia.

Virginia held her own fairly well with her five-year-old brother and his friends. But she screamed and cried when it was her turn to be the villain.

The way Virginia reacted to the possibility of being the villain showed her momentary confusion about the distinction between pretense and reality. She did not want to act like a bad person, perhaps because she feared that she might become that person. When she is older and surer of the line between pretense and reality, she will probably enjoy taking a turn at being the villain, monster, or robber.

Other examples illustrate children's confusion of pretense with reality. Young children usually insist that certain realities not be violated in their pretense (e.g., Allan did not allow his mother to pretend to drink green milk on their space ship "because milk is always white"). And young children often become worried if their pretend play goes too far beyond the bounds of what is allowed in their homes (e.g., Tina enjoyed the escalation of excitement in puppet play until she had her rabbit say, "Ka-ka in your pants," to her friend's monkey; after a shocked silence, both girls returned to calmer play).

Children between two and three years of age are not always confused about pretense and reality. Sometimes they say, "I'm making a pretend pie," or, "I'm pretending to eat sand." If playing with an infant, children at this age

▲ DEVELOPMENTAL ISSUES IN PRACTICE   9.5

STRATEGIES FOR FACILITATING DEVELOPMENT: ENCOURAGING PRETENSE

For Two-Year-Olds	
Characteristic	**How to Encourage**
Imitation of the actions of other people	Allow access to the sink to wash dishes, closet for dress-up, etc.
Enactment of familiar routines	Be patient with repetitive and sometimes inflexible activities.
Interest in realistic "props" for play	Provide "props" to engage their imaginations: keys, tools, kitchen and baby equipment, etc.
Seriousness	Laugh *with* them, if appropriate, but not *at* them (even if they have balls under their shirts or some other surprising outfits).

For Three-Year-Olds	
Characteristic	**How to Encourage**
Increased emphasis on language in pretense	Show interest in their ideas and sometimes extend them (e.g., "What else is he going to do?").
Preplanning	Help in gathering "props" that children feel are necessary for what they are doing.
Interest in pretend play with peers	Facilitate interactions of young children but realize that pretend episodes will be brief because of their inflexibility in handling differences of opinion.
Desire for expansion of ideas	Allow play to be extended in time and space (e.g., a line of chairs for a train, a closet for a store, a sofa for an airplane). Remember, too, that children of this age want to be near the center of family activity as they pretend.
Need to exert power and gain a sense of control	Be understanding of young children's assertions about what to do when in pretend play.

For All Ages
Provide open-ended play materials. A mechanical toy may have just one use, but a set of blocks can be used for many exciting purposes.
Provide a special place near the hub of family activity—a closet or cupboard or large cardboard box—to experience the world in miniature.

SOURCE: Adapted from *Just Pretending: Ways to Help Children Grow Through Imaginative Play* by M. Segal and D. Adcock, 1981, White Plains, NY: Mailman Family Press. Copyright 1981 by Mailman Family Press. Used with permission.

are appropriately shocked to see their companion actually eating the sand. At times, young children seem conscious of the framework of pretense that they are creating. They do not expect the mud to taste like cake; they are not surprised when the monster turns out to be harmless. Yet, at other times, young children show their uncertainty about the boundaries between pretense and reality.

Adults can help young children differentiate between pretense and reality and also retain their creativity. For example, when interacting with young children about television programs, books, or play experiences, adults can discuss what could happen and what could not. But adults can avoid seeming to disdain fantasy. Adults can help children develop their budding creativity if they say something like, "There aren't really monsters like that, but it makes an interesting story. The person who wrote the book used her good imagination!"

Peer Interactions and Play

Current research is not entirely consistent with the traditional view (derived from Parten, 1932–1933) of when young children develop certain skills in playing with each other. The traditional view gives an expected schedule for emergence of four main levels of play during the early childhood years. First, according to this view, solitary play takes place during the first two years of life. As the name implies, in **solitary play** children interact only with an object

Cooperative play encourages children to represent each other as active causal agents, capable of contributing to the game.

or with a familiar adult. Second, from two to three years of age, children participate in parallel play. Children involved in **parallel play** are near each other but remain independent of each other. Third, **associative play** begins around three to four years of age. In associative play, children participate together in small groups but have very limited sharing or interactions with each other. Fourth and finally, according to this traditional view, **cooperative play** starts at about four years of age. In cooperative play, children share ideas and roles and interact in increasingly more complex play. The traditional view was formulated when most research involved children whose interactions with peers were limited to occasional play groups and perhaps, at age four, to preschool programs that were only several hours in duration. Today, children spend more time than ever before in the company of peers in child care centers, family child care homes, and other programs. The changes in the amount of peer contact of young children necessitate reassessing the traditional age ranges given for the kinds of play in which young children take part.

Recent research shows that, given the opportunity to be with peers, even infants participate in parallel play, which had previously been considered to be absent from children's repertoires until the age of two. As early as 12 months of age, infants have been observed spending more time watching the activity of their peers than that of their mothers (Oden, 1982). Early parallel play usually centers on interest in the same toy or toys and often involves imitation of what another child is doing. Interaction is richer when the children are acquainted with each other. In one study, 12-month-old children were paired either with a friend with whom they had shared two earlier play sessions or with a stranger. Children were found to be more likely to touch, get close to, look at, and imitate the friend than the stranger (Oden, 1982).

Peer relationships in these early years give children important opportunities to practice social skills and to learn new ones. The research clearly shows that even preverbal children interact with their peers. Two- and three-year-olds who have frequent and sustained peer contacts engage in associative and cooperative play. For example, Ross and Lollis (1989) observed 20- and 30-month-old children over time in small peer group play sessions. They found that even at that young age, children formed relationships with individual friends that were qualitatively different from their interactions with other people. In addition, they found that these special relationships continued across a number of play sessions with surprising stability. These researchers observed the special relationships in the context of positive interactions. They point out that during the preschool years, special friendships are marked by quite a bit of conflict, which is an important part of the learning process in social interactions. In fact, conflict occurs most among friends. Ross and Lollis (1989) suggest that it is possible that positive interactions draw children into social relationships and that, once these relationships are established, conflict naturally emerges as a normal part of social development.

Caplan, Vespo, Pedersen, and Hay (1991) studied conflict in the peer relationships of 12- and 24-month-old toddlers. They examined the theory that conflict is due to frustration over play equipment and toys. They formed play groups and observed the toddlers under two conditions: one with a scarcity of toys and one with ample toys. In addition, they observed some of the groups with the condition of duplicate toys. They found that scarcity of toys was not related to conflict. Rather, it was the lack of duplicate toys that was related to conflict. The greatest amount of conflict occurred among 24-month-olds when there were scarce resources and no duplicate toys available. Among 12-month-olds there was a tendency to have less conflict. However, there was a specific type of conflict that occurred primarily at this early age. These very young toddlers showed a tendency to find a toy attractive if another child had it. This occurred even if there was another duplicate toy available in the room and sometimes even when the child was holding the duplicate toy. This behavior appeared to be a characteristic of the cognitive immaturity of the very young toddler.

Through play, children learn from each other. They give and receive information and get immediate, direct feedback about their ideas and overtures. Brownell and Carriger (1990) found that the ability to cooperate increased over the ages of 12 to 30 months. They found that at 12 months of age, no dyad could cooperate. At 18 months, the dyads cooperated, only infrequently and accidentally. The 24- and 30-month-old dyads cooperated frequently and repeatedly across the observation period. The authors theorized that the ability to engage in cooperative social interaction was related to the development of the child's ability to separate himself or herself from others cognitively. When the child is aware of the presence of other individuals, he or she can then cooperate with them. This is referred to as **self–other differentiation**. Brownell and Carriger (1990) measured this ability using the analysis by Fein (1981).

Fein found that at 12–15 months, toddlers represent themselves as **universal causal agents** and cannot represent others as having any ability to act independently. In addition, they cannot represent themselves and others as separate causal agents. Between 15 and 20 months, toddlers begin to recognize that others are distinct, but they view them as being passive recipients of the causal actions of the self, which is still seen as the universal causal agent. Between 20 and 24 months, the toddler acquires the ability to recognize that others can be autonomous agents who cause independent events to occur. Ultimately, the two-year-old can recognize interactions as two active agents working together, and cooperation becomes possible.

Brownell and Carriger (1990) found that cooperative play in the dyads was related to the ability of the child to represent the other as an active, causal agent. This supports the theory that cooperation is related to the cognitive development of self–other differentiation. This is important because it supports the theory of the development of autonomy, as discussed by Erikson.

Brownell (1990) extended this research to examine the younger and older peers by observing 18- and 20-month-old toddlers. Some had a same-aged peer and others had a younger or older peer. It was found that the groups that included a 24-month-old child tended to include more interactions, more complex imitations of interactions, and more socially positive interactions. Children from both age groups adjusted their behavior to conform to the behavior of a different age group. It appears that, even at this young age, children are aware of the differences in ability between age groups. The younger toddlers tended to use more complex social skills when interacting with older toddlers. Older toddlers were less active with younger children but used the most complex forms of initiation to play when paired with younger children. This was apparently done to draw the less skilled children into the play situation.

INFLUENCES OF THE FAMILY ENVIRONMENT

The family environment exerts critical influences on the psychosocial development of children from one to three years of age. These influences are wide-ranging, involving attachment and separation, prosocial behavior, and awareness of individual differences.

Attachment and Separation

The ability of young children to handle separations from parents and other special adults has a predictable cycle of ups and downs. Chapter 6 included a description of the first cycle of attachment behavior that often occurs between 9 and 11 months of age and can cause children to cling to parents and have difficulty separating from them. The second cycle of attachment behavior often peaks when children are between 20 and 22 months of age. Even children who seem to have made excellent adjustments to earlier separations may show a renewal of anxiety about separations and transitions.

Research on attachment and separation has shown that severe problems in attachment have been shown to be associated with maternal problems, such as mental illness, rather than child problems, such as deafness (van Ijzendoorn, Goldberg, Kroonenberg, & Frenkel, 1992). However, even in the normal situation, most children between one and three years of age show some distress when they are left by their parents, even for a short time. Children cry, call, follow, and stop their exploration all as responses to separation. But, despite the pervasiveness of the distress reaction, differences in how children handle separations have also been found.

Researchers in early childhood development have explained why some children are only mildly distressed at separations whereas others are very distressed. Through carefully controlled observation, they have found that children's responses to separation from their parents seem to be related to two differences in parent behaviors (Weintraub & Lewis, 1977). The first relevant parent behavior concerns the amount of contact that parents give children right before separation. The more parents hold and touch children and the less children play prior to parents' departure, the more distressed children are when parents leave. A similar study was done by Lollis (1990), in which she asked mothers to interact minimally or normally during a play session with their toddlers prior to separation. Toddlers whose mothers interacted minimally displayed stress sooner and played less with other toddlers after their mothers left. The most successful approach on the part of the mother appears to be to bring the child into the play environment to stimulate the child and help to establish play behavior before leaving. It is possible that excessive physical handling and sudden withdrawal both signal anxiety on the part of the mother, which sets off fear reactions.

The second relevant parent behavior involves the cognitive structure that parents give to children to help the children understand the separation and what should be done during that time. The more explicit parents are in explaining the departure and in giving suggestions about what to do in their absence, the more likely children are to play without crying. Toddlers have increased language ability, which provides a bridge to rely on during mother's absence. For example, an anxious boy can reassure himself by talking about what his mother has told him: "Mommy is going to see somebody and then she will be right back. She will just have some coffee and then she will be right back." This same kind of verbal cognitive structuring is important to children who must undergo relatively long separations, such as when hospitalized. It is recommended that parents remain with young children whenever possible, but, when separation is necessary, preparation is essential. T. Berry Brazelton (1974) has told a story of a hospitalized toddler who coped with parental separation by repeating over and over again, "My mommy said it would be this way."

Prosocial Behavior

Two-year-old Jackie toddled over to the crying child and stroked his cheek. When his crying continued, she fetched her "lovey" and gave it to him.

Jackie's behavior is called **prosocial,** defined as behavior intended to enhance the welfare of another person. Prosocial behavior represents a whole new area of study. Until the 1960s, researchers were concerned primarily with suppressing unwanted behavior. Research questions focused on how to prevent harmful or deceitful behavior. Now, however, researchers have begun to be more active in studying altruism and concern for others. The question for researchers today is how to encourage prosocial or positive behavior. Their findings offer important insights to those interested in early childhood development.

Research shows that parents and others can increase the probability of children's prosocial behavior by adopting certain patterns of child-rearing practices. A review of the research (Grusec, 1982) has indicated that parents who effectively elicit prosocial behavior from their children share the following three characteristics. First, these effective parents are models themselves of the sensitivity, self-control, responsiveness, and concern for others that they would like their children to exhibit. Research has repeatedly demonstrated the role of **modeling** in acquiring these positive behaviors as well as

Children who engage in pretense show many psychosocial and cognitive benefits.

potentially less acceptable aggressive behaviors. Second, these effective parents give reasons for the requests that they make and the limits that they impose. They explain to children how their misbehavior distresses others, and they show their own feelings about the behavior. They are clear and consistent in expressing their values and priorities. Third, these effective parents back up their reasoning with the threat of unpleasant consequences if children do misbehave. It seems that unpleasant consequences at a moderate level, such as a "time-out" period on a chair, provide the motivation for children to avoid certain behaviors. The explanations that parents have previously provided encourage children to attribute behavior to their internal decisions rather than to external pressures.

Awareness of Individual Differences

Learning about young children's awareness of individual differences provides intriguing insights into their psychosocial development. Young children putting themselves and others into gender or racial groups is, of course, related to their ability to form categories in general. And before they can develop a system of categories, children must be able to discriminate among people and objects and to note which differences are significant for classification. Gender and race are both used as early systems for classifying people into categories because the differentiating cues tend to be physical and easily observable. As soon as children begin to use labels, usually at about 18 months of age, they use "Mommy" accurately to refer to adult women and "Daddy" to refer to adult men. By the age of three, and perhaps sooner, children make different responses to variations in skin color and other racial cues (Katz, 1982). These early categories can be rather rigid, even in families with flexible gender roles and multiracial composition. Later, after children have established their systems of categories, the categories become more flexible.

Gender awareness.   The literature dealing with the understandings and behaviors of children with regard to gender is extensive. Before discussing the research, though, it is important to define some terms. **Gender identity** refers to what an individual person privately experiences as being male or female, including, for example, cognitive understanding, social perception, and emotional expression. **Gender role** is the public expression of gender identity. And **gender role stereotyping** refers to the labeling of certain behaviors as being appropriate or inappropriate for either boys or girls.

Gender identity seems to be formed early, but an understanding of just how early is inhibited by the inability to devise appropriate research strategies for children in the first year and a half of life. It is known, however, that young children use gender-related words to refer to themselves as soon as those words are in their vocabularies (Brooks-Gunn & Matthews, 1979). Kohlberg (1966) has pointed out that children know their own sex by the time they are two years old. When asked what sex they are, children can define themselves; however, they do not fully understand that their sexual identity is permanent and consistent. They tend to determine sexuality by external indicators, such as dress and activities. Very interesting research by Money and Ehrhardt (1972) confirms that by the age of two, children establish a personal sexual identity. This research is based on clinical and research work with individuals whose sexual identities were in doubt because of genetic and hormonal abnormalities that became evident at birth or shortly thereafter. The research indicates that, if a child was born with confusing sexual organs because of incomplete development, it was essential that the sexual confusion be eliminated before the age of two. Researchers found that it was very difficult to change a sexual identity after this age. In addition, it has been found that children can label gender correctly, using pictures, at around 29 months of age (Etaugh, Grinnell, & Etaugh, 1989).

Gender roles are probably influenced by a combination of biological differences between boys and girls and cultural and environmental differences in how they are treated. It can be demonstrated that by the time children are two years of age, boys have significantly higher activity levels than girls and that girls make better social use of language than boys. To what extent these differences and others result from biological variables or from cultural and social conditioning is not known. Money and Ehrhardt (1972) have emphasized that both are important. Sex is clearly determined by genetics, but the development of physical sexual characteristics occurs in the womb. Sexual hormones in the uterus impact the development of the brain as well. It is clear that these early hormonal patterns create differences that are part of the basic biological differentiation of males and females. Money and Ehrhardt argued that there is evidence for a biological basis for many of the differences between males and females from self-assertiveness and career preferences to sexual arousal and sexual preference. There is still a great deal of disagreement about this research, and most of the recent research has tended to emphasize the importance of environmental forces in shaping gender roles.

Gender roles are strongly influenced by parental expectations, but parents are rarely aware of how differently they treat boys and girls. Three examples confirm the existence of significant differences in treatment. First, in a number of studies it has been found that mothers interact more protectively with female infants than with male infants. They stay in closer proximity to infants who are girls than to those who are boys. Also, when one-year-olds fall down, mothers tend to encourage boys to dust themselves off and get back into action, whereas they tend to encourage girls to stay for holding and cuddling (Fagot, 1982; Fagot & Kronsberg, 1982). Second, parents reward girls and boys for different types of behavior. From the time that children are just one year of age, parents give girls more positive reactions for social responsiveness but boys get more positive reactions for their exploration (Fagot, 1982). Third, parents encourage what they consider to be gender-appropriate behavior. The types of play they choose for children are strongly determined by their perceptions of gender. When parents are playing with a boy, they present a toy train, but when they are playing with a girl, they present a doll (Brooks-Gunn & Matthews, 1979). Fathers are generally even more interested than mothers in promoting what they view as gender-appropriate play.

Stereotypes about gender roles develop early. In one study (Brooks-Gunn & Matthews, 1979), one-quarter of the two-year-old children could classify a majority of pictures of objects (e.g., lawn mower, purse, clothes dryer) according to common gender-typed groups. Also, by the time children are about two years of age, most of them have assigned different functions to the adults in their lives. If they live in two-parent families, they tend to prefer fathers for play and mothers for comfort in times of stress. Gender-role stereotyping seems to begin between two and three years of age. Gender stereotypes about emotions exist also, especially for anger, in that boys are more likely to be encouraged to express anger than are girls (Karbon, Fabes, Carlo, & Martin, 1992).

It must be stressed again that the classification ability of children is just developing and is likely to be fairly rigid. It is important for children to have experience with categorizing before they are able to become flexible in assigning roles. Parents and caregivers must be aware of this tendency; otherwise, the stereotyping behavior of toddlers could cause real concern. It is not likely that young children will drop their stereotypes until the end of the preschool period. Young children often argue, with a great deal of passion, in support of a particular sex role stereotype. It must be stressed that this does not represent a stereotype in the adult sense; rather, the child is making a case for a particular classification system that is tied to a general cognitive system, which is developmentally necessary and very important to the child. (See Chapter 10 for more coverage of this issue.)

Parents and other adults can help developing children become more flexible in their thinking about gender roles or can reinforce their stereotypes. Consider the effects of comments such as the following:

"Big boys don't cry."

"Keep your pretty dress clean."

"Boys don't play with dolls."

Such comments limit children's development. Many early childhood specialists believe that boys should be encouraged to have more experiences with nurturing others and expressing their own feelings and that girls should be encouraged to have more experiences with materials such as blocks that encourage logical and spatial thinking and active physical exploration. Girls have been found to enjoy dyadic interactions (i.e., between two people), whereas boys tend to prefer group interactions (Benenson, 1993). Society has been gradually moving away from practices that channel boys and girls into stereotyped occupational and personal choices. The goal should be to help children fulfill their greatest potential, regardless of gender. Books can be provided that offer a variety of options to boys and girls. In using such materials, one should be careful to avoid promoting peer pressure caused by the rigid gender categorization practiced by preschool children. For example, if a book recommends that boys should be allowed to play with dolls, and the issue is presented for discussion, the children are apt to reject the notion that boys can play with dolls. Group pressure could make it very difficult for any individual who happened to agree with the book's premise. Books such as this are best used in one-on-one situations.

Racial awareness.   In a diverse society, people of many racial and cultural backgrounds must find ways to live together in harmony. Within this context, the question of how and when children develop racial awareness is highly significant. In a review of the relevant literature, Phyllis A. Katz (1982) has observed that there are virtually no studies on the development of racial awareness before the age of three, yet evidence indicates that the process takes place in these first several years of life.

By three or four years of age, white children have positive associations to the color white and to the racial group labeled white. In years past, African American children showed a preference for white also, but in recent years they have shown either no preference or same-race preference in experimental situations (Katz, 1982). Generally it has been found that children from

By age three, children show awareness of racial differences; they also
show preferences in their play
activities.

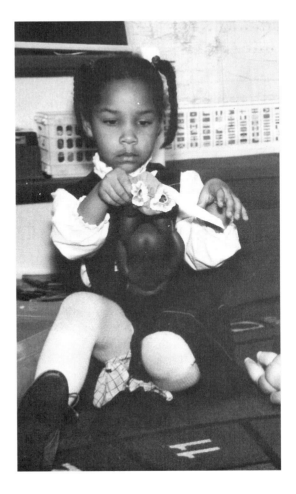

minority cultural groups are more sensitive to racial cues and develop racial awareness earlier than other children. For instance, in a study that asked children to discriminate among faces that were in various shades of black, white, and green, the performance of African American children was superior to that of other children. Younger children learned to discriminate faster when tested by a researcher of another race (Katz, 1982). With regard to this latter finding, the researchers concluded that, already by the time children reach three years of age, racial traits influence their perceptions and their learning processes. This finding has been supported by a recent study by Ramsey and Myers (1990) of preschool children in racially integrated classes. They found that race was a factor in children's categorization of people and in their choice of friends. The evidence seems to refute the hypothesis that young children are "color blind" with regard to racial differences.

Unless toddlers are from interracial families or have interracial child care arrangements, information about race comes from parents and others who are from the same background as the child. In neighborhoods that are

▲ **DEVELOPMENTAL ISSUES IN PRACTICE   9.6**

RACE IN CHILDREN'S LITERATURE

Jeanne Chall and her colleagues (1979) reported that only 14.4% of all children's books published between 1973 and 1975 had at least one black character. After analyzing later children's literature, Rudine Sims (1983) said that books with black characters can be divided into three main categories: (1) social conscience books, intended to encourage tolerance of black children among white children; (2) melting-pot books, showing by their illustrations that people are people but having in their text no specific references to race; and (3) culturally conscious books, told from the point of view of black characters. Sims is enthusiastic only about the third category, culturally conscious books.

The statistics reported by Chall and her colleagues and by Sims show that positive changes have taken place since the 1960s, when only 6.7% of books included even one black character in their text or illustrations and many of the portrayals of blacks were stereotypic or ridiculous (Larrick, 1965). Still, because of the paucity of culturally conscious books, Sims (1983, p. 653) has concluded that the "world of children's fiction . . .remains largely white in terms of the characters, the authors, and the audiences for whom the books are written. . . .We are no longer where we once were, but we are not yet where we ought to be."

not integrated, children under school age may have little acquaintance with racially different people except through television and books. If models from other racial groups are not available to children, misconceptions and oversimplifications may persist longer than those pertaining to gender, because models of both genders are accessible to children. Racial stereotypes are still found in the media and in children's books (see Developmental Issues in Practice 9.6), although the situation has improved much in the past decades.

Young children seem to evaluate more and make more judgments about race than about other areas of early learning; adults who value diversity should therefore be conscious of explicit and implicit messages given to children about racial and other differences. According to Katz (1982), after about the fourth grade, children do not rethink their racial attitudes unless their social environment changes significantly. Intervention on behalf of positive values, then, belongs in the earliest years of life.

SOCIAL INFLUENCES OUTSIDE THE FAMILY

It was previously thought that interactions outside the family assumed importance only when children enrolled in preschool, kindergarten, or first grade. Now, though, specialists in early childhood development have discovered that child care arrangements and television influence the lives of children in the earliest years of life.

Effects of Child Care

More than 50% of the children in the United States have mothers who work at least some time outside the home. Caruso (1992) found that 40% of toddlers of working mothers receive nonparental care. Parents worry about whether they are in any way harming their children. The anxiety of parents in this regard is heightened by researchers who still refer to studies conducted several decades ago with children who were full-time residents of institutions in which little warmth or stimulation was available. Alternate care during the work day is obviously not the same as long-term institutionalization. Current research offers insights into the effects of child care placement on one-, two-, and three-year-old children.

Most of the research on effects of daycare placement of very young children has been conducted in the context of well-funded, high-quality programs, often in university settings. The primary exception is the New York City Infant Day Care Study, which is discussed separately later. First, however, a summary of the findings from the majority of studies is given under three main headings: intellectual effects, emotional effects, and social effects.

Intellectual effects.   The research conducted so far indicates that scores on standardized intelligence tests neither go up nor go down for most young children who participate in child care programs (Greenstein, 1993). But children from low-income homes seem to benefit from involvement in child care programs. Specifically, enrollment of low-income children in daycare seems to halt the decline in intelligence test scores that ordinarily takes place between 18 and 36 months of age (Belsky, Steinberg, & Walker, 1982).

In a study (Carew, 1980) of one- and two-year-olds whose daily care was predominantly at home or in a child care center, it was found that stimulating environments at home and in daycare are dependent upon the efforts of adults. In both settings, about half (55% in the home study and 48% in the child care study) of the variation in intelligence at age three could be predicted from intellectual experiences provided by adults (see Table 9.1). These intellectually valuable experiences involve adults as active participants in labeling, describing, comparing, classifying, and questioning. There is a strong relationship between participation in these intellectually valuable experiences and the intellectual competence of children cared for at home and in child care centers. Olson, Bates, and Kaskie (1992) have confirmed the importance of nonrestrictive discipline style and verbal stimulation to later cognitive ability. They found that the relationship held in spite of variations in family social status, the child's temperament, or developmental status.

Emotional effects.   The available studies show few differences in attachment between children raised in a child care setting and those raised at home. Parent–child attachments do not seem to be weakened or changed when children are enrolled in daycare, even when daycare is initiated in these earliest years of life (Belsky & Steinberg, 1982). And when a child raised in a child care set-

Table 9.1. *Intellectually Valuable Experiences According to Carew (1980)*

Experience	Focus	Example
Language mastery	Naming, describing, defining, categorizing	A mother reads *school bus* from the side of a toy. The child repeats *school bus*.
Spatial, perceptual, fine motor mastery	Discriminating objects by characteristics or stacking, building or matching	A child tries to fit round figures in round holes and square figures in square holes.
Concrete reasoning and problem solving	Understanding physical regularities and solving problems	A child uses a cushion to make an incline and lets a vehicle roll down several times. The mother comments that the vehicle goes down by itself on a hill.
Expressive and artistic skill	Imagination, creativity	A child creates a conversation between imaginary children on a toy bus.

SOURCE: Adapted from "Experience and the Development of Intelligence in Young Children at Home and in Day Care" by J. V. Carew, 1980, *Monographs of the Society for Research in Child Development, 45*, no. 187. Copyright by The Society for Research in Child Development, Inc., at the University of Chicago Press. Adapted by permission.

ting is placed in a stressful situation with both the alternate caregiver and the mother present, the child consistently and overwhelmingly shows a preference for the mother (O'Connell, 1983).

In research conducted in Bermuda (McCartney, Scarr, Phillips, Grajek, & Schwarz, 1982), a relationship was found between quality of child care environment and emotional adjustment. Some children attended child care centers with good physical facilities and play materials but with less than the average amount of adult verbal interaction with children. Children in such centers were more emotionally maladjusted than children enrolled in centers with higher levels of verbal interaction. And at centers with low verbal interaction, emotional maladjustment was higher among children who entered in early infancy than among those who entered the same centers later.

Social effects. Of the many studies that have investigated peer social interactions in children raised in child care settings and those raised at home, most have found few differences. Some of the studies have reported more favorable behaviors from child care children; others have indicated that

Research shows that daycare centers can help to meet children's emotional needs by providing high levels of adult–child verbal interaction.

home-reared children are more adept socially. It has been suggested that social development may relate more to having the opportunity for interaction with a number of peers in a facilitative environment than to whether the interactions take place at a child care center or at home.

New York City Infant Daycare Study.　The New York Infant Daycare Study focused on the effects of publicly funded child care programs on children between six months and three years of age. The backgrounds of children in this study were more diverse than those in the research summarized earlier: 47% of the children in the New York study were black, 39% were Hispanic, and most were from working-class or low-income families (Stevens, 1982). Also, the New York study compared children in group child care centers with those who were enrolled in family child care homes (group child care centers are schools designed for young children, whereas family child care homes are residences in which several children receive care).

The findings of the New York study (Stevens, 1982) are consistent with those summarized earlier, and several additional insights were made possible by the design of the research. First, the children who received the most stimulation, either in centers or in homes, were later rated as more socially competent and more skillful in language use. Second, it was found that the physical environment, nutritional program, health care, and health surveillance of the group child care facilities were superior to those of the family child care programs. Third, children in group child care centers had higher scores on standardized intelligence tests than did children in family child care homes. The researchers were not able to detect variables in the two settings that would explain the differences in intellectual outcomes but noted that group child care workers usually had completed more education and more preparation in early education than people operating family child care homes.

Researchers do not yet have a full understanding of the effects of daycare on children, parents, and the family unit. However, the research already conducted does not give cause for alarm, provided that certain standards are maintained. All of the programs on which research has been conducted, including those in New York, have in common the maintenance of at least a one-to-five ratio of adults to children of these young ages. As discovered in the Carew and New York studies, high levels of cognitive/language and social/emotional stimulation by parents and teachers are positively related to the development of competence in children. Finding a personalized child care setting, staffed by adults with warm and stimulating interaction patterns, is an important challenge for parents of young children.

Effects of Television

True or false:

Children under four years of age do not sit still long enough to be influenced by television.

Young children are more likely to imitate a person in front of them than someone seen on television.

Television viewing is selective in most American homes.

False, false, false. And the implications of the facts underlying these statements require reevaluation of some current child-rearing practices. These three statements are considered, in question form, one at a time.

Are children under four years of age influenced by television? A comprehensive series of studies (McCall, Parke, & Kavanaugh, 1977) has shown that even one-year-old children imitate 28% of the simple behavior shown on television; two-year-olds imitate 76% of these behaviors. These findings clearly refute the hypothesis that young children are too active to be influenced by what is shown on television.

Are live models more effective than those who are televised? Three-year-olds were found to be as likely to imitate the actions of people on television as of people present in the room (McCall, Parke, & Kavanaugh, 1977). Before the age of three, imitation of a live model has been shown to be somewhat more accurate and frequent than is imitation of a televised model. Even with two-year-olds, a delay of one day between television viewing and a play session did not hinder the children's imitation of what they saw on television. Television is a powerful socializing force in the lives of even very young children.

Is American television viewing generally selective? The Nielsen Report on Television (1989) reported that the average family spent 6 hours and 55 minutes a day watching television. Young children in the home, then, are exposed to large amounts of television viewing, much of which is not planned or programmed particularly for their needs. What are they learning from soap operas, game shows, prime time programs, and children's cartoons? The answer to this question is still largely unknown.

However, two kinds of learning have been documented. First, children see a great deal of violence, and the most violence occurs on weekend programming for children, especially so-called children's cartoons (Huston, 1985). Children come to form attitudes about the acceptability of violent behavior. Alberta Siegel, a researcher at Stanford University, has said that research demonstrates the direct relationship between television violence and aggressive behavior in children (Dillon, 1982). Second, children receive messages from television about gender, cultural, and racial roles, which can encourage stereotyping in young, inexperienced viewers.

Research suggests that parents are not very effective in acting as interpreters or controllers of the television viewing of their young children. This is unfortunate because parents of toddlers are in a good position to control much of the impact of the environment, including television. First of all, parents underestimate the amount of time children spend watching television and do not enforce rules to limit what young children watch (Greenberg, Ericson, & Vlahos, 1972; Rossiter & Robertson, 1975). Furthermore, there is little evidence for parental interpretation or analysis of specific programming that children are watching (Mohr, 1979; Streicher & Bonney, 1974). Thompson and Slater (1983) have shown that parent–child coviewing was effective in influencing viewing behavior. However, less than half of their sample engaged in such behavior.

When young children are exposed to the world as portrayed by television without adult assistance to interpret and present alternative values, they can learn a great many things that are detrimental to their healthy growth and development. Greenberg, Abelman, and Cohen (1990) have found, however, that just giving parents the information about the negative impact of television did not change their behavior.

Parents can play an important role in determining the impact of television on young children. Research has shown that children are less affected by antisocial television when parents use reasoning and explanation rather than power-control disciplinary techniques (Desmond, Singer, Singer, Calam, & Colimore, 1985; Korzenny, Greenberg, & Atkin, 1979; Singer, Singer, & Rapaczynski, 1984). Abelman (1986) also found similar effects for children's responsiveness to prosocial television programming, with reasoning and explanation tending to enhance learning of prosocial content. When the networks used warnings to let parents know of objectionable material, 74% of those parents sampled said they were influenced by the warnings. Research showed that the parents who tended to act to control their children's viewing were those who usually regulated television programming in the home (Slater & Thompson, 1984).

Parents are expected to take responsibility for controlling television in the home. It is clear, however, that not all parents act responsibly. In addition, it is difficult for parents to fully control what is viewed, because they do not control programming decisions. The television broadcasters and advertisers have control over the content and timing of programming. Two federal agencies have responsibility for monitoring these private groups: the Federal Communications Commission (FCC) and the Federal Trade Commission (FTC), which is primarily interested in advertising issues. Both agencies have released numerous reports and recommendations; but these have been limited to policy recommendations, which the broadcasters were asked to implement through voluntary compliance (Kunkel, 1990).

In 1969, a public policy organization called Action for Children's Television was created to speak for the children's point of view. Under the organization's guidance, a number of policy statements were released, including one from the FCC that documented the danger of television violence to children. A second report from the FTC outlined the need for changes in advertising policies to protect children, who are cognitively limited in their ability to evaluate advertisements. However, in the early 1980s, government deregulation was instituted, resulting in a drop in children's programming, an increase in violent programming, an increase in the proportion of time given to advertisements, and more development of program-length commercials as part of children's television programming (Kunkel, 1990).

Research shows that television influences children in a negative way. What is known about the effects of television on young children should lead parents (and child care workers) to exercise great caution and selectivity in what they allow children to view. Public regulation would give parents great help in monitoring television; however, the fundamental responsibility still lies with the caregivers. Bob Keeshan (1983), Captain Kangaroo to millions of American children, has emphasized this by pointing out that American parents are willing to give their children things but they hold back on giving them time in the early years, when they need it most. If parents say to children, "I'm busy. Go watch television," in the morning when they are getting ready to go to work and in the evening when they return exhausted, they may be leaving much of their children's attitude formation to a questionable source: television.

SUMMARY

1. Achieving autonomy is the process of becoming a separate person with a separate will.
2. Erikson has said that children need to develop a strong sense of competence, with the desire to make decisions in an autonomous way, balanced by the possibility of experiencing shame and doubt.

3. The approach to handling the developmental crisis of autonomy versus shame and doubt varies by culture.

4. Oppositional behavior accompanies the establishment of autonomy and can be accompanied by defiance or self-assertion, depending on parental interactions with the toddler.

5. Young children with "difficult" or "slow-to-warm-up" temperaments need special handling during the years from one to three.

6. Temperamental style can be handled differently in various culture contexts and for the changing age of the child.

7. Transitional objects provide reliable comfort to young children.

8. Eight separate emotions are present by age two. All emotions are normal and of value to the child.

9. Adults can help children identify and label emotions and assist in training appropriate behavioral responses to emotions.

10. Fears develop at about 18 months of age, when children become able to form permanent mental images.

11. Two- and three-year-olds who have frequent and sustained peer contacts engage in more advanced forms of play than was previously expected.

12. Cooperative play among toddlers is related to the development of the cognitive understanding of the causal agent in others.

13. Children often experience a renewal of anxiety about separations and transitions in the months before their second birthdays.

14. Certain child-rearing practices increase the probability of children's prosocial behavior.

15. Children are aware of individual differences, such as gender and race, in the first few years of life.

16. Gender roles are the result of biological factors and cultural conditioning.

17. Child care placement of young children does not have adverse effects if adult–child ratios are maintained.

18. Research shows that although children learn from television and imitate it, parents provide relatively little guidance or direction for their toddlers' television viewing.

19. Action for Children's Television is a public policy organization designed to help promote television programming that is beneficial to children.

ACTIVITIES TO ENHANCE LEARNING

1. Assume that you are running a program for two-year-old children and the parents come to you for help in dealing with their children's oppositional behavior. Prepare an outline for a presentation on the so-called "no" stage in children.
   a. Include a discussion of Erikson's concept of autonomy.
   b. Include information on defiance and self-assertion.
   c. Include information on the parental role in avoiding defiant behavior in toddlers.
   d. Write a brief statement on the importance of children's oppositional behavior.

2. Assume that a parent is very upset because her toddler gets angry at her. Prepare an outline of the kinds of information you would use to explain to her the emotional needs of her child.

    a. Include information about children's emotional needs.

    b. Include information about how to handle temper tantrums.

3. A parent asks you to make a presentation to a group of parents with toddlers about choosing a good daycare program.

    a. Include information on the effects of social, emotional, and intellectual development of children.

    b. Include information on the importance of the program and staff of a center.

    c. Discuss the value to the child of play in peer interactions.

    d. Write a brief statement about the social benefits to the toddler of early peer interactions.

FOR FURTHER READING

Autonomy

Brazelton, T. B. (1974). *Toddlers and parents: A declaration of independence.* New York: Dell.

Erikson, E. H. (1982). *The life cycle completed.* New York: W. W. Norton.

Kaplan, L. I. (1978). *Oneness and separateness: From infant to individual.* New York: Simon & Schuster.

Emotions

Greenspan, S., & Greenspan, N. T. (1986). *First feelings.* New York: Penguin Books.

Smith, C. A. (1982). *Promoting the social development of young children: Strategies and activities.* Palo Alto, CA: Mayfield Publishing.

Play

Brittain, W. L. (1979). *Creativity, art, and the young child.* New York: Macmillan.

Garvey, C. (1990). *Play.* Cambridge, MA: Harvard University Press.

Trawick-Smith, J. (1993). *Interactions in the classroom: Facilitating play in the early years.* New York: Merrill/Macmillan.

Segal, M., & Adcock, D. (1981). *Just pretending: Ways to help children grow through imaginative play.* Englewood Cliffs, NJ: Prentice Hall.

Sutton-Smith, B., & Sutton-Smith, S. (1974). *How to play with your child (and when not to).* New York: Hawthorn.

CHAPTER 10

One- to Three-Year-Olds: Cognitive Development

▼ KEY IDEAS

Piaget's Stages of Intellectual Development
- ❑ Sensorimotor Substage 5
- ❑ Sensorimotor Substage 6
- ❑ Early Preoperational Thinking
- ❑ Criticisms of Piaget's Theory
- ❑ Applications of Piaget's Theory

Environments for Developing Cognition
- ❑ Differences in Home Environments
- ❑ Effects of Family Intervention Programs

Language Development
- ❑ Receptive Language
- ❑ First Words
- ❑ Phonetic Development
- ❑ Early Sentences
- ❑ Vocabulary Expansion

Language Learning Environments
- ❑ Cultural Differences: Black English
- ❑ Socioeconomic Differences in Language Learning Environments
- ❑ Parental Effects on Child Language Development

Cognitive development involves changes in mental processes, including problem solving and language usage. Children from one to three years of age make many striking advances in their cognitive development. This chapter describes advances in thinking by considering the theory of Jean Piaget and the views of those who differ from him. Information is also presented about language development, differences in language learning environments, and cultural differences in language.

PIAGET'S STAGES OF INTELLECTUAL DEVELOPMENT

According to Jean Piaget (Piaget & Inhelder, 1969), children complete the last two substages of sensorimotor thinking in the second year of life (see Table 10.1). Then, when they are about two years of age, children enter what Piaget has described as the preoperational stage of thinking.

This section begins with a description of the fifth and sixth sensorimotor substages and early preoperational thinking, which is represented by the preconceptual substage. The section ends with discussions of criticisms and applications of Piaget's theory of intellectual development.

Sensorimotor Substage 5

The fifth sensorimotor substage, typically extending from 12 to 18 months, is a time of mental growth. One of the hallmarks of this substage is the use of **tertiary circular reactions,** as illustrated by the behavior of Mary, age one:

Mary sits in her high chair and drops peas over the side of the tray. She pushes them off the edge with her spoon, releases them from her fingers, and then gets the idea of spitting them out. In each case she watches the path of the peas carefully.

According to Piaget, two elements differentiate Mary's behavior from what she did in earlier substages: Mary experiments with the peas rather than repeating just one action, and she shows an interest in understanding the nature of the unusual movements that she produces. Mary's process of finding novel trajectories for the peas takes her beyond her earlier secondary circular reactions, which would have focused on repetition of the original action.

Mary solves problems in a more sophisticated manner than earlier. Suppose that she wants to open a tightly closed cabinet. Now, as before, she first tries techniques that have obtained results in other situations. But, if she is not successful, she is able to change her behavior through trial and error until she reaches her goal. Piaget has said that behavior in the fifth substage is directed in two ways: by the goal and by earlier schemes that enable children to interpret what they are doing, based on past experiences.

More systematic imitation is another of Mary's new accomplishments in the fifth substage. Up to this point, her attempts at imitation were characterized by trial and error, and she usually took several movements before accu-

Table 10.1. Piaget's Sensorimotor Substages of Development

Sensorimotor Substage	Age	Accomplishments
Substage 1 (Reflexes)	Birth–1 month	Builds on reflexes
Substage 2 (Primary circular reactions)	1–4 months	Repeats interesting movements of the body (primary circular reactions) Anticipates familiar events (e.g., feeding) Coordinates senses
Substage 3 (Secondary circular reactions)	4–8 months	Repeats interesting actions on objects (secondary circular reactions) Imitates sounds and actions in repertoire Attempts search for hidden object
Substage 4 (Coordination of secondary schemes)	8–12 months	Uses goal-directed behavior Begins to be able to uncover a hidden object Imitates many behaviors
Substage 5 (Tertiary circular reactions)	12–18 months	Experiments with objects (tertiary circular reactions) Imitates accurately, needing little trial and error Searches for hidden objects where last seen
Substage 6 (Mental representations)	18–24 months	Works out solutions to problems mentally Defers imitation Comprehends object permanence and can imagine movements of unseen objects

rately duplicating an action. In the period from 12 to 18 months, however, Mary becomes able to imitate her father immediately and correctly. In a "monkey see" game, when he rubs his ear, she imitates him correctly by rubbing her ear also without trying her neck or cheek first.

Further developments in Mary's understanding of the permanence of objects are also notable in this substage. She has had enough experiences with relationships that she searches for a missing toy in the place where she last saw it. This search strategy contrasts with the one used in the fourth substage, when she would have looked in the place where she last was successful in finding the toy, even if the toy had not been near there since. Piaget would say that Mary is showing that she no longer connects objects with her motor

In the fifth sensorimotor substage, children solve problems in more sophisticated ways than earlier by changing behavior until the goal is reached.

experiences, such as her past success in finding the object, but she finally thinks of them as having permanence of their own. Still, Mary is not yet able to imagine movements of things. If a situation requires her to imagine how one of her toys might have been moved from place to place (rather than allowing her to follow the movements visually), Mary goes back to her former strategy of looking for the toy where she last found it.

Children's use of tertiary circular reactions, their problem-solving strategies, their more systematic imitation, and their expanded sense of object permanence make the fifth sensorimotor substage a dynamic period.

Sensorimotor Substage 6

In the sixth sensorimotor substage, children from approximately 18 months to two years of age begin to be able to work out solutions to problems mentally rather than relying only on sensory contact and physical manipulation of things. Note Jeff's strategy as he builds with blocks:

Jeff, age two, is an experienced builder with unit blocks. Today he is placing the blocks in a rectangular formation. When all pieces but one are in place, he stops work for a moment and looks around carefully at the remaining blocks, chooses one that will fit, and drops it confidently into position.

Jeff did not need to use trial and error to find the block that would fit. Instead of trying several blocks in the space, he thought about the problem. He drew upon his past experiences with blocks to help him in mentally comparing the size of the space to be filled with the sizes of blocks at hand. Piaget has described what happens in the sixth sensorimotor substage as providing a transition to symbolic thought. Children begin to use representations of objects to solve problems.

In this sixth and final substage of sensorimotor thought, Jeff's ability to imitate expands, too. Rather than relying on motor memory, he and other children of his age are able to retain a mental image of what they have seen and imitate it at a later time. Before this, Jeff would have had to do the imitation immediately in order to hold the action in motor memory. He demonstrated what Piaget called **deferred imitation** when he exactly duplicated the behavior of his older cousin two days after the family's return from a visit. He was able to defer the behavior.

Children at this substage can represent things symbolically. For example, during play, Jeff can use a block to represent a car or a box to represent the baby doll's bed. This ability to engage in the use of physical symbols has its counterpart in the use of verbal symbols, which will be discussed in the next section.

Another important development in this last sensorimotor substage involves object permanence. Piaget has noted that in this substage, children are finally able to understand completely the permanent qualities that objects possess. For instance, they can construct a mental map of a toy car's movement as it is moved from hiding places under different covers, such as a pillow, a towel, and finally a scarf. Children who have reached the end of their sensorimotor development can imagine that the object is being moved even though it is invisible because it is hidden within an adult's hand while being moved. They are capable of holding an abstract image of the object in their mind and can imagine the movement even though they can't see it. This is called **invisible displacement** because the object is moved invisibly and, as such, is the most abstract form of expression of the concept of object permanence. According to Piaget, these children show that they have become capable of a mature comprehension that things and people have permanent properties and continue to exist and function even when the child is not in sensorimotor contact with them; this comprehension provides a basis for all future cognitive development.

Piaget's theory has given structure to an account of the dramatic changes in children's thinking processes between birth and two years of age. Piaget has asserted that children are curious beings who seek out novelty and are mentally active in organizing and interpreting their experiences during the sensorimotor stage and in the preoperational stage that follows.

Early Preoperational Thinking

According to Piaget, the stage of preoperational thinking extends approximately from two through seven or eight years of age. This section focuses on the early part of the preoperational stage: ages two and three. This is the period Piaget called the preconceptual substage. The intuitive substage of the preoperational period is discussed in Chapter 13.

Preoperational thinking literally means "before operational or logical thinking." Piaget's most interesting contribution was to demonstrate that young children make unusual mistakes when they are asked to reason about simple things, such as the way to classify a group of differently colored blocks. However, this has led some people to think in terms of what children in this stage cannot do rather than in terms of their strengths. One of Jean Piaget's outstanding contributions to our knowledge of young children's thinking has been to demonstrate that there is a qualitative (not just a quantitative) difference in the thinking processes of young children, compared with older children and adults. But recognizing differences in young children's thinking need not lead to undervaluing the fascinating growth that takes place during the preoperational stage. We must remember that Piaget's theory of adaptation focuses on each behavior as adaptive for that particular stage.

Bjorklund and Green (1992) have shown that even so-called immature behaviors have an adaptive value. For example, egocentrism may have a value—research has shown that children remember things better when the material to be remembered is related to themselves personally. Possibly, the tendency of young children to relate everything to themselves enhances their ability to remember more things more effectively. If this is the case, then egocentrism, which is usually thought of as a liability, may in fact function as an adaptive quality.

One of the key developments in early preoperational thinking is the ability to use mental symbols. We will next describe such mental symbols, followed by a discussion of the patterns of thought that set young preoperational children apart from older children and adults.

Mental symbols. **Mental symbols** include words that represent things, actions that imitate adult roles, activities that use one thing as a symbol of another, and unconscious symbolizing (e.g., when dreaming). Using words to represent objects that are not visible is perhaps the most obvious sign that children are engaging in mental symbolism. "Ball," a child says, meaning either, "Where is the ball?" "There is the ball," "I want the ball," or "Here is the ball." The meaning can often be understood through context, but, whatever the meaning, the child is consistently using a culturally agreed-upon word to represent something in the environment.

Young children may use symbols that are unique to them and not culturally agreed upon. For example, "ba-ba" may refer to "bottle." It is a symbol if it is used consistently to refer to the same object. Usually, such idiosyncratic symbols become part of the communication within the family; they are accepted and used in a meaningful way. Piaget pointed out that young preoperational children use motor actions to symbolize words, as when Lucienne gave her father a box she couldn't open. She expressed her need to have him open it by opening her mouth.

Using words is not the only way that children share their mental symbols. At these ages, they usually begin to imitate adult roles that they have

Two-year-olds show use of mental symbols, such as a rock for money as this "truck driver" pays his toll.

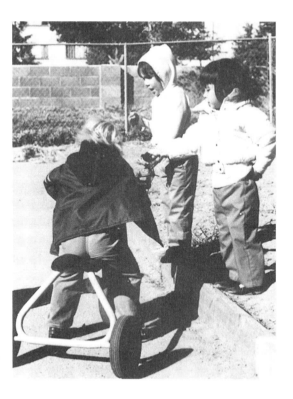

observed. One child ceremoniously gets out a sack, fills it with papers each morning after breakfast, and walks around the house in imitation of his mother and her always-stuffed briefcase. Another child drives a couch in a way that resembles the manner in which her father drives his moving van. These children have observed adult activities, formed and remembered mental symbols of essential elements, and acted out their versions at a later time.

In their play activities, children create and use mental symbols. Two sticks are crossed to form an airplane. An oatmeal container becomes a drum. Triangles and circles are combined to represent people in artwork. Dress-up clothes transform a child into an adult. A hat turns a three-year-old into an authentic fire fighter. By their actions, children provide evidence of the advances taking place in their thinking.

The discussion of psychosocial development in Chapter 9 mentioned that fearfulness sometimes results from unconscious symbolizing. Because preoperational children can retain and elaborate on mental symbols, they may develop fears of darkness, monsters, dogs, and other things. Parents are usually reassured to learn that their children's new fears are evidence of an advance in intellectual development and are normal at these ages. Parents who lack this information may blame themselves for some deed or omission that turned a previously confident child into a fearful one.

The early preoperational years bring with them many changes in abilities, and children themselves often seem invigorated by their new accomplishments. When children become capable of forming mental representations of objects or happenings, they can extend their thinking beyond the boundaries of the immediate time and place, an accomplishment of great value.

Thought patterns.   Piaget has shown that children are not just miniature, less experienced adults. The qualitative differences that set the thinking of young preoperational children apart from that of their older contemporaries include transductive reasoning, idiosyncratic concepts, and egocentrism.

Some of children's colorful comments illustrate what Piaget calls **transductive reasoning**. Transductive reasoning shows some or all of the following characteristics: it moves from effect to cause (e.g., the child kicks the tricycle after skinning his knee from falling off of it), focuses on only one of several variables (e.g., the child assumes that all four-legged animals are dogs), confuses general and specific cases (e.g., the child assumes that because his father has a beard, all fathers must have beards), and makes analogies to past events (e.g., the child assumes that because the family happens to be driving on the road that leads to the airport, Daddy is going out of town).

Transductive reasoning can lead to correct conclusions, but examples are more memorable when children use it to draw faulty conclusions. For instance, several days after Stephen, age two, was knocked to the floor and licked by a large but affectionate dog, he asked to be picked up when he saw the dog. He said, "Dog no eat." His mother, misunderstanding, said, "The dog is not eating." Stephen corrected her by saying, "Dog no lick; dog no eat me!" Stephen had apparently reasoned that the first licking was similar to tasting a new food and that eating would soon follow. Another example of transductive reasoning involves inaccurate conclusions about cause and effect, as when Peter is sure that Jake caused a toy to fall because Jake walked by at that moment.

Idiosyncratic concepts are concepts that seem general but convey meaning that relates only to personal experiences. Three-year-old Marian, for example, had learned that her grandparents live in Atlanta. When her family visited there, they all went out to dinner at a nearby restaurant. After dinner, Marian asked, "When are we going back to Atlanta?" meaning her grandparents' house rather than the city, which they had not yet left. In other cases, young children focus on only one variable in a situation. A child might say, "I know that Daddy is older because he is bigger." The focus is on size alone rather than on some attempt to coordinate size and age.

Characteristics of the thought of young children caused Piaget to label children **egocentric**. In this context, *egocentric* means "centered on self"—that is, the child views things from his own perspective and needs. For example, the child may go immediately to the toy department to select a gift for a parent. This is a normal characteristic of the thinking patterns of the preoperational child. It should not be confused with *egotism*, which has negative connotations for older children and adults (it is childish and inappropriate for adults to act like preoperational children). In his work, Piaget demonstrated

Egocentrism is expressed by the tendency of the preoperational child to expect that others (even the dog) will have the same needs as she does.

that young children are not as able as older children or adults to take the view or perspective of another person. For example, a child doing the hiding in a game of hide-and-seek may hide only her eyes, because she assumes that if she can't see the seeker, the seeker cannot see her. Or a child may get her favorite stuffed animal for her crying mother because it makes her feel better when she is sad and she assumes it will help her mother as well. Cognitive growth and experience in interactions with other people gradually diminish this egocentrism.

Transductive reasoning, idiosyncratic concepts, and egocentrism are all part of Piaget's view of young children's thinking during the early part of the preoperational stage of development. Although young children's thinking is not yet based on logic, it serves an important function. It is an essential stage in normal human development, which leads to mature, cognitive functioning.

Criticisms of Piaget's Theory

Toby, three years and two months old, pushed me into a cabinet and I hit my head on a corner. When she realized that I was hurt, she looked stricken and ran out of the room. Soon she returned, handed me her special Teddy, and stroked my leg gently.

Observations such as this one indicate that even young preoperational children are able to pay attention to how other people feel. Piaget said that young children are egocentric, but some contemporary researchers have criticized Piaget for underestimating the degree to which young children show awareness of and interest in what others are experiencing.

To understand some of the criticisms of Piaget's theory, it is first helpful to further understand Piaget's concept of egocentrism. He argued that children have an underlying structure for egocentrism and that it shows up in diverse areas of behavior. Children show egocentrism in spatial concepts where they fail to anticipate what others see from their perspective. Children also show egocentrism by failing to understand the feelings, thoughts, and needs of others. One of the ways Piaget gathered information was with the (now classic) "three mountain experiment" (Piaget & Inhelder, 1956). In this experiment, children are asked to sit on one side of a three-dimensional model of mountains. The mountains are distinguished by color, position, and placement of snow, a red cross, and a house. An adult puts a doll at different positions relative to the mountains and asks children to choose a picture that shows what the doll would see from its perspective. Children do not usually succeed in this experiment until they reach eight or nine years of age. Younger children often substitute their own perspective for that of the doll. Piaget used these findings as evidence of younger children's egocentrism: their inability to take a perspective other than their own.

However, other researchers believe that the nature of Piaget's experiment led young children to give more egocentric responses than they would in other situations. These researchers question both the appropriateness of this type of task and the generality of the conclusions that Piaget drew from his findings. This section presents research that questions the applicability of some of Piaget's findings. This current research is then used to analyze Piaget's theory and to give guidelines for creating growth-enhancing environments for young children.

Two sets of research findings have been selected from those that are critical of Piaget's conclusions about young children's egocentrism. In the first set of critical research findings, two researchers (Hood & Bloom, 1979) have shown that, under some circumstances, young children's understanding of causality is more advanced than Piaget indicated. According to Piaget, understanding of cause and effect does not develop until seven or eight years of age. However, Hood and Bloom found that even two- and three-year-olds understand causal relations and have the ability to express them. What explains the difference in findings? Piaget based his conclusions on interviews in which children talked about sequences of actions involving physical objects, but Hood and Bloom investigated spontaneous comments and responses to adult questions about causal relations in the psychological sphere. Hood and Bloom noted that even two-year-olds make causal statements involving events such as babies crying.

A second researcher to criticize Piaget is Borke (1983). Borke replicated Piaget and Inhelder's basic experimental design in the three mountain experiment and also made some substitutions so that the task would be more familiar to young children. Presented with a three mountain scene similar to Piaget and Inhelder's, only 42% of three-year-olds and 67% of four-year-olds were able to take the perspective of another person. But when Grover from "Sesame Street" parked and looked out of his car at toy objects such as boats and animals, three- and four-year-old children were highly accurate (80%) in predicting Grover's perspective. Borke (1983) concluded that the complexity and familiarity of tasks are critical variables in determining at what age children can take the perspective of another.

Should these studies cause rejection of Piaget's theory? It seems that the answer is no. To understand Piaget's explanation for his findings that preoperational children are egocentric, let's examine an earlier study by Borke (1971). She analyzed the responses of preschool children to stories about emotion-inducing events in the life of children. For example, she told the story of a child who loses a brand new puppy and asked the experimental population to identify the emotions the child would be feeling. Beginning at the age of three, most of the children could correctly identify the emotion. She concluded that children are less egocentric than Piaget claimed.

Borke's 1971 study was criticized by Chandler and Greenspan (1972). They pointed out that Piaget's definition of *egocentrism* involves "the ability to anticipate what someone else might think or feel precisely when those thoughts and feelings are different from one's own." To test for egocentrism using this definition, the subjects must have enough information to be able to organize their thinking and apply their structures to an analysis of someone else's motives and needs. To test for this capability, it is necessary to introduce conflicting or contradictory information to examine the child's ability to change answers to match the point of view of the target character.

Selman (1971) described the stages in the development of role-taking, which leads to true empathy:

1. Recognizing emotional states in others
2. Recognizing distinction between self and others
3. Projecting personal feelings onto others
4. Making socially accepted responses to others' needs
5. Fully understanding distinctive perspective of others

Stages 1–4 are egocentric stages, which the child must complete before attaining a nonegocentric orientation of true empathy at stage 5. This

To develop true empathy, egocentric toddlers must first go through a number of stages: recognize emotional states in others, distinguish between themselves and others, and project their own needs onto others.

approach helps us to understand Borke's findings. The children in her study were being asked only to identify feelings in others. It is quite possible that her subjects were at egocentric stage 1, which would be appropriate for two- and three-year-old children.

Another possibility is that Borke's subjects used projection to describe the feelings of the target child. This could be inferred if the children discussed their own experiences with losing a puppy at the same time as discussing the child in the story. A study by Hisrich and Franz (1980) in which children were encouraged to discuss their feelings about the stories corroborates this possibility. Another finding of the Hisrich study was the surprising discovery that the youngest children were likely to claim that the child in the story would be happy if the puppy ran away. In subsequent discussions with the children, it was found that these children believed that the puppy would not be lost. When the interviewer tried to explain that the puppy really was lost, the children refused to hear of it. They argued that the puppy would be found and the child would be happy. They were so egocentric that they couldn't accept the possibility of a bad outcome in such a happy picture—a child with a new puppy!

Note that the example given earlier of Toby's reaction to her teacher's distress is possible at Selman's stage 4. Toby recognizes the emotional state and behaves in a socially accepted way to console her sad teacher. She is behaving in an egocentric way because she projects onto her teacher her own needs by bringing her favorite stuffed toy. She cannot take the distinctive perspective of the teacher, who may be amused and pleased by the action but who will not get the same kind of comfort from the toy that the child has gotten in the past.

When researchers simplify the tasks, they are reaching to simpler structures. The younger children have structures that are sufficient to "pass" the task. These researchers have identified preliminary stages necessary to the development of the full structure. These findings do not contradict Piaget's theory but add to our understanding of the development of nonegocentric responses in children.

Applications of Piaget's Theory

Piaget's theory of cognitive development is rooted in the idea that changes occur as a result of an interaction of the child with the environment. Children acquire new abilities by solving problems to adapt to environmental demands. This is due to the child's need for equilibration, which is an innate desire to understand how to do things in the environment. If the child notices a new event that cannot be explained, he or she is thrown into disequilibrium and will work to return to equilibrium by solving the problem. When the child is in disequilibrium, he or she is ready to learn new things. Teachers and parents must watch for such opportunities of readiness. Teachers must also organize the learning environment so that such disequilibrium is encouraged.

▲ DEVELOPMENTAL ISSUES IN PRACTICE   10.1

PIAGETIAN ACTIVITIES FOR YOUNG CHILDREN

The following sensory activities have been designed for very young children or as a first step for older children. The basis for planning the activities is a Piagetian perspective, which views children as active agents in exploring and understanding their environments.

I See My World

To prepare: Find multiples of common objects (balls, dolls, shoes, spoons, blocks, large pop beads, plastic cups, rattles, plastic jars, receiving blankets, etc.). Put one of each object in a bag for yourself. Put the other objects in front of the child.

The activity: Choose one object from your bag. Ask, "What is this?" Use the label given by the child or supply the term if necessary. Ask, "Please find me another _____." Compare similar objects on the basis of color, size, shape, and other characteristics.

Concepts communicated: Visual discrimination, matching, description, naming

I Hear My World

To prepare: Collect familiar objects that make noises (rattle, bell, half-full tissue box, key chain and keys, piggy bank with coins, etc.). Let children look at and explore the objects and the sounds that they make.

Because children learn from interactions with their environment, there are many things that adults can do to encourage children's thinking by manipulating the environment. Developmental Issues in Practice 10.1 presents some ideas for organizing the environment in a way that contributes to the child's thinking processes. These strategies for facilitating development focus on the concrete world and involve the use of perceptual skills, the major tools with which preoperational children learn from the environment.

Piaget showed an interest in educational applications early in the development of his theory. He always stressed that the environment was essential for providing opportunities for learning. Piaget pointed out that the environment includes social relationships as well as the concrete, physical events that affect the child.

Piaget's most important contribution has been to provide support for the active role of the child in learning. As he points out, "To understand is to invent" (Piaget, 1973). The actions of invention and discovery are essential, but these need not be only physical actions; mental actions are equally important. In addition, to argue that a child should be active does not mean the child should be allowed to function in a wild, undisciplined way. Quite the

---

DEVELOPMENTAL ISSUES IN PRACTICE   10.1 (continued)

The activity: Demonstrate the sound that each object makes. Have children close their eyes or turn their bodies away from the objects. Shake an object and then ask the children to point to the correct thing. Supply the name of the object. Use descriptive terms such as "louder," "softer," "jingle," etc. Repeat with other objects.

Concepts communicated: Auditory discrimination, description, naming

I Touch My World

To prepare: Use a large sock to make a "feeling bag." Gather common objects (ball, large pop bead, nipple from a bottle, rattle, block, spoon, etc.). Allow children to examine the objects.

The activity: Away from children's lines of vision, place one object in the sock. Invite a child to put his or her hand in the sock to try to find out what the object is. Help the child supply descriptive terms for the tactile sensations (smooth, rounded, etc.) and a name for the object. Let the child see the object after a judgment has been made. Repeat with other objects.

In a more advanced variation, two objects can be put in the sock at the same time. You can give an instruction such as, "Find the thing that we use to eat with."

Concepts communicated: Tactile discrimination, description, naming

Adapted from S. Anselmo, Day Care and Early Education. Copyright 1980 by Human Sciences Press. Adapted by permission.

---

opposite—the child should be directed toward a more disciplined mental focus (Piaget, 1970).

Learning always involves action, so children must be given opportunities for action. The teacher's role is to provide interesting and stimulating situations to draw the child into activity. But the teacher's role is not entirely passive. He or she must guide and direct the child to engage in appropriate interactions. Developmental Issues in Practice 10.1 provides good examples of opportunities for teachers to present materials to the child. However, it is the child who manipulates the materials and it is the child's mind that constructs the new ideas. Developmental Issues in Practice 10.2 presents an example of Piaget's theory at work. It shows Jimmy using his knowledge of classification as a base on which to add new, more complex, classification concepts.

Children's ability to think proceeds through specific stages that are universally acquired in the same order. However, the speed (or rate) at which learning occurs varies widely among children and among cultures. It is clearly possible to accelerate learning through educational interventions. However, Piaget warned against excessive efforts at accelerating too quickly.

Young preoperational children learn best through their own experiences with a wide variety of materials.

He pointed out that after children learn something new, they need time to consolidate the information and restructure their thinking to incorporate the new information.

The appropriateness of learning tasks and classroom environments for young children has been evaluated by many interpreters of Piaget's theory (Bybee & Sund, 1982; Elkind, 1976, 1981; Furth, 1970; Kamii & DeVries, 1978; Labinowicz, 1980; Wadsworth, 1978). Because Piaget's emphasis was on theory rather than practice, these interpreters deserve much of the credit for showing parents, teachers, and others how to implement his theory.

ENVIRONMENTS FOR DEVELOPING COGNITION

The cognitive development of young children is influenced by the circumstances in which they live. Research findings provide data about how differences in home environments and family-based intervention programs can affect children's cognitive development.

▲ DEVELOPMENTAL ISSUES IN PRACTICE 10.2

AN EXAMPLE OF PIAGET'S THEORY AT WORK

Three-year-old Jimmy knows how to form classifications by putting things that look alike together. At his preschool he spends a lot of time with a set of blocks made up of red squares and blue triangles. He enjoys separating them into two sets. One day his teacher introduces some new blocks to the set, which include red triangles and blue squares. He is noticeably excited by the new blocks and immediately adds them to his collections. When the time comes to clean up, Jimmy's teacher asks him which blocks he wants to put away first. If he says, "The red ones," it gives the teacher an opportunity to ask whether there are different kinds of red ones. If Jimmy can explain that there are squares and triangles that are red, it is because he is beginning to understand a characteristic of multiple classification—that objects can have more than one characteristic simultaneously. The teacher has provided the materials and directed the activity, but Jimmy has acted on the materials and discovered their characteristics by himself. Jimmy should be given some time to play with the new set of blocks before a new intervention is planned.

Calvin and Hobbes　　　　　by Bill Watterson

Caregivers can help children to learn by encouraging disequilibration. However, the motivation to learn must come from the child's own questions and experience with the environment. Imposing information on children without regard for their developmental needs does not lead to learning.

Differences in Home Environments

Of the research projects that have investigated the relationship between differences in home environments and the cognitive development of one- to three-year-old children, two are particularly interesting. Information is presented about the findings of the Harvard Preschool Project and about effects of noise and confusion.

Harvard Preschool Project.   In the Harvard Preschool Project (White, 1978; White & Watts, 1973; White, Kaban, & Attanucci, 1979), 31 children below three years of age were intensively observed in their home environments to investigate the origins of competence. The researchers found that children's competence at age five could be predicted from parent–child interactions when children were one and two years of age and from children's social and cognitive abilities already emerging in the second year of life.

Some of the Harvard Preschool Project subjects, designated as "A" children in the study, were chosen because they were expected to attain very high levels of competence; the remainder, designated as "C" children, were chosen because they were expected to develop lower than average levels of competence. The children were also grouped by age and by occupation and income of parents.

The children were observed in their homes once every week for six months of each year. In addition, the children were given the Bayley Intelligence Test and tests of language ability, abstract thinking, and ability to sense discrepancies. Testing continued until children were five years of age.

The researchers found that "A" children experienced much more adult interaction than did "C" children. Mothers of "A" children who were 12–15

The Harvard Preschool Project found that some children experience more adult interaction and spontaneous teaching than others.

months and older used teaching techniques more often than did mothers of "C" children. And, between two and three years of age, about two-thirds of "A" children's experiences were encouraging, compared with the experiences of less than one-half of "C" children. Parents of "A" children were found to exhibit the following behaviors (White & Watts, 1973):

Talked frequently to children, at an appropriate level.

Made children feel that what they were doing was interesting.

Provided access to many objects and situations.

Helped and encouraged most, but not all, of the time.

Demonstrated and explained things to children, mostly on the children's instigation.

Prohibited certain activities with firmness and consistency.

Made imaginative associations and suggestions to children.

Gave children the feeling that it is good to do things well and completely.

Made children feel secure.

Strengthened children's motivation to learn.

The parents of "A" children did not often spend large blocks of time teaching their one- and two-year-olds. Instead, they frequently taught "on the fly," usually in response to an interest expressed by the children. Close social relationships with adults were prominent in the lives of the children who developed best.

Parents of "C" children, in contrast with those of "A" children, tended to restrict their children's exploration and curiosity. Playpens, high chairs, and cribs contained children for large parts of the day. The children who were thus restricted could not satisfy their curiosity, nor could they use their emerging physical skills. Usually the restrictions were for the purpose of avoiding the work, possible breakage, and physical danger posed by free mobility of a one-year-old. But children who were unable to build on their curiosity as one-year-olds were generally less curious children six months later.

The differences in environments of "A" and "C" children correlated with their high or low levels of competence at five years of age. The researchers (White, 1978) drew two main conclusions from the data. First, they concluded that the period between 10 and 18 months has critical importance in the development of competence. They found that children who attained high levels of competence at age five could already be differentiated from other children in the second year of life. Even before two years of age, these competent children were significantly more able than others to gain attention in socially acceptable ways, to use adults as resources after first trying a task, and to be proficient in their understanding of language. Second, these researchers concluded that a strong relationship exists between young children's competence and their parents' competence in performing three main functions: designing the world in a safe but interesting manner; being available to consult, comfort, and assist; and disciplining and controlling as necessary.

The Harvard Preschool Project was a landmark in educational research because it attempted to answer by direct observation the important question: How do the early environments of very competent and less competent children differ?

Effects of noise and confusion.   Appliances hum, people talk and shout, and the television roars in the corner. In homes with continuously high noise levels, 18-month-old children show deficiencies in conceptualizing about spatial relationships. In addition, 22-month-olds in these noisy environments lag behind peers in learning to talk (Wachs, 1982).

Researchers at Purdue University (Wachs, 1982) expected to find a linear relationship between the amount of stimulation and the rate of intellectual development in children. That is, they thought that there would be a higher rate of intellectual development when there was more stimulation. But when researchers repeatedly went into homes to observe various aspects of the home environment, they found that the relationship was actually in the form of an inverted U: both too much stimulation (in the form of high noise and confusion levels) and too little stimulation were detrimental to the cognitive development of very young children. The researchers have hypothesized that high levels of noise and confusion lead children to block out such noise and confusion; this blocking out, in turn, causes children to miss out on hearing things that are necessary to language development and on seeing things that give information about relationships in the environment.

The researchers also found that the development of some children is more negatively affected by noise and confusion than that of other children in similar environments. The two groups of children at highest risk are males and temperamentally difficult children. Males seem generally more vulnerable to the effects of all types of stress, and temperamentally difficult children seem more sensitive to noise and confusion because of low thresholds for aversive stimulation. Parents of boys and of sensitive children should give particular attention to the environments in which they place these children.

Effects of Family Intervention Programs

Researchers have attempted to intervene in the lives of families to influence the cognitive development of children from one to three years of age. Encouraging results have been obtained in research conducted at experimental Parent Child Development Centers (PCDCs). The U.S. Office of Education sponsored such experimental centers from 1970 to 1980. The PCDCs attempted to provide support to and intervene positively in the relationships between parents and children. Families were enrolled in PCDCs before children celebrated their first birthdays; they "graduated" when the children reached three years of age. To be eligible for the PCDCs, families were required to have incomes below those listed in federal guidelines.

There were three experimental sites for PCDCs: Birmingham, Houston, and New Orleans. Each PCDC site had its own distinctive program model, but all shared three key characteristics: (1) a stimulating educational program for children, who entered at 2 to 12 months of age, depending on the site; (2) a comprehensive curriculum for parents, including information on child development, child rearing, home management, personal development, nutrition, health, and government and community resources; and (3) extensive support systems, such as medical care and social services. At each site there were experimental groups, which participated in the PCDCs, and control groups, which were comparable to the experimental groups but did not participate. American Indian families were included in these programs.

Evaluations (Andrews et al., 1982) at the time of graduation showed that children whose families participated in PCDCs attained significantly higher scores than did controls on the Stanford-Binet Test. Parents in the program also differed from parents in the control group on all behaviors assessed. For example, compared with controls, parents at the Birmingham PCDC site used language less to restrict and control and more to provide information, gave more instructions and praise in teaching situations, and asked more questions. Compared with controls, parents at the Houston PCDC site were more emotionally responsive to children, provided appropriate play materials and greater variety in daily routines, gave more affection and less criticism, and encouraged verbalizations more. Compared with controls, parents at the New Orleans PCDC site were more sensitive to, more accepting of, and less interfering with their children; and parental interactions had a higher informational content. PCDC children and parents maintained their advantages over the control groups in testing and observation conducted one year later, although the differences were not as large.

Research at Parent Child Development Centers demonstrated that family-based intervention can result in cognitive benefits to children in this age group. It must be emphasized that the intervention was quite extensive, as it was designed to change the family's entire life-style, including parent–child interactions, health care, and family support networks.

LANGUAGE DEVELOPMENT

> This [language learning] is doubtless the greatest intellectual feat any one of us is ever required to perform. (Bloomfield, 1933, p. 29)

Adults who have nurtured young children during the language-learning years usually share Leonard Bloomfield's awe of the human capacity required in language learning. Bloomfield (1933) was a linguist whose work dominated the field until Noam Chomsky (1965) redirected the energies of language researchers. Although their approaches differ significantly, both Bloomfield and Chomsky have said that the mystery of language learning centers on two characteristics of human language: it is governed by rules, and it is also creative. In other words, most speech forms have regular grammatical patterns, but there are almost infinite numbers of word combinations, some of which may never have been uttered. These two characteristics would seem to make language learning nearly an impossible task, which makes it all the more amazing that every normal child masters one or more languages in a few years' time.

Most linguists hold some variation of Chomsky's view about how children manage to learn the languages spoken in their environments (Gleitman & Wanner, 1982). Chomsky has asserted that all languages share universal properties and that human infants are biologically programmed to master the rules of the languages they hear.

Human language consists of three components: phonetics, semantics, and syntax. **Phonetics** is the development of the sound system (we have already discussed the early development of phonetics in Chapter 7 in the sections on cooing and babbling). **Syntax** refers to the development of an understanding of grammar—the way words are combined into meaningful statements. **Semantics** refers to the meanings attached to words. Chomsky was especially interested in the development of grammar. He maintained that the capacity to understand the rules of grammar is species universal and species specific—that is, language is an innate biological trait that occurs in all humans.

Chomsky has noted that children usually receive no formal instruction about the rules that underlie adult language. Instead, they hear a specific set of utterances, different from those heard by the children next door or across the world. Chomsky has said that, from these utterances and the circumstances in which they are heard, children organize and build a workable grammar. The effect is that the children learn the grammar rules found in their native language(s). They use this grammar when they communicate with words, combinations of words, and sentences. In groundbreaking research, Bloom (1970) showed that even the earliest two-word utterances of young children are regular and consistent in the ways words are used and combined. Of course, children cannot discuss the rules of this grammar and are not even aware of it. But researchers feel sure that a mental structure must exist to govern language learning and usage.

All language is based on the human capacity for and need to communicate. Children's efforts at learning language are motivated by this need. No matter how immature a child's speech is, what is most important to the child is that others can understand him or her.

The language development of a fictitious child, Jana, is chronicled as an example of how a child might progress in language learning. The ages at which Jana attains certain milestones represent the ages at which the majority of children attain them (averages are derived from Owens, 1984, and Garvey, 1984). But other children may reach these milestones somewhat later or earlier than Jana and still be within the range of what is called normal.

Jana established the two key bases for speech during her first year of life. First, she developed and continues to develop sensorimotor intelligence, giving her some ideas about how the environment operates and responds. Second, she had experience in prespeech communication, giving her an understanding of turn-taking, reciprocity, and other aspects of interacting with people. On these bases, Jana broadens her understanding and use of language.

Receptive Language

A dramatic linguistic milestone for Jana is the increase in her understanding of language around the time of her first birthday. The term **receptive language** is used to denote language that is received and understood. Receptive language is contrasted with **expressive language,** which is produced by children themselves.

Jana's parents are delighted when their 12-month-old begins to be able to follow simple one-step requests like, "Get the teddy bear," "Give me the cup," and "Show the block." The gestures that adults use to accompany their speech are the primary cues used by the child at this age to understand adult speech and to follow directions (Allen, 1991). By 16 months of age, Jana points to body parts—tummy, nose, eyes, mouth, ears—when asked to do so. Jana understands and responds appropriately and enthusiastically to these and similar requests.

First Words

Jana's first word is *mama,* uttered meaningfully when she is 12 months old. In her first year, she practiced making the *m* sound, but that sound was nonspecific and did not stand for any one person. Now, however, when she says "mama" she refers to the special person in her life. By her second birthday, Jana has added other words to her verbal repertoire: *no, more, baby, ball, up, juice,* and *bottle.* Most of her words are substantive, referring to classes of objects. A few words in her vocabulary are function forms (e.g., *no, more, up*), and these latter words are used frequently.

Nelson (1973) studied the origins of the first 50-word vocabularies of a group of infants. She found a striking similarity among the words first learned by children. She observed that the objects described by children in their first symbol use were not necessarily the ones most commonly found in the infant's environment. For example, children rarely use the words *diaper* and *crib* at this early stage. Rather, we see words such as *keys, cup, ball,* and *book.* These are the objects the child manipulates. It appears that the sensorimotor contact with objects is one of the experiences that prompts early labeling. This provides further support for the theory that the child needs opportunities to explore and manipulate objects. There is also some evidence that the first words produced are the ones most frequently used by parents (Hart, 1991). This provides support for the theory that parents need to describe objects and events to the child. Developmental Issues in Practice 10.3 presents an example of a typical child diary kept by the mother of two brothers. It reflects their speech at the same age (16 months). Note that there are many identical words that both children used. There is also a number of words that were acquired as part of the unique language environment provided by the family at that time in the child's life.

▲ DEVELOPMENTAL ISSUES IN PRACTICE   10.3

ANALYZING CHILD LANGUAGE DIARIES

Child diaries kept on brothers made it possible to compare the brothers' expressive vocabularies at 16 months of age. Their mother was fascinated by the similarities and differences in these first words. Nine of the brothers' first 20 words were identical, another cluster of words referred to food or eating, and the remainder of the words reflected individual interests and preferences.

	C's Words	*D's Words*
Identical words	mama	mama
	dada	dada
	eye	eye
	hi	hi
	bye	bye
	Papa (Grandfather)	Baba (Grandfather)
	ba(ll)	ba(ll)
	mou (th)	mou (th)
	door	doo(r)
Food-related words	e(gg)	mo (more)
	ba-ba (bottle)	yuk
	aa-ba (apple)	bow(l)
	all done	
Other	bu(g)	no
	baby	ya (yes)
	airplane	na-na (night-night)
	bath	no(se)
	do(g)	boo(k)
	bu (tton)	moo (for cow)
	ho-ho (What we say	baa (lamb)
	at Christmas)	Nanna (Nanny)

Many of Jana's early words refer to obvious features of her current environment. Karmiloff-Smith (1979) has proposed that one of the functions of early language for children like Jana is to show that these children separate their actions from objects in the environment. For example, when Jana knows the various actions that she can perform with her bottle (e.g., suck, bang, roll), she can attach the language label, "bottle," to show that the bottle has a continuity beyond the current action that she is performing with it.

As Jana communicates, seven separate functions or uses of words can be identified (Garvey, 1984). The first uses are often instrumental to satisfy wants and needs; regulatory, to control the behavior of others; interactional, to establish and maintain contact with others; and personal, to assert and express oneself. Gradually, language is also used in a heuristic manner, to find out about the world; imaginatively, to create images and pleasurable effects; and representationally, to inform others and express information.

Some of Jana's one-word utterances carry the meaning found in full adult sentences. When she says, "Juice!" she might mean, "I want more juice," "There's the juice," or "The juice spilled." The context of the utterance and the gestures that accompany Jana's words help adults understand her meaning. Linguists use the term **holophrases** to refer to single-word utterances that embody meaningful ideas.

Phonetic Development

Jana's parents notice that she mispronounces the first words she uses. This is normal, and Jana's parents should not worry that this trait will affect her language development. Some evidence from twin studies (Locke & Mather, 1989) indicates that the speed with which correct forms are acquired is due in part to genetics. There may be wide variation in children's speech accomplishments, which reflect individual, inborn patterns. There is no evidence that correct pronunciation is associated with language proficiency.

Once we have learned one language, we tend to assume we know all about language sounds. It is often not until we attempt to learn a second language that we discover how difficult it is to add new sounds to our phonetic abilities. We have difficulty discriminating some sounds as different because we don't routinely use them in our own language. Small children do not have that problem. They can easily adapt to any number of languages. They have the capacity to learn to say all sounds. With age, that flexibility is lost.

Each language uses only a small portion of the speech sounds possible, and only certain combinations are acceptable. For instance, in English, *br, gl, str,* and *tl* are acceptable consonant combinations, referred to as **consonant clusters**. An example of an unacceptable combination in English is *tlngt*. We don't know how to say this combination. However, it happens to be the name of a North American Indian group and is an acceptable combination of sounds for them. English-speaking people generally pronounce this name by adding vowel sounds: *Tlingit*. This produces consonant clusters that are acceptable in English. The child's job in acquiring a language is to learn which sounds are meaningless and to correctly pronounce the sounds that have meaning in the language being learned.

Sounds are produced by passing air through the throat and mouth. **Vowel** sounds are made by passing the air through the voice box, or **larynx,** and out of the mouth. By raising and lowering the tongue, and by moving the tongue from front to back in the mouth, a variety of different sounds is produced. Table 10.2 shows the vowel sounds in English using common words. Try saying these sounds and noticing the position of the tongue on your upper mouth.

Table 10.2.   *The Vowels of English*

	Place of Articulation in Mouth		
	Front	**Center**	**Back**
High	beat		cooed
	b*i*t		could
	ba*i*t	roses	code
	bet		cawed
Low			
	bat	b*u*t	cod

From Philip S. Dale, *Language Development, Structure, and Function*, p. 198. New York: Holt, Rinehart & Winston, 1976. Used by permission.

Consonant sounds are made by causing the air to be temporarily stopped or restrained by touching the tongue to the top of the mouth. When the air is completely stopped, such sounds are called **stops**. Examples of stops include *p* and *d*. If the air is partially stopped, the sound made is called a **fricative,** such as *z,* or an **affricative,** such as *ch* and *j*. Any sound can be nasalized by allowing air to simultaneously pass through the nasal passage. In English there are three nasalized sounds: *n, m,* and *ng*. Sounds can be either **voiced** or unvoiced. **Voicing** occurs when the larynx is activated. In English the general case is that sounds are used in pairs—voiced and unvoiced—except for nasals, all of which are voiced. Table 10.3 shows the consonants of English by place of articulation in the mouth and voicing. Once again, experiment with saying the sounds and observing the location of your tongue as it touches the top of your mouth.

In addition, there are **liquids** (*r* and *l*), which are difficult to learn and acquired late in development, and **glides** (*w* and *y*), which are easy to learn and acquired early. Phonetic development proceeds in clear stages according to the complexity of producing the sound; such development is unrelated to the amount of occurrence in any given language. These normal developmental patterns give rise to common phonemic errors made by children. Examples of some of these errors are presented in Developmental Issues in Practice 10.4. Children spend their preschool years perfecting most sounds, but some phonemes, such as *r* and *th,* may not be acquired until the first years of school. Parents and teachers should not be alarmed by these errors. They are not related to intelligence and will drop out naturally if normal communications are maintained.

Early Sentences

By the end of her second year, Jana is producing her first multiword sentences. At this point, Jana begins to learn to use syntax—the grammar of a language is needed only when words are combined into sentences. Brown

Table 10.3.   *The Consonants of English*

	Bilabial	Labiodental	Dental	Alveolar	Palatal	Velar	Glottal
				Place of Articulation			
	Two lips	Upper teeth on lower lips	Tongue on upper teeth	Tongue on alveolar ridge	Tongue on palate ridge	Tongue on velar ridge	Tongue on glottis
Stops							
Voiceless	*paste*			*tear*		*came*	
Voiced	*baste*			*dare*		*game*	
Fricatives							
Voiceless		*file*	*thin*	*seal*	*hash*		*heat*
Voiced		*vile*	*that*	*zeal*	*rouge*		
Affricatives							
Voiceless				*cheap*			
Voiced				*jeep*			
Nasals							
Voiced	*me*			*no*		*walking*	

From Philip S. Dale, *Language Development, Structure, and Function,* p. 200. New York: Holt, Rinehart & Winston. Used by permission.

(1973) has placed early sentences into 10 main categories that express universal concepts. These categories and examples of Jana's early sentences follow:

1. Nomination, such as "That book."
2. Notice, such as "Hi belt."
3. Recurrence, such as "More juice."
4. Nonexistence, such as "Allgone rattle."
5. Attributive, such as "Big truck."
6. Possessive, such as "Mine doggie."
7. Locative, such as "Walk street" or "Sweater chair."
8. Agent-action, such as "Mommy go."
9. Agent-object, such as "Mommy shoe."
10. Action-object, such as "Put book."

Some of these early two-word sentences depend on gestures, intonation, word order, and context cues for interpretation.

Chomsky argued that all humans have an innate understanding of a basic sentence form made up of "agent-action-dative-object-locative." Brown (1973) demonstrated that children automatically use this basic format, even when they are in the two-word stage of language use. They drop out the less

▲ DEVELOPMENTAL ISSUES IN PRACTICE   10.4

COMMON PHONETIC ERRORS MADE BY YOUNG CHILDREN

Children find it difficult to form words with many consonants, so they engage in *consonant reduction*:

> **pajama** becomes **jama** or **jamy**
>
> **bottle** becomes **ba** or **baba**

Children find it difficult to form consonant clusters, so they engage in *cluster reduction*:

> **spoon** becomes **poon**
>
> **truck** becomes **tuck**

Children find it difficult to produce liquids (*r* and *l*), so they drop the liquid and replace it with a glide (*w* and *y*):

> **little rabbit** becomes **witte wabbit**

Or they use the same or similar sound as found in other parts of the word, sometimes called *backward assimilation*:

> **Roger** becomes **Goge**
>
> **truck** becomes **guck**

Many common phonemic errors made by children have become institutions, as in Elmer Fudd's *wascally wabbit*. Some of the errors are so common that new words have been created that are culturally meaningful, such as the word *jamy* for children's pajamas. Children have a variety of utterances they use for the word *grandmother*, which is difficult to pronounce because it contains two *r* sounds, two consonant clusters, and three syllables. There are many culturally accepted alternative words for *grandmother*, which correspond to phonemic adaptations made by children (e.g., *nanny*, *nona*, *oma*, and, of course, *granny* and *grandma*. In addition, children may have more or less difficulty saying their own names depending on the phonetic form their name takes. For example, *Gregory* is obviously much harder to say than is *Tony*.

important words but always retain the correct order. See Table 10.4 for examples of sentences derived from the basic sentence form.

Linguists have shown that these two-word sentences are universal. Examples of such combinations can be found in every language. This is important because it substantiates Chomsky's theory that these grammatical fundamentals are universal and inborn in humans. These rules produce early sentences that are grammatically incorrect, but they represent an early organized attempt to master the complex rules of language. This is a primitive grammar, which informs the listener of "who did what to whom" by the word

Table 10.4.   *Sentence Combinations Derived from the Basic Sentence Form*

Ordered Combinations	Example
Agent-action	Mommy fix.
Agent-object	Mommy pumpkin.
Agent-locative	Baby table.
Action-dative	Give doggie.
Action-object	Hit ball.
Action-locative	Put floor.
Agent-action-object	I ride horsie.
Agent-action-locative	Tractor go floor.
Action-dative-object	Give doggie paper.
Action-object-locative	Put truck window.
Agent-action-object-locative	Jana put it box.
Agent-action-dative-object-locative	Mama give Jana lunch kitchen.

Reprinted by permission of the publishers from *A First Language: The Early Stages* by Roger Brown, Cambridge, Mass.: Harvard University Press, Copyright 1973 by the President and Fellows of Harvard College.

order. The actor or agent is always first. In addition, uttering these sentences fills Jana with a sense of power because she can communicate her ideas in words.

Vocabulary Expansion

By Jana's third year, her receptive and expressive vocabulary expands. She shows that she can follow two-step requests (e.g., "Get your shoes and take them to Nanny"). She can even point to objects that are described by use (e.g., "Show me something that we use to brush hair"). By the time Jana is four, she has mastered the basic grammar of her language. Brown (1973) demonstrated that, as children develop, they acquire the ability to deal with increasingly complex grammatical expressions. He defined the smallest unit of grammar as the **morpheme**. A morpheme is a single word, such as *mommy, cup,* and *go,* or a single grammatical marker, such as *ed, s,* and *ing.*

Initially, young children do not use any grammatical markers to provide meanings to the words in the sentence. They rely entirely on word order, as was shown by the use of the basic sentence in the earlier section. As children mature, they add grammatical markers in a specific developmental order. See Table 10.5 for the specific order.

During this developmental period, an interesting phenomenon occurs, which demonstrates how Jana actively seeks to organize her language experiences. Earlier, Jana correctly used past tenses of most verbs. But suddenly she begins to say, "I singed a song," and "I bringed it with me." Linguists say that Jana is **overregularizing** a rule about verb endings. They refer to this phenomenon as evidence that language learners like Jana attempt to apply

Language development is encouraged by shared experiences.

the rules they have learned. *Bring* and *sing* have an irregular past form, so one overregularizes to form the past using the regular form of *-ed*. So firmly entrenched is Jana's need to regularize that attempts at correction are unnoticed. Her mother responds to her statements by attending to the content of the message and by using the correct form in her reply. Here is one of their interchanges:

Table 10.5. *Development of Grammatical Morphemes of English*

Morpheme	Order of Acquisition	Semantic Dimensions
Present progressive *(ing)*	1	temporary duration
on	2.5	support
in	2.5	containment
Plural *(s, es)*	4	number
Past irregular	5	earlierness
Possessive *('s)*	6	possession
Uncontractible copula *(be)*	7	number
Articles *(a, an, the)*	8	specificity
Past regular *(-ed)*	9	earlierness

Reprinted by permission of the publishers from *A First Language: The Early Stages* by Roger Brown, Cambridge, Mass.: Harvard University Press, Copyright 1973 by the President and Fellows of Harvard College.

J:	I singed "Old McDonald."
M:	Oh, you sang it by yourself?
J:	I singed it all!

Jana uses overregularizations in the past tense on verbs (*-ed*), the third person singular of verbs (*s*), the plural on nouns (*s*), and the possessive on nouns (*'s*). Examples of Jana's overregularizations are listed in Table 10.6. After several years of overregularizing, Jana constructs a more comprehensive grammatical rule for irregular verb and noun endings and uses the past tense in the way that the adults around her do.

It is important to have an understanding of the developmental expectations for various ages to recognize children who have developmental delays. Developmental Issues in Practice 10.5 gives an example of a validated screening test for language abilities. It is also useful as a general guide for the ages when some major language milestones are acquired by most children.

LANGUAGE LEARNING ENVIRONMENTS

Cultural Differences: Black English

Some young African American children learn to speak a dialect of Standard English that linguists have called **Black English.** These children learn Black English because people in their families and neighborhoods speak it, just as many middle-class children learn Standard English because people in their families and neighborhoods speak it. Most linguists agree that Black English is a highly developed language system. Black English differs from Standard English, but both are structurally equal—both have grammatical, vocabulary,

Table 10.6.   *Overregularizations of Words*

Inflection	Example
Verb *-ed* (past tense)	falled
	growed
	throwed
	waked up
	hurted
Verb *-s* (third person)	doos
	fells
Noun *-s* (plural)	deers
	mans
	peoples
	feets
Noun *-s* (possessive)	mines
	hims

▲ **DEVELOPMENTAL ISSUES IN PRACTICE   10.5**

LANGUAGE SCREENING

Adults who work with young children often wish for a language screening device to ascertain the possible presence of developmental disabilities. Most tests for children under three years of age either lack standardization and validation or require considerable specialized training to administer. Now, however, Copian and colleagues (1982) have developed a brief language assessment suitable for use by pediatricians and other professionals working with young children. The Early Language Milestone (ELM) scale is sensitive and specific as a detector of developmentally delayed children, when compared with more formal tests given by clinical psychologists and speech pathologists. The developers of the ELM believe that young children who show delayed language milestones should undergo formal assessment instead of waiting to see whether they "grow out of it."

The ELM includes 41 language items divided into three groups of behaviors: auditory expressive, auditory receptive, and visual. Sample items from the first parts of the ELM are as follows:

Milestone	Months at Which 90% of Children Attain Milestone
Auditory Expressive	
Mama/dada: correct usage	14.0
First word beyond mama/dada	17.0
Uses 4–6 single words	23.5
Uses 2-word sentences	23.2
Uses 50 or more single words	25.6
Holds brief conversations	34.3
Gives name and use of two objects	34.4
Correct use of pronoun I	>36
Auditory Receptive	
Follows one-step commands	13.5
Points to one or more body parts	20.8
Follows two-step commands	25.1
Points to named object	27.0
Points to objects described by use	32.6

From R. Copian, R. Gleason, M. G. Burke, and M. L. Williams, "Validation of an Early Language Milestone Scale in a High Risk Population." *Pediatrics, 70* (1982): 677–683. Used by permission of American Academy of Pediatrics.

and sound systems that are internally consistent. (See Table 10.7.) Black English is a distinct dialect; it is not deficient nor incorrect Standard English.

Linguists believe that as long as sociocultural differentiation exists within the larger society, there will be dialect variation. Black English and other dialects promote solidarity within ethnic or cultural groups and present a barrier to outsiders. Most individuals feel a conscious or unconscious allegiance to the language of their own group.

The language development of young speakers of Black English parallels that of young speakers of Standard English. Language development is enhanced for all young children if the communicative aspects of language are emphasized. Children speak freely and fluently if they feel that their backgrounds and language are accepted and acceptable. People who work with young African American children should understand some of the characteristics of Black English so they can respond appropriately to the content of children's and parents' messages.

Socioeconomic Differences in Language Learning Environments

Researchers (Schachter, 1979; Schachter & Strage, 1982) studied 24,192 speech acts of mothers and toddlers and found extensive differences in the social and emotional components of communication. The study involved 30 mother/toddler pairs divided into three groups: black disadvantaged, black advantaged, and white advantaged. *Advantaged* was defined in terms of the level of education of the mother, which averaged below high school graduation for the disadvantaged group and included one year of graduate school for the advantaged groups. The study was designed specifically to separate black ethnicity and disadvantaged status; other studies have confounded these two characteristics by comparing black disadvantaged individuals with white advantaged individuals. The researchers hoped that analysis of the speech of advantaged mothers and their young children would help special-

Table 10.7. *Selected Characteristics of Black English*

Characteristic	Language Sample
Noun possessives of common nouns are indicated by word order.	It the girl book.
Suffix *-s* or *-es* to mark the third-person singular is absent.	She walk.
Is may be absent in contexts where it is contractible in Standard English.	She a bad girl.
Are tends to be used infrequently.	You nice.
Verb phrases with *might, should,* or *could* may contain two of these three words.	You might should do it.
The past tense ending *-ed* is not pronounced.	He finish dinner.
Done may be combined with a past tense form to indicate that an action was started and finished at some point in the past.	She done tried that.
Be may be used as a main verb.	Today she be busy.

Adapted from E. H. Wiig and E. Semel, *Language Assessment and Intervention for the Learning Disabled* (2nd ed.), pp. 368–369. New York: Merrill/Macmillan, 1984. Copyright 1984 by Bell & Howell Company. Adapted by permission.

ists in early childhood development understand how adults contribute to the language development of young children.

The researchers found no observable racial difference in the everyday speech acts of mothers and toddlers in their homes. The black and white advantaged groups responded to their toddlers in the same ways. But significant and consistent differences were observed between the advantaged groups and the disadvantaged group. For instance, advantaged mothers talked twice as much to their children as did disadvantaged mothers. There was no difference in the amount of spontaneous talk or in the percentage of verbalizations involving teaching and learning; the dramatic difference was that the speech of advantaged mothers was three times as likely as the speech of disadvantaged mothers to be responsive to interests and desires expressed by children. Showing an awareness of developmental levels, advantaged mothers delayed the teaching of letters and numbers until speech and concepts were established, whereas disadvantaged mothers put more focus on these readiness skills at early ages. Similarly, advantaged mothers supported their children's individuality during a time when the assertion of autonomy is important, whereas disadvantaged mothers worried about spoiling young children if strict limits were not communicated and enforced.

The researchers concluded that a unifying theme seemed to integrate the differences in the everyday talk of advantaged and disadvantaged mothers to their toddlers. Educated mothers, both black and white, support and facilitate the actions of their young children. This conclusion led researchers to wonder whether outreach programs would be effective in helping parents to be more responsive to their children's language, more sequential in their teaching strategies, and more positive in their methods of control. Further research has been designed to ascertain whether such intervention programs with parents and young children can positively influence the course of language development.

Parental Effects on Child Language Development

Parents do not consciously work to encourage syntactic development in their children. They appear to be too busy just trying to communicate. However, there is evidence that parents do influence the language development of their children. Cazden (1981) puts forward the theory that children figure out the meaning of sentences by paying attention to what is said and the context in which it is said. Then they determine what rules control the process of converting the events into meaningful sentences. The way parents interact with their children can be more or less helpful to this process.

Vygotsky (1962) points out that communicating with someone using language involves a **shared meaning**. The parent and the child have to share an understanding of the events, meaning of words, and the syntax of the sentence. A very young child just acquiring language must have a meaningful referent, which Vygotsky calls a **shared referent**. If the parent uses the word *keys* in the sentence as the keys are given to the child, the referent *keys* is like a peg on which to hang the sentences while the child engages in manipulation of the keys. For example, as the parent gives the keys to the child she may say, "Here are the keys. . . .Did you drop the keys? . . .Where are the keys? . . .I see the keys." The child can then use the context and the gestures made by the parent to help build up the "rules" that make each of the sentences syntactically correct. In this way, the child can develop the ability to participate in a shared meaning with the parents.

Note that the sentences mentioned here are simpler in their grammatical form than would be used in adult conversation, but they are typical of the way that parents talk to their very young children. Parents appear to adapt their speech; these adaptations are referred to as **motherese** and **fatherese**. More than 100 alterations of ordinary adult speech have been identified, including use of a higher pitch, simplified grammar and shorter sentences, repetition of words, avoidance of words that change in meaning ("Mommy's doing it" rather than "I'm doing it"), and inclusion of only those topics of conversation that are happening at the moment (Schachter & Strage, 1982).

The adaptations that adults make occur gradually. Mervis and Mervis (1982) showed that mothers of 9-month-olds label objects for their children in an adult manner. But mothers of 13-month-olds have changed their labeling behavior in response to their children's increased interest in language. Instead of using adult categories, they choose labels for objects according to their predictions of what would be the most meaningful to their children. For instance, they take into account that leopards and house cats would be perceived as being the same by young children. This suggests that the parent is learning to make adaptations in speech to communicate with the young child.

Wells and Robinson (1982) have concluded that three critical components of the adult speech environment contribute to the speech development of the child: (1) clear and intelligible adult speech, (2) adult speech related to the child's interests at the moment, and, to some extent, (3) the amount of such speech. Two types of speech allow the adult to focus on the child's interests at the moment. One of these is **expansions** of the child's speech. When the child produces a simple two-word statement, it is important for the parents to respond to such a communication attempt. They can acknowledge their understanding of the statement and, at the same time, expand the statement into a syntactically correct English sentence by adding the missing words. Examples of expansions include the following:

Child's statement	*Mother's expansion*
Daddy come.	Daddy is coming in.
Mommy tea.	Mommy drank her tea.
Sat chair.	She sat in the chair.
Throw Jana.	Throw the ball to Jana.
Give keys.	Give the keys to Mommy.

This has been found to be a highly effective way of increasing speech competency in young children (Cazden, 1981).

A second way of focusing on the child's interests is to use **extensions,** which are sentences that extend the discussion by referring to the previous sentence topics. This, of course, is what is normally meant when one refers to conversation. However, many adults don't feel that it is necessary to carry on conversations with children. For example, when the child says, "Want milk," parents can respond by saying, "You must be thirsty," or, "Does it taste good?" These extensions encourage responses from the child and thus allow the conversation to be carried on.

Nelson, Denninger, Bonvillian, Kaplan, and Baker (1984) have shown that a combination of expansions and extensions used with 22-month-old children increased language competence at 27 months, whereas changing the subject and responding in a very complex way was detrimental to language development. Hoff-Ginsberg (1990) supports these findings in a study that compared a number of maternal speech characteristics to see which ones were most related to improving syntactic development in the children. The most important factors were the ability of the mother to engage the child in linguistic interaction (i.e., converse) and to provide examples for the child of the speech structures that the child was acquiring.

If conversation is so important to language development, then the ability to sustain conversations is essential. Tomasello, Conti-Ramsden, and Ewert (1990) found that mothers functioning as the primary caregivers had fewer communicative breakdowns than did fathers who functioned as the secondary caregivers. The researchers assumed this was due to the greater opportunity for the primary caregiver to communicate with the child during the day. They argued that fathers can be viewed as providing opportunities for children to experience the kinds of communication problems that are likely to occur with less familiar adults in other social settings. In effect, fathers fulfill an important social role in giving the child practice for extrafamilial social contacts.

SUMMARY

1. According to Jean Piaget, children complete the last two substages of sensorimotor thinking in the second year of life and then begin preoperational thinking.
2. The fifth sensorimotor substage is characterized by use of tertiary circular reactions, accurate imitation, and search strategies that allow the child to find hidden objects where they were last seen.
3. The sixth sensorimotor substage is characterized by the ability to work out solutions to problems mentally, to defer imitation, to find objects involving complex hiding places, and to imagine movements of unseen objects.
4. Early preoperational thinking, during the preconceptual substage, is characterized by the ability to use mental symbols and by thought patterns such as transductive reasoning, idiosyncratic concepts, and egocentrism.

5. Critics of Piaget's theory have demonstrated that in meaningful contexts involving basic human communication, young children can demonstrate the ability to engage in simple behaviors. Studies have provided added depth to our understanding of the development of children's cognitive abilities.

6. According to Piaget, effective learning environments for young children should encourage the child's active interaction with a developmentally appropriate environment and systematic adult-directed interventions.

7. The cognitive development of young children is influenced by the home environments in which they live.

8. Children's competence at age five has been predicted from parent–child interactions at one and two years of age and from children's social and cognitive abilities already emerging in the second year of life.

9. In homes with continuously high noise levels, 18-month-old children show deficiencies in conceptualizing about spatial relationships and 22-month-olds lag behind peers in learning to talk.

10. Educational intervention in the lives of families with children below three years of age has facilitated change in parents and cognitive growth in children beyond that experienced by parents and children who did not participate in special programs.

11. Language acquisition involves the creative use of rules and is made up of three components: phonetics, syntax, and semantics. Language milestones in the first 18 months include understanding of receptive language and use of meaningful words, including holophrases.

12. Phonetic development includes the ability to control air through the larynx so as to produce vowels, consonants, and consonant clusters.

13. Syntactic development includes the ability to produce variations on the basic sentence form and to combine morphemes into meaningful sentences.

14. The child's understanding of basic grammar rules is demonstrated in the use of overregularizations.

15. Mothers who have a high level of education have been found to be more responsive to their children's language, more appropriate in their teaching strategies, and more positive in their methods of control than mothers who have lower levels of education.

16. Black English is a distinct dialect learned by children whose families and neighbors speak it. Those who work with young black children should understand characteristics of Black English to respond appropriately to the content of communications.

17. Parents contribute to language development by providing shared referents to assist the child in acquiring shared meanings in communication and by using expansions and extensions.

ACTIVITIES TO ENHANCE LEARNING

The following exercises are designed to help students apply what has been learned and to increase understanding about cognitive development between one and three years of age. To complete these exercises, it will be necessary to make observations of young children. If friends or neighbors do not have one- to three-year-olds, the following are some possible ways to arrange observations: visit a public place that attracts families, such as a busy store, park, or zoo; request permission to observe at a daycare center, family daycare home, or preschool that enrolls children from one to three years of age. These exercises require the use of observational techniques discussed in Chapter 2. Plan to review the relevant section before beginning the observations.

1. Narrative Observation. Write down everything that a one- to three-year-old does for a 10-minute period. Repeat the observation at approximately the same time each day for three days. (Remember to use descriptive, nonjudgmental language.) Answer the following questions about the child's behavior:

   a. Define in technical terms the cognitive and language behavior you see.
   b. What patterns of language and cognitive behavior occur over the three time periods?
   c. What differences occur in each time period?
   d. What stage of cognitive functioning characterizes your subject?

2. Vignettes. Plan a one-hour observation time with a particular child. During the time period, watch for examples of specific cognitive or language functioning. Decide in advance which aspects of the child's cognitive functioning you will transcribe (egocentric behavior, transductive reasoning, two-word sentences, holophrases, etc.). Write down as many of the target behaviors as you observe. Answer the following questions about the child's behavior:

   a. Define in technical terms the cognitive or language behavior you see.
   b. Is the child engaging in behavior appropriate for his or her age?
   c. What would you tell the parent about the child's functioning, based on the vignettes recorded?

3. Child Diaries. Maintain a daily diary of your child's speech patterns. Write down either the vocabulary or the sentences, depending on the child's age. If you are recording vocabulary:

   a. Make a listing of the words the child knows.
   b. Count the number of words in the child's vocabulary.
   c. Organize the words according to categories (see Developmental Issues in Practice 10.3). If you are recording sentences:
      1. Count the number of two-, three-, four-, or more-word sentences you have recorded.
      2. Find examples of each of the different sentence forms, as described in this chapter.

4. Checklists. Prepare a developmental checklist for either language or cognitive functioning. Use the information in this chapter to make up the list of behaviors in developmental order. The checklist should be appropriate for the age of the child being observed. Observe the child and use the checklist to assess performance.

   a. Did the child perform as expected based on his or her age?
   b. Is the child functioning at the appropriate developmental level?

5. Interviews. Design a questionnaire and use it to interview the parent of a one- to three-year-old about the child's ability to show empathy and understanding of another's feelings. Answer the following questions:

   a. Based on the interview, is the child's egocentric functioning appropriate to his or her age?
   b. At what level is the child functioning?

c. How do the parents interpret the child's behavior?

d. Do the parents have a correct perception of the child's egocentric functioning?

6. Time Sampling. Adapt the recording form given as an example in Chapter 2 (Developmental Issues in Practice 2.6) for either cognitive or language development. Use the recording form to observe a child between one and three years of age. Write a few paragraphs describing what you learned about the child's functioning.

7. Event Sampling. Adapt the recording form given as an example in Chapter 2 (Developmental Issues in Practice 2.7) for either cognitive or language development. Use the recording form to observe a child between one and three years of age. Write a few paragraphs describing what you learned about the child's functioning.

FOR FURTHER READING

Language Development

Anisfeld, M. (1984). *Language development from birth to three*. Hillsdale, NJ: Lawrence Erlbaum Publishers.

Bloom, L. (1991). *Language development from two to three*. New York: Cambridge University Press.

Brown, R. (1973). *A first language*. Cambridge, MA: Harvard University Press.

Wood, B. S. (1981). *Children and communication: Verbal and nonverbal language development* (2nd ed.). Englewood Cliffs, NJ: Prentice Hall.

Cognitive Activities

Kamii, C., & DeVries, R. (1978). *Physical knowledge in preschool education: Implications of Piaget's theory*. Englewood Cliffs, NJ: Prentice Hall.

Maxim, G. W. (1990). *The sourcebook*. New York: Merrill/Macmillan.

Weiser, M. G. (1991). *Infant/toddler care and education* (2nd ed.). New York: Merrill/Macmillan.

Interpreters of Piaget's Theory

Bybee, R. W., & Sund R. B. (1982). *Piaget for educators* (2nd ed.). New York: Merrill/Macmillan.

Labinowicz, E. (1980). *The Piaget primer: Thinking, learning, teaching*. Menlo Park, CA: Addison-Wesley.

Wadsworth, B. J. (1984). *Piaget's theory of cognitive and affective development* (3rd ed.). New York: Longman.

PART IV

Early School Years (Ages Four through Eight): Exploring the World

In a daycare center that offers both full-day and after-school care, children eat an afternoon snack. Four-year-old Shawna and five-year-old Wilma use their orange peels to cover their teeth and make monster noises for some giggling younger children. Six-year-old Jason sits near the teacher and earnestly describes his reactions to his first spelling test. "It was cinch-o. They were so easy. I got 'em all. I know I did," he says, watching Mrs. Madera's eyes, seeming to wait for a confirming response. Eight-year-olds Tom and Chico huddle apart from the others, alternately eating and drawing plans for a fort. They speak to each other in low, conspiratorial tones. When a seven-year-old, Alexa, tries to approach them, they sing out, almost in unison, "Up your nose with a rubber hose. Scat, rat!"

The behavior and appearance of these children gives testimony to the existence of considerable physical, psychosocial, and cognitive development in the early school years. In physical development, children in these years refine their large and small muscle skills and develop the ability to participate in sports. They acquire an understanding of their bodies and bodily functions. In psychosocial development, children attain a sense of initiative and then enter the stage of industry. This stage ends with the acquisition of a sense of social relationships and the ability to understand the needs of others. In cognitive development, children begin the period with the entrance into Piaget's second substage of preoperational thought and complete it with the full transition into concrete operational thought.

This part is divided into three chapters devoted to information about physical, psychosocial, and cognitive development. Educational applications are stressed throughout the chapters, and practical applications are also included. Chapter 11 presents information on the milestones of physical development, disabilities, and the formation of a positive physical image and healthy habits. Chapter 12 includes information on Erikson's concept of psychosocial development, the development of a concept of the self, emotional development, prosocial and antisocial behavior, the influences of family and culture, and a discussion of childhood stress. Chapter 13 covers information on the development of logic, perceptual development, language development, the continuing role of play, and the effects of early education programs.

CHAPTER 11

Early School Years (Ages Four through Eight): Physical Development

▼ KEY IDEAS

Milestones of Physical Development
- ❏ Large Muscle Skills
- ❏ Motor Development
- ❏ Small Muscle Skills
- ❏ Drawing and Writing
- ❏ Perceptual–Motor Integration
- ❏ Gender Differences

Disabilities
- ❏ Hearing Impairment
- ❏ Visual Impairment
- ❏ Mental Retardation
- ❏ Emotional Disturbance
- ❏ Specific Learning Disabilities
- ❏ Hyperactivity
- ❏ Speech and Language Impairment
- ❏ Public Law 94-142
- ❏ Disabilities and Cultural Background

Forming a Positive Physical Image
- ❏ Sexuality
- ❏ Concepts of the Body and Illness

Forming Healthy Habits
❑ Eating Habits
❑ Health Care
❑ Fitness
❑ Safety

This chapter was written with James William Younge, Ed.D., Western Illinois University.

The Williams children include Brian, age four; Steven, age six; and Melody, age eight. On one Saturday afternoon, Brian rode his three-wheeled "hot cycle" around the playground of the nearby school, Steven practiced on his two-wheeler with training wheels, and Melody and her friends experimented with popping wheelies and doing other stunts with their two-wheelers. Later when they returned home to make birthday cards for their mother, Brian painted a colorful design, Steven drew a picture of his mother opening her presents, while Melody composed and carefully printed a poem. The children's different activities show not only their individuality but also some of the physical developments that take place during the early school years.

Children change in many ways during the early school years. The four major topics presented in this chapter are intended to clarify the differences in physical capabilities between the youngest and oldest Williams children. The first topic, milestones of physical development, includes large muscle skills, motor development, small muscle skills, drawing and writing, perceptual–motor integration, and gender differences. The second section of this chapter gives information about various disabilities that affect development, legislation on the education of children with disabilities, and the relationship between disabilities and cultural background. The third section focuses on factors that affect the development of a positive physical image: sexuality and concepts of body and illness. The fourth and final topic concerns the formation of healthy habits of eating, health care, fitness, and safety. These four discussions give insights into the complexity and importance of physical developments taking place during the early school years.

MILESTONES OF PHYSICAL DEVELOPMENT

For most children the early school years are an active time during which considerable physical development takes place. Children gain skill in using their large muscles to balance, hop, skip, run, and jump. They also grow more proficient in using their small muscles to reach, grasp, and manipulate objects.

The growth trend of the early school years is slow and constant. Slow, steady growth, rather than growth spurts, allows for practice and refinement of motor skills without the frustration of adjusting to structural changes. However, although growth is gradual, the improvements in coordination and skill are dramatic. Refined sensory systems result in perceptual–motor integration. Children benefit tremendously by having ample time to practice and refine their motor skills and body management capabilities.

The first three parts of this section describe milestones of physical development as experienced by two hypothetical children, Bruce and Paula. These three parts describe changes in large muscle skills, small muscle skills, and the ability to draw and write during the early school years. The fourth part gives information about perceptual–motor integration. The final part describes gender differences in physical development.

Large Muscle Skills

The development of large muscle skills in the early school years is shown through the feats of a hypothetical child, Bruce. The ages at which Bruce is said to attain certain milestones reflect accepted norms (adapted from Sanford & Zelman, 1981) but must be viewed as approximate for other children. Some normal children will develop more slowly and some more quickly than Bruce.

Four to five years.   One of the most notable changes in Bruce during the year from age four to five is his improved sense of balance. He can carry a cup filled with water from the kitchen sink to the table located 10 feet away without spilling. He can walk around a four-foot circle without stepping off the line, walk heel-to-toe for four or more steps along a line, and stand on one foot for five seconds. In other developments, Bruce can hop on one foot, skip 10 steps, pedal his tricycle skillfully around obstacles and sharp corners, and hang from a bar by his hands. He likes to play ball with a neighbor and has become adept at throwing and catching. When Bruce throws now, he turns his nondominant shoulder toward his target and steps with opposition as he throws. His catching has improved, too—he receives the ball away from his body in his hands with palms facing each other.

Five to six years.   Bruce loves a parade and has become able to coordinate his marching with the music on his favorite records. As was the case last year, his balance continues to improve. He stands on tiptoes for 10 seconds, stands on one foot for 8 seconds, swings each leg separately for five swings, and walks backward heel-to-toe for four steps or more. He can also touch his toes with both hands without bending his knees. Jumping has progressed to two-foot takeoff and two-foot landing, with a preliminary crouch and swing of the arms from back to front. In ball play, he can walk up and kick a stationary ball with a full swing of the leg and compensating use of the arms to aid in balance. Bruce runs a 35-yard dash in 10 seconds or less.

Six to seven years.   Bruce is eager to help with household routines and is now able to carry a 10-pound sack of groceries the 50 feet from the car to the apartment. In the time between his sixth and seventh birthdays, he refines other large muscle skills. He rides his two-wheel bike without training wheels, jumps rope three or more times in a row, chins himself on the bar at school, and stands on each foot alternately with his eyes closed. In ball play,

During the early school years, as part of their gross motor development, children develop the ability to control objects.

he catches a tennis ball with one hand, bounces it with one hand, and catches it again with both hands. He is able to jump 38 inches or more from a standing position, jump from a standing position over a yardstick that is held eight inches off the floor, and jump and do a complete about-face. Bruce now enjoys activities that help him improve and refine the basic motor skills. Activities that combine movements such as catching while running begin to lead Bruce toward specialized sport skills.

Seven to eight years.   In the years from seven to eight, Bruce's growth slows and his body control continues to improve. He becomes skillful in maneuvering his bike and in using adult tools such as hammers, saws, rakes, and shovels. He learns to swim and skate and participates in group games such as soccer with competency, understanding, and great enjoyment. Changes in Bruce's physical growth, body structure, and physiological development combine to produce higher levels of performance (Gabbard, 1992). Bruce's large muscle skills have improved significantly since his fourth birthday. Sport-specific skills are now a part of most of the games and activities in which he participates. With continued proper instruction and ample practice time, Bruce will become competent and enjoy his participation in sport activity (e.g., sport participation is positively associated with throwing skill) (Butterfield & Loovis, 1993).

Motor Development

During the early school years, children acquire the ability to engage in all basic movement skills. It is important that children feel a sense of accomplishment, which will encourage them to continue to work at motor development and participate in activities that in turn strengthen physical fitness. Gilliom (1970) has shown that such skills can be acquired and that there is a number of teaching approaches that enhance learning of motor skills. She is concerned with teaching basic movement education skills to teachers. She defines *basic movement education* as follows (Gilliom, 1970, p. 6):

> The foundational structure and process portion of physical education which is characterized by the experiential study of
> 1. time, space, force, and flow as the elements of movement,
> 2. the physical laws of motion and the principles of human movement which govern the human body's movement, and
> 3. the vast variety of creative and efficient movements which the human body is capable of producing through manipulation of movement variables.

Gilliom believed that it is possible to identify the basic movements that are important to performing all physical activity, including those occurring in dance, sport, games, and so forth. She also believed that children can be taught to use basic themes in a variety of contexts and skill areas and that what children learn in one area enhances skills in other areas. Although physical education is generally associated with sports activities, it is important for children to first learn basic skills before they can perform well in sports. In addition, basic skills can benefit fine motor coordination. Gilliom was concerned with the following themes.

1. *Where can you move?* (space)   This theme involves an understanding of **self space** (i.e., the space that the child can reach by extending the body to its greatest reach in all directions) and **general space** (i.e., the space that includes relationships with other people and objects). The child must be able to use the space by becoming skilled at moving in different directions, moving at different levels, moving in different ranges and changing bodily forms (e.g., rolled up like a ball), moving in air (flight), and moving in different pathways.

2. *What can you move?* (body awareness)   This theme includes the skills of identifying body parts, moving different body parts, and learning about the changing relationships of body parts to each other and to other objects.

3. *How do you move?* (force, balance weight transfer)   This theme involves the skills of creating force, absorbing force, moving on-balance and off-balance (gravity), transferring weight (rocking, rolling, and sliding on adjacent parts), and transferring weight, which involves steplike movements using many different parts of the body, not just the feet.

4. *How can you move in a better way?* (time, flow)   This theme includes teaching children to move at different speeds and to move rhythmically, which means being able to vary movements to changing pulse beats. Ultimately, children learn to create movement sequences.

Thus, Gilliom's educational program seeks to teach children the following basic information: Our bodies move in *space*, in *time*, with *force*, and with *flow*. These teaching components are summarized in Table 11.1, which identifies the various curriculum components that Gilliom developed for use by physical education teachers.

Gilliom's curriculum plans provide teachers with ideas for encouraging children to experiment with their bodies so that they discover for themselves the ways they can stretch their abilities and skills (Gilliom, 1970). Gilliom believes that there is never a wrong way to move, if the movement themes are general and presented as problems to be solved. For example, children can be asked to move over a line or a rope on the floor. Children are asked to go over the ropes in different ways. Then the teachers can give suggestions, such as, "Can you move forward and backward and sideward over the ropes?" "Can you change direction each time you go over a rope?" "Have you gone over the rope backward?" In this way, children discover different ways of moving in space and are given ideas for the great variety of movements available to them (Gilliom, 1970). Developmental Issues in Practice 11.1 presents one of Gilliom's curriculum modules for the early school years; it demonstrates her technique and methods.

Table 11.1.   *Movement Chart*

My body.	moves.	in space.	in time and with force.	and with flow. . . . . .
Body parts	**By transfer of weight**	**Division of space**	**Time**	**Dimensions of flow**
1 Head	50 Steplike actions	57 Self space	79 Speed	98 Free flow
2 Neck	51 Rocking	58 General space	80 Slow	99 Bound flow
3 Etc., to 25	52 Rolling		81 Medium	100 Movement sequences
	53 Sliding	**Dimensions of space**	82 Fast	
Body surfaces	54 Flight		83 Accelerating	**Smooth series of movements**
26 Front		59 Directions	84 Decelerating	
27 Back	**By balancing (active stillness)**	60 Forward	85 Rhythm	**Beginning and ending**
28 Sides		61 Backward	86 Pulse beats	
	55 Balancing weight on different body parts	62 To one side	87 Phrases	**Preparation, action, and recovery smoothly linked**
Body shapes		63 To the other side		
29 Curved	56 Balancing on different numbers of parts (4, 3, 2, 1)	64 Up	**Degrees of force**	**Transitions**
30 Straight and narrow		65 Down	88 Strong	
31 Straight and wide		66 Levels	89 Medium	
32 Twisted		67 High	90 Weak	
		68 Medium		
Body relationships: body part to body part		69 Low	**Qualities of force**	
		70 Ranges	91 Sudden, explosive	
33 Near to each other (curled)		71 Large	92 Sustained, smooth	
34 Far from each other (stretched)		72 Medium		
35 Rotation of one part		73 Small	**Creating force**	
		74 Planes	93 Quick starts	
Relationship of body parts to objects: on, off, over, around, across, under, near to, far from		75 Pathways (floor or air)	94 Sustained, powerful movements	
		76 Straight	95 Held balances	
		77 Curved		
		78 Zigzag	**Absorbing force**	
36 Walls, floor			96 Sudden stops on-balance	
37 Boxes, benches, beams			97 Gradual absorption ("give")	
Manipulating				
38 Balls—bouncing, catching, tossing, pushing				
39 Ropes, hoops, etc.				
Relationship of one person to another or others				
40 Near to				
41 Far from				
42 Meeting				
43 Parting				
44 Facing				
45 Side by side				
46 Shadowing				
47 Mirroring				
48 Leading				
49 Following				

SOURCE: From B. C. Gilliom, *Basic movement education for children*, p. 8. New York: Random House, 1970. Used by permission of McGraw-Hill.

CURRICULUM FOR TEACHING MOTOR MOVEMENT THEMES

MAJOR PROBLEM 72

Beginning Grade

"On the signal, find a self space and try to <u>keep your hands on the floor in one spot</u> while you <u>move your feet around</u> in different ways."

"....Can you find ways to take some of your weight on your hands while your feet are moving around?...are your hands part of your base of support? ...how many places can you take your feet?...into different levels?...have you tried different ways of jumping or hopping your feet around as well as running them around your hands?... how many different ways can your feet meet and part?...have you tried to have your stomach up toward the ceiling part of the time?...can you keep moving s-m-o-o-t-h-l-y all the time?... how strong can you make your arms so that gravity won't pull you down?... how many ways can you move if your base of support is very big?...hands far apart, and at least one foot far from your hands?...how many ways can you move if your base of support is very small?...hands close together, and at least one foot close to your hands?... find a way to move in which you are very stable, very much on balance."

Note: The major problem, in bold-face type, is to be stated by the teacher while the children are still.

Note: The subproblems, in light type, are to be stated by the teacher, while children are working on the major problem, only if needed to "bump" individuals or the group into finding more structural relation-ships within the major problem.

From B. C. Gilliom, *Basic Movement Education for Children*, p. 30. New York: Random House, 1970. Used with permission of McGraw-Hill.

Small Muscle Skills

To illustrate the changes that occur in small muscle skills between four and eight years of age, the development of an imaginary child, Paula, is described. The ages at which Paula is able to do certain things are adapted from Sanford and Zelman (1981) and represent average ages for attainment of the various milestones. However, some children may develop at a somewhat different pace and still be perfectly normal.

Four to five years.   Paula increases in her ability to dress and feed herself. Her most recent accomplishments include putting on socks, pull-up garments, belts, shirts that button in the front, and clothes with zippers. By her fifth birthday, she can dress herself with some help from a parent. At the table, she serves herself food and feeds herself with her spoon and fork much more neatly than in the past.

In her Head Start classroom, Paula has learned to use scissors to cut a piece of paper in half along a line. She can fold and crease paper horizontally, vertically, and diagonally as demonstrated by an adult. In fingerpainting, Paula uses broad movements of her fingers, hands, and arms. When she learns to complete a three-piece jigsaw puzzle, she proudly shows her technique to anyone who will look. She handles one-inch-long pegs with ease and is able to put 10 of them into a bottle with a three-quarter-inch opening.

Five to six years.   By her sixth birthday, Paula can dress and undress herself without any assistance. She also has learned to spread food with a table knife, to tie knots that hold, and to wind thread on a spool. She has become more skillful with scissors and now can use them to cut out a square, staying on the lines. She inserts prefolded papers into envelopes and inserts paper into a three-ring binder. At school she makes recognizable shapes out of clay and presents them as gifts to family members.

Six to seven years.   Paula becomes able to help with food preparation in many ways, including scraping carrots, cutting, mixing, and measuring. At mealtime, she now cuts her food with a table knife and uses a fork. She bathes herself with some assistance and supervision. She is perhaps proudest of learning to tie her own shoelaces.

Seven to eight years.   The end of the early school years is a time of consolidation and further rapid development of Paula's small muscle skills. She uses these skills frequently on school tasks (described in the next section) and is able to do hand sewing and knitting under the tutelage of her grandmother. She greatly enjoys crafts and projects of all kinds and can complete them capably and carefully. Eight-year-old Paula uses her small muscles skillfully.

Drawing and Writing

Because of their importance for school success, drawing and writing are described separately from other small muscle skills. Research by Sanford and

Zelman (1981), Lamme (1984), and Brittain (1979) provides information about the typical ages at which children attain various milestones.

Four to five years.   Paula begins to hold her paintbrush with her thumb and fingers instead of her fist, and she holds the paper in place with the hand opposite from the one in which she is holding the paintbrush. She is able to copy a cross, a square, and a simple word such as *cat*.

In her drawing, Paula enters a stage called **the naming of scribbling stage** (Brittain, 1979). She may not start drawing with a particular intent, but her work takes on meaning as she goes along. Moving toward her fifth birthday, she begins the **early representational stage** of drawing (Brittain, 1979). Objects and people appear in her drawings in what seem to be shorthand representations—that is, as symbols rather than as portrayals of the way she actually sees them. Her drawings of people often have just two body parts—a head and legs—and she does not try to portray space but draws in just two dimensions.

Five to six years.   In her kindergarten year, Paula is able to copy triangles, rectangles with diagonals, and her first name. She prints the alphabet, using uppercase and lowercase letters, and writes the numerals from 1 to 9. In drawing, Paula enters the **preschematic stage** (Brittain, 1979). She draws recognizable pictures, often adding ground and sky and attending to size relationships. Objects do not usually float around in space as before, and her people may have as many as six or seven distinct body parts.

The four-year-old who drew this picture is at the "naming of scribbling" stage. He began with no apparent plan but later designated family members.

The four-year-old who drew this picture has entered the early representational stage. She uses shorthand symbols (heads and legs) for people.

A kindergartner created this preschematic drawing at an easel.

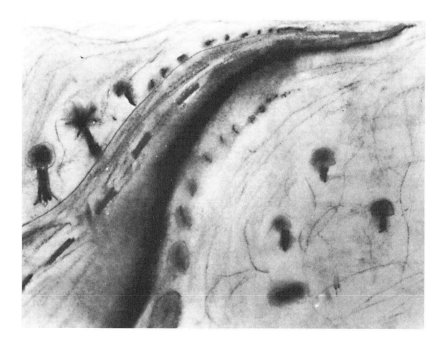

Seven- and eight-year-olds can employ perspective in their schematic drawings if they are helped to be keen observers of nature and the work of other artists.

Six to seven years.   In first grade, Paula is able to copy a diamond shape, print her first and last name, and write the numerals from 1 to 19. She uses her new skills to record her ideas in stories and to do arithmetic computations. Her drawings become more detailed and more **representational.**

Seven to eight years.   The longer Paula is in school, the more she uses her writing skills. She can think of and record longer stories and do more complex computations. In third grade, she begins to write in cursive script. Her drawings enter the **schematic stage,** showing attention to design, balance, and perspective. Great changes characterize Paula's drawing and writing over the course of the early school years.

It has long been known that children make systematic errors in their drawings (Piaget & Inhelder, 1956; Werner, 1957). For example, children tend to draw chimneys rising at an angle from the roof because they are perpendicular to the sloping roof, not the ground (see Figure 11.1). Pemberton (1990) has identified three types of errors: **simplifications, schematizations,** and **orientation biases.** (See Figure 11.2 for examples of good drawings, systematic errors, and other errors.) The presence of these systematic errors is evidence that children follow a sophisticated rule system. The simplification error involves using fewer lines to draw the picture. Paula's drawing, during the preschool years, of only a few body parts to represent people is an example of such an error. Schematization errors involve bringing a schema for drawing another object into the new object—for example, when a child gives

Figure 11.1 *Drawing of House Showing Orientation Error in the Chimney*

animals or cars human characteristics. Orientation bias requires that the child attempt to orient everything toward the perpendicular—for example, when the chimney of the house rises from the slanted roof as though the roof were a flat surface.

Pemberton (1990) found that all three errors decrease with age between 4 and 10 years. The simplification error drops off to nearly nothing, with the schematization error very close behind. However, the orientation error drops slightly from 4 to 6 years and then remains steady through age 10. The cause of the orientation error is not fully understood. It has been suggested that it is due to a number of different factors, including inherent tendencies; production biases; perceptual, motor, and social constraints; and individual style. Whatever the cause, we can expect to see such errors in children until well into the school years. It is possible to use intervention programs to increase

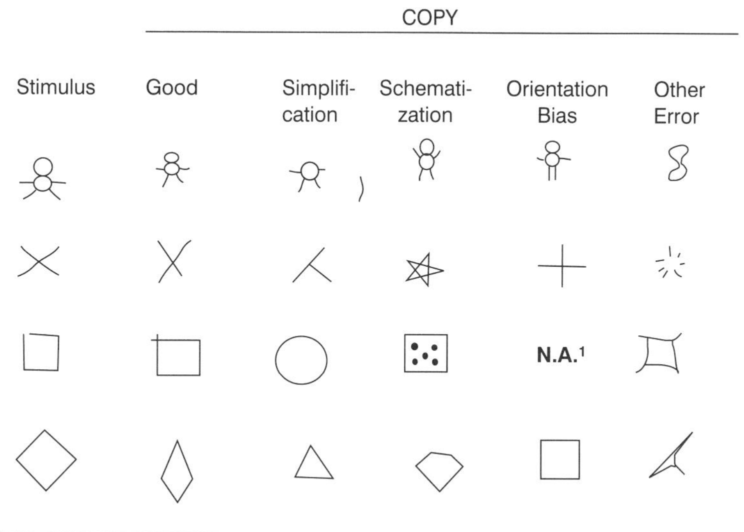

		COPY			
Stimulus	Good	Simplifi-cation	Schemati-zation	Orientation Bias	Other Error

Figure 11.2 *Examples of Good Drawings, Systematic Errors, and Other Errors*

[Figure showing drawings: stimulus figures with corresponding good drawings and various error types across four rows — a stick figure person, an X shape, a square, and a diamond — each shown in Good, Simplification, Schematization, Orientation Bias, and Other Error columns. The Orientation Bias cell in the third row is marked N.A.[1]]

[1]Not Applicable

SOURCE: From E. F. Pemberton, "Systematic errors in children's drawings." *Cognitive Development, 5* (1990): 398. Used with permission.

the skill level of drawing shapes in preschool children. However, the improvement occurs only for those forms just beyond the child's developmental competence (Stiles, Wendy, & Whipple, 1990). This supports the theory that drawing ability is related to cognitive developmental processes.

Perceptual–Motor Integration

Many tasks in the early school years can be accomplished successfully only if children guide their body movements with their perceptions. Playing ball games, drawing, and writing are examples of tasks requiring **perceptual–motor integration**. According to a perspective first expressed by Kephart (1971), perceptual–motor integration follows a developmental progression. The first steps involve control of the whole body (discussed in Chapter 8). The next steps establish control of the arm and hand. Coordination of eye and hand follows, but only after large muscle activities are mastered.

To establish control of the arm and hand, children need practice in using their hands as extensions of their arms. Children can be asked to throw a ball or other object at a target. To hit the target, children must coordinate the movement of their arms both with the grasping and releasing done by their hands and with perceptual data from the target. Developmental Issues in Practice 11.2 gives some additional ideas for movement exploration activities that are helpful in facilitating perceptual–motor integration.

Eye–hand coordination begins when children's eyes can be guided to follow low movements of their hands. Children can be encouraged to observe their actions while they push a train along a track or while they move a

---

▲ **DEVELOPMENTAL ISSUES IN PRACTICE   11.2**

MOVEMENT EXPLORATION FOR PERCEPTUAL–MOTOR INTEGRATION

Many movement exploration activities are helpful in facilitating perceptual motor–integration. The following activities were devised by Sullivan (1982a):

The Tunnel (for four-year-olds)

Objectives: To help create a special space for others.

Directions: "I would like everyone to sit down. When I call your name, come here and put your body like this." Put your body in a crawling position. "Angela, you come first. OK, Marius you're next. You go right next to Angela." Continue until all of the children are in a line, shoulder to shoulder. "Each one of you is going to get to crawl through this long, dark tunnel that your bodies make. It is very important that you not move and that you take good care of the people going through. Angela, you're first. That's right, you get to crawl under all those bodies right through to the other end. OK, Angela, now you need to help make the tunnel here at this end. And it's Marius's turn." Continue until all of the children have had a chance to go through the tunnel. (pp. 67–68)

Mirrors (for five- to eight-year-olds)

Objectives: To become aware of the shape of the body. To understand the role of the leader and to be responsible for another body's movement.

Consideration: Can be done in a limited space.

Directions: The total class should face you. "I am going to do some movements and I would like you to copy me exactly." Do simple movements that can be easily followed.

---

crayon across a large sheet of paper. After their eyes can successfully follow movements of their hands, children can use visual information to guide their movements, such as when they draw around a metal form, trace figures, or complete mazes.

Various aspects of perceptual–motor integration lead to interaction between visual, auditory, and tactile-kinesthetic modalities. Games such as "Statues," in which the leader's position is copied by children in the group, use visual–motor translation; that is, children use visual cues to decide how they should position their bodies. Activities such as marching to a drum beat or playing musical chairs require children to make an auditory–motor match; children use the sounds they hear to control their movements.

DEVELOPMENTAL ISSUES IN PRACTICE   11.2 (continued)

"Now, choose a partner. Sit facing each other. One person will be the leader and the other person will follow. The person who leads needs to move only one or two body parts at a time. You want your partner to be able to follow." After a time, switch leaders.

Extensions: Once the children can lead and follow with only one or two body parts moved, they can begin to lead with their whole body.

Note: Attention span is limited for this intense activity. (pp. 126–127)

Places (for five- to eight-year-olds)

Objective: To acquire an awareness of a point in space and a point in time.

Considerations: Ample space is required. A drum is useful. This activity is appropriate for older children.

Directions: "Pick out a place in the room with your eyes. Now walk to that place. Look around. Can you remember exactly where you are? Now pick out another place in the room with your eyes. Walk to that place. Freeze. Look around. Remember this place. Now walk back to the first place. Freeze. Now walk back to the second place. Freeze in a shape when you are there. Now I will count to 5 and I want you to arrive at Place 1 exactly when I reach 5, not before or after. 1, 2, 3, 4, 5. Freeze! Now move to your other place backward while I count to 5. Not before or after. 1, 2, 3, 4, 5. Freeze! (p. 116)

SOURCE: From M. Sullivan, *Feeling Strong, Feeling Free: Movement Exploration for Young Children*. Washington, DC: National Association for the Education of Young Children, 1982. Copyright 1982 by Molly Sullivan. Used by permission.

Gender Differences

Parents, teachers, and others who interact with children in the early school years often note gender differences in the attainment of physical milestones. According to Gesell Institute data (Ames, Gillespie, Haines, & Ilg, 1979), girls attained certain milestones up to six months earlier than did boys. The differences seemed particularly prominent in tasks requiring use of small muscles. For instance, 61% of girls and only 48% of boys could copy a square at four years and six months of age; 77% of girls but only 45% of boys could draw a person with eight body parts at five years of age; and 88% of girls but only 53% of boys could print their first names at five years of age. Males tend to improve in skills as their developing strength becomes a factor in skill perfor-

▲ **DEVELOPMENTAL ISSUES IN PRACTICE   11.3**

CATEGORIES OF CHILDREN WITH DISABILITIES: PUBLIC LAW 94-142

Public Law 94-142 defines categories of children with disabilities as including the following:

Deaf means a having a hearing impairment that is so severe that the child is impaired in processing linguistic information through hearing, with or without amplification, which adversely affects educational performance.

Deaf-blind means having a concomitant hearing and visual impairment, the combination of which causes such severe communication and other developmental and educational problems that such children cannot be accommodated in special education programs solely for deaf or blind children.

Hard of hearing means having a hearing impairment, whether permanent or fluctuating, that adversely affects a child's educational performance but is not included under the definition of *deaf* in this section.

Mentally retarded means having significantly subaverage general intellectual function along with deficits in adaptive behavior and manifested during the developmental period, which adversely affects a child's educational performance.

Having multiple disabilities means having various impairments (such as being mentally retarded and blind, mentally retarded and orthopedically impaired, and so on), the combination of which causes such severe educational problems that these children cannot be accommodated in special education programs solely for one of the impairments. The term does not include *deaf-blind* children.

Orthopedically impaired means having a severe orthopedic impairment that adversely affects a child's educational performance. The term includes impairments caused by congenital anomaly (e.g., clubfoot, absence of some member), impairments caused by disease (e.g., poliomyelitis, bone tuberculosis), and impairments from other causes (e.g., cerebral palsy, amputations and fractures, or burns that cause contractures).

Health impaired in other ways means having limited strength, vitality, or alertness due to chronic or acute health problems (such as a heart condition, tuberculo-

mance. Boys have been found to engage in more high-intensity, large muscle activity than girls (Butterfield & Loovis, 1993; Poest, Williams, Witt, & Atwood, 1989). This interest contributes to the tendency of males to excel in sports-related skills. Females tend to peak in skills at age 14 and then level off or decrease in performance. Males have longer arms and gradually develop wider shoulders, producing the leverage and rotation torque needed to forcefully propel objects. Females have more body fat, less muscle mass, and gradually develop wider hips (Gabbard, 1992). Differences in ability between boys and girls depend on the motor task involved and the opportunities for

DEVELOPMENTAL ISSUES IN PRACTICE   11.3 (continued)

sis, rheumatic fever, nephritis, asthma, sickle-cell anemia, hemophilia, epilepsy, lead poisoning, leukemia, and diabetes), which adversely affects a child's educational performance.

Seriously emotionally disturbed means having a condition that exhibits one or more of the following characteristics over a long period of time and to a marked degree, which adversely affects educational performance: (1) an inability to learn, which cannot be explained by intellectual, sensory, or health factors; (2) an inability to build or maintain satisfactory interpersonal relationships with peers and teachers; (3) inappropriate types of behavior or feelings under normal circumstances; (4) a general pervasive mood of unhappiness or depression; (5) a tendency to develop physical symptoms or fears associated with personal or school problems. The term includes children who are schizophrenic or autistic; it does not include children who are socially maladjusted, unless it is determined that they are seriously emotionally disturbed.

Having a specific learning disability means having a disorder in one or more of the basic psychological processes involved in understanding or using language, spoken or written, which may manifest itself in an imperfect ability to listen, think, speak, read, write, spell, or do mathematical calculations. The term includes children with such conditions as perceptual disabilities, brain injury, minimal brain dysfunction, dyslexia, and developmental aphasia. The term does not include children who have learning problems that are the result primarily of visual, hearing, or motor disabilities; the result of mental disabilities; or the result of environmental, cultural, or economic disadvantage.

Having a speech disorder means having a communication disorder such as stuttering, impaired articulation, language impairment, or a voice impairment, which adversely affects a child's educational performance.

Having a visual disability means having a visual impairment that, even with correction, adversely affects a child's educational performance. The term includes both partially seeing and blind children.

---

instruction and practice; however, the largest overriding factor among males and females is individual variability (Haywood, 1986).

DISABILITIES

Disabilities affect the psychosocial, physical, and cognitive development of children. According to federal guidelines, children are defined as "disabled" if they fall into one of the following categories: deaf, deaf-blind, hard of hearing, mentally retarded, having multiple disabilities, orthopedically impaired, health impaired in other ways, seriously emotionally disturbed, having a specific learning disability, having a speech disorder, or having a visual disability

(U.S. Office of Education, 1977). The categories of disabilities, as described here, have been amended based on the "Guidelines for Reporting and Writing About People with Disabilities." Thus, the terms are not identical with the way they were used in the 1977 law. However, it is important to use the newer, more appropriate terminology when talking and writing about children with disabilities. Developmental Issues in Practice 11.3 defines these categories.

Until recently, the care and education of three- to five-year-old children with disabilities were the full responsibility of their families, and older children with disabilities were sometimes also excluded from receiving public education. Since the implementation of **Public Law 94-142,** passed in 1977, however, free and appropriate education must be provided for all children with disabilities from 3 to 21 years of age. Public Law 94-142, renamed in 1990 as the Individuals with Disabilities Education Act, makes free public education mandatory for children over five years of age and subject to state laws for three- to five-year-old children. Over half of the state legislatures have been persuaded of the importance of educating three- to five-year-old children with disabilities and have made provisions for either mandatory or permissive programs.

In this section, the following clusters of disabilities are described: hearing impairment, visual impairment, mental retardation, emotional disturbance, specific learning disabilities, hyperactivity, and speech and language impairment. For each disability, symptoms and effects are noted (adapted from Lerner, Mardell-Czudnowksi, & Goldenberg, 1981; Patton, Payne, Kauffman, Brown, & Payne, 1987; and Bailey & Wolery, 1984). The section ends with further discussion of the provisions of Public Law 94-142 and consideration of disabilities in relation to cultural background.

Hearing Impairment

The symptoms of **hearing impairment** may be either prominent or subtle, depending on the severity of the impairment and the age of the child. Hearing impairment should be suspected if children do not seem to respond to nearby sounds or voices when their backs are turned; if they need demonstrations before they understand directions; if they do not speak clearly; if they consistently speak more loudly or softly than is usual; if they are very attentive to lip movements and facial expressions; if they have frequent ear infections, allergies, or upper respiratory infections; and if they have had scarlet fever, measles, meningitis, or severe head injury.

When hearing impairment is suspected, physicians or audiologists use special equipment to measure the loudness and pitch of sounds that a child can hear. Any hearing impairment may vary in degree from severe to mild. Children with the most severe impairments are typically called deaf and usually cannot understand speech even if it is amplified by hearing aids. Children with milder hearing impairments may be able to understand some speech and may be helped by the use of hearing aids. Children who lose hear-

These children are deaf, as defined by Public Law 94-142.

ing before developing speech and language usually show delays in both skills. Special educators believe that children who can benefit from wearing hearing aids should be fitted with them as early as possible. Whether they wear hearing aids or not, children with hearing impairments and their families need to work cooperatively with special educators to select an appropriate system of communication. Options include the use of sign language, lip reading, finger spelling, and various combinations of these approaches.

Visual Impairment

Behavioral symptoms of **visual impairment** include squinting, rubbing the eyes, having difficulty in judging distance, covering one eye to see something, and losing one's place while reading. Children may also have crusty, red, or watery eyes, sensitivity to light, and headaches or dizziness. Even in the absence of such symptoms, the Society for the Prevention of Blindness advocates vision screening for all children between three and five years of age.

Visual impairment ranges from moderate conditions to **blindness,** defined as the ability to see only at 20 feet what the normally sighted person can see at 200 feet. Children with any degree of visual impairment should be under the care of a physician.

Blind children may develop distinctive habits, such as poking their fingers in their eyes, rocking, and making strange noises. These behaviors usually diminish when children are guided in receiving stimulation from their other senses. All visually impaired children have a narrower potential range of experiences than other children, so they may lack confidence in their movements and be slow to develop body image. These children need help in finding alternatives to visual ways of exploring their environments and feeling comfortable with their bodies. Later, when readiness for reading instruction is established, visually impaired children often require either books with large type or Braille books.

Mental Retardation

The definition of **mental retardation** has recently been broadened to include both low intellectual functioning (usually measured by intelligence tests) and deficits in functioning in the community. Children who cannot master school tasks but who display appropriate self-help skills and social responsibility are not considered mentally retarded under the current definition.

Symptoms of mental retardation include general delays in attaining developmental milestones, slowness in controlling the body, and problems with the development of language, speech concepts, and social adaptation. Children with severe mental impairment are often identified in infancy, but children with mild retardation may not be identified until the early school years.

The effects of mental retardation vary with the severity of the individual impairment. In the early school years, these children respond well to stimulating, structured environments. They require many repetitions of learning tasks and work best with actual objects rather than symbols or pictures.

Emotional Disturbance

Emotional disturbance can occur when children are involved in conflict with themselves or others. Symptoms include hostility, depression, unhappiness, withdrawal, lack of satisfying interpersonal relationships with adults and peers, and disruptive or other inappropriate behavior. These children often have a lack of academic and social success that cannot be attributed to intellectual or other factors. They manifest atypical behaviors and poor coping skills over a significant period of time.

Because of the disruptive symptoms these children exhibit, these children are difficult to manage. The effects of emotional disturbance are as diverse as the symptoms. Most children with emotional disturbance need structured opportunities to learn appropriate social skills and to practice them with adults and children. They and their families require a variety of individualized support services.

Specific Learning Disabilities

The most recently defined category of disabilities is called **specific learning disabilities**. The *Report to the U.S. Congress* on learning disabilities prepared by the Interagency Committee on Learning Disabilities (1987) describes current research in this field. This condition is often confused with hyperactivity because hyperactivity and other attentional disorders are the major indicators of learning disability. However, it is possible to control hyperactivity without improving learning in children. In addition, it has been found that there are at least two different types of specific learning disability: one that includes hyperactivity and one that does not. For these reasons, hyperactivity is discussed in a separate section.

Children with specific learning disabilities have significant difficulties in learning but are not eligible for other special education services. These children fail to master specific academic skills such as reading skills, arithmetic skills, language skills, and writing skills, but they are not impaired in vision, hearing, or general mental processes and are not emotionally disturbed. Some neurological dysfunction or problem with the central nervous system is usually assumed, but such dysfunction is difficult to diagnose in medical examinations. There is a definite genetic link in children with specific learning problems and there is strong evidence of chemical imbalances in the brain.

The effects of specific learning disabilities extend beyond academic achievement; children's sense of self-esteem can be undermined. Children who try hard but do not succeed begin to see themselves as failures and losers. These children have difficulty making friends and show a high level of social dysfunction. It is unfortunate that children with learning disabilities who do not also demonstrate hyperactive tendencies are often incorrectly diagnosed and do not receive remedial treatment. Children who have difficulties in learning need to be identified early and given programs that are individualized to meet their needs. When such intervention is not forthcoming, these children may be at the highest risk for developing social and personality problems. More girls than boys tend to suffer from specific learning disabilities without the addition of hyperactivity, and they may be at the highest risk of inattention from the school systems (Berry, Shaywitz, & Shaywitz, 1985).

Hyperactivity

Jeff, age six, seems to be in constant motion in his classroom. Given a worksheet, he prints the first letters of his name vigorously—so vigorously that he rips the paper. A noise from the group next to him attracts his attention and he joins in what becomes a loud disruption. When removed from the group by the teacher, Jeff first laughs and then kicks and hits at the restraining adult.

Children in the early school years show a wide range of activity levels. Some children with low activity levels and long attention spans seem perfectly suited to school environments. Jeff and other children who have very high activity levels seem unable to stay quietly in one place long enough to take part in school activities. Children such as Jeff are often labeled **hyperactive**. Hyperactive children display some or all of the following characteristics: high activity level, short attention span, inability to sit still, impulsiveness, inability to wait, distractibility, unexpected shifts in mood, and frequent touching of objects and people. Hyperactive children are often intelligent but unable to concentrate and learn. More boys than girls suffer from **hyperactivity,** also called **attention deficit disorder.**

Treatment for hyperactive children includes one or more of three approaches: changes in diet, changes in environment, and use of medication. Feingold (1974) is the best known advocate of treating hyperactivity by removing foods with additives from children's diets. He suggested that hyperactive children avoid foods with artificial coloring and flavoring, the preservatives BHT and BHA, and aspirin. These additives are contained in most baked goods, cereals, relishes, toothpastes, frozen meals, and medicines. He also recommended that some children not eat foods containing natural salicylates (e.g., apples, oranges, strawberries, and cucumbers). Testimony about the effectiveness of the Feingold diet comes from parents who describe dramatic changes in their children after diet modifications. However, researchers have been unable to reproduce Feingold's results and believe that more evidence is necessary to draw conclusions about the relationship between diet and hyperactivity.

A second approach to the treatment of hyperactivity involves changing the home and school environments of children. Some hyperactive children respond well to a simple, predictable routine in a setting where as many distractions as possible are eliminated. Behavioral techniques reinforce children's appropriate actions. Research (Pelham, Schnedler, Bologna, & Contreros, 1980) shows that behavioral therapists and parents can be effective in devising and implementing intervention to modify specific problems of hyperactive children.

A third approach to the treatment of hyperactivity is the use of psychostimulant drugs such as amphetamines. These drugs enable as many as 60–90% of hyperactive children treated to increase their goal-directed, on-task behaviors (Whalen & Henker, 1980). That makes the use of drug treatment the single most effective intervention for hyperactivity. However, the evidence that drug treatment has an effect on cognition, conduct, and social behavior is less clear. In recent years, evidence has emerged that the side effects are minimal. However, psychostimulant drugs should be prescribed only after a complete evaluation of a specific case by educators, psychologists, and physicians. Short-term side effects of psychostimulants can include appetite and sleep disturbances as well as increased heart rate and blood pressure. Growth retardation can result from long-term use of psychostimulant drugs. Longitudinal research indicates that behavior changes from the use of psychostimulant drugs do not continue into adolescence when the medication is stopped (Whalen & Henker, 1980). Psychostimulant drugs can be very beneficial to certain children, but they should be prescribed and administered with care.

To determine which approach(es) to use for treatment, professionals should evaluate hyperactive children as early as possible in their school years. Otherwise, the children's inability to attend to school tasks can interfere with learning and with forming a positive self-image.

Speech and Language Impairment

Speech impairment. Speech impairment exists when children's speaking patterns interfere with the communication process. Types of speech impairment include articulation disorders, in which children add, omit, distort, or substitute speech sounds; voice disorders, in which children use unusual pitch, quality, and intensity; and rhythm defects, including stuttering, blocking, or repeating. It is important for the caregivers of children to be aware of the differences between impaired speech and normal language development. Children learn to pronounce words in a systematic way throughout the early school years. They will not have full control of all speech forms until well into the school years. Caregivers should not worry about these normal developmental patterns, as they will improve with maturation. See Developmental Issues in Practice 11.4 for a discussion of these normal patterns.

Children with **speech and language impairments** may feel frustrated by being unable to communicate fully with others. Their reliance on nonverbal communication limits the nuances of meaning that they can convey. Children with speech and language disorders need early diagnosis and treatment to attain their full potential.

An orthopedically handicapped child and his teacher work to meet an objective from his individual education program (IEP).

▲ DEVELOPMENTAL ISSUES IN PRACTICE   11.4

NORMAL PHONEMIC DEVELOPMENT

Adults are very sensitive to language errors, and children's errors of pronunciation can cause great concern. It is important to realize that children continue to make errors in pronunciation until well into the early school years. Such errors are normal and should not be a source of concern. They can often lead to confusion, as illustrated in the following vignette.

> A developmental psychologist speaks at a community center to a group of parents. An anxious mother explains her concern about her son because he is three years old and never says his own name. His name is Gregory. At what age is it expected that he will be able to say it correctly? she asks.

(See the tables for normal developmental patterns.)

Obviously, *Gregory* is a difficult name to say, and the child will likely not say it correctly until after he enters school. This is an example of misplaced parental concern. It is important for Gregory's mother to understand that her son is developing normally. It is possible that he has tried to say his name but that she has failed to notice his efforts because he didn't produce the correct form that she is expecting. For this reason, it is important that she not discourage his attempts by trying to force only the correct form on him. At three years of age he will most likely say "Geg" or "Geggy."

Developmental Emergence and Mastery of Consonants

Age (years/ months)	Consonants Customarily Produced (+50% correct)	Consonants Mastered (+90% correct)
Before 2/0	p, b, m, n, w, h	
2/0	t, d, k, g, ŋ	
3/0	f, s, r, l, j	p, m, n, w, h
4/0	v, z, ʃ, tʃ, dʒ	b, d, k, g, f, j
5/0	θ, ð	
6/0		t, ŋ, r, l
7/0	ʒ	θ, ʃ, tʃ, dʒ, z
8/0		v, ð, s, ʒ

SOURCE: From C. Stoel-Gammon and C. Dunn, *Normal and Disordered Phonology in Children*, p. 31. Baltimore: University Park Press, 1985. Used with permission.

Language impairment.   Children demonstrate impaired language when vocabulary use and sentence construction are delayed or limited. **Dyslexia,** limited reading ability, is the most common of such problems. According to the Interagency Committee on Learning Disabilities (1987), there are two major deficits involved in dyslexia: slow verbal retrieval and difficulty in developing syllables (or the "chunks") that underlie fluent word identifica-

---

DEVELOPMENTAL ISSUES IN PRACTICE   11.4 (continued)

Developmental Mastery (75% Correct) of Speech–Sound Clusters

Age (years/months)	Initial Clusters	Final Clusters
4/0	pl, bl, kl, gl pr, br, tr, dr, kr tw, kw sm, sn, sp, st, sk	mp, mpt, mps, ŋk lp, lt, rm, rt, rk pt, ks ft
5/0	gr, fl, fr, str	lb, lf rd, rf, rn
6/0	skw	lk rb, rg, rθ, rdʒ, rst, rtʃ nt, nd, nθ
7/0	spl, spr, skr sl, sw	sk, st, kst lθ, lz dʒd
8/0		kt, sp

SOURCE: From M. C. Templin, "Norms on a Screening Test of Articulation for Ages Three Through Eight." *Journal of Speech and Hearing Disorders, 18* (1953): 323–331. Used with permission.

---

tion. In addition, dyslexics appear to have difficulty making visual representations that are necessary in fluent reading.

Public Law 94-142

Public Law 94-142, the Individuals with Disabilities Education Act, requires that free public education be provided for all children between 3 and 21 years of age. A key provision of this legislation is the development of an **Individual Education Plan (IEP)** for all children identified as having disabilities. The IEP must include the following information (U.S. Office of Education, 1977):

Statement of child's present levels of educational performance

Statement of annual goals, including short-term objectives

Statement of special education and services to be provided and the extent to which the child will participate in regular education programs

Dates of initiation and duration of services

Evaluation procedures and schedules to determine whether short-term objectives are being achieved

The IEP is planned by the child's teacher in collaboration with a special educator, parents, and possibly other resource people. Public Law 94-142 requires that all testing be conducted in the child's language and provides for **due process** safeguards, including legal procedures, to protect the rights of children. These safeguards include the requirement for parental consent

Some children benefit from mainstreaming—that is, receiving educational services in a regular classroom.

before a child is evaluated or placed in special education, the right of parents to inspect all of a child's school records, and the requirement that parents be notified of any changes in identification or placement.

Public Law 94-142 requires professionals to consider the concept of least restrictive environment when making decisions about placement of children with disabilities. The **least restrictive environment** provision was designed to stop the exclusion of children with disabilities from public school classrooms.

Sometimes, but not always, the least restrictive environment for a particular child is the regular classroom. Providing educational services to children with disabilities in regular classrooms is called **mainstreaming.** Some children with disabilities benefit from mainstreaming for all or part of a day, and others need educational services that can be provided only in special classrooms. Members of the IEP team work together to determine appropriate placement for each child. When children are mainstreamed into regular classrooms, they are thrown together with normal children. It is important for those children who do not have experience with children with disabilities to be able to learn and play together with such children. Developmental Issues in Practice 11.5 lists recommended children's books on disabilities. It is important to expose children to such information to help alleviate tensions and fears.

Disabilities and Cultural Background

Public Law 94-142 requires that assessments for special education placement be culturally fair. In the past, special education classrooms included some students who didn't have disabilities as now defined in Public Law 94-142 but

▲ DEVELOPMENTAL ISSUES IN PRACTICE　11.5

CHILDREN'S BOOKS ABOUT DISABILITIES

Books read to or by children can facilitate their understanding of disabilities. Ideally, these books show children with disabilities as being active participants, not observers, and as being multifaceted. One facet is their disability, but the disability is not their complete existence. Some excellent children's books about disabilities are listed here.

Introduction to Differences

Simon, N. (1976). *Why am I different?* Chicago: Whitman.

Hearing Impaired

Glazzard, M. (1978). *Meet Camille and Danille: They're special persons.* Lawrence, KS: H & H Enterprises.

Peterson, J. W. (1977). *I have a sister—My sister is deaf.* New York: Harper.

Cerebral Palsy

Mack, N. (1976). *Tracy.* Milwaukee, WI: Raintree Editions.

Physical Disabilities

Fanshawe, E. (1977). *Rachel.* Scarsdale, NY: Bradbury.

Fassler, J. (1975). *Howie helps himself.* Chicago: Whitman.

Lasker, J. (1980). *Nick joins in.* Chicago: Whitman.

Mentally Retarded

Brightman, A. (1976). *Like me.* Boston: Little, Brown.

Glazzard, M. (1978). *Meet Lance: He's a special person.* Lawrence, KS: H & H Enterprises.

Learning Disabilities

Glazzard, M. (1978). *Meet Scott: He's a special person.* Lawrence, KS: H & H Enterprises.

Multiple Disabilities

Glazzard, M. (1978). *Meet Danny: He's a special person.* Lawrence, KS: H & H Enterprises.

SOURCE:　From M. Sapon-Shevin, "Teaching children about differences: Resources for teaching," *Young Children, 38* (1983): 24–31. Washington, DC: National Association for the Education of Young Children, 1983. Copyright 1983 by the National Association for the Education of Young Children. Used by permission.

who were culturally different from the majority group. This occurred, in part, because the tests being used were culturally biased in favor of the majority population and children from other cultures were more apt to fail the tests. In the 1970s, lawsuits challenged the testing procedures being used then. For instance, Larry P. v. Riles was a class action suit filed on behalf of black students who were put in classes for the mentally retarded when that placement was not appropriate. Larry P. was decided in favor of the plaintiffs, and the decision was upheld on appeal. A related lawsuit, Diana v. State of California, gave Hispanic children an out-of-court settlement of the same issue raised in the Larry P. case. The results of these cases forced educators to provide culture-fair tests, so that social/cultural differences cannot be used as an excuse to place children in special classrooms. These students deserve the education that meets their individual needs, just as much as children from the majority culture deserve such education.

Special education classrooms have never been intended for students who do not have disabilities as defined in Public Law 94-142. However, minority children are overrepresented in special education programs (Killalea Associates, 1980), and part of the problem may still lie in the discriminatory testing procedures. Patton et al. (1987) noted two problems in tests used for special education placement of students from diverse cultures. First, some tests have norms obtained from mostly white, middle-class groups; these norms are not valid for application to children from other groups. Second, some tests use linguistic styles or require information typical of the majority group but not necessarily of minority cultures. An example of this second problem is from the Peabody Individual Achievement Test (PIAT). The question "What do we call the last car on a freight train?" is meant to assess general knowledge but might be unfair to children from locations such as Southeast Asia or Hawaii. Special education placement is appropriate for culturally different students who have disabilities defined in Public Law 94-142, but fair identification of these children requires the use of nondiscriminatory assessments that are administered with sensitivity.

FORMING A POSITIVE PHYSICAL IMAGE

In the early school years, children's image of their bodies is influenced by a number of factors, including their understanding of sexuality and concepts of illness. By understanding these influences, adults can help children feel positive about their bodies and themselves.

Sexuality

Part of the physical image formed by children comes from their feelings about sexuality. In Chapter 8, information was presented about early gender awareness and identity; through the early school years and beyond, children continue the process of understanding themselves as male or female and developing attitudes about their biological sexuality and organic sensations. The sensitivity with which adults interact with children and respond to their questions and concerns helps determine the way children feel about their sexuality.

In this section, two major issues relating to sexuality are presented. The first continues from Chapter 8 the discussion of sex education and children's levels of understanding reproduction. The second issue deals with the problem of sexual abuse of children.

Sex education. In a public affairs pamphlet, Gordon and Dickman (1981) advise that sex education be provided to children under two conditions: when they ask and when they do not. Often, children in the early school years ask many questions about their bodies, about where babies come from, and about the birth process. It is desirable that they find out that no questions are considered wrong and that the important adults in their lives want to create an atmosphere of open communication.

Children develop understanding and positive attitudes when their questions are answered factually with correct terminology. If children do not ask questions, it is usually not because they do not wonder about these things. Somehow they may have decided that certain topics are inappropriate or embarrassing to others. Because children are sensitive to these attitudes, the way that adults handle questions may be as important as the information conveyed. If children have not asked questions by the early school years, adults should share information about sexuality, read appropriate books to them, and take advantage of teachable moments such as when one sees an obviously pregnant woman.

Even when children receive sex education in a supportive atmosphere, their ability to comprehend it is limited. Research on stages of understanding reproduction has been conducted by Bernstein and Cowan (1981) and confirmed by Goldman and Goldman (1982). At each stage, children incorporate from explanations of reproduction what they are able to understand, and they ignore or reject the rest. Accordingly, children revisit the same information over a period of years before they can develop a mature understanding of sex and reproduction. Adults who provide this information must have the patience to answer the same kinds of questions many times.

Stages 1 and 2 are part of the preoperational period from three to seven years. Bernstein and Cowan (1981) labeled stage-1 children "geographers" because their question "Where do I come from?" refers to geographic place of origin. The child really intends to ask "What town was I born in?" Stage-2 develops sometime during the preschool years. Children at this stage were named "manufacturers" because of the mechanical, concrete way they think about things. They are incapable of understanding the complex, organic process of development. Rather, they think of a baby being put together like a doll on an assembly line.

During this stage, children often express an animistic view of reproduction (see Chapter 10 for a discussion of animism). Children assign humanlike qualities to the sperm and/or egg, as in this description by a child of four and a half years (Bernstein & Cowan, 1981):

Adult:	Where does the egg come from?
Child:	From the daddy.
Adult:	Then what happens?
Child:	It swims in; into the penis and then it . . .I think it makes a little hole and then it swims into the vagina.
Adult:	How?
Child:	It has a little mouth and it bites a hole. (p. 166)

Children's views of everything are very concrete at this age, and their understanding of human sexuality is no different. If they are told that "Daddy plants a seed," children will naturally think of gardening. Such simple statements by adults may be the cause of the colorful ideas we attribute to preschool children (e.g., finding babies in the cabbage patch). The idea that "Daddy plants a seed in the mother" may give rise to unusual ideas about plants growing inside the mother (these prelogical concepts are discussed in greater detail in Chapter 13).

During stage 3, which begins at around six years, children increase their understanding of the role of genitals in intercourse, as in this description by a child of six years and two months: "[The father] puts his penis right in the place where the baby comes out. . . .It seems like magic sort of" (Bernstein & Cowan, 1981). Obviously, this child still has poor understanding of the processes governing conception and is in the transitional stage leading to logical understanding.

Children in stage 3 have grown in their understanding of physical causes for conception and birth, but there are still similarities to earlier stages. They reject animism in their ideas about conception, but they still lack the ability to grasp logical, nonconcrete explanations. For example, they do not see why the participation of both parents is necessary to create a baby. The following interview is with a child of seven years and nine months (Bernstein & Cowan, 1981):

Adult:	Why do the seed and the egg have to come together?
Child:	Or else the baby, the egg, won't really get hatched very well.
Adult:	How does the baby come from the egg and the seed?
Child:	The seed makes the egg grow. It's just like plants; if you plant a seed a flower will grow.
Adult:	Can the egg grow into a baby without the seed?
Child:	I don't think so.
Adult:	Can the seed grow into a baby without the egg?
Child:	I don't know. (p. 223)

Only later in the school years do children refer to sexual intercourse as the beginning of fertilization.

Sexual abuse.   Sexual abuse of children is a major problem. Experts estimate that one in four girls below age 18 is sexually abused. Many boys are also, and incest occurs in 1 in 10 families. Children are often warned against vague dangers presented by strangers, yet strangers pose the least risk: 85% of children who are sexually abused are victims of someone they know and trust (Colao & Hosansky, 1983).

Children depend on adults for food, clothing, and housing and attention, love, and protection. When adults abuse children sexually, the relationship is coercive because of the imbalance of power. Children submit to sex with adults for a variety of reasons: they have been taught to obey adults; they do not know what else to do; they are told that it is OK or that everyone does it; they need affection and it is not offered under other circumstances; they are afraid that they or someone else will be hurt if they refuse; they fear disruption of the only family unit they know (Bass & Thornton, 1983). When children are sexually abused and instructed not to tell anyone, they learn that the world is full of shameful sex, that they are powerless, and perhaps that some people entrusted with their care will betray them. They may carry into adulthood painful, unresolved feelings, such as those expressed by a woman who was sexually abused by her father 30 years earlier (Bass & Thornton, 1983, p. 90):

> Betrayal is a basic theme in my life. . . .I am sure it is a hurt that goes back to my father. What a terrible betrayal. My father is a fine man who prides himself on his high moral principles. How he could have betrayed a child, his child, is still overwhelming to me.

Counseling can help victims of sexual abuse deal with their feelings. However, often sexually abused children do not tell anyone or seek the help they need. Their silence is a heavy burden, but they maintain it for several reasons: they are dependent on the abuser; their safety (or someone else's) has been threatened; they have been told that it happened because they were bad and they feel guilty; they fear that they will not be believed, either because the adult is known and trusted or because they have no proof; or they do not have the words to explain what happened and no one accurately interprets what they mean when they say they have been "bothered" or "teased" (Colao & Hosansky, 1983).

Children who have been taught to be "good"—that is, compliant with adults—are easy prey for abusive adults. Children need information about what parts of their bodies are private and about their right to refuse uncomfortable advances. Children have the right to say no to unwanted touch or affection; they have the right to say no to adult demands and requests; and they have the right to run, scream, and make a scene if they feel threatened. These rights apply whether the advances are from relatives, teachers, religious leaders, coaches, other authority figures, or strangers.

Children need to know accurate terms for their body parts and they need help in communicating their experiences. Sometimes children who are victims of sexual abuse can be observed for changes in behavior or what seem to be excessive expressions of anxiety about interactions with certain adults. Here is an example of a misunderstood communication from a seven-year-old child to a parent (from Colao & Hosansky, 1983):

Jane:	Uncle Joe always teases me, especially when he is baby-sitting for me.
Mother:	Oh, that's part of growing up. My uncle used to tease me, too.
Jane:	[Eyes widening and filling with tears] But, Mommy, how could you stand it?
Mother:	Well, I just learned to live with it, I guess.
Jane:	[Bursts into tears] (p. 49)

Six months later, Jane was diagnosed as having gonorrhea of the throat. If Jane's mother had explored what was meant by "teasing" and why Jane burst into tears, the sexual abuse could have been stopped sooner. Here is how her mother might have helped Jane to communicate:

Jane:	Uncle Joe always teases me, especially when he is baby-sitting for me.
Mother:	Does it bother you?
Jane:	Yes, I hate it.
Mother:	Does he tickle you or say things that upset you?
Jane:	Well, sometimes he wants to play funny games and I don't want to.
Mother:	What kinds of games? (p. 49)

By probing in this way, the mother could have helped Jane to articulate the fact that her uncle was sexually abusing her.

Children who are victims of sexual abuse have specific needs. First and most important, they need to understand that they are not to blame for the abuse. The problem is with the adults, who can have confused feelings that lead them to hurt children. Adult abusers are in control, and, no matter what children do, the children are not at fault. Second, children need to be assured that they are believed and that it is right to tell about the abuse. Third, they need to know that they deserve help and will get it and that a trusted adult will stay with them. They need medical care and afterwards they and their families need counseling by experienced, sensitive professionals.

There is evidence that pornographic material is associated with child sexual abuse. Lanning and Burgess (1989) point out that pedophiles (people who desire sex with children) always collect some kinds of pornography, often with child models. Any evidence of such collections should be viewed as highly suspicious. In addition, pedophiles never use force, as with rape. They tend to reward and praise their victims at first and then use threats later to keep them from telling. If children have been traumatized by such a relationship, they usually show the following types of symptoms, which can be identified fairly easily:

Somatic: headache, stomachache

Enuresis and urinary tract infection

Sexually explicit behavior

Social withdrawal and difficulty with peers

Mood changes

Multiple personality, depression, and psychosis

Marshall (1989) points out that rapists report having been exposed to pornography during the age range from 6 to 10 years. He suggests that early exposure during the child's formative years may create aberrant sexual needs. Thus, it is important to protect children from early contact with sexually explicit material.

Concepts of the Body and Illness

Children's conceptions of illness are important to the development of their concepts of their body. Bibace and Walsh (1981) described the prelogical thinking of the preschool child. At first, these children use "phenomenism" as an explanation. They blame an outside event, usually the most recently occurring phenomenon, however illogical. Later, they subscribe to the concept of "contagion," where mere proximity to bad influences in a magical way causes one to become sick. At school age, children begin to understand a primitive concept of "contamination," where illness is caused by contact with bad things or by bad behavior.

Obviously, young children have a poor concept of illness and will not be able to grasp technical explanations. In addition, they will not understand the value and intent of treatments. It will be hard for a child to appreciate why he or she must endure painful and tedious medical intervention. Logical explanations will not help make it easier. A real danger at this age is chil-

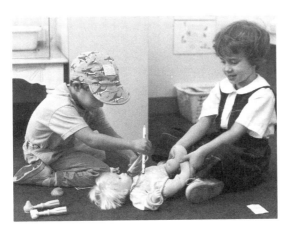

Young children have a poor concept of illness and cannot understand complex and technical explanations.

dren's tendency to use immanent justice—that is, to blame themselves (i.e., their own behavior) for their illness and pain. It is important to be alert for such tendencies in sick and hospitalized children to help them avoid the development of poor self-concepts. Springer and Ruckel (1992) have shown that most preschool children blame illness on contagion and not the notion of immanent justice. In either case, hospitalization can be very difficult for young children. For this reason, the Association for the Care of Children's Health has developed guidelines for the Child Life Programs, which provide care for hospitalized children. See Developmental Issues in Practice 11.6 for the Child Life position statement.

Children cannot understand the mechanisms by which illness occurs, in part because they do not have a concept of their body interiors. It is not until school age that children name interior organs (Crider, 1981). However, even at this age, children only assign one function to each organ, and they do not understand the complex physiological functions that govern the working of the body. For example, they may be able to name the stomach as the place where food is digested. However, they will not understand that digestion begins from the time food is placed in the mouth, that digestion involves the breakdown of food into basic elements, or that these elements are taken up for use by the body.

FORMING HEALTHY HABITS

Habits established during the early school years can affect development at this time as well as later in middle childhood, adolescence, and adulthood. Of particular importance for positive physical development are the eating, health care, fitness, and safety habits practiced by young children.

Eating Habits

Eating habits are established in the early years. They are influenced by internal factors, such as hunger and growth rate, and by external factors, such as cultural and family practices. This section considers both internal and external factors. Information is presented about nutrition, typical growth patterns, and childhood obesity. With such information, adults can be better able to encourage children to form positive eating habits, which are fundamental for healthy life.

Nutrition and growth patterns.   Changes in growth patterns and appetites are found in the early school years. Most four-year-olds have relatively slow rates of growth, small appetites, and continuation of some of the eating problems discussed in Chapter 8. However, by five or six years of age, children usually enter a period of steady growth accompanied by increased appetite (Pipes, 1981), and they generally show fewer eating problems than earlier. However, children in the early school years may carry over some eating idiosyncrasies, such as refusing to eat foods mixed with others and preferring plain, warm (not hot) foods (Whitney & Rolfes, 1993).

CHILD LIFE POSITION STATEMENT

Association for the Care of Children's Health

CHILD LIFE ACTIVITY STUDY SECTION POSITION PAPER

Child Life Programs in health care settings strive to promote optimum development of children, adolescents and families, to maintain normal living patterns and to minimize psychological trauma. As integral members of the health care team in both the ambulatory care and inpatient settings, child life staff provide opportunities for gaining a sense of mastery, for play, for learning, for self-expression, for family involvement and for peer interaction.

I. RATIONALE FOR CHILD LIFE PROGRAMS

- Excessive anxiety and stress related to illness, separation, hospitalization, and medical encounters can be emotionally damaging to an infant, child or adolescent as well as interfere with his or her optimal response to medical treatment and care.
- Major interruptions of normal life experiences can jeopardize growth and development.
- Physical limitations of illness and hospitalization invite dependency and can erode self-esteem.
- Compared to the general population, children and adolescents in health care settings are more likely to have previously experienced excessive social, familial and environmental stress.
- A child's hospitalization can at times be a positive growth experience when truly comprehensive care is given. Such comprehensive care by definition includes child life services staffed by appropriately trained personnel. These services are derived from the ACCH policy statement with a particular focus on the following:

II. ESSENTIAL GOALS OF CHILD LIFE PROGRAMS

A. Minimizing Stress and Anxiety for the Child and Adolescent

1. Provide abundant play opportunities and other experiences which encourage expression of feelings and promote a sense of mastery and understanding of medical experiences. This necessitates qualified personnel, provision of suitable play materials and opportunities for medical play.

2. Increase the familiarity of surroundings and events.

3. Maintain the child's relationship with parents and other family members.

4. Provide supportive relationship for patients and parents characterized by warmth, empathy, respect and understanding of developmental stages.

B. Provision of Essential Life Experiences

C. Providing Opportunities to Retain Self-Esteem and Appropriate Independence

III. STANDARDS FOR PERSONNEL

A. Child Life Specialist

Academic preparation at the Bachelor's Degree level with supervised experience in the health care setting and competence in the following areas: growth and development, family dynamics, play and activities, interpersonal communication, developmental observation and assessment, the learning process, group process, behavior management, the reactions of children to hospitalization and to illness, interventions to prevent emotional trauma, collaboration with other health care professionals, basic understanding of children's illnesses and medical terminology, supervisory skills.

B. Child Life Assistant

Such a person (to work only under the direct supervision of a Child Life Specialist) would generally hold a diploma or a degree from a two year college in an appropriately related field and have personal qualifications similar to the above.

SOURCE: Child Life Position Statement. Association for the Care of Children's Health. Used with permission.

The early school years present children with new social, physical, and cognitive challenges, and children require good nutrition to meet these challenges. Undernourished children are unable to summon the prolonged effort necessary to deal effectively with school activities. They are susceptible to infection, miss school frequently, and have low levels of school achievement. Research demonstrates a relationship between children's nutrition problems and fatigue, boredom, low motivation, and low concentration (Goldsmith, 1980). Undernourished children have lower than expected growth rates and may have difficulty establishing a sense of industry in the early school years.

To be adequately nourished, children in the early school years should be offered a variety of nutritious foods and few empty-calorie items such as candy, chips, and soda. Dietary recommendations include two servings daily of lean meat, fish, poultry, and eggs; the equivalent of about one quart of milk per day; three or more servings of vegetables; two or more servings of fruit; and six or more servings of breads and cereals (Queen & Wilson, 1987). Preschool children will eat the amount of food that is appropriate for their size. As discussed in Chapter 8, it is important that caregivers don't demand that young children eat the large amounts of food appropriate for adults. A rule of thumb for serving sizes for children in the early school years is one level tablespoon per year of age for each food (Whitney & Rolfes, 1993).

Childhood obesity.   About 16 of every 100 children are obese; unless their eating habits change, they tend to be at high risk for certain diet-related diseases, such as hypertension and diabetes (Wishon, Bower, & Eller, 1983). **Obesity** is a health hazard, and obese children are also less able to participate in physical activities and more likely to be teased and ridiculed than their peers.

Childhood obesity results from an interaction of factors. Wishon, Bower, and Eller (1983) have reviewed literature that shows the effects of both hereditary and environmental factors. Genes seem to influence the rate of metabolism and the accumulation of fatty tissue, and the environment seems to govern the nature of eating habits and the rate of physical activity. In some cases, extreme obesity in preschool children is associated with psychosocial dysfunction in the family (Christoffel & Forsyth, 1989).

The atmosphere in which food is served and eaten seems to affect children's eating habits and their attitudes about nutrition and eating. Overeating can be unintentionally encouraged by using desserts or other foods as rewards for good behavior; by giving food as a symbol of affection ("If you love me, you'll eat"); and by eating while engaged in other activities, such as watching television. Also, many children learn poor habits by substituting eating for expressing anger or dealing with boredom.

Proper nutrition is an important cornerstone of good health, and it is most likely to be achieved when children eat light, nutritious snacks and three nutritious meals in an environment of pleasant family conversation. Children need sensitive adult assistance in dealing with their emotional needs separately from issues of nutrition and hunger, and obese children should receive a registered dietitian's services (Whitney & Rolfes, 1993).

Lack of regular physical activity is characteristic of most obese children in the early school years. If they have little exercise, they use only a few calories and store the rest in fatty deposits. Obese children often watch excessive amounts of television and need guidance and encouragement to take part in moderate, regular physical activity. After consultation with a health professional, they should work toward 15- to 20-minute sessions of walking, swimming, bicycle riding, or playing active games. Exercise, combined with limited intake of food, can improve the fitness of obese children. And, if overeating is a response to boredom or stress, exercise can provide a positive way to deal with both of these factors.

Adults tend to think of children as being naturally fit. However, with today's life-styles, which involve riding in cars rather than walking and watching television for long periods, children's fitness programs have become more important (Carson, 1982, 1986). In the early school years, families and schools can work together to help obese children change their eating habits and activity levels. Nutrition education and fitness programs at school can be enhanced by family encouragement at home.

Health Care

The social interactions, activity level, and learning patterns of young children are influenced by their state of health. To maintain optimal health, children in the early school years require regular health care. At least once each year, they should receive a complete physical examination, including tuberculin skin test, urinalysis, blood tests, hearing and vision screening, and necessary vaccinations or booster shots. Yearly physical examinations, along with visits to the doctor for any illnesses during the year, make it possible to monitor, prevent, and treat conditions that might interfere with children's development.

In addition to physical examinations, two specialized types of health care gain increased importance in the early school years: dental care and vision screening. The importance of dental care is underscored by the appearance of the first permanent teeth; the importance of vision screening is emphasized by the highly visual presentation of many learning experiences in the early school years. In this section, dental care and vision screening are described.

Dental care.　Patterns of good dental care should be established well before the early school years, but the appearance of the first permanent teeth often heightens the motivation of families to provide this care. Permanent teeth begin to come in when children are about six years of age. Simultaneously, the six-year molars erupt and the two lower front teeth (lower central incisors) become loose. Gradually, the permanent incisors push up from underneath, destroying the roots of the first teeth until they fall out. The permanent teeth replace the first teeth in the same order in which the first teeth appeared: incisors, molars, and then canines (the sharp teeth between incisors and molars). The substitution is usually complete by the time children are 12 or 13 years of age.

The appearance of the permanent teeth makes good oral hygiene especially important. Ideally, teeth should be brushed after every meal; at a minimum, they should be carefully brushed in the morning and in the evening. In areas without fluoride in the water supply, supplementation should continue until all permanent teeth are in.

Children should establish a habit of visiting a dentist every six months from the time they are three or four years of age. The dentist can provide feedback about dental care and anticipate the need for orthodontia, which corrects crooked and misaligned teeth. Modern methods of orthodontia may require that the procedures begin in the early school years. Removable appliances called crozats apply mild pressure to the teeth and bones to make room for all the teeth. Orthodontia improves appearance, but a more important goal is often less well understood: orthodontia improves occlusion, or bite. Chewing causes a force of as much as 200 on the teeth; to withstand this pressure without problems, the teeth need to be properly aligned and in correct relationship to each other. Otherwise, damage can be done to the bone structure and nervous system, causing pain and headaches. Orthodontia can correct the incorrect alignment and prevent a lifetime of discomfort.

Vision screening.   Many learning experiences in the early school years involve vision, and subtle difficulties in vision can interfere with children's ability to learn. The well-known Snellen chart measures vision only at a distance of 20 feet; although the information gained from using this chart is helpful, it does not identify some visual difficulties that create reading and other problems. One such difficulty is **amblyopia** (pronounced am-blee-OH-pee-uh)—seeing well with one eye but poorly with the other. Amblyopia begins when children use only their good eye and not their poor eye. If untreated, it can lead to permanent loss of vision. Amblyopia can be discovered by a simple screening procedure in which each eye is tested with the other eye covered. This screening can be conducted by parents or volunteers from community groups who are trained by specialists at their local health districts or at the Society for the Prevention of Blindness. To be most effective, screening should take place early and treatment should begin by the time children are four years of age.

Even more subtle visual difficulties can be diagnosed by ophthalmologists trained in children's developmental vision. They examine a wide range of visual performance skills, including tracking of moving objects, focusing, converging when looking at near objects, depth perception, visual acuity at distances and nearby, and range of readability. These ophthalmologists also may investigate children's balance, coordination, spatial perception, and figure–ground discrimination (Ames, Gillespie, Haines, & Ilg, 1979). By conducting a complete examination of children's visual behavior, developmental ophthalmologists can first determine whether children have any visual problems that could interfere with school performance and then provide necessary treatment.

Fitness

Children in the early school years often seem to be in perpetual motion. In the past, many educators assumed that playing games would provide a foundation for later fitness. Now it is realized that education for fitness must be part of the formal and informal curriculum. As they play, children can be taught about their bodies, conditioning, and the role of exercise in lifelong fitness.

The definition of **fitness** includes six components: strength, power, muscular endurance, cardiovascular endurance, flexibility, and body fatness. Strength is the ability to exert force. Power is the ability to exert considerable force over a very short period of time. Muscular endurance is the ability to exert force continuously over a long period of time. Cardiovascular

Fitness training is important for early school-age children because it provides conditioning and teaches them about their bodies.

▲ **DEVELOPMENTAL ISSUES IN PRACTICE   11.7**

TEACHING SAFETY RULES

The American Red Cross has developed curriculum materials for teaching children in the early school years about safety (Robbins, 1984). These materials help teachers plan learning experiences to improve behavior, understanding, and attitudes of young children about safety. Here are examples of suggested activities:

- ❏ Make cartoons illustrating rules of safety for riding in automobiles.
- ❏ Make posters illustrating school bus rules and display them on bulletin boards or in school buses.
- ❏ Dramatize jaywalking situations and their results.
- ❏ Make puppets and conduct a puppet show on walking and riding safety.
- ❏ Identify hazards that interfere with safe walking and riding and tell how such hazards can be avoided.
- ❏ Make bright yellow kerchiefs and beanies that can be readily seen by motorists.
- ❏ Make traffic signals and use them in role-playing safety situations.
- ❏ Compose safety songs and safety games.
- ❏ Prepare for and take field trips to places concerned with safety practices and promotion of safety.
- ❏ Demonstrate how to fasten and unfasten a safety belt.
- ❏ Demonstrate bicycle safety rules.

Contact a local chapter of the American Red Cross for more information about curriculum materials on safety.

SOURCE: From E. Robbins, "American Red Cross teaches safety rules to children," *Day Care and Early Education, 12* (1984): 32–33. Used by permission of Human Sciences Press.

endurance or stamina is the ability of the lungs, heart, and circulatory system to carry oxygen and nutrients to the cells of the body. There is some evidence that the majority of young children engage in such low levels of physical activity that they fail to promote cardiovascular health (Poest, Williams, Witt, & Atwood, 1989). Flexibility is the ability of the joints to move through their entire normal range of motion. Body fatness is the proportion of fat cells to other body tissue.

Attaining physical fitness is an individual matter that involves exercising to improve the levels of the six components just described. The results of fitness programs should be noted in changes in specific children over time; comparisons among children are not relevant. Programs encouraging basic fitness that are designed with developmentally appropriate activities for children in the early school years have been shown to be effective (Carson, 1982, 1986).

In 1992 the President's Council on Physical Fitness and Sport and the American Alliance for Health, Physical Education, Recreation and Dance combined the Physical Best and President's Challenge programs. The new fitness program will be called the President's Youth Fitness Program. The new fitness education program will be designed for students in kindergarten through 12th grade and will include the best of each former program. It will include education information and assessment of aerobic endurance, body composition, flexibility, muscular endurance, and muscular strength.

Safety

Children in the early school years and through the age of 14 experience the lowest rate of death of any period from birth to age 24. Children of these ages have successfully survived many of the early childhood and birth-related diseases and have not yet entered the older age group that has a high incidence of work-related and motor vehicle accidents. Still, in the early school years, accidents are the leading cause of death, accounting for over half of the deaths at this age (U.S. Bureau of Census, 1980). During this age, as children mature and learn to care for themselves, safety is attained by changing the focus from protection to education (Surveyer, James, & Burns, 1985). Safety education should have a high priority in homes and schools. Developmental Issues in Practice 11.7 presents methods for teaching safety rules to children.

Because children in the early school years have a high degree of mobility and a wide range of activities, they need safety education that focuses on the home, school, and wider community. Children require guidance and constant reinforcement to become safety conscious at home and at school and to become responsible pedestrians, cyclists, and riders of school buses and public transportation. Outside experts such as fire fighters and police officers may be effective in motivating children to be safe and aware.

SUMMARY

1. Children develop many new physical competencies during the early school years.
2. Regarding large muscle skills, children between the ages of four and eight improve in balancing, hopping, skipping, running, and jumping.
3. Regarding small muscle skills, children gain proficiency in reaching, grasping, and manipulating objects.
4. From four to eight years of age, children learn to control writing and drawing implements and add considerable representational detail to their drawings.
5. Young school-age children make systematic errors when drawing, which include simplifications, schematizations, and orientation bias.

6. Perceptual–motor integration progresses from control of the whole body to control of the arm and hand to coordination of the eye and hand.

7. Girls are somewhat ahead of boys in reaching physical milestones, especially those using small muscle skills.

8. The development of children in the early school years is affected by such disabilities as hearing impairment, visual impairment, mental retardation, emotional disturbance, specific learning disabilities, and speech and language impairment.

9. Public Law 94-142 requires that free public education be provided for all children, even those with disabilities, between 3 and 21 years of age.

10. Children from minority cultural backgrounds are overrepresented in special education classrooms; nondiscriminatory assessment is necessary to determine which children need these services.

11. Hyperactive children, often intelligent but unable to concentrate and learn, are treated by changes in diet, changes in environment, or use of medication.

12. Sexuality and concepts of body and illness influence children's physical images of themselves.

13. Sex education should be provided to answer children's implicit or explicit questions; children also need preparation for the possibility of being sexually abused, which is a major problem.

14. Concepts of the human body and illness are poorly developed in young school-age children.

15. By age five or six, children enter a period of steady growth accompanied by increased appetite; nutritious choices should be made available to them. Both environment and heredity contribute to childhood obesity.

16. Physical examination, dental care, and vision screening are important aspects of health care in the early school years.

17. Specific attention should be given to physical fitness. Children should exercise to increase levels of strength, power, muscular endurance, cardiovascular endurance, and flexibility and to maintain an appropriate percentage of body fat.

18. Accidents are the leading cause of death in the early school years. Safety education is very important.

ACTIVITIES TO ENHANCE LEARNING

1. Assume that you are running a program for three-year-old children and the parents come to you to ask you to initiate a program to teach the children how to participate in sports. Prepare an outline of the kinds of information you would use to explain to the parents why most three-year-olds are not ready to learn sports skills.
   a. Include information on the developmental limitations of the motor skills of three-year-olds.
   b. Include information on the importance of learning basic motor skills first.
   c. Write a brief statement on the importance of general motor ability in young children.

2. Assume a parent is very upset because her preschool child doesn't seem to understand how sex and reproduction work. Prepare an outline of the kinds of

information you would use to explain to her the developmental level of preschool children.

    a. Include information on children's understanding of sexual issues.

    b. Include information on children's understanding of how their own bodies function.

    c. Include information on the importance of being sensitive to children's cues that they are victims of unwanted sexual attention.

3. A parent asks you to make a presentation to a group of parents about the kinds of programs available to children with disabilities.

    a. Include information on the various kinds of disabilities and the importance of defining the conditions correctly.

    b. Include information on Public Law 94-142 and the requirement for Individual Education Plans.

    c. Discuss the importance of programs for children with disabilities.

FOR FURTHER READING

Movement Experiences

Kamii, C., & DeVries, R. (1980). *Group games in early education: Implications of Piaget's theory.* Washington, DC: National Association for the Education of Young Children.

Sullivan, M. W. (1982a). *Feeling strong, feeling free: Movement exploration for young children.* Washington, DC: National Association for the Education of Young Children.

Children with Disabilities

Patton, J. R., Payne, L. S., Kauffman, L. M., Brown, G. B., & Payne, R. A. (1987). *Exceptional children in focus* (4th ed.). New York: Merrill/Macmillan.

Child Abuse

Besharov, D. J. (1990). *Recognizing child abuse: A guide for the concerned.* New York: Free Press.

Colao, F., & Hosansky, T. (1983). *Your children should know: Teach your children the strategies that will keep them safe from assault and crime.* Indianapolis: Bobbs Merrill.

Nutrition

Endres, J. B., & Rockwell, R. E. (1993). *Food, nutrition, and the young child* (4th ed.). New York: Merrill/Macmillan.

Satter, E. (1987). *How to get your child to eat . . .But not too much.* Palo Alto, CA: Bull Publishing.

Videotape Presentation on Motor Development

Carson, L. (Producer). (1992). *KinderSkills, Ages 3, 4, 5.* Morgantown, WV: PlaySkills Videos.

CHAPTER 12

Early School Years (Ages Four through Eight): Psychosocial Development

Influences and Adjustments Outside the Family
❑ Peer Relationships
❑ Effects of Television
❑ Culture and School Adjustment
❑ Multicultural Understanding

Childhood Stress
❑ Differences in Coping Processes
❑ Developmental Changes in Reactions to Stress
❑ Protective Factors

To understand the psychosocial development of children in the early school years, changes in children as well as influences on them must be considered. This chapter begins with a description of children's development of a sense of self, referred to as self-concept. One important aspect of self-concept is that of developing an awareness of personal identity. This chapter will begin by looking at Erikson's theory of the psychosocial changes in children as they try to attain a sense of initiative and then a sense of industry.

A second important aspect of self-concept is the development of self-awareness and self-control. The chapter describes emotional development and then social cognitive development of children, including both prosocial and antisocial behaviors. This is followed by an examination of various external influences on the psychosocial development of young children. These influences include children's families, parenting styles, adjustments outside the family, and childhood stress. This chapter deals with the important psychological and personality issues of the early school years with a recognition that the development of children's self-concept is always affected by the children's social interactions, and vice versa, so that both affect each other.

ERIKSON'S CONCEPT OF PSYCHOSOCIAL DEVELOPMENT

According to the theory of Erik Erikson (1982), children's self-concept is rooted in his theory of personal identity. Developing a positive self-identity in the early school years requires success in two important psychosocial tasks. During the preschool years (approximately 3 to 5 years old), children are challenged to either take initiative or suffer the effects of guilt; during the school years (approximately 6 to 12 years old), they learn either industry or inferiority. The ability to take initiative is necessary for whatever humans do; the ability to become industrious has a decisive effect on school life and on later entrance into the world of work. Children who achieve positive resolutions of these psychosocial tasks attain a sense of purpose and a sense of competence. In this section, Erikson's concepts of **initiative versus guilt** and **industry versus inferiority** are described.

Erikson's Concept of Initiative

Four- and five-year-old children show a vigorous, imaginative, and playful unfolding. They use toys to re-create past experiences, anticipate future roles, and work out the range of activities open to them. They are eager to learn, to work with other children to plan and build, to listen to teachers, and to model the behavior of admired figures. They are curious and easily engaged in the excitement of new undertakings. Their initiative extends to include their expanding social, physical, and cognitive prowess.

Achieving a sense of initiative leads to the basic human strength of purpose. However, pure, unbridled initiative can result in acts of aggression, manipulation, and coercion. Children can misdirect their physical energies in activities that are discouraged by adults or harmful to others, such as running on the sofa, climbing the furniture, or pushing playmates. Children can use their verbal abilities to hurt people, telling family and friends, "I hate you," or, "I'm not inviting you to my birthday party." Children can use language to shock and offend, displaying a knowledge of vulgar words that surprises even their parents. Initiative refers to the intention to engage in specific behaviors, such as those just described. When negative consequences occur as a result of specific negative actions, children feel a sense of guilt. This sense of guilt is at the opposite end of a continuum from initiative and helps to balance children's behavior. Children gradually establish a moral sense that restricts the horizon of permissible behavior. Children look for opportunities to use initiative without feeling too much guilt.

Initiative adds to autonomy the quality of planning and taking on tasks for the sake of being active. Initiative is an important human quality and needs to be nurtured. Children at ages four and five should have many opportunities to initiate social interactions, active physical movement, and imaginative play. According to Erikson's theory, children's sense of initiative is validated when adults respect and give encouragement to their interests and respond positively to their frequent questions, which are indicators of intellectual initiative. Though the possibility of feeling guilt provides a safeguard against the misuses of initiative, the danger remains that children can be made to feel too heavy a burden of guilt. If guilt overwhelms initiative, children lack the sense of purpose that helps them find success in future endeavors. It is for this reason that children at this age must have the opportunity to engage in useful and effective acts of initiative. Parents must endeavor to insulate the child from extensive failure, which can create a self-concept dominated by feelings of guilt. Developmental Issues in Practice 12.1 provides some guidelines for encouraging initiative in preschool children.

Erikson's Concept of Industry

Children from first grade through the elementary years are ready to channel their energy into producing things. Children at these ages become excited by projects such as building forts, sewing, cooking, and making collections and models (the more ambitious the better). Children's sense of industry is enhanced when their efforts are encouraged and their completed projects noticed and rewarded. Elkind (1970) has called this the Robinson Crusoe age

▲ DEVELOPMENTAL ISSUES IN PRACTICE   12.1

DISCIPLINE TECHNIQUES THAT PRESERVE INITIATIVE

Four-year-old children have tremendous amounts of energy and desire to use initiative; however, they also need a lot of help in staying out of trouble and using good judgment. Maria felt that she was "on" her four-year-old son, Raimundo, nearly all the time: "Get off the table!" "If I hear you say that word again . . .Not at the dinner table!" Raimundo clearly needed redirection and help in learning appropriate behavior, but Maria could sense that Raimundo's self-concept was being wounded after a day of many such commands. Maria wondered whether she could guide Raimundo in more positive and less guilt-inducing ways. At a parent discussion group, she learned about discipline techniques that preserve children's initiative. Instead of resorting to threats and orders, Maria began to follow these steps:

1. State expectations clearly and positively. For instance, when Raimundo climbed on the table, Maria said, "The table is for eating or working."

2. Give alternatives, if appropriate. "You can work at the table or climb in the yard."

3. Give a limited choice in cases of continued inappropriate behavior. "Climb down from the table yourself or I'll lift you down."

4. If necessary, give sanctions for continuation of inappropriate behavior. "If you climb on the table again, I'll know that you need a few minutes of time out." (Note: "Time out" consists of up to five minutes spent sitting in a chair away from the hub of family activity. Maria sets a hand timer so that Raimundo knows when he can return.)

Maria found that following these steps made her feel more in control and less harassed. In addition, she felt that Raimundo was happier and less guilt-ridden about his activities. Now, if Raimundo's behavior is inappropriate, Maria presents him with choices that allow him to exercise his sense of initiative. Raimundo can understand his mother's expectations better and see the relationship between decisions and consequences. He feels that he can make plans that are acceptable, and he has a more positive self-concept.

because the enthusiasm and detail with which Crusoe described his activities also characterizes children's own unfolding sense of industry.

In all societies, children at these ages receive some systematic instruction. In U.S. society, the fundamentals of technology are developed in schools, where great emphasis is placed on literacy and basic education for a wide variety of jobs and careers. Children often participate in a wide range of clubs (Scouts, 4-H, religious organizations) and take classes in a wide range of subjects (music, art, dance, sports). In the elementary years, goals are expected to gradually supersede the whims and wishes of play. Children become eager, absorbed participants in productive situations.

Achieving a sense of industry leads to a self-concept that includes the important component of competence. Children who feel competent are able to attempt new individual tasks and carry out their parts in cooperative efforts. But not all children have experiences in and out of school that contribute to the development of a sense of industry. At the opposite end of the continuum from a sense of industry lies a sense of inferiority. Children develop a sense of inferiority when their projects are viewed as a nuisance and when their work is seen as inadequate. They feel unable to live up to external and internal expectations of social interaction, physical feats, or mental discipline. Children's personality development can be disrupted if their predominant feeling during the elementary years is inferiority rather than industry. That is why school success is so important and so pervasive in the concerns of a child. It is important for children to be successful in one field of endeavor: academics, athletics, dance, music, and so on. They need opportunities for such experiences and support for their successes. In addition, both the individual and the society are threatened if children begin to feel that they are being evaluated according to the color of their skin or the nature of their background rather than their competence.

Erikson (1982) has said that the resolution of this psychosocial crisis is decisive in determining children's attitudes about themselves and about what they can do in later years. No one can achieve mastery in every situation, but the balance of children's experiences at the end of a day or week or month should allow them to feel successful about human interactions, physical performances, and cognitive tasks. To develop a sense of industry, children need sensitive parents, teachers, recreation leaders, and others who can individualize expectations.

Enhancing children's self-concept is an important priority in the early childhood years.

DEVELOPMENT OF SELF-CONCEPT

The roots of the development of a **self-concept** lie in infancy and involve the many interactions the child has with the social environment as development progresses. However, children enter the preschool years at approximately age three with the cognitive and social skills to begin a new phase of self-awareness.

This self-awareness will make possible the development of **self-esteem,** which can be defined as the affective (or emotional) side of self-concept; that is, it is the emotional assessment of how children feel about themselves. To be able to have an emotional response to the self, it must first be possible to evaluate the self. Self-evaluation appears to begin in the preschool years (Stipek, Recchia, & McClintic, 1992). As children develop a sense of competence, it becomes possible to assess their self-esteem (Harter, 1982, 1985), beginning in middle childhood. This section will examine some of the different kinds of research that have given us information about the roots of self-esteem, including studies on **self-knowledge,** self-awareness and self-control.

Broughton's Concept of Self-Knowledge

Broughton (1978) believed that, to have an understanding of oneself, it is necessary to develop self-consciousness. He reasoned that one could ask children to talk about their understanding of the self and the mind and, from the answers, it would be possible to analyze the limits of children's understanding. The questions he asked were quite complex and included asking the children to define *reality, knowledge, truth, mind,* and *thoughts.* Probably most of us would have to really think about these questions before giving an answer. According to Broughton, children at the same age levels gave surprisingly similar kinds of answers to the questions. He found that there was a definite developmental progression in the way the questions were answered. He organized the answers in two levels: (1) objective, which included children from ages 4 to 7; and (2) empirical, which included children from ages 8 to 12.

Children at the objective level believed that "reality" was an absolute thing associated with physical, concrete objects that could be "known" directly. Children thought of their minds as a part of their physical bodies and believed that thoughts simply flowed through the whole body. At this level, children had no sense of the reality of feelings, needs, personality, and so on. In addition, they had no understanding of thoughts being produced in a specific part of the body, the brain. Indeed, they had a very poor concept of the interiors of their bodies (this issue is discussed at greater length in Chapter 11).

At around eight years of age, children begin to enter the empirical level. This stage was so named because it refers to the ability to obtain information from the environment. At this level, children came to understand the importance of perception in providing information about reality, and they came to believe that knowledge was acquired through the senses (i.e., reality was whatever you could see, hear, touch, etc.). They understood that they each have a brain and that thoughts and images come from the brain or mind.

▲ DEVELOPMENTAL ISSUES IN PRACTICE   12.2

THE USE OF ROLE-PLAYING WITH EARLY SCHOOL-AGE CHILDREN

Research has shown that children develop their concept of themselves and others over the years from three to eight. This concept limits their ability to take on the role of another person. Thus, role-playing as an activity will have a different value and meaning to children at different ages.

For example, a teacher wants to help a child to understand the value of a prosocial behavior, such as cooperation. If Valerie has just taken a toy away from Suzy, the teacher can ask Valerie, "How do you think Suzy feels when her toy is taken away?" Such a question forces Valerie to use her concept of self and others and to attempt to understand the meaning of her aggressive action. This technique will work to varying degrees depending on Valerie's age and development. The development can be summarized by age, and the implications for role-playing vary by age.

Using the example of Valerie's aggressive behavior, the responses she gives will be very different depending on how old she is. Following is a list of the different developmental stages by age along with a discussion of what kinds of role-playing ability can be expected at each stage.

❑ Ages 2–3:   Valerie is egocentric and assumes that everyone has the same knowledge she has about herself and others. Valerie has no concept of Suzy as a separate person. She assumes everyone has the same view of the world that she has. She would answer the teacher's question by saying that she should have the toy because she wants it. She would have no concept of Suzy's separate and distinct feelings about the toy.

❑ Ages 4–6:   Valerie's self-knowledge is based on physical action and concrete events. Valerie still has problems with egocentrism; however, she will judge

Selman's Concept of Self-Awareness

Selman (1980) used a story, rather than direct questions, to find out about children's **self-awareness**. He gave the children the following problem:

Eight-year-old Tom is trying to decide what to buy his friend, Mike, for a birthday party. By chance, he meets Mike on the street and learns that Mike is extremely upset because his dog, Pepper, has been lost for two weeks. In fact, Mike is so upset that he tells Tom, "I miss Pepper so much that I never want to look at another dog again." Tom goes off, only to pass a store with a sale on puppies. Only two are left, and these will soon be gone.

Selman then asked the children whether Tom should buy Mike the puppy. This dilemma allowed Selman to ask questions about the children's understanding of people and interpersonal relations (e.g., "Can you ever fool yourself into thinking that you feel one way when you really feel another?" and "Is there an inside and an outside to a person?").

DEVELOPMENTAL ISSUES IN PRACTICE 12.2 (continued)

the situation by concrete actions and events. She would answer the teacher's question by saying that Suzy gave up the toy in the face of aggression, so she doesn't really want it. Valerie may willingly return the toy under such circumstances, if that is the school rule. But she does this only because she understands it to be the generally accepted practice, not because she understands the reasons behind the action.

❑ Ages 6–8:   Valerie's self-knowledge includes an awareness of psychological components, but she assumes that the psychological and physical realities will be consistent. Valerie begins to be aware of the need to assess the psychological reality of the situation. At this age, she will be aware of Suzy's desire for the toy and disappointment at losing it. For the first time, Valerie will be able to address Suzy's feelings and will be aware that what she has done has caused her friend sadness. She will be able to apply her own awareness of such feelings to Suzy and sympathize in the true sense with her loss of the toy.

❑ Ages 8–12:   Valerie's self-knowledge includes an awareness of psychological components and the understanding that psychological issues—such as needs, beliefs, and values—can be different from the physical reality of words and actions. Valerie will be able to use relatively complex analyses of Suzy's psychological state to determine how to react to the situation. She may be able to ascertain that Suzy doesn't really like the toy that much and would be willing to part with it, or she may be aware that Suzy's sadness is put on in order to get the teacher's sympathy. At this age, Valerie can apply complex issues of context and personal psychological need to problem solving. Thus, true role-playing really becomes possible at eight years of age.

Selman found that the answers allowed him to formulate a theory of self-awareness with three developmental levels. Level 1, physicalistic conception of self, is like Broughton's first level. Selman found that children at this level thought of themselves only in terms of physical acts. They reasoned that Mike said he didn't want another puppy, so that was the reality. These children could not grasp the possibility that Mike's psychological state might be different from what he said it was. Selman stated that, at this level, children "often report that their mouth tells their hand what to do or that their ideas come from their tongue" (Selman, 1980, p. 176).

As with Broughton's theory, Selman found that there is a developmental change in early grade school, so that children begin to recognize the presence of inner, subjective states, including feelings, needs, and thoughts that are different from the outer, physical reality. However, Selman believes that this developmental change occurs in two stages: one beginning at age six and the other at age eight. At age six, Level 2, Selman found that children were aware that there were two "realities": the inner, subjective reality and the outer, objective one. However, at this level, the children still thought that the two parts of a person would be consistent. It was only at Level 3, at age eight, that the children came to understand that the two parts of a person could be in contradiction. By age eight, children could understand that Mike might really want to have another dog and that it was possible to fool someone else into misunderstanding one's real desires. They also understood that it is possible to fool oneself.

Thus, there is good evidence that preschool children have a physical awareness of themselves, whereas school-age children develop both a physical and a psychological sense of the self. This notion was further refined by Keller, Ford, and Meachum (1978). They asked children to answer questions about themselves by completing sentences, such as: "I am a _____. I am a boy/girl who _____." It was found that preschool children are most apt to represent themselves in terms of physical activities. Statements about body image, such as size and color of eyes and hair, were very rare. Thus, the physical concept of self at this age may be based specifically on physical actions. It is for this reason that motor development is so important to young children, and success in motor activities probably is instrumental in the development of positive self-concept (this issue is addressed in Chapter 11).

All the research suggests that there is a major shift in self-concept at around the age of eight, when an awareness of the psychological self is developed. An additional characteristic of that awareness is that children begin to show the ability to compare themselves with others. In a study by Secord and Peevers (1974), children responded to questions about themselves in relative terms. For example, younger children would say, "I ride a bike." On the other hand, third graders began to say, "I ride a bike better than my little brother." This response suggests that third graders are beginning to refine their sense of self to include evaluations of their performance in terms of others. This observation demonstrates the importance of social relationships to the development of the self-concept. It also suggests that such social relationships become more important to self-concept as children mature and may be somewhat less important in the preschool years, when children still have a poorly developed concept of themselves.

These facts about children's self-knowledge and self-awareness are important when considering the use of role-playing as a technique for teaching children about themselves and others. If children have a poorly developed sense of their psychological selves, role-playing may have a different value at different ages. Developmental Issues in Practice 12.2 discusses the use of role-playing with young school-age children.

The Blocks' Concept of Self-Control

The Blocks' research consisted of a longitudinal study of personality development, using subjects from three to seven years of age (Block & Block, 1980). The research was based on Freud's theory of the ego as the primary unit of

Ego control refers to the part of the personality that manages impulses, needs, and desires and allows children to be in charge of themselves.

personality (see Chapter 1 for more discussion of this theory). It is one thing to have some level of self-awareness, but it is children's level of self-control that is of greatest interest to those around them. This is the focus of the Blocks' research. According to this theory, the ego is the part of the personality that allows an individual to interact rationally and logically with reality. The ego is responsible for controlling impulses and desires to enable the person to act responsibly in interpersonal relationships and within social organizations. Two aspects of ego functioning emerged from the research findings: **ego control** and **ego resiliency**.

Ego control refers to the part of the personality that manages impulses, needs, and desires. It is possible for a child to function on a range of control from extreme undercontrol to extreme overcontrol. Undercontrollers were described as being expressive, spontaneous, distractible, unable to delay gratification, and having many but relatively short-lived enthusiasms and interests. Overcontrollers were described as constrained, inhibited, showing minimal expression of emotion, nondistractible, less exploratory, relatively conforming with narrow and unchanging interests, organized, and having difficulty with ambiguous situations. Obviously, it would be most functional for someone to be in the middle range between these two extremes.

Ego resiliency refers to the ability of a person to modify the level of ego control to meet the demands of changing situations. That is, the person is adaptable. It was found that a person who could respond with flexibility to life's demands had higher ego resiliency and was more functional than someone with lower ego resiliency.

Together these two personality characteristics determine the amount of self-control that an individual will have. The important finding of the research was that children tend to develop a definite pattern of ego control and ego resiliency by the age of three and that the pattern developed at this early age is remarkably stable into the early school years. In addition, the pattern of ego development at the age of three can predict specific patterns of behavior in middle childhood.

The research found that extreme ego undercontrollers are highly active (Buss, Block, & Block, 1980). Such children at the age of seven tend to be more aggressive, more assertive, less compliant, less shy, and less inhibited in their play than more controlled children. In addition, ego undercontrollers demonstrated later negative interpersonal behavior, including teasing, manipulativeness, and aggression (Block & Block, 1980). Ego resiliency, on the other hand, was related to later positive interpersonal behavior, including empathy, social responsiveness, and protectiveness. The most adaptive pattern for later functioning was that of high ego control and high ego resiliency. This pattern produced children who were in charge of themselves and at the same time were able to function with an absence of anxiety and intimidation. High ego control combined with low ego resiliency was a maladaptive combination; children with this combination appeared immobilized, anxious, and overwhelmed by a world to which they could not adapt (Block & Block, 1980). The research suggests that ego control and ego resiliency are determined largely by the style of interaction provided by the parents (this will be discussed at greater length in the section on the family).

EMOTIONAL DEVELOPMENT

Chapter 9 discussed different types of emotions and some of the important considerations adults should have in dealing with children's emotions. This section will further define emotions and discuss the importance of the environment in generating them. This will be followed by a discussion of some important considerations in providing education about emotions.

Definition of Emotions

Emotions are important to us because they serve as messengers, energizers, and a source of bonding between individuals (Coleman & Hammen, 1974). They signal to us our actual response to a situation; they mobilize us to act in appropriate ways, such as in self-protection or in joy; and they help us bond to people through communication. In other words, emotions provide a link between ourselves and the environment (Plutchik, 1980). It is through emotions that we are able to make contact between our "self" and the world around us.

Emotions occur as a result of our interpretation of the world around us. They help us cope with our environment by helping us accurately define what is happening to us. As long as we have an accurate response to our environment, we are responding rationally and appropriately. However, incorrect or irrational responses can be destructive of a person's personality; for example, if a person has a fear of something that doesn't exist, it would be very damaging for the person to organize his or her life around such an irrational fear.

Research into the developmental changes in children's emotions demonstrates that preschool children have more irrational emotions than do children in the elementary school years (Bauer, 1976). It is most likely, for this reason, that preschool children have a tendency to have nightmares; this appears to be due to the lack of cognitive understanding of so many environmental events, which is typical of preschool children. They fail to understand what is happening in the environment and so they give incorrect emotional responses. However, during the school years, children show a decrease in irrational fears and other incorrect emotional responses. This is a sign of emotional maturity, which can be enhanced by effective adult intervention and encouragement. Children can learn to recognize and interpret their emotions if given correct feedback from the social environment. The next section will deal with methods for facilitating such education efforts.

Education About Emotions

Emotional development can be facilitated with proper adult intervention and is important for a number of reasons (Smith, 1982). First, what we teach children about the environment directly influences emotions; children learn to fear things because they lack correct information about them. For example, children's fears of the dark are based on the fact that darkness precludes information. A child's theory about the dark could be stated as, "What I can't see probably can hurt me." Children can fill in the dark spaces with the products of their own imaginations. The more that children know about objects like snakes and spiders, the less they fear them.

Second, adults can help children understand themselves and others by focusing on children's emotions. They can help children recognize the emotions they are feeling. In addition, adults can help children understand how others are feeling and functioning.

Third, adults can help children organize appropriate responses to emotions. It is common to find that adults try to ignore children's emotions, especially if they are "negative" emotions, such as anger or sadness. This does not help children to formulate healthy responses to events in their lives.

Smith (1982) has established a set of emotional skills that children need to learn. They are set up in approximate order of their occurrence in a learning sequence (see Table 12.1) and are as follows:

1. Becoming aware of feelings. This is the process of learning to recognize and describe feelings. This must be mastered before a child can learn to manage feelings.

Table 12.1. *Emotional Education for Early School-Age Children*

Skill	Definition	Social/Cognitive Processes	
1. Becoming aware of feelings	1. The ability to recognize, describe, and accept feelings associated with joy, liking, fear, surprise, sadness, disgust, anger, and curiosity *Example:* A five-year-old describes sadness as feeling like "... there are tears in your heart."	Defining *Joy* *Happy* *Like* *Affection* *Fear* *Brave* *Surprise*	*Sad* *Lonely* *Disgust* *Bored* *Anger* *Curious*
2. Understanding the relationship between emotions and social behavior	2. The ability to identify experiences that influence emotions, the possible consequences of emotional reactions, and appropriate responses to emotional reactions; to discriminate between potentially harmful forms of emotional behavior *Examples:* A four-year-old says, "When I feel sad sometimes I cry." A seven-year-old comments, "When you get mad it doesn't do any good to hit—they might hit you back."	Deciding	
3. Constructively communicating feelings	3a. The ability to describe how one feels through (a) direct identification, (b) the use of metaphors, or (c) stating the kind of action the feelings urge you to do *Examples:* A three-year-old announces during a frightening TV sequence, "I'm *scared!*" A five-year-old states after a playground collision with another child, "I feel like a bug that's being squashed!" A seven-year-old describes how she felt during a school play: "I was *so* embarrassed. I just wanted to disappear!"	Acting	
	3b. The ability to take action appropriate to how one feels without harming one's self or others *Examples:* When the TV show becomes frightening, the three-year-old changes the channel. When he finds his pet canary dead, a seven-year-old cries.	Acting	
4. Developing a sensitivity to the feelings of others	4. The ability to recognize and describe how another feels; the ability to communicate this understanding to others *Examples:* A three-year-old points to another child who is angry and says, "He's sad." A seven-year-old approaches his father, who is having a difficult time with a woodworking task, and says, "You frustrated Dad? Can I hold something for you?"	Sensing	

Used with permission from Charles A. Smith, *Promoting the Social Development of Young Children.* Palo Alto, CA: Mayfield Publishing, 1982.

2. Understanding the relationship between emotions and social behavior. This is the process of coming to recognize that there are social causes for emotions and that behavior based on emotions can have consequences.

3. Constructively communicating feelings. This is the process of learning to express feelings in a way that allows the child relief from the stress of "bottling up" feelings yet does not do damage to interpersonal relationships.

4. Developing a sensitivity to the feelings of others. This is the process of learning to recognize the feelings of others. This particular step is most dependent on the cognitive development of the child. As we have seen earlier in this chapter, children may have incorrect conclusions, based on immature cognitive functioning. However, it is important for children to recognize the need to attend to the feelings of others, which must be developed before children can learn to accurately perceive these feelings. With time, a sensitive child will establish a more accurate understanding, but that will never be possible if the sensitivity is not encouraged first.

Developmental Issues in Practice 12.3 presents an example of an emotional education activity developed by Smith (1982).

PROSOCIAL AND ANTISOCIAL BEHAVIOR

Most adults are very concerned about the expression of aggression and other negative behaviors in children. However, it is equally important to encourage the expression of positive, or prosocial, behaviors, including cooperation and altruism.

Prosocial Behavior

Cognitive psychologists have pointed out that children's **prosocial** behavior is to some extent based on the development of their understanding of themselves and others and their ability to understand the emotions and inner personal needs of others. Shantz (1975) summarized this theory as the child's ability to conceptualize others. She stressed that all the different types of social cognitive functioning are supported by the same developmental abilities and therefore tend to occur at the same developmental stages. For example, preschool children have difficulty conceptualizing the inner, psychological needs of themselves and others. It is not until the concrete operational stage, around six years of age, that children overcome their egocentrism, and it is not until around eight years old that a full appreciation of inner psychological states becomes possible. This is true whether the child is judging the feelings, thinking, or understanding of the other person. Shantz (1975) reported high correlations between social cognitive abilities and demonstrated that role-playing ability was linked as well.

▲ **DEVELOPMENTAL ISSUES IN PRACTICE   12.3**

EXAMPLE OF EMOTIONAL EDUCATION ACTIVITY FOR EARLY SCHOOL-AGE CHILDREN

Feeling Peeling (four years +)

Purpose	To help children become aware of feelings and the relationship between emotions and social behavior. Key concepts are *afraid, happy, angry, affectionate,* and *sad.*
Setting	Community group arrangement or individual conversation
Materials	None
Activity	This activity involves asking questions that encourage children to think about the causes and consequences of various emotions. They are more appropriate for verbal children who are capable of engaging in this type of discussion. Some suggested questions follow. Emotions like *happy, angry, affection,* and *sad* can be substituted for *afraid.*

What do you do when you are afraid?

What would you like to do when you are afraid?

What would you like other people to do for you when you are afraid?

What are some of the things that give you an afraid feeling?

What do you think is going to happen when you [see, smell, touch, feel, hear, or taste] _____ [fill in with response from previous question]

What are some things that people get afraid of? What do they do when they become afraid?

How do you feel when someone is afraid of you?

What feeling is difficult to tell other people about?

This list is only the beginning of a large number of potential questions that will encourage children to explore their emotions. *Remember to respect the child's desire not to disclose how he or she feels. Do not pressure any child to respond.*

SOURCE: From Charles A. Smith, *Promoting the Social Development of Young Children.* Palo Alto, CA: Mayfield Publishing, 1982. Used with permission.

Cooperation.   **Cooperation** is highly valued and often discussed as an important behavior to develop in children. However, cooperation and competition are clearly mutually exclusive behaviors (Smith, 1982). That is, it is not possible to have both kinds of behaviors existing together because they are incompatible. If two children are fighting over a toy, they cannot simultaneously cooperate. On the other hand, if two children are working together on a pro-

When children cooperate on projects it helps break down egocentric behavior and train social skills.

ject, they cannot work separately. Although we express a desire for cooperative activities, our culture is, in reality, very competitive. We tend to reward individuals for separate accomplishments and not for helping behaviors. In school, we tend to expect children to do their own work and receive their own rewards.

There is, however, very good evidence that working cooperatively on a project brings about favorable attitudes toward those in the group and that working competitively can encourage negative attitudes. Thus, we have a strong incentive to encourage cooperation to facilitate the development of friendships. Bronfenbrenner (1970) has argued that cooperation encourages a "we" mental set, whereas competition encourages an "I" mental set. The most effective way to encourage cooperation is to reinforce for it. This can be done by providing rewards for individual acts of cooperation and by providing rewards to entire groups for group accomplishments. For example, a group can work together on a project and each member of the group then receives the same grade for the product, which is the result of a cooperative effort.

Altruism.   **Altruism** is defined as behavior that does not benefit the actor but does benefit others. True altruism requires that the action be done in secret so as to eliminate the possibility that the act is done in the hope of impressing others. This makes it somewhat difficult to study (Shaffer, 1988).

Bryan (1975) has described one method of studying altruism. It involves bringing children into a laboratory setting and allowing them to earn candy by participating in an experimental program. At the end of the program, the children are told that there is a box of candy to be given to poor children who don't have any candy and the children are invited to contribute candy from their own supply. The experimenter then leaves the room and the child is invited to drop the candy through a small hole in the opening of the box. After the child leaves, the experimenter counts the amount of the donation.

This research has demonstrated that the single most important factor in encouraging donation behavior is the presence of a model who donates. If the experimenter, acting as the model, first donates some candy, there is a much greater tendency on the part of children to donate. This is especially true if the model expresses great pleasure in having the opportunity to donate. The warm, kind behavior of the model toward the children did not affect the children's tendency to donate. Elementary school children are more apt to donate than are preschool children. Sex is usually not a factor, but it has been found that girls are more apt to donate than are boys. Reminders to the child did not encourage donation behavior. Even when the model was hypocritical, saying one thing but doing another, the children were still strongly affected by what the model did. This appears to be one example of children imitating adults by "doing as they do, not as they say" (Shaffer, 1988).

Aggression

Research conducted by Eron (1982a) and colleagues (Huesmann & Eron, 1984) over 30 years has shown that early manifestations of aggression predict adult aggression and antisocial behavior. In 1960 the researchers studied nearly 900 eight-year-olds and interviewed their parents. Children's aggression was measured by asking all children in classes to rate all other children on a series of specific aspects of aggressive behavior, aggression anxiety, and popularity. In 1981 the researchers studied over 400 of the original subjects, now at the average age of 30. They also obtained data about criminal offenses, traffic violations, and state hospital admissions of these 400 subjects and over 200 others from the Division of Criminal Justice Services, Division of Motor Vehicles, and Department of Mental Hygiene. In some cases, data were obtained from three generations of informants: subjects and their spouses, subjects' parents, and subjects' children.

Analysis of data from this longitudinal study has indicated that aggressive eight-year-olds are likely to become aggressive adults who engage in antisocial and criminal behavior. Specifically, male subjects viewed by peers as more aggressive at age eight rated themselves as more aggressive at age 30, were rated by their wives as more aggressive, had more convictions in the criminal justice system, committed more serious crimes, had more moving traffic violations, and had more convictions for driving while intoxicated than males who were viewed as being less aggressive. Female subjects viewed by peers as more aggressive at age eight rated themselves as more aggressive at age 30 and rated their punishment of their children as more severe than did females who were viewed as being less aggressive. Data from parents and children of both male and female subjects showed that aggressive parents have aggressive children.

It is interesting that the teacher ratings did not correctly predict the aggressive individuals. This suggests that adults do not have adequate infor-

It is important to help children to learn alternative behaviors to replace aggression, as there is no evidence that children simply grow out of it.

mation about ongoing aggressive activity in their classrooms. Teachers often only notice aggression after a fight has broken out. At this point, the apparent aggressor may be the child who is responding to an initial aggressive attack. Other factors were found to predict aggression in adults, including parenting styles of discipline and extensive viewing of violent television programming. These issues will be addressed under separate sections later in this chapter.

Aggressive behavior seems to be stable across time and generations. Researchers attribute the stability of aggression to both the continuity of constitutional factors (genetic, hormonal, and neurological) and the continuity of environmental factors. The patterns of behavior established in the early school years seem to have lifelong influences. For this reason, it is important to recognize that aggression in children during the early school years is serious and deserving of attention, as it might signal a future problem. There is no evidence to suggest that children will simply outgrow this behavior.

INFLUENCES OF THE FAMILY

Even though children in the early school years have increasing numbers of experiences outside their homes, they continue to be greatly influenced by their families. Children learn and refine social, physical, and cognitive skills within the family context, and they note the extent to which family members value their qualities and activities. Family relationships usually have a continuity not present in other relationships.

An ecological approach to the study of children examines various influences on their development. This section reports research data on the influences of the family, including characteristics of strong families and the effects of different kinds of parenting styles. We will also examine the way children conceptualize the notion of authority, which is so important to understanding how they respond to attempts by parents to impose discipline. This section will end with a discussion of sibling relationships.

Characteristics of Strong Families

The family is the primary social institution in our society. Whether the family is functioning well or poorly can be expected to influence young children developing within that environment. Recently, researchers have undertaken the task of describing qualities shared by families that are perceived by members to be functioning effectively.

These researchers believe that too little attention has been given to publicizing the strengths that make family life satisfying. In an attempt to understand what is "right" with some families, Stinnett, Sanders, and DeFrain (1981) surveyed 283 families from throughout the United States. Individuals volunteered to participate in the study because they perceived themselves to be members of strong family units. Most participants were white, middle-class Protestants; thus, the findings of the study cannot be generalized beyond that group.

Strong families show appreciation for each other, have good communication, and spend time together.

The researchers found many similarities among their sample of strong families. Strong families seem to spend time together, have good patterns of communication, show appreciation for each other, worship together, and demonstrate commitment to the family group.

1. Spend time together. Members of strong families spend time together pleasantly. They work together in the yard or on household tasks, they eat together, and they spend time together outdoors away from distractions. In untroubled times, families build up a reserve of good feelings, which can then help them through difficult times.

2. Have good patterns of communication. Members of strong families are able to share their feelings. They spend a good deal of time talking with each other and are able to get conflicts out in the open. Life is not always tranquil in these families, but problems are dealt with as they appear rather than allowed to build.

3. Show appreciation for each other. Individuals in strong families report that they are able to show and accept appreciation from each other. They feel good about each other and express their feelings in ways that are supportive and loving.

4. Worship together. Members of strong families tend to express and act on strong religious beliefs. Sharing religious beliefs seems to be one way for families to attain a sense of unity and common purpose and to learn values.

5. Demonstrate commitment to the family group. Members of strong families report that they retain their commitment to the family group even at the worst of times. At times of crisis or stress, they reduce involvement in work or social life to give higher priority to their families.

This study found that one sample of strong families shares more than an absence of pathology—these families, describing themselves as strong, have distinctive positive characteristics that set them apart from more troubled families. Further research is needed on strong families from a wide variety of other cultural, socioeconomic, and religious groups.

Secure and Insecure Attachment

Chapter 8 discussed the importance of early attachment on later social behaviors of children. A number of studies have been found to confirm the expectation that secure attachments between mother and child in infancy predict successful social interactions in the preschool years. Turner (1991) found that preschool boys with insecure attachments to mothers were more aggressive, disruptive, assertive, controlling, and attention-seeking than securely-attached boys. Insecure-attached girls were more dependent, showing less assertive and controlling behavior than securely-attached girls. Interestingly, the securely-attached boys and girls did not differ. Park and Waters (1989) found that when four-year-olds played with their best friends, securely-attached dyads were more harmonious, less controlling, more responsive and happier than insecurely-attached dyads. Securely-attached preschoolers were also shown to be more emotionally open to appropriate negative feeling and showed greater ability to tolerate distress than insecurely-attached children (Shouldice & Stevenson-Hinde, 1992).

Parenting Styles

Children growing up in some families are more likely than children in other families to demonstrate prosocial behaviors such as sharing possessions with other children, showing sympathy to children who need help, and cooperating with group routines. Baumrind (1967, 1977) has collected research evidence that shows that children whose parents have authoritative parenting styles are more likely to exhibit prosocial behaviors than are children whose parents have authoritarian or permissive parenting styles. **Authoritative** parents are consistent, loving, conscientious, and secure in handling their children; they set firm rules, communicate clearly their expectations for responsible performance, and are warm and unconditionally committed to serving the best interests of their children. In comparison with authoritative parents, **authoritarian** parents are less nurturing and involved with their children; they exercise firm control but offer little support and affection. **Permissive** parents behave in a much less controlling manner than authoritative or authoritarian parents, are insecure in their ability to influence their children, and expect less of their children than do authoritative or authoritarian parents.

Baumrind (1977) has said that authoritative parents are effective in developing prosocial behavior because their children achieve a balance between self-assertiveness and conformity with group standards. She has expressed her belief that both authoritarian control and permissive noncontrol minimize opportunities for children to interact with people, by suppression of dissent or discussion in the case of authoritarian control and by indulgence and distraction in the case of permissive noncontrol.

Authoritative parents are consistent, loving, set firm rules, and clearly communicate their expectations for responsible behavior.

Research of parental impact on ego development supports the findings of Baumrind. Block (1971) found that ego overcontrol is encouraged when families emphasize structure and order. On the other hand, ego undercontrol is more common in families that are conflict-ridden and undemanding of the child. Ego resilience is fostered by families that are communicative and philosophically and morally oriented and in which parents are loving, patient, and competent. Nonresilience, however, is fostered by conflictual, discordant families that have few philosophical and moral concerns (Sigelman, Block, Block, & Van Der Lippe, 1970). Thus, children with well-developed self-control (high ego overcontrol and high ego resilience) are apt to have families that emphasize structure but at the same time are communicative and loving.

Children's Concept of Authority

One of the most important parts of the relationship between parents and children is that of the authority of the parent over the child. This becomes an issue in the area of discipline and is of great importance to the adults who must socialize the child. Damon (1977, 1980) developed hypothetical stories and presented them to children from the ages of 4 to 12. An example of one of the stories follows:

This is Peter ["Michelle" for girl subjects], and here is his mother, Mrs. Johnson. Mrs. Johnson wants Peter to clean up his own room every day, and she tells him that he can't go out and play until he cleans his room up and straightens out his toys. But one day Peter's friend Michael comes over and tells Peter that all the kids are leaving right away for a picnic. Peter wants to go, but his room is a big mess. He tells his mother that he doesn't have time to straighten his room right now, but he'll do it later. She tells him no, that he'll have to stay in and miss the picnic.

A number of follow-up questions were developed to obtain information about parental authority—specifically, the legitimacy of the leadership and the rationale for obedience. Legitimacy deals with the perception of the person's right to lead or command; for example, what qualities make a person suited for leadership? The rationale for obedience has to do with the reasons one should obey another's commands; for example, what would happen if Peter disobeyed his mother and went to the picnic without cleaning his room?

Table 12.2 summarizes Damon's developmental analysis of the changes in children's understanding of these two authority issues. He found that there were three levels of development. The first, found in preschool-age children, was based on the egocentric beliefs of children at this age. Children reported that if they wanted to obey, they did. Parents were obeyed if they wanted the child to do something the child already wanted to do. Commands that conflict with the child's desires don't have to be obeyed. There are two substages: the first is based on momentary, illogical self-desire and the second involves the child's attempts to use obedience to maximize the self's desires. At this stage, parents will obviously be most successful if they can place commands in a positive context to maximize the attractiveness of obedience. Support for this interpretation comes from a study by Lay, Waters, and Park (1989) on compliance in four-year-olds. It was found that a generally positive mood produced more compliance than did a negative mood. Adults need to help children "want to" comply.

Damon's second level was found in children from five to nine years of age. This level is marked by a tendency of children to give authority figures all-encompassing power and great personal strength. It is as if the child rea-

Table 12.2.   *The Development of the Concept of Authority*

Level	Approximate Age Range	Authority Legitimized By	Basis for Obedience
0–A	4 years and under	Love; identification with self	Association between authority's commands and self's desires
0–B	4–5 years	Physical attributes of persons	A means for achieving self's desires
1–A	5–8 years	Social and physical power	Respect for authority figure's power
1–B	7–9 years	Attributes that reflect special ability, talent, or actions of authority figure	Authority figure deserves obedience because of superior abilities or past favors
2–A	8–10 years	Prior training or experience with leadership	Respect for authority figure's leadership abilities; awareness of authority figure's concern for subordinate's welfare
2–B	10 years and above	Situationally appropriate attributes of leadership	Temporary and voluntary consent of subordinate; spirit of cooperation between leader and led

SOURCE: Based on W. Damon, "Patterns of change in children's social reasoning: A two-year longitudinal study." *Child Development 51* (1980): 1011. Used with permission. Copyright by The Society for Research in Child Development, Inc.

sons that because parents are authority figures they must have the necessary qualifications; the children do not have the capacity to evaluate the person's qualifications for themselves. In the second substage of this level, children begin to look for attributes that will logically legitimize authority. However, adults have such attributes naturally, such as size, strength, control of resources, and so on. At this level, adults find it relatively easier to assert authority than with younger children. Early school-age children are naturally prepared to respect authority in adults.

Damon's third level begins at approximately age eight and occurs because of the ability of children at this age to accurately evaluate the characteristics of others. At this level, children are capable of evaluating the attributes that are necessary for an authority figure, and respect for authority is based on their perception of the person's ability and respect for the welfare of the individual child. In the second substage of this level, children come to appreciate situationally appropriate attributes of leadership and they establish a pattern of mutual cooperation between authority figures and themselves. This pattern doesn't emerge until the middle school years. At this stage, adults must "earn" the right to be an authority figure by demonstrating superior knowledge and skill but also by demonstrating concern for the well-being of the child. This is probably the reason that authoritative parenting styles that take account of the child's needs are so successful in establishing compliance and mutual regard between parent and child.

Sibling Relationships

Traditional views of early childhood development have emphasized the influence of parents on their children and, more recently, the reciprocal influence between parents and children. However, Bronfenbrenner (1979) and others have replaced these traditional views with an ecological view of the family as a complex social system within which all family members influence each other and are influenced by outside forces (Bronfenbrenner, 1979). Researchers who hold an ecological view of the family have begun to investigate the developmental significance of relationships between siblings. Findings about sibling interactions in early childhood, children who have no siblings, and cultural differences in sibling relationships are presented next.

Sibling interactions.   Current societal conditions are believed to be causing siblings to have more contact with each other and to have a higher level of emotional interdependence than was previously the case (Bank & Kahn, 1982). These conditions include geographic mobility, divorce and remarriage, parental stress, shrinking family size, and alternate child care because of maternal employment. Children need contact, constancy, and permanency in their relationships with other human beings and turn to siblings for satisfaction of these needs if parents are not available.

Siblings seem to be intensely involved with each other in the early childhood years, and their relationships appear to be full ones, with a broad range of social interactions. Researchers (Abramovich, Pepler, & Corter, 1982) found that pairs of siblings initiated over 60 interactions per hour when first observed and over 80 interactions per hour when observed 18 months later. Researchers had expected to find aggressive behavior between siblings but were surprised at the high degree of prosocial behavior. Siblings were cooperative, helpful, and affectionate as well as aggressive. During the first set of observations, older siblings, as compared with younger siblings, initiated significantly more prosocial behavior, including cooperation and help, comfort, and praise; 18 months later the younger siblings had increased their proportion of prosocial interactions to 42% from 35%. At both observations, younger children imitated their older siblings significantly more than the reverse. Although not as predominant as expected, aggression was observed. Older children initiated more verbal arguments at the time of both observations and more physical aggression at the time of the first set of observations; but by the time of the second set of observations, younger siblings started fights and engaged in physical aggression just as much as their older siblings. Other studies (most recently, Hoff-Ginsberg & Krueger [(1991]) of language interaction between siblings have found that older siblings modify their speech to younger siblings by simplifying it to enhance communication. Even preschool children were capable of doing this, but older children were more effective at it.

The intense involvement of siblings with each other in early childhood and their patterns of interaction undoubtedly affect other social interactions and the course of the children's psychosocial development. Researchers were surprised at what they did not find in studying the interactions of young siblings: neither the age interval between siblings nor the gender composition of pairs of siblings had the expected effect. Researchers have speculated that sibling interactions may be unique and not subject to comparison with other peer relationships (Abramovich, Pepler, & Corter, 1982).

"Only" children (children with no siblings).   The general societal view of children who have no siblings (i.e., "only" children) tends to be negative. Growing up without siblings is thought to make children maladjusted, self-centered, and unlikable. Reviewing research on "only" children, Falbo (1982) found mixed results: "only" children seem to excel in achievement, as do first-borns, but data about peer relationships, self-esteem, and marital success are conflicting. Falbo (1982) concluded that generalizations about the development of "only" children growing up today cannot be made from research conducted in other generations. "Only" children who grew up during the depression, when such children were common, had a different milieu than "only" children who grew up during the postwar baby boom, when such children were less common. Of the current crop of "only" children, those of single parents may develop differently from "only" children of two-parent families.

Most people focus on the difference between "only" children and others as being the lack of siblings, but the many distinctive attributes of parents with only one child probably contribute to any distinctive attributes of the children. More research is needed on "only" children and their families. This question has been investigated in China, where the one-child policy has led to large numbers of families with only one child. Falbo and Poston (1993) found that there were few differences between the "only" children in China and those from families with more children. The primary differences tended to favor the "only" children, because they received a greater share in the resources and were healthier than children who had siblings.

Cultural differences.   A cross-cultural view (Weisner, 1982) of sibling relationships has given a broader perspective than the Western focus on concerns such as achievement, status, and rivalry. Siblings in South Asian, Polynesian, and most other non-Western societies around the world participate throughout their life spans in activities essential to survival, reproduction, and transmission of cultural and social values. In these societies, responsibilities are shared. Goals involve assistance to others rather than personal development, and help is forthcoming from the group when needed.

Family systems in these societies encourage sibling cooperation, solidarity, and authority of older members over younger members. Sibling caregiving is part of a larger pattern of childhood experiences that emphasizes interdependence. From the end of infancy, children are placed in the care of slightly older siblings, moving gradually out of direct involvement with their mothers. Children cared for by other children learn by imitation rather than through the highly verbal modes used by Western parents. Children in sibling care grow up to be highly peer oriented and tend to be uncomfortable in intensive one-to-one interactions with adults. The interaction patterns developed by these children may not match the patterns used by teachers who have been educated in another tradition.

INFLUENCES AND ADJUSTMENTS OUTSIDE THE FAMILY

During the early school years, children have many experiences that do not include their families. As they explore the world, children are influenced by their involvement with other children and by media presentations; they make adjustments to school and to living in a pluralistic society. Among the topics of interest described next are peer relationships, effects of television, culture and school adjustment, and multicultural understanding.

Peer Relationships

Peer relationships assume increasing importance as children move through the early school years. Children form friendships, reflect on obligations friends have to each other, and develop strategies for interacting with peers. They affect the prosocial behavior of peers by the behaviors they notice and the reactions they show. And they develop different goals, values, and social behavior patterns, depending on their gender. A consideration of peer relationships is a vital part of the study of early childhood development.

Children's friendships.   Friends are defined as people who spontaneously seek each other's company without social pressure to do so. Selman (1981) has found that even young children are able to reflect on and express their understanding of friendship. He divided young children's descriptions of what friendship entails into three overlapping stages.

At Stage 0, from approximately age 3 to 7, children see friends as being children who live nearby or go to the same school and are frequent playmates. Children at Stage 0 view fights as relating to specific toys or space rather than as conflicts over personal feelings.

At Stage 1, spanning the years from approximately 4 to 9, children believe that friends are important because they perform specific activities. Close friends are seen as sharing more than convenient proximity. They know each other's likes and dislikes and they engage in shared activities.

At Stage 2, from approximately 6 to 12 years of age, children express a new awareness of the two-way nature of friendship. Children show a concern for coordinating the likes and dislikes of both people rather than unilaterally expecting the behavior of friends to conform to preconceived ideas. However, specific arguments or disagreements are seen as severing the relationship; the idea of continuity in friendship develops in later stages.

Peer relationships assume increasing importance as children move through the early school years.

Smollar and Youniss (1982) asked six- and seven-year-old children how two strangers would become friends. Children responded that friendship would result if the strangers performed activities together or shared or helped each other. Children further said that the strangers would become best friends if they increased the amount of time they spent together or extended it to settings outside of school. In other words, six- and seven-year-olds seemed to identify friendship with interaction. When asked about the obligations of friendship, most six- and seven-year-olds made comments that would be classified as part of Stage 2; they indicated that cooperation is of paramount importance and that mutual needs are as significant as those of either individual.

Children with few friends.   Some young children have many friends and some have few. Children with few friends can be categorized into two groups. Isolates in one group appear to take the position voluntarily, possibly as an expression of temperament, and are quite content. The majority of these children, however, tend to be at higher risk than more socially accepted peers for low achievement in school, learning difficulties, delinquency, and emotional and mental health problems in adulthood (Putallaz & Gottman, 1981). In an observational study, Best (1983) found that third-grade boys who were not accepted by their peers seemed to lose motivation to achieve academically. Whereas the reading scores of the "in" third-grade boys improved, the scores of the "out" boys stayed the same or declined. This influence of peer acceptance on academic performance operated only among second- and third-grade boys. Among girls and younger boys, a warm, supportive teacher seemed to have more to do with success in school than did peer group acceptance.

Research has also discovered a relationship between children's friendships and prosocial development. Boys with a good friend have demonstrated higher levels of cooperation with others than boys without a good friend. And children who belong to more social organizations have higher moral judgment scores than those who belong to fewer organized groups (Zahn-Waxler, Iannotti, & Chapman, 1982).

Researchers have tried to determine whether children with few friends behave differently from children with many friends. Already in the preschool-age range, there is evidence that children can correctly assess their actual peer acceptance (Pagioa & Hollett, 1991). When preschool children were measured for likability, emotion knowledge, and prosocial and aggressive behavior, emotion knowledge and prosocial behavior were direct predictors of likability (Denham, McKinley, Couchoud, & Holt, 1990).

A series of studies (Putallaz & Gottman, 1981) has shown that popular and unpopular second and third graders are differentiated by their strategies of interacting with each other and of joining ongoing groups. Popularity was determined by adding up the number of times children were nominated by peers as friends. In one-to-one interactions, popular children agreed more and disagreed less with other children than did unpopular children. Closer examination of the data also showed differences in the way that popular children and unpopular children disagreed. Popular children tended to provide a constructive alternative action along with their disagreement, making escalation of the disagreement less likely. Unpopular children expressed disagreement in the form of commands that did not give any alternative. Researchers described unpopular children as "bossy" in their disagreement.

In joining ongoing groups, unpopular children hovered at first. They took longer than popular children to make their first bid to enter the group, used more bids, and took more time for entry. Unpopular children used disagreement and three other entry strategies—self-statements, feeling statements, and informational questions—more than popular children. These strategies were usually unsuccessful, leading the unpopular children to be rejected or ignored. Popular children, in contrast, first determined the "frame of reference" common to members of the group they were approaching and then established themselves as sharing in this frame of reference by agreeing with statements and exchanging relevant information. Peer networks have been found to change with age from early to middle childhood (Feiring & Lewis, 1991); however, the network characteristics were related to school competence only for the girls.

Researchers believe that there is potential for intervention on behalf of children with few friends. There is some evidence that a mother's warmth and affection can serve as a protective factor against adjustment difficulties associated with peer rejection (Patterson, Cohn, & Kao, 1989). Such findings need follow-up research on more effective strategies of intervention.

Peers and prosocial behavior.   Parental caregiving and discipline practices that influence children's prosocial behavior were discussed in Chapter 9 and earlier in this chapter. Researchers (Zahn-Waxler, Iannotti, & Chapman, 1982) have cited three reasons for believing that peers are also important in children's prosocial development. First, mutual influence is likely among children because they are more equal in power than are adults and children. Second, children have numerous natural opportunities to share materials and cooperate in pretense and other forms of play. And third, children's rough-and-tumble play often leads to expressions of distress, to which others respond.

Friendship seems to provide a context within which peers exhibit prosocial behavior. In a naturalistic study of best friends between two and nine years of age, observers noted sympathy and sensitivity in interactions between the children (Gottman & Parkhurst, 1980). It is not known whether the reciprocity of friendship leads children to increase prosocial behavior or whether children who exhibit prosocial behavior are the ones who form close friendships. Most likely the relationship between friends and prosocial behavior is complex and multidimensional.

Peers can help children modify aggressive impulses and show concern for others. Prosocial behaviors in classrooms can be increased if peers are asked to note and report prosocial behaviors that occur. And peer groups can successfully use role-playing procedures to learn about awareness of the motivations and feelings of others (Zahn-Waxler, Iannotti, & Chapman, 1982). Further study of the conditions that lead to early prosocial experiences with peers is needed.

Gender differences in friendship.   Boys and girls differ in the goals, values, and social behavior patterns that they bring to possible friendships. Children may not realize that these differences exist and may not be aware that others are using familiar terms to mean unfamiliar things. Children may consequently make harsh judgments about behavior that varies from their own, mistakenly assuming that others share goals and values but choose to defy them.

Different goals, values, and social behavior patterns may be related to many kinds of differences in background. Dweck (1981) has developed the hypothesis that the self-segregation of girls and boys creates obstacles to successful friendships. According to Dweck's review of the research literature, segregation of boys and girls begins at the start of the early school years and intensifies by third grade. Urberg and Kaplan (1989) found that, as early as the preschool age, same-age and same-sex play partners occurred at a greater rate than expected by chance. Furthermore, it has been found that sex role flexibility and prosocial behavior are related among boys but not among girls (Doescher & Sugawara, 1990). This study provides partial support for Dweck's hypothesis that boys function more effectively if they can avoid rigid segregation from girls.

In the school setting, both boys and girls respond to warmth and support from teachers through the first-grade year. In second grade, however, boys begin to show lower dependence on teachers and more reliance on peers. (Girls tend to remain dependent on teacher approval and acceptance until fourth grade or later.) Beginning in second grade, then, boys increasingly defy teachers and other adult authorities because of the promise of support from peers. They segregate themselves from girls whenever possible and establish a hierarchy of dominance and authority within their groups. By the third grade, male peer groups are well established, distinguishing themselves by trading secrets, giving in-group names, being exclusive, and engaging in occasional antiestablishment activities to show solidarity against adults (Best, 1983).

The ostracism of girls by boys in early school years is not the only social behavior pattern that leads to segregation and diverging experiences (Dweck, 1981). Girls tend to engage in small-group games in small spaces and spend time refining social rules and roles. Traditional girls' games such as jumping rope and playing hopscotch are turn-taking games in which competition is indirect: one child's success is not related to another's failure. These experiences give girls few opportunities to resolve disputes; instead, they learn about close personal relationships. Meanwhile, boys are developing their own culture by engaging in larger-group games that are more physically active and wide ranging. In the early school years, much of the outdoor play space is usually reserved for ball games and other action games. Boys' games tend to have explicit rules that move them toward defined goals. Boys' experiences lead them to learn about elaboration of rules, fair procedures for handling conflict, competition, and achievement of goals. According to Dweck (1981), the separate cultures of boys and girls are based on different interests, values, and goals. With segregation, the cultures grow increasingly far apart and there are more barriers to friendship.

Best (1983) found that third-grade boys and girls have very different ideas about how to coordinate devotion to friends and competitive instincts. She presented the following hypothetical situation to boys:

> *Suppose . . .that Dennis and Randy, two very good friends, decided to compete against one another for the quarterback position on the football team. Dennis knows that Randy wants to win that position more than he wants anything in the whole world, but Dennis has stronger legs and can run faster than Randy. He also has stronger arms and can throw a ball farther than Randy. And, although Dennis would like to play the quarterback position, it isn't as important to him as it is to Randy. So, should he let Randy win the competition? (p. 83)*

Boys responded that Dennis should not let Randy win because pride takes priority over a friend's happiness. They attached importance to whether others would know about their greatness if they did not win. Chad summed up the discussion by saying, "Your guys won't like you as much if you lose your pride" (p. 83). In contrast, Best found that for girls the point of games is found in the companionship and interaction and not in winning or losing. Girls sometimes let a friend win in order to enhance the relationship, and they seemed under much less pressure than boys to prove themselves.

Gilligan (1982) has concluded that masculinity is defined through separation and competition and femininity is defined through attachment and relationships. She illustrated the differences by analyzing the responses of eight-year-old girls and boys when asked to describe a situation in which they were not sure about the right thing to do. Typical responses, those of Jeffrey and Karen, follow:

Jeffrey:	When I really want to go to my friends and my mother is cleaning the cellar, I think about my friends, and then I think about my mother, and then I think about the right thing to do. [But how do you know it's the right thing to do?] Because some things go before other things.
Karen:	I have a lot of friends, and I can't always play with all of them, so everybody's going to have to take a turn, because they're all my friends. But like if someone's all alone, I'll play with them. [What kinds of things do you think about when you are trying to make that decision?] Um, someone all alone, loneliness. (pp. 32—33)

In Gilligan's (1982) view, both children struggle with the same issues: exclusion and priority created by choice. But Jeffrey thinks about a hierarchy of desire and duty and what goes first; Karen focuses on who is left out in a network of relationships that includes all of her friends. Looking at psychological theory from a female perspective, Gilligan has drawn the following conclusion: "In the different voice of women lies the truth of an ethic of care, the tie between relationship and responsibility" (p. 173). She and Best (1983) have both said that many researchers, educators, and parents have operated from the assumption that there is a single norm of social experience and interpretation—the male norm. Evaluating female decision making from a male perspective has led to a failure to see the different reality of females' lives. According to these researchers, the time has not yet arrived when male and female experiences converge.

The differences in male and female values and interests lead to differing experiences and eventually to different views of the world and areas of competence. Therefore, a socially skilled boy and a socially skilled girl might not understand each others' perspectives or relate to each other successfully as friends. To bridge group differences and facilitate friendships, children can be sensitized to the myriad of reasons for behavior different from their own and the many possible interpretations of events.

Effects of Television

Television plays an important part in children's lives. First graders, for instance, watch television for an average of three hours per day (Honig, 1983). In 1987 the average number of television sets per household was 1.83 (Andreasen, 1990). This suggests that family members may be watching television alone, without the opportunity for family consultation. Research cited in Chapter 9 showed that television influences the behavior of children under the age of four and that caregivers can have a positive effect on the impact of television. The research presented in this section demonstrates that television continues to affect children's behavior through the early school years and beyond. Attention is given to the effects on children of both violent and prosocial content of television programming.

Violent content.   Many television programs are highly violent, and substantial numbers of young children (one-fourth of boys and one-third of girls interviewed) say that they are frightened by this violence (Honig, 1983). There is evidence that television violence has changed over time. Pena, French, and Doerann (1990) analyzed the heroes from two time periods: Roy Rogers of the 1950s and Brave Starr of the 1980s. The results indicated that the modern hero and his followers appeared to be more fearful and self-critical than their 1950s counterparts, and the modern villain and his followers expressed more hostility toward others and made more negative references about others. Bandura (1977) and other social learning theorists have repeatedly shown that children exposed to aggressive, violent models in laboratory situations increase their own aggressive, violent behavior. Research in naturalistic settings has added a new perspective to the understanding of the effects of violent television.

The most striking finding of recent research is that some children are more highly susceptible than others to behavior changes as a result of watching televised violence. Highly susceptible children include those who are rated as aggressive and children below eight years of age.

In a study of children with different initial levels of aggression, Gouze (1979) divided the children into low- and high-aggression groups depending on their ideas about how to resolve conflicts. Children in both groups heard stories that had negative consequences for aggression after viewing an aggressive television program. Children in the low-aggression group decreased in aggression, but children in the high-aggression group increased in aggression.

In a study of the long-term effects of viewing violent television programs, Eron (1982b) investigated the television viewing habits of eight-year-old children and then reinterviewed some of them 10 years later. The surprising finding was that there was a much higher correlation between viewing violent television programs at age 8 and being characterized as aggressive at age 18 than between viewing violent television at age 18 and being characterized as aggressive at that same age. Eron (1982b) has said that children up to eight years of age may be especially susceptible to the effects of watching televised violence.

Prosocial content.   Some television programs are not only nonviolent, they consciously present prosocial content. Friedrich and Stein (1973) examined the effects on children of watching one such program with prosocial content, "Mister Rogers' Neighborhood." The researchers showed young children 15-minute episodes with such themes as cooperation, sharing, sympathy, affection, friendship, control of aggression, coping with frustration, and delay of gratification. The greatest gains in prosocial interpersonal behaviors were made by low-income children who increased their levels of cooperative play,

For school to be a positive experience for children, their various language patterns must be understood and respected.

▲ **DEVELOPMENTAL ISSUES IN PRACTICE   12.4**

MISTER ROGERS' PHILOSOPHY

In the journal *Young Children,* Fred Rogers, the originator of "Mister Rogers' Neighborhood," discussed his ideas about communicating prosocial values to children. Here is an excerpt from that article (Rogers, 1984):

> One main thing I try to do through my television work is to give the children one more honest adult in their life experience. In fact, I feel that honesty is closely associated with freedom. "The truth will make us free" we've heard for a long time. I've tried to translate that into a song. It's a song for all ages:
>
> The Truth Will Make You Free
>
> *What if I were very, very sad*
> *And all I did was smile?*
> *I wonder after a while*
> *What might become of my sadness?*
> *What if I were very, very angry,*
> *And all I did was sit*
> *And never think about it?*
> *What might become of my anger?*
> *Where would they go*
> *And what would they do*
> *If I couldn't let them out?*
> *Maybe I'd fall, maybe get sick, or doubt.*
> *But what if I could know the truth*
> *And say just how I feel?*
> *I think I'd learn a lot that's real about freedom.*
> *I'm learning to sing a sad song when I'm sad.*
> *I'm learning to say I'm angry when I'm very mad.*
> *I'm learning to shout, I'm getting it out.*
> *I'm happy, learning exactly how I feel inside of me.*
> *I'm learning to know the truth.*
> *I'm learning to tell the truth.*
> *Discovering truth will make me free.*

Discovering the truth about ourselves is a lifetime work, but it's worth the effort.

SOURCE: From Fred Rogers, "The Past and Present Is Now." *Young Children, 29* (March 1984): 16. Copyright by Fred M. Rogers. Used with permission.

nurturance, and verbalization of feelings. (See Developmental Issues in Practice 12.4 for a statement by Fred Rogers about his philosophy of children's programming.)

In addition, researchers found that viewing prosocial episodes is related to increased task persistence and self-control, whereas viewing violent programming is related to decreased self-control. This finding is extremely

▲ DEVELOPMENTAL ISSUES IN PRACTICE   12.5

GUIDELINES FOR USING TELEVISION POSITIVELY

Nearly all homes have at least one television set. The following guidelines can help make television a positive force in the lives of young children.

1. Limit children's television viewing to programs with prosocial and educational content.

2. Set a daily time limit for television viewing. Balance children's interest in television with time for play, exploring, socializing, studying, and reading.

3. Discuss misleading and coercive television advertising. Discuss the ways children are manipulated by advertising and the motivations of the advertisers.

4. Talk with children about television plots and characters. Explain your own values and show disapproval of violence, stereotyping, and negative portrayals of societal groups.

5. Explain and extend words and concepts introduced on educational television.

SOURCE: Adapted from A. S. Honig, "Research in Review: Television and Young Children." *Young Children, 38* (1983): 63–76. Copyright 1983 by the National Association for the Education of Young children. Used by permission.

important because self-control is essential for a child to succeed in school-work and to join in harmonious family life. The damage done by violent programming may have wider ramifications than just the relationship with aggressive behavior. Additional research has demonstrated that excessive television viewing in kindergarten children, regardless of content, is associated with less advanced moral judgments (Rosenkoeter, Huston, & Wright, 1990). Thus, while prosocial programming can be shown to benefit children, excessive viewing of general programming can have negative implications for very young school-aged children. It is important for parents and child care workers to monitor television viewing. Developmental Issues in Practice 12.5 gives some suggestions for such monitoring.

Culture and School Adjustment

In the early school years, children use language in ways that are consistent with experiences that they have had in their cultural groups. There may or may not be much overlap between the verbal repertoire of young children and the language used in the classrooms they enter. A key factor in the school adjustment of young children is the understanding that school personnel have of language patterns used by cultural groups represented in the school.

Hymes (1980) has cited problems that native American children have in adjusting to their early school experiences. Many of these children speak only

English when they enter school; yet they have problems because of differences in patterns of language usage. Native American children have become accustomed to distinctive ways of answering questions, taking turns during conversations, speaking or not speaking, and giving instructions.

Such distinctive patterns of language usage can cause misunderstanding and confusion in the early school years. Hymes (1980) has given several examples of difficulties caused by these differences. First, patterning of expression can cause misinterpretation of personality. Mesquaki Fox children in Iowa interpreted their teachers' loudness of voice and verbal directness as "meanness" and a "tendency to get mad." Second, patterning of speech situations can reflect complex and long-standing customs. A teacher of Navajo children did not understand that boys might not be able to speak to some girl classmates because of kinship relationships existing between them. And third, patterning of attitudes can reflect cultural values and outlooks, as with Tewa-speaking children whose loyalty to the dialect has had a separatist and unifying role for their group. Whether teachers are knowledgeable about the language patterns used in native American and other cultural groups affects the adjustment of children to school.

Multicultural Understanding

Multicultural understanding is essential for citizens in a pluralistic society. Research indicates that attempts to influence children's basic racial and cultural attitudes must start in the early years when those attitudes are forming. In the early school years, the educational system begins to join the family in providing experiences that enhance children's cultural identities and their concern and respect for others. Such experiences, designed to emphasize the universal human experiences as well as the richness of cultural diversity, are included in discussions on multicultural education.

Multicultural education is built on continuous assessment of children's cultural attitudes and identities. Appropriate multicultural experiences vary, depending upon the composition of a given community and the needs of individual children. If children's cultural backgrounds are diverse, multicultural education might focus on helping children understand the extent of similarities and the nature of differences. If children's backgrounds are monocultural, the focus might be on helping children see diversity within the group and on grasping the idea that there are many other cultures and ways of life (Ramsey, 1982).

Ramsey (1982) has suggested three broad goals for multicultural education in the early school years: enhancing self-concept and cultural identity, developing social skills and responsibility, and broadening the base of cultural understanding. Each of these goals is described in turn.

Enhancing self-concept and cultural identity.   Enhancing children's self-concepts is an important priority in the early childhood years. Studying literature and art, discussing feelings and competencies, and performing other activities provide vehicles for children to develop awareness of the ways all people's lives are similar and yet unique. Multicultural education is as much a perspective as it is a curriculum. Teachers who share this perspective take advantage of spontaneous occurrences as well as planned activities to incorporate each child's cultural, racial, and ethnic identity into the classroom in the early school years. Children from minority groups retain a sense of the value of their culture when they perceive genuine interest in and respect for their life-styles and families. Children from monocultural communities learn that people are both similar and different in appearance, experiences, and family composition. If teachers are thinking only in terms of planning a curriculum, they might produce many activities that run counter to these goals. For example, a section on native Americans can end by being only a series of cliches: feathered head-dresses and buffalo. Instead of fostering genuine multicultural experiences, such programs end by detracting from the opportunity to learn about the uniqueness and value of the culture in question.

Developing social skills and responsibility.   The ability of children to see the perspective of others develops over the course of the early school years (Shantz, 1975). This developmental process can be enhanced and encouraged when multicultural education is used to motivate children to practice and expand their skills in seeing others' perspectives. To do so, teachers can make provisions for frequent social interaction, both spontaneous and planned. Planned activities are those that require cooperation, such as science observations that are recorded by teams and movement experiences that must be synchronized. Teachers also consistently call attention to the existence and validity of other points of view in curriculum content areas as well as in the psychosocial domain.

Broadening the base of cultural understanding.   In broadening the base of children's cultural understanding, the goal is not to teach children facts, figures, geography, and historical details about other cultural groups. Ample evidence shows that young children do not grasp concepts such as that of *country*, cannot read maps, and cannot coordinate abstract lists of similarities and differences (Anselmo, 1979). An emphasis on cognitive content can lead to memorization without context or understanding. Instead, the goal of broadening the base of cultural understanding is for children to realize that there are many acceptable languages, points of view, and life-styles. In pluralistic situations, experiences and materials reflect the cultural groups of children in the classroom. By sharing with classmates and observing each other, children see that people look, speak, eat, cook, and so on in different ways. In monocultural situations, experiences, pictures, and visitors are used to introduce children to some of the differences among people. For instance, children can explore the many ways that people carry things on their backs, hips, and heads and in many types of containers and thus take a step toward developing a flexible, open approach to people whose appearances and customs are unfamiliar to them. Multicultural education has great potential in enriching the lives and increasing the understanding of children in a pluralistic society.

CHILDHOOD STRESS

Many adults mistakenly assume that early childhood is a time of joy with few pressures. However, young children are often victims of stress. **Stress** is caused by environmental changes that provoke a high degree of emotional tension and interfere with normal patterns of response (Janis & Leventhal, 1968). Children experience stress from changes brought about by events such as hospitalization, birth of a sibling, and parental divorce (see Developmental Issues in Practice 12.6 for a description of the kinds of stress a child can feel while experiencing the divorce of the parents). Children sometimes gain strength and sometimes suffer as a result of stress. Variability in children's responses to stress can be understood by examining the topics in this section: differences in coping processes, developmental changes in reactions to stress and protective factors.

Differences in Coping Processes

Children experience stress not so much because of specific events but because of resultant changes in patterns of family interaction and relationships. Such changes extend over time, and children's **coping** processes must likewise be continuous. Coping involves efforts to manage environmental and internal demands that tax or exceed a person's resources (Rutter, 1983).

Research (Rutter, 1983) has found that coping processes are influenced by individual differences in characteristics such as age, gender, and style of appraising the situation. Age influences children's ability to cope with the stress of hospitalization and the birth of siblings, but not the stress of divorce. When hospitalization is necessary, children between six months and four years of age have the most difficulty coping with the stress that occurs. Below six months of age children have not formed selective attachments, and above four years they have the cognitive skills to know that separation is not the same as abandonment and to understand the need for medical treatment. When siblings are born, younger children are more likely than older children to show some form of disturbed behavior as evidence of problems in coping with stress.

Research on gender influences on coping processes indicates that boys are less able than girls to cope with effects of stressful events. Significantly more boys than girls show adverse reactions to hospitalization, withdrawal behavior when siblings are born, and severe and prolonged disturbance after their parents divorce (Rutter, 1983).

Children's appraisals of the implications of an event influence their ability to cope with any resulting stress. Research (Rutter, 1983) has found that boys tend to respond with greater effort if given feedback that they are failing, but girls tend to give up. Boys seem to be socialized to attribute failure to

▲ DEVELOPMENTAL ISSUES IN PRACTICE   12.6

A CHILD'S VIEW OF DIVORCE

Because of their cognitive limitations, young children are especially susceptible to blaming themselves for problems. They are egocentric and cannot conceptualize the inner psychological needs of others. They have only themselves as a referent. Adults must be alert for danger signs that a child is suffering from unnecessary guilt. It is important to address the issue with the child and provide reassurance. The tendency of young children to blame themselves for stressful changes in their lives is illustrated by excerpts from an interview with Gillian, then seven years of age (Berger, 1984):

> Sometimes I think I made Mommy and Daddy get a divorce, because I wasn't a good child. I mean, I think I could have done better, like try to keep my room clean. I used to get into lots of trouble, like once I painted my sister's hand blue, and it got all yucky. It took a long time for Mommy to get all the paint off. And once I went out with friends and didn't ask permission. So I think I gave Mommy and Daddy more things to worry about. Maybe if I didn't give them so much to worry about, we'd all still be together in our house in Charlotte. (p. 12)

By the next year, with help, Gillian began to understand her blamelessness in the situation (Berger, 1984):

> Mommy gave me this book to read called *Divorce* or something like that. I read it with my sister, Emma. It's a children's book, and it says don't blame yourself because it wasn't your fault your parents weren't happy with each other. That helped. It made me think maybe it wasn't my fault Mommy and Daddy got divorced, even if I was bad sometimes. (p. 13)

not trying hard enough, whereas girls seem to be socialized to attribute failure to their lack of ability. See Developmental Issues in Practice 12.7 for a copy of the Childhood Stress Test. This gives some indication of the types of problems that lead to stress in children.

Developmental Changes in Reactions to Stress

Maccoby (1983) has examined research relating to children's reactions to stress and has proposed some hypotheses about developmental changes that take place. Six of these hypotheses have particular relevance to early childhood development.

First, she has proposed that the younger the child, the more important is environmental structure and predictability. Stress builds for young children if too many elements in the environment change at once.

Second, she has proposed that the younger the child, the more likely is extensive behavioral disorganization as a response to stress. Research indi-

▲ **DEVELOPMENTAL ISSUES IN PRACTICE 12.7**

STRESS IN CHILDHOOD

Saunders and Remsberg (1984) have attempted to rank the various stresses of childhood. This test shows how stressful events compare in their impact on a child.

This is a scale to check the amount of stress in your child's life. Add up the points for items that have touched your child's life in the last 12 months. If your child scored below 150, he or she is carrying an average stress load. If your child's score is between 150 and 300, he or she has a better-than-average chance of showing some symptoms of stress. If the child's score is above 300, his or her stress load is heavy and there is a strong likelihood he or she will experience a serious change in health or behavior:

☐ Death of a parent	100	☐ Sibling going away to school	29
☐ Divorce of parents	73	☐ Winning school or community	
☐ Separation of parents	65	awards	28
☐ Parent's jail term	63	☐ Mother or father going to work	
☐ Death of a close family		or quitting work	26
member	63	☐ School beginning or ending	26
☐ Personal injury or illness	53	☐ Family's living standard	
☐ Parent's remarriage	50	changing	25
☐ Suspension/expulsion from		☐ Change in personal habits	
school	47	(bedtime, homework, etc.)	24
☐ Parents' reconciliation	45	☐ Trouble with parents	23
☐ Long vacation	45	☐ Change in school hours,	
☐ Parent or sibling illness	44	schedule	23
☐ Mother's pregnancy	40	☐ Moving to a new house	20
☐ Anxiety over sex	39	☐ New sports, hobbies,	
☐ Birth or adoption of baby	39	recreation activities	20
☐ New school, classroom, or		☐ Change in church activities	19
teacher	39	☐ Change in social activities	18
☐ Money problems at home	38	☐ Change in sleeping or nap	
☐ Death or moving away of close		habits	16
friend	37	☐ Change in number of family	
☐ Change in studies	36	get-togethers	15
☐ More quarrels with parents	35	☐ Change in eating habits	15
☐ Change in school		☐ Vacation	13
responsibilities	29	☐ Christmas	12
☐ Family quarrels with		☐ Breaking a rule	11
grandparents	29	TOTAL	

SOURCE: From Antoinette Saunders and Bonnie Remsberg, *The Stress-Proof Child*. New York: Holt, Rinehart & Winston, 1984. Used with permission.

cates that maturation of the nervous system contributes to children's ability to maintain behavioral organization.

Third, she has proposed that with increasing age, children have an increasing repertoire of coping behaviors. Young children's coping behaviors center on going to the attachment figure in case of threat. After age 11, children usually rely less on adults and more on other strategies for dealing with stress.

Fourth, she has proposed that an obedient stance toward adult authority gives young children a buffer against stress that is not available in adolescence. If young children carry out the instructions of trusted adults, they feel less anxiety about the outcomes of their actions and less stress when there are negative outcomes than if they are acting autonomously.

Fifth, she has proposed that the nature of distress caused by the disruption of peer friendships changes with age. In the preschool and early school years, friends are people with whom children play and share activities, so children feel the loss of these activities when friendships are disrupted. Later, in middle childhood, friends share confidences, trust, and thoughts, and loss of friendships means loss of children's emotional support.

Sixth and finally, she has proposed that with age comes an increasing sensitivity to the reactions of others to the self. Stressors then become more individualized, depending on the identity the individual has chosen to project and the emotional territory the individual has chosen to defend.

Protective Factors

Researchers have been interested in the development of children who become competent despite lives that involve high levels of stress brought about by poverty, family instability, and sometimes parents' serious mental health problems. Even in the most difficult home situations, some children develop healthy personalities and display **resilience,** defined as the ability to adjust easily to or recover from continuing high levels of stress (Werner, 1984). Researchers have asked, "What is right with these children?" and have tried to draw conclusions from their lives to help other children become less vulnerable to stress.

Researchers in England, in American urban ghettos, and in Hawaii (summarized in Garmezy, 1983, and Werner, 1984) have all found that children who "make it" despite problems and obstacles differ from others by three types of protective factors. These protective factors lie within the children themselves, within their families, and outside their families.

Resilient children tend to have characteristics of temperament that cause others to react positively to them (Garmezy, 1983). In infancy and early childhood these children have personalities and temperaments that are described as "active," "socially responsive," and "autonomous." They often find satisfaction and self-esteem in hobbies and creative interests. Their hobbies and senses of humor provide refuge when the levels of stress in their lives rise (Werner & Smith, 1982). These children somehow manage to maintain the faith that things will work out. And they translate their faith into action by taking on responsibilities for siblings or the household beyond what might be considered appropriate for their young ages. According to Werner (1984), these acts of required helpfulness lead to enduring positive changes in the children.

Within the family, most resilient children have the opportunity to form a close bond with at least one person during the first year of life (Werner, 1984). This nurturing allows them to establish a basic sense of trust. These children seem to be adept at actively seeking out surrogate parents, grandparents, other relatives, child care personnel, parents of friends, or neighbors.

Most resilient children have strong external sources of support—peers, ministers, teachers, or older friends—for their coping processes. They tend to be liked by classmates and to have close friends (Werner & Smith, 1982). They often do well in school, in academics, and in extracurricular activities, and they seem to make school a refuge from their chaotic households. Early childhood programs and favorite teachers can act as buffers against stress (Werner, 1984).

Research on resilient children (Garmezy, 1983; Rutter, 1983; Werner & Smith, 1982) seems to show that the long-term effects of stress do not depend on the number of incidents of stress but rather on how the children deal with stress. The same event can be followed by successful adaptation, humiliating failure, or no long-term consequence whatsoever. Certain stresses are inevitable, and one of the developmental tasks of childhood is to learn positive coping processes. Caring adults can provide valuable support if they do the following:

Accept children's temperamental idiosyncrasies and allow them some experiences that challenge, but do not overwhelm, their coping abilities.

Convey to children a sense of responsibility and caring and in turn reward them for helpfulness and cooperation.

Encourage children to develop a special interest, hobby, or activity that can serve as a source of gratification and self-esteem.

Encourage children to reach out beyond their nuclear family to a beloved relative or friend. (Werner, 1979, 1984)

The lives of resilient children show that faith can be sustained even in adverse circumstances, if children find people in their lives who demonstrate commitment and caring.

SUMMARY

1. Erik Erikson has described two psychosocial tasks of the early school years: learning to take initiative and learning to become industrious.
2. Four- and five-year-old children display initiative in social, physical, and cognitive ways. Initiative is balanced by the possibility of feeling guilty.

3. Elementary-age children begin to channel their energy into being industrious. If they do not succeed in school and other tasks, they can feel inferior.

4. According to Broughton, early school-age children develop self-awareness at two levels: the objective and the empirical.

5. According to Selman, early school-age children have a self-awareness that develops in three stages: a physicalistic conception, a conception of an inner self, and an awareness that the inner and outer self can be in conflict.

6. The Blocks studied personality from the perspective of self-control and defined two types of control: ego control and ego resiliency.

7. Emotions are messengers, energizers, and a source of bonding between individuals.

8. Young children have more irrational emotional responses to events than do older children. Smith has demonstrated four levels of learning of emotions.

9. Cooperation is incompatible with competition.

10. Altruism is present in young preschool children and appears to be enhanced by modeling.

11. Eron found that aggression present by the age of 8 years is apt to be stable over the next 10 years.

12. Family influences remain strong during the early school years.

13. One group of strong families shares many characteristics: spending time together, communicating, appreciating each other, worshiping together, and sharing commitment to the family group.

14. Children with secure attachments to parents tend to have better peer relations and to be happier and more well adjusted than children without secure attachments to parents.

15. Parents with authoritative parenting styles are more likely than those with authoritarian styles to have children who exhibit prosocial behaviors.

16. Children's concept of authority changes in three stages. First they are obedient because obedience is self-desired; then they show obedience to authority figures; and then they show obedience to those with qualifications to demand it.

17. Siblings mutually influence development by their intense involvement with each other in the early childhood years.

18. Characteristics of "only" children depend upon attributes of their parents and not just upon the absence of siblings.

19. In many cultural groups, siblings care for each other within a context of interdependence; sibling care has effects on children's ability to engage in one-to-one interactions with adults.

20. Children are influenced by forces outside the family, such as peers and television, and they make adjustments to attending school and living in a pluralistic society.

21. Friendships of young children characteristically move through three stages and show increasing reciprocity.

22. Children with few friends have distinctive approach and interaction patterns.

23. Peers influence the prosocial behavior exhibited by children; the lack of peer relationships leads to problem behavior in children.

24. There are gender differences in peer relationships.

25. Young children are vulnerable to the effects of televised violence and benefit from prosocial television content.

26. Cultural differences in children's language patterns can influence their adjustment to school.

27. Multicultural understanding can be enhanced by multicultural education having several goals: enhancing self-concept and cultural identity, developing social skills and responsibility, and broadening the base of cultural understanding.

28. Young children feel stress, differ in their ability to cope with it, and show developmental trends in adapting to it.

29. Resilient children have certain personal characteristics, family support, and support from outside the family, all of which tends to protect them from the effects of stress.

ACTIVITIES TO ENHANCE LEARNING

The following exercises are designed to help students apply what has been learned and to increase understanding about psychosocial development between four and eight years of age. To complete these exercises, it will be necessary to make observations of young children. If friends or neighbors do not have three- to eight-year-olds, the following are some possible ways to arrange observations: visit a public place that attracts families, such as a busy store, park, or zoo; request permission to observe at a daycare center, family daycare home, or preschool that enrolls children who are three to six years old. These exercises require the use of observation techniques discussed in Chapter 2. Plan to review the relevant section before beginning the observations.

1. Narrative Observation. Find a child with a sibling and observe the children together. Write down everything that the target child does in a 10-minute period. Repeat the observation at approximately the same time each day for three days. (Remember to use descriptive, nonjudgmental language.) Answer the following questions about the child's behavior:
   a Describe the social interaction behavior that you see, noting both prosocial and aggressive behaviors.
   b. What patterns of social interaction occur over the three time periods?
   c. What differences occur in each time period?
   d. Summarize your impression of the sibling interactions. Were the interactions positive or negative?

2. Vignettes. Plan a one-hour observation time with a particular child. During the time period, watch for examples of specific emotions. Decide in advance which aspects of the child's emotional functioning you will transcribe (joy, happiness, sadness, fear, surprise, etc.). Write down as many of the target behaviors as you observe. Answer the following questions about the child's behavior:
   a. Describe the reason for the expression of emotion.
   b. Is the child engaging in behavior appropriate for the particular situation?
   c. Does the child show evidence of understanding the relationship of the emotional functioning to the social environment?
   d. Does the child appear to be aware of the feelings being expressed?
   e. Is the emotional communication destructive or constructive for the particular situation?

3. Child Diaries. Maintain a daily diary of the child's responses to friends.
   a. Based on your observations, at what level does the child understand the meaning of friendship?

    b. Discuss the child's behavior in developmental terms and determine whether the child is functioning on the appropriate level.

4. Checklists. Prepare a developmental checklist for social interactions appropriate to the child's age level. Use the information in this chapter to make a list of behaviors in developmental order. Observe the child and use the checklist to assess performance.
    a. Did the child perform as expected based on his or her age?
    b. Is the child functioning at the appropriate developmental level?

5. Interviews. Design an interview with the child, making use of either the questions or the stories in this chapter to assess self-concept or self-knowledge.
    a. Based on the interview, is the child's functioning appropriate to his or her age?
    b. At what level is the child functioning?

6. Time Sampling. Adapt the recording form given as an example in Chapter 2 (Developmental Issues in Practice 2.6) for aggressive behaviors. Use the recording form to observe a child between four and eight years old. Write a few paragraphs describing what you learned about the child's functioning.

7. Event Sampling. Adapt the recording form given as an example in Chapter 2 (Developmental Issues in Practice 2.7) for either social or emotional development. Use the recording form to observe a child between four and eight years old. Write a few paragraphs describing what you learned about the child's functioning.

FOR FURTHER READING

Prosocial Behavior

Damon, W. (1990). *The moral child: Nurturing children's natural moral growth.* New York: Free Press.

Gonzalez-Mena, J. (1993). *The child in the family and thecommunity.* New York: Merrill/Macmillan.

Emotional Development

Jensen, L. C., & Wells, M. G. (1979). *Feelings: Helping children understand emotions.* Provo, UT: Brigham Young University Press.

Hildebrand, V. (1990). *Guiding young children* (5th ed.). New York: Macmillan.

Smith, C. A. (1982). *Promoting the social development of young children: Strategies and activities.* Palo Alto, CA: Mayfield Publishing.

Using Television Positively

Singer, D. G., Singer, J. L., & Zuckerman, D. M. (1981). *Teaching television: How to use television to your child's advantage.* New York: Dial.

Communicating Multicultural Understanding

Williams, L. R., & DeGaetano, Y. (1985). *ALERTA: A multicultural bilingual approach to teaching young children.* Menlo Park, CA: Addison-Wesley.

CHAPTER 13

Early School Years (Ages Four through Eight): Cognitive Development

There has been an increased tendency for children to enter school environments at earlier ages. One reason is the push for children to prepare for elementary school by acquiring school skills. A second reason is the need for child care for children of working parents. The result is that more and more children these days are in nursery school and daycare, where education interventions are under way as early as three and four years of age.

Children in the early school years face a multitude of new experiences outside the confines of their homes. Their initial reactions to these experiences often include exuberant curiosity and eagerness. Whether their positive reactions are maintained depends on their success in school, which in turn is influenced by the cognitive development that takes place during the early school years.

This chapter describes cognitive development from age four to age eight by considering the following topics: the development of logic, including preoperational and concrete operational stages, and using logic, such as philosophical thinking and moral development; perceptual development, including perceptual processes, reading ability, and educational applications; language development, including linguistic milestones and bilingualism; the continuing role of play, including gender differences and humor; and the effects of early education programs, including programs for low-income children, programs for advantaged children, and social and intellectual competence.

THE DEVELOPMENT OF LOGIC

There are striking differences between the reasoning of most four-year-olds and that of most eight-year-olds. Typically, four-year-olds base many of their judgments on their perceptions, focusing on just one variable in complex situations. Eight-year-olds, however, have often attained the ability to reason logically, coordinating several variables to make decisions. The following vignette provides an illustration of the contrast of perceptual and logical orientations between the two ages:

> *The mother of two children is handing them cookies from the package. Four-year-old Chuck receives a whole cookie, while his older sister, Sarah, receives one that is broken into two pieces. Chuck complains that his sister has received more because she has two cookies. She understands the problem he is having and corrects it by breaking his cookie into two pieces. "Now we have the same," she says. Chuck is satisfied and happily eats his two pieces.*

Chuck's behavior reflects prelogical thinking. He believes that if the cookie is in two pieces it appears to be more and, therefore, it is more. In contrast, the behavior of eight-year-old Sarah reflects logical thinking. She understands that different arrangements of the parts of the cookie still contain the same amount of cookie to eat. Piaget and Inhelder (1969) have said that thinking such as Chuck's is at the **preoperational stage** and thinking such as Sarah's is at the **concrete operational stage**. The transition from preoperational thinking to concrete operational thinking occurs between six and seven years and is usually completed by the time a child is eight years old. This is the developmental period discussed in this chapter.

To explain the development of logic in the early school years, this section begins with a description of Piaget's theory of thinking in the preoperational and concrete operational stages. (For a discussion of interpretations that differ from Piaget's, refer to Chapter 10.) The section ends by exploring children's development of philosophical thinking and moral reasoning.

Preoperational and Concrete Operational Stages

During most of the preschool years, children continue to function at the preoperational stage in their thinking, according to the theory of Jean Piaget (Piaget, 1960a, 1960b, 1964; Piaget & Inhelder, 1969). They continue to use strategies already described in Chapter 10, such as transductive reasoning and egocentrism. Although their thinking is not yet based on logic, what happens during the preoperational stage provides an important basis for the later attainment of logical thought. Throughout the preoperational stage, children become proficient in mentally working through solutions to problems. They learn to classify ideas and events and to order and organize numbers, time, and space. Performing these mental activities and developing the language to represent them efficiently is an essential step in the development of logical thinking.

Concrete operational thinkers are able to reason logically as long as problems are within the realm of their direct experiences. That is why this type of reasoning is called "concrete." Concrete operational thinking represents an important change from preoperational thinking, but it still has limitations if compared with a subsequent, more abstract type of logical thinking, formal operational thought, which is attained by many individuals in adolescence.

Piaget has described a number of fundamental differences between the thinking of children at the preoperational and concrete operational stages (Piaget, 1960a, 1960b, 1964). The differences can best be presented by contrasting responses to situations involving cause and effect, classification (including matching, grouping, and recognizing common relations), seriation (including size ordering and temporal ordering), and conservation. Implications for interactions with children in the early school years can then be drawn. Developmental Issues in Practice 13.1 contains a table describing the long-term, school-related benefit to children of mastering each of these abilities in the preschool years. Clearly, it is important to encourage cognitive functioning during the early school years.

Cause and effect.   Children at the preoperational stage seem to produce a steady stream of questions: "Where did the moon go?" "Why is the grass green?" "Why is it raining?" Their frequent questions reflect their view that things do not happen by chance but instead are influenced in ways that can

LINKS BETWEEN MENTAL ABILITIES AND LATER SCHOOL-RELATED SKILLS

Ability	Value
Matching: Can identify which things are the same and which things are different *Basic question:* Can you find the pair that is exactly the same?	The ability to discriminate is crucial to development of other mental abilities. An important aspect of gaining literacy: discriminate between letters (such as "m" and "w"). Promotes understanding of equality. Encourages skill in figure and ground perception (separating a significant figure from the background).
Grouping: Can identify common property that forms a group or class *Basic question:* Can you show me the things that belong to the same family?	Fosters mathematical understanding: set theory and equivalency. Children must discriminate, reason, analyze, and select in order to formulate groups. Regrouping encourages flexibility of thought. Depending on manner of presentation, may foster divergent thinking—more than one way to group items. Requires use of accommodation and assimilation. Classification is a basic aspect of life sciences: allows people to organize knowledge.
Common relations: Can identify common property or relationship between a *nonidentical pair* *Basic question:* Which thing goes most closely with what other thing?	Fosters mathematical understanding: one-to-one correspondence. Fosters diversity of understanding concepts: many kinds of pairs (opposites, cause-effect congruent). Can teach use of analogies and riddles.
Cause and effect: Can determine what makes something else happen: a special case of common relations *Basic question:* What makes something else happen?	Basis for scientific investigations. Conveys sense of order of world. Conveys sense of individual's ability to be effective: act on his world and produce results, make things happen. Encourages use of prediction and generation of hypotheses. Introduces child to elementary understanding of the scientific method.
Seriation: Can identify what comes next in a graduated series *Basic question:* What comes next?	Fosters mathematical understanding. Relationship between quantities: counting (enumeration) with understanding, one-to-one correspondence, equivalency, estimation. If teacher presents series going from left to right, fosters basic reading skill.
Temporal ordering: Can identify logical order of events occurring in time *Basic question:* What comes next?	Fosters mathematical understanding. Conveys a sense of order and a sense of time and its effect. Relationship between things: cause-and-effect and other relationships. Prediction. Requires memory: what happened first, then what happened?
Conservation: Can understand that a substance can return to its prior state and that quantity is not affected by mere changes in appearance *Basic question:* Are they still the same quantity?	Idea of constancy (reversibility) is fundamental as a foundation for logical reasoning, basic for scientific understanding; it is also the basis for mathematical calculations involving length, volume, area, and so forth.

SOURCE: From J. Hendrick, *The Whole Child: Developmental Education for the Early Years* (4th ed.). New York: Merrill/Macmillan, 1988. Used with permission.

be discerned. Their attempts to find simple explanations for complex phenomena lead to interpretations that often surprise adults. For instance, in explaining the change from night to day, egocentric children at the preoperational stage might say, "It gets light to wake me up." On the other hand, it has been found that children learn more when they have asked questions about a topic. In a study by Pierce (1990), the number of questions asked by children predicted how well they remembered the answers. This finding confirms the idea that children need to be able to integrate information into their own structure, or concept of the world, in order for them to learn. When they ask questions, they are in a position to direct the analysis of cause and effect.

Children at the preoperational stage also tend to ascribe human, animate characteristics to inanimate objects such as dolls, stuffed animals, and trees. This type of thinking is called **animism**. An adult gave the following account of her ideas about the tree outside the window in her early school years:

> During the day I knew it to be an innocent and harmless apple tree. But at night it was backlighted and cast an ominous shadow on my white window shade. I saw its arms reaching out to get me and developed ways of placating the tree so that it would not. If I had to get out of bed at night, I would only get out of one side. If I forgot and went out the other side, I had a little ritual that I would go through. Years later, I told my mother about the tree and she was upset that I never came to her about it. I didn't tell anyone because I thought that my view of the tree was common knowledge shared by everyone else.

Preoperational thinkers view cause and effect very differently than do concrete operational thinkers. Concrete operational thinkers do not seem driven to explain all events with a sentence or two. When some justification seems called for, their explanations reflect an increased understanding of the world. They are more logical but still have difficulty accounting for complicated events, such as the action of waves. They are fascinated by physical events and love to explore such things as the way water flows, the impact of gravity, and other aspects of physics. As the assignment of animism to inanimate objects decreases, children develop a clearer understanding of life and death, bodily functions, and reproduction.

In their groundbreaking research on children's understanding of reproduction, Bernstein and Cowan (1981) described the stages of the preoperational and concrete operational thinkers. The preoperational period included two types of approaches to the question "Where do babies come from?" They called the first type "geographers" because children's questions were basically aimed at finding out what town they were born in, the answer to their question being the place of birth. The second type were called "manufacturers" because these children had a very mechanical approach to the notion of reproduction and human growth and development. They described the baby as being assembled, much like a doll on an assembly line: "First you take a body and add the head, then arms and legs,. . . ." This approach to human growth contains many of the characteristics of the thinking of preoperational children. It reflects animism, in that the baby is treated like an animate doll. It also contains elements of **artificialism,** in which the child attempts to find a technical, artificial explanation for everything. This approach is also very concrete, in that the explanations are limited to the characteristics of simple, concrete processes that can be visualized from experiences with dolls. The concrete understanding of reproduction is beautifully expressed by the following vignette of a four-year-old:

Sally had just met a family friend who was pregnant. The friend explained to Sally that her baby was "growing inside my stomach." At dinner that night Sally expressed her approval that the baby was inside the mother's stomach because "when the mother eats, the baby can get the food and eat too!" A member of the family then patiently explained the difference between a uterus and a stomach. During the explanation, Sally became increasingly agitated until she blurted out, "But, if the food doesn't fall on the baby, how is the baby going to eat?"

To appreciate this vignette, it is necessary to realize that the child was trying to incorporate a complex new idea into her understanding of people and their needs. Obviously the baby would need to eat, and the concrete and mechanical thinking of the child naturally leads to the ingenious explanation. Once such structures of understanding have been formed, it is very difficult to change them, as Sally's family found. Parents and teachers should not worry about this because as the child's ability to think changes naturally with time, the ideas will evolve into correct explanations. Furthermore, there is an element of truth in her statement, since what the mother eats is ultimately available to the baby. It is only the process that the child misunderstands. Often, it is better to go along with the child's thinking to encourage intellectual processing to occur. A negative response would discourage the child from future efforts at thinking about the environment.

The concrete operational child can imagine the complex development, even though it is invisible inside the mother's body. After around the age of seven, most children go through a "transition" stage, when they begin to accept and learn about the technical explanations of reproduction and can begin to formulate theories about how reproduction occurs. However, it will not be until adolescence that an accurate understanding of complex biological processes can be fully understood. (See Chapter 11 for more discussion of this issue.)

Classification. **Classification** is the grouping of objects or people on the basis of similar characteristics. The ability to make classes is of great importance because it is the basis for all thinking. To make sense out of our world, we must understand when things belong together because of similar characteristics. Very young children often begin to classify using color as the criterion. Macario (1991) has shown that this is especially true when the objects classified are food items. When the objects to be classified are play items, the children tended to classify by shape. With maturity, preschool children can incorporate many criteria in a set of objects and manipulate them into hierarchies. This skill develops with increasing complexity across the preoperational period. Following are descriptions of some of the classification skills in order of their acquisition:

Graphic collections: arranging the objects into a picture rather than into groupings

Incomplete classification: putting the objects into inconsistent groups (e.g., beginning to sort by color and then switching to size)

Single classification: putting objects in a group according to one characteristic but being unable to recognize that the objects can have more than one characteristic (such as being both red and small)

Multiple classification: putting objects into a matrix involving two characteristics simultaneously (putting the large red square in the intersection of large objects and red objects)

Class inclusion: recognizing that subclasses can be arranged into hierarchical groupings (tulips and daisies are both members of the superordinate class of flowers)

Three classification tasks are described next. In each case, the interviewer sits opposite the child and places the objects on the table. The purpose of the interviews is to observe the way the child arranges the objects and the level of logic used in answering the questions.

Classification Interview for Single Classification

Materials: Squares of paper in the following distribution: four large yellow, four small yellow, four large red, four small red, four large blue, four small blue, four large green, four small green

Request 1: "Please put these in groups so that the ones in the group are the same as each other and different from the other groups."

Request 2: After children have classified the squares one way, say, "Now mix them up. Find another, different way to put them into groups."

Classification Interview for Multiple Classification

Materials: Cardboard with a matrix containing blue shapes along the bottom horizontal axis and a row of different-colored circles along the right vertical axis, with a space in the lower right corner where the blue circle should go; a collection of cards to fit the empty space containing a variety of colored shapes, blue shapes, and the correct card: the blue circle (see Figure 13.1)

Request: "Look at this card. You can see that we have two rows. This one has lots of blue things in it and this one has many colored circles. But there's a space here that belongs to both rows. Can you find a picture that will go here that will match both rows?"

Multiple Classification

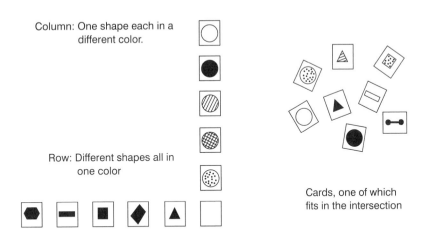

Column: One shape each in a different color.

Row: Different shapes all in one color

Cards, one of which fits in the intersection

Figure 13.1   *Multiple Classification Task*
A matrix with one row containing pictures of different shapes (all the same color) and a column containing pictures of one object (a circle) in many different colors. The cards contain pictures of objects to go in the blank space, which is the intersection of the row and the column.

Classification Interview for Class Inclusion

Materials: 25 wooden beads, of which 22 are red and 3 are yellow

Request: "Here are some beads. They are all wooden. Can you see that they are all wooden? Some are red and some are yellow. Can you tell me if there are more red beads or more wooden beads?"

Some of the problems encountered by preoperational children center on classification difficulties, as shown by a vignette that was recorded at a nursery school of four-year-olds:

A female pediatrician came to talk to the children about visiting the doctor. She wore her white coat and stethoscope. When she was finished talking about medical issues, she asked the children whether any of them wanted to grow up to be doctors. Only the boys raised their hands. She asked whether any of the girls wanted to become doctors, and they all assured her that boys become doctors and girls become nurses. They proceeded to argue with her about this, even though she pointed out that she was a "girl."

The children had established their classification of medical personnel based on their personal experience, and they would not accept an alternative system. This rigidity in thinking is common in preschool children, and it is not until they reach concrete operations that they have the mental flexibility to allow for exceptions to the single classification rule based on gender. During the preoperational period, this misconception is not based in sexist thinking but simply reflects the limited analytical ability of children at this age.

In contrast, children at the concrete operational stage form categories consistently. They may classify the same set of materials first by color, then by shape, and then by some other variable. They understand that objects can form hierarchies (e.g., from living things to animals to farm animals to cows), and they deal with the relationships between objects and people at different levels of the hierarchy. They can comprehend more easily than earlier the multiple roles that any one individual may have, regardless of gender. Freund, Baker, and Sonnenschein (1990) have shown that preschool children cannot modify their classification procedures to accommodate new task demands. It is not until they can form concrete operations that children are ready to accept a flexible classification system that allows for objects and gender to be defined in a number of different ways.

Seriation.   **Seriation** is putting objects into ordered relationships, such as from large to small. Seriation is essential as a basis for all mathematical understanding. Developmental Issues in Practice 13.2 presents a readiness inventory specifying the abilities necessary for children to have before they can begin to study mathematics as part of a school curriculum. Note that the abilities involve seriation and classification skills discussed in this chapter.

Seriation is also very important to daily living, because children must be able to order their time, activities, money, and so on. Preschool children often show a poor ability to organize and plan their daily activities. Friedman (1990) has shown that by age five, children can put their daily activities into a correct order, into a backward order, and into a forward order from multiple

Seriation involves putting objects into ordered relationships, such as from large to small.

▲ DEVELOPMENTAL ISSUES IN PRACTICE   13.2

A MATHEMATICS READINESS INVENTORY

1. **Ability to Count**
   Give a child 10 beads. Ask the child to count the number of beads on the table. Encourage child to discuss ways of finding out how many beads there are. Child may be able to tell without touching the beads, but if not, ask child to touch the beads as he or she counts. If child loses the one-to-one correspondence before arriving at 10, then record the last number in correct association.

2. **Ability to Recognize Number Quantities**
   Counters are arranged in sets. As each set is shown, ask, "How many counters do you see?" Record the answer.

3. **Ability to Select a Designated Number Group**
   The ability to select a designated number of counters from a larger set indicates an understanding of a number idea. Ask children to give you three counters, or any other number of counters, and record the answer.

4. **Ability to Compare Through Noting Changes in Size and Amount**
   Present objects that are easily handled and arrange into two sets. Vary the sets and ask children: "Which is more?" "Which is the same?" "Which is different?" "Which is less?"

5. **Ability to Use Ordinals**
   Arrange five counters in a line. Ask the child to show you the first, last, second, and so on.

6. **Ability to Arrange Counters into Sets**
   Ask the child to tell you which sets are equal, which are pairs, which could be partners.

7. **Ability to Match Number Symbols**
   Ability to match numerals precedes the ability to recognize and write the figure. A 9-inch square card marked with 3-inch squares is prepared. In each of the nine smaller squares one of the numerals from 1 to 9 is written. They are out of sequence. Corresponding numerals should then be written on separate 3-inch squares to be used in matching the figures. Ask children to take the smaller squares and say, "Put this numeral over the same one on the big card."

8. **Ability to Recognize Number Symbols**
   Referring to Number 7, use the same cards, and ask the child to give you the 4, and so on.

9. **Ability to Match Number Symbols to Number Groups**
   Arrange groups of counters in different ways. Ask the child to place the correct numeral by a set. Give children numerals and ask them to arrange counters to match the numerals.

10. **Ability to Recognize and Perform Simple Operations**
    a. *Oral demonstration:* Ask the child to arrange a given number of counters and tell or demonstrate about a number, say, 3. Children may respond, "Two and one are three," "one and two are three," and so on.
    b. *Reading and manipulation of symbols:* When the children can complete oral demonstration of simple operations, give them cards with the symbols $+$, $-$, $=$, $>$, and $<$ on them. Ask them to arrange the numbers using these symbols and tell about them.

SOURCE: From C. Seefeldt and N. Barbour, *Early Childhood Education: An Introduction* (2nd ed.), p. 390. New York: Merrill/Macmillan, 1990. Used with permission.

reference points (e.g., events happening after lunch as opposed to after breakfast). By age seven the children in Friedman's study could also order events backward from different reference points. However, Arlin (1990) has shown that preschool children's understanding of time is still limited because they express the belief that the clock goes slower at night than in the daytime. This perception appeared to reflect children's egocentric assumption that time is not constant but goes faster or slower in response to their own behavior. Between seven and nine years of age, the children acquired a correct understanding of time constancy.

Sequential planning ability has been studied by Casey, Bronson, Tivnan, Riley, and Spenciner (1991). They demonstrated that this is a separate skill, unrelated to general intellectual functioning. Thus, seriation ability is an important acquisition of the preschool years. It develops in a systematic way across the preoperational period. Children respond to seriation tasks in the following developmental pattern:

Making random arrangements or setting down pairs of objects that ignore other relationships

Making one correct seriation but not being able to incorporate an "extra" piece after the initial seriation is completed

Simultaneously placing two seriations together (as in the multiple seriations found in the story "The Three Bears")

Later, at the concrete operational level, children employ a system for comparing each item with all others rather than using trial and error. They can coordinate two dimensions, such as color and size, in a matrix. And they can be shown two objects, one of which is then removed, and use that information to explain the relationship with a third object. A seriation task follows.

Seriation Interview

Materials: Nine construction paper strips, in a single color, ranging in length from 1 inch to 9 inches

Preparation: Place the longest and the shortest strips of paper on the table with a large space between them. Withhold one strip of intermediate length.

Request 1: "Please put these pieces of paper [a randomly arranged pile of six strips] where they belong."

Request 2: After the child has made an arrangement, say, "Here's an extra one. Would you put it where it belongs?"

Conservation. **Conservation** involves the understanding of the constancy of characteristics such as number, length, mass, or area, despite changes in appearance. The ability to correctly understand conservation is the most important characteristic of the concrete operational child and is the method used most in testing for the presence of concrete operational thought. Different conservations are acquired in a logically inherent order across the entire

A child studies checkers in a conservation-of-number interview.

stage of concrete operations. The first to be understood by most children at around six years of age is number. Length, liquid and substance quantity, and area are usually acquired by eight years of age.

All interviews about conservation use the same sequence: (1) establishing equivalence (Request 1); (2) showing some change in appearance of one of the equivalent objects; (3) asking for another judgment of equivalence; and (4) asking why the child thinks that way. If a child does not establish initial equivalence, the interviewer does not proceed. The most important part of the task is that of asking for the child's explanation. This explanation must be characterized by logic in order to be certain that concrete operational strategies are being used. Only one of the many conservation tasks is presented here. (Conservation of number is described in Chapter 2.)

Conservation of Liquid Quantity

Materials: Two clear glasses of identical size and shape; one clear glass that is taller and narrower than the pair; one pitcher of water

Preparation: Fill the identical glasses with water.

Request 1: "If this glass is yours and this glass is mine [pointing], would you have more to drink or would I have more to drink or would we have the same?"

"Now watch what I do." [Pour the water from one of the identical glasses into the tall, narrow glass. Remove the empty glass.]

Request 2: "Would you have more to drink or would I have more to drink or would we have the same?"

Request 3: "Why do you think so?"

Children at the preoperational stage usually respond that the tall glass has more "because it is so high." This response occurs because the children are failing to use compensation, which would enable them to compare the height and width of the glasses and compensate for changes in one direction. Children at the concrete operational stage are often surprised that they would be asked such a silly question. "Of course they're still the same; you haven't added any water or taken any away."

It is important to note that the conservation tasks about which children are interviewed have no inherent significance. These types of tasks were chosen by Piaget because they require logical responses that are not usually directly taught at home or school.

Children at the preoperational stage of development are unable to conserve. They base their judgments on perceptual cues (e.g., "Because it's so high"; "Because it sticks out on this end"), focus on one variable (height) rather than coordinating several (both height and width), do not mentally reverse their thinking to consider the original state ("You just moved it"), and do not recognize that nothing has really been changed ("You didn't add any").

At the concrete operational stage, however, children are able to conserve. They are no longer rigidly concrete but justify their conserving responses logically. These justifications refer to **reversibility** (mentally returning objects to the original position or state), **compensation** (seeing that one variable, such as height, is balanced by another, such as width), or **identity** (recognizing that nothing has been added or taken away).

Educational implications.   Four important implications can be drawn from descriptions of thinking at the preoperational and concrete operational stages. First, children have their own unique perspectives and less flexibility than adults to change perspectives. Especially at the preoperational stage, they may be structuring information in a different way than does someone else with whom they are communicating. For instance, while an adult is talking about a hierarchical arrangement of elements, some children might be capable only of simple classifying. Because knowing the focus of a given child, particularly in a group situation, is not easy, information on concepts must be presented in as many different ways as possible.

The way that adults communicate with children helps to enhance many of these skills. Sigel and Cocking (1977) have developed some practical suggestions for enhancing children's cognitive functioning using language, which they call "distancing" (see Developmental Issues in Practice 13.3 for a discussion of this approach).

The second educational implication of the concrete and preoperational thinking stages is that children at these stages of development need experiences with **concrete objects** in order to learn to reason about their properties. Often, children in the early school years are given worksheets that depict objects, but they need first to explore the actual objects using all their senses. Children in the early school years learn best when they have the actual objects to manipulate.

Third, children need to have opportunities to organize information and integrate it into existing knowledge. Their interests in activities can signal a readiness to learn. Children must also be given an opportunity to "play" with new information before rushing on to new concepts. If they show a desire to continue to work on something, it may be that they need additional time to fully assimilate the new knowledge.

Fourth and finally, children can be observed and interviewed to assess their levels of logical thinking and to match these levels with appropriate experiences. Children who do not conserve numbers (e.g., they believe that one row of eight objects can be more than another row of eight) have not yet built an appropriate foundation for mathematics (refer again to Developmental Issues in Practice 13.2). To be sure, these children may be able to memorize number facts, but their understanding of the operations is limited. Some mathematics programs, such as Mathematics Their Way (Baratta-Lorton, 1976), take into account the special needs of children at the preoperational and early concrete operational stages.

Using Logic

Piaget has often asked children questions that philosophers would recognize as belonging in their domain. For instance, in his book *The Child's Conception of the World*, Piaget (1960b) asked children questions such as the following:

What is thinking?

What is the relationship between a word and its meaning?

What things are alive?

Piaget's purpose in asking these questions and in analyzing the responses was to provide evidence of the inherent logic of the children's thinking. Children's answers sometimes seem "wrong" to adults; however, Piaget emphasized that the process of thinking and reasoning would always be appropriate to the developmental level of the child. What is lacking in children's analysis is the advanced level of structural development found in adults. Children do not have the capacity to organize (or "structure") the information in the same complex way that adults can. This chapter has discussed the nature of the structural development of the preoperational and concrete operational child. This section will apply some of what has been presented by looking at philosophical thinking and moral development.

▲ **DEVELOPMENTAL ISSUES IN PRACTICE   13.3**

DISTANCING STRATEGIES

Sigel and Cocking (1977) pointed out that an important developmental goal for preschool children is to lessen their concrete and perception-based tie to the environment and develop a more logical and symbolic strategy for environmental interactions. Any strategy that helps to create that distance for the child would facilitate cognitive growth.

They proposed that there are language strategies that can help one accomplish this goal by encouraging cognitive analysis of the concrete situation and by encouraging thinking to occur. They called these "distancing strategies." They are intended to be used as part of the normal verbal communication between adults and children, and many parents and teachers use them naturally. However, Sigel and Cocking (1977) proposed that children would benefit if adults learned to use these strategies efficiently.

Following are the examples developed by Sigel and Cocking. The first column contains the cognitive benefit, or outcome, of using the strategy. The second column provides a detailed demonstration of what the adult should say and do. Note that these strategies involve the child in thinking about such cognitive skills as cause and effect, classification, seriation, and conservation.

Observing	Examining or asking the child to examine: "Watch. . . . This is how. . . ." Teacher demonstrating also: "Look at what I'm doing."
Labeling	Naming a singular object or event (to be distinguished from concept labeling): "What is that called?". Identifying—for example, "What do you call what she is doing?"
Describing	Providing elaborated information of a single instance: "This is how it works." "It is . . .," "Appears like . . .," "Looks like . . . ." Also describing inner states of self, "How does it make you feel?" and actions, "What are you doing?"
Interpretation	To attribute or explain meaning, such as "What do you mean?" "What does it mean to be something?"
Demonstrating	Showing primarily through action or gestures that something is to be done: "Show me how . . ."
Sequencing	Temporal ordering of events, as in a story or carrying out a task. Steps articulated, as "next," "afterwards," "start," "begin," "last."

Philosophical thinking.   Children attempt to understand all the complex issues around them, as has been demonstrated in the discussion earlier in this chapter of the child's attempts to understand reproductive processes. These concerns include issues of life and death as well. The following discussion was overheard in a supermarket:

> Five-year-old Olivia and seven-year-old Robert were discussing whether a plastic flower attached to a container of room deodorant was "alive" or not. Olivia was

DEVELOPMENTAL ISSUES IN PRACTICE   13.3 (continued)

Reproducing	Construct previous experiences; the dynamic interaction of events; interdependence; functional understanding: "How was it done?" "How did it happen?"
Comparing	
Describing similarities	Noting common characteristics (perceptual analysis): "Are those the same?"
Describing differences	Noting differences among instances (perceptual analysis): "Which ones are different?"
Proposing alternatives	Using key words: "other," "another," "something different from before"
Combining	
Classifying	Recognition of commonalities of a class: "How are these alike?"
Counting	Counting objects in the class
Synthesizing	Reconstructing components into a unified whole: "Which ones belong together here?"
Evaluating	
Consequences	Assess quality of outcome: "Is this right or wrong?" "Is this a good thing to happen?"
Affect	Assess personal liking, opinion: "Do you like the way it looks?" "How do you feel about feeling sad?"
Inferring	Nonapparent, unseen relationships
Cause/effect	Prediction of causal relationships: "How will this work?" "Why should we do it?"
Feelings	Prediction of how persons will feel: "How do you think that will make her feel?"
Effects	Predictions of what will happen (without articulation of the causality): "What will happen?"
Resolving conflict	Presentation of contradictory or conflicting information and resolution: "What would happen if you tried . . . ?"
Generalizing	Application of knowledge to other settings or objects: "It's just like the one at home." "We've done this before."
Transforming	Pointing out changes in the nature, function, or appearance of something: "See how different it looks (feels, seems)."
Planning	Arranging conditions to carry out a set of actions in an orderly way: "Let's talk about what we will do now." "What do you think we need in order to do that?"
Concluding	Relating actions, objects, or events by summarizing: "What has happened to it?" "I guess it is now . . ."

SOURCE: From Irving E. Sigel and Rodney R. Cocking, *Cognitive Development from Childhood to Adolescence: A Constructivist Perspective.* New York: Holt, Rinehart & Winston, 1977. Used with permis-

certain that it was alive because, she said, "It looks alive, feels alive, and smells alive." Her older brother, at the concrete operational level of thinking, could tell that it was only plastic and was not alive. However, every argument he produced was countered by the concrete and animistic thinking of his younger sister, who had the evidence of her perception to prove that it clearly appeared to be "alive." Finally Robert came up with an argument that was acceptable to Olivia's preoperational approach to the problem. He said, "It's not alive because it can't die."

▲ DEVELOPMENTAL ISSUES IN PRACTICE   13.4

ADVANCING CHILDREN'S PHILOSOPHIC THINKING

The Institute for the Advancement of Philosophy for Children (Montclair State College, Upper Montclair, NJ), under the direction of Matthew Lipman, has developed curriculum materials for children and guides for teachers in developing philosophical thinking. The early childhood materials include the books *Rio and Gus* (Lipman, 1982) and *Pixie* (Lipman, 1981), as well as the accompanying teachers' guides. These novels and related activities help children examine philosophical concepts of great interest to them: friendship, goodness, fairness, reality, truth, being a person. The vehicle for learning is discussion, and children learn to reason together. In so doing, they attain some of the following thinking skills (Philosophy for Children, 1984):

Analyzing value statements

Classifying and categorizing

Constructing hypotheses

Defining terms

Developing concepts

Discovering alternatives

Drawing inferences from hypothetical syllogisms

Drawing inferences from single premises

Drawing inferences from double premises

Finding underlying assumptions

Formulating causal explanations

Formulating comparisons as relationships

This example demonstrates a number of points. First of all, neither of the children was "wrong." Both had a different way of analyzing and structuring the problem; that is, they each had different structures available to them. Given their individual structures, each one was thinking quite correctly. Second, to help change the structures of children, it is necessary to seek out the inconsistencies in thinking that, once exposed, lead to disequilibration and restructuring. Clearly, Olivia knew that the flower was plastic and would not die, but she had not integrated that information into her perceptions of life and death. This particular philosophical discussion led to a reorganization of her structures and an increase in knowledge. Third, Robert's ability to seek and find the appropriate argument to help in Olivia's disequilibration may be due, in part, to the fact that at his age he has more recently dealt with such concerns himself. Adults often realize that they have trouble finding an appropriate argument because it has been so long since they themselves were preoperational and they have difficulty putting themselves into the child's position and understanding his or her needs.

DEVELOPMENTAL ISSUES IN PRACTICE   13.4 (continued)

Formulating questions

Generalizing

Giving reasons

Grasping part–whole and whole–part connections

Identifying and using criteria

Knowing how to deal with ambiguities

Knowing how to treat vagueness

Looking out for informal fallacies

Making connections

Making distinctions

Predicting consequences

Providing instances and illustrations

Recognizing contextual aspects of truth and falsity

Recognizing differences of perspective

Recognizing interdependence of means and ends

Seriation

Standardizing ordinary language sentences

Taking all considerations into account

Using ordinal or relational logic

Working with analogies

Working with consistency and contradiction

Philosophical questions raised by children in the early school years have the potential of helping children learn to think independently, logically, and ethically. Research with older children (fifth through eighth graders) has shown that children with experience in philosophical thinking made significant gains in reading, mathematics, and creativity when compared with children without that experience (Alvino, 1980). Because of such impressive research findings, it has been suggested that philosophy be made a part of the school curriculum even in the early school years. Developmental Issues in Practice 13.4 presents a list of some of the thinking skills that have been attributed to curricula designed to enhance philosophical thinking.

The importance of philosophical thinking involves the nature of the discipline itself. Philosophy gives a methodology for inquiring about fundamental assumptions. The aims and objectives of teaching philosophy to children include the following (Alvino, 1980):

1. To increase children's reasoning skills as well as their abilities to draw valid inferences

2. To help children see connections and make distinctions

3. To develop creative as well as logical abilities

4. To help children discover alternatives, the need for objectivity and consistency, and the importance of giving reasons for beliefs (p. 54)

The basic techniques of questioning and using dialogue in teaching philosophy help children recognize that learning and understanding are cooperative functions. Children experience what is "right" and "fair," develop standards and rules, and discover the differences between truthfulness and lying and cheating. For example, Strichartz and Burton (1990) studied the recognition of truth and lies by examining children's understanding of (1) the factuality of a statement, (2) the speaker's belief in the statement, and (3) the speaker's intent to deceive the listener. They found that the fifth grade marked a transition of increased understanding, with younger children performing significantly less well than those above the fifth-grade level. However, studies have demonstrated that children as young as three years old can predict the behavior of story characters acting under the influence of a false belief (Siegal & Beattie, 1991). On the other hand, the ability of three-year-olds to perform well in these tasks is affected by a number of different factors, including the clarity of the language used in the task (Lewis & Osborne, 1990; Robinson & Mitchell, 1992) and the opportunity to use simple hide-and-seek strategies to cause the deception (Freeman, Lewis, & Doherty, 1991).

This research demonstrates that starting at the age of three, children begin to construct an idea of the mind and can begin to recognize that people can act on the basis of a false belief about something. In a related ability, research has shown that preschool children have difficulty telling the difference between the appearance of a person and the actual moral intent of the person (Flavell, Lindberg, Green, & Flavell, 1992). This ability to tell the difference is essential to the self-protective actions of children dealing with strangers. Older preschool children are more capable of assessing the actual intent of a stranger and ignoring the mere appearance.

Moral development.   Philosophical thinking prepares the way for moral development reasoning. The concept of moral development involves a wide range of developmental components. The three components discussed here include rule following, moral reasoning, and conventional behavior. One of the first theorists to study the structural characteristics of moral functioning was Jean Piaget. His approach was to analyze the behavior of children as they played games governed by rules. He found that children's conception of rules changes systematically with age (Piaget, 1964). The first stage is descriptive of preschool children until approximately the age of five years. It is characterized by a tendency to use idiosyncratic rules. That is, the children feel free to change rules at any time, to invent rules as they go along in the game, and to allow their own private needs and desires to govern what the rules will be. The structure governing the functioning of children at this stage is egocentrism. There is no evidence of collective effort or cooperative intent. The second stage in Piaget's analysis is characterized by a decline in egocentrism and a tendency to view rules as handed down by a higher authority. Rules at this stage are characterized by being permanent, unchangeable, and nearly sacred.

At both of these stages, children put more emphasis on the consequences of their actions than on the intentions governing their behavior. This has been studied by presenting children with a set of stories involving children's moral behavior. For example, in one story the subject is told that a child has two different experiences. In the first experience, the child accidentally knocks over an entire tray of 12 of Mother's best glasses while helping her. In the second experience, the child purposely breaks one of the glasses out of anger at the mother. The subject is then asked to explain which incident represents the worst behavior. Most preschool children are overwhelmed by the 12 broken glasses and report that the accidental breaking of the glasses is more negative than the intentional breaking of only one glass. As children enter the early school years, they begin to put more importance on the issue of **intentionality.**

Another characteristic of moral thinking at this age level is that of **moral realism,** which Piaget defined as the confusion between moral and physical laws. This involves the child's belief that negative or sinful behaviors will be immediately followed by a punishing consequence. For example, if a child tells a lie, he or she might fear being punished immediately by being hit, for example, by a falling tree. This is also referred to as **imminent justice** because the justice is given out immediately, or imminently, following the transgression. Jose (1990) has shown that this orientation is associated with children's belief in a just world. Thus, children expect that justice will prevail and that their transgressions will be punished.

Kohlberg followed Piaget's original theory about moral development but expanded the research by creating moral dilemmas to test the subject's ability to reason about moral issues of right and wrong. The moral dilemmas required the subject to justify some type of moral behavior. Kohlberg (1981) found that the ability to analyze moral issues developed in a systematic way with age. His theory of a stage-based developmental pattern of moral development was confirmed by a subsequent longitudinal study (Colby, Kohlberg, Gibbs, & Lieberman, 1993). Kohlberg called the stage of the preschool age group **preconventional morality**. It is made up of two substages. The first substage is characterized by strategies of punishment–avoidance. That is, children at this stage level determine right and wrong by whether they are in danger of being punished. They ignore the content of the actions involved and judge that "might makes right." They reason that if they can get away with it then it is the right behavior. The second substage is characterized by strategies of maximizing pleasure. Children at this stage follow the maxim "If it feels good, do it."

During the early school years, Kohlberg found that children enter the stage of **conventional morality** in moral development, so called because children functioning at this stage are governed by the conventional norms of the social group. It is characterized by a social orientation and a desire to please others. Good moral behavior for this stage means doing what everyone else would do. At this stage, the children are still unable to analyze the content of the moral issues. Rather, they rely on modeling the behavior of others. Turiel (1966) confirmed Kohlberg's stages and showed that children could be trained to learn more mature behavior if the training program was developed to expand on the stage in which the child was already functioning. This theory is intended not to predict the behavior of the child but rather to analyze the reasoning process used by the child in making moral decisions.

Many additional factors determine the actual moral behavior of children. Asendorpf and Nunner-Winkler (1992) found, for example, that being temperamentally inhibited was an important determiner of the moral behavior of six- and seven-year-old children. Richards, Bear, Stewart, and Norman (1992) demonstrated that both the lowest and the highest levels of moral reasoning among school children were associated with good behavior in the classroom. In other words, both punishment-avoiding reasoning and socially principled reasoning were used most often in explaining good behavior.

Turiel (1978) was able to demonstrate that moral issues are different from **social conventions** and that they represent two independent factors in cognitive reasoning. Social conventions include such things as manners, etiquette, and proper dress; these are important social behaviors but do not contain the serious implications of moral issues of right and wrong, which are characteristic of Kohlberg's moral dilemmas. For example, it might be considered improper to wear play clothes to church but it doesn't do lasting harm to anyone. Turiel found that children don't understand the distinction between social conventions and moral issues until they enter the conventional stage of moral functioning at around six or seven years of age. They treat conventions in much the same way as rules, considering them to be unchangeable and uniform for all people. By eight or nine years of age, children begin to recognize that conventions are not compulsory. At this stage, children understand that social conventions serve a social function and are arbitrary.

PERCEPTUAL DEVELOPMENT

We tend to assume that once a child's eyes and ears are fully formed in infancy, the ability to learn through these sense organs is fully mature. However, it is important to realize that the ability to perceive accurately requires that two separate events occur. First, the sense organs must pick up the sight or sound, and second, the brain must evaluate and interpret it. This ability is important in many areas of the child's life, but it is particularly necessary when learning to read. In our culture, it is essential that everyone learn to read, and families and schools are likely to emphasize it. Because of the danger of overemphasizing it as a critical skill, it is important to understand something about the perceptual basis for reading ability.

The ability to read is based on a wide range of developmental skills acquired during the preschool years. One critical component is perception. Research (Bruce, 1964) suggests that the average age for reading readiness is 6.5 years, which falls at a time that most children are in the first grade. This is the traditionally accepted time for reading to begin. However, many children learn to read either earlier or later than this average. There has been a tendency for us to label children who start later as deficient and to put great pressure on children to acquire reading skills at earlier ages. It is important to stress that any attempts to encourage reading should be based on what we know about the developmental abilities of the particular child involved. This section will begin with a discussion of perceptual processes, which will be discussed from the point of view of reading acquisition, and the section will end with a discussion of educational applications.

Perceptual Processes

To understand the kind of problems that children can have with perception, consider the child who sees his father give his mother a "love pat." The child evaluates it as a spanking and interprets the event as a fight. Another example is that of the child mistaking a "b" for a "d." Research on language difficulties (Vellutine, 1987) has shown that this problem with letter identification involves not the eyes but the brain's processing of the language system.

Gibson and Levin (1975) have argued that preschool children will naturally exhibit some of these problems because their perceptual skills have not fully matured. These researchers have presented a wide range of study to show that perceptual judgments develop between three and eight years of age. They argue that the maturity of these skills is essential to the ability of the child to read. There are three areas of interest that pertain directly to the development of reading ability: discrimination, attention, and recognition of distinctive features.

Discrimination. First is the child's **discrimination** ability, which is the ability to recognize differences in forms. This research is done by asking the child to match one picture from a set to a sample picture. Although the child's eyes can see the picture as well as any adult, the child cannot quickly come up with a strategy for eliminating the characteristics that don't help the child find the match.

In practical terms, two of the forms that children frequently confuse are "b" and "d." Adults make the discrimination by noting whether the circle is on the left side or right side of the vertical line. As we've already discovered in the section on spatial development, preschool children have difficulty distinguishing right from left (see Chapter 8 for a discussion of laterality). Consequently, they will be unable to make the discrimination required to tell the difference between the two letters. The child's interpretation for both letters may be to describe them as a "ball with a stick." Obviously, this description fits both "b" and "d" and does not help the child to discriminate between the two letters.

Attention.   One reason for children's perceptual problems is that, as they mature, they learn to attend to things more efficiently. Adults can generally focus on the one thing of importance in the environment and block out all interfering events, thus attending directly to the task at hand. Preschool children have trouble with distractions from competing events. This has been called **obligatory attention.** For example, if the child is trying to pay attention to a teacher's instructions but another child is also talking, the preschool child is more apt to miss some of the teacher's words, even if the child wants to hear them.

The child's attentional abilities should be taken into account when designing teaching materials. The more colorful and complex a picture is, the harder it is for very young preschool children to identify all the parts and draw conclusions from it. They need to begin with simple drawings of specific objects.

A second important factor in attention ability is the **search strategy** used by the child. The ability to visually scan an object in an efficient way increases with age and reaches maturity at approximately 6–7 years (Vurpillot, 1968). Research has shown that the search strategies of the very young child are characterized by certain problems: (1) the failure to examine the contours of the object, (2) the failure to seek out the important features of an object, and (3) the tendency to linger on one spot for long periods of time. (See Figure 13.2 for a comparison of children's scanning abilities at different ages.)

Thus, it is clear why the younger children obtain less information from their search activities than those who are perceptually more mature. Children need a lot more time to implement a successful search strategy. The same limitations are true of children's attempts to scan letters. Research on the scanning of letters has shown that, as with forms, the older children have a better chance of identifying the letters.

However, a third critical factor, **context use,** affects attentional skills. It involves the context in which the perceptions must be interpreted. Smith (1928) has described the limitations of visual information processing. It takes one second for a person to process and identify four to five unrelated letters. However, in the same period of time, the same person can process and identify an entire sentence made up of many letters formed into words. A great deal more information can be processed if it is embedded in a meaningful context. Smith (1983) has made a strong case that language skills, including reading, are embedded in meaningful communication. Fast, accurate com-

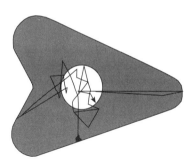

Trajectory of eye movements
of three year old in familiarization with figure (20 seconds)

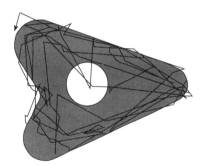

Trajectory of eye movements
of six year old in familiarization
with figure (20 seconds)

Figure 13.2 *Samples of Scanning Ability in Children by Age*
The lines represent the successive eye movements performed by a child during the comparison of the two stimulus figures. The younger subject fails to examine the contour of
the figure, seek out important characteristics, or move quickly around the figure.
SOURCE: From V. P. Zinchenko, Van Chzihi-Tsin, & V. V. Tarakonov, "The Formation and Development of Perceptual Activity," *Soviet Psychology & Psychiatry, 2,* (1963): 3–12. Reported in E. J. Gibson, *Principles of Perceptual Learning & Development.* New York: Prentice Hall, 1969, p. 457. Used
with permission.

prehension of language is enhanced by a thorough familiarity with the context in which it is embedded. Research on "functional print" in preschool
children (McGee, Lomax, & Head, 1988) confirms the tendency of children to
read more material when it is embedded in meaningful contexts, such as a
page of listings from *TV Guide*, a letter, newspaper headlines, a map, and a
grocery store coupon. Accuracy was significantly better for readers than for
nonreaders. However, all the children responded to the task by attempting to
decipher meaningful words, using the context of the particular reading material for clues to meaning.

Recognition of distinctive features.   The last major area of perceptual development concerns the preschool child's ability to recognize the **distinctive features** of objects. There are a few key features we usually come to associate
with each object. For example, most adults quickly associate long ears with a
rabbit. If an adult sees a partial picture of an animal with long ears, he or she
will immediately guess that it is a rabbit. It takes longer for a preschool child
to recognize this "clue," and the child will need more pictures with more
information before he or she will be able to guess correctly what the picture
is about.

   All these factors help explain why children are so fascinated with cartoons. Cartoons have all the characteristics that make visualization easier for
preschool children. They are usually simple, contain only the most important

information, are of a few specific images, and include only the most distinctive features of the object.

A variation of this skill is the child's ability to identify **invariants** in the
objects they see. An invariant is anything that always stays the same in an
object in spite of superficial changes in appearance. For example, as we
learned in the section on cognitive development, there can be an identical
amount of liquid in two differently shaped glasses. A preschool child will frequently not recognize his or her teacher if the teacher is seen in a different
place, such as a shopping mall, or dressed in different clothing. Another
example involves the difficulty that preschool children have recognizing
someone after they have a haircut or if they are wearing a Halloween costume. This explains the fear children sometimes exhibit when they come to
school to find all their teachers in costume for Halloween. They may feel that
they are surrounded by strangers.

As these examples show, a major reason for the difficulty in recognizing
distinctive features is that the child relies heavily on the context for making
accurate identifications. A teacher in a shopping mall or a Halloween clown
in nursery school are out of context from the child's usual experiences. In
addition, the unusual dress of the teachers in these examples produces the
incorrect context for the person the child has come to know. Such experiences can be very helpful to the child in providing important information
about which distinctive features a child should be using to identify people; for
example, clothing is not a good feature for children to rely on. Children can
begin to learn to use other features when they are confronted with such experiences.

Reading Ability

In reading, children must first learn to recognize the distinctive features of
letters. Smith (1928) has pointed out that there are probably at least six distinctive features for each letter of the English alphabet necessary to distinguish one letter from the other. It is important for very young children to
learn to make these distinctions and identify the letters of the alphabet. However, in reading, it would be impossible for anyone to attend to all the distinctive features of each letter of every word being read. It is clear that, once
learned, reading does not rely on distinctive features of letters to identify
words. Rather, reading involves the complex integration of large pieces of
previously learned facts about letters and words to satisfy the desire to understand the information being communicated.

Smith (1928) has described the concept of **tunnel vision** in discussing
this issue. He points out that tunnel vision involves focusing on the smallest
distinctive feature possible. Children must first learn to use the distinctive
features. In reading, however, the goal is to overcome tunnel vision and focus
on comprehending the meaning of the whole written material. Nodine and
Lang (1971) found that proficient readers at the age of eight years are much
faster at scanning material being read than are preschool-age children. The

The ability to read is based on a wide range of developmental skills that are acquired during the preschool years.

proficient readers scan too fast to be focusing on the distinctive features of each letter and each word. This is presumably because they have learned to use the context of the written material to avoid tunnel vision. Ehri and Wilce (1987b) trained kindergarten children in phonemic segmenting. This is a process of encouraging the children to learn to recognize clusters of letters (such as st, sn, sl, ts, etc.) and to understand that letters can have a number of different sounds. The intention is to assist in word recognition by eliminating tendencies toward tunnel vision; phonemic segmenting is thus helpful in increasing word recognition.

Mann (1993) also found that phoneme awareness is important. She found that a high level of awareness predicted the successful reading ability of first-grade children.

Educational Applications

It should be clear from reviewing this material that young preschool children have a great deal to learn before they will be ready to read. Parents tend to be very eager to have their children read, mistakenly believing that early reading is a benefit to their child. In fact, early reading could be detrimental. If the child is perceptually unprepared for reading, pressure to acquire the skills involved could lead to frustration and fear of the whole subject. These experiences could cause the child to reject the whole idea of reading, which would have exactly the opposite effect from the one desired by the parent. Gibson and Levin (1975) have stressed the need to respect the developmental level of children; they suggest providing prereading training and waiting until children are individually ready to begin to read.

Language/thinking programs (Anselmo, Rollins, & Schuckman, 1986; Hendrick, 1990) provide preschool children with training in prereading skills. In addition, Neuman and Roskos (1991) have found that literacy could be enhanced by incorporating literary objects into preschool children's spontaneous free play activities. These are some of the ways to encourage a sense of success in the preschool child, which can induce a feeling of the joy in anticipation of reading.

Ehri and Wilce (1987a) have proposed that there is a developmental process for acquiring reading skills, which begins late in the preschool years. They suggest three stages in the process:

1. Visual cue reading: finding visual stimuli in the words to give cues to the meaning; for example, using the curl in the last letter of the word *dog* to remind the child of the dog's tail

2. Phonetic cue reading: using pronunciation and spelling as cues for reading words

3. Cipher reading: learning the alphabet, acquiring phonemic segmenting skills, internalizing spelling rules, and understanding the systematic relation between spelling and pronunciation

Ehri and Wilce argue that visual cue reading begins in the preschool years but that beginning readers switch to phonetic cue reading at the beginning of the school years. Frank Smith (1983) has argued that children use such skills as part of their subconscious effort to obtain meaning from reading. He suggests that it is important to allow children to acquire the skills naturally by engaging in reading but to limit the teaching of these specific skills, because the tendency is for our teaching methods to destroy the natural learning process. He points out that only five minutes of every teaching hour, on average, is actually spent in reading.

Smith (1983) recommends that beginning readers be given as much information as possible to establish the context of the story material being read. For example, pictures and previous familiarity with the story can be used to give the child an opportunity to guess at the meaning of words. Smith argues that the important thing to emphasize for beginning readers is comprehension of the meaning of the written material; correction for details, such as pronunciation and correct word usage, can wait until after children begin to read with comprehension. He particularly argues that it is essential not to deaden the children's desire to read by emphasizing drills of material that lead to tunnel vision rather than comprehension.

Marie Clay's (1967) research has supported Smith's claims. She studied the reading ability of school children and found that effective readers were self-motivated to engage in risk taking and were able to learn from their own errors. Don Holdaway's (1979) reading theory stresses the socially satisfying aspect of reading by encouraging a naturalistic approach, using large-print books in group settings.

To be prepared for formal reading, children must first acquire a number of abilities. Table 13.1 provides a checklist for observing beginning literacy in early childhood education programs. This table compares the level that children can generally attain on their own with the performance that can be expected when children read with adult help. The checklist summarizes the many skills that are part of beginning literacy and also suggests the value of appropriate adult stimulation to encourage reading without the use of worksheets and drills, which dull interest in the subject.

LANGUAGE DEVELOPMENT

Children's ability to use their native language is essentially complete by the early school years. Research has demonstrated, however, that some aspects of children's language development continue during the early school years. Owens (1984) has said of this age group: "Having acquired much of the 'what' of language form, the child turns to the 'how' of language use" (p. 263). A description of language development in the early school years covers two important topics: linguistic milestones and bilingualism.

Linguistic Milestones

During the preoperational stage, language use is affected by the egocentrism and concreteness characterized by preoperational thought. As the child enters the stage of concrete operations at six to seven years of age, various important changes occur. Most of these linguistic milestones are necessary for the child's success in schoolwork. Linguistic milestones of children in the early school years include advances in their ability to derive words, use complex noun and verb phrases, use sentences of varied types, produce speech sounds, use a larger vocabulary, reflect on their own use of language, and achieve complexity in language. Each of these milestones is discussed in terms of relevant research, and then suggestions are given for appropriate adult assistance.

Word derivation.   Research reviewed by Owens (1984) showed a qualitative increase in word derivation skills around the age of seven. Children become able to add the suffixes *-er*, *-man*, and *-ist* to words to make nouns that may previously have been unfamiliar to them. For instance, they can produce the word *experimenter* from the phrase *person who experiments*. Similarly, at about the same age, they learn to add *-ly* to make adverbs.

Use of noun and verb phrases.   Children in the early school years increasingly differentiate among subject pronouns such as *I*, object pronouns such as *me*, and reflexive pronouns such as *myself*. They struggle with determining the referents of pronouns and with mastering adjective ordering (Richards, 1980). Gentner (1982) has shown that the use of verb phrases poses problems for children in the early school years. For example, there are several ways to reverse verb actions: using *un-* as in *untie*, using particles as in *pull on* and

Table 13.1.   Checklist for Beginning Literacy

Type	Independent Level	Level with Adult Help
Ages 3–4		
Storybook		
Interest	Has one or two very favorite books and poems; knows them well, so recognizes when they are "misread"	Can become interested in new stories; asks questions
Story understanding	Can relate sequence of events	Can tell about a story in its absence
Story seeking	Is happy to participate in storytime	Is eager to help an adult find books
Notions about reading		
Print and picture	Can point to where story is contained	Can verbalize difference in what picture and print show
Purpose for reading	When asked, can find newspaper, book, etc.	Talks about the kind of reading done in various media
Parts of stories	Can answer question about sequence	Talks about parts of story explicitly
Notion of word	Picks out word in title	Can identify where words begin and end
Writing		
Practice	"Writes" (scribbles) when asked	Is eager to show "writing" to an appreciative adult
Words	For example, has notion that big people ought to have big names	Talks about ideas regarding print
Letter	Learns letters of own name	Learns letters of name and asks for more
Ages 4–5		
Storybook		
Familiarity	Knows several storybooks by name	Has specific things to say about several books
	Knows passages of at least one book	Knows several book segments by heart
Routine	Experiences a school and a home reading routine	Can be explicit about routines for reading
Preference	May have preference for one type of book	Is beginning to like certain types of storybooks
Purposes	Is quite specific about various reasons for reading	Can identify several purposes for reading

pull off, and using separate words such as *open* and *close.* Children must learn that some of these reversals are appropriate only for certain verbs.

Use of varied sentence types.   Owens (1984) has reported an improvement in the early school years of comprehension of the linguistic relationships in sentences using passive voice or temporal sequences. Before the age of five or six years, children are still using the basic sentence structure: agent-action-

Table 13.1. *Checklist for Beginning Literacy (continued)*

Type	Independent Level	Level with Adult Help
Notions about books and print		
Books	Knows which way to hold a book, where beginning and end, pages, title, etc. are	Can describe how to handle a book for reading, and uses terms well
Reading terms	Points correctly to page, sentence, word, and letter; says sound	Uses terms correctly; page, sentence, word, letter, and sound
Notions about reading		
Print	Has no confusion about where a story comes from	
Stability	Knows that a story is always the same because of the print	Can explain why print tells the story
Words	Is familiar with terms and words and can point to printed words	Can identify oral and written forms and tries to describe the difference
Printed words	Has observed and spoken of the way words are printed with the same letters	Knows that words are written with the same letters and sequence each time
Sequence	Participates in talk about oral and written sequences in writing	Can identify how oral and written sound/symbol sequences occur
Letters		
Letters	Knows several letters in different settings	Can name many letters in different settings
Notion about alphabetic principle	Puzzles about word size and consistency of use for sounds	Begins to talk about stability of letters in different words to represent sounds
Writing		
Name	Writes name (possibly uses magnetic letters, but pencil use is preferred)	Asks for help to write other names
Practice	"Writes" when asked; makes signs and labels	"Writing" may take on spontaneous spelling; has a variety of writing purposes

SOURCE: From S. W. Pflaum, *The Development of Language and Literacy in Young Children* (3rd. ed), pp. 138–139. New York: Merrill/Macmillan, 1986. Used with permission.

object-locative. Consequently, they don't understand any sentences that transform the basic form into a more complex one, such as passive sentences ("The window was broken by the ball"). Six- and seven-year-olds begin to understand passive constructions at about the same time that they begin to understand seriation and conservation. Other examples of the ability to transform sentences at this time include using temporal sequences introduced by words such as *because, so,* and *therefore*—these transformations require comprehension of relationships and timing. Only after about the age of seven can children understand what happened first, for example, if someone said, "I went because I was asked" (Owens, 1984, p. 287).

Production of speech sounds.   By the age of eight, most children can produce all the English speech sounds accurately. (See Chapter 11 for a discussion of pronunciation problems.) Children become interested in rhyming and other playful variations on the sounds of words and begin to understand the basis of sound similarity in rhyming words. And, by around six years of age, children learn to divide words into syllables and sentences into words. These abilities are believed to be important prerequisites for reading success (Watson, 1984).

Vocabulary growth.   Throughout the early school years, children increase the size and range of their vocabularies. Between the ages of 7 and 11, they gain improved comprehension of relationships of space, time, and logic (Owens, 1984). In about second grade, children also move from using single-word definitions with individual meanings to complex definitions with socially shared meanings (Wehren, DeLisi, & Arnold, 1981). And between five and seven years of age, most children become more able to interpret figurative expressions such as "Hit the road."

Reaction on language use.   Children in the early school years increase their ability to judge the grammatical acceptability of sentences (Owens, 1984) and to react separately to the content and structure of language. This ability to reflect on language use is called **metalinguistic awareness.** By the age of seven, most children can effectively use indirect requests (e.g., saying "It sure is a cold day to walk to school" to a parent who is getting in the car to drive to work).

Complexity of language.   Owens (1984) has asserted that the most important linguistic growth in the early school years involves the growing subtlety and complexity of language. The conversational abilities of children in the early school years expand. As egocentric tendencies lessen, they are increasingly able to clarify messages and to be successful in adapting their speech to the needs of different listeners (McDevitt, Spivey, Sheehan, Lennon, & Story,

Vocabulary growth is facilitated when children learn new words and concepts within a context encouraging relationship with the environment. The children looking at these pictures later walked in the neighborhood to find arches and other structural components.

1990). By the age of eight, children can recognize when information has been implied but not given explicitly. At about the same time, language rituals assume importance in asserting interpersonal control, as shown by the following exchange:

David:	I'm first.
Chris:	No, I called it.
David:	Changes. My turn, forever no changes, forever no changes.

David, having lost first place to Chris, invoked "changes" and then guaranteed his position with "forever no changes." The words used are assumed to carry the power to control others.

Appropriate adult assistance. Schiefelbusch (1984) has reviewed research findings and concluded that adults can assist children in the early school years in acquiring competence in communication. To be effective, adult assistance can be in the form of **semantically contingent responding,** defined as relating adult speech to the meaning of the preceding speech of the child; creating environments for communicating; and providing instruction. By responding directly or indirectly to children's talk, adults allow children to determine topics and take the initiative in communication. According to Schiefelbusch (1984), it is also important for adults to provide social contexts with both peers and adults where children can be active, successful participants in meaningful communication. And, although instruction is important, it is often most salient if indirect, as when children model, imitate, and respond to adult storytelling and role-playing.

Bilingualism

Many children learn one language and later learn another, either formally or informally. Other children learn two or more languages simultaneously in the early childhood years because they grow up in bilingual families or communities. A considerable body of research has investigated the effects on cognitive development and school achievement of learning two languages rather than one in childhood.

Early studies of the relationship between bilingualism and cognition reported that bilingualism stood in the way of cognitive development (Saville-Troike, 1982). However, these early studies did not control for socioeconomic status and often used tests in the bilingual children's weaker language. These early studies have now been discounted by most researchers, according to Saville-Troike (1982).

Recent evidence is mixed on the effect of second-language learning on cognitive development and school achievement, especially if exposure to the second language begins after four or five years of age. The variability in research findings has been partially explained by a distinction first made by Lambert (1975) between **additive bilingualism** and **subtractive bilingualism.**

A puppet production of a classic tale reinforces listening comprehension, oral language expression, and vocabulary comprehension for performers and audience.

Additive bilingualism takes place when children are members of the majority social class, speak the majority language, and receive positive feedback from families and communities for continued use of the first language. In cases of additive bilingualism, the second language is usually successfully added with no negative effects on first-language competence. Examples of additive bilingualism are Canadian programs to teach French to English-speaking children. In contrast, subtractive bilingualism takes place when children are members of minority groups and do not receive support outside of their families for continued use of the first language. In cases of subtractive bilingualism, the second language is often not successfully added and there may also be lack of growth in first-language competence. Examples of subtractive bilingualism are U.S. programs to teach English to minority-language children, such as Hispanics.

Research on bilingualism in the United States is particularly susceptible to these problems, and the results from these studies range from highly positive to negative (Galambos & Goldin-Meadow, 1990; Lambert, 1975; Saville-Troike, 1982; Verhoeven, 1990). Any problems with cognitive development and academic success seem unlikely to be due to second-language learning per se. For example, Umbel, Pearson, Fernandez, and Oller (1992) found that both bilingual and Spanish-speaking-only Hispanic children performed equally well in the Spanish language, demonstrating that being bilingual does not necessarily interfere with speaking ability in the original language. Rather, such problems may have their basis in social status, identity, and attitudinal variables associated with being a member of a minority group. Saville-Troike (1982) has said that the school success of minority children, now in situations of subtractive bilingualism, depends on a change in the negative feedback they are receiving about their native languages and cultures.

Hakuta (1988) has made the point that in Canada, where the bilingual pattern is an additive one, there is a great deal of literature to suggest that the addition of a second language is beneficial to the cognitive and language development of children. Thus, there is evidence that a bilingual environment would be inherently beneficial if it were not for the social problems associated with being a member of a language minority.

THE CONTINUING ROLE OF PLAY

Play continues to have an important role in the lives of children in the early school years. Vygotsky (1976) proposed that playing is an important way for children to develop their symbolic abilities. In social play, children use actions to symbolize the rules of social interactions. For example, in acting out the role of the father, a child may take an authoritarian approach, ordering children to do something or risk being punished. The words and actions used are symbols of the father's authority, not the words their own father would necessarily use. For this reason, Vygotsky suggested that high levels of social play would result in high levels of language and cognitive functioning in children.

Play continues to have an important role in the lives of children in the early school years.

Vygotsky said that although children can teach themselves many things, at some point, adult involvement becomes necessary for learning to progress. He emphasized that children should be encouraged to teach themselves as much as possible before adults were required to intervene and provide assistance. He referred to the material that children could learn on their own as belonging to the **zone of proximal development**. He stressed that social, creative play gave children access to the zone of proximal development. This theory may explain why creative play during the early school years enhances intellectual functioning.

Research reviewed by Hoot (1984) affirms the importance of play opportunities to higher levels of thinking, problem solving, and school performance. Pellegrini (1980) has asserted that young children's ability to play predicts achievement, and that skills used in higher modes of play are required in reading and writing. Schrader (1989) has shown that five-year-old children use reading and writing skills in their sociodramatic play, and Taharally (1991) has demonstrated that encouraging fantasy play in nursery school children causes significant gains in scores in language ability. This section views the role of play from the perspective of gender differences and humor.

Gender Differences

From the age of three and onward, boys and girls play in distinctively different ways (Etaugh & Liss, 1992; Fagot & Kronsberg, 1982). Girls engage in more doll and domestic play, art activities, and dancing. Toys intended for girls encourage imitative play and the learning of existing social roles. Boys, in contrast, engage in more play with transportation toys, woodworking materials, and blocks. Boys are more apt to be involved in rough-and-tumble play and verbal and physical aggression. And boys are also significantly more likely than girls to take physical risks (Ginsburg & Miller, 1982). Toys intended for boys encourage exploration and flexible use of materials. With few changes over time, these findings have been replicated many times since the 1930s in observational studies of children in natural settings (Etaugh & Liss, 1992; Fagot & Kronsberg, 1982). Furthermore, children are more apt to be given requested toys by their parents if the toys conform to gender distinctions (Etaugh & Liss, 1992).

As early as three years of age and continuing through childhood, most children play in same-gender groups. Children consequently receive social reactions mainly from their peers of the same gender. Research shows that peers tend to give children more positive feedback when they engage in gender-typical behaviors and more negative feedback when they engage in behaviors typical of the other gender (Fagot & Kronsberg, 1982). This is undoubtedly the reason that sex-typical behaviors occur more often in school-age children than preschool children and more often in same-gender groupings than mixed-gender groupings (Leaper, 1991; Wall, Pickert, & Gibson, 1989). Peer groups are conservative in their gender-role expectations, and boys are more likely than girls to conform to toy and activity stereotypes (Eisenberg, Murray, & Hite, 1982; Etaugh & Liss, 1992).

Boys conform more to gender stereotypes than do girls.

Etaugh and Liss (1992) observed 245 children from ages five to eight years. They found that with increasing age, the number of requests by girls for female-typed toys tended to decrease, and requests for neutral toys tended to increase. This was not true of boys, which confirms earlier findings that boys conform more to gender-based male expectations. Toy and play preferences are important—Etaugh and Liss (1992) found that they are related to occupational choices by both boys and girls.

Humor

Researchers consider **humor** as a subset of the broader category of play (McGhee, 1984). Humor is considered to be a form of intellectual play—that is, play with ideas. Incongruous ideas (those that are somehow inconsistent with children's knowledge or experience) are a necessary but not sufficient condition for humor. McGhee (1984) has described four stages of humor development, parallel to stages of cognitive development. His description is based on more than a decade of individual and collaborative research on children's humor.

The first three stages of humor begin before the early school years. Stage 1 involves **incongruous actions toward objects** and appears in the context of pretend play with objects in the second year of life. Children playfully substitute one object for another and laugh at having created a set of conditions known to be at odds with reality. Stage 2 humor centers on **incongruous labeling of objects and events** and takes place later in the second year, when children are developing new language skills. Children may laugh uproariously at calling a mouth an eye or a car an airplane. Most of the humor of two- and three-year-old children involves some combination of stages 1 and 2. Even in the early school years, humor at stages 1 and 2 continues to be enjoyed.

At about three years of age, children experience a new form of humor. Stage 3 humor is built on **conceptual incongruity**. When language begins to be used to refer to classes of objects with common characteristics, children find it humorous to alter the defining features of the concept. Instead of just imagining a dog to be a cow or calling it a cow, children in stage 3 may find humor in talking about milking a dog or having a dog "moo." Distortion of familiar sights and sounds, including rhyming and nonsense words, is a source of humor at this stage. Language is often important in stage 3 humor, but much humor is also based on violations of perceptual appearances of things. Seeing someone with a large nose or watching clowns be clumsy at things even children do easily can be humorous to young children.

In a series of studies, McGhee (1984) found that incongruities need to occur in a fantasy context in order to produce humor; the same incongruities in a reality context interfere with humor. For example, if a clown had an exaggerated nose, children would perhaps laugh. If, however, a person on the street had a realistic ear in the usual position of her nose, humor would likely be replaced by discomfort.

The humor of young children changes dramatically when they realize that words sometimes have ambiguous meanings. At stage 4, children find humor in multiple meanings. Even if they know two meanings of a word, children are usually unable to keep both meanings in mind until they begin to attain concrete operational thinking toward the end of the early school years. Riddles and knock-knock jokes such as the following become popular sources of humor at stage 4:

"What did the rug say to the floor?"
"Don't move. I've got you covered."

"Knock-knock."
"Who's there?"
"Lettuce."
"Lettuce who?:
"Lettuce in; it's cold out here."

Children also develop their own plays on words at stage 4. McGhee (1984) reported on research to find out whether the degree of cognitive challenge contributes to the level of humor experienced. The researchers developed jokes based on violations of the concepts of conservation and class inclusion. Jokes similar to the following were told to young children:

Suzy wanted to eat an apple for a snack. Her mother asked whether she wanted it cut into four or eight pieces. Suzy said, "Four. I'm not hungry enough for eight."

Researchers found that first-grade children who had acquired conservation and class inclusion concepts found the jokes funnier than both first graders who had not acquired the concepts and older children who had probably understood the concepts for some time. There seems to be an optimal amount of cognitive effort that maximizes humor.

Mahony and Mann (1992) also found that word riddles are popular among second graders. In addition, they found that both IQ scores and reading ability are associated with children's ability to solve the riddles and find them funny.

EFFECTS OF EARLY EDUCATION PROGRAMS

The term *early education programs* as used in this chapter refers to group educational experiences before the age of compulsory school attendance. The numbers of young children enrolled in these early education programs have increased steadily in the past decades (U.S. Bureau of the Census, 1990). Many children enter these programs when they are four years of age or younger because their parents anticipate favorable long-term consequences for intellectual or social development. Whether there are such consequences has been widely debated, and now longitudinal data can give the debate an empirical foundation. These data indicate that high-quality early education programs positively affect the development of individuals at least into adolescence. The data allow cautious optimism about the possibility of making positive changes in the lives of young children by providing appropriate early education programs.

In this section, data are presented from three sources: Project Head Start, the Consortium for Longitudinal Studies, and Brigham Young University. The first two sources provide data about the effects of early education on low-income children. The third source provides data about the effects of early education on educationally advantaged children.

Programs for Low-Income Children

Since the 1960s, the United States has instituted early education programs designed to equalize educational opportunity for children from low-income families. A government-sponsored educational effort started in 1965, Project Head Start is the best known of the programs for low-income children and continues to receive funding. In 1988, an additional project, Even Start, received funding. This project is family focused, including integrated educational programs for families, adult basic skills training, and parenting training. The evaluations of the effectiveness of Even Start are currently being undertaken and data are not yet available. On the other hand, Project Head Start and a consortium of 12 other programs begun in the 1960s have collected data on program participants, some of whom are now young adults. Thus, it is possible to evaluate the influence of early education programs on the lives of these children.

Research shows that Head Start children perform better than matched peers on measures of later school success.

Project Head Start.   In 1965, Head Start funds were sent to community action agencies around the country to establish summer programs for low-income children. However, it became clear that one summer was a short time for intervention, and the transition from summer to year-round programs took place from 1969 to 1972. Planned curricular variations were also introduced in the late 1960s and early 1970s.

Summarizing the findings of Head Start research reported in 1,400 documents, Hubbell (1983) has concluded that participation in Head Start has positive effects on children's social competence. Head Start children score higher than controls on some measures of task orientation, and task orientation correlates with cognitive test scores. Head Start children are rated as showing levels of social development comparable with that of the general elementary school population and have been found to be more sociable and assertive than their low-income peers without Head Start experience. The self-esteem of Head Start children has been found to decline once they enter public school, but children from some types of Head Start curricula continue to show higher levels of social participation through the second grade.

Research reviewed by Hubbell (1983) has shown mixed findings on the persistence of academic and intellectual gains produced during the Head Start program year. About half of the relevant studies have indicated that Head Start children maintain achievement test differences into the later school years and the remainder of the studies show that these differences are not maintained. However, research results have also demonstrated that Head Start children perform better than their low-income peers on global measures of school success, such as graduating from high school, placement in regular classrooms rather than special education, staying in school, and passing each grade. Research results have revealed as well that Head Start children display more reflective and less impulsive cognitive styles than do comparable low-income children without Head Start experience. Participation in Head Start also improves language development, especially in the case of bilingual children. Children's achievement is positively related to parental involvement in Head Start.

Research has also demonstrated that because needed nutrition services, health screening, immunizations, dental care, and health treatment are provided for Head Start children, these children are more likely to be of normal height and weight than comparable low-income children (Hubbell, 1983). They also perform well on physical tests and are less likely to be absent from school. Head Start children improve in hemoglobin levels, dental health, general physical development, and motor control during the Head Start year.

Consortium for Longitudinal Studies.   The Consortium for Longitudinal Studies was formed in 1975 to answer questions about whether early education programs had measurable long-term effects on low-income children. The consortium is made up of all but one of the major large-scale studies of early education begun in the 1960s: the Early Training Project, Perry Preschool Program, Gordon Parent Education Infant and Toddler Program, five University of Illinois approaches, the Louisville Experiment, the Harlem Study, Verbal Interaction Project, the Micro-Social Learning Environment, New Haven Project, the Philadelphia Study, and the Institute for Developmental Studies Program (Condry, 1983).

In all these programs, children in the program (the experimental group) were carefully matched with children who had similar backgrounds but who did not enroll in early education programs. The development of the nonenrolled, low-income children (the control group) could then be compared with that of children enrolled in early education programs. The independence of the separate studies makes the findings highly reliable; they are similar statistically to multiple, independent replications (Lazar, 1983). The consortium has provided convincing, ecologically valid evidence that these programs have been effective in enhancing the lives of low-income children through adolescence and young adulthood (Condry, 1983).

Research compiled by the consortium has substantiated the conclusion that appropriate early education programs increase the intelligence test scores of low-income children. Data show that program children had a 5.80-point IQ advantage over control children at the start of first grade. Furthermore, the gains in IQ scores of low-income children enrolled in early education programs have remained significant for up to three or four years after the program (Royce, Darlington, & Murray, 1983).

The use of intelligence test scores in early education programs is controversial, but these scores do predict scholastic achievement and provide a uniform basis for the assessment of cognitive growth. Consortium researchers have said that cultural bias against some children is unlikely because the children's backgrounds were relatively homogeneous: 94% of the children were black and nearly all were low-income (Royce, Darlington, & Murray, 1983).

Follow-up research by the consortium has shown that children enrolled in early education programs have increased achievement motivation, school competence, and educational attainment when compared with similar low-income children (Royce, Darlington, & Murray, 1983).

Consortium data have also demonstrated that early education programs improve later competence in school. Progression through the school system was examined as a measure of children's competence in adapting to the role requirements of the school. Two categories of failure to progress were interpreted as evidence that students were not meeting school expectations: placement in special education classes and retention in grade. In analysis at the seventh-grade level (eight programs) and at the time of high school graduation (four programs), program children were significantly less likely to have been placed in special education or to be retained in grade. At the seventh-grade level, the average rate of special education placement was 14.5% for program children and 34.9% for control children. The average rate of retention in grade was 19.8% for program children and 32.0% for control children. Findings were similar in the projects that had records through the end of high school at the time of the 1980 follow-up. Program children were also significantly more likely to have completed high school (Royce, Darlington, & Murray, 1983).

Recent results from the Perry Preschool Project (Wiekart, 1989) indicate that long-term life skills are enhanced for the children in the intervention group. More of the members of the preschool education group completed high school; more attended college or job training programs; and more now hold jobs, support themselves, and report satisfaction with their paid work. There has clearly been an overall social benefit of the early intervention programs.

Zigler, Taussig, and Black (1992) have analyzed results of the studies from the consortium. They concluded that an unexpected benefit of these programs is that they have acted as a preventative for juvenile delinquency. These data provide strong support for the cost benefit of early childhood education. Zigler et al. (1992) concluded that these positive benefits may occur because the programs were intensive, comprehensive, and long term. Although such programs are expensive, they are cost effective because of the great reduction in social services costs to the community.

Data available to the consortium were analyzed to ascertain whether different types of programs had different effects. There were no differences in school outcomes between early education programs taught in centers and those taught in homes. And later school outcomes showed no significant differences related to the type of curriculum used. All curricula were successful in reducing school failure, and all the curricula used in consortium programs were superior to no early education program at all. An analysis of data indicates that program effectiveness can be enhanced by a combination of five components:

Intervention begun as early as possible

Services provided to parents as well as to the child

Frequent home visits

Involvement of parents in the instruction of the child

As few children per teacher as possible. (Royce, Darlington, & Murray, 1983, p. 442)

Programs for Advantaged Children

A longitudinal study at Brigham Young University has been designed to investigate the effect of school enrollment on "advantaged" children between 42 months and five years of age (Larsen, Draper, & Hite, 1984). Advantaged children are defined as those whose parents have a high level of educational attainment and middle-income status. Until this time, research with middle-income children usually has focused on curricular comparisons rather than the long-term influences on children.

The main finding from the first complete analysis of the data was that scores on intelligence tests were related to early school enrollment. The program children had a mean IQ of 131.7 and the comparison children had a mean IQ of 127.1. This finding of immediate IQ gains from attendance in early education programs is similar to what has been found in studies of low-income children. The researchers speculate that school enrollment may create unique benefits in the years before age five, regardless of the quality of home environments (Larsen, Draper, & Hite, 1984). Recent research by Brand and Welch (1989) and Warash (1991) has confirmed the findings of the Brigham Young study. They provide continued support for the merits of school-based education for advantaged children under the age of five.

Social and Intellectual Competence

Researchers at Harvard University (White & Watts, 1973), attempted to answer the question, "What is human competence in six-year-old children?" They compiled a list of abilities that seemed to distinguish children with high overall competence from those with low competence. Based on extensive independent observations by 15 staff members and the children's teachers and also on children's performance on the Wechsler and other tests, children were divided into two groups: those who were the most competent and those who were the least competent. White and Watts (1973) found that children judged to be highly competent were more likely than others to be able to do the following:

1. Get and maintain adult attention in positive ways

2. Use adults to help meet goals

3. Communicate feelings to adults and peers

4. Both direct and follow peers

5. Compete with peers

6. Show pride in accomplishments

7. Take adult roles

8. Show linguistic competence
9. Show intellectual competence
   - note discrepancies
   - anticipate consequences
   - deal with symbols and concepts
   - take others' perspectives
   - make interesting associations
   - make and execute multistep plans
   - attend to two things simultaneously

In the early school years, these social and intellectual competencies were related to successful functioning, as defined by teachers and independent observers. It is clear that social as well as intellectual abilities are necessary to competent functioning. Our culture tends to put great stock in intellectual development, and professionals who work with children are in the best position to help educate parents and others of the importance of interaction between the two domains of functioning. They are both essential to an effective adaptation to early school experiences by the age of eight years. This adaptation forms the base for later academic success.

SUMMARY

1. Children in the early school years move from the preoperational to the concrete operational stage of intellectual development, changing in their orientation to cause and effect, classification, seriation, and conservation tasks.
2. During the preoperational period, children use animism, artificialism, egocentrism, and concreteness in understanding cause and effect.
3. Classification is the method used to organize the environment; it develops in a consistent way across the period of the early school years.
4. Seriation is the strategy we use to organize our world according to a logical order. It is the basis for mathematics and sequential planning and develops in a consistent way across the period of the early school years.
5. Conservation is a Piagetian task designed to measure the entrance of children into the stage of concrete operations. It is characterized by mental structures of reversibility, compensation, and identity.
6. Philosophical thinking can develop logical thinking and problem-solving ability.
7. Moral development consists of the components of rule following, moral reasoning, and social conventions reasoning.
8. Perceptual development during the early school years involves changes in discrimination, attention, and recognition of distinctive features.
9. Perception has important implications for the development of reading.
10. Children advance in the following areas of language during the early school years: word derivation, noun and verb phrase use, use of varied sentence types, production of speech sounds, vocabulary growth, reflection on language use, and complexity of language. Appropriate adult assistance involves responding contingently, providing communication settings, and instructing.

11. Research is mixed on the effects of bilingualism. The mixed results are partially explained by the concepts of additive and subtractive bilingualism.
12. Play has a continuing role in the early school years as it allows children to expand their zone of proximal learning.
13. Creativity is enhanced through play and involves divergent thinking skills.
14. Humor is based on the notion of incongruity; its essence changes as children continue to develop.
15. Data on the effects of early education programs demonstrate that positive changes will occur in the lives of young disadvantaged children. Even advantaged children benefit intellectually.
16. School success is influenced by both social and intellectual competence.

ACTIVITIES TO ENHANCE LEARNING

1. Assume that you are running a program for four-year-old children and the parents come to you to ask you to initiate a program to teach the children to read. Prepare an outline of the kinds of information you would use to explain to the parents why most four-year-olds are not ready to learn to read.
   a. Include information on perceptual development.
   b. Include information on prereading skills to be acquired first.
   c. Write a brief statement on the role of reading in the overall development of the preschool child.

2. Assume that a parent is very upset because her preschool child doesn't seem to understand why it is wrong to tell lies and to try to "get away" with improper behavior. Prepare an outline of the kinds of information you would use to explain to her the moral developmental level of the average preschool child.
   a. Include information about moral reasoning at the preconventional level.
   b. Include information about children's understanding of intentionality.
   c. Include information on children's use of false belief in interaction with others.

3. A parent asks you to make a presentation to a group of parents with preschool children about preparing their children for success in school. Prepare an outline of the kinds of information you would include in such a presentation.
   a. Include information about the importance of social issues.
   b. Include information about child-rearing patterns that appear to encourage success in school.
   c. Discuss the importance of language preparation for school and give suggestions for parents to enhance language development.

FOR FURTHER READING

Thinking Activities

Anselmo, S., Rollins, P., & Schuckman, R. (1986). *R is for rainbow: Developing young children's thinking skills through the alphabet.* Menlo Park, CA: Addison-Wesley.

Baratta-Lorton, M. (1976). *Mathematics their way.* Menlo Park, CA: Addison-Wesley.

Emerging Literacy

McGee, L. M., & Richgels, D. J. (1990). *Literacy's beginnings: Supporting young readers and writers.* Needham Heights, MA: Allyn and Bacon.

Strickland, D. S., & Morrow, L. M. (Eds.). (1989). *Emerging literacy: Young children learn to read and write.* Newark, DE: International Reading Association.

Creativity

Edwards, L. C. (1990). *Affective development and the creative arts: A process approach to early childhood education.* New York: Merrill/Macmillan.

Isenberg, J. P., & Jalongo, M. R. (1993). *Creative expression and play in the early childhood curriculum.* New York: Macmillan.

Early Childhood Education

Feeny, S., Christensen, D., & Moravcik, E. (1991). *Who am I in the lives of children?* New York: Merrill/Macmillan.

Seefeldt, C., & Barbour, N. (1990). *Early childhood education: An introduction.* New York: Merrill/Macmillan.

Epilogue: Middle Childhood

L ooking at eight-year-olds, about to step over the invisible line separating early and middle childhood, one is struck by how far they have come since their lives began. This book has offered a chronicle of their physical, psychosocial, and cognitive development. It concludes with a brief glance toward middle childhood.

Middle childhood was once defined as beginning at school entrance and ending at puberty. Using this framework, many texts gave the age boundaries as 6 and 12 years. Now, however, the traditional domain of middle childhood has been eroded by societal and physical changes. Societal changes, such as the growing number of mothers in the labor force and a greater emphasis on the importance of early educational experiences, have combined to ensure that most children enter an educational setting before age 6. Physical changes, believed to be brought about by better nutrition and living conditions, have lowered the range of ages for the onset of puberty to a point below the age of 12 years. Since 6 is not the age of school entrance, nor is 12 the age of onset of puberty, new boundaries have evolved for the levels of development. The boundaries of early childhood development have been adjusted upward to acknowledge the continuity from birth through age 8 in physical, psychosocial, and cognitive development. And the terms *preteen* and *preadolescent* have been coined to recognize how much children younger than 12 have in common with adolescents.

Defined in this way, middle childhood (ages 9–12) is a period of consolidation. In physical development, the rate of increase in size is usually regular until the onset of puberty, with females maturing earlier. Children gradually take greater responsibility for their own health and fitness. They begin to have the coordination and interactional skill to participate in sports.

In psychosocial development, children continue to work to establish a sense of industry. They internalize standards and expectations for their own behavior and make the transition from describing themselves in terms of concrete attributes and actions to referring to themselves by more abstract qualities of disposition. They begin to have a mature ability to understand the needs of others and can learn to engage in role-playing. Feedback from the school environment becomes increasingly important to how children feel about themselves. In effect, school achievement is important to both psychosocial and cognitive development of the middle childhood years.

In cognitive development, children make the transition to concrete operations, applying operational thought to increasingly complex areas, including space, weight, and volume. School provides formal opportunities to acquire and use knowledge involving academic content and societal values. Less formal sources of knowledge continue to be important in children's lives; for example, children in middle childhood watch more television than either younger or older children.

In physical, psychosocial, and cognitive development, middle childhood is a time of building on foundations laid in the years of early childhood. It is the transition into adolescence.

Glossary of Key Terms

Accommodation A way of processing new information in which the new information causes a restructuring of thinking. Accommodation is a principle in the theory of Jean Piaget. (Ch. 1)

Achievement test A tool for measuring proficiency by testing performance in a given field. (Ch. 2)

Active awake A state in the infant characterized by restlessness and bodily activity. (Ch. 5)

Active intermodal mapping A process in which infants use equivalences between gestures they see and gestures they perceive themselves to be making. This process may explain early infant imitation and language skills. (Ch. 7)

Additive bilingualism Second-language learning that takes place when children who speak a minority language belong to the majority social class, speak the majority language, and receive positive feedback for continued use of their first language. (Ch. 13)

Affricative A consonant sound made by touching the tongue to the roof of the mouth so that it only partially stops the air as it flows through the mouth (e.g., *ch* and *j*). (Ch. 10)

Altruism Behavior, which can be learned through modeling, that benefits persons other than oneself.

Amblyopia A vision problem in which one eye sees well and the other sees poorly. If untreated, it can result in loss of vision. (Ch. 11)

Amniocentesis Extraction and analysis of the amniotic fluid in the uterus for the purpose of prenatal detection of chromosomal disorders. (Ch. 3)

Analgesics Drugs, including tranquilizers and sedatives, that reduce the intensity of pain. (Ch. 4)

Anesthetics Drugs that are used to eliminate pain. General anesthetics affect the whole body; local anesthetics are injected into a part of the body. (Ch. 4)

Animism Preoperational stage of logic in which the child ascribes human, animate characteristics to inanimate objects, such as stuffed animals, moons, and spoons. (Ch. 13)

Anoxia A loss of oxygen to the brain. (Ch. 4)

Anxious/avoidant One of three types of attachment (observed by Ainsworth) characterized by relatively little distress at separation but no pleasure at mother's return; a child who is anxious/avoidant is capable of being comforted by any adult. (Ch. 6)

Anxious/resistant One of three types of attachment (observed by Ainsworth) characterized by little interest in exploring, greatest distress upon separation, and the inability of the mother to comfort the child upon her return. (Ch. 6)

Apgar score A score that rates newborns' functioning in five areas: appearance (skin color), pulse (heart rate), grimace (reaction to slight pain), activity (motor responsiveness and tone), and respiration (breathing adequacy). The scale was devised by Dr. Virginia Apgar. (Ch. 4)

Artificialism Preoperational stage of logic in which the child finds technical, artificial explanations for everything, including biological processes. (Ch. 13)

Assimilation A way of processing new information in which the new information is integrated with the existing organization of thought. Assimilation is a principle in the theory of Jean Piaget. (Ch. 1)

Associative play Play in which children participate together but demonstrate limited sharing and cooperation. (Ch. 9)

Attachment Strong bonds of affection directed from children to significant people in their lives. (Ch. 6)

Attachment-in-the-making The second stage in the attachment process, occurring from 12 weeks to six months. During this stage, infants begin to discriminate among people, showing more social excitement when around the primary caregivers. (Ch. 6)

Attention deficit disorder See *Hyperactivity*. (Ch. 11)

Authoritarian A style of parenting described by Baumrind as involving the exercise of firm control but with little support or affection. (Ch. 12)

Authoritative A style of parenting described by Baumrind as involving firm rules in a context of clear communication and warm commitment. (Ch. 12)

Autonomy The sense of being self-directed. (Ch. 9)

Autonomy versus shame and doubt The second of Erik Erikson's eight stages of psychosocial development. In this stage, two- and three-year-olds balance their assertion of self with feelings of shame and doubt. (Ch. 1, 9)

Babbling Production of both vowel and consonant sounds (such as *ma* and *da*), often beginning toward the end of the first six months of life. (Ch. 7)

Behavioral theory A view of learning that focuses on changes in actions or observable behavior. There are three distinct types of behavioral theories: classical conditioning, operant conditioning, and social learning theory. (Ch. 1)

Being needs Values such as truth, honesty, beauty, and goodness (according to the theory of Abraham Maslow). (Ch. 1)

Bilingual Able to use two languages with approximately equal fluency. (Ch. 13)

Black English A dialect of Standard English with internally consistent grammar, vocabulary, and sound system. (Ch. 10)

Blindness Ability to see only at 20 feet what the normally sighted person sees at 200 feet. (Ch. 11)

Bonding A complex psychological tie from parent to infant. (Ch. 4)

Bottle-mouth syndrome Severe childhood dental decay that results when children frequently go to sleep with a bottle containing anything but water. This decay is caused by the pooling of milk or juice against the teeth. (Ch. 8)

Brazelton scale A scale that assesses 16 reflexes and 27 behavioral items, which together simulate a variety of situations faced by newborns. The primary developer was Dr. T. Berry Brazelton. (Ch. 4)

Carrier The person who carries a hereditary trait as a recessive gene that is not part of the person's own expressed inheritance but may be passed on to the offspring. (Ch. 3)

Case study A strategy for summarizing and organizing many observations into a coherent overview of a given child. (Ch. 2)

Center of gravity The point in the body at which there is equally as much body mass above as below the point. Because the center of gravity is high in the bodies of infants and toddlers, these young children are unstable and prone to falling over. (Ch. 8)

Cephalo-caudal A principle that states that growth proceeds generally from the head (*cephalo*) to the tail (*caudal*) area. (Ch. 1, 5)

Cervix The opening of the uterus. (Ch. 4)

Checklist An observation tool used to record children's behavior. Individual children's behavior is compared with a list of target or expected behaviors. (Ch. 2)

Child abuse Nonaccidental action by an adult that threatens a child's health or welfare. (Ch. 5)

Child diary An observation tool used for recording children's behavior. Regular entries chronicle the day-to-day milestones in the lives of young children. (Ch. 2)

Chromosome A part of the nucleus of all cells of human beings and other living things. It contains genetic information. (Ch. 3)

Classical conditioning A process of learning discovered by Ivan Pavlov (1849–1936). Animals as well as people learn to link an event, such as the ringing of a bell, with another event, such as feeding; after conditioning, the same response is given to both events. (Ch. 1)

Classification Logical grouping based on similar characteristics. (Ch. 13)

Cognitive development The aspect of development that deals with thinking, problem solving, intelligence, and language. (Ch. 7, 10, 13)

Cognitive theory A view of learning, described by Jean Piaget, that focuses on internal thought processes. (Ch. 1)

Collective symbolism The second of two levels of early pretend play, following Piaget's solitary symbolic play. By the latter part of the third year, young children use collective symbolism as they interact with others in playing roles. (Ch. 9, 10)

Colostrum The fluid available in the mother's breasts during the first days after birth before the milk comes in. It contains important material for the health of the newborn baby. (Ch. 5)

Compensation A characteristic of logical thinking whereby change in one variable is seen to be balanced by change in another variable. (Ch. 13)

Conceptual incongruity The third stage in the development of humor, beginning at about age three, when children alter the defining features of a concept (e. g., to talk about cats barking). (Ch. 13)

Conceptus See *Zygote*. (Ch. 3)

Concrete objects Tangible things that children can experience with more than one sense. Young children usually learn better from experiences with concrete objects, such as apples, than from abstractions, such as pictures of apples or the written word *apple*. (Ch. 13)

Concrete operational stage The third of Jean Piaget's four stages of intellectual development. Between about seven years of age and adolescence, children begin to use logical reasoning rather than perceptions to justify judgments. (Ch. 1, 13)

Conditioned response A response, such as salivation, brought about through conditioning. A conditioned stimulus (e.g., ringing of a bell) is associated with an event (feeding) to produce a conditioned response (salivation), even in the absence of the object related to the event (food). (Ch. 1)

Conditioned stimulus According to the theory of classical conditioning, a previously unmeaningful event (e.g., the ringing of a bell) that is associated with another event (e.g., feeding). (Ch. 1)

Congenital malformations Structural or anatomical abnormalities present at birth. (Ch. 3)

Conservation The understanding of the constancy of certain attributes, such as number or area, despite changes in appearance. (Ch. 13)

Consonant clusters Combinations of consonants that are acceptable in a given language. In English, these include such clusters as *st, str, tr, cl, dr, gl, gr*, etc. (Ch. 10)

Consonants Sounds in the human language system made by limiting the movement of air through the mouth and throat. (Ch. 10)

Construction The action of learning by creating structures from interaction with the environment. Construction is a part of Piaget's theory of cognitive development. (Ch. 1)

Contextual characteristics of child abuse Historical and ongoing conditions of parents' lives that put them at risk of being child abusers. (Ch. 8)

Context use Ability to apply an understanding of language to anticipate what word makes sense in a given context. (Ch. 13)

Continuous development The theory of the process of development whereby change occurs without any apparent change in the kind of behavior exhibited but with change in the amount and efficiency of the behavior exhibited. Continuous development is associated with learning theories. (Ch. 1)

Continuous schedule Reinforcement schedule according to which reinforcement is delivered each time a certain behavior is emitted. (Ch. 1)

Controlled scribbling Basic shapes and lines made while children observe the movement of the drawing instrument. The wrist is more flexible than in random scribbling, and writing implements are held in a grip more similar to that used by adults. Controlled scribbling characterizes drawings from 30 months to four years of age. (Ch. 8)

Conventional morality The concrete operational stage of moral understanding during which children become aware of the social aspects of moral functioning and base their behavior on the functional norms of the social group. (Ch. 13)

Cooing Production of vowel sounds, often in response to a human face or voice, beginning usually in the second month of life. (Ch. 7)

Cooperation Learned behavior based on a "we" mental set. (Ch. 12)

Cooperative play Play in which children share ideas and roles in complex interaction. (Ch. 9)

Coordination of secondary schemes The fourth substage in Piaget's sensorimotor stage, occurring at approximately 8 to 12 months. (Ch. 7)

Coping A process whereby one uses efforts to manage environmental and internal demands and stresses that threaten to overwhelm one's resources. (Ch. 12)

Cross-modal transfer of information The ability of the infant to use a number of sensory modes to process the same information (e.g.,

examining an object with the eyes, hands, and mouth). (Ch. 7)

Crying A state in the infant characterized by loud, unpleasant vocalizations. (Ch. 5)

Deaf Having a severe hearing problem, which impairs the processing of linguistic information. (Ch. 11)

Deferred imitation Retention of a mental image of something and imitation of it at a later time. The ability to defer imitation is said by Piaget to occur at the end of the sensorimotor stage. (Ch. 10)

Defiance Behavior of toddlers aimed at resisting the adult and associated with abuse and insecure attachment. (Ch. 9)

Deprivation needs Physiological, safety, belongingness, and esteem needs that, according to Abraham Maslow, must be met before higher values can be pursued. (Ch. 1)

Desensitization The act of lowering the level of an emotionally conditioned response by introducing stimuli in closer and closer approximations to the conditioned stimulus so that new associations can be formed. (Ch. 1, 9)

Developmental assessment Test measuring the level of achievement appropriate for a given age or stage of development. (Ch. 2)

Diagnostic test Test given for a specific purpose to determine, or diagnose, a particular disability or learning problem so that appropriate interventions can be established. (Ch. 2)

Directionality The projection beyond the body of the laterality that is perceived. Directionality allows differentiation of the letters *p* and *q*, for example. (Ch. 8)

Discontinuous development The theory of development that holds that changes occur in discrete units resulting in the emergence of distinctly new and different behaviors. (Ch. 1)

Discrimination The ability to recognize differences in forms, a necessary skill for reading. (Ch. 13)

Distinctive features, recognition of The ability to find and use the few distinctive features that allow correct identification of objects. Cartoons are examples of drawings that rely only on the distinctive features of objects, so they can be rendered in simpler form than, say, realistic drawings. (Ch. 13)

Dizygotic   Referring to fraternal twins, formed when two ova are fertilized by different sperm. These twins do not share any more inherited characteristics than do any other siblings. (Ch. 3)

DNA (deoxyribonucleic acid)   The substance of which genes are composed. DNA contains information allowing formation of chains of protein leading to new tissue and organs, control of other genes, and regulation of body processes. (Ch. 3)

Domains   The specific content areas of standardized tests, such as measures of IQ, altruism, and sibling rivalry. (Ch. 2)

Dominant trait   A trait that appears when it is paired genetically with a recessive trait. (Ch. 3)

Drowsiness   A state in the infant characterized by a glazed, unfocused look in preparation for sleep. (Ch. 5)

Due process   Safeguards to protect the rights of children, required under provisions of Public Law 94-142. (Ch. 11)

Dynamical systems theory   A theory of motor development (established by Ray and Delprato) based on the idea that a person uses all systems collectively to accomplish coordination of a task. (Ch. 5)

Dynamic balance   One of three large muscle skills, involving the ability to maintain balance while moving (includes such actions as walking, running, and climbing). (Ch. 8)

Dyslexia   Limited reading ability involving slow verbal retrieval and difficulty in developing syllables. (Ch. 11)

Early childhood development   The orderly psychosocial, physical, and cognitive changes that take place between the prenatal months and eight years of age. (Ch. 1)

Early intervention programs   Programs that provide support, instruction, and help to chil-

dren with certain needs and their families. (Ch. 7)

Early representational stage   A stage of drawing described by Brittain as beginning around age five. At this stage, children depict people and objects in simplified renditions. (Ch. 11)

Eclectic approach   An approach that incorporates methods, ideas, and research findings from a spectrum of theoretical positions. (Ch. 1)

Ecological environment   A concept involved in Bronfenbrenner's (1979) approach to studying three levels of influence on young children: immediate family, intermediate environments such as parental work sites, and more distant societal forces. (Ch. 13)

Egocentricity   Characteristic of preoperational thinking, indicating a relative inability to take the view or perspective of others. (Ch. 10)

Ego control   The Blocks' theory of the personality whereby impulses, needs, and desires are managed and measured from extreme undercontrol to extreme overcontrol. (Ch. 12)

Ego resiliency   The Blocks' theory of the personality that focuses on the ability to modify the level of ego control to meet the demands of changing situations (also called adaptability). (Ch. 12)

Embryo   The developing life form, from the time of implantation in the uterus until the end of the eighth week after fertilization. (Ch. 3)

Emergent literacy   Early behaviors that are the basis for later reading and writing but do not appear to have relevance for these skills (such as visual tracking). (Ch. 7)

Emotional disturbance   A condition involving problems in personal/social behavior that adversely affect educational performance and cannot be explained by intellectual, sensory, or health factors. (Ch. 11)

En face   A position for holding a baby so the caregiver's face is aligned directly with the baby's face. (Ch. 4)

Engrossment   The absorption and interest of fathers in their infants. (Ch. 4)

Episiotomy A small incision made in the back of the opening of the vagina to widen the outlet to allow easier delivery of the baby and to prevent tearing, which is thought to heal less well than a cut. (Ch. 4)

Equilibration The counterpart of the biological concept of homeostasis, proposed by Jean Piaget. Equilibration refers to the internal mental process of establishing balance (equilibrium) in thinking. According to Piaget's theory, a sense of disequilibrium precedes mental growth. (Ch. 1)

Ethics of science A set of standards delineating the responsibilities of researchers. In early childhood development, these ethics assert that children's rights supersede those of parents or guardians before any research can be undertaken. (Ch. 2)

Event sampling A strategy of observation in which predefined information is recorded when a predefined event or type of behavior occurs. (Ch. 2)

Expansions Strategies used for enhancing language development in children. Adults enlarge, or expand, a statement made by the child so that it more closely resembles adult speech. (Ch. 10)

Expressive language Language that is spoken (often contrasted with receptive language). (Ch. 10)

Extensions Sentences that extend children's words into a conversation by making reference to topics in the previous sentence they spoke. (Ch. 10)

Extinguish To remove a response by eliminating reinforcement of it. (Ch. 1)

Extrinsic motivation Desire for participation coming from wanting to receive approval or reward. (Ch. 9, 10)

Fatherese Adaptations of adult (i.e., father's) speech to the needs of young children who are learning language. Alterations include simplification, repetition, and limitation of topics. (Ch. 10)

Fertilization Contact between sperm and ovum, beginning a new life. At the time of fertilization, paternal and maternal chromosomes intermingle. (Ch. 3)

Fetal alcohol syndrome A condition involving retardation, heart disease, and other abnormalities present at birth in cases in which excessive amounts of alcohol were consumed by the mother during pregnancy. (Ch. 3)

Fetal monitor A machine used to monitor the heart rate of the fetus during labor to watch for distress. (Ch. 4)

Fetus The developing life form, from the ninth week after fertilization until birth (derived from the Latin word meaning "offspring"). (Ch. 3)

Fitness Physical well-being, including strength, power, muscular endurance, cardiovascular endurance, flexibility, and body fatness. (Ch. 11)

Fontanelles Open spaces between the bones of the fetal skull that allow for compression of the head during delivery. The appearance of fontanelles can result in a misshaped head at birth, which will correct itself within a few weeks after birth. (Ch. 5)

Formal operational The last of Jean Piaget's four stages of intellectual development. Beginning in adolescence, young people learn to think symbolically and hypothetically, using abstract thinking and concepts. (Ch. 1)

Fricative A consonant sound made by touching the tongue to the top of the mouth and only partially stopping the air as it flows through (e.g., *z*). (Ch. 10)

Full term The normal length of human gestation. A full-term birth occurs around 38–40 weeks. (Ch. 4)

Gastrulation The event occurring soon after implantation when the developing embryo undergoes a major change in form. After this period, the cells appear to be committed to becoming specific kinds of cells. (Ch. 3)

Gender One's sexual identity, determined by the kind of sperm (X- or Y-bearing) that fertilizes an ovum (which contains only X chromosomes). If an ovum is fertilized by an X-bearing sperm, a female (XX) will develop; if an ovum is fertilized by a Y-bearing sperm, a male (XY) will develop. (Ch. 3)

Gender identity   An individual's understanding of self as male, female, or ambivalent. (Ch. 3, 9)

Gender role   The public expression of gender identity. (Ch. 3, 9)

Gender role stereotyping   The labeling of certain behaviors according to their appropriateness for either males or females. (Ch. 9)

Gene   A part of the chromosomes located at the nucleus of all cells of human beings and other living things. Genes control the transmission of hereditary characteristics. (Ch. 3)

Generalization   An extension of a concept or behavior to situations different from that in which the concept or behavior was first learned. (Ch. 1)

General space   The space that the child can occupy by moving in different directions, levels, ranges, shapes, and pathways and in the air. This includes relationships with other people and objects. (Ch. 11)

Genetic code   A person's total inheritance contained in the genes and passed on in each cell of the body. (Ch. 3)

Genetic counseling   Counseling about the risk of occurrence or recurrence of genetic handicaps. (Ch. 3)

Genotype   Totality of a human's genetic heritage, including all genes inherited from both parents. (Ch. 3)

Gestational age   A measurement of fetal and newborn age based on actual time since conception; the true age of the child. (Ch. 3, 4)

Glides   Sounds made by the human language system that are easy to say and learned early in development (e.g., *w* and *y*). (Ch. 10)

Goal-corrected partnership   The fourth stage in the attachment process, occurring after the child's second birthday. Child's behavior becomes more flexible in response to parental plans, allowing for cooperative interactions. (Ch. 6)

Habituated   Accustomed to a sight or sound so that it no longer seems novel or interesting. The principle of habituation has been used in research with infants. (Ch. 7)

Hearing impairment   A difficulty in hearing that adversely affects educational performance. (Ch. 11)

Helping professions   Professions that provide human services (e.g., early childhood teaching, parent education, social work, nursing, music therapy, and recreation). (Ch. 1)

Heritability   The mathematical estimate of the relative amount of genetic versus environmental effect determining a given trait. (Ch. 1)

Heritability rate   A statistic computed to represent the relative impact of genetic and environmental effects for a given trait. (Ch. 3)

Hierarchical   A characteristic of stages in which each new stage is integrated into the old stages so that nothing is lost. (Ch. 1)

Holophrase   Single-word utterance that embodies the meaning found in full adult sentences (e.g., "Juice!" meaning "I want juice"). (Ch. 10)

Homeo box   The genetic material that acts as a "master switch" to control the timing of the activation of different genes, thus controlling the course of development. (Ch. 3)

Humanist   Referring to a theory of development that emphasizes values, human choices, relationships, and actualization of self. (Ch. 1)

Humor   A form of intellectual play with ideas. (Ch. 13)

Hyperactivity   A condition with some or all of the following characteristics: high activity level, short attention span, inability to sit still or to wait, impulsiveness, and distractibility (also called attention deficit disorder). (Ch. 11)

Identity   A characteristic of preoperational thinking; the child fails the conservation task because he or she doesn't recognize that nothing has been added or taken away. (Ch. 13)

Idiosyncratic concepts   Concepts of preoperational children that are used generally even though they are based on specific, personal experiences. (Ch. 10)

I-message A technique of communication proposed by Gordon. I-messages contain three parts: how the parent feels, what the child did to make the parent feel that way, and why the behavior is upsetting. (Ch. 1)

Imminent justice The egocentric stage of moral understanding in which the child believes that the punishment for wrongdoing is inherent in the act itself, so that punishment follows immediately from wrongdoing. (Ch. 13)

Immune factors Protective factors in the blood that prevent the development of illness. Immune factors are present in colostrum and are passed on to the infant during nursing. (Ch. 5)

Implantation The embedding of the zygote in the uterus, where it can be nourished and grow. (Ch. 3)

Incongruous actions toward objects The first stage in the development of humor, taking place during pretend play in the second year of life. (Ch. 13)

Incongruous labeling of objects and events The second stage in the development of humor, taking place when two- and three-year-olds purposely misname objects. (Ch. 13)

Indirect genetic effects Behaviors that occur because direct genetic effects cause the environment to respond in specific ways to a particular trait. (Ch. 3)

Individual Education Plan (IEP) A provision of Public Law 94-142 calling for preparation of a personalized plan for each child who has a disability. Each IEP is prepared by a team, including parent(s), and must be signed by all members of the team. (Ch. 2, 11)

Industry versus inferiority The fourth of Erik Erikson's eight stages of psychosocial development. In this stage, children of elementary school age balance feelings of competence with those of failure. (Ch. 1, 12)

Initiative versus guilt The third of Erik Erikson's eight stages of psychosocial development. In this stage, four- and five-year-olds balance the exercise of new verbal and physical prowess with guilt feelings because of having gone too far. (Ch. 1, 12)

Intentional communication Communication as a goal in itself. Infants begin to develop goal-directed behavior by the end of the first year, and slowly communication is conveyed through motor actions, such as pointing. (Ch. 7)

Intentionality Concrete operational understanding of moral issues involving the idea that the intention of those involved is important in assessing blame. (Ch. 13)

Intermittent schedule A schedule of reinforcement according to which the reinforcement is not delivered every time the behavior occurs. Behaviors reinforced according to an intermittent schedule will not extinguish as easily as those established through continuous schedules. (Ch. 1)

Interview A one-to-one verbal interaction, usually structured by a list of questions. (Ch. 2)

Intrinsic motivation Desire for participation coming from within oneself; an internal desire to be effective. (Ch. 9, 10, 13)

Invariant A characteristic of preoperational thinking; the child fails the conservation task because he or she fails to identify those aspects of the task that remain the same. (Ch. 13)

Invisible displacement An accomplishment of Piaget's last substage of sensorimotor development whereby the child can follow the movement of an object that has been hidden, say, in a box or a hand. Thus, the child can visualize or imagine the presence of the invisible object. (Ch. 10)

Kwashiorkor Severe malnutrition that results when food intake is deficient in protein even if it is adequate in calories. Kwashiorkor develops most frequently when children between one and two years are weaned. (Ch. 8)

Labor The birth process, often divided into three stages: opening of the cervix, delivery of the infant, and delivery of the placenta. (Ch. 4)

Lamaze method A method of childbirth using conditioning principles to teach the mother to control pain by breathing in certain patterns. (Ch. 3, 4)

Language impairment See *Speech and language impairment.*

Lanugo A white, greasy substance that collects on the body of the fetus to protect it from the amniotic fluid. It can often be seen on the body of the newborn baby at birth. (Ch. 5)

Large muscle skills Physical skills that make use of large body movements. These skills include dynamic balance, used in walking, running, and climbing; static balance, used in standing on one foot; projecting, used in jumping; and throwing and catching. (Ch. 11)

Larynx The human voice box, located in the throat. When air is passed through the larynx, a sound is made, called voicing. Consonants may be voiced or unvoiced (e.g., *b* is voiced, *p* is unvoiced). (Ch. 7, 10)

Laterality Internalized awareness of the two sides of the body and their differences. (Ch. 8)

Learning Changes that occur in behavior as the result of experience. (Ch. 1)

Least restrictive environment A concept set forth by Public Law 94-142, designed to ensure that children with disabilities are placed in educational environments with as few deviations from the "normal" as are individually appropriate. (Ch. 11)

Leboyer method A method of childbirth designed to ease the transition from within to outside the uterus by using soft lights and other soothing techniques. (Ch. 4)

Liquids Sounds in the human speech system that are difficult to say and are learned late in development (e.g., *r* and *l*). (Ch. 10)

Locomotion One of the three categories of infant motor skills involving movement of the infant, which can occur at various levels (e.g., crawling, scooting, walking). (Ch. 5)

Mainstreaming The practice of placing children with disabilities in "normal" classrooms for all or part of the day. (Ch. 11)

Manipulation One of the three categories of infant motor skills, involving the ability to use the hands in the process of exploration (e.g., reaching, grasping, releasing). (Ch. 5)

Marasmus A condition that occurs in the first year of life and is caused by an inadequate total food intake. Symptoms include growth failure and wasting of muscles. (Ch. 5)

Maturationist A theoretical position that emphasizes the role of genetically determined growth patterns and deemphasizes the role of environmental stimulation in early childhood development. (Ch. 1)

Meiosis Process by which a cell divides during reproduction; meiosis occurs in the germ cells when conception occurs. (Ch. 3)

Mendelian laws of heredity The laws developed by Gregor Mendel in 1866 to explain the way genetic traits are passed on as either dominant or recessive. (Ch. 3)

Menstrual age A measurement of fetal age based on the date of the mother's missed menstrual period, thus giving an estimated age that is older than the actual gestational age. (Ch. 3, 4)

Mental retardation General intellectual functioning that is significantly below average, combined with deficits in adaptive behavior. (Ch. 11)

Mental symbols Words that represent things, actions that imitate adult roles, activities that use one thing as a symbol of another, and unconscious symbolizing (manifestations of thought found at the beginning of the preoperational stage of development). (Ch. 10)

Metalinguistic awareness Ability to reflect on language usage (i.e., to separate content and structure of language). (Ch. 13)

Méthode clinique The clinical method by which Jean Piaget (and others) asked questions of children to discover how they think and why they respond as they do. (Ch. 1, 2)

Middle childhood An artificial division of a person's life extending from the end of early childhood to the onset of adolescence (i.e., from about 9 to 12 years of age).

Mitosis Process by which a cell reproduces by dividing into an exact duplicate of the original. (Ch. 3)

Modeling Ability to take in the values, beliefs, and behaviors of a valued model (such as a parent). Modeling accounts for much of the child's acquisition of prosocial and aggressive behaviors. (Ch. 9)

Monozygotic Referring to identical twins, formed when a zygote splits and the two identical halves develop independently. Such a twin shares identical inherited characteristics. (Ch. 3)

Moral realism The preoperational stage of understanding of moral issues in which moral and physical laws are confused and the child assumes that wrongdoing will automatically be punished by physical events. (Ch. 13)

Morpheme The smallest unit of grammar (e.g., a single word or a grammatical marker, such as *ed*, *s*, and *ing*). (Ch. 10)

Motherese Adaptations of adult (i.e., mother's) speech to the needs of young children learning language. Alterations include simplification, repetition, and limitation of topics. (Ch. 10)

Multicultural education Education that involves learning experiences designed to emphasize universal human experiences as well as the richness of cultural diversity. (Ch. 12)

Naming of scribbling stage A stage of drawing described by Brittain. At around four years of age, children may begin to draw with no particular intent but may ascribe meaning during the process. (Ch. 11)

Narrative observation A strategy of observation that gives an account of behavior as it occurs, using descriptive, nonjudgmental language. (Ch. 2)

Nature versus nurture issue The dispute about the relative impact of heredity (nature) and environment (nurture) on development. Most experts agree that nature and nurture interact with each other. (Ch. 1)

Neglect The absence of adult action toward a child, resulting in harm to the child's health and welfare. (Ch. 5)

Neonatal abstinence syndrome (NAS) A condition that occurs in newborn babies whose mothers were addicted to drugs during pregnancy. The NAS baby is born addicted and suffers from withdrawal symptoms. (Ch. 4)

Neonatal intensive care unit (NICU) A specialized unit in the hospital designed to care for sick and premature newborns. (Ch. 4)

Neonatal period The first four weeks of life, during which adjustments are made to life outside the uterus. (Ch. 5)

Nonorganic failure to thrive Poor development of an infant due to neglect and characterized by low weight and developmental delay, with no organic cause. (Ch. 5)

Norms Average ages of attainment of psychosocial, physical, and cognitive milestones. (Ch. 1)

Obesity Overweight condition that inhibits physical and social interaction; obesity is caused by a combination of genetic and environmental factors. Extreme obesity can be associated with family pathology. (Ch. 11)

Object permanence The understanding that things and people continue to exist even though they are not in view. Object permanence is established during Piaget's sensorimotor stage of development, from birth to age two. (Ch. 7)

Obligatory attention The tendency of children in the early school years to have difficulty blocking out competing information in order to focus on the task at hand. (Ch. 13)

Ontogenetic Development associated with individual life experiences not found in all members of the species. (Ch. 5)

Operant conditioning Learning whereby a voluntary response is strengthened when reinforced. Operant conditioning was first described by B. F. Skinner. (Ch. 1)

Oppositional behavior Behavior in toddlers that is in opposition to behavior of others. Such behavior ranges from active rejection (saying "no") to passive failure to act when ordered. (Ch. 9)

Orient What an infant does to indicate that he or she is paying attention to a stimulus (e.g., turns toward, looks, quiets, and brightens). (Ch. 4, 5)

Orientation bias An error in drawing that occurs when the child orients everything toward the perpendicular (e.g., drawing a chimney on a house so that it is perpendicular to the roof, not to the ground). Orientation bias is one of the systematic errors observed by Pemberton. (Ch. 11)

Overregularize The tendency of young children to misuse a newly learned grammatical rule and apply it in an irregular case that has an exceptional form (e.g., "hurted"). (Ch. 10)

Oxytocin A drug used to induce labor that is associated with developmental deficits in the baby. (Ch. 4)

Parallel play Play in which children locate near one another but remain engaged in independent activity. (Ch. 9)

Parent–infant rhythms Mutual coordination and adjustment of behavior to sustain interaction between parents and infants. (Ch. 6)

Perceptual–motor integration Linkage between taking in and processing information and making the appropriate movement in response. (Ch. 8, 11)

Permissive A pattern of parenting characterized by warmth and very low levels of control. (Ch. 12)

Phenotype A person's actual traits, resulting from the environment as well as the interaction of genes with each other. (Ch. 3)

Phonetics The sound system in language learning. (Ch. 10)

Phylogenetic Behaviors characteristic of a whole species (e.g., in humans, sitting, crawling, and walking). Phylogenetic behaviors are not easily changed by early practice. (Ch. 5)

Physical development The aspect of development dealing with growth patterns, coordination, and body image. (Ch. 5, 8, 11)

Placenta The organ within the uterus that permits the exchange of materials carried in the bloodstreams of a pregnant woman and the developing fetus. (Ch. 3)

Play Activity characterized by intrinsic motivation, attention to means rather than ends, nonliteral behavior, freedom from external rules, exploration, and active engagement. (Ch. 9)

Polygenic Caused by the interaction of many genes and not just a pair. Complex human characteristics such as intelligence are polygenic. (Ch. 3)

Preattachment The first stage in the attachment process, occurring from birth to 8–12 weeks of age. During this stage, infants respond with interest to all adults. (Ch. 6)

Preconventional morality The preoperational stage of moral functioning, which is based on prerational and egocentric functioning, not on the rules of conventional morality. (Ch. 13)

Predefined behaviors Behaviors defined in advance, for purposes of designing observational tests. (Ch. 2)

Preoperational stage The second of Jean Piaget's four stages of intellectual development. Between about two and seven years of age, children at this stage think intuitively and base their judgments on perception. (Ch. 1, 10, 13)

Preschematic stage A stage of drawing described by Brittain as usually beginning after five years of age. At this stage, children draw recognizable pictures, sometimes with ground and sky. (Ch. 11)

Pretense Play that is not literal, in an "as if" mode. (Ch. 9)

Preterm birth Birth that occurs before the expected full term for gestation. (Ch. 3, 4)

Primary circular reaction Active reproduction of an action that an infant first produced by chance. Part of Piaget's description of sensorimotor intelligence, primary circular reactions first occur between one and four months of age. (Ch. 7)

Projecting One of three large muscle skills, involving the ability to direct the body through the air, as in jumping and hopping, or to hurl other objects, as in throwing and kicking. (Ch. 8)

Proprioceptive The ability to sense feeling in the body to provide information on what the body is doing. (Ch. 7)

Prosocial Behavior intended to enhance the welfare of another person. (Ch. 9, 12)

Protein-calorie malnutrition A condition resulting from a lower than necessary intake of protein or calories. (Ch. 5)

Protest, despair, detachment The sequence of reactions shown by infants who are separated from adults to whom they have formed attachment. (Ch. 6)

Proximo-distal A principle that holds that development proceeds generally from the body to the extremities. (Ch. 1, 5)

Psychoanalytic theory Theory originated by Freud and adapted by Erikson emphasizing the importance of development and unconscious control of behavior. (Ch. 1)

Psychosexual theory A Freudian theory based on the idea that personality development is driven by psychosexual urges. (Ch. 1)

Psychosocial development The aspect of development dealing with feelings, self-concept, and interactions within a broad social context. (Ch 6, 9, 12)

Psychosocial theory Erikson's theory based on the idea that personality development happens as a result of the crisis that occurs in response to social interactions at each stage of development. (Ch. 1, 6, 9, 12)

Public Law 94-142 Legislation known as the Individuals with Disabilities Education Act, which makes free public education mandatory for children over five years of age and subject to state laws for three- to five-year-old children. (Ch. 11)

Punishment The inflicting of painful events in response to behavior, which has the effect of reducing the behavior. (Ch. 1)

Quiet A state in the newborn baby of alertness indicative of attention to environmental events. (Ch. 4)

Quiet awake state One of six different states in the newborn, when infants are attentive to outside stimuli. This is an alert state, when learning can occur (it occurs during only 10% of the day in a newborn baby). (Ch. 5)

Random scribbling Definite dots and lines made with simple, whole-arm movement. Random scribbling characterizes the drawings of children from one to two and a half years of age. (Ch. 8)

Readiness test An achievement test given in advance for the purpose of predicting the ability of a child to perform successfully, usually in school tasks. (Ch. 2)

Receptive language Language that is received and understood. (Ch. 10)

Recessive gene A gene that influences phenotype only if it is not paired with a dominant gene. (In contrast, dominant genes influence phenotype no matter how they are paired.) (Ch. 3)

Recessive trait A trait determined by genes that is not apparent in the person's genetic inheritance because it is masked by a dominant trait, which is apparent. Recessive traits can be passed on to the next generation. (Ch. 3)

Reflexes Actions not under voluntary control. Reflexes can be viewed as part of the competence of newborns. (Ch. 5)

Reinforce To increase the likelihood that a given response will be repeated. (Ch. 1)

Reliability The consistency with which different observers record behavior (this term is more generally used to denote a characteristic of tests that give similar results under different conditions). (Ch. 2)

REM (rapid eye movement) A state of sleep characterized by electrical brain discharges associated with dreaming and measured by rapid movements of the eyes under the closed lids. (Ch. 5)

REM sleep One of six levels of alertness of infants. In rapid eye movement (REM) sleep, which alternates with sound sleep, infants are restless and easily roused. (Ch. 5)

Representational stage of drawing A stage during which drawings contain more detail, so that they represent the objects being drawn. (Ch. 11)

Resilience Ability to adjust to or recover from continuing high levels of stress. (Ch. 12)

Resilient children Children who have very positive developmental outcomes in spite of living in very negative environments. (Ch. 12)

Respiratory distress syndrome (RDS) A life-threatening condition in the preterm baby that is due to the inability of the premature lungs to function correctly. (Ch. 4)

Reversibility A characteristic of logical thinking in which something is mentally returned to the original position or state. (Ch. 13)

Rh factor A component in red blood cells that, when lacking in the mother and present in the father and the fetus, can cause damage to the fetus. Treatment exists for Rh incompatibility. (Ch. 3)

Schematic stage A stage of drawing described by Brittain. Around eight years of age, children show attention to design, balance, and perspective in their drawings. (Ch. 11)

Schematization bias The use of systems for drawing one object incorrectly in drawing a second object (e.g., when a child uses human features in drawing vehicles or animals). Schematization bias is one of the systematic errors observed by Pemberton. (Ch. 11)

Scheme See *Structure*. (Ch. 1, 5)

Screening test Test given for the purpose of selecting subjects who may require further testing. (Ch. 2)

Search strategy The ability to visually scan an object in a fast and efficient manner. (Ch. 13)

Secondary circular reaction Repetition of interesting actions involving objects, such as rattles. These reactions, described as part of Piaget's theory of sensorimotor intelligence, first occur between four and eight months of age. (Ch. 7)

Securely attached One of the three types of attachment observed by Ainsworth, characterized by extensive, exploratory behavior; quick recovery from absence; and relatively little distress. (Ch. 6)

Self-actualized Referring to individuals who, according to the theory of Abraham Maslow, have met deprivation needs and being needs and have become creative, productive members of society. (Ch. 1)

Self-assertion Behavior of toddlers intended to express autonomy (not defiance) and associated with developmentally mature children who engage in negotiation with caregivers and are securely attached. (Ch. 9)

Self-awareness A characteristic of personal awareness of the self, which develops from a physicalistic conception to a psychological conception during the early years. (Ch. 12)

Self-concept The understanding the child develops about the self, based on self-knowledge, self-awareness, and self-control. (Ch. 12)

Self-esteem The child's personal, emotional assessment of the self, based on self-awareness and self-knowledge. (Ch. 12)

Self-knowledge The child's conscious understanding of body, mind, and consciousness. (Ch. 12)

Self–other differentiation The toddler's developing awareness of the peer as a separate person with separate needs, which lays the groundwork for cooperation to take place. (Ch. 9)

Self space The space a child can occupy by extending the body to its greatest reach in all directions. (Ch. 11)

Semantically contingent responding Relating parental speech to the preceding remarks by a child. (Ch. 13)

Semantics The development of the understanding of the meanings attached to words. (Ch. 10)

Sensorimotor The first of Jean Piaget's four stages of intellectual development. Generally occurring before two years of age, the sensorimotor stage is characterized by learning through the senses and through activity. (Ch. 1, 7, 10)

Sequential Stages of development that occur in a logically predictable order. (Ch. 1)

Seriation A logical organization of objects into ordered relationships, such as from tall to short. (Ch. 13)

Shared meaning Vygotsky's theory that learning language requires that the adult and the child share an understanding of the meaning of events, words, and so on. (Ch. 10)

Shared referent   Vygotsky's theory that learning language requires that the adult and the child share an understanding of what is being referred to. (Ch. 10)

Siblings   Individuals with the same parents. (Ch. 4)

Simplification bias   The use of fewer lines in drawing, which is one of the systematic errors identified by Pemberton. (Ch. 11)

Skill assessments   Tests measuring readiness for, or achievement of, specific skills and abilities. (Ch. 2)

Small for date   Born after a pregnancy of normal length but without having grown as would be expected. (Ch. 3)

Small muscle skills   Physical skills using small body movements (e.g., drawing, eating, and bead stringing). (Ch. 8, 11)

Social cognition   The process by which individuals understand and perceive other people. (Ch. 6)

Social learning theory   A behavioral theory that proposes that learning occurs through imitation. (Ch. 1)

Solitary play   Play in which children interact only with an object or familiar adult but not with peers. (Ch. 9)

Solitary symbolic play   The first of two levels of early pretend play, beginning between 12 and 18 months and centering on the child's pretense. (Ch. 9)

Sound sleep   One of six levels of alertness of infants. During sound sleep, infants have regular breathing patterns and are unaware of the sights and sounds of the environment. (Ch. 5)

Spatial perceptual awareness   The ability to control the movement of the body in space (general space) and have a sense of personal space (that of the child's own body). (Ch. 8)

Specific learning disabilities   Disorders of the basic processes involved in learning that cannot be attributed to another handicapping condition. (Ch. 11)

Speech and language impairment   A communication disorder that adversely affects learning and interaction. (Ch. 11)

Speech entrainment   The ability of even newborn babies to respond to human speech with continuous motor movements, in rhythm to the adult speech. (Ch. 7)

Stability   One of three infant motor skills that involves gaining control of body parts and muscles to allow them to work against gravity. (Ch. 5)

Standardized measure   Test that has adequate norms, rules for administration, and data on reliability and validity. (Ch. 2)

State   A cycle of six different conditions in the neonate (e.g., crying, deep sleep, etc.) that determine the way the infant will respond to stimulation. (Ch. 5)

Static balance   One of three large muscle skills that involves the ability to maintain balance, including such skills as standing on one foot. (Ch. 8)

Stop   A consonant sound made by completely stopping the air as it flows through the mouth by placing the tongue against the roof of the mouth (e.g., *p, b, t, d*). (Ch. 10)

Stranger anxiety   Reactions typical of fear, beginning at eight or nine months of age, that may be directed at people who are unfamiliar to the infant. (Ch. 6)

Stress   A high degree of emotional tension, brought about by environmental changes and interfering with normal patterns of response. (Ch. 12)

Structure   Organized elements of thought, described in the theory of Jean Piaget. (Ch. 1)

Subtractive bilingualism   Second-language learning that takes place when children are members of minority groups and do not receive societal support for continued use of their first language. (Ch. 13)

Surfactant   The material that completes the final maturation of the lining of the lungs immediately before birth. It is possible to artificially stimulate the development of surfactant with an injection when a premature delivery is threatened. (Ch. 4)

Synaptogenesis   Increases in the synapses (electrochemical connections between the cells of the brain) when new behaviors occur. All behavior depends on these synapses, and the greater their density, the greater the repertoire of the person. (Ch. 7)

Syntax The development of the understanding of grammar. (Ch. 10)

Tabula rasa A state, hypothesized by John Locke (1632–1704), in which the mind is completely blank and awaiting the imprint of experience. (Ch. 1)

Tantrums Bursts of anger in response to a loss of autonomy or control. (Ch. 9)

Temperament An individual's unique, inborn way of dealing with people and situations; the "how" of behavior. (Ch. 6, 9, 12)

Temporal perceptual awareness The ability to control the speed of the body's movements, including the coordination of different body parts, which is also referred to as rhythm and expressed in dance. (Ch. 8)

Teratogens Drugs, viruses, and other environmental factors that increase the incidence of congenital malformations. (Ch. 3)

Tertiary circular reactions Activities of infants that show experimentation, not just repetition, and search for understanding. Part of Piaget's description of sensorimotor intelligence, these reactions usually first occur between 12 and 18 months of age. (Ch. 10)

Theory An organized system of hypotheses or statements, based on observations and evidence, that explains or predicts something. (Ch. 1)

Time sampling A strategy of observation that documents the frequency (and sometimes the duration) of predefined behaviors by recording during specified time intervals. (Ch. 2)

Transductive reasoning The sometimes inaccurate reasoning of preoperational children that confuses specific cases with general cases and fails to recognize the transition between events. (Ch. 10)

Transitional objects Objects, such as blankets and teddy bears, to which children form special attachments. Psychologists view these objects as facilitating transition from parents and home to the larger world. (Ch. 9)

Triggering events of child abuse Events responsible for the immediate act of abuse.

These will trigger abuse only if there are contextual factors present as well. (Ch. 8)

Trust versus mistrust The first of Erik Erikson's eight stages of psychosocial development. In this stage, infants develop a sense of the degree to which their worlds are comfortable and trustworthy. (Ch. 1, 6)

Tunnel vision A technique used in reading in which the child focuses on the smallest distinctive features rather than using the entire context and finding the chunks of material that provide the most information. Tunnel vision leads to slow, ineffective reading. (Ch. 13)

Ultrasound Sound with frequencies above the range of human hearing. Ultrasonic images of a fetus can be used to diagnose fetal problems. (Ch. 3)

Universal causal agent The tendency for toddlers to think of themselves as the only ones with the ability to act independently. At approximately two years, toddlers recognize the ability of others to act independently, thus making possible self–other differentiation. (Ch. 9)

Validity A characteristic of standardized tests that demonstrates that the test can measure the construct it purports to measure. (Ch. 2)

Vicarious reinforcement Indirect reinforcement in which behavior develops because of the modeling of actions of others, who receive pleasure or power. (Ch. 1)

Vignette An observational tool that is used to record accounts of events believed to be meaningful in children's development. (Ch. 2)

Visual impairment A difficulty in the ability to see; visual impairment adversely affects educational performance. (Ch. 11)

Visual information processing The ability to learn using visual analysis. In infants it is observed by studying attentional abilities, as measured by speed of habituation. (Ch. 7)

Visual preference Preference for certain visual stimuli. From birth, infants prefer to look at dark/light and complex patterns, indicating the presence of innate visual capabilities. (Ch. 7)

Voicing   Sounds made in the human language system when air is passed through the larynx (e.g., *b, d, g*). (Ch. 10)

Vowels   Sounds in the human language system that are made by changing the shape of the opening of the mouth and throat, so that air passing through will take on a different sound. (Ch. 10)

Zone of proximal development   The material that children can teach themselves, using social, creative play, without adult intervention (based on Vygotsky's theory). (Ch. 13)

Zygote   The first cell of a developing human being, resulting from the fusion of sperm and ovum. (Ch. 3)

References

Abelman, R. (1986). Children's awareness of television's prosocial fare: Parental discipline as an antecedent. *Journal of Family Issues, 7,* 51–66.

Abramovich, R., Pepler, D., & Corter, C. (1982). Patterns of sibling interaction among preschool-age children. In M. E. Lamb & B. Sutton-Smith (Eds.), *Sibling relationships: Their nature and significance across the lifespan.* Hillsdale, NJ: Lawrence Erlbaum.

Achermann, J., Dinneen, E., & Stevenson-Hinde, J. (1991). Clearing up at 2.5 years. *British Journal of Developmental Psychology, 9,* 365–376.

Ainsworth, M. D. S. (1967). *Infancy in Uganda: Infant care and the growth of love.* Baltimore: Johns Hopkins University Press.

Ainsworth, M. D. S. (1978). Infant–mother attachment. In M. Richards (Ed.), *The child's integration into the social world.* New York: Cambridge University Press.

Ainsworth, M. D. S., & Bell, S. M. (1970). Attachment, exploration, and separation: Illustrated by the behavior of one-year-olds in a strange situation. *Child Development, 41,* 49–67.

Ainsworth, M. D. S., Bell, S. M., & Stayton, D. J. (1971). Individual differences in strange situation behavior of one-year-olds. In H. R. Schaffer (Ed.), *The origins of human social relations.* New York: Academic Press.

Ainsworth, M. D. S., Bell, S. M., & Stayton, D. J. (1974). Infant–mother attachment and social development: Socialization as a product of reciprocal responsiveness to signals. In M. P. M. Richards (Ed.), *The integration of a child into a social world.* London: Cambridge University Press.

Allen, R. (1991). Integration of communicational cues by very young children. *Journal of Psycholinguistic Research, 20,* 389–402.

Almy, M., Monighan, P., Scales, B., & Van Hoorn, J. (1984). Recent research on play: The perspective of the teacher. In L. G. Katz (Ed.), *Current topics in early childhood education* (Vol. 5). Norwood, NJ: Ablex.

Alvino, J. (1980, March). Philosophy for children. *Teacher, 97,* 53–57.

American Academy of Pediatrics. (1987). Neonatal anesthesia. *Pediatrics, 80,* 446.

Ames, L. B., Gillespie, C., Haines, J., & Ilg, F. L. (1979). *The Gesell Institute's child from one to six.* New York: Harper & Row.

Anderson, J. (1986). Sensory intervention with the preterm infant in the neonatal intensive care unit. *The American Journal of Occupational Therapy, 40,* 19–26.

Andersson, B. (1992). Effects of day-care on cognitive and socioemotional competence of thirteen-year-old Swedish schoolchildren. *Child Development, 63,* 20–36.

Andreasen, M. S. (1990). Evolution in the family's use of television: Normative data from industry and academe. In J. Bryant (Ed.), *Television and the American family.* Hillsdale, NJ: Lawrence Erlbaum.

Andrews, S. R., Blumenthal, J. B., Johnson, D. L., Kahn, A. J., Ferguson, C. J., Lasater, T. M., Malone, P. E., & Wallace, D. B. (1982).

The skills of mothering: A study of Parent Child Development Centers. *Monographs of the Society for Research in Child Development, 47* (6, Serial No. 198).

Anisfeld, E., Casper, V., Nozyce, M., & Cunningham, N. (1990). Does infant carrying promote attachment? An experimental study of the effects of increased physical contact on the development of attachment. *Child Development, 61,* 1617–1627.

Anisfeld, E., Curry, M. A., Hales, D. J., Kennel, J. H., Klaus, M. H., Lipper, E., O'Connor, S., Siegel, E., & Sosa, R. (1983). Maternal–infant bonding: A joint rebuttal. *Pediatrics, 72,* 569–571.

Anisfield, M. (1984). *Language development from birth to three.* Hillsdale, NJ: Lawrence Erlbaum Publishers.

Anselmo, S. (1979). A Piagetian perspective on multicultural experiences in early childhood education. In M. K. Poulsen & G. I. Lubin (Eds.), *Piagetian theory and its implications for the helping professions.* Los Angeles: University of Southern California Press.

Anselmo, S. (1980, Fall). Children learn about their senses. *Day Care and Early Education, 8,* 42–44.

Anselmo, S., Rollins, P., & Schuckman, R. (1986). *R is for rainbow: Developing young children's thinking skills through the alphabet.* Menlo Park, CA: Addison-Wesley.

Arlin, M. (1990). What happens to time when you sleep? Children's development of objective time and its relation to time perception. *Cognitive Development, 5,* 71–88.

Arnold, J. H., & Gemma, P. B. (1983). *A child dies: A portrait of family grief.* Rockville, MD: Aspen Systems.

Asendorpf, J. B., & Nunner-Winkler, G. (1992). Children's moral motive strength and temperamental inhibition reduce their immoral behavior in real moral conflicts. *Child Development, 63,* 1223–1235.

Autti-Ramo, I., & Granstrom, M. L. (1991). The psychomotor development during the first year of life of infants exposed to intrauterine alcohol of various duration: Fetal alcohol exposure and development. *Neuropediatrics, 22,* 59–64.

Autti-Ramo, I., Korkman, M., Hillakivi-Clarke, L., Lehtonen, M., Halmesmaki, E., & Granstrom, M. L. (1992). Mental development of 2-year-old children exposed to alcohol in utero. *Journal of Pediatrics, 120,* 740–746.

Azrin, N. H., & Foxx, R. M. (1981). *Toilet training in less than a day.* New York: Pocket Books.

Bagley, C. R. (1991). Factor structure of temperament in the third year of life. *Journal of General Psychology, 118,* 291–297.

Bailey, D. B., Jr., & Wolery, M. (1984). *Teaching infants and preschoolers with handicaps.* Columbus: Charles E. Merrill.

Bailey, J. M., & Revelle, W. (1991). Increased heritability for lower IQ levels? *Behavior Genetics, 21,* 397–404.

Bailey, R. A., & Burton, E. C. (1982). *The dynamic self: Activities to enhance infant development.* St. Louis: C. V. Mosby.

Bamford, F. N., Bannister, R. P., Benjamin, C. M., Hillier, V. F., Ward, B. S., & Moore, W. M. O. (1990). Sleep in the first year of life. *Developmental Medicine and Child Neurology, 32,* 718–724.

Bandura, A. (1977). *Social learning theory.* Englewood Cliffs, NJ: Prentice Hall.

Bandura, A., Ross, D., & Ross, S. A. (1963). Imitation of film-mediated aggressive models. *Journal of Abnormal and Social Psychology, 66,* 3–11.

Bank, S. P., & Kahn, M. D. (1982). *The sibling bond.* New York: Basic Books.

Baratta-Lorton, M. (1976). *Mathematics their way.* Menlo Park, CA: Addison-Wesley.

Barbero, G. J. (1975). Failure to thrive. In M. H. Klaus, T. Leger, & M. A. Trause (Eds.), *Maternal attachment and mothering disorders: A round table.* Sausalito, CA: Johnson & Johnson.

Bass, E., & Thornton, L. (Eds.). (1983). *I never told anyone: Writings by women survivors of child sexual abuse.* New York: Harper & Row.

Battelle, P. (1981, February). The triplets who found each other. *Good Housekeeping, 192,* 74–83.

Bauer, D. H. (1976). An exploratory study of developmental changes in children's fears. *Journal of Child Psychology and Psychiatry, 17,* 69–74.

Bauer, G., Ewald, L. S., Hoffman, J., & Dubanoski, R. (1991). Breastfeeding and cognitive development of three-year-old children. *Psychological Reports, 68,* 1218.

Baumrind, D. (1967). Child care practices anteceding three patterns of pre-school behavior. *Genetic Psychology Monographs, 75,* 43–88.

Baumrind, D. (1977). Some thoughts about childrearing. In S. Cohen & T. J. Comiskey (Eds.), *Child development: Contemporary perspectives.* Itasca, IL: F. E. Peacock.

Bax, M. (1981). The intimate relationship of health, development, and behavior in young children. In C. C. Brown (Ed.), *Infants at risk: Assessment and intervention.* Skillman, NJ: Johnson & Johnson.

Beaty, J. J. (1993). *Observing development of the young child* (3rd ed.). New York: Merrill/Macmillan.

Bell, S. M., & Ainsworth, M. D. S. (1972). Infant crying and maternal responsiveness. *Child Development, 43,* 1171–1190.

Belsky, J. (1988). The effects of infant day care reconsidered. *Early Childhood Research Quarterly, 3,* 235–272.

Belsky, J., Lerner, R. M., & Spanier, G. B. (1984). *The child in the family.* Reading, MA: Addison-Wesley.

Belsky, J., Rovine, M. J., & Taylor, D. G. (1984). The Pennsylvania infant and family development project: III. The origins of individual differences in infant–mother attachment: Maternal and infant contributions. *Child Development 55,* 718–728.

Belsky, J., & Steinberg, L. D. (1978). The effects of day care: A critical review. *Child Development, 49,* 929–949.

Belsky, J., & Steinberg, L. D. (1982). The effects of day care: A critical review. In J. Belsky (Ed.), *In the beginning: Readings on infancy.* New York: Columbia University Press.

Belsky, J., Steinberg, L. D., & Walker, A. (1982). The ecology of day care. In M. E. Lamb (Ed.), *Nontraditional families: Parenting and child development.* Hillsdale, NJ: Lawrence Erlbaum.

Benenson, J. F. (1993). Greater preference among females than males for dyadic interaction in early childhood. *Child Development, 64,* 544–555.

Benirschke, K., Carpenter, G., Espstein, C., Fraser, C., Jackson, L., Motusky, A., & Nyhan, W. (1976). Genetic diseases. In R. L. Brent & M. I. Harris (Eds.), *Prevention of embryonic, fetal and perinatal disease.* Bethesda, MD: National Institutes of Health.

Berger, S. (1984, July 1). Sometimes I feel bad: Divorce as seen through one child's eyes. *Parade Magazine,* 12–13.

Berman, C. P. (1992). Part H coordinators: Stresses, satisfactions, and supports. *Zero to Three, 12,* 13–18.

Bernstein, A. C., & Cowan, P. A. (1981). Children's conceptions of birth and sexuality. In R. Bibace & M. E. Walsh (Eds.), *Children's conceptions of health, illness, and bodily functions.* New Directions for Child Development series. San Francisco: Jossey-Bass.

Berry, C. A., Shaywitz, S. E., & Shaywitz, B. A. (1985). Girls with attention deficit disorder: A silent minority? A report on the behavioral and cognitive characteristics. *Pediatrics, 76,* 801–809.

Besharov, D. J. (199). *Recognizing child abuse: A guide for the concerned.* New York: Free Press.

Best, R. (1983). *We've all got scars: What boys and girls learn in elementary school.* Bloomington, IN: Indiana University Press.

Bibace, R., & Walsh, M. E. (1981). Children's conceptions of illness. In R. Bibace & M. E. Walsh (Eds.), *Children's conceptions of health, illness, and bodily functions.* New Directions for Child Development series. San Francisco: Jossey-Bass.

Bijou, S. W., & Baer, D. M. (1961). *Child development* (Vol. 1). New York: Appleton-Century-Crofts.

Bithoney, W. G., McJunkin, J., Michalek, J., Snyder, J., Egan, H., & Elpstein, D. (1991). The effect of a multidisciplinary team approach on weight gain in nonorganic failure-to-thrive children. *Journal of Developmental and Behavioral Pediatrics, 12,* 254–258.

Bjorklund, D. F., & Green, B. L. (1992). The adaptive nature of cognitive immaturity. *American Psychologist, 47,* 46–54.

Block, J. H. (1971). *Lives through time.* Berkeley, CA: Bancroft Books.

Block, J. H., & Block, J. (1980). The role of ego-control and ego-resiliency in the organization of behavior. In W. A. Collins (Ed.), *Development of cognition, affect, and social relations* (Minnesota Symposium on Child Psychology, Vol. 13). Hillsdale, NJ: Lawrence Erlbaum.

Bloom, L. (1970). *Language development: Form and function in emerging grammars.* Cambridge, MA: MIT Press.

Bloom, L. (1991). *Language development from two to three.* New York: Cambridge University Press.

Bloomfield, L. (1933). *Language.* New York: Henry Holt. (Reprinted 1961).

Borke, H. (1971). Interpersonal perception of young children. *Developmental Psychology, 5,* 263–269.

Borke, H. (1983). Piaget's mountains revisited: Changes in the egocentric landscape. In M. Donaldson, R. Grieve, & C. Pratt (Eds.), *Early childhood development and education: Readings in psychology.* New York: Guilford.

Bornstein, M. H. (1985). Infant into adult: Unity to diversity in the development of visual categorization. In J. Mehler & R. Fox (Eds.), *Neonate cognition: Beyond the blooming buzzing confusion.* Hillsdale, NJ: Lawrence Erlbaum.

Bornstein, M. H., Tamis-LeMonda, C. S., Tal, J., Ludemann, P., Toda, S., Rahn, C. W., Pecheux, M., Azuma, H., & Vardi, D. (1992). Maternal responsiveness to infants in three societies: The United States, France, and Japan. *Child Development, 63,* 808–821.

Bower, T. G. R. (1977). *The perceptual world of the child.* Cambridge: Harvard University Press.

Bower, T. G. R. (1977). *A primer of infant development.* San Francisco: W. H. Freeman.

Bower, T. G. R. (1982). *Development in infancy* (2nd ed.). San Francisco: W. H. Freeman.

Bowlby, J. (1958). The nature of a child's tie to his mother. *International Journal of Psychoanalysis, 39,* 350–373.

Bowlby, J. (1982). *Attachment and loss* (2nd ed.). New York: Basic Books.

Boyd, C. J., & Mieczkowski, T. (1990). Drug use, health, family and social support in "crack" cocaine users. *Addictive Behaviors, 15,* 481–485.

Boyle, R. J. (1993). Use of surfactant in premature infants: How it affects health and developmental outcomes. *Infants and Young Children, 6,* 21–25.

Brand, H. J., & Welch, K. (1989). Cognitive and social-emotional development of children in different preschool environments. *Psychological Reports, 65,* 480–482.

Brazelton, T. B. (1962). A child-oriented approach to toilet training. *Pediatrics, 29,* 121–128.

Brazelton, T. B. (1973). *Neonatal Behavioral Assessment Scale.* Philadelphia: J. B. Lippincott.

Brazelton, T. B. (1974). *Toddlers and parents: A declaration of independence.* New York: Dell.

Brazelton, T. B. (1979). Behavioral competence of the newborn infant. *Seminars in Perinatology, 3,* 35–44.

Brazelton, T. B. (1981). *On becoming a family: The growth of attachment.* New York: Delacorte/Seymour Lawrence.

Brazelton, T. B. (1982). Behavioral assessment of the premature infant: Uses in intervention. In M. H. Klaus & M. O. Robertson (Eds.), *Birth, interaction, and attachment: A round table.* Skillman, NJ: Johnson & Johnson.

Bredekamp, S., & Rosegrant, T. (Eds.). (1992). *Reaching potentials: Appropriate curriculum and assessment for young children* (Vol. 1.). Washington, DC: National Association for the Education of Young Children.

Brett, D. (1988). *Annie stories: A special kind of storytelling.* New York: Workman Publishing.

Brittain, W. L. (1979). *Creativity, art, and the young child.* New York: Macmillan.

Bromwich, R. (1981). *Working with parents and infants: An interactional approach.* Austin, TX: PRO-ED, Inc. (Originally published by University Park Press, Baltimore, MD.)

Bronfenbrenner, U. (1970). *Two worlds of childhood.* New York: Russell Sage.

Bronfenbrenner, U. (1979). *The ecology of human development: Experiments by nature and design.* Cambridge, MA: Harvard University Press.

Brooks-Gunn, J., Klebanov, P. K., Liaw, F., & Spiker, D. (1993). Enhancing the development of low-birthweight, premature infants: Changes in cognition and behavior over the first three years. *Child Development, 64,* 736–753.

Brooks-Gunn, J., & Matthews, W. S. (1979). *He and she: How children develop their sex-role identity.* Englewood Cliffs, NJ: Prentice Hall.

Broughton, J. (1978). Development of concepts of self, mind, reality, and knowledge. *New Directions for Child Development, 1,* 75–100.

Brown, C. C. (Ed.). (1981). *Infants at risk: Assessment and intervention. An update for health care professionals and parents: A round table.* Skillman, NJ: Johnson & Johnson.

Brown, R. (1973). *A First Language.* Cambridge, MA: Harvard University Press.

Brownell, C. A. (1990). Peer social skills in toddlers: Competencies and constraints illustrated by same-age and mixed-age interaction. *Child Development, 61,* 838–848.

Brownell, C. A., & Carriger, M. S. (1990). Changes in cooperation and self–other differentiation during the second year. *Child Development, 61,* 1164–1174.

Bruce, D. J. (1964). An analysis of word sounds by young children. *British Journal of Educational Psychology, 34,* 158–170.

Brumback, R. A., Bodenstein, J. B., & Roach, S. (1990). Support groups for pediatric neurological disorders. *Journal of Child Neurology, 5,* 344–349.

Bryan, J. H. (1975). Children's cooperation and helping behaviors. In E. M. Hetherington (Ed.), *Review of child development research* (Vol. 5). Chicago: University of Chicago Press.

Burchinal, M., Lee, M., & Ramey, C. (1989). Type of day-care and preschool intellectual development in disadvantaged children. *Child Development, 60,* 128–137.

Burgess, B. J. (1980). Parenting in the native-American community. In M. O. Fantini & R. Cardenas (Eds.), *Parenting in a multicultural society.* New York: Longman.

Burtoff, B. (1982, December 30). Child's "security blanket" OK. *Stockton* (California) *Record,* p. 11.

Buss, D., Block, J. H., & Block, J. (1980). Preschool activity level: Personality correlates and developmental implications. *Child Development, 51,* 401–408.

Butte, N. F., Jensen, C. L., Moon, J. K., Glaze, D. G., & Frost, J. D. (1992). Sleep organization and energy expenditure of breast-fed and formula-fed infants. *Pediatric Research, 32,* 514–519.

Butterfield, S. A., & Loovis, M. (1993). Influence of age, sex, balance and sport participation on development of throwing by children in grades K-8. *Perceptual and Motor Skills, 76,* 459–464.

Bybee, R. W., & Sund, R. B. (1982). *Piaget for educators* (2nd ed.). New York: Merrill/Macmillan.

Calkins, S. D., & Fox, N. A. (1992). The relations among infant temperament, security of attachment, and behavioral inhibition at twenty-four months. *Child Development, 63,* 1456–1472.

Callaghan, J. W. (1981). A comparison of Anglo, Hopi, and Navajo mothers and infants. In T. M. Field, A. M. Sostek, P. Vietze, & P. H. Leiderman (Eds.), *Culture and early interactions.* Hillsdale, NJ: Lawrence Erlbaum.

Campos, J. J., & Stenberg, C. R. (1981). Perception, appraisal and emotion: The onset of social referencing. In M. E. Lamb & L. R. Sherrod (Eds.), *Infant social cognition: Empirical and theoretical considerations.* Hillsdale, NJ: Lawrence Erlbaum.

Camras, L. A., & Sachs, V. B. (1991). Social referencing and caretaker expressive behavior in a day care setting. *Infant Behavior and Development, 14,* 27–36.

Capian, F. (1978). *The first 12 months of life.* New York: Bantam.

Caplan, M., Vespo, J., Pedersen, J., & Hay, D. F. (1991). Conflict and its resolution in small groups of one- and two-year-olds. *Child Development, 62,* 1513–1524.

Carew, J. V. (1980). Experience and the development of intelligence in young children at home and in day care. *Monographs of the Society for Research in Child Development, 45* (Serial No. 187).

Carmichael, L. (1970). Onset and early development of behavior. In P. H. Mussen (Ed.), *Carmichael's manual of child psychology* (3rd ed.). New York: John Wiley & Sons.

Carpenter, G. C., Tecce, J. J., Stechler, G., & Friedman, S. (1970). Differential visual behavior to human and humanoid faces in early infancy. *Merrill-Palmer Quarterly, 16,* 91–107.

Carson, L. (1982). KinderSkills: A motor development program for parent and child. *Journal of Health, Physical Education, Recreation, and Dance, 53,* 96–47.

Carson, L. (1986). Intergenerational motor development instruction. *Journal of Health, Physical Education, Recreation, and Dance, 57* 45–48.

Carter, D., & Mason, L. (1989). Health visitors' perceptions of normal infant behavior. *Health Visitor, 62,* 56–59.

Cartwright, S. (1988). Play can be the building blocks of learning. *Young Children 43,* 44–47.

Caruso, G. L. (1992). Patterns of maternal employment and child care for a sample of two-year-olds. *Journal of Family Issues, 13,* 297–311.

Casey, M. B., Bronson, M. B., Tivnan, T., Riley, E., & Spenciner, L. (1991). Differentiating preschoolers' sequential planning ability from their general intelligence: A study of organization, systematic responding, and efficiency in young children. *Journal of Applied Developmental Psychology, 12,* 19–32.

Catherwood, D., Crassini, B., & Freiberg, K. (1990). Infant response to stimuli of similar hue and dissimilar shape: Tracing the origins of the categorization of objects by hue. *Child Development, 60,* 752–762.

Cazden, C. B. (Ed.). (1981). *Language in early childhood education* (rev. ed.). Washington, DC: National Association for the Education of Young Children.

Cazden, C. B. (1984). Effective instructional practices in bilingual education. NIE contract #400-81-0004.

Cazden, C. B. (1988). Environmental assistance revisited: Variation and functional equivalence. In F. S. Kessel (Ed.), *The development of language and language researchers: Essays in honor of Roger Brown.* Hillsdale, NJ: Lawrence Erlbaum.

Chall, J., Radwin, E., French, V. W., & Hall, C. R. (1979). Blacks in the world of children's books. *Reading Teacher, 32,* 527–533.

Chandler, M. J., & Greenspan, S. (1972). Ersatz egocentrism: A reply to H. Borke. *Developmental Psychology, 7,* 104–106.

Chappell, P. A., & Steitz, J. A. (1993). Young children's human figure drawings and cognitive development. *Perceptual and Motor Skills, 76,* 611–617.

Chasnoff, I. J., Griffith, D. R., Freier, C., & Murray, J. (1992). Cocaine/polydrug use in pregnancy: Two-year follow-up. *Pediatrics, 89,* 284–289.

Chasnoff, I. J., Griffith, D. R., MacGregor, S., Dirkes, K., & Burns, K. A. (1989). Temporal patterns of cocaine use in pregnancy. *Journal of the American Medical Association, 261,* 1741–1744.

Chess, S., Thomas., A., & Birch, H. G. (1972). *Your child is a person: A psychological approach to parenthood without guilt.* New York: Viking Press.

Chomsky, N. (1965). *Aspects of the theory of syntax.* Cambridge, MA: MIT Press.

Christoffel, K. K., & Forsyth, B. W. C. (1989). Mirror image of environmental deprivation: Severe childhood obesity of psychosocial origin. *Child Abuse & Neglect, 13,* 249–256.

Clarke-Stewart, K. A. (1988). The "Effects of infant day care reconsidered" reconsidered: Risks for parents, children, and researchers. *Early Childhood Research Quarterly, 3,* 293–318.

Clay, M. (1967). The reading behaviour of five year old children: A research report. *New Zealand Journal of Educational Studies, 2,* 11–31.

Cohn, J. F., Campbell, S. B., & Ross, S. (1991). Infant response in the still-face paradigm at 6 months predicts avoidant and secure attachment at 12 months. *Development and Psychopathology, 3,* 367–376.

Colao, F., & Hosansky, T. (1983). *Your children should know: Teach your children the strategies that will keep them safe from assault and crime.* Indianapolis, IN: Bobbs-Merrill.

Colby, A., Kohlberg, L., Gibbs, J., & Lieberman, M. (1983). A longitudinal study of moral judgment. *Monographs of the Society for Research in Child Development, 40*(1–2, Serial No. 200).

Coleman, J. C., & Hammen, C. L. (1974). *Contemporary psychology and effective behavior.* Glenview, IL: Scott, Foresman.

Colombo, J., Mitchell, D. W., Coldren, J. T., & Freeseman, L. J. (1991). Individual differences in infant visual attention: Are short lookers faster processors or feature processors? *Child Development, 62,* 1247–1257.

Condon, W. S., & Sander, L. W. (1974). Neonate movement is synchronized with adult speech: Interactional participation and language acquisition. *Science, 183,* 99–101.

Condry, S. (1983). History and background of preschool intervention programs and the Consortium for Longitudinal Studies. In Consortium for Longitudinal Studies, *As the twig is bent . . .Lasting effects of preschool programs.* Hillsdale, NJ: Lawrence Erlbaum.

Connelly, C. D., & Straus, M. A. (1992). Mother's age and risk for physical abuse. *Child Abuse & Neglect, 16,* 709–718.

Cooper, R. P., & Aslin, R. N. (1990). Preference for infant-directed speech in the first month after birth. *Child Development, 61,* 1584–1595.

Copian, J., Gleason, J. R., Ryan, R., Burke, M. G., & Williams, M. L. (1982). Validation of an early language milestone scale in a high-risk population. *Pediatrics, 70,* 677–683.

Cratty, B. J. (1986). *Perceptual and motor development in infants and children.* Englewood Cliffs, NJ: Prentice Hall.

Crider, C. (1981). Children's conceptions of the body interior. In R. Bibace & M. E. Walsh (Eds.), *Children's conceptions of health, illness, and bodily functions.* New Directions for Child Development series. San Francisco: Jossey-Bass.

Crockenberg, S., & Litman, C. (1990). Autonomy as competence in 2-year-olds: Maternal correlates of child defiance, compliance, and self-assertion. *Developmental Psychology, 26,* 961–971.

Crockenberg, S., & Litman, C. (1991). Effects of maternal employment on maternal and two-year-old child behavior. *Child Development, 62,* 930–953.

Crockenberg, S., & McCluskey, K. (1982). Caring for irritable babies: A research report. *Human Relations, 7,* 1–3.

Cryan, J. R. (1986). Evaluation: Plague or promise? *Childhood Education 62,* 344–350.

Damon, W. (1977). *The social world of the child.* San Francisco: Jossey-Bass.

Damon, W. (1980). Patterns of change in children's social reasoning: A two-year longitudinal study. *Child Develoment, 51,* 1010–1017.

Damon, W. (1983). *Social and personality development: Infancy through adolescence.* New York: W. W. Norton.

Damon, W. (1990). *The moral child: Nurturing children's natural moral growth.* New York: Free Press.

Dawe, H. C. (1934). An analysis of two hundred quarrels of preschool children. *Child Development, 5,* 139–157.

Day, N. L., & Richardson, G. A. (1991). Prenatal alcohol exposure: A continuum of effects. *Seminars in Perinatology 15,* 271–279.

Day, N. L., Richardson, G. A., Robles, N., Sambamoorthi, U., Taylor, P., Scher, M., Stoffer,

D., Jasperse, D., & Cornelius, M. (1990). Prenatal alcohol exposure: A continuum of effects. *Pediatrics 85*, 748–752.

DeCasper, A. J., & Fifer, W. P. (1980). Of human bonding: Newborns prefer their mothers' voices. *Science, 208*, 1174–1176.

de LaCoste, M. C., Horvath, D. S., & Woodward, D. J. (1991). Possible sex differences in the developing human fetal brain. *Journal of Clinical and Experimental Neuropsychology, 13*, 831–846.

Demany, L., McKenzie, B., & Vurpillot, E. (1977). Rhythm perception in early infancy. *Nature, 266*, 718–719.

Denham, S. A., McKinley, M., Couchoud, E. A., & Holt, R. (1990). Emotional and behavioral predictors of preschool peer ratings. *Child Development, 61*, 1145–1152.

Dennis, W. (1940). The effect of cradling practices upon the onset of walking of Hopi children. *Journal of Genetic Psychology, 56*, 77–86.

Desmond, R. J., Singer, J. L., Singer, D. G., Calam, R., & Colimore, K. (1985). Family mediation patterns and television viewing: Young children's use and grasp of the medium. *Human Communication Research, 11*, 461–480.

Dillon, M. (1982, November). Kids' TV: 18 violent acts per hour; Doesn't anyone care? *Stanford Observer* (Stanford University), p. 4.

Dinkmeyer, D., & McKay, G. D. (1976). *Systematic training for effective parenting (STEP)*. Circle Pines, MI: American Guidance Services.

DiPietro, J. A., & Porges, S. W. (1991). Relations between neonatal states and 8-month developmental outcome in preterm infants. *Infant Behavior and Development, 14*, 441–450.

Dixon, S. D. (1989). Effects of transplacental exposure to cocaine and methamphetamine on the neonate. *Western Journal of Medicine, 150*, 436–442.

Dobzhansky, T. (1973). *Genetic diversity and human equality*. New York: Basic Books.

Doescher, S. M., & Sugawara, A. I. (1990). Sex role flexibility and prosocial behavior among preschool children. *Sex Roles, 22*, 111–123.

Dreikurs, R., & Soltz, V. (1964). *Children: The challenge*. New York: Hawthorn Books.

Dunn, J., & Kendrick, C. (1982). Siblings and their mother: Developing relationships within the family. In M. E. Lamb & B. Sutton-Smith (Eds.), *Sibling relationships: Their nature and significance across the lifespan*. Hillsdale, NJ: Lawrence Erlbaum.

Dunst, C. J., Trivette, C., & Deal, A. (1988). *Enabling and empowering families: Principles and guidelines for practice*. Cambridge, MA: Brookline Books.

Dweck, C. S. (1981). Social-cognitive processes in children's friendships. In S. R. Asher & J. M. Gottman (Eds.), *The development of children's friendships*. Cambridge: Cambridge University Press.

Eaton, W. O., & Saudino, K. J. (1992). Prenatal activity level as a temperament dimension? Individual differences and developmental functions in fetal movement. *Infant Behavior and Development, 15*, 57–70.

Edwards, L. C. (1990). *Affective development and the creative arts: A process approach to early childhood education*. New York: Merrill/Macmillan.

Egeland, B., Kalkoske, M., Gottesman, N., & Erickson, M. F. (1990). Preschool behavior problems: Stability and factors accounting for change. *Journal of Child Psychology and Psychiatry and Allied Disciplines, 31*, 891–909.

Egland, B., & Stroufe, L. A. (1981). Developmental sequelae of maltreatment in infancy. *New Directions for Child Development, 11*, 77–92.

Ehrhardt, A. A., & Meyer-Bahlburg, H. F. L. (1981). Effects of prenatal sex hormones on gender-related behavior. *Science, 211*, 1312–1318.

Ehri, L. C., & Wilce, L. S. (1987a). Cipher versus cue reading: An experiment in decoding acquisition. *Journal of Educational Psychology, 79*, 3–13.

Ehri, L. C., & Wilce, L. S. (1987b). Does learning to spell help beginners learn to read words? *Reading Research Quarterly, 22*, 47–65.

Eisen, L. N., Field, T. M., Bandstra, E. S., Roberts, J. P., Morrow, C., Larson, S. K., & Steele, B. M. (1991). Perinatal cocaine effects on neonatal stress behavior and performance on the Brazelton scale. *Pediatrics, 88,* 477–480.

Eisenberg, N., Murray, E., & Hite, T. (1982). Children's reasoning regarding sex-typed toy choices. *Child Development, 53,* 81–86.

Elkind, D. (1970, April 5). Erik Erikson's eight ages of man. *New York Times Magazine,* pp. 21–34.

Elkind, D. (1976). *Child development and education: A Piagetian perspective.* New York: Oxford University Press.

Elkins, T. E., Stovall, T. G., Wilroy, S., & Dacus, J. V. (1986). Attitudes of mothers of children with Down Syndrome concerning amniocentesis, abortion, and prenatal genetic counseling techniques. *Obstetrics and Gynecology 68,* 181–184.

Elkins, V. H. (1976). *The rights of the pregnant parent.* New York: Schocken Books.

Emde, R. N., Plomin, R., Robinson, J., Corley, R., DeFries, J., Fulker, D. W., Reznick, J. S., Campos, J., Kagan, J., & Zahn-Waxler, C. (1992). Temperament, emotion, and cognition at fourteen months: The MacArthur longitudinal twin study. *Child Development, 63,* 1437–1455.

Endres, J. B., & Rockwell, R. E. (1993). *Food, nutrition, and the young child* (4th ed.). New York: Merrill/Macmillan.

Erikson, E. H. (1963). *Childhood and society* (2nd ed.). New York: W. W. Norton.

Erikson, E. H. (1977). *Toys and reasons: Stages in the ritualization of experience.* New York: W. W. Norton.

Erikson, E. H. (1982). *The life cycle completed.* New York: W. W. Norton.

Eron, L. D. (1982a). The consistency of aggressive behavior across time and situations. In *Consistency of aggression and its correlates over twenty years.* Symposium presented at the meeting of the American Psychological Association, Anaheim, California.

Eron, L. D. (1982b). Parent-child interaction, television violence, and aggression of children. *American Psychologist, 37,* 197–211.

Etaugh, C., Grinnell, K., & Etaugh, A. (1989). Development of gender labeling: Effect of age of pictured children. *Sex Roles, 21,* 769–773.

Etaugh, C., & Liss, M. B. (1992). Home, school, and playroom: Training grounds for adult gender roles. *Sex Roles, 26,* 129–147.

Fagot, B. I. (1982). Sex role development. In R. Vasta (Ed.), *Strategies and techniques of child study.* New York: Academic Press.

Fagot, B. I., & Kronsberg, S. J. (1982). Sex differences: Biological and social factors influencing the behavior of young boys and girls. In S. G. Moore & C. R. Cooper, (Eds.), *The young child: Reviews of research* (Vol. 3). Washington, DC: National Association for the Education of Young Children.

Fajardo, B. F., Browning, M., Fisher, D., & Paton, J. (1992). Early state organization and follow-up over one year. *Developmental and Behavioral Pediatrics, 13,* 83–88.

Fajardo, B. F., & Freedman, D. G. (1981). Maternal rhythmicity in three American cultures. In T. M. Field, A. M. Sostek, P. Vietze, & P. H. Leiderman (Eds.), *Culture and early interactions.* Hillsdale, NJ: Lawrence Erlbaum.

Falbo, T. (1982). Only children in America. In M. E. Lamb & B. Sutton-Smith (Eds.), *Sibling relationships: Their nature and significance across the lifespan.* Hillsdale, NJ: Lawrence Erlbaum.

Falbo, T., & Poston, D. L. (1993). The academic, personality, and physical outcomes of only children in China. *Child Development, 64,* 18–35.

Fantz, R. (1961). The origin of form perception. *Scientific American, 204,* 66–72.

Farel, A. M. (1980). Effects of preferred maternal roles, maternal employment, and sociodemographic status on school adjustment and competence. *Child Development, 51,* 1179–1186.

Feeny, S., Christensen, D., & Moravcik, E. (1991). *Who am I in the lives of children?* New York: Merrill/Macmillan.

Fein, G. G. (1981). Pretend play in childhood: An integrative review. *Child Development, 52,* 1095–1118.

Feingold, B. F. (1974). *Why your child is hyperactive.* New York: Random House.

Feiring, C., & Lewis, M. (1981). Middle class differences in the mother–child interaction and the child's cognitive development. In T. M. Field, A. M. Sostek, P. Vietze, & P. H. Leiderman (Eds.), *Culture and early interactions.* Hillsdale, NJ: Lawrence Erlbaum.

Fernald, A., & Morikawa, H. (1993). Common themes and cultural variations in Japanese and American mother's speech to infants. *Child Development, 64,* 637–656.

Field, T., & Goldson, E. (1984). Pacifying effects of non-nutritive sucking on term and preterm neonates during heelstick procedures. *Pediatrics, 74,* 1012–1015.

Field, T. M., & Widmayer, S. M. (1981). Mother–infant interactions among lower SES Black, Cuban, Puerto Rican and South American immigrants. In T. M. Field, A. M. Sostek, P. Vietze, & P. H. Leiderman (Eds.), *Culture and early interactions.* Hillsdale, NJ: Lawrence Erlbaum.

Finnegan, L. P. (1984). Neonatal abstinence. In M. Nelson (Ed.), *Current therapy in neonatal and perinatal medicine.* St. Louis: C. V. Mosby.

Fischer, K. W. (1987). Relations between brain and cognitive development. *Child Development, 58,* 623–632.

Fish, M., Stifter, C. A., & Belsky, J. (1991). Conditions of continuity and discontinuity in infant negative emotionality: Newborn to five months. *Child Development, 62,* 1525–1537.

Flavell, J. H., Lindberg, N. A., Green, F. L., & Flavell, E. R. (1992). The development of children's understanding of the appearance-reality distinction between how people look and what they are really like. *Merrill-Palmer Quarterly, 38,* 513–524.

Fonagy, P., Steele, H., & Steele, M. (1991). Maternal representations of attachment during pregnancy predict the organization of infant–mother attachment at one year of age. *Child Development, 62,* 891–905.

Food and Nutrition Board. (1992). *Nutrition during pregnancy.* Washington, DC: National Academy Press.

Fowler, W. (1980). *Curriculum and assessment guides for infant and child care.* Boston: Allyn and Bacon.

Fraiberg, S. (1977). *Every child's birthright: In defense of mothering.* New York: Basic Books.

Franz, W. K. (1981). Fetal development: A novel application of Piaget's theory of cognitive development. In T. W. Hilgers, D. J. Horan, & D. Mall, (Eds.), *New perspectives on human abortion.* Fredrick, MD: Alltheia Books, University Publications of America.

Freeman, N. H., Lewis, C., & Doherty, M. J. (1991). Preschoolers' grasp of a desire for knowledge in false-belief prediction: Practical intelligence and verbal report. *British Journal of Developmental Psychology, 9,* 139–157.

Freund, L. S., Baker, L., & Sonnenschein, S. (1990). Developmental changes in strategic approaches to classification. *Journal of Experimental Child Psychology, 49,* 343–362.

Friedman, W. J. (1990). Children's representations of the pattern of daily activities. *Child Development, 61,* 1399–1412.

Friedrich, L. K., & Stein, A. H. (1973). Aggressive and prosocial television programs and the natural behavior of preschool children. *Monographs of the Society for Research in Child Development, 38*(4, Serial No. 151).

Fullard, W., McDevitt, S. C., & Carey, W. B. (1978). *Toddler Temperament Scale.* (Available from W. Fullard, Department of Educational Psychology, Temple University, Philadelphia, PA 19122).

Fullard, W., McDevitt, S. C., & Carey, W. B. (1984). Assessing temperament in one- to three-year-old children. *Journal of Pediatric Psychiatry, 9,* 205–217.

Furth, H. G. (1970). *Piaget for teachers.* Englewood Cliffs, NJ: Prentice Hall.

Gabbard, C. (1992). *Lifelong motor development.* Dubuque, IA: William C. Brown.

Galambos, S. J., & Goldin-Meadow, S. (1990). The effects of learning two languages on levels of metalinguistic awareness. *Cognition, 34,* 1–56.

Galinsky, E. (1981). *Between generations: The six stages of parenthood.* New York: Times Books.

Galinsky, E. (1990). Government and child care. *Young Children, 45,* 2–3, 76–77.

Gallahue, D. L. (1989). *Understanding motor development: Infants, children, adolescents.* Indianapolis, IN: Benchmark Press.

Ganz, M. (1983, January 30). Retarded boy's right to live: Who decides? (San Francisco) *Sunday Examiner and Chronicle,* pp. A1, A6.

Gardner, E. J. (1983). *Human heredity.* New York: John Wiley & Sons.

Garmezy, N. (1983). Stressors of childhood. In N. Garmezy & M. Rutter (Eds.), *Stress, coping, and development in children.* New York: McGraw-Hill.

Garvey, C. (1977). *Play.* Cambridge, MA: Harvard University Press.

Garvey, C. (1984). *Children's talk.* Cambridge, MA: Harvard University Press.

Gelles, R. J. (1982). Problems in defining and labeling child abuse. In R. H. Starr, (Ed.), *Child abuse prediction: Policy implications.* Cambridge, MA: Harper & Row.

Gentner, D. (1982). Why nouns are learned before verbs: Linguistic relativity vs. natural partitioning. In S. Kuczaj (Ed.), *Language development.* Vol. 2. *Language, thought, and culture.* Hillsdale, NJ: Lawrence Erlbaum.

George, G., & Main, M. (1979). Social interactions of young abused children: Approach, avoidance, and aggression. *Child Development, 50,* 306–518.

Gesell, A., & Ilg, F. G. (1949). *Child development: An introduction to the study of human growth.* New York: Harper.

Gibson, E. J., & Levin, L. (1975). *The psychology of reading.* Cambridge, MA: MIT Press.

Gil, D. G. (1973). *Violence against children: Physical child abuse in the United States.* Cambridge, MA: Harvard University Press.

Gilligan, C. (1982). *In a different voice: Psychological theory and women's development.* Cambridge, MA: Harvard University Press.

Gilliom, B. C. (1970). *Basic movement education for children: Rationale and teaching units.* Reading, MA: Addison-Wesley.

Ginott, H. (1965). *Between parent and child.* New York: Macmillan.

Ginsburg, H., & Opper, S. (1988). *Piaget's theory of intellectual development* (3rd ed.). Englewood Cliffs, NJ: Prentice Hall.

Ginsburg, H. J., & Miller, S. M. (1982). Sex differences in children's risk-taking behavior. *Child Development, 53,* 426–428.

Gleitman, L. R., & Wanner, E. (1982). Language acquisition: The state of the state of the art. In E. Wanner & L. R. Gleitman (Eds.), *Language acquisition: The state of the art.* Cambridge: Cambridge University Press.

Glover, M. E., Preminger, J. L., & Sanford, A. R. (1978). *The early learning accomplishment profile for developmentally young children, birth to 36 months.* Winston-Salem, NC: Kaplan Press.

Goldberg, S., & Divitto, B. A. (1983). *Born too soon: Preterm birth and early development.* San Francisco: W. H. Freeman.

Goldfield, B. A. (1993). Noun bias in maternal speech to one-year-olds. *Journal of Child Language, 20,* 85–99.

Goldman, R. J., & Goldman, J. D. G. (1982). How children perceive the origin of babies and the roles of mothers and fathers in procreation: A cross-national study. *Child Development, 53,* 491–504.

Goldsmith, R. H. (1980). *Nutrition and learning.* Bloomington, IN: Phi Delta Kappa Educational Foundation.

Gonzalez-Mena, J. (1993). *The child in the family and the community.* New York: Merrill/Macmillan.

Gordon, J. W., & Ruddle, F. H. (1981). Mammalian gonadal determination and gametogenesis. *Science, 211,* 1265–1272.

Gordon, S., & Dickman, I. R. (1981). *Sex education: The parents' role.* New York: Public Affairs Pamphlets (No. 549).

Gordon, T. (1975). *P.E.T.: Parent effectiveness training.* New York: Wyden.

Gottman, J. M., & Parkhurst, J. T. (1980). A developmental theory of friendship and acquaintanceship processes. In W. A. Collins

(Ed.), *Development of cognition, affect, and social relations* (Minnesota Symposium on Child Psychology, Vol. 13). Hillsdale, NJ: Lawrence Erlbaum.

Gould, J. B., & LeRoy, S. (1988). Socioeconomic status and low birth weight: A racial comparison. *Pediatrics, 82,* 896–904.

Gouze, K. (1979) Does aggressive television affect all children the same way? *Early Report, 6.*

Grace, C., & Shores, E. F. (1991). *The portfolio and its use: Developmentally appropriate assessment of young children.* Little Rock, AK: Southern Association of Children Under Six.

Graven, S. N., Bowen, F. W., Brooten, D., Eaton, A., Graven, M. N., Hack, M., Hall, L. A., Hansen, N., Hurt, H., Kavalhuna, R., Little, G. A., Mahan, C., Morrow, G., Oehler, J. M., Poland, R., Ram, B., Sauve, R., Taylor, P. M., Ward, S. E., & Sommers, J. G. (1992). The high-risk infant environment. Part 2. The role of caregiving and the social environment. *Journal of Perinatology, 12,* 267–275.

Gray, D. B., & Yaffe, S. J. (1986). Prenatal drugs and learning disabilities. In M. Lewis (Ed.), *Learning disabilities and prenatal risk.* Chicago: University of Illinois Press.

Greenberg, B. S., Abelman, R., & Cohen, A. (1990). Telling children not to watch television. In R. J. Kinkel (Ed.), *Television and violence: An overview.* Detroit, MI: Mental Health Association of Michigan.

Greenberg, B. S., Ericson, P. M., & Vlahos, M. (1972). Children's television behavior as perceived by mother and child. In E. A. Rubinstein, G. A. Comstock, & J. P. Murray (Eds.), *Television and social behavior.* Vol. 4. *Television in day-to-day life.* Washington, DC: U.S. Government Printing Office.

Greenberg, M., & Morris, N. (1974). Engrossment: The newborn's impact upon the father. *American Journal of Orthopsychiatry, 44,* 520–531.

Green-McGowan, K. (1985). Community management of the profoundly handicapped. In J. Bopp (Ed.), *Human life and health care ethics.* Frederick, MD: University Publications of America.

Greenough, W. T., Black, J. E., & Wallace, C. S. (1987). Experience and brain development. *Child Development, 58,* 539–559.

Greenspan, S., & Greenspan, N. T. (1986). *First feelings.* New York: Penguin Books.

Greenstein, T. N. (1993). Maternal employment and child behavioral outcomes. *Journal of Family Issues, 14,* 323–354.

Grogaard, M. B., Lindstrom, D. P., Parker, R. A., Culley, B., & Stahlman, M. (1990). Increased survival rate in very low birth weight infants (1500 grams or less): No association with increased incidence of handicaps. *Journal of Pediatrics, 117,* 139–146.

Grusec, J. E. (1982). Prosocial behavior and self-control. In R. Vasta (Ed.), *Strategies and techniques of child study.* New York: Academic Press.

Gustafson, G. E., & Harris, K. L. (1990). Women's responses to young infants' cries. *Developmental Psychology, 26,* 144–152.

Haight, W., & Miller, P. J. (1992). The development of everyday pretend play: A longitudinal study of mothers' participation. *Merrill-Palmer Quarterly, 38,* 331–349.

Hakuta, K. (1988). Why bilinguals? In F. S. Kessel (Ed.), *The development of language and language researchers: Essays in honor of Roger Brown.* Hillsdale, NJ: Lawrence Erlbaum.

Harding, C. G. (1983). Setting the stage for language acquisition: Communication development in the first year. In R. M. Golinkoff (Ed.), *The transition from prelinguistic to linguistic communication.* Hillsdale, NJ: Lawrence Erlbaum.

Harlow, H. F. (1961). The development of affectional patterns in infant monkeys. In B. M. Foss (Ed.), *Determinants of infant behavior* (Vol. 1). London: Methuen.

Harlow, H. F., & Zimmerman, R. R. (1959). Affectual responses in the infant monkey. *Science, 130,* 421–432.

Harris, M. B., Simons, C. J. R., Ritchie, S. K., Mullett, M. D., & Myerberg, D. Z. (1990). Joint range of motion development in premature infants. *Pediatric Physical Therapy, 2* 185–191.

Hart, B. (1991). Input frequency and children's first words. *First Language, 11,* 289–300.

Harter, S. (1982). The perceived competence scale for children. *Child Development, 53,* 87–97.

Harter, S. (1985). *Self-perception profile for children.* Denver, CO: Department of Psychology, University of Denver.

Harwood, R. L. (1992). The influence of culturally derived values on Anglo and Puerto Rican mothers' perceptions of attachment behavior. *Child Development, 63,* 822–839.

Haseltine, F. P., & Ohno, S. (1981). Mechanisms of gonadal differentiation. *Science, 211,* 1272–1278.

Haswell, K. L., Hock, E., & Wenar, C. (1982). Techniques for dealing with oppositional behavior in preschool children. *Young Children, 37,* 13–18.

Haywood, K. M. (1986). *Life span motor development.* Champaign, IL: Human Kinetics Publishers.

Heber, R. (1968). *Rehabilitation of families at risk for mental retardation.* Madison, WI: University of Wisconsin Regional Rehabilitation Center.

Heins, M. (1984). The "battered child" revisited. *Journal of the American Medical Association, 251,* 3295–3298.

Helfer, R. (1982). The relationship between lack of bonding and child abuse and neglect. In M. H. Klaus, T. Leger, & M. A. Trause (Eds.), *Maternal attachment and mothering disorders: A round table* (2nd ed.). Skillman, NJ: Johnson & Johnson.

Henderson, L. W. (1991). *Parental involvement in the developmental screening of young children: A multiple risk perspective.* Doctoral dissertation, University of Michigan, Ann Arbor.

Hendrick, J. (1990). *Total learning: Developmental curriculum for the young child* (3rd ed.). New York: Merrill/Macmillan.

Hendrick, J. (1992). *The whole child: Developmental education for the early years* (5th ed.). New York: Merrill/Macmillan.

Hildebrand, V. (1990). *Guiding young children.* (5th ed). New York: Macmillan.

Hirshberg, L. (1990). When infants look to their parents. II. Twelve-month-olds' response to conflicting parental emotional signals. *Child Development, 61,* 1187–1191.

Hirshberg, L. M., & Svejda, M. (1990). When infants look to their parents. I. Infants' social referencing of mothers compared to fathers. *Child Development, 61,* 1175–1186.

Hisrich, S., & Franz, W. (1980). *A study of the cognitive processes used by the preschool child in predicting the emotional responses of others.* Presented at the Southeastern Conference on Human Development, Alexandria, Virginia.

Hofferth, S. L. (1989). What is the demand for and supply of child care in the United States? *Young Children, 44,* 28–33.

Hoff-Ginsberg, E. (1990). Maternal speech and the child's development of syntax: A further look. *Journal of Child Language, 17,* 85–99.

Hoff-Ginsberg, E., & Krueger, W. M. (1991). Older siblings as conversational partners. *Merrill-Palmer Quarterly, 37,* 465–482.

Hoffman, M. (1991). How parents make their mark on genes. *Science, 252,* 1250–1251.

Hoffman-Plotkin, D., & Twentyman, C. T. (1984). Multimodal assessment of behavioral and cognitive deficits in abused and neglected preschoolers. *Child Development, 55,* 794–802.

Holdaway, D. (1979). *The foundations of literacy.* Sydney: Ashton Scholastic.

Holden, C. (1980). Identical twins reared apart. *Science, 207,* 1323–1328.

Holditch-Davis, D. (1990). The development of sleeping and waking states in high-risk preterm infants. *Infant Behavior and Development, 13,* 513–531.

Holmes, D. L., Reich, J. N., & Pasternak, J. F. (1984). *The development of infants born at risk.* Hillsdale, NJ: Lawrence Erlbaum.

Honig, A. S. (1983, May). Research in review: Television and young children. *Young Children, 38,* 63–76.

Honzik, M. (1983). Value and limitations of infant tests: An overview. In M. Lewis (Ed.), *Origins of intelligence: Infancy and early childhood.* New York: Plenum.

Hood, L., & Bloom, L. (1979). What, when, and how about why: A longitudinal study of early expressions of causality. *Monographs of the Society for Research in Child Development, 44*(6, Serial No. 181).

Hooker, D. (1939). *A preliminary atlas of early human fetal activity.* Ladd Laboratory of the Department of Anatomy, University of Pittsburgh School of Medicine. Self-published.

Hoot, J. (1984). Caution: A decrease in play may be hazardous to children's school success. *Texas Child Care Quarterly, 8,* 10–13.

Hostler, S. L. (1991). Family-centered care. In J. M. Blackman (Ed.), *The Pediatric Clinics of North America, 38,* 15–60.

Hoy, E. A., Sykes, D. H., Bill, J. M., Halliday, H. L., McClure, B. G., & Reid, M. M. (1992). The social competence of very-low-birthweight children: Teacher, peer, and self-perceptions. *Journal of Abnormal Child Psychology, 20,* 123–150.

Hubbell, R. (1983). *A review of Head Start research since 1970.* Washington, DC: U.S. Government Printing Office.

Huesmann, L. R., & Eron, L. D. (1984). Cognitive processes and the persistence of aggressive behavior. *Aggressive Behavior, 10,* 243–251.

Huston, A. (1985). Television and human behavior. Paper presented at the Science and Social Policy Seminar, Federation of Behavioral, Psychological and Cognitive Sciences, Washington, DC.

Hymes, D. (1980). *Language in education: Ethnolinguistic essays.* Washington, DC: Center for Applied Linguistics.

Illuzzi, L. (1991). Preschool aquatic program: An analysis of aquatic motor patterns. *National Aquatic Journal, 7,* 3–6.

Interagency Committee on Learning Disabilities. (1987). *Learning disabilities: A report to the U.S. Congress.* Washington, DC: U.S. Government Printing Office.

Isabella, R. A. (1993). Origins of attachment: Maternal interactive behavior across the first year. *Child Development, 64,* 605–621.

Isabella, R. A., & Belsky, J. (1991). Interactional synchrony and the origins of infant–mother attachment: A replication study. *Child Development, 62,* 373–384.

Isabella, R. A., Belsky, J., & von Eye, A. (1989). The origins of infant–mother attachment: An examination of interactional synchrony during the infant's first year. *Developmental Psychology, 25,* 12–21.

Isenberg, J. P., & Jalongo, M. R. (1993). *Creative expression and play in the early childhood curriculum.* New York: Macmillan.

Izard, C. E., Haynes, O. M., Chisholm, G., & Baak, K. (1991). Emotional determinants of infant–mother attachment. *Child Development, 62,* 906–917.

Jablow, M. M. (1982). *Cara: Growing with a retarded child.* Philadelphia: Temple University Press.

James, W. (1890). *The principles of psychology.* New York: Holt.

Janis, I. L., & Leventhal, H. (1968). Human reactions to stress. In E. F. Borgatta & W. W. Lambert (Eds.), *Handbook of personality theory and research.* Chicago: Rand McNally.

Jensen, A. R. (1969). How much can we boost I. Q. and scholastic achievement? *Harvard Educational Review, 39,* 1–123.

Jensen, L. C., & Wells, M. G. (1979). *Feelings: Helping children understand emotions.* Provo, UT: Brigham Young University Press.

Johnson, C. M. (1991). Infant and toddler sleep: A telephone survey of parents in one community. *Journal of Developmental and Behavioral Pediatrics, 12,* 108–114.

Johnson, E. P., & Peckover, R. B. (1988). The effects of play period duration on children's play patterns. *Journal of Research in Childhood Education, 3,* 123–131.

Johnson, J. E., Ershler, J., & Lawton, J. T. (1982). Intellective correlates of preschoolers' spontaneous play. *Journal of General Psychology, 106,* 115–122.

Johnson, M. H., Dziurawiec, S., Ellis, H., & Morton, J. (1991). Newborns' preferential tracking of face-like stimuli and its subsequent decline. *Cognition, 40,* 1–19.

Johnson, S. R., Winkleby, M. A., Boyce, W. T., McLaughlin, R., Broadwin, R., & Goldman, L. (1992). The association between hemoglobin and behavior problems in a sample of low-income Hispanic preschool children. *Developmental and Behavioral Pediatrics, 13,* 209–214.

Jose, P. E. (1990). Just-world reasoning in children's immanent justice judgements. *Child Development, 61,* 1024–1033.

Jusczyk, P. W., Bertoncini, J., Bijeljac-Babac, R., Kennedy, L. J., & Mehler, J. (1990). The role of attention in speech perception by young infants. *Cognitive Development, 5,* 265–286.

Kaler, S. R., & Kopp, C. B. (1991). Compliance and comprehension in very young toddlers. *Child Development, 61,* 1997–2003.

Kamii, C. (Ed.). (1990). *Achievement testing in the early grades.* Washington, DC: National Association for the Education of Young Children.

Kamii, C., & DeVries, R. (1978). *Physical knowledge in preschool education: Implications of Piaget's theory.* Englewood Cliffs, NJ: Prentice Hall.

Kamii, C., & DeVries, R. (1980). *Group games in early education: Implications of Piaget's theory.* Washington, DC: National Association for the Education of Young Children.

Kaplan, L. I. (1978). *Oneness and separateness: From infant to individual.* New York: Simon & Schuster.

Karbon, M., Fabes, R. A., Carlo, G., & Martin, C. L. (1992). Preschoolers' beliefs about sex and age differences in emotionality. *Sex Roles, 27,* 377–390.

Karmel, M. (1959). *Thank you Dr. Lamaze: Painless childbirth.* Philadelphia: J. B. Lippincott.

Karmiloff-Smith, A. (1979). *A functional approach to child language: A study of determiners and reference.* London: Cambridge University Press.

Katz, P. A. (1982). Development of children's racial awareness and intergroup attitudes. In L. G. Katz (Ed.), *Current topics in early childhood education* (Vol. 4). Norwood, NJ: Ablex.

Keeshan, B. (1983). Families and television. *Young Children, 38,* 46–55.

Keller, A., Ford, L. H., & Meachum, J. A. (1978). Dimensions of self-concept in preschool children. *Developmental Psychology, 14,* 483–489.

Kelley, S. J., Walsh, J. H., & Thompson, K. (1991). Birth outcomes, health problems and neglect with prenatal exposure to cocaine. *Pediatric Nursing, 17,* 130–136.

Kellogg, R. (1969). *Analyzing children's art.* Palo Alto, CA: National Press Books.

Kempe, C. H., Silverman, F. N., Steele, B. F., Droegemueller, W., & Silver, H. K. (1962). The battered-child syndrome. *Journal of the American Medical Association, 181,* 17–24.

Kennell, J. H., & Klaus, M. H. (1971). Care of the mother of the high risk infant. *Clinical Obstetrics and Gynecology, 14,* 926–954.

Kennell, J. H., Trause, M. A., & Klaus, M. H. (1975). *In parent-infant interaction.* Ciba Foundation Symposium 33. Amsterdam: Elsevier Publishing.

Kephart, N. C. (1971). *The slow learner in the classroom* (2nd ed). Columbus, OH: Merrill.

Killalea Associates. (1980). *State, regional, and national summaries of data from the 1978 civil rights survey of elementary and secondary schools.* Prepared for the U.S. Office of Civil Rights. Alexandria, VA: Killalea Associates.

Klaus, M. H. (1987). The frequency of suckling: A neglected but essential ingredient of breastfeeding. *Obstetrics and Gynecology Clinics of North America, 14,* 623–633.

Klaus, M. H., Jerauld, R., Kreger, N., McAlpine, W., Steffa, M., & Kennell, J. H. (1972). Maternal attachment: Importance of the first postpartum days. *New England Journal of Medicine, 286,* 460–463.

Klaus, M. H., & Kennell, J. H. (1976). *Maternal–infant bonding.* St. Louis: C. V. Mosby.

Klaus, M. H., & Kennell, J. H. (1982). *Parent–infant bonding* (2nd ed.). St. Louis: C. V. Mosby.

Klaus, M. H., Kennell, J., Berkowitz, G., & Klaus, P. (1992). Maternal assistance and support in labor: Father, nurse, midwife, or doula? *Clinical Consultations in Obstetrics and Gynecology, 4,* 211–217.

Klaus, M. H., Leger, T., & Trause, M. A. (Eds.). (1982). *Maternal attachment and mothering disorders: A round table* (2nd ed.). Skillman, NJ: Johnson & Johnson.

Klaus, M. H., & Robertson, M. O. (Eds.). (1982). *Birth, interaction, and attachment: A round table.* Skillman, NJ: Johnson & Johnson.

Kohlberg, L. (1966). A cognitive-developmental analysis of children's sex-role concepts and attitudes. In E. Maccoby (Ed.), *The development of sex differences.* Stanford, CA: Stanford University Press.

Kohlberg, L. (1981). *Essays on moral development.* Vol. 1. *The philosophy of moral development: Moral stages and the idea of justice.* New York: Harper & Row.

Kolata, G. B. (1979). Sex hormones and brain development. *Science 205,* 985–987.

Korzenny, F., Greenberg, B. S., & Atkin, C. K. (1979). Styles of parental disciplinary practices as a mediator of children's learning from antisocial television portrayals. In D. Nimmo (Ed.), *Communication Yearbook 3.* New Brunswick, NJ: Transaction Books.

Kuhl, P. K. (1980). Perceptual constancy for speech-sound categories in early infancy. In G. H. Yeni-Komshian, J. F. Kavanagh, & C. A. Ferguson (Eds.), *Child phonology.* Vol. 2. *Perception.* New York: Academic Press.

Kuhl, P. K. (1985). Categorization of speech by infants. In J. Mehler & R. Fox (Eds.), *Neonate cognition: Beyond the blooming buzzing confusion.* Hillsdale, NJ: Lawrence Erlbaum.

Kunkel, D. (1990). Child and family television regulatory policy. In J. Bryant (Ed.), *Television and the American family.* Hillsdale, NJ: Lawrence Erlbaum.

Labinowicz, E. (1980). *The Piaget primer: Thinking, learning, teaching.* Menlo Park, CA: Addison-Wesley.

Lacey, J. I., Kagan, J., Lacey, B. C., & Moss, H. (1962). The visceral level: Situational determinants and behavioral correlates of auto-

nomic response patterns. In P. J. Knapp (Ed.), *Expression of emotions in man.* New York: International University Press.

Laegreid, L., Hagberg, G., & Lundberg, A. (1990). The effect of benzodiazepines on the fetus and the newborn. *Neuropediatrics, 23,* 18–23.

Lamb, M. E. (1981). The development of social expectations in the first year of life. In M. E. Lamb & L. R. Sherrod (Eds.), *Infant social cognition: Empirical and theoretical considerations.* Hillsdale, NJ: Lawrence Erlbaum.

Lamb, M. E. (1982). Maternal employment and child development: A review. In M. E. Lamb (Ed.), *Nontraditional families: Parenting and child development.* Hillsdale, NJ: Lawrence Erlbaum.

Lamb, M. E., Hopps, K., & Elster, A. B. (1987). Strange situation behavior of infants with adolescent mothers. *Infant Behavior and Development, 10,* 39–48.

Lamb, M. E., & Sutton-Smith, B. (Eds.). (1982). *Sibling relationships: Their nature and significance across the lifespan.* Hillsdale, NJ: Lawrence Erlbaum.

Lamb, M. E., Thompson, R. A., & Frodi, A. M. (1982). Early social development. In R. Vasta (Ed.), *Strategies and techniques of child study.* New York: Academic Press.

Lambert, W. E. (1975). Culture and language as factors in learning and education. In A. Wolfgang (Ed.), *Education of immigrant students.* Toronto: Ontario Institute for Studies in Education.

Lamme, L. L. (1984). *Growing up writing.* Washington, DC: Acropolis Books.

Langendorfer, S. (1989). Aquatic experiences for young children: Evaluating risks and benefits. *Pediatric Exercise Science, 1,* 230–243.

Lanning, K. V., & Burgess, A. W. (1989). Child pornography and sex rings. In D. Zillmann & J. Bryant (Eds.), *Pornography: Research advances & policy considerations.* Hillsdale, NJ: Lawrence Erlbaum.

Larrick, N. (1965, September). The all-white world of children's books. *Saturday Review,* pp. 63–65, 84–85.

Larsen, J. M., Draper, T. W., & Hite, S. J. (1984). Preschool does make a difference for educationally advantaged children: Longitudinal student update. Paper presented at the conference of the National Association for the Education of Young Children, Los Angeles.

Lay, K., Waters, E., & Park, K. A. (1989). Maternal responsiveness and child compliance: The role of mood as a mediator. *Child Development, 60,* 1405–1411.

Lazar, I. (1983). Discussion and implications of findings. In Consortium for Longitudinal Studies, *As the twig is bent . . .Lasting effects of preschool programs.* Hillsdale, NJ: Lawrence Erlbaum.

Lazar, I., & Darlington, R. (1982). Lasting effects of early education: A report from the Consortium for Longitudinal Studies. *Monographs of the Society for Research in Child Development, 47*(2–3, Serial No. 195).

Leaper, C. (1991). Influence and involvement in children's discourse: Age, gender, and partner effects. *Child Development, 62,* 797–811.

Leboyer, F. (1975). *Birth without violence.* New York: Knopf.

Lecuyer, R. (1989). Habituation and attention, novelty and cognition: Where is the continuity? *Human Development, 32,* 148–157.

Legerstee, M. (1990). Infants use multimodal information to imitate speech sounds. *Infant Behavior and Development, 13,* 343–354.

Leifer, A. D., Leiderman, P. H., Barnett, C. R., & Williams, J. A. (1972). Effects of mother–infant separation on maternal attachment behavior. *Child Development, 43,* 1303–1318.

Lerner, J., Mardell-Czudnowski, C., & Goldenberg, D. (1981). *Special education for the early childhood years.* Englewood Cliffs, NJ: Prentice Hall.

Leslie, L. A., Anderson, E. A., & Branson, M. P. (1991). Responsibility for children: The role of gender and employment. *Journal of Family Issues, 12,* 197–210.

Lester, B. M., & Brazelton, T. B. (1982). Cross-cultural assessment of neonatal behavior. In D. A. Wagner & H. W. Stevenson (Eds.), *Cul-*

tural perspectives on child development. San Francisco: W. H. Freeman.

Lester, B. M., Corwin, M. J., Sepkoski, C., Seifer, R., Peucker, M., McLaughlin, S., & Golub, H. L. (1991). Neurobehavioral syndromes in cocaine-exposed newborn infants. *Child Development, 62,* 694–705.

Levy, J. (1973). *The baby exercise book for the first fifteen months.* New York: Pantheon.

Lewis, C., & Osborne, A. (1990). Three-year-olds' problems with false belief: Conceptual deficit or linguistic artifact? *Child Development, 61,* 1514–1519.

Lewis, M. (1983). The nature of intelligence: Science or bias. In M. Lewis (Ed.), *Origins of intelligence: Infancy and early childhood.* New York: Plenum.

Lewis, M., & Brooks-Gunn, J. (1979). *Social cognition and the acquisition of self.* New York: Plenum.

Lewis, M., & Brooks-Gunn, J. (1981). Visual attention at three months as a predictor of cognitive functioning at two years of age. *Intelligence, 5,* 131–140.

Lewis, M., Wilson, C. D., Ban, P., & Baumel, M. H. (1970). An exploratory study of resting cardiac rate and variability from the last trimester of prenatal life through the first year of postnatal life. *Child Development, 41,* 799–811.

Lipman, M. (1981). *Pixie.* Montclair, NJ: First Mountain Foundation.

Lipman, M. (1982). *Kio and Gus.* Montclair, NJ: First Mountain Foundation.

Lipsitt, L. P., Engen, T., & Kaye, H. (1963). Developmental changes in the olfactory threshold of the neonate. *Child Development, 34,* 371–376.

Lloyd-Still, J. (1976). *Malnutrition and intellectual development.* Lancaster, England: M.T.P. Press.

Locke, J. L., & Mather, P. L. (1989). Genetic factors in the ontogeny of spoken language: Evidence from monozygotic and dizygotic twins. *Journal of Child Language, 16,* 553–559.

Lollis, S. P. (1990). Effects of maternal behavior on toddler behavior during separation. *Child Development, 61,* 99–103.

Londerville, S., & Main, M. (1981). Security of attachment, compliance and maternal training methods in the second year of life. *Developmental Psychology, 17,* 289–299.

Lozoff, B. (1989). Nutrition and behavior. *American Psychologist 44,* 231–236.

Lynn, R. (1989). A nutrition theory of the secular increases in intelligence: Positive correlations between height, head size and I.Q. *British Journal of Educational Psychology, 59,* 372–377.

Macario, J. F. (1991). Young children's use of color in classification: Foods and canonically colored objects. *Cognitive Development, 6,* 17–46.

Maccoby, E. E. (1983). Social-emotional development and response to stressors. In N. Garmezy & M. Rutter (Eds.), *Stress, coping, and development in children.* New York: McGraw-Hill.

Macfarlane, A. (1977). *The psychology of childbirth.* Cambridge, MA: Harvard University Press.

MacLusky, N. J., & Naftolin, F. (1981). Sexual differentiation of the central nervous system. *Science, 211,* 1294–1303.

Mahony, D. L., & Mann, V. A. (1992). Using children's humor to clarify the relationship between linguistic awareness and early reading ability. *Cognition, 45,* 163–186.

Mangelsdorf, S., Gunnar, M., Kestenbaum, R., Lang, S., & Andreas, D. (1990). Infant proneness-to-distress, temperament, maternal personality, and mother–infant attachment: Association and goodness of fit. *Child Development, 61,* 820–831.

Mann, V. A. (1993). Phoneme awareness and future reading ability. *Journal of Learning Disabilities, 26,* 259–269.

Marean, G. C., Werner, L. A., & Kuhl, P. K. (1992). Vowel categorization by very young infants. *Developmental Psychology 28,* 396–405.

Marshall, W. L. (1989). Pornography and sex offenders. In D. Zillmann & J. Bryant (Eds.),

Pornography: Research advances & policy considerations. Hillsdale, NJ: Lawrence Erlbaum.

Maslow, A. H. (1968). *Toward a psychology of being.* Princeton, NJ: Van Nostrand.

Maslow, A. H. (1970). *Motivation and personality* (2nd ed.). New York: Harper & Row.

Maxim, G. W. (1990). *The sourcebook.* New York: Merrill/Macmillan.

McCall, R. B., & Carriger, M. S. (1993). Recognition memory performance as predictors of later IQ. *Child Development, 64,* 57–79.

McCall, R. B., Parke, R. D., & Kavanaugh, R. D. (1977). Imitation of live and televised models by children one to three years of age. *Monographs of the Society for Research in Child Development, 42*(5, Serial No. 173).

McCartney, K., Scarr, S., Phillips, D., Grajek, S., & Schwarz, J. C. (1982). Environmental differences among day care centers and their effects on children's development. In E. F. Zigler & E. W. Gordon (Eds.), *Day care: Scientific and social policy issues.* Boston: Auburn House.

McCarton, C., Vaughan, H., & Golden, R. (1988). Can neurobehavioral outcomes be predicted by perinatal variables? In P. M. Vietze & H. G. Vaughan (Eds.), *Early identification of infants with disabilities.* Boston: Allyn and Bacon.

McClearn, G. E. (1970). Genetic influences on behavior and development. In P. H. Mussen (Ed.), *Carmichael's manual of child psychology* (Vol. 1, 3rd ed.). New York: John Wiley & Sons.

McCormick, M. C., Gortmaker, S. L., & Sobol, A. M. (1990). Very low birth weight children: Behavior problems and school difficulty in a national sample. *Journal of Pediatrics, 117,* 687–693.

McDevitt, T. M., Spivey, N., Sheehan, E. P., Lennon, R., & Story, R. (1990). Children's beliefs about listening: Is it enough to be still and quiet? *Child Development, 61,* 713–721.

McEwan, M. H., Dihoff, R. E., & Brosvic, G. M. (1991). Early infant crawling experience is reflected in later motor skill development. *Perceptual and Motor Skills, 72,* 75–79.

McEwen, B. S. (1981). Neural gonadal steroid actions. *Science, 211*, 1303–1312.

McGee, L. M., Lomax, R. G., & Head, M. H. (1988). Young children's written language knowledge: What environmental and functional print reading reveals. *Journal of Reading Behavior, 20*, 99–118.

McGee, L. M., & Richgels, D. J. (1990). *Literacy's beginnings: Supporting young readers and writers.* Needham Heights, MA: Allyn and Bacon.

McGhee, P. E. (1984). Play, incongruity, and humor. In T. D. Yawkey & A. D. Pellegrini (Eds.), *Child's play: Developmental and applied.* Hillsdale, NJ: Lawrence Erlbaum.

McGraw, M. B. (1935). *Growth: A study of Johnny and Jimmy.* New York: Appleton.

McGraw, M. B. (1963). *The neuromuscular maturation of the human infant.* New York: Hafner.

McLane, J. B., & McNamee, G. D. (1991). The beginnings of literacy. *Zero to Three, 12*, 1–8.

McNeese, M. C., & Hebeler, J. R. (1977). The abused child: A clinical approach to identification and management. *Clinical Symposia, 29.* Summit, NJ: CIBA Pharmaceutical.

Mehler, J. (1985). Language related dispositions in early infancy. In J. Mehler & R. Fox (Eds.), *Neonate cognition: Beyond the blooming buzzing confusion.* Hillsdale, NJ: Lawrence Erlbaum.

Meltzoff, A. N., & Moore, M. K. (1985). Cognitive foundations and social functions of imitation and intermodal representations in infancy. In J. Mehler & R. Fox (Eds.), *Neonate cognition: Beyond the blooming buzzing confusion.* Hillsdale, NJ: Lawrence Erlbaum.

Mervis, C. B., & Mervis, C. A. (1982). Leopards are kitty-cats: Object labeling by mothers for their thirteen-month-olds. *Child Development, 53*, 267–273.

Michelsson, K., Rinne, A., & Paajanen, S. (1990). Crying, feeding and sleeping patterns in 1 to 12-month-old infants. *Child Care, Health and Development, 116*, 99–111.

Mizukami, K., Kobayashi, N., Ishi, T., & Iwata, H. (1990). First selective attachment begins in early infancy: A study using thermography. *Infant Behavior and Development, 13*, 257–271.

Mohr, P. J. (1979). Parental guidance of children's viewing of evening television programs. *Journal of Broadcasting, 23*, 213–228.

Molfese, D. L., Burger-Judisch, L. M., & Hans, L. L. (1991). Consonant discrimination by newborn infants: Electrophysiological differences. *Developmental Neuropsychology, 7*, 177–195.

Money, J., & Ehrhardt, A. A. (1972). *Man and Woman, Boy and Girl.* Baltimore: Johns Hopkins University Press.

Moon, C., & Fifer, W. P. (1990). Syllables as signals for 2-day-old infants. *Infant Behavior and Development, 13*, 377–390.

Moore, K. L., & Persand, T. V. H. (1992). *The Developing Human* (5th ed.). Philadelphia: W. B. Saunders.

Moore, T., & Haig, D. (1991). Genomic imprinting in mammalian development: A parental tug-of-war. *Trends in Genetics, 7*, 45.

Morisset, C. E., Barnard, K. E., Greenberg, M. T., Book, C. L., & Spieker, S. J. (1990). Environmental influences on early language development: The context of social risk. *Development and Psychopathology, 2*, 127–149.

Morse, J. M., & Bottorff, J. (1989). Intending to breastfeed and work. *Journal of Obstetric, Gynecologic and Neonatal Nursing, 13*, 493–500.

Myers, B. J. (1982). Early intervention using Brazelton training with middle-class mothers and fathers of newborns. *Child Development, 53*, 462–471.

National Swimming Pool Safety Committee. (1987). *Operation: Water watch fact sheet on child drowning.* Washington, D.C.: United States Consumer Product Safety Commission.

Nelson, K. (1973). Structure and strategy in learning to talk. *Monographs of the Society for Research in Child Development, 38* (Serial No. 149).

Nelson, K. E., Denninger, M. M., Bonvillian, J. D., Kaplan, B. J., & Baker, N. (1984). Maternal input adjustments and non-adjustments as related to children's linguistic advances and to language acquisition theories. In A. D. Pellegrini & T. D. Yawkey (Eds.), *The development of oral and written language in social contexts*. Norwood, NJ: Ablex.

Neuman, S. B., & Roskos, K. (1991). Literacy objects as cultural tools: Effects on children's literacy behaviors in play. *Reading Research Quarterly, 24*, 203–225.

Neumann, C., McDonald, M. A., Sigman, M., & Bwibo, N. (1992). Medical illness in school-age Kenyans in relation to nutrition, cognition, and playground behaviors. *Developmental and Behavioral Pediatrics, 13*, 392–398.

Newman, V., Lyon, R. B., & Anderson, P. O. (1990). Evaluation of prenatal vitamin-mineral supplements. *Clinical Pharmacy, 6*, 770–777.

Newton, N. (1973). Interrelationships between sexual responsiveness, birth, and breast feeding. In J. Zubin & J. Money (Eds.), *Contemporary sexual behavior: Critical issues in the 1970's*. Baltimore: Johns Hopkins University Press.

Nicolson, S., & Shipstead, S. G. (1994). *Through the looking glass: Observations in the early childhood classroom*. New York: Merrill/Macmillan.

Nielsen Report on Television 1989. (1989). Northbrook, IL: A. C. Nielsen.

Nilsson, L., Ingelman-Sundberg, A., & Wirsen, C. (1981). *A child is born*. New York: Dell/Seymour Lawrence.

Nodine, C. F., & Lang, N. J. (1971). The development of visual scanning strategies for differentiating words. *Developmental Psychology, 5*, 221–232.

Nowlis, G. H., & Kessen, W. (1976). Human newborns differentiate differing concentrations of sucrose and glucose. *Science, 191*, 865–866.

O'Brien, W. F. (1984). Mid-trimester genetic amniocenteses: A review of the fetal risks. *Journal of Reproductive Medicine, 29*, 59–63.

O'Connell, J. C. (1983, January). Children of working mothers: What the research tells us. *Young Children, 38*, 62–70.

Oden, S. (1982). Peer relationship development in childhood. In L. G. Katz (Ed.), *Current topics in early childhood education* (Vol. 4). Norwood, NJ: Ablex.

Olson, S. L., Bates, J. E., & Kaskie, B. (1992). Caregiver–infant interaction antecedents of children's school-age cognitive ability. *Merrill-Palmer Quarterly, 38*, 309–330.

Overton, W. F., & Reese, H. W. (1973). Models of development: Methodological implications. In J. R. Nesselroade & H. W. Reese, (Eds.), *Life-span developmental psychology*. New York: Academic Press.

Owens, R. E. (1984). *Language development: An introduction*. New York: Merrill/Macmillan.

Pagioa, L. P., & Hollett, N. (1991). Relations between self-perceived and actual peer acceptance among preschool children. *Perceptual and Motor Skills, 72*, 224–226.

Park, K. A., & Waters, E. (1989). Security of attachment and preschool friendships. *Child Development, 60*, 1076–1081.

Parke, R. D. (1982). Theoretical models of child abuse: Their implications for prediction, prevention, and modification. In R. H. Starr (Ed.), *Child abuse prediction: Policy implications*. Cambridge, MA: Harper & Row.

Parke, R. D., & Collmer, C. (1975). *Child abuse: An interdisciplinary analysis*. Chicago: University of Chicago Press.

Parten, M. (1932–1933). Social participation among preschool children. *Journal of Abnormal and Social Psychology, 27*, 243–269.

Patterson, C. J., Cohn, D. A., & Kao, B. T. (1989). Maternal warmth as a protective factor against risks associated with peer rejection among children. *Development and Psychopathology, 1*, 21–38.

Patton, J. R., Payne, L. S., Kauffman, L. M., Brown, G. B., & Payne, R. A. (1987). *Exceptional children in focus* (4th ed). New York: Merrill/Macmillan.

Pederson, D. R., Moran, G., Sitko, C., Campbell, K., Ghesquire, K., & Acton, H. (1990). Maternal sensitivity and the security of infant–mother attachment: A Q-sort study. *Child Development, 61,* 1974–1983.

Pelham, W. E., Schnedler, R. W., Bologna, N. C., & Contreros, J. A. (1980). Behavioral and stimulant treatment of hyperactive children: A therapy study with methylphenidate probes in a within-subject design. *Journal of Applied Behavior Analysis, 13,* 221–236.

Pellegrini, A. D. (1980). The relationship between kindergarteners' play and achievement in pre-reading, language and writing. *Psychology in the Schools, 17,* 530–535.

Pellegrini, A. D. (1986). Communicating in and about play: The effect of play centers on preschoolers' explicit language. In G. Fein & M. Rivkin (Eds.), *The young child at play: Reviews of research* (Vol. 4). Washington, DC: National Association for the Education of Young Children.

Pemberton, E. F. (1990). Systematic errors in children's drawings. *Cognitive Development, 5,* 395–404.

Pena, S., French, J., & Doerann, J. (1990). Heroic fantasies: A cross-generational comparison of two children's television heroes. *Early Childhood Research Quarterly, 5,* 393–406.

Philosophy for Children. (1984). Upper Montclair, NJ: Institute for Advancement of Philosophy for Children.

Piaget, J. (1960a). *The child's conception of physical causality.* Totowa, NJ: Littlefield, Adams. (Originally published 1927.)

Piaget, J. (1960b). *The child's conception of the world.* Totowa, NJ: Littlefield, Adams. (Originally published 1926.)

Piaget, J. (1962). *Play, dreams, and imitation in childhood.* New York: W. W. Norton. (Originally published 1946.)

Piaget, J. (1963). *The origins of intelligence in children.* New York: W. W. Norton. (Originally published 1952.)

Piaget, J. (1964). *Judgment and reasoning in the child.* Totowa, NJ: Littlefield, Adams. (Originally published 1924.)

Piaget, J. (1970). *Science of education and the psychology of the child.* New York: Orion Press. (Originally published 1969.)

Piaget, J. (1973). *To understand is to invent.* New York: Grossman. (Originally published 1948.)

Piaget, J. (1976). *The psychology of intelligence.* Totowa, NJ: Littlefield, Adams.

Piaget, J., & Inhelder, B. (1956). *The child's conception of space.* London: Routledge & Kegan Paul.

Piaget, J., & Inhelder, B. (1969). *The psychology of the child.* New York: Basic Books.

Pierce, J. W. (1990). The more they ask, the more they remember: Variables related to preschoolers' memory for answers to their own questions. *Child Study Journal, 20,* 279–286.

Pinyerd, B. J., & Zipf, W. B. (1989). Colic: Ideopathic, excessive, infant crying. *Journal of Pediatric Nursing, 4,* 147–154.

Pipes, P. L. (1981). *Nutrition in infancy and childhood* (2nd ed.). St. Louis: C. V. Mosby.

Pless, I. B., Cripps, H. A., Davies, H. M. C., & Wadsworth, M. E. J. (1989). Chronic physical illness in childhood: Psychological and social effects in adolescence and adult life. *Developmental Medicine & Child Neurology, 31,* 746–755.

Plutchik, R. (1980, February). A language for the emotions. *Psychology Today,* 68–78.

Poest, C. A., Williams, J. R., Witt, D. D., & Atwood, M. E. (1989). Physical activity patterns of preschool children. *Early Childhood Research Quarterly, 4,* 367–376.

Pollitt, E., Gorman, K. S., Engle, P. L., Martorell, R., & Rivera, J. (1993). Early supplementary feeding and cognition. *Monographs of the Society for Research in Child Development, 58*(7, Serial No. 235).

Pollitt, E., & Wirtz, S. (1981). Mother–infant feeding interaction and weight gain in the first month of life. *Journal of the American Dietetic Association, 78,* 596–601.

Porter, F., Miller, S. M., & Marshal, R. E. (1987). Local anesthesia for painful procedures in the sick newborn. *Pediatric Research, 21,* 374A.

Porter, R. H., Makin, J. W., Davis, L. B., & Christensen, K. M. (1992). Breast-fed infants respond to olfactory cues from their own mother and unfamiliar lactating females. *Infant Behavior and Development, 15,* 85–93.

Poulson, C. L., Kymissis, E., Reeve, K. F., Andreatos, M., & Reeve, L. (1991). Generalized vocal imitation in infants. *Journal of Experimental Child Psychology, 51,* 267–279.

Practical Applications of Research. (1983, June 5). Newsletter of Phi Delta Kappa's Center on Evaluation, Development, and Research.

Putallaz, M., & Gottman, J. M. (1981). Social skills and group acceptance. In S. R. Asher & J. M. Gottman (Eds.), *The development of children's friendships.* Cambridge: Cambridge University Press.

Queen, P. M., & Wilson, S. E. (1987). Growth and nutrient requirements of infants. In R. J. Grand, J. L. Sutphen, & W. H. Dietz, Jr. (Eds.), *Pediatric nutrition.* Boston: Butterworths.

Ramsey, P. G. (1982, January). Multicultural education in early childhood. *Young Children, 37,* 13–24.

Ramsey, P. G., & Myers, L. C. (1990). Salience of race in young children's cognitive, affective, and behavioral responses to social environments. *Journal of Applied Developmental Psychology, 11,* 49–67.

Raver, A. (1991). *Strategies for teaching at-risk and handicapped infants and toddlers: A transdisciplinary approach.* New York: Merrill/Macmillan.

Ray, R. D., & Delprato, D. J. (1989). Behavioral systems analysis: Methodological strategies and tactics. *Behavioral Science, 34,* 81–127.

Raymond, C. A. (1987). Birth defects linked with specific level of maternal alcohol use, but abstinence still is the best policy. *Journal of the American Medical Association, 258,* 177–178.

Reed. G., & Leiderman, P. H. (1981). Age-related changes in attachment behavior in polymatrically reared infants: The Kenyan Gusii. In T. M. Field, A. M. Sostek, P. Vietze, & P. H. Leiderman (Eds.), *Culture and early interactions.* Hillsdale, NJ: Lawrence Erlbaum.

Reese, H. W., & Overton, W. F. (1970). Models of development and theories of development. In L. Goulet & P. Baltes, (Eds.), *Life-span developmental psychology.* New York: Academic Press.

Reidy, T. J. (1977). Aggressive characteristics of abused and neglected children. *Journal of Clinical Psychology, 120,* 439–446.

Reinisch, J. M. (1977). Prenatal exposure of human foetuses to synthetic progestin and oestrogen affects personality. *Nature, 266,* 561–562.

Rende, R. D. (1993). Longitudinal relations between temperament traits and behavioral syndromes in middle childhood. *Journal of the American Academy of Child and Adolescent Psychiatry, 32,* 287–290.

Rhoden, N. K. (1986). Treating Baby Doe: The ethics of uncertainty. *Hastings Center Report, 16,* 34–42.

Richards, H. C., Bear, G. G., Stewart, A. L., & Norman, A. D. (1992). Moral reasoning and classroom conduct: Evidence of a curvilinear relationship. *Merrill-Palmer Quarterly, 38,* 176–190.

Richards, M. (1980). Adjective ordering in the language of young children: An experimental investigation. *Journal of Child Language, 6,* 253–277.

Richardson, G. A., & Day, N. L. (1991). Maternal and neonatal effects of moderate cocaine use during pregnancy. *Neurotoxicology and Teratology, 13,* 455–460.

Robbins, E. (1984, Fall). American Red Cross teaches safety rules to children. *Day Care and Early Education, 12,* 32–33.

Robinson, B. E., & Barret, R. L. (1986). *The developing father: Emerging roles in contemporary society.* New York: Guilford Publications.

Robinson, E. J., & Mitchell, P. (1992). Children's interpretation of messages from a speaker with a false belief. *Child Development, 63*, 639–652.

Rodning, C., Beckwith, L., & Howard, J. (1989). Characteristics of attachment organization and play organization in prenatally drug-exposed toddlers. *Development and Psychopathology, 1*, 277–289.

Roe, K. V. (1991). Short-term stability of three-month-old infants' vocal response to mother vs stranger. *Perceptual and Motor Skills, 73*, 419–424.

Rogers, C. R. (1961). *On becoming a person.* Boston: Houghton Mifflin.

Rogers, C. S., Rahman, Y., & Casertano, M. A. (1991). Social experiences and stranger anxiety among infants of working and non-working mothers. *International Journal of Early Childhood, 23*, 59–68.

Rogers, F. (1984, March). The past and the present is now. *Young Children, 39*, 13–18.

Rose, S. A. (1981). Predicting cognitive development from infancy measures. In P. M. Vietze & H. G. Vaughan (Eds.), *Early identification of infants with disabilities.* Boston: Allyn and Bacon.

Rose, S. A., Feldman, J. F., & Wallace, I. F. (1992). Infant information processing in relation to six-year cognitive outcomes. *Child Development, 63*, 1126–1141.

Rosenblith, J. F., & Sims-Knight, J. E. (1985). *In the beginning: Development in the first two years.* Monterey, CA: Brooks/Cole.

Rosenkoeter, L. I., Huston, A. C., & Wright, J. C. (1990). Television and the moral judgment of the young child. *Journal of Applied Developmental Psychology, 11*, 123–137.

Ross, H. S., & Lollis, S. P. (1989). A social relations analysis of toddler peer relationships. *Child Development, 60*, 1082–1091.

Rossiter, J., & Robertson, T. S. (1975). Children's television viewing: An examination of parent–child consensus. *Sociometry, 38*, 308–326.

Royce, J. M., Darlington, R. B., & Murray, H. W. (1983). Pooled analysis: Findings across studies. In Consortium for Longitudinal Studies, *As the twig is bent . . .Lasting effects of preschool programs.* Hillsdale, NJ: Lawrence Erlbaum.

Rubin, R. T., Reinisch, J. M., & Haskett, R. F. (1981). Postnatal gonadal steroid effects on human behavior. *Science, 211*, 1318–1324.

Rue, V. M. (1985). Death by design of handicapped newborns: The family's role and response. *Issues in Law and Medicine, 1*, 201–225.

Ruiz, F. J., & Cravioto, A. (1989). Factors which affect the duration of breast feeding in a cohort longitudinally followed of urban mothers. *Boletin Medico Del Hospital Infantil De Mexico, 46*, 705–708.

Russell, M. J. (1976). Human olfactory communication. *Nature, 260*, 520–522.

Rutter, M. (1983). Stress, coping and development: Some issues and some questions. In N. Garmezy & M. Rutter (Eds.), *Stress, coping, and development in children.* New York: McGraw-Hill.

Sabotta, E. E., & Davis, R. L. (1992). Fatality after report to a child abuse registry in Washington state, 1973–1986. *Child Abuse & Neglect, 16*, 627–635.

Saltz, E., Dixon, D., & Johnson, J. (1977). Training disadvantaged preschoolers on various fantasy activities: Effects on cognitive functioning and impulse control. *Child Development, 48*, 367–380.

Salzinger, S., Feldman, R. S., & Hammer, M. (1993). The effects of physical abuse on children's social relationships. *Child Development, 64*, 169–187.

Sameroff, A. J. (1981). Longitudinal studies of preterm infants: A review of chapters 17–20. In S. L. Friedman & M. Sigman (Eds.), *Preterm Birth and Psychological Development.* New York: Academic Press.

Sanford, A. R., & Zelman, J. G. (1981). *Learning accomplishment profile.* Winston Salem, NC: Kaplan.

Satter, E. (1991). *Child of mine: Feeding with love and good sense.* Palo Alto, CA: Bull Publishing.

Satter, E. (1984). Developmental guidelines for feeding infants and young children. *Food & Nutrition News, 56,* 21–24.

Satter, E. (1987). *How to get your child to eat . . .But not too much.* Palo Alto, CA: Bull Publishing.

Saudino, K. J., & Eaton, W. O. (1991). Infant temperament and genetics: An objective twin study of motor activity level. *Child Development, 62,* 1167–1174.

Saunders, A., & Remsberg, B. (1984). *The stress-proof child.* New York: Holt, Rinehart and Winston.

Saunders, S. E., & Carroll, J. (1988). Post-partum breast feeding support: Impact on duration. *Journal of the American Dietetic Association, 88,* 213–215.

Saville-Troike, M. (1982). The development of bilingual and bicultural competence in young children. In L. G. Katz (Ed.), *Current topics in early childhood education* (Vol. 4). Norwood, NJ: Ablex.

Schachter, F. F. (1979). *Everyday mother talk to toddlers: Early intervention.* New York: Academic Press.

Schachter, F. F., & Strage, A. A. (1982). Adults' talk and children's language development. In S. G. Moore & C. R. Cooper (Eds.), *The young child: Reviews of research* (Vol. 3). Washington, DC: National Association for the Education of Young Children.

Scher, A. (1991). A longitudinal study of night waking in the first year. *Childcare, Health and Development, 17,* 295–302.

Schiefelbusch, R. L. (1984). Assisting children to become communicatively competent. In R. L. Schiefelbusch & J. Pickar, (Eds.), *The acquisition of communicative competence.* Baltimore: University Park Press.

Schieffelin, B. B., & Ochs, E. (1983). A cultural perspective on the transition from prelinguistic to linguistic communication. In R. M. Golinkoff (Ed.), *The transition from prelinguistic to linguistic communication.* Hillsdale, NJ: Lawrence Erlbaum.

Schiff, M., Duyme, M., Dumaret, A., Stewart, J., Tomkiewicz, S., & Feingold, J. (1978). Intellectual status of working-class children adopted early into upper-middle-class families. *Science, 200,* 1503–1504.

Schmidt, R. A. (1991). *Motor learning and performance: From principles to practice.* Champaign, IL: Human Kinetics Publishers.

Schneider-Rosen, K., & Cicchetti, D. (1984). The relationship between affect and cognition in maltreated infants: Quality of attachment and the develoment of visual self-recognition. *Child Development, 55,* 648–658.

Schrader, C. T. (1989). Written language and use within the context of young children's symbolic play. *Early Childhood Education Research Quarterly, 4,* 225–244.

Schutter, S., & Brinker, R. (1992). Conjuring a new category of disability from prenatal cocaine exposure: Are the infants unique biological or caretaking casualties? *Topics in Early Childhood Special Education, 11,* 84–111.

Scrimshaw, N. S. (1991, October). Iron deficiency. *Scientific American,* 46–52.

Secord, P., & Peevers, B. H. (1974). The development and attribution of person concepts. In T. Mischel (Ed.), *Understanding other persons.* Totowa, NJ: Rowman & Littlefield.

Seefeldt, C., & Barbour, N. (1990). *Early childhood education: An introduction.* New York: Merrill/Macmillan.

Segal, M., & Adcock, D. (1981). *Just pretending: Ways to help children grow through imaginative play.* Englewood Cliffs, NJ: Prentice Hall.

Selman, R. L. (1971). Taking another's perspective. Role-taking development in early childhood. *Child Development, 42,* 1721–1734.

Selman, R. L. (1980). *The growth of interpersonal understanding.* New York: Academic Press.

Selman, R. L. (1981). The child as friendship philosopher. In S. R. Asher & J. M. Gottman (Eds.), *The development of children's friendships.* Cambridge: Cambridge University Press.

Shaffer, D. R. (1988). *Social and personality development* (2nd ed.). Pacific Grove, CA: Brooks/Cole.

Shantz, C. U. (1975). The development of social cognition. In E. M. Hetherington (Ed.), *Review of child development research* (Vol. 5). Chicago: University of Chicago Press.

Shapiro, D. (1979). *Parents and protectors.* New York: Research Center, Child Welfare League of America.

Sherrod, L. R. (1981). Issues in cognitive-perceptual development: The special case of social stimuli. In M. E. Lamb & L. R. Sherrod (Eds.), *Infant social cognition: Empirical and theoretical considerations.* Hillsdale, NJ: Lawrence Erlbaum.

Shonkoff, J. P. (1992). Early intervention research: Asking and answering meaningful questions. *Zero to Three, 12,* 7–9.

Shonkoff, J. P., Hauser-Cram, P., Krauss, M. W., & Upshur, C. C. (1992). Development of infants with disabilities and their families. *Monographs of the Society for Research in Child Development, 57*(Serial No. 230).

Shouldice, A., & Stevenson-Hinde, J. (1992). Coping with security distress: The separation anxiety test and attachment classification at 4.5 years. *Journal of Child Psychology and Psychiatry, 33,* 331–348.

Siegel, E. (1982). A critical examination of studies of parent–infant bonding. In M. H. Klaus & M. O. Robertson (Eds.), *Birth, interaction, and attachment: A round table.* Skillman, NJ: Johnson & Johnson.

Siegel, M., & Beattie, K. (1991). Where to look first for children's knowledge of false beliefs. *Cognition, 38,* 1–12.

Sigel, I. E., & Cocking, R. R. (1977). *Cognitive development from childhood to adolescence: A constructivist perspective.* New York: Holt, Rinehart and Winston.

Sigelman, E., Block, J., Block, J. H., & Van der Lippe, A. (1970). Antecedents of optimal psychological adjustment. *Journal of Consulting and Clinical Psychology, 35,* 283–289.

Sigman, M., Cohen, S. E., Beckwith, L., Asarnow, R., & Parmelee, A. H. (1991). Continuity in cognitive abilities from infancy to 12 years of age. *Cognitive Development, 6,* 47–57.

Simopoulos, A. P. (1986). Nutrition in relation to learning disabilities. In M. Lewis (Ed.), *Learning disabilities and prenatal risk.* Chicago: University of Illinois Press.

Sims, R. (1983). What has happened to the "all-white" world of children's books? *Phi Delta Kappa, 64,* 650–653.

Singer, D. G., Singer, J. L., & Zuckerman, D. M. (1981). *Teaching television: How to use television to your child's advantage.* New York: Dial.

Singer, D. G., Zuckerman, D. M., & Singer, J. L. (1980). Helping elementary children learn about television. *Journal of Communication, 30,* 84–93.

Singer, J. L., Singer, D. G., & Rapaczynski, W. S. (1984). Family patterns and television viewing as predictors of children's beliefs and aggression. *Journal of Communication, 34,* 73–89.

Skinner, B. F. (1974). *About behaviorism.* New York: Knopf.

Slater, A., Mattock, A., & Brown, E. (1990). Size constancy at birth: Newborn infants' responses to retinal and real size. *Journal of Experimental Child Psychology, 49,* 314–322.

Slater, A., Mattock, A., & Brown, E. (1991). Form perception at birth: Cohen and Younger (1984) revisited. *Journal of Experimental Child Psychology, 51,* 395–406.

Slater, D., & Thompson, T. L. (1984). Parental discretion advised: Televised warning statements and parental attitudes. Paper presented at the Speech Communication Association Conference, Chicago, IL.

Smeriglio, V. L. (Eds.). (1981). *Newborns and parents: Parent-infant contact and newborn sensory stimulation.* Hillsdale, NJ: Lawrence Erlbaum.

Smith, A. E. A., & Knight-Jones, E. V. (1990). The abilities of very low-birthweight children and their classroom controls. *Developmental Medicine and Child Neurology, 32,* 590–601.

Smith, C. A. (1982). *Promoting the social development of young children: Strategies and activities.* Palo Alto, CA: Mayfield Publishing.

Smith, F. (1928). *Comprehension and learning: A conceptual framework for teachers.* New York: Holt, Rinehart and Winston.

Smith, P. B., & Pederson, D. R. (1988). Maternal sensitivity and patterns of infant–mother attachment. *Child Development, 59,* 1097–1101.

Smollar, J., & Youniss, J. (1982). Social development through friendship. In K. H. Rubin & H. S. Ross (Eds.), *Peer relationships and social skills in childhood.* New York: Springer-Verlag.

Smotherman, W. P. (1982). Odor aversion learning by the rat fetus. *Physiology & Behavior, 29,* 769–771.

Snow, C., DeBlauw, A., & Van Roosmalen, G. (1979). Talking and playing with babies: The role of ideologies in childrearing. In M. Bullowa (Ed.), *Before speech.* Cambridge: Cambridge University Press.

Sontag, L. W. (1970). Prenatal determinants of postnatal behavior. In H. A. Waisman & G. K. Kerr (Eds.), *Fetal growth and development.* New York: McGraw-Hill.

Sontag. L. W., & Wallace, R. F. (1934). A study of fetal activity: A preliminary report of the Fels Fund. *American Journal of the Disabled Child, 48,* 1047–1050.

Sontheimer, D. (1989). Visual information processing in infancy. *Developmental Medicine & Child Neurology, 31,* 787–796.

Spelke, E. S. (1985). Perception of unity, persistence, and identity: Thoughts on infants' conceptions of objects. In J. Mehler & R. Fox (Eds.), *Neonate cognition: Beyond the blooming buzzing confusion.* Hillsdale, NJ: Lawrence Erlbaum.

Spelt, D. K. (1948). The conditioning of the human fetus in utero. *Journal of Experimental Psychology, 38,* 338–346.

Springer, K., & Ruckel, J. (1992). Early beliefs about the cause of illness: Evidence against immanent justice. *Cognitive Development, 7,* 429–443.

Staff. (1983, July 18). Big jump in U.S. birth defects. *San Francisco Chronicle,* p. 1.

Stevens, J. H., Jr. (1982, January). Research in review: The New York City infant day care study. *Young Children, 37,* 47–53.

Stevens, J. H., Jr., & Baxter, D. H. (1981, May). Malnutrition and children's development. *Young Children, 36,* 60–71.

Stickrod, G., Kimble, D. P., & Smotherman, W. P. (1982). In utero taste/odor aversion conditioning in the rat. *Physiology & Behavior, 28,* 5–7.

Stifter, C. A., Fox, N. A., & Porges, S. W. (1989). Facial expressivity and vagal tone in 5- and 10-month-old infants. *Infant Behavior and Development, 12,* 127–137.

Stifter, C. A., & Moyer, D. (1991). The regulation of positive affect: Gaze aversion activity during mother–infant interaction. *Infant Behavior and Development, 14,* 111–123.

Stiles, J., Wendy, T., & Whipple, T. (1990). Facilitative effects of labeling on preschool children's copying of simple geometric forms. *Perceptual and Motor Skills, 70,* 663–672.

Stinnett, N., Sanders, G., & DeFrain, J. (1981). Strong families: A national study. In N. Stinnett, J. DeFrain, K. King, P. Knaub, & G. Rowe (Eds.), *Family strengths 3: Roots of well-being.* Lincoln: University of Nebraska Press.

Stipek, D., Recchia, S., & McClintic, S. (1992). Self-evaluation in young children. *Monographs of the Society for Research in Child Development, 57*(1, Serial No. 226).

Streicher, L. H., & Bonney, N. L. (1974). Children talk about television. *Journal of Communication, 24,* 54–62.

Streissguth, A. P. (1986). Smoking and drinking during pregnancy and offspring learning disabilities: A review of the literature and development of a research strategy. In M. Lewis (Ed.), *Learning disabilities and prenatal risk.* Chicago: University of Illinois Press.

Streissguth, A. P., Landesman-Dwyer, S., Martin, J. C., & Smith, D. W. (1980). Teratogenic effects of alcohol in humans and laboratory animals. *Science, 209,* 353–361.

Strichartz, A. F., & Burton, R. V. (1990). Lies and truth: A study of the development of the concept. *Child Development, 61,* 211–220.

Strickland, D. S., & Morrow, L. M. (Eds.). (1989). *Emerging literacy: Young children learn to read and write.* Newark, DE: International Reading Association.

Students with Disabilities and Special Education, 10th ed. (1993). Rosemount, MN: Data Research, Inc.

Sullivan, M. W. (1982a). *Feeling strong, feeling free: Movement exploration for young children.* Washington, DC: National Association for the Education of Young Children.

Sullivan, M. W. (1982b). Reactivation: Priming forgotten memories in human infants. *Child Development, 53,* 516–523.

Surveyer, J. A., James, S. R., & Burns, M. (1985). Prevention of injury. In S. R. Mott, N. F. Fazekas, & S. R. James (Eds.), *Nursing care of children and families: A holistic approach.* Menlo Park, CA: Addison-Wesley.

Sutton-Smith, B., & Roberts, J. M. (1981). Play, toys, games and sports. In H. C. Triandis & A. Heron (Eds.), *Handbook of developmental cross-cultural psychology* (Vol. 4). Boston: Allyn and Bacon.

Sutton-Smith, B., & Sutton-Smith, S. (1974). *How to play with your child (and when not to).* New York: Hawthorn.

Taharally, L. C. (1991). Fantasy play, language and cognitive ability of four-year-old children in Guyana, South America. *Child Study Journal, 21,* 37–56.

Takahashi, K. (1990). Are the key assumptions of the "strange situation" procedure universal? A view from Japanese research. *Human Development, 33,* 23–30.

Tamis-LeMonda, C. S., & Bornstein, M. H. (1990). Language, play, and attention at one year. *Infant Behavior and Development, 13,* 85–98.

Tanzer, D., & Block, J. L. (1976). *Why natural childbirth?* New York: Schocken Books.

Tengbom, M. (1989). Grief for a season. Minneapolis, MN: Bethany House Publishers.

Thoman, E. B., & Ingersoll, E. W. (1989). The human nature of the youngest humans: Prematurely born babies. *Seminars in Perinatology, 13,* 482–494.

Thomas, A., & Chess, S. (1981). The role of temperament in the contributions of individuals to their own development. In R. M. Lerner & N. A. Busch-Rossnagel (Eds.), *Individuals as producers of their development: A life-span perspective.* New York: Academic Press.

Thomas, A., & Chess, S. (1984). Genesis and evolution of behavioral disorders: From infancy to early adult life. *American Journal of Psychiatry, 141,* 1–9.

Thompson, P. E., Harris, C. C., & Bitowsk, B. E. (1986). Effects of infant colic on the family: Implication for practice. *Issues in Comprehensive Pediatric Nursing, 9,* 273–288.

Thompson, T. L., & Slater, D. (1983). Parent–child co-viewing and parental monitoring of television: Their impacts and interaction. Paper presented at the Speech Communication Association Conference, Washington, DC.

Timor-Tritsch, I. E., Peisner, D. B., & Raju, S. (1990). Sonoembryology: An organ-oriented approach using a high-frequency vaginal probe. *Journal of Clinical Ultrasound, 18,* 286–298.

Timor-Tritsch, I. E., & Rottem, S. (1988, April). High-frequency transvaginal sonography: New diagnostic boon. *Contemporary Ob/Gyn,* 111–113.

Toda, S., Fogel, A., & Kawai, M. (1990). Maternal speech to three-month-old infants in the United States and Japan. *Journal of Child Language, 17,* 279–294.

Tomasello, M., Conti-Ramsden, G., & Ewert, B. (1990). Young children's conversations with their mothers and fathers: Differences in breakdown and repair. *Journal of Child Language, 17,* 115–130.

Toth, S. L., Manly, J. T., & Cicchetti, D. (1992). Child maltreatment and vulnerability to depression. *Development and Psychopathology, 4,* 97–112.

Townsend, J. W., Klein, R. E., Irwin, M. H., Owens, W., Yarbrough, C., & Engle, P. L. (1982). Nutrition and preschool mental development. In D. A. Wagner & H. W. Stevenson

(Eds.), *Cultural perspectives on child development*. San Francisco: W. H. Freeman.

Trause, M. A., & Irvin, N. A. (1982). Care of the sibling. In M. H. Klaus & J. H. Kennell, (Eds.). *Parent–infant bonding* (2nd ed.). St. Louis: C. V. Mosby.

Trawick-Smith, J. (1993). *Interactions in the classroom: Facilitating play in the early years*. New York: Merrill/Macmillan.

Trehub, S. E., Endman, M. W., & Thorpe, L. A. (1990). Infants' perception of timbre: Classification of complex tones by spectral structure. *Journal of Experimental Child Psychology, 49,* 300–313.

Tulkin, S. R. (1977). Social class differences in maternal and infant behavior. In P. H. Leiderman, S. R. Tulkin, & A. Rosenfeld (Eds.), *Culture and infancy: Variations in the human experience*. New York: Academic Press.

Turiel, E. (1966). An experimental test of the sequentiality of developmental stages in the child's moral judgments. *Journal of Personality and Social Psychology, 3,* 611–618.

Turiel, E. (1978). The development of concepts of social structure: Social convention. In J. Glick & A. Clarke-Stewart (Eds.), *The development of social understanding*. New York: Gardner.

Turner, P. J. (1991). Relations between attachment, gender, and behavior with peers in preschool. *Child Development, 62,* 1475–1488.

Umbel, V. M., Pearson, B. Z., Fernandez, M. C., & Oller, D. K. (1992). Measuring bilingual children's receptive vocabularies. *Child Development, 63,* 1012–1020.

Urberg, K. A., & Kaplan, M. G. (1989). An observational study of race, age, and sex-heterogeneous interaction in preschoolers. *Journal of Applied Developmental Psychology, 10,* 299–311.

U.S. Bureau of the Census. (1990). Who's minding the kids? Child care arrangements, 1986–87. *Current Population Reports*, Series P-70, No. 20. Washington, DC: U.S. Government Printing Office.

U.S. Bureau of the Census. (1991). *Statistical abstract of the United States 1990* (110th ed.), p. 747.

U.S. Department of Transportation, National Highway Traffic Safety Administration. (1980). *Child restraint systems for your automobile*. Washington, DC: U.S. Government Printing Office.

U.S. Office of Education. (1977, August 23). Education of handicapped children. *Federal Register* (Part II). Washington, DC: Department of HEW.

U.S. Office of Education. (1977, December 29). Assistance to states for education of the handicapped: Procedures for evaluating specific learning disabilities. *Federal Register* (Part III). Washington, DC: Department of HEW.

Uzgiris, I. C., & Hunt, J. McV. (1975). *Assessment in infancy*. Urbana, IL: University of Illinois Press.

Valentine, D. (1982). Adaptation to pregnancy: Some implications for individual and family mental health. *Children Today, 11,* 17–20, 36.

Van Buren, A. (1982, November 16). Dear Abby. *San Francisco Chronicle*, p. 41.

Van den Bergh, B. R. H. (1990). The influence of maternal emotions during pregnancy on fetal and neonatal behavior. *Pre- and Peri-Natal Psychology, 5,* 119–130.

van Hoorn, J. L. (1982). *Games of infancy: A cross-cultural study*. Unpublished doctoral dissertation, University of California, Berkeley.

van Ijzendoorn, M. H., Goldberg, S., Kroonenberg, P. M., & Frenkel, O. J. (1992). The relative effects of maternal and child problems on the quality of attachment: A meta-analysis of attachment in clinical samples. *Child Development, 63,* 840–858.

van Ijzendoorn, M. H., & Kroonenberg, P. M. (1990). Cross-cultural consistency of coding the Strange Situation. *Infant Behavior and Development, 13,* 469–485.

Vasta, R. (1979). *Studying children: An introduction to research methods*. San Francisco: W. H. Freeman.

Vellutine, F. R. (1987). Dyslexia. *Scientific American, 256,* 34–41.

Verhoeven, L. T. (1990). Acquisition of reading as second language. *Reading Research Quarterly, 25,* 90–114.

Verny, T., with Kelly, L. (1981). *The secret life of the unborn child.* New York: Summit Books.

vom Saal, F. S., & Bronson, F. H. (1980). Sexual characteristics of adult female mice are correlated with their blood testosterone levels during prenatal development. *Science, 208,* 597–599.

Vurpillot, E. (1968). The development of scanning strategies and their relation to visual differentiation. *Journal of Experimental Child Psychology, 6,* 632–650.

Vygotsky, L. S. (1962). *Thought and language.* Cambridge, MA: MIT Press.

Vygotsky, L. S. (1976). Play and its role in the mental development of the child. In J. Bruner, A. Jolly, & K. Sylva (Eds.), *Play: Its role in development and evolution.* New York: Basic Books.

Vygotsky, L. S. (1978). *Mind in society: The development of higher psychological functions.* Cambridge, MA: Harvard University Press.

Wachs, T. D. (1982). Relation of home noise-confusion to infant cognitive development. Paper presented at the meeting of the American Psychological Association, Washington, DC.

Wachs, T. D., & Gruen, G. E. (1982). *Early experience and human development.* New York: Plenum.

Wadsworth, B. J. (1978). *Piaget for the classroom teacher.* New York: Longman.

Wadsworth, B. J. (1984). *Piaget's theory of cognitive and affective development* (3rd ed.). New York: Longman.

Wald, E. R., Guerra, N., & Byers, C. (1991). Frequency and severity of infections in day care: Three-year follow-up. *Journal of Pediatrics, 118,* 509–514.

Walker, L. O., & Best, M. A. (1991). Well-being of mothers with infant children: A preliminary comparison of employed women and homemakers. *Women & Health, 17,* 71–89.

Walker-Andrews, A. S., & Lennon, E. (1991). Infants' discrimination of vocal expressions: Contributions of auditory and visual information. *Infant Behavior and Development, 14,* 131–142.

Wall, S. M., Pickert, S. M., & Gibson, W. B. (1989). Fantasy play in 5- and 6-year-old children. *The Journal of Psychology, 123,* 245–256.

Walters, C. E. (1965). Prediction of postnatal development from fetal activity. *Child Development, 36,* 801–808.

Warash, B. (1991). *The effects of preschool experiences on advantaged children.* Doctoral dissertation, West Virginia University.

Warren, K. R., & Bast, R. J. (1988). Alcohol-related birth defects: An update. *Public Health Reports, 103,* 638–642.

Wasserman, G., Graziano, J. H., Factor-Litvak, P., Popovac, D., Morina, N., Musabegovic, A., Vrenezi, N., Capuni-Paracka, S., Lekic, V., Preteni-Redjepi, E., Hadzialijevic, S., Slavokovich, V., Kline, J., Shrout, P., & Stein, Z. (1992). Independent effects of lead exposure and iron deficiency anemia on developmental outcome at age 2 years. *Journal of Pediatrics, 121,* 695–703.

Waters, E., Matas, L., & Sroufe, L. A. (1975). Infants' reactions to an approaching stranger: Description, validation, and functional significance of wariness. *Child Development, 46,* 348–356.

Watson, A. J. (1984). Cognitive development and units of print in early reading. In D. Valtin & R. Valtin (Eds.), *Language awareness and learning to read.* New York: Springer-Verlag.

Watson, J. B. (1928). *Psychological care of infant and child.* New York: W. W. Norton.

Watson, J. D. (1968). *The double helix.* New York: Atheneum.

Wehren, A., DeLisi, R., & Arnold, M. (1981). The development of noun definition. *Journal of Child Language, 8,* 165–175.

Weikert, D. P. (1989). Quality preschool programs: A long-term social investment. Occasional Paper No. 5, Ford Foundation Project on Social Welfare and the American Future. New York: Ford Foundation.

Weintraub, M., & Lewis, M. (1977). The determinants of children's responses to separation. *Monographs of the Society for Research in Child Development, 42*(4, Serial No. 172).

Weiser, M. G. (1991). *Infant/toddler care and education* (2nd ed.) New York: Merrill/Macmillan.

Weisner, T. S. (1982). Sibling interdependence and child caregiving: A cross-cultural view. In M. E. Lamb & B. Sutton-Smith (Eds.), *Sibling relationships: Their nature and significance across the lifespan.* Hillsdale, NJ: Lawrence Erlbaum.

Wells, C. G., & Robinson, W. P. (1982). The role of adult speech in language development. In C. Fraser & K. F. Scherer (Eds.), *The social psychology of language.* Cambridge: Cambridge University Press.

Werner, E. E. (1979) *Cross-cultural child development: A view from the planet earth.* Monterey, CA: Brooks/Cole.

Werner, E. E. (1984, November). Resilient children. *Young Children, 40,* 68–72.

Werner, E. E., & Smith, R. S. (1982). *Vulnerable, but invincible: A longitudinal study of resilient children and youth.* New York: McGraw-Hill.

Werner, H. J. (1957). The conception of development from a comparational and organismic point of view. In D. Harris (Ed.), *The concept of development* (pp. 125–148). Minneapolis, MN: University of Minnesota Press.

Westinghouse Learning Corporation–Ohio University. (1973). The impact of Head Start: An evaluation of the effects of Head Start on children's cognitive and affective development. In L. Frost (Ed.), *Revisiting early childhood education.* New York: Holt, Rinehart & Winston.

Whalen, C. K., & Henker, B. (1980). The social ecology of psychostimulant treatment: A model for conceptual and empirical analysis. In C. K. Whalen & B. Henker (Eds.), *Hyperactive children: The social ecology of identification and treatment.* New York: Academic Press.

White, B. L. (1978). *Experience and environment: Major influences on the development of the young child* (Vol 2). Englewood Cliffs, NJ: Prentice Hall.

White, B. L. (1990). *The first three years of life.* New York: Prentice Hall.

White, B. L., Kaban, B. T., & Attanucci, J. S. (1979). *The origins of human competence: The final report of the Harvard Preschool Project.* Lexington, MA: Lexington Books.

White, B. L., & Watts, J. C. (1973). *Experience and environment: Major influences on the development of the young child* (Vol 1). Englewood Cliffs, NJ: Prentice Hall.

Whitener, C. B., & Kersey, K. (1980). A purple hippopotamus? Why not! *Childhood Education, 57,* 83–89.

Whitney, E. N., & Rolfes, S. R. (1993). *Understanding nutrition.* Minneapolis: West Publishing.

Will, G. F. (1983, January). The poison poor children breathe. *Young Children, 38,* 11–12.

Williams, L. R., & DeGaetano, Y. (1985). *ALERTA: A multicultural bilingual approach to teaching young children.* Menlo Park, CA: Addison-Wesley.

Williamson, P. S., & Williamson, M. L. (1983). Physiologic stress reduction by a local anesthetic. *Pediatrics, 71,* 36–40.

Wilson, J. D., George, F. W., & Griffin, J. E., (1981). The hormonal control of sexual development. *Science, 211,* 1278–1285.

Winick, M. (1976). Maternal nutrition. In R. L. Brent & M. I. Harris (Eds.), *Prevention of embryonic, fetal and perinatal disease.* Bethesda, MD: National Institutes of Health.

Wishon, P. M., Bower, R., & Eller, B. (1983). Childhood obesity: Prevention and treatment. *Young Children, 39,* 21–27.

Wolff, P. H. (1959). Observations of newborn infants. *Psychosomatic Medicine, 21,* 110–118.

Wolfner, G. D., & Gelles, R. J. (1993). A profile of violence toward children: A national study. *Child Abuse & Neglect, 16,* 197–212.

Wood, B. S. (1981). *Children and communication: Verbal and nonverbal language develop-*

ment (2nd ed.). Englewood Cliffs, NJ: Prentice Hall.

Woodard, C. Y. (1986). Guidelines for facilitating sociodramatic play. In J. L. Frost & S. Sunderlin (Eds.), *When children play*. Proceedings of the International Conference on Play and Play Environments. Wheaton, MD: Association for Childhood Education International.

Woods, N. S., Eyler, F. D., Behnke, M., & Conlon, M. (1991). *Cocaine use: Maternal depressive symptoms and neonatal neurobehavior over the first month*. Poster presented at the biennial meetings of the Society for Research in Child Development, Seattle, WA.

Wood-Shuman, S., & Cone, J. D. (1986). Differences in abusive, at-risk for abuse, and control mothers' descriptions of normal child behavior. *Child Abuse & Neglect, 10*, 397–405.

Wortham, S. C. (1990). *Tests and Measurement in Early Childhood Education*. New York: Merrill/Macmillan.

Writers Guild of America, West, Inc. et al., v. FCC. 423 F. Supp. 1134 (U.S.D.C., Central District of California, 1976).

Yamane, R. (1989). Integrating process of communicative mode in demanding situation during preverbal period. *Japanese Journal of Educational Psychology, 37*, 345–352.

Yang, P. K. (1981). Maternal attitudes during pregnancy and medication during labor and delivery: Methodological considerations. In V. L. Smeriglio (Ed.), *Newborns and parents: Parent–infant contact and newborn sensory stimulation*. Hillsdale, NJ: Lawrence Erlbaum.

Zahn-Waxler, C., Iannotti, R., & Chapman, M. (1982). Peers and prosocial development. In K. H. Rubin & H. S. Ross (Eds.), *Peer relationships and social skills in childhood*. New York: Springer-Verlag.

Zaslow, M. J., Pederson, F. A., Suwalsky, J. T. D., & Rabinovich, B. A. (1989). Maternal employment and parent–infant interaction at one year. *Early Childhood Research Quarterly, 4*, 49–78.

Zeanah, C. H., Benoit, D., Barton, M., Regan, C., Hirshberg, L. M., & Lipsitt, L. P. (1993). Representations of attachment in mothers and their one-year-old infants. *Journal of the American Academy of Child and Adolescent Psychiatry, 32*, 278–286.

Zelazo, P. R., Weiss, M. J., Papageorgiou, A. N., & Laplante, D. P. (1989). Recovery and dishabituation of sound localization among normal-, moderate-, and high-risk newborns: Discriminant validity. *Infant Behavior and Development, 12*, 321–340.

Zepp, F., Bruhl, K., Zimmer, B., & Schumacher, R. (1993). Battered child syndrome: Cerebral ultrasound and CT findings after vigorous shaking. *Neuropediatrics, 23*, 188–191.

Zigler, E., Taussig, C., & Black, K. (1992). Early childhood intervention: A promising preventative for juvenile delinquency. *American Psychologist, 47*, 997–1006.

Name Index

Subject Index